The Cavell Reader

BLACKWELL READERS

In a number of disciplines, across a number of decades, and in a number of languages, writers and texts have emerged which require the attention of students and scholars around the world. United only by a concern with radical ideas, *Blackwell Readers* collect and introduce the works of pre-eminent theorists. Often translating works for the first time (Levinas, Irigaray, Lyotard, Blanchot, Kristeva) or presenting material previously inaccessible (CLR James, Fanon, Elias) each volume in the series introduces and represents work which is now fundamental to study in the humanities and social sciences.

The Lyotard Reader
Edited by Andrew Benjamin

The Irigaray Reader
Edited by Margaret Whitford

The Kristeva Reader
Edited by Toril Moi

The Levinas Reader
Edited by Sean Hand

The CLR James Reader
Edited by Anna Grimshaw

The Wittgenstein Reader
Edited by Sir Anthony Kenny

The Blanchot Reader
Edited by Michael Holland

The Elias Reader
Edited by S. Mennell

The Lukács Reader
Edited by Arpad Kardakay

The Cavell Reader
Edited by Stephen Mulhall

Forthcoming:
The Benjamin Reader
Edited by Drew Milne

The Fanon Reader
Edited by Homi Bhabha

The Cavell Reader

Edited by
Stephen Mulhall

BLACKWELL
Publishers

Copyright © Blackwell Publishers Ltd, 1996

First published 1996

2 4 6 8 10 9 7 5 3 1

Blackwell Publishers Inc
238 Main Street
Cambridge, Massachusetts 02142,
USA

Blackwell Publishers Ltd
108 Cowley Road
Oxford OX4 1JF
UK

Library of Congress Cataloging-in-Publication Data
Cavell, Stanley, 1926–
    [Selections. 1996]
    The Cavell reader / edited by Stephen Mulhall.
        p. cm. – (Blackwell readers)
    Includes index.
    ISBN 0–631–19742–7 (alk. paper). – ISBN 0–631–19743–5 (pbk. alk. paper)
    1. Philosophy. 2. Criticism. I. Mulhall, Stephen, 1962–
    II. Title. III. Series.
    B945.C273C382   1996
    191–dc20   95–36051
                                                                                           CIP

British Library Cataloguing in Publication Data
A CIP catalogue record for this book is available from the British Library.

Typeset in 10 on 12 pt Plantin
by Pure Tech India Ltd, Pondicherry
Printed in Great Britain

This book is printed on acid-free paper

Contents

Acknowledgments

I would like to thank those of my colleagues who took the time to offer me their thoughts on my proposed selection of extracts for this collection – Jay Bernstein, Richard Eldridge, Michael Fischer, Karen Hansen, Michael Payne, and of course Stanley Cavell. The usefulness of this volume was, I am sure, much enhanced as a result. I am also grateful to Peter Fosl, for his generosity in allowing me to include a portion of the results of his ongoing bibliographical work on Cavell; it is, and will continue to be, an important scholarly resource. Finally, I would like to thank Alison Baker, who knows why.

Introduction

> In philosophizing, I have to bring my own language and life into imagination. What I require is a convening of my culture's criteria, in order to confront them with my words and life as I pursue them and as I may imagine them; and at the same time to confront my words and my life as I pursue them with the life my culture's words may imagine for me: to confront the culture with itself, along the lines in which it meets in me.
>
> This seems to me a task that warrants the name of philosophy.
>
> Stanley Cavell, *The Claim of Reason* (p. 125)

The burden of Stanley Cavell's philosophy is the acknowledgment of human finitude. His writing attempts to comprehend three interrelated sets of limits or conditions: those of human existence, of the existence of philosophy in modernity, and of its own existence as words written by a particular human being at a particular time and place in the history of modern philosophy. The first set includes such phenomena as embodiment, language, other people, and the world; the second embraces the problematic of skepticism, the absence of God, the politics and morality of liberalism, and the competing claims of neighboring cultural practices – science, literature, theatre, cinema, psychoanalysis; and the third – fixed by its author's understanding of himself as a twentieth-century American musician-turned-philosopher – includes a sensitivity to modernism in the arts and elsewhere, to both the English and the Franco-German traditions of philosophy, and to Emersonian Transcendentalism.

Prose that is continuously responsive to these multiple, complex, and idiosyncratic conditions, the conditions of its own possibility (and what philosophical writing can avoid this responsibility?), is bound to offer obstacles as well as pleasures; and these obstacles – the juxtaposition of texts usually assigned to very different disciplines, a tendency to read texts from one discipline in terms drawn from another, a style that owes as much to literature and psychoanalysis as to philosophy, and an unembarrassed propensity for continuous self-reference – are likely to be much more obtrusive than the rewards consequent upon overcoming them. My aim in this introduction is to offer some preliminary help in finding one's way around those obstacles, by highlighting the structure – and so the intrinsic importance and interest – of the intellectual project that throws them up. Providing a synoptic surview of that project is not possible in so short a space;[1] so I will confine myself to touching upon some central and intersecting themes in Cavell's work.

1 Modernism and Modernity

At several points in Cavell's first collection of essays, *Must We Mean What We Say?*, he acknowledges the significance of his intellectual comradeship and dialogue with the art historian and critic, Michael Fried – one of the most significant theorists of the modernist project in the arts. Fried built upon the work of Clement Greenberg, who claimed that the advent of the Enlightenment, with its attack upon the influence of the church over society and its championing of individual autonomy, had initiated a process in which the various facets of human culture – science, morality, politics – separated themselves out from one another, attempting to establish their autonomy by unearthing or developing the founding principles of their own unique role in the cultural economy. For art, the removal of any external underpinning for aesthetic activity threatened its annihilation or (what comes to the same thing) its transformation into entertainment unless principles unique to its own practice could be discovered; and the same urgent need impelled the various arts making up this sphere each to establish their autonomy by testing their limits, exploring their own conditions of possibility and foregrounding those which were shared with no other art. According to Greenberg, this project began to achieve full self-consciousness in painting by the middle of the nineteenth century; by the mid-twentieth century, serious painters had isolated the flatness of the support as the pure or distinctive condition of their own endeavor, and begun systematically to explore the implications of this discovery for the continuation of their tradition. In so doing, they inverted the traditional order of priority between the two-dimensionality of the painted canvas and the optical or pictorial space made visible by the placement of pigment on that canvas. Whereas traditional painters had worked to ensure that the viewer would pass over the two-dimensionality of the canvas in favour of the depicted (usually three-dimensional) space of the painting, the painters championed by Greenberg – such as Jackson Pollock – made paintings which, without abandoning the responsibility of creating and controlling a pictorial space, exercised it in ways which ensured that they were seen first and primarily as marks on canvas, and so as acknowledging in their pictorial substance the distinctively painterly conditions of their own possibility as works of art.

Modernism thus appears as a condition in which serious painters are no longer able to rely upon agreed conventions inherited from their tradition to establish that what they produce is indeed painting – a contribution to that same tradition of artistic endeavor. Because the issue of what is to count as a painting is at stake in each painting, and because each painting can therefore alter our understanding of what a painting is, the success or failure of a painting is at stake in a new way, putting in question its representation of the living present of the tradition it aims to inherit. Fried accepted much of Greenberg's analysis of the modernist predicament, but he came to reject Greenberg's implicit assumption that what successful modernist paintings uncover is the timeless essence of painting. Artistic success and failure – particularly with reference to the work of Stella, Noland, and Olitski – were discussed in terms of new artistic solutions to problems posed in and by the development of an art; and this came to be expressed as a matter of acknowledging the conditions of the art.

The specific trajectories and outcomes of these discussions are of great intrinsic interest; but there is no necessity to rehearse them in great detail here, since my aim is only to provide a sketch of one possible intellectual context for Cavell's own work. It may, however, be worth noting that the emergence in this context of a concept of acknowledgment, as in something like a contestation with a concept of theatricality, might perhaps be viewed as the first fruits of the complex intellectual dialogue between Cavell and Fried that commenced with Cavell's arrival at Harvard in 1963.[2]

By that time, Cavell had already begun developing an anti-essentialist understanding of the condition of modernism that he not only drew from but also applied to philosophy, crucially through his study of Wittgenstein's *Philosophical Investigations*. He can thus be seen to be engaged in closing the circle opened by Greenberg's application to the arts of a Kantian conception of Enlightened philosophy as essentially critical and self-critical. Cavell therefore defined himself, an American attempting to write philosophy in the 1960s, as one for whom the relation between the past of his enterprise and its present has become problematic. For him, but not just for him (drawing upon philosophy's usual arrogance – but without being able to thematize or ground the issue until his *Pitch of Philosophy*, nearly thirty years later – Cavell takes himself to be representative in some not-yet determined degree), it is no longer clear what will count as a continuation of that enterprise; but since he is not prepared to reject it as an inheritance, he can only carry it forward by writing in a way which explores the present conditions of its possibility – testing the limits of what we are prepared to acknowledge as philosophical prose, and thereby unearthing its present constraints and opportunities. An essentially modern commitment to purified autonomy is thereby transmuted into an essentially modernist concern with (re)defining the integrity of philosophy as one amongst other spheres of human cultural endeavor, and with establishing the distinctiveness of the American inheritance of European philosophy in the mid-twentieth century.

The former concern underlies Cavell's abiding interest in acknowledging the otherness of science and of the other humanities to philosophy. With respect to science, his fear is that philosophy will be subsumed within it, in accordance with an abiding desire of the Anglo-American tradition, so his primary aim is to establish a healthy distance between the two; with respect to other humanistic disciplines or practices – especially literature and literary criticism, cinema and theatre, and psychoanalysis – his aim is more to overcome the prevalent Anglo-American denial that a relationship even exists between philosophical and artistic or therapeutic impulses. This is one motive for his incisive interpretations of the essential differences between scientific and philosophical modes of authority, of the determining conditions of the media of theatre and film,[3] and of the fundamental purposes governing the work of specific artists (Shakespeare,[4] the English Romantics), therapists (Freud, Lacan), and philosophers (Wittgenstein, Heidegger).

Cavell's concern with the distinctiveness of American philosophy creates a more complex mapping of assumptions and themes. In so far as any serious philosophy must address perennial philosophical issues in their distinctively modern guises, Cavell investigates the nature of human existence – the relations between mind and body, subject and objective world, fact and value, individual and community, thought and language – through the lens of a characteristically modern preoccupation which places each of those relations in question: the threat of skepticism. He also asks how the post-Enlightenment concern with autonomy, with human freedom and equality in the aftermath of the decline in the authority of God and of Kings, inflects our best understandings of the human being as a moral agent and as a citizen.[5] But Cavell understands his position as an American philosopher to pose two further challenges – that of maintaining relations with European philosophy in both its English and Franco-German forms, and that of establishing or recovering a distinctively American contribution to that tradition. The first challenge requires that he write in a way that attempts to heal – or at least to acknowledge the suffering presently inflicted by – the split between analytical philosophy (centrally inspired by Frege, Russell, and logical positivism, and dominant in most philosophy departments in America) and what is commonly called "Continental philosophy" (drawing upon phenomenology, existentialism, and deconstruction, and represented most forcefully in some American literature departments). The second challenge led him to the writings of Emerson and Thoreau, and – in a series of highly influential and highly idiosyncratic readings – to reclaim them as philosophers rather than "merely" edifying essayists.

The perspective from which Cavell attempts to meet these complex and interrelated challenges is his inheritance of the tradition of ordinary language philosophy, as represented in the work of Austin and Wittgenstein. He understands their writings to be fundamentally responsive to the threat of skepticism, and takes their constant but radically critical therapeutic engagement with analytical philosophy to provide a potentially fruitful bridge between the two halves of the European philosophical mind; and he suggests that their uncompromising openness to the resources of ordinary language, their perception of it as both cause and cure of the skeptical and metaphysical impulse in philosophy, needs to be underwritten by Emerson's and Thoreau's faith in what they call "the ordinary, the common, the low." To understand Cavell's appropriation of ordinary language philosophy, it is, accordingly, essential to grasp his reading of the Wittgensteinian notion of criteria.

2 Criteria and Skepticism

The modern skeptic denies that we can know that the humanoid creatures around us have a mind or inner life like our own, or that a world external to our own mind exists at all. Most Wittgensteinian philosophers claim that skepticism can be refuted or rejected on the ground that the criteria bequeathed to us by ordinary language can confer certainty on our judgments of the inner states of others and the objects of our world. Cavell's Wittgenstein claims that skepticism can neither be refuted nor accepted; the criteria of ordinary language are and must be open to repudiation in the way favored by the skeptic, but such repudiation does not reveal the limitations of human knowing – it denies the conditions for the possibility of human knowledge and human existence.

What are criteria? They are the linguistic specifications in terms of which competent speakers judge whether something falls under a specific concept; they therefore link human beings with one another and align them with the world. But criteria do not simply control the way we talk about objects: they also determine their essential nature. Many things we wish to know about the world can only be unearthed by empirical investigation, but any such endeavor presupposes the prior alignment of words and world that criteria facilitate; in their absence, we would not know what to look for in our investigation of the facts. We cannot discover whether the liquid in a given bottle is water unless we know what would constitute its being water, what has to be the case for it to count as water – and that is a matter of knowing when to say of something that it is water. This criterial or grammatical structure can and must be investigated from our armchairs, by drawing upon our competence as speakers, our ability to apply words to the world; and since criteria determine what is is for something to be water, a boat, a chair and so on – since essence is expressed by grammar, as Wittgenstein has it – a grammatical investigation can tell us as much about the world as it does about language.

Cavell thinks of this as criteria telling us what counts – but in a dual sense of that word. First, criteria are criteria of individuation: in determining what counts *as* a chair or a table, they determine what differentiates a chair from a table. Second, criteria make manifest what counts *for* human beings: by determining how human beings individuate things, they trace the distinctions and connections which matter to them – the ones which count. The structure of our concepts is thus an expression of human interests, of which aspects of the world we deem significant enough to wish to get a grip on; and the agreement in criteria upon which that structure rests is an expression of the ways in which our interests in and reactions to the things of the world are attuned. To agree in criteria means that we share routes of interest and feeling, modes of response, a sense of similarity, significance, outrageousness and so on – that we share in forms of life.[6]

Since our ability to make judgments about the world depends upon our agreeing in criteria, it is hardly surprising that the skeptical philosopher should be anxious about the reliability of the judgments they facilitate; if our connection with the world is most fundamentally a matter of certain linguistic conventions and attunements, why should we believe that such fragile and seemingly anthropocentric agreements connect us with the world as it really is? What Cavell calls the truth in skepticism lies here. For the skeptic rightly rejects the common-sense view that our grip on the world is most fundamentally cognitive – that the connection between pain and behavior expressive of pain is something we believe to hold, or that the existence of material objects is something that we know for certain. The truth is that, since criteria are the condition for the possibility of knowledge-claims, they cannot themselves be items of knowledge. Criteria specify what must be the case if something is to count as an instance of a certain kind, but they do not claim that any given thing is of that kind, or even that there is such an instance anywhere in the world; they determine the grammar of a word, they do not employ that word to make a claim about reality.

Consequently, the skeptic's final position is no better than the common sense view. For in so far as she simply denies that we ever know that

someone is in pain or that material objects exist, she continues to treat
the issue as if it were cognitive (merely reversing the signs from positive
to negative, as it were); whereas, if our relationship to the world is
fundamentally criterial, it cannot intelligibly be assessed in terms of truth
and falsity. The (behavioral) criteria for pain cannot get the true nature
of pain wrong, because they fix what is to count as "pain;" anything that
fails to fit those criteria will not be an instance of pain, and anything that
does, will. So, unhesitating belief in the truth of criteria and skeptical
doubts about it are equally misplaced. Nevertheless, since criteria are
based on agreement, a skeptical repudiation of such agreement is a
standing human possibility; anything essentially conventional must be
vulnerable to the withdrawal of consent. So it can never be right to
combat skepticism either by claiming that criteria confer certainty, or by
denying the possibility of their repudiation. What must rather be shown
is the true cost of that repudiation; for if criteria determine the use, and
so the meaning, of our words, to refuse them is to deprive oneself of the
power of coherent speech. The skeptic's predicament is that she finds
herself compelled either to say something other than she meant, or to say
nothing meaningful at all.[7]

But is this really what happens when someone denies the reality of
other minds or the external world? What, for example, goes linguistically
awry when the skeptic attempts to generate doubts about whether another can ever know my pain with the certainty that is available to me by
claiming that "others can learn of my sensations only from my behavior?"
Wittgenstein points out that the word "only" is here being employed in
the absence of its usual criteria; for if it were being used normally, it
would imply the existence of another, superior route to this knowledge –
and since there is no such alternative available to third parties, it must be
one utilized by the person whose sensation it is. But this amounts to
implying that a person in pain typically *learns* that she is in pain – a use
of the word "learn" that is highly aberrant, and that distances the person
from her own sensations in just the way that the original claim was meant
to contradict (effectively eliminating the difference between first-person
and third-person perspectives). Cavell adds that our puzzlement about
why otherwise competent speakers should misuse "only" in this way may
be alleviated by noting that the misuse seems expressive of the speaker's
disappointment with behavior – not with some particularly ambiguous
twitch or wince but with behavior as such, as if she sees her body as
standing in the way of other people's knowledge of her mind. Picturing
the body as an impenetrable integument rather than as the field of
expression of a soul misrepresents the nature of human embodiment,
repudiating our grasp of what it is to be one human creature amongst
others; and it does so in a way which satisfies a need to place the human

mind beyond reach. For such a fantasy of necessary inexpressiveness lets me think of myself as powerless to make myself known, and thus simultaneously absolves me of any responsibility to make myself known and removes the fear that I am really or fully known by others.[8]

The above case exemplifies what one might call a local repudiation of criteria, an attempt to speak outside those language games which involve concepts of mind and body. But for Cavell, all philosophical problems and confusions have the same general physiognomy – all involve repudiating criteria of one kind or another; and if so, the question arises: what human need does the satisfaction of that *general* skeptical impulse serve? What is it about criteria as such (rather than, say, specifically psychological criteria) that sometimes compels otherwise competent speakers to refuse them? Cavell offers two interlinked answers.

First: if criteria always both determine kinds of object and attribute value or interest to those kinds, any philosopher who repudiates them loses the capacity to discriminate between and to respond to the phenomena of the world. Unable to distinguish one thing or event or mood from another, she annihilates the differences between those things – which amounts to annihilating the world that they make up. And she refuses her participation in the modes of interest and response to which criteria give expression; by speaking outside the structure of our language games, she denies that the phenomena of the world matter to her in any way, and so withdraws her investment of interest in it. In short, violating the criteria of words strips the world of its variegated specificity and value. The philosopher annihilates the world by annihilating its capacity to elicit her interest; she is driven past caring for it, it goes dead for her and recedes from her grasp. On this interpretation, philosophical skeptics bring about the death of their world and of their interest in it (which means the death of a part of themselves); hence Cavell's interest in the various representatives of Romanticism, who endlessly claimed that this was the state into which human life is endlessly bringing itself and its habitat.

Second: on this account, criteria constitute the limits or conditions of the human capacity to know, think, or speak about the world and the various things that are in it – they are that without which human knowledge of the world would not be possible; but it is fatally easy to interpret limits as limitations, to experience conditions as constraints. And of course, this is how the skeptic often understands her own motives: she repudiates our ordinary reliance upon criteria because she regards what we ordinarily count as knowledge as nothing of the kind, as failing to put us into contact with the world as it really is. But it would only make sense to think of the conditions of human knowledge as limitations if we could conceive of another cognitive perspective upon the world that did not require them; but philosophers from Kant onwards have variously striven to show that there is no such perspective – that the absence of the concepts or categories in terms of which we individuate objects would not clear the way for unmediated knowledge of the world, but would rather remove the possibility of anything that might count as knowledge. In other words, what the skeptic understands as a process of disillusionment in the name of true knowledge, Cavell interprets as an inability or refusal to acknowledge the fact that human knowledge – the knowledge available to finite creatures, subjective agents in an objective world – is necessarily conditioned. But, as Cavell finds himself having to remind us, nothing is more human than the desire to deny the human, to interpret limits as limitations and to repudiate the human condition of conditionedness or finitude in the name of the unconditioned, the transcendent, the inhuman. On Cavell's understanding of the matter, philosophical skepticism – flourishing in a culture conditioned by the death of God and the rise of the new science – is a modern inflection of the prideful human craving to be God, of the perennial human desire to deny one's own humanity.

3 The Human Form of Life: Language, Gender, Identity

Since Cavell identifies himself with the Wittgensteinian therapeutic project of attempting serially to overcome the innumerable particular manifestations of this endemic skeptical impulse, much of his later writing can be seen as investigating the various ways in which that project might best be carried out. Since, however, he sees skepticism as endemic to modernity rather than simply to philosophy, Cavell often pursues this investigation in non-philosophical dimensions of modern culture – particularly literature, psychoanalysis, and cinema. And in so doing, he develops a highly distinctive understanding of the modern significance of three defining conditions of human existence – language, gender, and selfhood.

His inheritance of Wittgenstein leads him to give a prominent role to language in this therapeutic project. As we have already seen, philosophical skepticism takes the form of refusing criteria, which constitute the grammatical framework of language; accordingly, to refuse to succumb to the skeptical impulse demands a capacity to recall criteria, to remind oneself of what counts in both senses of that term – what Wittgenstein calls a grammatical investigation. We will thus be reminded not only of what counts as a certain kind of object, but of our attributions of a certain kind of interest or value to that object; and in so doing, we will be reminded of the true nature of objects and of our own life with those objects – we will at once acknowledge language, the world, and our humanity instead of attempting to deny them. In so doing, of course, we will trace out the multifarious ways in which our words are woven into our practical activities, social institutions, and culture – into our form of life. "Form of life" thus has both a social and a biological sense: it refers to the differences between one particular cultural practice and another, and to that which distinguishes human life forms from those of other species. Our species-specific endowment centrally includes the capacity to acquire and deploy language – talking is the human form of life; but that capacity can be variously realized, with each human being speaking some particular language and inhabiting some particular modification of society and culture that the talking form of life makes possible.[9]

Accordingly, when the skeptic refuses the limits of language as such, she refuses a defining condition of her own humanity; but when Wittgenstein talks of grammatical investigations as returning us to the ordinary or the everyday, or as requiring that we accept forms of life as given, he need not be counselling an acceptance of the particular inflection of our interests, capacities, and needs that prevails at a given historical juncture. On the contrary: the actual everyday may have to be overthrown if the eventual everyday – the real possibilities of the distinctively human life form that are covered over by particular cultural formations as well as by enactments of skeptical thinking – are to be realized. For example, a grammatical investigation of psychological concepts can show that our common belief that no other person could have exactly the same pain as me depends upon (incoherently) treating the possessor of a pain as a property of the pain itself, and so manifests a false sense of our separateness as persons by forcing a non-existent uniqueness upon our experience; but the skepticism of which this belief is the intellectual expression is also something that pervades our ordinary lives – we exist within this mislocated sense of our separateness and commonality, we live our skepticism.

The form of philosophical practice that is required to oppose skepticism therefore need not be a reactionary reiteration of whatever happens to be the case, but might rather revolutionize our ordinary life with language. Recalling criteria leaves everything as it is, but not in the sense that it requires cultural or linguistic conservatism; the passivity it demands is a species of forbearance, a refusal of the all-too-human desire for the linguistically (and so socially and biologically) unconditioned, a refusal to impose (philosophical and cultural) preconceptions upon language, the world it opens up for us, and the life we lead within it. It asks us to let our words teach us the present and possible place of each specific thing in our form of life, and so the present and possible configurations of our life form; and then it calls us actively to maintain or enact the best of those possibilities, in the name of a world worthy of the investment of our interest and desire.

Many of Cavell's readings of specific plays, poems, stories, and films focus upon enactments of this struggle with skepticism. In Shakespearian tragedies, the poems and stories of English, German, and American Romantics, and the genre of Hollywood movies Cavell labels "comedies of remarriage,"[10] he follows out the fates of human beings caught up in relationships with others in which skepticism about other minds is lived out and stands as exemplary of skepticism in general. In terms made familiar by Romanticism, the human capacity to revive self and world by recovering an interest in its autonomous yet environing life is figured by the capacity of these couples to acknowledge one another as separate and yet related; the vicissitudes of their weddedness to one another symbolize the vicissitudes of human weddedness to the world. And on a different level, the continued telling of tales capable of exploring such issues with sophistication and control indicates a continuing human ability to maintain genres and forms of cultural production worthy of the investments of human significance they inherited and continue to claim. But Cavell does not regard such texts as non-philosophical illustrations of independently derived philosophical theses. The fact that their central concern is recognizably skepticism rather suggests an unsettling of any received wisdom about the placing of borders between the philosophical and that which lies outside it; and the details of their treatment of skeptical issues is often Cavell's primary motivation for refining or redirecting his more obviously philosophical investigations of those issues.[11]

The most significant instance of this illumination of philosophy by the non-philosophical is Cavell's sudden realization that skepticism is inflected by gender. Given that so many of the relationships examined in the texts he has studied are between a man and a woman, an insight of this kind or order seems predictable in retrospect; but it was first sparked through his reading of *The Winter's Tale*. In that play, Leontes represents the skeptic, with his sudden and calamitous collapse into jealousy about Hermione's faithfulness appearing as a virtual transcription of Descartes' *Meditations*. But the precise form of his skeptical doubt (a worry about whether his child is his own) is simply not available to a woman; it is the doubt of a father, a man's anxiety. This exclusivity or restriction was entirely consonant with Cavell's long-held suspicion about the couples in the Hollywood comedies of remarriage; despite his intuition that these films bear up under the burden of assigning prime responsibility for the success of the relationship to the man's capacity to re-educate the woman's desires as well as his own, Cavell sensed a taint of villainy in even the best of these men (Spencer Tracy eating his [liquorice] gun in *Adam's Rib* is perhaps the signature moment of this anxiety). But it remained unclear what the implications of this insight might be. Did it signal that skepticism as such was no business of women – to their cost as well as their benefit? Or that certain forms of skepticism are peculiar to the male – and so, that there are others which are the prerogative of the female? Or did it signify that the skeptical impulse in modernity and the impulse to overcome skepticism draw upon aspects or conditions of the human mind and heart that might illuminatingly be conceptualized as male and female respectively?

Cavell's work on psychoanalysis made an important contribution to the task of answering these questions.[12] As well as utilizing its discoveries about and conceptualizations of human motivation to illuminate his readings of literature and philosophy, he interpreted the creation and development of this cultural practice as a stage in the battle against skepticism in modern Western culture. The Freudian project can be characterized as an attempt to render humanly comprehensible certain modes of pathological behavior with no evident psychological meaning, and so to extend and deepen the human capacity to acknowledge seemingly aberrant behavior as a part (however twisted a part) of our shared human world; it thus helps to flesh out what it might mean to acknowledge the sheer humanity of the other – a traditional anti-skeptical aspiration of Romanticism. From the viewpoint of philosophy, psychoanalysis embodies the intuition that there are regions of the mind that go beyond consciousness; so its practical success is a proof of the existence of the unconscious mind, and so a practical proof of the mind's existence (as unconscious) that avoids the fate of Descartes' famous attempted proof by denying his denial of the existence of those regions of the mind. Understood in this way, the fact that Freudian clinical practice is founded upon his studies of primarily female case histories signifies that this mode of acknowledging human existence in the face of skepticism is to be thought of as essentially female.

Women attain such centrality in the founding case histories because of what Freud calls their capacity for hysterical conversion – a psycho-physical aptitude for allowing very large sums of excitation to find bodily expression rather than being transposed into consciousness or discharged into practice. This can be thought of as a talent for communication, a capacity to enact one's existence by acknowledging one's body, and the specific body of one's expressions, as one's own; it thereby vanquishes skeptical anxieties about the reality of the embodied human psyche. But of course, although women might possess this capacity to a distinctive degree, it is available to every psycho-physical being, and so cannot be unavailable to men. Indeed, since Freud's therapeutic project presupposes his capacity to see the life of the mind in hysterical symptom-formation, since his practice depends upon his capacity to let the meaning of such bodily modifications find expression in his interpretations, psychoanalysis as such depends for its efficacy upon the therapist's capacity to adopt or accept the position of the woman. When this capacity is lacking – when, for example, the woman is interrogated in a manner which suggests (along lines classically associated with skepticism about other minds) that her certainty about her own existence depends upon her possession of some piece of knowledge that men lack and jealously desire – the therapist adopts the position of the man and thereby forces psychoanalysis to betray its most central promise. But either way, the implication is that the gender-inflection of skepticism and its overcoming should be read as relating not to men and women but to the male and female sides of a broader human character.

By thinking of hysterical conversion as feminine and coercive interrogation as masculine, Cavell implicitly commits himself to a highly contestable, morally and politically fraught association of feminity with passivity and masculinity with activity. But its fruitfulness or sterility depends critically upon how the terms "activity" and "passivity" are to be understood; and their meaning for Cavell is in crucial part fixed by their significance in non-psychoanalytic domains – for example, in the Wittgensteinian understanding of skepticism. The practice of recounting criteria – the capacity to allow one's know-how as a competent speaker to recall the true significance of words and world, to allow oneself to be known in the body of one's expressions – is clearly analogous to the feminine capacity for hysterical conversion; but the passivity of this mode of thinking takes a peculiarly active inflection (demanding revolutionary revisions of our conception of ourselves and our world, and radical action to enact them), and is of course highly valued as the way to overcome skepticism. By contrast, skepticism itself, the fate which the human intellect struggles to avoid, appears as a form of active thinking, a jealous interrogation of the world – although with a peculiarly passive inflection (its violent attempts to clutch at reality alternating with a deadened, apathetic acceptance of its inevitable recession from the human grasp). If passivity and activity are defined by reference to these paradigms, then their association with feminity and masculinity is more likely to unsettle than to entrench orthodox understandings of the sharp differences between, and the relative worth of, the male and female aspects of human character.

In order to accommodate his sense of the human mind and heart as perennially torn between its active and passive sides – between masculinity and femininity, between the conscious will and unconscious drives, between skepticism and its overcoming – Cavell has utilized the tradition of distinctively American thinking founded by Emerson and Thoreau (the tradition of Emersonian perfectionism) to develop a conception of the self as ineluctably split or doubled.[13] To be a self, a human individual, one must be capable of relating to oneself in a variety of ways (love, hate, knowledge, ignorance), including that of adopting a detached or impartial perspective upon oneself; one can thereby take an interest in oneself as having attained a particular state and as capable of moving beyond that state. When that capacity is active, the self becomes engaged in an endless process of self-development – endless because every attained state of the self neighbors a further, unattained but attainable state which forms its horizon, its possible future. However, that capacity need not be active; it may even be entirely eclipsed, whether by the settled attractions of remaining in the state one has already attained or by the efforts of oneself and others to disguise the attractions of one's neighboring, unattained but attainable self. But the eclipse of that openness to the unattained future amounts to the eclipse of the self's capacity to grow, to change itself in the name of a better or higher state of self and of society; and the loss of that capacity is the loss of an essential aspect of selfhood – the capacity to set and pursue, but particularly to revise, one's conception of the good.

This perfectionist notion of the self as conditioned by an ineliminable internal doubleness is clearly indebted to the early Heidegger's understanding of human existence as always thrown from the past into the present and projecting into the future, and as necessarily either mired in inauthenticity or authentically free to attain genuine individuality. It is also figured in Cavell's early contrast between cinema and theatre: the dominance of actor over character in movies represents the self's fatedness to its own existence, whereas the dominance of character over actor in plays represents its journeying from state to state.[14] But – as the last sentence of the preceding paragraph implies – it can also be thought of as underlying the characteristically modern liberal moral and political concern with individual autonomy.[15]

This seemingly self-directed concern with one's spiritual well-being has critical implications for the essentially other-directed concerns of morality and politics, because it is only by cultivating a sensitivity to the claims of one's unattained self that one develops a responsiveness to the genuine needs of others. To put matters in Kantian terms: the essentially other-directed moral law must be not only followed but internalized – it must be addressed to the self by the self, become an expression of the self's autonomy rather than its conformity to external coercion. But then the proper enactment of that law presupposes that those who apply it are genuinely autonomous, that they have a living, genuine self from which and to which that law is delivered; and the cultivation of such genuine selfhood precisely requires a concern for one's unattained self. The consequences of abandoning that cultivation are dramatized in the Hollywood melodramas of the unknown woman, which trace the struggles of women whose openness to self-development is variously stifled or tri-vialized by the men in their lives and the society in which they find themselves, and in which that society's moral and political health de-pends upon the women's capacity to maintain their sense of outrage and society's capacity to nurture individuals able to respond to that outrage as expressive of a generalized injustice. What Cavell sees in liberal political theorists (specifically Rawls) are the consequences of losing touch with that responsiveness: an excessively contractualized under-standing of the social contract, in which the inability to ground a cry of injustice in accepted principles of right political action licenses a refusal to respond to that cry rather than an acknowledgment that our principles as they stand might fail fully to capture our sense of what justice de-mands.

4 Cavell Reading

Since the intellectual project whose main landmarks have just been adumbrated is driven from beginning to end by Cavell's interpretations of specific texts, and since it is modern philosophy's obligation endlessly to explore the conditions of its own possibility, it seems fitting to bring this introduction to an end by exploring the defining conditions of the Cavellian genre of textual interpretation. I will touch upon three of those conditions: his conception of words and language, his conception of authorial intention, and his conception of the relation between writers and readers of perfectionist texts.

Whether reading philosophical or literary texts, Cavell's interpretations implicitly assume that the words which comprise them are governed by criteria that can be elucidated in ordinary ways – in other words, that their significance can be computed with the resources that any compe-tent speaker who has lived an unremarkable human life is capable of bringing to bear. This approach clearly grows from his allegiance to Wittgenstein's philosophical faith in ordinary language. But Cavell does not interpret this as a trust in the verities of common sense or some specifiable sector of language as such; it is a reliance upon natural language as opposed to formal languages or logical calculi, and upon criteria as opposed to their skeptical rejection. The words of ordinary language are therefore not the repository of a certainty to which the skeptic is wilfully blind; rather their criterial foundation is the condition for the possibility of skepticism. Accordingly, Cavell is not complacent about the security or obviousness of the conclusions that his reminders or recountings of criteria generate; he acknowledges from the outset that these reminders test the limits of our agreement in criteria rather than presupposing that this agreement is limitless. Moreover, in so far as recounting criteria presupposes that Cavell allows his competence as a speaker to teach him what he has overlooked but cannot quite never have known, it entails that he stand as an other to his own self; and this means that the criteria his investigations elicit may surprise himself as much as they do others. In particular, they may elicit a surprising account of what counts as "language;" they might uncover an often-unacknowledged grammar for the word "word."

In fact, Cavell has come to attribute a certain autonomy to the life of words. He has, for example, taken up Austin's dictum that words come trailing clouds of etymology – that their history is still operative in their present lives; and he has also become inclined to decompose words into elements which possess a meaning that is not evidently operative in the words they inhabit, but which appear to have significance in the texts that those words make up.[16] Nevertheless, the very real autonomy he thereby attributes to words and their parts is essentially relative; for these ranges of signification are never entirely beyond human acknowledgment, but can be recovered by careful readings – as must be the case if words have criteria that are ultimately determined by the uses to which they are put in human forms of life. He is therefore not inclined to endorse the post-structuralist perception that linguistic meaning is essentially beyond human control. Such perceptions typically appear in Cavell's work as over-reactions to admittedly incoherent metaphysical theses; in their reactiveness, they participate in the very metaphysical impulse they claim to overcome. On Cavell's view, for example, Derrida's emphasis upon the iterability of words (their capacity to be cited in an indefinite number of contexts) underlines a grammatical point about the concept of a word (since nothing incapable of being reused in new contexts could be used to say something meaningful); it therefore justifies the rejection of meta-physical assumptions that word-meaning is fixed for example by self-present mental images, but it does not license the equally metaphysical conclusion that words uttered in a specific context cannot have a specific and recoverable meaning.

Beyond these more recent developments, however, Cavell's work both early and late has staked the claim that human languages have the three following conditions. A language is totally and systematically meaningful – its words invite projection into certain contexts and refuse others, each in accord with its utterly specific criteria; words are meant by human beings – they express or conceal the beliefs and convictions of the person who ordered them; and the saying of something as and when it is said is as significant as the meaning and ordering of the words said.[17] These conditions shape Cavell's readings of texts from the very beginning (as he acknowledges in the prologue to his reading of *King Lear*, "The Avoidance of Love"). They license his attentiveness to every line and phrase as a potentially significant contribution to the meaning of the text as a whole – and so his tendency to treat individual texts as integral wholes. They underwrite his assumption that the meanings of words spoken by characters in texts are a function of their significance as words and the significance of their being uttered at a given time by a given individual. And they ground his overarching presupposition that the significance of the orderings of words which comprise a given text is something meant or intended by its author.

Naturally, Cavell takes the notion of "intention" with which he is working to be the ordinary, familiar one; so he takes recent critical attempts to dissuade us from so employing it to be based on metaphysical misinterpretations of this concept. Some critics reject critical references to the artist's intentions because they picture an intention as existing in the artist's head and having only a causal relation to the artwork; they thereby fail to see that intention and outcome are internally related – that nothing is more visible than what was and was not meant by a certain action, visible in the correctly executed action or in the slip or mistake that marred it. Invoking intentions does not therefore drive us outside the artwork, but further into it; it does not focus on the artist's biography, but on what she has succeeded in realizing in her chosen medium – and since what she does achieve may either go beyond or diverge significantly from what she initially understood herself to be aiming for, the true nature of her actual success may come as much as a surprise to her as to the critic who first identifies it to her. Limiting the artist's authority over her intentions in this way does not make Cavell's references to her intentions otiose, for preoccupations of the mind and the independence of the world entail that human actions typically have consequences that may outrun the agent's initial foresight. This does not mean that she flatly is or flatly isn't responsible for those consequences; it means rather that she is then flatly responsible for determining her relation to them – whether and how to claim them as unforeseeable or simply unforeseen, to accept them as meant or excuse them as unintended. The artist's dialogue with her critic is one way in which such determinations are made out in the case of actions which celebrate the fact that human beings can intend the things they do. And since, on Cavell's view, the first fact about works of art is that they are meant – that is, that they are the sort of thing that people make in order to elicit a certain sort of interest from other people – a refusal to relate to artworks in these terms would amount to a refusal to relate to them as works of art.[18]

One can think of such factors as the meaningfulness of language and the intendedness of human action as conditions for the possibility of textual production, and so as inevitably thematic for readers and writers in the condition of modernism. Cavell's readings of texts foreground those conditions because he believes that they must be acknowledged in any texts produced by writers who understand themselves as searching for ways to inherit the enterprise of serious human uses of language. Since that enterprise is central to his understanding of what it might mean to fight against the skeptical impulse in modernity, to engage in it amounts to committing oneself to maintaining the possibility of human progress from our present, attained state of culture – with its deadened responses to nature, self, and world – to unattained but attainable states in which we might find ourselves capable of reinvesting our interest in our worldly life with words. In so far as the texts Cavell studies hold out this prospect to their readers, they specify their author as exemplifying the eclipse of the attained self by the unattained self, and their reader as exemplifying the inverse condition; and their orderings of words appear as designed to liberate their reader's unattained self. The conception of the relation between author and reader that they embody thus mirrors the conception of internal duplexity that perfectionism identifies as a condition of human existence, and does so with the aim of shifting the balance in the inner economy of their readers.[19]

This vision of a certain sort of reading as essentially redemptive draws heavily upon Cavell's understanding of the relation between analyst and patient in psychoanalytic therapy; in effect, that vision is one in which the perfectionist text takes up the position of analyst rather than analysand. The reader does not interpret, but rather is interpreted by, the (author of the) text; exemplifying a mode of active passivity, the text invites transferences from its reader, projections of unconscious thoughts, fears, and desires, with the ultimate aim of responding to that onslaught in ways that disrupt its mechanical, fixated effects on the reader's interpretations of her own existence and world. This response will itself be shaped by counter-transference; the text will contain an image or fantasy of itself and its readers, one that guides its questioning and working through of the unacknowledged material elicited by the transference, and which ultimately aims at encouraging a process of mourning in its reader – a detachment from an outmoded pattern of desire in favour of new possibilities, the transformation of nostalgia into freedom. The process of reading thus becomes a process of reorienting desire: the reader submits to the seduction of the text in order to be seduced away from her fixated desires and restored to a desire to live her own life. Its end-point cannot therefore be a new fixation on the text; the text must conclude its seductions by repelling its reader from any such concrete identification – its voice is exemplary of the reader's unattained self, but it cannot dictate the content of her new, autonomously willed state. This is why Cavell's readings inculcate a sense that the text under interpretation delivers up thoughts that are his, but that he did not know he had – thoughts hitherto unacknowledged as his own returning with an uncanny sense of familiarity.

Since, on Cavell's account, the psychoanalyst works with the analysand in these ways to give expression to the conditions that condition the latter's utterly specific life, then to think of perfectionist texts as adopting the position of the analyst and himself – their reader – that of the analysand entails that the writings in which he develops the tuition those texts provide will give expression to the conditions of his own, utterly specific, life of thought. This is why Cavell's writing is inevitably and increasingly self-referential in style; it is why, for example, his most recent writing to date has taken an explicitly autobiographical turn. Methodologically, that reflexivity is an acknowledgment of the reliance of the ordinary-language philosopher upon a species of self-knowledge; to recall criteria is to speak of "what we say when," and so presumes that the philosopher's imaginings of what she would say or do can be representative of other speakers. In other words, the authority of ordinary language philosophy is autobiographical; modes of self-reference empower everything it does. When, therefore, Cavell offers endlessly revised accounts of the conditions of his own intellectual project, or his life as a thinker, this does not necessarily amount to narcissism or self-indulgence (although it necessarily runs those risks); he is utilizing autobiography to ground his authority to speak for philosophy and the intellectual life. He is testing, essaying, the degree to which his inheritance of this method and these interests are representative or exemplary of what it is to inherit the life of thought as such, here and now.

If, however, the perfectionist or psychoanalytic model correctly specifies Cavell's relations to the texts he reads, it should also exemplify our relation to the texts he writes. Their author declares himself to have been converted to this task by his own heroic writers; but the task itself leads him to picture his readers in his own image – as capable of, but standing in need of the same kind of help if they are to realize, the openness of the genuinely autonomous self. This openness is to a future state of self, words, and world in which the best possibilities of the human form of life are recovered from repression, in which the axis of our explorations is reoriented around the fixed point of our real needs, and in which the various aspects of human culture can more responsibly acknowledge the finitude of the creature whose psycho-physical being is sufficiently complex for it to be burdened with language. It is a daunting invitation – but also an exhilarating one.

On such an understanding of what it means to be a reader of Cavell, however, it is not just permissible but obligatory for me to conclude this introduction on a more autobiographical note. In one sense, of course, this book – taken as a whole – inevitably strikes such a note; to offer an organized selection of Cavell's texts as a *Cavell Reader* is to lay out in great (if largely implicit) detail my personal interpretation of his *oeuvre*, and so amounts to specifying my (doubtless idiosyncratic) relation to those texts. But one facet of my self-understanding as a reader of Cavell may be worth underlining. I talked just now of deriving from Cavell an idea of openness as part of what is involved in the possession of a genuinely autonomous self; and I want to stress how pertinent that concern is for those who take Wittgenstein's writing as an exemplary achievement in philosophy. For it is, I think, commonly believed that one of the most baleful of the many dangerous aspects of Wittgenstein's influence is that he deprives his readers of any sense of a future for philosophy – that the *Philosophical Investigations* closes off any possibility of their continuing to philosophize. This danger is real: it was certainly the position in which I found myself during my graduate studies. After working on Wittgenstein for three or four years, I took myself to have learned that the Anglo-American philosophical tradition in its contemporary forms could not survive Wittgenstein's critique; I had stopped trying to deny my strong interest in French and German philosophy, but could see no way in which their grounding assumptions might survive a Wittgensteinian critique either; and I could not find a way of writing philosophy that was true to Wittgenstein's basic insights without merely (more or less competently) reproducing them – whether by reiterating those insights or by mechanically applying his general methodological principles to areas of the subject upon which he did not explicitly comment. It was not clear to me then that such a way of proceeding might amount to a failure to inherit Wittgenstein's thought as a living tradition; but it was clear that such a way of proceeding would not satisfy me, because it left out too much of my self – too many of the interests and desires that led me to philosophy in the first place.

Then, in 1984, I read *The Claim of Reason*; and it showed me that a love of Wittgenstein did not necessarily go together with a loss of interest in philosophy. By taking seriously Wittgenstein's uncertainty over the inheritability of his thought, by connecting that anxiety with the question of how the form of his writing related to its content, and by showing how to write recognizably philosophical prose that was at once indebted to Wittgenstein's own and yet responsive to an independent constellation of (philosophical and not obviously philosophical) interests, that book demonstrated that the future of philosophy after Wittgenstein was still open and that there was a place in it for me. Perhaps most importantly, however, it showed that taking up that place, finding a philosophical opening, meant relating to other philosophers and other philosophical traditions in a manner which enabled rather than inhibited one's individuality; it exemplified the difference between taking a text as exemplary or representative, and taking it as definitive or coercive. In short, Cavell's writing showed me how to go on from my particular inheritance as a philosopher; and it is my hope that this selection of his texts will be similarly enabling for its readers.

Notes

1 Those interested in such an account should refer to my *Stanley Cavell: Philosophy's Recounting of the Ordinary* (Oxford: Oxford University Press, 1994).
2 Further developments or consequences of this dialogue are recorded in Cavell's acknowledgments of Fried's influence in Essays 5 and 6 of this collection. For an account by one of Fried's students of certain phases of these exchanges, see "Mutual Facing: A Memoir of Friedom" by Steven Z. Levine, in J. Beaulieu, M. Roberts, and T. Ross (eds) *The Writings of Michael Fried* (University of Indiana Press, forthcoming).
3 See Essay 8 for theatre, and Essay 9 for film.
4 See Essay 11.
5 For Cavell's views on religion, see especially Essay 7, and – obliquely – Essay 4.
6 See Essay 1.
7 See Essay 4.
8 See Essays 2 and 3.
9 See Essay 16.
10 See Essay 10.
11 See Essay 15.
12 See Essay 12.
13 See Essay 14.
14 A point I owe to Howard Caygill; see Essay 9.
15 See Essay 17.
16 See Essay 15.
17 See Essay 14.
18 See Essay 6.
19 See Essay 17.

Prologue: The Avoidance of Love (The Abdication Scene)

Placing this early passage from Cavell's earliest and most influential reading of a Shakespeare play at the opening of this selection of his writings seems essential. The other passages from "The Avoidance of Love" that appear here deal with themes that are central to *King Lear*; but they take us away from the detailed texture of the play, and so offer a misleading impression of Cavell's interpretative approach. His reading of the abdication scene perfectly exemplifies his favored mode of attention to the words of a literary work, and indeed of any text: one directed to the voice that says them, and through that to the phenomenology of the straits of mind in which only those words said in that order will suffice. Here, we can see one central affinity between Cavell's literary-critical and his philosophical attunements. His interpretations of Lear and Cordelia in effect answer the question of why they say what they say when they say it; their words and deeds appear as the actions of ordinary human beings in the everyday contexts of familial intimacy and emotional stress from which other interpretations – however unintentionally – have dislocated them.

In effecting this restoration, Cavell shows us what it might mean for a father to fail to acknowledge his daughter; his fear of the demands that her love seems to make upon him forces them both into a situation where that love is incapable of being given expression. Here, the seemingly vague concept of "acknowledgment" – so central to Cavell's early work – is seen to have a strong internal logic: failures of acknowledgment feed upon themselves and devour both the person who initiates them and the one who suffers them. Moreover, the wider context of the essay makes it clear that, for Cavell, appreciating the logic of acknowledgment and its failures is the key to understanding skepticism – both within philosophy and outside it. Less explicitly, Cavell's reading of this scene already raises questions of skepticism and gender identity or identification. Is it purely

Originally published in *Must We Mean What We Say? A Book of Essays*, by Stanley Cavell (Cambridge: Cambridge University Press, 1969), pp. 285–93. Reprinted by permission.

coincidental that this failure of acknowledgment – what Cavell thinks of as living out the skeptical impulse – is orchestrated by a man and victimizes a woman? In recalling his readers to this obvious fact about the abdication scene, is Cavell drawing upon a capacity to acknowledge some aspect of himself in the King, or in the king's daughter? And if – as Cavell's autobiographical reflections explicitly acknowledge (cf. chapter 1 of *A Pitch of Philosophy*) – the aspect of himself he drew upon involved his relations with his father, what does this say about the relations between critical and clinical matters, between the universal and the personal registers of the human voice? In this sense, the main phases of Cavell's intellectual project were always already discernible in his understanding of the divisions of Lear's kingdom; from these recountings, his intellectual fate unfolded.

We now have elements with which to begin an analysis of the most controversial of the *Lear* problems, the nature of Lear's motivation in his opening (abdication) scene. The usual interpretations follow one of three main lines: Lear is senile; Lear is puerile; Lear is not to be understood in natural terms, for the whole scene has a fairy tale or ritualistic character which simply must be accepted as the premise from which the tragedy is derived. Arguments ensue, in each case, about whether Shakespeare is justified in what he is asking his audience to accept. My hypothesis will be that Lear's behaviour in this scene is explained by – the tragedy begins because of – the same motivation which manipulates the tragedy throughout its course, from the scene which precedes the abdication, through the storm, blinding, evaded reconciliations, to the final moments: by the attempt to avoid recognition, the shame of exposure, the threat of self-revelation.

Shame, first of all, is the right kind of candidate to serve as motive, because it is the emotion whose effect is most precipitate and out of proportion to its cause, which is just the rhythm of the *King Lear* plot as a whole. And with this hypothesis we need not assume that Lear is either incomprehensible or stupid or congenitally arbitrary and inflexible and extreme in his conduct. Shame itself is exactly arbitrary, inflexible and extreme in its effect. It is familiar to find that what mortifies one person seems wholly unimportant to another: think of being ashamed of one's origins, one's accent, one's ignorance, one's skin, one's clothes, one's legs or teeth. . . . It is the most isolating of feelings, the most comprehensible perhaps in idea, but the most incomprehensible or incommunicable in fact. Shame, I've said, is the most primitive, the most private, of emotions; but it is also the most primitive of *social* responses. With the discovery of the individual, whether in Paradise or in the Renaissance, there is the simultaneous discovery of the isolation of the individual; his presence to himself, but simultaneously to *others*. Moreover, shame is felt not only toward one's own actions and one's own being, but toward the actions and the being of those with whom one is identified – fathers, daughters, wives . . . the beings whose self-revelations reveal oneself. Families, any objects of one's love and commitment, ought to be the places where shame is overcome (hence happy families are all alike); but they are also the place of its deepest manufacture, and one is then hostage to that power, or fugitive. – L. B. Campbell, in *Shakespeare's Tragic Heroes*,[1] collects valuable examples of Renaissance "doctrine," and sorts them perspicuously around Shakespeare's topics. But she follows a typical assumption of such investigations – that if Shakespeare's work is to be illuminated by these contemporary doctrines, he must illustrate them. For example:

> It must be evident, then, that there was in Shakespeare's day an old and firmly founded philosophy of anger, finding its sources in ancient medicine and ancient philosophy and in the mediaeval makings-over of those ancient sources as well. According to this philosophy, pride or self-esteem is the condition in which anger takes its rise, vengeance becomes its immediate object, and some slight, real or imagined, is its cause. Anger is folly; anger brings shame in its train. The sequence of passions is pride, anger, revenge, and unless madness clouds the reason altogether, shame.

But in *King Lear* shame comes first, and brings rage and folly in its train. Lear is not maddened because he had been wrathful, but because his shame brought his wrath upon the wrong object. It is not the fact of his anger but the irony of it, specifically and above all the *injustice* of it, which devours him.

That Lear is ashamed, or afraid of being shamed by a revelation, seems to be the Fool's understanding of his behavior. It is agreed that the Fool keeps the truth present to Lear's mind, but it should be stressed that the characteristic mode of the Fool's presentation is *ridicule* – the circumstance most specifically feared by shame (as accusation and discovery are most feared by guilt). Part of the exquisite pain of this Fool's comedy is that in riddling Lear with the truth of his condition he increases the very cause of that condition, as though shame should finally grow ashamed of itself, and stop. The other part of this pain is that it is the therapy prescribed by love itself. We know that since Cordelia's absence "the fool hath much pin'd away" (*I, iv*, 78), and it is generally assumed that this is due to his love for Cordelia. That need not be denied, but it should be obvious that it is directly due to his love for Lear; to his having to see the condition in Lear which his love is impotent to prevent, the condition moreover which his love has helped to cause, the precise condition therefore which his love is unable to comfort, since its touch wounds. This is why the Fool dies or disappears; from the terrible relevance, and the horrible irrelevance, of his only passion. This is the point of his connection with Cordelia, as will emerge.

I call Lear's shame a hypothesis, and what I have to say here will perhaps be hard to make convincing. But primarily it depends upon not imposing the traditional interpretations upon the opening events. Lear is puerile? Lear senile? But the man who speaks Lear's words is in possession, if not fully in command, of a powerful, ranging mind; and its eclipse into madness only confirms its intelligence, not just because what he says in his madness is the work of a marked intelligence, but because the nature of his madness, his melancholy and antic disposition, its incessant invention, is the sign, in fact and in Renaissance thought, of genius; an option of escape open only to minds of the highest reach. How then can we understand such a mind seriously to believe that what Goneril and Regan are offering in that opening scene is love, proof of his value to them; and to believe that Cordelia is withholding love? We cannot so understand it, and so all the critics are right to regard Lear in this scene as psychologically incomprehensible, or as requiring a psychological make-up – *if* that is, we assume that Lear believes in Goneril and Regan and not in Cordelia. But we needn't assume that he believes anything of the kind.

We imagine that Lear *must* be wildly abused (blind, puerile, and the rest) because the thing works out so badly. But it doesn't *begin* badly, and it is far from incomprehensible conduct. It is, in fact, quite ordinary. A parent is bribing love out of his children; two of them accept the bribe, and despise him for it; the third shrinks from the attempt, as though from violation. Only this is a king, this bribe is the last he will be able to offer; everything in his life, and in the life of his state, depends upon its success. We need not assume that he does not know his two older daughters, and that they are giving him false coin in return for his real bribes, though perhaps like most parents he is willing not to notice it. But more than this: there is reason to assume that the open possibility – or the open fact – that they are *not* offering true love is exactly what he wants. Trouble breaks out only with Cordelia's "Nothing," and her broken resolution to be silent. – What does he want, and what is the meaning of the trouble which then breaks out?

Go back to the confrontation scene with Gloucester:

> If thou wilt weep my fortunes, take my eyes.

The obvious rhetoric of those words is that of an appeal, or a bargain. But it is also warning, and a command: If you weep for me, the same thing will happen to me that happened to you; do not let me see what you are weeping for. Given the whole scene, with its concentrated efforts at warding off Gloucester, that line says explicitly what it is Lear is warding off: Gloucester's sympathy, his love. And earlier:

> GLOU.   O! Let me kiss that hand.
> LEAR.   Let me wipe it first, it smells of mortality.
>   (*IV, vi*, 134–135)

Mortality, the hand without rings of power on it, cannot be lovable. He feels unworthy of love when the reality of lost power comes over him. That is what his plan was to have avoided by exchanging his fortune for his love at one swap. He cannot bear love when he has no reason to be loved, perhaps because of the helplessness, the passiveness which that implies, which some take for impotence. And he wards it off for the reason for which people do ward off being loved, because it presents itself to them as a demand:

> LEAR.   No. Do thy worst, blind Cupid; I'll not love.
>   (*IV, vi*, 139)

Gloucester's presence strikes Lear as the demand for love; he knows he is being offered love; he tries to deny the offer by imagining that he has been solicited (this is the relevance of "blind Cupid" as the sign of a brothel); and he doesn't want to pay for it, for he may get it, and may not, and either is intolerable. Besides, he has recently done just that, paid his all for love. The long fantasy of his which precedes this line ("Let copulation thrive' . . . "There is the sulphurous pit – burning, scalding, stench, consumption . . .") contains his most sustained expression of disgust with sexuality (ll. 116ff.) – as though furiously telling himself that what was wrong with his plan was not the debasement of love his bargain entailed, but the fact that love itself is inherently debased and so unworthy from the beginning of the bargain he had made for it. That is a maddening thought; but still more comforting than the truth. For some spirits, to be loved knowing you cannot return that love, is the most radical of psychic tortures.

*   *   *   *   *

This is the way I understand that opening scene with the three daughters. Lear knows it is a bribe he offers, and – part of him any way – wants exactly what a bribe can buy: (1) false love; and (2) a public expression of love. That is: he wants something he does not have to return *in kind*, something which a division of his property fully pays for. And he wants to *look* like a loved man – for the sake of the subjects, as it were. He is perfectly happy with his little plan, until Cordelia speaks. Happy not because he is blind, but because he is getting what he wants, his plan is working. Cordelia is alarming precisely because he *knows* she is offering the real thing, offering something a more opulent third of his kingdom cannot, must not, repay; putting a claim upon him he cannot face. She threatens to expose both his plan for returning false love with no love, and expose the necessity for that plan – his terror of being loved, of needing love.

Reacting to over-sentimental or over-Christian interpretations of her character, efforts have been made to implicate her in the tragedy's source, convicting her of a willfullness and hardness kin to that later shown by her sisters. But her complicity is both less and more than such an interpretation envisages. That interpretation depends, first of all, upon taking her later speeches in the scene (after the appearance of France and Burgundy) as simply uncovering what was in her mind and heart from the beginning. But why? Her first utterance is the aside:

> What shall Cordelia speak? Love, and be silent.

This, presumably, has been understood as indicating her decision to refuse her father's demand. But it needn't be. She asks herself what she can say; there is no necessity for taking the question to be rhetorical. She wants to obey her father's wishes (anyway, there is no reason to think otherwise at this stage, or at any other); but how? She sees from Goneril's speech and Lear's acceptance of it what it is he wants, and she would provide it if she could. But to pretend publicly to love, where you do not love, is easy; to pretend to love, where you really do love, is not obviously possible. She hits on the first solution to her dilemma: Love, and be silent. That is, love *by being* silent. That will do what he seems to want, it will avoid the expression of love, keep it secret. She is his joy; she knows it and he knows it. Surely that is enough? Then Regan speaks, and following that Cordelia's second utterance, again aside:

> Then poor Cordelia!
> And yet not so; since I am sure my love's
> More ponderous than my tongue.
>
> (*I, i*, 76–78)

Presumably, in line with the idea of a defiant Cordelia, this is to be interpreted as a re-affirmation of her decision not to speak. But again, it needn't be. After Lear's acceptance of Regan's characteristic out-stripping (she has no ideas of her own, her special vileness is always to increase the measure of pain others are prepared to inflict; her mind is itself a lynch mob) Cordelia may realize that she will *have* to say something. "More ponderous than my tongue" suggests that she *is* going to move it, not that it is immovable – which would make it more ponderous than her love. And this produces her second groping for an exit from the dilemma: to speak, but making her love seem less than it is, out of love. Her tongue will move, and obediently, but against her condition – then poor Cordelia, making light of her love. And yet *she* knows the truth. Surely that is enough?

But when the moment comes, she is speechless: "Nothing my lord." I do not deny that this can be read defiantly, as can the following "You have begot me, bred me, lov'd me" speech. She is outraged, violated, confused, so young; Lear is torturing her, claiming her devotion, which she wants to give, but forcing her to help him betray (or not to betray) it, to falsify it publicly. (Lear's ambiguity here, wanting at once to open and to close her mouth, further shows the ordinariness of the scene, its verisimilitude to common parental love, swinging between absorption and rejection of its offspring, between encouragement to a rebellion they failed to make, and punishment for it.) It may be that with Lear's active violation, she snaps; her resentment provides her with words, and she levels her abdication of love at her traitorous, shameless father:

> Happily, when I shall wed,
> That lord whose hand must take my plight shall carry
> Half my love with him . . .
>
> (*I, i*, 100–102)

The trouble is, the words are too calm, too cold for the kind of sharp rage and hatred real love can produce. She is never in possession of her situation, "her voice was ever soft, gentle and low" (*V, iii*, 272–273), she is young, and "least" (*I, i*, 83). (This notation of her stature and of the quality of her voice is unique in the play. The idea of a defiant *small* girl seems grotesque, as an idea of Cordelia.) All her words are words of love; to love is all she knows how to do. That is her problem, and at the cause of the tragedy of King Lear.

I imagine the scene this way: the older daughters" speeches are public, set; they should not be said to Lear, but to the court, sparing themselves his eyes and him theirs. They are not monsters first, but ladies. He is content. Then Cordelia says to him, away from the court, in confused appeal to their accustomed intimacy, "Nothing" – don't force me, I don't know what you want, there is nothing I can say, to speak what you want

I must not speak. But he is alarmed at the appeal and tries to cover it up, keeping up the front, and says, speaking to her and to the court, as if the ceremony is still in full effect: "Nothing will come of nothing; speak again." (*Hysterica passio* is already stirring.) Again she says *to him*: "Unhappy that I am, I cannot have my heart into my mouth" – not the heart which loves him, that always has been present in her voice; but the heart which is shuddering with confusion, with wanting to do the impossible, the heart which is now in her throat. But to no avail. Then the next line would be her first attempt to obey him by speaking publicly: "I love your Majesty according to my bond; no more no less" – not stinting, not telling *him* the truth (what is the true *amount* of love this loving young girl knows to measure with her bond?), not refusing him, but still trying to conceal her love, to lighten its full measure. Then her father's brutally public, and perhaps still publicly considerate, "How, how, Cordelia! Mend your speech a little, lest you may mar your fortunes." So she tries again to divide her kingdom (". . . that lord whose hand must take my plight shall carry half my love with him . . ."). Why should she wish to shame him publicly? He has shamed himself and everyone knows it. She is trying to conceal him; and to do that she cuts herself in two. (In the end, he faces what she has done here: "Upon such sacrifices, my Cordelia. . . ." Lear cannot, at that late moment, be thinking of prison as a sacrifice. I imagine him there partly remembering this first scene, and the first of Cordelia's sacrifices – of love to convention.)

After this speech, said in suppression, confusion, abandonment, she is shattered, by her failure and by Lear's viciousness to her. Her sisters speak again only when they are left alone, to plan. Cordelia revives and speaks after France enters and has begun to speak *for* her:

> Sure, her offence
> Must be of such unnatural degree
> That monsters it, or your fore-vouch'd affection
> Fall into taint; which to believe of her,
> Must be a faith that reason without miracle
> Should never plant in me.
>
> (*I, i*, 218–223)

France's love shows him the truth. Tainted love is the answer, love dyed – not decayed or corrupted exactly; Lear's love is still alive, but expressed as, colored over with, hate. Cordelia finds her voice again, protected in France's love, and she uses it to change the subject, still protecting Lear from discovery.

A reflection of what Cordelia now must feel is given by one's rush of gratitude toward France, one's almost wild relief as he speaks his beautiful trust. She does not ask her father to relent, but only to give France some explanation. Not the right explanation: What has "that glib and oily art" got to do with it? That is what her sisters needed, because their task was easy: to dissemble. Convention perfectly suits these ladies. But she lets it go at that – he hates me because I would not flatter him. The truth is, she *could* not flatter; not because she was too proud or too principled, though these might have been the reasons, for a different character; but because nothing she could have done would have *been* flattery – at best it would have been *dissembled flattery*. There is no convention for doing what Cordelia was asked to do. It is not that Goneril and Regan have taken the words out of her mouth, but that here she cannot say them, because for her they are true ("Dearer than eye-sight, space and liberty . . ."). She is not disgusted by her sister's flattery (it's nothing new); but heart-broken at hearing the words she wishes she were in a position to say. So she is sent, and taken, away. Or half of her leaves; the other half remains, in Lear's mind, in Kent's service, and in the Fool's love.

Note

1 New York: Barnes and Noble, Inc., 1966; the quotation which follows is from pp. 181–2 of this edition. The book was first published in 1930 by the Cambridge University Press.

1

The Normal and the Natural

This extract forms the concluding third of the last chapter of Part One of *The Claim of Reason*; in it, Cavell develops one fundamental aspect of the distinctive understanding of Wittgenstein's later philosophy which will ground his treatment of skepticism and related matters in the remaining three parts of the book, as well as all the topics and texts with which his writings engage. Fundamental to this philosophy is a particular vision of language, of the human capacity to apply words to the world – a capacity that Wittgenstein sees as controlled by criteria, which determine what counts as an instance of a given kind of thing. We learn the criteria-governed use of words in certain contexts, and are then expected to project them into further contexts, but nothing *insures* that this will happen (not books of rules, and not universals); the fact that it does happen is a matter of our sharing routes of interest and feeling, a sense of similarity and disparity, seeing the pattern or point in going on with words in a certain way – all the whirl of organism that Wittgenstein calls "forms of life." For Cavell, human speech and activity, sanity and community, rest on nothing more and nothing less than this attunement in our natural reactions or responses to reality.

In developing this vision of the dependence of language and rationality upon forms of life, Cavell touches upon Wittgenstein's "anthropological" conception of necessity in a way which prefigures his later critique of Kripke's account of Wittgenstein's rule-following considerations (cf. chapter 2 of *Conditions Handsome and Unhandsome*). But his central concern is with the ways in which grounding the normative in the natural alters our understanding of what happens when language is taught or acquired. He highlights the sense in which a child can acquire words only by entering into the forms of cultural life of which they are a part, the ways in which an adult is both empowered and powerless to teach the correct use of words, the fact that the teaching of language (which means the inheritance of a culture) is not guaranteed by anything other than the

Originally published in *The Claim of Reason: Wittgenstein, Skepticism, Morality, and Tragedy*, by Stanley Cavell (Oxford: Clarendon Press, 1979), pp. 111–25. Copyright © 1979 by Oxford University Press, Inc. Reprinted by permission.

human capacity to recognize oneself in another, to recognize another's responses as exemplary or representative, to judge the right times and places for authority to be claimed over or ceded to the autonomy of the other. Such alterations in our understanding of what is familiar exemplify the work of philosophy, what Cavell here calls education for grown-ups, the task of confronting one's culture with itself along the lines in which it lives in me; but they also implicitly raise the question of whether such a conception of philosophy (Wittgenstein's, and so Cavell's) is itself teachable, inheritable by and for our culture. Here we can see one source of Cavell's sense that philosophy is in the condition of modernism.

From the time of the *Brown Book* (1934–35), Wittgenstein's thought is punctuated by ideas of normality and abnormality. It goes with a new depth in the idea that language is *learned*, that one *becomes* civilized. And in the recognition of how little can be *taught*; how, so to speak, helpless or impotent the teaching is, compared with the enormity of what is learned. As though he sees philosophical disputes as exemplifying this concurrent outsideness and fatedness to a culture. Or as dramatizing, recapitulating, the original facts of this asymmetry between teaching and learning. (Then the motive to philosophy can be thought of as a desire to true this asymmetry.) The mind cannot be led at every point; teaching (reasons; my control) comes to an end; then the other takes over. And the object of my instruction (my assertions, questions, remarks, encouragements, rebukes) is exactly that the other shall take over, that he or she shall be able to go on (alone). But correctly; that is, that the other do what I would do, make what I make of it. The differences between normality and abnormality are philosophically not as instructive as their fundamental unity – that both depend upon the same fact of civilization, that it expects complete acceptance and understanding from its natives. And yet it can *say* so little about itself in achieving its acquisition. In both cases you have to go on alone; in the one case toward acceptance, in the other toward isolation.

A certain tribe has a language of the kind (2). [A language of kind (2) is essentially that of §§1–2 of the *Investigations:* It contains "demonstrative teaching" of names of building blocks, and a series of numerals learnt by heart.] . . . The children of the tribe learn the numerals this way: They are taught the signs from 1 to 20 . . . and to count rows of beads of no more than 20 on being ordered, "Count these". When in counting the pupil arrives at the numeral 20, one makes a gesture suggestive of "Go on", upon which the child says (in most cases at any rate) "21". Analogously, the children are made to count to 22 and to higher numbers. . . . The last stage of the training is that the child is ordered to count a group of objects, well above 20, without the suggestive gesture being used. . . . If a child does not respond to the suggestive gesture, it is separated from the others and treated as a lunatic. (*Brown Book*, p. 93)

Imagining this makes me rather anxious. I feel: These people are in a great hurry to separate out lunatics. Why is open-ended counting so important to them? And their evidence for lunacy is so slim: the picking up of a mere gesture, and an indefinite one at that! But then I feel: What is *ample* evidence for lunacy? Not being able to keep up in school over a period of years? We may not call it lunacy, our gradations are not so crude; but the children are certainly treated differently because of it, and set apart. And sometimes the ostracism is based on the way a member dresses or on what he does not possess or on the words he uses. Is this more rational? How does it happen?

> . . . B has been taught a use of the words "lighter" and "darker". . . Now he is given the order to put down a series of objects, arranging them in the order of their darkness. He does this by laying out a row of books, writing down a series of names of animals, and by writing down the five vowels in the order u, o, a, e, i. We ask him why he put down that latter series, and he says, "Well, o is lighter than u, and e lighter than o". – We shall be astonished at his attitude, and at the same time admit that there is something in what he says. Perhaps we shall say: "But look, surely e isn't lighter than o in the way this book is lighter than that". – But he may shrug his shoulders and say, "I don't know, but e *is* lighter than o, isn't it?"
> We may be inclined to treat this case as some kind of abnormality, and to say, "B must have a different sense, with the help of which he arranges both colored objects and vowels". (*Brown Book*, pp. 138–9)

When we hear the diatonic scale we are inclined to say that after every seven notes the same note recurs, and, asked why we call it the same note again one might answer, "Well, it's a c again". But this isn't the explanation I want, for I should ask "What made one call it a c again?" And the answer to this would seem to be "Well, don't you hear that it's the same note only an octave higher?". . . .

If we had made this experiment with two people A and B, and A had applied the expression "the same note" to the octave only, B to the dominant and octave, should we have a right to say that the two hear different things when we play to them the diatonic scale? – If we say they do, let us be clear whether we wish to assert that there must be some other difference between the two cases besides the

one we have observed, or whether we wish to make no such statement. (*Ibid.*, pp. 140–1)

If we say "They hear different things" this might mean "There is something in what B hears" (the dominant, as doubling interval, say in plain
song, is "closer" to the octave than any other interval); or it might mean
"B has a different way of hearing". On the former interpretation we take
B's reaction as a natural one, only it is not ours (we may even think his
response is historically more primitive, and that ours has lost something
in its sophistication; we might *try* hearing his way); on the latter interpretation, our words may simply mean "B does not hear as we do", where
"simply" means that we have neither any notion of *how* he hears (what
else this abnormality goes with) nor of some way in which ours is special.
– But why do we want any words at all in such places? Why not just say
"B doesn't hear the thing we hear, the uniqueness of the octave", without
trying to make up an explanation of this discrepancy? Why do we attach
such importance to this that we have to make of one or other of us an
outcast, or make sure that there is room in the world for both? About
music, most people may let it go without explanation; but in some
families, not hearing the uniqueness of the octave might be sufficient
evidence for idiocy. To an outsider this treatment will seem not merely
severe, but altogether unjust, the merest personal decision that a person
be treated in a special way; not merely unjust, but irrational.

After the set of cases including the series of darker to lighter vowels and
the diatonic scale, Wittgenstein continues: "All the questions considered
here link up with this problem: Suppose you had taught someone to write
down series of numbers according to the form: Always write down a
number *n* greater than the preceding." And then he goes on to produce his
case in which, upon the order "Add 1" the subject does what you expect
up to 100; after which he starts, as we would say, adding 2; and after 300
adding 3; etc. Then, upon your reprimand, he insists that he is doing what
you asked, doing the same thing after 200 and 300 as after 100.

> You see that it would get us no further here again to say "But don't
> you see . . . ?", pointing out to him again the rules and examples we
> had given to him. We might, in such a case, say that this person
> naturally understands (interprets) the rule (and examples) we have
> given as we should understand the rule (and examples) telling us:
> "Add 1 up to 100, then 2 up to 200, etc.'
> (This would be similar to the case of a man who did not naturally
> follow an order given by a pointing gesture by moving in the
> direction shoulder to hand, but in the opposite direction. And
> understanding here means the same as reacting.)

(This last conjunction of examples appears in the *Investigations* at §185, where they are reasserted as similar.)

These examples are all very upsetting. Is it because these people are not really intelligible to us? No doubt we cannot communicate with them – at least in certain areas. But that is not an unfamiliar fact, even with our friends. What is the content of "not really intelligible" in these upsetting cases? I can understand *what he does* (e.g., "He adds 1 up to 100; 2 up to 200; 3 up to . . . well, as far as it will go in the 200's; etc."). I don't know *why* he does it that way. But is that necessary here? What could count as "knowing *why*"? Before Bach, we are told, keyboard performers did not use their thumbs in playing. Why didn't they? Did they fail to see that there was greater efficiency to be had, lying at hand? But for many virtuosi it probably wouldn't be more efficient, at least at first. Or suppose that for 10,000 years men made ax heads by chipping only at one side of a stone to get an edge. Did they fail to see the advantage in turning the stone over and grading both sides toward a common edge? For 10,000 years? Eventually people began doing it the new way. That may or may not be because it was thought to be better, more advantageous or efficient. Maybe the followers of the old way just stopped playing or working because it wasn't done their way any longer; and the followers of the new never think about *comparing* their way with another. We know very little about our pupil; maybe in 10,000 minutes he will find his way to our way. But we know two things about him as matters stand. We know that he is not completely unintelligible to us; we feel he *must* be able to follow our directions. And we know we are impotent in this moment to get him to. The cause of our anxiety is that *we cannot make ourselves intelligible* (to him). But why does this create anxiety? Is it that we read our unintelligibility to him as our unintelligibility as such? What gives him this power over us? Why have we given it?

Our ability to communicate with him depends upon his "natural understanding", his "natural reaction", to our directions and our gestures. It depends upon our mutual attunement in judgments. It is astonishing how far this takes us in understanding one another, but it has its limits; and these are not merely, one may say, the limits of knowledge but the limits of experience. And when these limits are reached, when our attunements are dissonant, I cannot get below them to firmer ground. The power I felt in my breath as my words flew to their effect now vanishes into thin air. For not only does he not receive me, because his natural reactions are not mine; but my own understanding is found to go no further than my own natural reactions bear it. I am thrown back upon myself; I as it were turn my palms outward, as if to exhibit the kind of creature I am, and declare my ground occupied, only mine, ceding yours.

When? When do I find or decide that the time has come to grant you secession, allow your divergence to stand, declare that the matter between us is at an end? The anxiety lies not just in the fact that my understanding *has* limits, but that I must *draw* them, on apparently no more ground than my own.

We have come across some people who sell wood not according to what *we* call "the amount of wood" in a pile, but according to the amount of ground covered by the pile, regardless of its height:

> How could I show them that – as I should say – you don't really buy more wood if you buy a pile covering a bigger area? – I should, for instance, take a pile which was small by their ideas and, by laying the logs around, change it into a "big" one. This *might* convince them – but perhaps they would say: "Yes, now it's a *lot* of wood and costs more" – and that would be the end of the matter. (*Remarks on the Foundations of Mathematics*, I, §149)

Why is *that* the end? Are we convinced that their way is all right? And if not, is there no further interest we have in these people? Perhaps we were merely looking for recruits for our lumber company, and clearly these people will not serve, anyway not as sellers or buyers. As cutters perhaps. I may not care to understand more than that. But couldn't I? (I am prompted to this example by Barry Stroud's "Wittgenstein and Logical Necessity".)

We have varying criteria according to which we measure cost; and various reasons and possibilities for making "profits" and for "sacrificing" goods. If we are *convinced* that those wood sellers cannot have in mind any coherent mode of "calculating a proportionate price" we can make all sorts of difficulties for them, make them quite unintelligible to us, decide they are unlike us. But suppose our attitude is that we are *inclined to suppose* that they are quite coherent, even in our terms (they more or less seemed to be, until this last step about selling according to area covered). There are details which may then become relevant to learn: Does wood, given the way trees are felled and wood cut and stacked and transported in that place, "naturally" involve standard piles, so that logs are more trouble, i.e., more costly, to store and to load if they are strewn around; if for no other reason than that they have first to be piled, or piled again, before delivery? Then "a lot of wood" means something like "a bunch of wood", a "non-pile". And what do their buildings look like? It needn't be true that you can "build more or bigger" buildings with more wood rather than less. All buildings may have the same amount of wood in them. Bigger buildings – i.e., ones covering a greater area – have the wood spaced differently; instead of what we call log cabins, the logs are used as columns, with cloth or strings of vines stretched between. – "But obviously "build more or bigger" means "more or bigger *of the same kind*". You can build either more or bigger cabin structures *or* more or bigger temple structures with a greater amount of wood." – It was not obvious. And maybe it is irrelevant: each member is permitted to build only one structure, and he has simply to choose which; or maybe their architectural skills limit them to types of structures which will not accept more than a certain amount of wood for each structure. (For example, they can't lay logs horizontally on top of one another to a point higher than the tallest logs, which, placed vertically, are used as retainers.) If a great architect rises up among them, he or she may teach them to notch the logs into one another so as to get much greater heights; then a member will have to choose not just which kind of structure he wants, but what size; and maybe pay accordingly. Now they will have a use for the expression "more wood" which is like ours, because then they will also have a use for the expression "bigger cabin" and even for "more cabin". Of course there will be new possibilities for cheating in this tribe, ones new to us. An entrepreneur may surreptitiously go around nudging strewn logs closer together and buy terrific amounts of non-pile wood at pile prices; more than he can build his structure with. Either he likes to have lots of unbuilt wood on his premises, or he has found that he can build more structures than he can inhabit and sell them to others. Suppose this is not against their law: the law hadn't envisioned that someone would have a reason for building a structure he would then part with. And the wood sellers may even know the man means to cheat them, but they don't mind; they think he is crazy to expend labour nudging logs closer together for the sole purpose of getting more wood than he can use for his house in order to accumulate more money to buy more wood with. This need not at all mean that they do not demand payment for their wood. Payment is essential for these people because it is the open sign that you *own* the thing you paid for, that it is yours to do with as you please, and be responsible for.

Nor need calculation enter in at all, even where we will still call what they do "selling" rather than "giving". If there is just one price for piles of wood and one other price for non- piles, what would there *be* to *calculate*? (Nor is it necessary to assume that the piles all happen to contain the same quantity of wood. You pay your money and take your choice, as happens with us in certain sales or in buying Christmas trees when the good ones have been taken or when the time for selling them is running out.) I once knew a man who coveted a particular old automobile owned by a mutual friend. For a year he coveted it but thought its owner would not sell it or that she would ask more than he could pay. One day the owner, who knew he wanted it, offered it to him for $100.

He immediately accepted, but having paid so little for it he never quite took it seriously again, and let it deteriorate. In a few months it was beyond repair; but the former owner, not knowing this, offered the man $500 to buy it back. She said that when she sold it to him she needed just $100 so that is what she asked; and now that she had more money she could afford to pay him what it would bring on the used car market. He was overcome with a sense of loss; not mere financial loss, but shame; and apparently with guilt toward the *car*. – She didn't calculate when she sold it (at least she didn't calculate the worth of the car, only the amount of her need then); she estimated or perhaps calculated when she wanted to buy it back, but then from *his* point of view, since the car was then his. He didn't calculate when he bought the car, but he accepted its asking price as if it were the result of calculation, a serious measure of its real worth. – Who is crazy? I do not say no one is, but must somebody be, when people's reactions are at variance with ours? It seems safe to suppose that if you can describe any behavior which I can recognize as that of human beings, I can give you an explanation which will make that behavior coherent, i.e., show it to be imaginable in terms of natural responses and practicalities. Though *those* natural responses may not be mine, and those practices not practical for me, in my environment, as I interpret it. And if I say "They are crazy" or "incomprehensible" then that is not a fact but my fate for them. I have gone as far as my imagination, magnanimity, or anxiety will allow; or as my honor, or my standing cares and commitments, can accommodate. I take it that this is what Wittgenstein's Swiftian proposal about separating out the child and treating it as a lunatic is meant to register.

It is not necessary that human beings should have come to engage in anything we would call calculation (inferring, etc.). But if their natural history has brought them to this crossroads, then only certain procedures will count as calculating (inferring, etc.) and only certain forms will allow those activities to proceed. It is not necessary that the members of a group should ever have found pleasure and edification in gathering together to hear the stories of their early history related; but if they do, then only certain kinds of stories, in certain structures, will provide (what we can comprehend as) that pleasure and edification. "There must be agreement not only in definitions but also . . . in judgments. This seems to abolish logic, but does not do so." In particular, I take it: It is not necessary that we should recognize anything as "logical inference"; but if we do, then only certain procedures will count as drawing such inferences, ones (say) which achieve the universality of agreement, the teachability, and the individual conviction, of the forms of inference we accept as logic. There is no logical explanation of the fact that we (in general, on the whole) will agree that a conclusion has been drawn, a rule applied, an instance to be a member of a class, one line to be a repetition of another (even though it is written lower down, or in another hand or color); but the fact is, those who understand (i.e., can talk logic together) do agree. And the fact is that they agree the *way* they agree; I mean, the ways they have of agreeing at *each* point, each *step*. For example: "Assume the negation is true (and they agree it has been written down): we know that X (and they write down another line); and substituting we get Y (Right?); and applying R we get Z (Right?) . . .'

Wittgenstein's view of necessity is, as one would expect, internal to his view of what philosophy is. His philosophy provides, one might say, an anthropological, or even anthropomorphic, view of necessity; and that can be disappointing; as if it is not really *necessity* which he has given an anthropological view of. As though if the a priori has a history it cannot really be the a priori in question. – "But something can *be* necessary whatever *we* happen to take as, or believe to be, necessary." – But that only says that we have a (the) concept of necessity – for it is part of the meaning of that concept that the thing called necessary is *beyond our control*. If the wish were not mere father but creator of the deed, we would have no such concept. If upon doing a calculation I could wish, and my wish bring it about, that the figures from which I "started" become altered, if necessary, in order that the result of my calculation prove correct; and if I could wish, and my wish bring it about, that the world alter where necessary so that the altered figures are still *of* what they are supposed to be; then the sense of necessity (standing over myself, at any rate) is not likely to be very strong in me. What we take to be necessary in a given period may alter. It is not logically impossible that painters should now paint in ways which outwardly resemble paintings of the Renaissance, nor logically necessary that they now paint in the ways they do. What is necessary is that, in order for us to have the form of experience we count as an experience of a painting, we accept something as a painting. And we do not know a priori what we will accept as such a thing. But only someone outside such an enterprise could think of it as a manipulation or exploration of mere conventions.

Very little of what goes on among human beings, very little of what goes on in so limited an activity as a game, is *merely* conventional (done *solely* for convenience). In baseball, it is merely conventional for the home team to take the field first or for an umpire to stand behind the catcher rather than behind the pitcher (which might be safer). In the former instance it is convenient to have such a matter routinely settled one way or the other; in the latter instance it must have been found more convenient for the task at hand, e.g., it permits greater accuracy in calling pitches, and positions an official so that he is on top of plays at home plate and faces him so that his line of sight crosses those of the other

umpires. More or less analogous advantages will recommend, say, the
Gerber convention in bridge. But it can seem that really *all* the rules of a
game, each act it consists of, is conventional. There is no necessity in
permitting three strikes instead of two or four; in dealing thirteen cards
rather than twelve or fifteen. – What would one have in mind here? That
two or four are just as good? Meaning what? That it would not alter the
essence of the game to have it so? But from what position is this supposed
to be claimed? By someone who does or does not know what "the essence
of the game" is? – e.g., that it contains passages which are duels between
pitcher and batter, that "getting a hit", "drawing a walk", and "striking a
batter out" must have *certain* ranges of difficulty. It is such matters that
the "convention" of permitting three strikes is in service of. So a justification for saying that a different practice is "just as good" or "better" is
that it is *found* just as good or better (by those who know and care about
the activity). But is the *whole* game in service of anything? I think one may
say: It is in service of the human capacity, or necessity, for play; because
what *can be played*, and what play can be watched with that avidity, while
not determinable a priori, is contingent upon the given capacities for
human play, and for avidity. (It should not be surprising that what is
necessary is contingent upon something. Necessaries are means.) It is
perhaps not derivable from the measurements of a baseball diamond and
of the average velocities of batted baseballs and of the average times
human beings can run various short distances, that 90 feet is the best
distance for setting up an essential recurrent crisis in the structure of a
baseball game, e.g., at which the run and the throw to first take long
enough to be followed lucidly, and are often completed within a familiar
split second of one another; but seeing what happens at just these
distances will sometimes strike one as a discovery of the a priori. But also
of the utterly contingent. There is no necessity that human capacities
should train to just these proportions; but just these proportions reveal
the limits of those capacities. Without those limits, we would not have
known the possibilities.

To think of a human activity as governed throughout by mere conventions, or as having conventions which may as well be changed as not,
depending upon some individual or other's taste or decision, is to think
of a set of conventions as tyrannical. It is worth saying that conventions can be changed because it is essential to a convention that it be in
service of some project, and you do not know a priori which set of
procedures is better than others for that project. That is, it is internal to
a convention that it be open to change *in convention*, in the convening of
those subject to it, in whose behavior it lives. So it is a first order of
business of political tyranny to deny the freedom to convene. What that
prevents is not merely, as (say) Mill urges, the free exchange of truths

with partial truth and with falsehoods, from the fire of which truth rises. That *might* happen in an isolated study. It prevents the arising of the issue for which convening is necessary, viz., to see what we do, to learn our position in what we take to be necessaries, to see in what service they are necessary.

The internal tyranny of convention is that only a slave of it can know how it may be changed for the better, or know why it should be eradicated. Only masters of a game, perfect slaves to that project, are in a position to establish conventions which better serve its essence. This is why deep revolutionary changes can result from attempts to conserve a project, to take it back to its idea, keep it in touch with its history. To demand that the law be fulfilled, every jot and tittle, will destroy the law as it stands, if it has moved too far from its origins. Only a priest could have confronted his set of practices with its origins so deeply as to set the terms of Reformation. It is in the name of the idea of philosophy, and against a vision that it has become false to itself, or that it has stopped thinking, that such figures as Descartes and Kant and Marx and Nietzsche and Heidegger and Wittgenstein seek to revolutionize philosophy. It is because certain human beings crave the conservation of their art that they seek to discover how, under altered circumstances, paintings and pieces of music can still be made, and hence revolutionize their art beyond the recognition of many. This is how, in my illiteracy, I read Thomas Kuhn's *The Structure of Scientific Revolutions*: that only a master of the science can accept a revolutionary change as a natural extension of that science; and that he accepts it, or proposes it, in order to maintain touch with the idea of that science, with its internal canons of comprehensibility and comprehensiveness, as if against the vision that, under altered circumstances, the normal progress of explanation and exception no longer seem to him to be science. And then what he does may not seem scientific to the old master. If this difference is taken to be a difference in their *natural* reactions (and Kuhn's use of the idea of a "paradigm" seems to me to suggest this more than it suggests a difference in conventions) then we may wish to speak here of conceptual divergence. Perhaps the idea of a new historical period is an idea of a generation whose natural reactions – not merely whose ideas or mores – diverge from the old; it is an idea of a new (human) nature. And different historical periods may exist side by side, over long stretches, and within one human breast.

We were led, and I take Wittgenstein to be similarly led, to those recent more or less mathematical examples, from within a need to follow out an idea of normality. Why is this? I am not competent to quarrel with or to affirm Wittgenstein's ideas about logic and the foundation of mathematics. But mathematical-looking fragments make their appearance as integral to the thought of the *Investigations*, and I cannot to that extent ignore them. What is their function?

Their general background is an idea that the primitive abilities of mathematics (e.g., counting, grouping, adding, continuing a series, finding quantities equal or smaller) are as natural as any (other) region of a natural tongue, and as natural as the primitive abilities of logic (e.g., drawing an inference, following a rule of substitution). The implication is that ordinary language no more *needs* a foundation in logic than mathematics does. More specifically, he uses the picture of "continuing a series" as a kind of figure of speech for an idea of the meaning of a word, or rather an idea of the possession of a concept: to know the meaning of a word, to have the concept titled by the word, is to be able to go on with it into new contexts – ones we accept as correct for it; and you can do this without knowing, so to speak, the formula which determines the fresh occurrence, i.e., without being able to articulate the criteria in terms of which it is applied. If somebody could actually produce a formula, or a form for one, which generated the schematism of a word's occurrences, then Wittgenstein's idea here would be more than a figure of speech; it would be replaced by, or summarize, something we might wish to call the science of semantics.

Most immediately for us, the examples of "knowing how to continue" give, as I was suggesting earlier, a simple or magnified view of teaching and learning, of the transmission of language and hence of culture. It is a view in which the idea of *normality*, upon which the strength of criteria depends, is seen to be an idea of *naturalness*. It isolates or dramatizes the inevitable moment of teaching and learning, and hence of communication, in which my power comes to an end in the face of the other's separateness from me.

Wittgenstein's idea of naturalness is illustrated in his interpretation of taking a thing to be *selbstverständlich*.

> The rule can only seem to me to produce all its consequences in advance if I draw them as a *matter of course*. (§238)

I know the series, I can continue with a word, when, for me, the continuity is a matter of course, a *foregone* conclusion. In the series of words we call sentences, the words I will need meet me half way. They speak for me. I give them control over me. (Maybe that is what a "sentence" is; or rather "a complete thought".) That is what happens to my power over the pupil; I give it over to the thing I am trying to convey; if I could not, it would not be that thing. No conclusion is more foregone for me than that *that* is human suffering, that *that* is the continuation of the series "1, 2, 3, . . .", that *that* is a painting, a sentence, a proof. *What*

I take as a matter of course is not itself a matter of course. It is a matter of history, a matter of what arrives at and departs from a present human interest. I cannot *decide* what I take as a matter of course, any more than I can decide what interests me; I have to find out.

The course is not always smooth. What I took as a matter of course (e.g., that that is a proof, that that is not a serious painting) I may come to take differently (perhaps through further instruction or examples or tips or experience, which it may be a matter of course for me to seek or to deny). What I cannot now take as a matter of course I may come to; I may set it as my task. "I am not used to measuring temperatures on the Fahrenheit scale. Hence such a measure of temperature '*says*' nothing to me" (§508). I know more or less how to go about getting used to another measuring system, that it takes repeated practice; and it may or may not work in my case – a fever of 39 degrees centigrade may never come to *look* high. Taking counts, like cursing, is familiarly deep in a native tongue; someone fluent in a foreign language may revert to the native for *just* such purposes, as though he can't be sure they have *taken effect* otherwise.

If it is the task of the modernist artist to show that we do not know a priori what will count for us as an instance of his art, then this task, or fate, would be incomprehensible, or unexercisable, apart from the existence of objects which, prior to any new effort, we do count as such instances as a matter of course; and apart from there being conditions which our criteria take to define such objects. Only someone outside this enterprise could think of it as an exploration of mere conventions. One might rather think of it as (the necessity for) establishing new conventions. And only someone outside this enterprise could think of establishing new conventions as a matter of exercising personal decision or taste. One might rather think of it as the exploration or education or enjoyment or chastisement of taste and of decision and of intuition, an exploration of the kind of creature in whom such capacities are exercised. Artists are people who know how to do such things, i.e., how to make objects in response to which we are enabled, but also fated, to explore and educate and enjoy and chastise our capacities as they stand. Underlying the tyranny of convention is the tyranny of nature.

Some children learn that they are disgusting to those around them; and they learn to make themselves disgusting, to affect not merely their outer trappings but their skin and their membranes, in order to elicit that familiar natural reaction to themselves; as if only that now proves to them their identity or existence. But not everyone is fated to respond as a matter of course in the way the child desperately wishes, and desperately wishes not, to be responded to. Sometimes a stranger does not find the child disgusting when the child's parents do. Sometimes the stranger is a doctor and teaches the child something new in his acceptance of him. This is not accomplished by his growing *accustomed* to the disgusting creature. It is a *refusing* of foregone reaction; offering the other cheek. The response frees itself from conclusions. If the freedom in saintliness were confined to saints, we would not recognize it.

Wittgenstein's stories using mathematical imagery – about the group of wood sellers, and others about people "measuring" with lax rulers, making unsystematic lists, not caring whether they are cheated or not, "calculating" by asking someone to let a number come to mind – read, from a step away, as though their characters are children. It is appropriate, in writing so fundamentally about instruction, and in which a central character is the child, that we have dramatized for us the fact that we begin our lives as children. Those tribes of big children can put us in mind of how little in each of us gets educated; and make us wonder how we ever have fresh recruits for our culture. I could have explained the reactions of the wood sellers, had I taken them as actual children, by saying "When they take the area covered as a measure of amount, they are interpreting "amount of wood" as something like "amount of water", in estimating which they take fat cylinders to contain more water than thin ones, no matter how tall the thin ones are; and about which they "know" that a greater area is covered by more water, when it is spilled, than by less water". I may say such a thing out of a genuine desire to learn about the child's construction of reality, or as a way of dismissing the reaction, reminding myself of my advancement, saying in effect that they will grow out of the habit. (The fat-thin cylinder case is, I seem to remember from Piaget, the reverse of what he found. That doesn't matter for my example. I would think of it in that case as an explanation of abnormality.) Children's intellectual reactions are easy to find ways to dismiss; anxiety over their "errors" can be covered by the natural charms of childhood and by our accepting as a right answer the answer the child learns we want to hear, whether or not he or she understands what we think of as the content of our instruction. By the time the charm fades, their education takes place out of our sight. So we may have no continuing measure of how far we are prepared to go on "making encouraging gestures" to our familiar stranger.

When my reasons come to an end and I am thrown back upon myself, upon my nature as it has so far shown itself, I can, supposing I cannot shift the ground of discussion, either put the pupil out of my sight – as though his intellectual reactions are disgusting to me – or I can use the occasion to go over the ground I had hitherto thought foregone. If the topic is that of continuing a series, it may be learning enough to find that I *just do*; to rest upon myself as my foundation. But if the child, little or big, asks me: Why do we eat animals? or Why are some people poor and others rich? or

What is God? or Why do I have to go to school? or Do you love black people as much as white people? or Who owns the land? or Why is there anything at all? or How did God get here?, I may find my answers thin, I may feel run out of reasons without being willing to say "This is what I do" (what I say, what I sense, what I know), and honor that.

Then I may feel that my foregone conclusions were never conclusions *I* had arrived at, but were merely imbibed by me, merely conventional. I may blunt that realization through hypocrisy or cynicism or bullying. But I may take the occasion to throw myself back upon my culture, and ask why we do what we do, judge as we judge, how we have arrived at these crossroads. What is the natural ground of our conventions, to what are they in service? It is inconvenient to question a convention; that makes it unserviceable, it no longer allows me to proceed as a matter of course; the paths of action, the paths of words, are blocked. "To imagine a language means to imagine a form of life" (cf. §19). In philosophizing, I have to bring my own language and life into imagination. What I require is a convening of my culture's criteria, in order to confront them with my words and life as I pursue them and as I may imagine them; and at the same time to confront my words and life as I pursue them with the life my culture's words may imagine for me: to confront the culture with itself, along the lines in which it meets in me.

This seems to me a task that warrants the name of philosophy. It is also the description of something we might call education. In the face of the questions posed in Augustine, Luther, Rousseau, Thoreau . . . , we are children; we do not know how to go on with them, what ground we may occupy. In this light, philosophy becomes the education of grownups. It is as though it must seek perspective upon a natural fact which is all but inevitably misinterpreted – that at an early point in a life the normal body reaches its full strength and height. Why do we take it that because we then must put away childish things, we must put away the prospect of growth and the memory of childhood? The anxiety in teaching, in serious communication, is that I myself require education. And for grownups this is not natural growth, but *change*. Conversion is a turning of our natural reactions; so it is symbolized as rebirth.

2

Knowing and Acknowledging

This essay – taken from Cavell's first collection – provides an example of his general approach to skepticism, as that finds expression in the philosophical discourse of modernity. Cavell deploys a dense weave of argument, fully imagined thought-experiments, and textual exegesis to develop his sense that, whilst Wittgenstein's approach to skeptical anxieties about the existence of other minds offers the best hope of overcoming or undermining those anxieties, the lessons drawn by some of his best-known commentators not only fail correctly to identify that approach, but end by opposing skeptical denials of knowledge with claims to certainty that are as misplaced – as pervaded by misuses of ordinary language – as those of the skeptic. In its most general terms, Cavell's assumption is that the mere reiteration of criteria cannot amount to a refutation of skepticism. Since criteria determine the identity of something rather than guaranteeing its reality or existence, they cannot exclude the possibility that pain-behavior is feigned or expressive of something other than pain; and since our agreement in criteria rests upon our sharing forms of life, criteria are necessarily vulnerable to skeptical withdrawals from the shared routes of interest and response that help constitute those forms of life. In an impeccably professional manner, Cavell here begins to carve out a distinctive interpretation of Wittgensteinian method, and a distinctive understanding of the peculiar economy of truth and nonsense in philosophical skepticism.

This essay also introduces Cavell's signature concept of acknowledgment. Central to his understanding of modernist art (cf. Essay 6 in this collection), and pivotal in his readings of Shakespeare (cf. the Prologue to this collection), Cavell here shows how it emerges as an apt summation of Wittgenstein's remarks on the place of knowledge and doubt in relation to the grammar of psychological concepts. For Cavell, the human individual's relation to another's pain is best characterized in terms of acknowledgment rather than knowledge; as the embodiment of the latter term in the former suggests, acknowledgment is not something

Originally published in *Must We Mean What We Say? A Book of Essays*, by Stanley Cavell (Cambridge: Cambridge University Press, 1969), pp. 238–66. Reprinted by permission.

other than knowledge but an inflection of it – a way of emphasizing the fact that another's pain makes a claim upon me. I need not respond to that claim with sympathy; but if I do not, then what happens is not a cognitive failure (a piece of ignorance, an absence) but a refusal to act which itself reveals something (indifference or exhaustion, a spiritual emptiness). And for Cavell, this same dimension of evaluation applies to our relation to our own minds; the form that my knowledge of my own pain takes is that of acknowledging it or of failing to do so. Wittgenstein is usually held to deny that it makes sense to say that I know my own pain; Cavell's Wittgenstein is concerned rather to reject overly cognitive pictures of self-knowledge.

It is, I believe, generally assumed – certainly it is natural to assume – that the philosophical appeal to ordinary language constitutes some sort of immediate repudiation of traditional philosophy, in particular of that continuous strain or motive within traditional philosophy which is roughly characterizable as skepticism (a strain or motive which most clearly includes elements of Cartesianism and of British Empiricism). This formulation is vague enough, and the assumption I refer to, if I am right that it is there, is itself vague enough. It would be the latest in the long history of altering relations which philosophy, as it alters, will draw between itself and common sense or everyday belief or the experience of the ordinary man. And the specific terms of criticism in which one philosophy formulates its opposition to another philosophy or to everyday beliefs is as definitive of that philosophy as any of the theses it may produce. I wish in what follows to suggest that so far as the appeal to what we should ordinarily say is taken to provide an immediate repudiation of skepticism, that appeal is itself repudiated.

The usefulness, not to say the authority, of appeals to what we should ordinarily say, *as philosophical data*, depends upon their being met in independence of any particular philosophical position or theory. (This is, I take it, what the phrase "ordinary language" meant to its Oxford coiners: a view of words free of philosophical preoccupation.) It looks as if this is what is happening in appealing to ordinary language against skepticism: the skeptic has a particular philosophical view which positions his words oddly, whereas the ordinary language critic makes use only of what any unprejudiced man can see to be the straight truth. But this is partial, because it assumes that the skeptic need not be counted among those who can see that their words are in apparent conflict with what is ordinarily said and that he is not in full authority to settle, or account for, that conflict in ordinary terms.

The partiality of these ideas shows two ways: (1) They assume that the skeptic is for some reason less perfect a master of (say) English than his critic. Put this way, the assumption is patently incredible. But what else are we given to believe? That he misuses words or changes their meanings? (For no reason? Or out of perversity? Or guile?) Or that he cannot really mean what he says? (Because it is obviously not true?) But what reason is there to believe such claims? (2) When the skeptic repudiates something we would all say is the correct thing to say (for example, when he denies that I am certain that there is a table here or that I can see it) he immediately goes on to concede, for example, that "for practical purposes" I am certain and that "in a sense" I can see it (I see it "indirectly") – concessions which exactly register his knowledge that his conclusions are incompatible with what should ordinarily be said, and which leave what is ordinarily said quite intact, if somewhat abashed.

These concessions may themselves seem forced, or seem empty; but to show this you have to show that a master of English, who knows everything you know, has no real use for them. And how could this be shown? An essential step in showing it would be to convince the skeptic – that is, the skeptic in yourself – that you know what he takes his words to say. (Not exactly what he takes them to *mean*, as though they had for him some special or technical meaning.) Understanding from inside a view you are undertaking to criticize is sound enough practice whatever the issue. But in the philosophy which proceeds from ordinary language, understanding from inside is methodologically fundamental. Because the way you must rely upon yourself as a source of what is said when, demands that you grant full title to others as sources of that data – not out of politeness, but because the nature of the claim you make for yourself is repudiated without that acknowledgment: it is a claim that no one knows better than you whether and when a thing is said, and if this is not to be taken as a claim to expertise (a way of taking it which repudiates it) then it must be understood to mean that you know no better than others what you claim to know. With respect to the data of philosophy our positions are the same. This is scarcely a discovery of ordinary language philosophy; it is the latest confirmation of what the oracle said to Socrates. The virtue of proceeding from ordinary language is that it makes (or ought to make) this message inescapably present to us.

In particular, it provides the message with three methodological morals: (1) The appeal to ordinary language cannot directly repudiate the skeptic (or the traditional philosopher generally) by, for example, finding that what he says contradicts what we ordinarily say or by claiming that he cannot mean what he says: the former is no surprise to him and the latter is not obviously more than a piece of abuse. What the appeal can and ought directly to do is to display what the skeptic does or must mean, even how he can mean what he says. What other way is there to take him seriously? And if his critic has not taken him seriously, why should he listen to what he is told? He knows he is not understood. (2) This means that the appeal to what we should ordinarily say does not constitute a defense of ordinary beliefs or common sense. One could say: We can disagree in many of our beliefs, but that very disagreement implies that we agree in the use of the words which express those beliefs. (If the *words* meant something other than they seemed to mean, the skeptic would not even seem to conflict with ordinary beliefs when he says, for example, "I cannot know that another man is in pain because I cannot have his pain.") One could also say: The issues over which philosophers conflict with one another or with common sense are not "beliefs" which each has about the world. The *Investigations* has this: "I am not of the *opinion* that he has a soul" (p. 178). Nor am I of the opinion that there is a world, nor that the future will be like the past, etc. If I say that such ideas are the ground upon which any particular beliefs I may have about the world, or the others in it, are founded, this does not mean that I cannot find this ground to crack. (This is why the skeptic's knowledge, should we feel its power, is devastating: he is not challenging a particular belief or set of beliefs about, say, other minds; he is challenging the ground of our beliefs altogether, our power to believe at all.) Proceeding from what is ordinarily said puts a philosopher no closer to ordinary "beliefs" than to the "beliefs" or theses of any opposing philosophy, e.g., skepticism. In all cases his problem is to discover the specific plight of mind and circumstance within which a human being gives voice to his condition. Skepticism may not be sanity, but it cannot be harder to make sense of than insanity, nor perhaps easier, nor perhaps less revealing. And the first fact it reveals is that an appeal to what we should say is not the same as a piece of testimony on behalf of what we all believe. That the appeal sometimes presents itself as a piece of such testimony is what makes it natural to assume that the appeal is inherently anti-skeptical. But my interest in finding what I would say (in the way that is relevant to philosophizing) is not my interest in preserving my beliefs. (Of course I have not said what "in the way that is relevant to philosophizing" means. The point of these remarks is exactly that this requires investigation. The sentences which immediately precede this parenthesis might serve as beginning points in such an investigation.) My interest, it could be said, lies in finding out what my beliefs mean, and learning the particular ground they occupy. This is not the same as providing evidence for them. One could say it is a matter of making them evident. And my philosophical interest in making them evident is the same as my interest in making evident the beliefs of another man, or another philosophy. And I do not know what my interest in them would be, nor how I could make them evident, if I did not or could not share them. (3) It will seem that these remarks put the ordinary language critic at the mercy of his opposition – that a test of

his criticism must be whether those to whom it is directed accept its
truth, since they are as authoritative as he in evaluating the data upon
which it will be based. And that is true. But what it means is not that the
critic and his opposition must come to *agree* about certain proposition
which until now they had disagreed about (for just as we do not *believe*, for
example, that the world exists, so it would be empty to *agree* that it exists
– you might as well *decide* that it exists). What this critic wants, or needs,
is a possession of data and descriptions and diagnoses so clear and
common that apart from them neither agreement nor disagreement
would be possible – not as if the problem is for opposed positions to be
reconciled, but for the halves of the mind to go back together. This
ambition frequently comes to grief. But it provides the particular satisfaction, as well as the particular anguish, of a particular activity of philosophizing.

Two admirable articles have recently appeared which, it seems to me,
harbor more or less definite ideas of the skeptic and share the sense that
appeals to ordinary language constitute (what I have been calling) direct
repudiations of skepticism concerning our knowledge of other minds.[1] In
what follows I will use several passages from each as a way of exemplifying concretely several of the claims I have been making. These papers
are congenial in their recognition that the skeptic's position needs accounting for if criticism against him is to be formidable. Both, however,
are hasty in their conviction that this position has been correctly drawn,
and to that extent their counter-assertions lack force. My object here is
not to answer the questions, "What, or who, is the skeptic? What is the
power of his position?"; it is an attempt to show why those questions are
worth asking.

* * * * *

The question of the privacy of pain, according to Professor Malcolm, is
"the idea that it is impossible that two people should have (or feel) the
same pain" (p. 138). Against this idea he cites Wittgenstein's remark: "In
so far as it makes *sense* to say that my pain is the same as his, it is also
possible for us both to have the same pain." The point here is that
different kinds of objects have different criteria of identity. With a sensation – as with a color, style, disease, etc. – the criterion of identity, that
in terms of which various instances count as *one*, is given by a description
of it; with other objects – material objects, points? – the criterion may be
identity of location.

Some philosophers might take this as a sufficient refutation of the
skeptical idea that two people cannot have the same pain, so it is worth

noticing that it is not. If, as it stands, it were a refutation, it must further be true that when an object's criterion of identity is a description, then we *only* count in terms of that description. But this also depends on the kind of object it is. To say we own the same car (that is, are partners) is to say that there is one car we own. (What makes it the same one is its physical integrity, so to speak.) To say we have the same car is to say that my car is the same as yours (both are 1952 MG-TD's). That they are the same means that they are not different, anyway not different *makes*. I do not know whether we will say they are different *cars*, but it cannot be denied that I have mine and you have yours – that there are two. That the cars are counted as the same does not mean that there are not two of them. This may lead one to wonder: How can two things be the same thing? It may calm the wonder to be told: (1) where it makes sense to say that one thing is the same as another, it makes sense to say they are the same thing. It may flatly answer the wonder to be told: (2) there *aren't* two things, there is only one. This will be the answer with respect to colors or gaits, for example. If the color of that block fits the same description as the color of this block (say, #314 of the Universal Color Chips) then the color of the blocks is the same, period. If you ask, "But aren't there still two colors?", then unless you mean that one of them seems closer to #315 or #313, you don't know what "color" or "same" means, what *a* color is.

Which of these answers would one like to give to the question: How can two pains be one and the same pain? I think it is fair to say that Malcolm gives, or suggests, both answers, but it is not clear to me that this can coherently be done. Because the first answer seems clearly to imply that it also makes sense to say there are two pains, *two the same*; whereas the second answer denies flatly that it makes sense to say there are two at all. It seems that with pains, as with cars, but not with colors, we can say: In a sense there are two, but in a sense there is only one. And we see, or seem to see, what these senses are: philosophers have called them "qualitative identity" and "numerical identity." Malcolm therefore, wanting to deny that there is a good sense in which (descriptively) identical pains can be said to be *two*, properly undertakes to show that the notion of "numerical identity and difference" *has no application* to sensations. How is this made out?

"Given that the description of your image, feeling or emotion is the same as mine, there cannot be a *further* question as to whether yours is *different* from mine" (p. 144). But this can be said of our twin cars as well: they are not different. But there are two. *Why*, with respect to pains described the same, can there be no further question? Because "the same" *means* "descriptively the same"? Obviously it doesn't. Because "the same" *applied to pains* can only mean "descriptively the same"? But why shouldn't the skeptic at this point simply feel that this begs the question? Is there no further question because saying "the same" *settles* the question? But is this true? With cars the question *is* settled, in favor of two; with colors the question is also settled, in favor of one. How is it settled in the case of pain?

Malcolm finds (p. 142) that while "the temptation is great (indeed, overwhelming) to suppose that there is a sense of 'same sensation' in which two people *cannot* have the same," nevertheless "the case is really no different from that of styles, colors, opinions, and sudden thoughts." Sticking to color, how is this assimilation to be established? Or, what perhaps comes to the same, how can one share Malcolm's confidence that what the skeptic is expressing can only be "an overwhelming temptation" and cannot be an insight, or fact? Earlier Malcolm had said:

> Surface A and surface B have exactly the same color, i.e., they are "identical" or "indistinguishable" in color. Can there be a further question as to whether the color of A is numerically identical with the color of B? What would it mean? Given that the color of one area is indistinguishable from the color of another area, what more can be asked? Despite what we are tempted to think, there is not a sense of "same color" such that the color of one place *cannot* be the same as the color of another place. It is one of the most truistic of truisms that the very same shade of color can be many places at the same time. (p. 141)

This seems to show how *different* colors are from, say, headaches. I can't offhand answer – offhand it means nothing to ask – whether the identically colored objects have numerically identical colors. But I *can* answer the question whether my headache is numerically identical with his. The answer is, Of course not! (though it's true we've compared notes and discovered that we suffer the same frightful headache, the one Dr Ewig describes as part of Ewig's Syndrome). I may not like the question, or quite see its point, but it seems I have to answer as I answered – "have to answer" in the sense that if I do not the skeptic would seem justified in feeling that I was *avoiding* the answer, avoiding the truth. Whereas in the case of color, I simply and truly *have no answer*. "Despite what we are tempted to think . . ." Malcolm says. But I do not find that I am a bit tempted to think that there is some sense of "same color" such that the color of one object *cannot* be the same as the color of another.

What Malcolm's assimilation of pain to color shows is solely that color and pain are alike in this respect: both are counted or identified in terms of descriptions. But in this respect both of them are also like 1952 MG-TD's. Colors cannot be counted in any other way, but it is not *plain* that pains cannot be counted any other way. If pressed at this point I find I would say that in this respect pains are more like objects than like colors. We may both have Dr Ewig's Syndrome, with its headache, but I have mine and you have yours, I express or suppress mine, and you yours. If we are both given identical blue headbands, then while I have my headband and you have yours, I don't have my blue and you yours. There *could* be a blue which was my blue (one I alone know how to mix, or characteristically wear), but it would be different from your blue (if you had one); that's the point of saying "my" here, the point of associating it with me in particular – though you may copy or adopt it. But if a headache is (described as) my headache, the point of associating it with me is not necessarily to distinguish it from yours. It is not generally important whether it is different from yours, if you happen to have one; though we may try to determine whether we hurt in the same place, or as much, perhaps because that will help diagnose its cause, but perhaps because misery loves company. There is as much or as little point in associating it with me as there is point in showing that I have one. "My headache is worse" is as much an *expression* of the headache as "I have a headache" is. And it is striking that the point of locating *exactly* where the child hurts, while it is in part, or first, to see what needs to be done, is also, and often wholly, to be able to sympathize more relevantly. One could say: Our interest in pain is different from our interest in color. The fundamental importance of someone's having pain is *that* he has it; and the nature of that importance – namely, that he is suffering, that he requires *attention* – is what makes it important to know where the pain is, and how severe and what kind it is (among a very few kinds, e.g., throbbing, dull, sharp, searing, flashing . . .). These are the ways we have of identifying pains; and so you can say, if you like, that if one pain gets identified by these criteria with the same results as another does (same place, same degree, same kind) then it is the same pain. But it also seems to me not *quite* right, or these criteria of identity are not quite enough, to make fully intelligible saying "the same."

These criteria are meant to show, to the extent possible, that the two pains (I mean, this man's pain and that man's pain) are physically identical (or indistinguishable); but exact physical similarity is not in every case enough to establish the application of "(descriptively) the same." (Physical integrity is sufficient in the case of re-identifying an object as the same one you saw yesterday, or used when you were there last year. . . .) Unless there is a *standard* description of an object in terms of which specific features are antecedently established as securing the application of the description, and thereby securing that various instances count as the same, then "(descriptively) the same" is not fully justified. And generally: physical identity (that is, empirical indistinguishability) is neither sufficient nor necessary to justify "(descriptively) the same." It is not sufficient: for two peas in a pod may be empirically indistinguishable (apart from their difference of location, on a particular occasion) but that would not lead us to say that the peas are one and the same (unless, perhaps, they are together being contrasted with a third pea of a different variety). It is not necessary: for if there *is* some standard description (or some striking feature in terms of which a description is constructed) which secures the application of "(descriptively) the same" to each of two instances, then we tolerate an indefinitely wide physical discrepancy between the instances. My MG-TD may be badly battered and yours freshly hammered out and repainted, but we still have the same car; my headache may be causing a twitch in my eyelid, or go with a mild nausea, but if both meet Dr Ewig's criteria then we have the same headache. (Perhaps these considerations explain why Wittgenstein says merely "*in so far as* it makes sense to say my pain is the same as his . . ."; he does not say that it always makes sense, nor even that it ever does fully.) We could say: Our normal interest in saying "descriptively the same" is the interest in the standards in terms of which instances are counted the same (e.g., an interest in their cost or consequences or treatment or the taste they express), not an interest in their physical identity (which comes up when the point is, for example, to *match* objects, in order to get one of the right weight or color, or determine one of the right proportion . . .). So it looks as if, whether or not the skeptic has falsely taken "numerical identity or difference" to be applicable to sensations, the philosopher opposing skepticism is led to apply "descriptively the same" apart from its normal criteria – as though he has no real use for the concept (except to refute the skeptic).

The skeptic comes up with his scary conclusion – that we can't know what another person is feeling because we can't have the same feeling, feel his pain, feel it the way he feels it – and we are shocked; we must refute him, he would make it impossible ever to be attended to in the right way. But he doesn't *begin* with a shock. He begins with a full appreciation of the decisively significant facts that I may be suffering when no one else is, and that no one (else) may know (or care?); and that others may be suffering and I not know, which is equally appalling. But then something happens, and instead of pursuing the significance of these facts, he is enmeshed – so it may seem – in questions of whether we can have the same suffering, one another's suffering. But whether or not one senses that the issue has become deflected in the course of his investigation, his motivation in it is still stronger, even more comprehensible, than that of the anti-skeptic. I mean: it is clear why the skeptic has to consider whether we can feel (have) the (same) experience another person feels (has). He has, or seems to himself to have, discovered that unless we can share or swap feelings, we can't know what that person is experiencing (if anything). I do not say this is a perfectly unobjectionable idea, but I am far from confident that I know what is objectionable about it. And I am confident that if I *have to consider* the question "Can I have the same feeling he does?", consider it seriously, not knowing as it were what the answer *must* be, then the honest answer must be, No. Let me be as clear as I can: it may turn out that the question is badly conceived, and that the honest answer collects merely an illusion of honesty and provides only the illusion of an answer. But I do not see that this has been *shown*. It is *assumed*, I think it is clear, that the skeptic *cannot* be serious, that he has discovered nothing which his words are trying, perhaps slightly forced, to convey. But what justification is there for such assumptions? That his conclusion conflicts with common sense? He knows that, and he accounts for it. That in practical situations he does not practice his skepticism? He knows that, and he accounts for it. That there is a sense in which we *can* have the same feeling? He knows that, too: that is exactly *why* he says that we do not have *literally* the same, *numerically* the same, feeling – conceding as it were that we have descriptively the same. Now again, he may here have been pushed into a distorted utterance, contracted the illusion of a discovery. But this cannot be shown by insisting that we do or can have the same.

To offer that as an answer to the skeptic (and what other reason is there for *insisting* upon it?) is fatal. It is (1), as was said, inaccurate; or, where accurate, disappointingly limited. It is (2) empty, because the skeptic's use of the qualification "literally or numerically" means exactly that he is not denying that the feelings may be descriptively the same. This accounts for the way (3) the skeptic's supposed discovery is *stronger* than the anti-skeptic's supposed fact (which appears as a fact, even an arbitrary fact, about language); because the obvious fact that we can (or can be said to) have the same is *undercut* by the discovery that we cannot have literally or numerically the same. (His discovery makes our ordinary use of "the same" seem a *façon de parler*, and makes the ordinary language philosopher's *appeal* to this use seem willful ignorance or superficiality.) The underlying reason for this is that the skeptic's problem, unlike the anti-skeptic's, is directed to what I spoke of earlier as our natural interest in the occurrence of pain, namely, *that* a given man has it. It reveals (4) that the anti-skeptic's motivation is at least as questionable as the skeptic's. For what is at stake for the anti-skeptic in insisting that we *can* have the same? Suppose we *can*, now, have the same (descriptively the same, the same in the sense in which it makes sense to say "the same") pain as anyone else can have – say a headache localized over the right eye. Does *he* have this particular pain? Granted that he can, does he? Can we know here and now that he does? And faced with that question, *my* pain is obviously irrelevant (it may even make it harder for me to find out whether he has the pain). Someone may even be led now to suppose that, apart from my pain, I need (a replica of) his in order to know whether he has it. And we don't know how to grant *that*. If this is the way things are, we don't know whether he has the pain or not; we never can.

But of course it will be objected: "You make it seem that being unable to imagine having (or to grant that we may have) literally or numerically the same pain as he has (i.e., have his pain) describes a real or intelligible experience. But it is a complete confusion; there is nothing we need or need to grant. You have tolerated the idea of "numerical or literal identity," but that is what is incoherent. There is no such thing to grant; the wish for it is a wish for nothing; not a real wish." But why isn't this hysterical? What I have said is this: To meet the skeptic by saying that we *can* have the same feeling, fails; in failing, it perpetuates the idea that whether we have the same feeling is *relevant* to whether we can know what another is feeling; but if this is taken as relevant, it is discovered that the sense in which we can have the same feeling is insufficient for knowing whether another person feels what I feel, or feels anything at all. A gap has (apparently) been revealed which must be closed if we are to know whether another is in pain, a gap described in terms of "having numerically or literally the same pain he has."

If this is not perfectly intelligible, it is not perfectly unintelligible either. (That is the trouble with skepticism; and the skeptic has an explanation of it. For example, he may speak of knowing something which he cannot believe.) To say it is completely unintelligible is something which has to be made out, and it is not clear what making it out will have to consist in. The *words* aren't unintelligible. (If, as I began by arguing, comparing the skeptic's words with their everyday use does not automatically show that he means nothing, but rather shows what he *must* mean, or *does* mean, then the question is, (how) can he? It is a *question*.) One wants to say: What it *envisions* is unintelligible. But *what* is envisioned which is unintelligible? It looks as if to make out that it is unintelligible you have to do exactly what the person who claims to envision it has to do – say what is envisioned. But it is exactly your point that this cannot be done. Does your inability prove your point, or defeat it? If you take it to prove your point, what you are assuming is that your inability has, so to speak, the same significance as the skeptic's – that is, you assume that if what he envisions is intelligible he has to be able to say what it is; or rather, you assume that the fact that he can't means that he can't show it to be intelligible. But there will seem to him to be *this* asymmetry between his inability and yours: he doesn't need to show its intelligibility – because, perhaps, he knows he means the words, they have *that* much intelligibility, and it doesn't matter that they do not describe an envisionable state of affairs; they are the only (they are the *right*) words for meeting the situation he has found himself in. (If not, so much the worse for his words.) Whereas you *do* need to show its unintelligibility, since, so to speak, you have no other use for the words than that. What you then need to do is show that *he* has no real use for them either, that their intelligibility is illusory, that he can't *really* mean them, that he has merely the *impression* of saying something.[2] How is this to be done?

Take a different case. At a certain point in his investigation, a traditional epistemologist will say: You can't see the back of the object, nor its inside, so all you see, at most, is the front surface. Is this unintelligible? Suppose one tries to make this out as follows: "*What* can't I do? I don't know what it would be like if I *could* see the back half while standing in front of it! It's as if you envision a situation in which seeing an object would be having one's sight penetrate through an infinite layer of surfaces. That is what is not intelligible. And until you make that intelligible, it makes no sense to say I can't do it." But is that true? And doesn't it seem to increase the hysteria it wishes to oppose? And why can't the skeptic here simply feel: "You don't understand what I mean. My words are intelligible, it's obvious what they mean, and your suggestion of a situation which cannot be envisioned just shows you don't understand. Your idea simply indicates that you have no use for those words, and the reason you have no use for them is that you do not appreciate what I have discovered." The anti-skeptic will now want to show the skeptic that he sees no real problem either, has no real use for the words either. But how? Presumably by finding out what the source of the apparent intelligibility is, what gives the impression of meaning something; in a word, by diagnosis. – But we know the source of the intelligibility: the words themselves, the fact that *they* are intelligible, i.e., that in some contexts they carry full meaning. "You can't see the back half, so you don't know it's red all over" – there is no trouble finding a practical context in which that is a fact (namely, one in which it is of practical importance that the object be (say) red all over and in which you cannot in fact see the part not facing you). And now comes the objection: The skeptic uses a form of words that makes perfect sense in certain contexts and then applies it to a case in which it makes no sense. He takes a context in which the back half of an object is in fact hidden from view and uses that as the model for seeing objects generally.

The problem with this objection is that it cuts two ways: it does show that the skeptic is shifting contexts, but it also shows why what he says *is intelligible.* (If not fully, still not fully not.) That these words are not ordinarily used in such contexts doesn't mean they can't naturally be given application in them. (Using language depends on this ability to give application in new contexts.) Whether his words mean what they say here, or only produce in him the impression of a meaning, depends on whether they have been given application. And it doesn't seem obvious that an object can't (and even oughtn't to) be taken to be something whose front ineluctably conceals its back. This is, of course, not all the skeptic wants. He wants us to see the rightness, the inevitability of his application; and given that, his conclusion comes fast. But it is *no* argument against his application to say that if he is allowed it an unwelcome conclusion follows.

Similarly with "we cannot have literally or numerically the same feeling as another." Malcolm says that "If the distinction between 'the same' and 'numerically the same' *were* to be given an application to sensations, then we should have to *make up* criteria for it" (p. 145). He takes the case of the Siamese twins with a common hand and notes our conflict in deciding whether to call a pain in that hand one pain or two. But we don't need the common hand to bring out this conflict. If each of us has the pain (caused, say, by a hammer blow) in the same place on our left hands (say, under the nail of the thumb), then asked "Are there one or two pains?" we will be pulled in the same directions as in the case of the Siamese twins. This may mean that such a case is not of the right kind for giving the distinction its application. It might even be that what produced the Siamese twins as the right kind of case is a particular picture of what "having numerically the same pain" would be, if so to speak it had a use – a picture in which the pain is located in numerically the same place. But is this the right, or a necessary, picture?

Take a case adapted from that of the Corsican Brothers, one of whom, call him Second, suffers everything which happens to his brother First. Whip First and Second writhes with him (not in sympathy, *seeing* what's happening; but even miles away, not knowing what is happening). Add to this the fact that Second never suffers unless First does: whip Second himself and he doesn't feel it. I assume further that there is no physical trauma produced in Second by what First undergoes. What I wish the example to create is the sense that Second feels pain because First *feels* it – so that, for example, if First is anaesthetized, Second equally feels nothing. Therefore it is crucial to the example that First be something we treat as a living body. (It is not unimaginable that it be a dummy or a doll which has some peculiar causal connection with Second. But that would not be a case of "feeling because another feels it.") – I think one finds that the usual philosophical remark to the effect that "Any pain one feels will be one's own" is, though said to be logically necessary, simply false here. Second *has* no pain of his own; he has only First's pain. And doesn't it describe this situation to say: His pain is not just descriptively the same as First's, it is numerically the same?

So here we have a pain in *this* body and a pain in *that* body and it is numerically the same pain, literally the same. The thing which looked unintelligible, was so, only given a certain picture. What has happened to make the situation intelligible is this: while we still have pain in two bodies, we no longer have, so to speak, two *owners* of pain. That is, the pain in Second's body is not Second's pain. (This is not a case of "feeling pain in another's body.") It is not clear whether Second will express his pain by saying "I am in pain" or "He (First) is in pain"; nor whether he will locate the pain in his leg *on* his leg or on First's. What is significant is that he can do either. Which he will do will depend on the point of expressing and locating the pain in a given context. It is not that he is in doubt whether he (or, for that matter, First) is in pain; but that expressing and locating pain can be said to have a different point than they now have. (His pain won't be relieved unless you attend to First; but he may nevertheless be comforted if you attend to him (Second).)

Does this give the skeptic what he took to be necessary in order to know that another is in pain? Surely it cannot be denied that Second *knows* that First is in pain, knows what he feels, and knows it *because* he feels it, because he *has* that pain?

The skeptic, on this realization of his wish, has got more than he bargained for. Let us ask: Does First know what Second feels, that Second is in pain? I think one will be pulled in opposite directions. One of them will be: Since they have numerically the same pain, First *must* know. But another will be: What *can* First know other than his own pain? That's the *only* pain he has. That it is the only pain *Second* has is perhaps irrelevant here; for even if one insists that Second is feeling something separate from First, and that First's feeling tells him that, First's feeling, as it were, drowns it out. Every pain First feels is *his*. (This now means something in contrast to Second, none of whose feelings are his.) First knows *what* Second feels (and when and where he is feeling it) – but so can we know those things. I would like to say that First's knowledge of Second's pain – if based on his own pain – is somehow too intellectual to be called "knowledge that Second is in pain"; he indeed has, I feel like saying, a model of Second's pain, but the primary fact for him is that *he* feels it, as if there is no way around it to appreciate the individuality of Second's pain (though First may sympathize, in moments of saintliness or calm, with Second's *position* with respect to him). If First's knowledge is not based on his own pain, then he knows, or fails to know, the way anyone would. The numerical identity of his pain with Second's is unusable for just the thing for which it seemed indispensable. The skeptic's wish is granted, but it does not – or ought not to – satisfy him.

Nor does it – nor ought it to – satisfy him in the case of Second's knowing First's pain. Here what emerges is not so much that the wish is insufficient as that it is a wish for the wrong thing. We admitted that Second has not only numerically the same pain as First, but has First's pain, and that he knows First is in pain on the basis of his having it. But I find that while it may not wholly be wrong to say "Second knows First is in pain," this again is not what *we* mean by "knowing someone is in pain." Not because I (in Second's position) do not know that the pain I have is *his*, had by him (First). (That was true of the case in which I gave myself descriptively the same pain; and perhaps it is true of First's position.) It is rather that *his* pain no longer contrasts with *my* pain, his has no further content, so to speak; "his pain" no longer differentiates what he feels from what I feel, him from me; he is not *other* in the relevant sense. I said that in the former case (First knowing Second) First's knowledge is "too intellectual"; even though he has the same pain as Second, he still has to "infer" (or remember?) that Second is in pain. So the phenomenological pang in having to say that knowing another mind is a matter of inference – something shared by the skeptic and the anti-skeptic – remains after we have granted what seemed to be lacking in our knowledge of the other. In the latter case (Second knowing First), Second's knowledge is "too immediate"; his "having" First's pain is, one might say, an effect of that pain, not a response to it – a different phenomenological pang. But how shall we understand this wish for a *response* to my expressions (of pain, of any region of the mind)? Does it suggest that our concept of my knowledge of another is bound up with the concept of my freedom, an independence from the other, from all others – which I may or may not act upon? What is this "knowing a person"?

* * * * *

What does it mean to say, "I know he is in pain," and how does that differ from saying, "I know I am in pain'? It will perhaps be thought that I should have asked these questions before submitting to the skeptic's wish to "know another's pain the way he does," because that wish can be shown to be incoherent quite directly, namely by showing that one does not *know* one's own pain at all, or, as it may be put, that the statement "I know I am in pain" is senseless. So the whole idea that he knows something I do not know is senseless.

I claimed earlier that the attempt to answer the skeptic's denial that two people can have the same pain, by the head-on assertion that they *can*, puts the anti-skeptic in a weaker position than the skeptic; where "weaker" means "weaker in conviction or motivation" and "no better in faithfulness to what we all believe" – so that our ordinary beliefs seem subject either to open repudiation or to faint-hearted defense. Something similar is happening here.

At some stage the skeptic is going to be impressed by the fact that my knowledge of others depends upon their *expressing themselves*, in word and conduct. That is surely an essential fact to be impressed by. And then he realizes that the other may not in fact express himself, or that his expression may be falsified (deliberately or in some other way); and that again is undeniable. It follows that in such a case I would not know what is going on in the other. So the skeptic adds, supposing himself to express that fact, "But still *he* knows." And if *now* the anti-skeptic digs in his heels, he must seem to the skeptic simply perverse. The only obvious reason for digging in one's heels here is that in another moment it will turn out that *I* can *never* know; and we don't want that. So again, if that is the reason, then the skeptic must suppose that you are just avoiding the truth. There is a fact there to be recorded. The skeptic records it by saying "He knows what he is feeling." There is, I take it, no suggestion that the skeptic can't speak English as well as another man, so why assume that he is mis-speaking here? Because that *isn't* what the words "He knows he's in pain" record? Two questions arise: (1) What *does* record that fact? And (2) What does "He knows he's in pain" record? The anti-skeptic goes on to answer the second of these questions, but the skeptic will not be much impressed; it will seem like quibbling about words. Because *his* fact needs recording, and until you can show what records it you have no grip against his conviction that, whatever else "He knows he's in pain" records, it also records this fact. This is another way of saying what I meant by calling the anti-skeptic's position weaker: the skeptic has a fact which needs noticing and recording; the anti-skeptic has no fact of his own to compete with that, he has only some words to think about, and his words keep looking like they *deny the facts*.

"I know I am in pain" is senseless, Malcolm says. Well, the skeptic realizes that *something* is odd about it, but since he needs it he diagnoses why it seems odd (e.g., it is so trivially true as not to be worth saying – except to someone trivial enough to deny it) and then goes on using it. If the anti-skeptic is to penetrate this defense, it can't be enough to show that it is odd, even very odd, or that the skeptic's diagnosis of its oddness is wrong. He has to show that its oddness prevents it from recording that fact. Is that what showing that it is "senseless" accomplishes?

How is its senselessness made out? Malcolm argues that the "I know" in "I know I'm in pain" "cannot do any of its normal jobs" (p. 148). He cites three normal jobs: claiming grounds, authority, and privileged position. But are there no other relevant functions of "I know'? Here are three more: (1) There is "I know New York (Sanskrit, the signs of the Zodiac, Garbo, myself)." To know in such cases is to have become acquainted with, or to have learned, or got the hang of. (2) There is, again, "I know I am a nuisance," "I know I am being childish," "I know I am late." To (say you) know in these cases is to admit, confess, *acknowledge*. (3) There is, again, the use of "I know" to *agree* or confirm what has been said, or to say I *already* knew. – Can it be shown that none of these additional uses exemplifies a (the) relevant use of "I know" in "I know I'm in pain"? They are not obviously irrelevant. So what accounts for Malcolm's having taken the uses of "I know" he cites as alone relevant, suggesting that if it has a genuine use with respect to first person present tense statements about pain, it must be one of these?

The uses Malcolm cites are ones connected with the idea of certainty; in them "I know" contrasts with "I believe"; all claim that one is in a position to know, and someone who uses them competently must be prepared to document his claim. It is true that "I know I'm in pain" hasn't the function of claiming certainty. Professor Cook puts this by saying that it is not an "expression of certainty" (p. 287). We might put it by saying. "I know I'm in pain does not mean "I'm certain I'm in pain" – there is no condition short of certainty which the claim to certainty would be excluding. Cook allows *a* use of "I know I'm in pain" (Malcolm allows a similar use of "I know I have a toothache"), one related to the final use of "I know" I added to Malcolm's three, the one in which I *agree*. But this use is not, as Cook correctly and usefully says, an expression of certainty; it is an expression of *exasperation* (p. 285); and the implication is that this use is not going to help the argument that I know something which no one else can know. – It is worth noticing that it is not *because* it is an expression of exasperation that it *can't* be an expression of certainty (i.e., senseless as an expression of certainty). "I *know* Washington never told a lie" expresses certainty; and it *also* can express exasperation (say in a context in which you go on refusing to believe me; or one in which you tell *me* about George Washington, as if it's news, when it was I who told you). Its exasperation does not compete, so to speak, with its other potentialities of expression.

It is obvious enough, but unremarked, that "I know I'm in pain" (containing as its assertible factor "I am in pain") is an *expression of pain* (accepting Wittgenstein's view that "I am in pain" is such an expression). It may also be an expression of exasperation. And it has the form ("I know I . . .") of an *acknowledgment* (the second use of "I know" which I added to Malcolm's three). As an acknowledgment (admission, confession) it is perfectly intelligible. It won't be one which is used very often, perhaps; it requires a context in which, for some reason, I wish to conceal my pain – say because to admit it would be shameful, or would look like an excuse – and the person to whom I say "I know I . . ." here is trying to get me to admit it.

Does *this* use of ":I know I'm in pain" also repudiate the skeptic's argument, i.e., does it fail to record his fact? What he wanted to say was "Only *he* knows whether he's in pain; I do not know." One is fully entitled to say "Only he can acknowledge his pain; I can't"; and it can be said with exasperation (which would not prevent it from being true) and as an expression of certainty. It is not, it seems, in fact what the skeptic does say; he says that the other alone *knows*, not that the other alone *can acknowledge*. But what is the difference? It isn't as if being in a position to acknowledge something is *weaker* than being in a position to know it. On the contrary: from my acknowledging that I am late it follows that I know I'm late (which is what my words say); but from my knowing I am late, it does not follow that I acknowledge I'm late – otherwise, human relationships would be altogether other than they are. One could say: Acknowledgment goes beyond knowledge. (Goes beyond not, so to speak, in the order of knowledge, but in its requirement that I *do* something or reveal something on the basis of that knowledge.)

Is it, then, a suppressed premise of the skeptic's that "If he can acknowledge he's in pain then he knows whether he is in pain'? And would we deny this premise? – "Still, this does not alter the fact that if he says "I know I'm in pain" he will not be expressing certainty, and *this* is what the skeptic needs." – Perhaps he will not be expressing *certainty*; but why can one not say, what his words say, that he is expressing *knowledge*? And isn't *that* what the skeptic needs? But then, if the philosopher really stuck to the idea of another person's failing to *acknowledge* his experiences, he would never become a skeptic; that is, the philosopher's fact would simply be the ordinary fact that sometimes we just do not know the experiences of others: they often, even more often than not, conceal them. This does not lead to his unleashed conclusion that we can *never* know, that the feelings of another are ineluctably concealed from us because we cannot *have* them.

Maybe the situation is like this: the fact that another person may now be in pain yet not acknowledge that he is in pain, is the same as, or seems to entail, the fact that he now knows that he is in pain; and this turns into the (imagined?) fact – or is read as the (imagined) fact – that he is now *certain* that he is in pain. And from *this* point, the rest of the argument is forced upon us, seems undeniable: How does he know (what is his certainty based on)? Because he feels (has) it (the fact that he feels (has) it). But obviously I can't feel it, I can't have the same feeling he has, his feeling; so I can never be certain another person is in pain. Moreover, even if he tells me, he might only be feigning, etc., etc.

This argument may be incoherent, or have incoherent presuppositions; but it does not *begin* incoherently, and it is not clear, once begun, that any given step is avoidable. Any formidable criticism, I take it, must be as compelling as the argument itself is. I have suggested in particular that neither of two criticisms are strong enough to place much confidence in: neither "We *can* have the same pain" (which denies the truth of one of the steps) nor "The form of words "I know I am in pain" is senseless, as an expression of certainty" (which takes a presupposition to be incoherent). Our choice seems to be this: either we accept the anti-skeptic's *analysis* of the several statements made by the skeptic, which explain why they make no sense, or are false; or we hold on to the obvious facts which they seem to record, and conclude that the offered analysis cannot be correct, has not followed the argument.

*   *   *   *   *

The head-on effort to defeat skepticism allows us to think we have explanations where in fact we lack them. More important, in fighting the skeptic too close in, as it were, the anti-skeptic takes over – or encourages – the major condition of the skeptic's argument, viz., that the problem of knowledge about other minds is the problem of certainty. At the same time, he neglects the fundamental insight of the skeptic by trying single-mindedly to prove its non-existence – the insight, as I wish to put it, that *certainty is not enough*. What I mean can perhaps be brought out this way: In concentrating on the skeptic's apparently impossible demands (and neglecting what may be the insight which produces those demands) the anti-skeptic concentrates on the first-person half of the problem of other minds, to the neglect of the third person, as though half believing the skeptic's repudiation of the third person. When he does consider that person, it is in contrast to the first person, and largely only to the extent of saying that such statements as "I know (am certain) he is in pain," "I doubt whether he is in pain" *make sense* as opposed to their first person analogues (cf. Malcolm, p. 146). Obviously they do make sense in this opposition – that is, as expressions of certainty. But in *this* sense they raise no special problems about our knowledge: sometimes we are certain, sometimes we know we are not; and on various obvious grounds – we heard it over the radio, or someone told us, or we went upstairs and saw for ourselves, or we heard him cry out, or we saw opened medicine bottles on his night table, etc. But there *are* special problems about our knowledge of another; *exactly the problems the skeptic sees*. And these problems can be said to invoke a special concept of knowledge, or region of the concept of knowledge, one which is not a function of certainty. This region has been pointed to in noticing that a first person acknowledgment of pain is not an expression of certainty but an expression of pain, that is, an exhibiting of the *object* of knowledge.

There is an analogue to this shift in the case of third person utterances about pain.

I said: Third person utterances about sensations – where they express certainty – raise no special problems about our knowledge of others. I could also have said: They are not *basic* to the problem of other minds, the way "I see it" is basic to establishing claims to know the external world. The gamekeeper may have told me, or I figured it out for myself, or I have noticed footprints in the sand – but unless I see (or sense) the bittern in the garden, the basic way of knowing has not been forthcoming, and when it comes it takes precedence: unless somebody has actually witnessed the thing, the whole structure of reports may collapse. (It is exactly when *my* witnessing of the thing, under the best possible conditions, does (seem to) collapse that I know the entire structure of reports about the external world collapses.) Similarly, unless there is someone who knows (there is a way of knowing) at first hand, or directly, that another person is in pain, the whole structure of reports about another is left up in the air. – But there *is* someone who knows, there is a position which is totally different from mine in the matter of knowing whether he is in pain, different not only in being better (as if certain factors in my position were increased in accuracy or range) but in being decisive, making the best position I can be in seem second hand: namely, *his* position. I do not mean to insist upon the validity of this idea of "position," but phenomenologically, as a datum, it seems to me undeniable. I think everyone recognizes the experience which goes with it, that it is some terrible or fortunate fact, at once contingent and necessary, that *I* am not in that position; the skeptic merely comes to concentrate upon it. And it is not obviously invalid.

Cook offers this repudiation of such an idea: the idea that I cannot know another's feeling because I cannot *have* that feeling

> . . . makes out the difference between first-and third-person sensation statements to rest on a matter of circumstance (like being unable to see my neighbor's crocuses), whereas Wittgenstein has made us realize that the difference resides in the language game itself. The difference does not rest on some circumstance, and therefore . . . [the idea] which purports to name such a circumstance with the words "being unable to feel another's sensations", is inherently confused. (p. 291)

Why is "being unable to feel another's sensation" not a circumstance? Because, I take it, it is not something that can coherently be imagined to be other than it is; it does not describe an *inability* of ours, but a general fact of (human) nature. (This is, one assumes, the force of saying "the difference resides in the language game itself".) But why can't a general fact of nature be thought of, accurately, as a circumstance, a permanent circumstance? The circumstance is, I feel like saying, *him*. The problem, that is, may be that the formulation "inability to feel" tries but fails to capture my experience of separation from others. This does not make it inherently confused but, one might say, much too weak – as though words are in themselves too weak to record·this fact. If the skeptic does not recognize this failure of (his) words, then *this* is the correct criticism of him here (though we do not yet know how serious a criticism it is). But to apply an inaccurate term of criticism to him (to say of him, falsely, that his idea is inherently confused) further deflects the truth to which he is responding.

What wishes to express itself as an "inability" might vanish if I could become clear what my *abilities* are in this domain and in this way make clear what it seems to me they are insufficient to accomplish. It may look as if that is just what the analogy of the neighbor's crocuses makes clear, that I am regarding my inability to enter my neighbor's mind as something like an inability to enter his garden; only, as it were, it is a permanent inability, the garden is sealed or charmed out of reach. And then, shown this, I am to realize that this is a bad analogy and to conclude that there is nothing I cannot do. – But *is* this my impression, when, that is, I am under the impression that there is something I cannot know about my neighbor? And why should I conclude that it is wrong – as the expression of an impression, for which words are too weak anyway? (For it isn't as if the *words* "enter into the minds of others" are themselves senseless. It is only a way of *taking* the words, a "picture" of their application, that is being called senseless; and it looks as if the senseless way of taking them is expressed by the analogy of entering a garden. But that is the question: *Is* that the way they are, or need to be, taken? And isn't there a way of taking "enter his garden" which makes it a correct (figurative) description of what I do when I enter his mind?) I would express my feeling, rather, simply as one of inability; that is, one of being *powerless*. And I do not see that I have to accept the question, "Powerless to do *what*?"; any more than if I sometimes express a particular sense of being defenseless or dependent I have to specify, in order to substantiate the validity of this feeling, what it is I am defenseless against or dependent upon. Of course I do not claim that the sense of powerlessness is to be taken at face value, as though it itself, so to speak, shows what it is I am powerless to do; on the contrary, it is my point that it does not claim to do this. The feeling needs accounting for, as dependence and defenselessness do. And it is not clear a priori that in accounting for it one will not be contributing to an investigation of our knowledge of other minds. What is certain is that a false or forced account of it will not show it to be irrelevant to such an investigation.

Adapting another remark from the *Philosophical Investigations*, we might say: We know what the word "know" means, and we know what the words "a pain" mean, so we think we must know – or it must be obvious – what the combination "knowing a pain" means. Here the skeptic does seem impressed by a particular picture: a man's knowing his pain is something he is doing continuously (the eye turned inward and staring); which makes it unlike any other familiar kind of knowing. One feels here like saying to the skeptic: What is continuous is the sensation itself, and saying that a man *knows* this sensation adds nothing to saying that the sensation is *there*. But is that true? What it adds is the fact that the sensation is not *here*, that it is not continuous in me, so that even if I can be said to know he is in pain, I do not know it continuously, hence not the way he knows it. You may wish to say that "knowing continuously" is not *knowing* at all. But this has yet to be made out – for no one has denied that he can be *said* to know he is in pain (as a joke, for example); and if he knows then mustn't he know continuously? And the picture has at least this significance: it shows something of the inaccuracy of the neighbor's garden as a diagnosis of our impressions. For that analogy captures the impression that I am sealed *out*; but it fails to capture the impression (or fact) of the way in which *he* is sealed *in*. He is not in a position to walk in that garden as he pleases, notice the blooms when he chooses: he is *impaled* upon his knowledge.

The skeptic may not record that fact accurately, and he will come to the point of saying that we do not know this. But *this* is what we do not know, according to his picture (if my filling in of that picture is right as far as it goes). And this seems to me to be the right picture; and it is not false to say we do not know what it pictures. For what it pictures is the fact that behavior is *expressive* of mind; and this is not something we know, but a way we *treat* "behavior." The skeptic in effect goes on to say that we have no *reason* to treat behavior in this way. And is that false? – But what he turns out to mean is that behavior is one thing, the experience which "causes" or is "associated" with it is something else. That is, he stops treating behavior as expressive of mind, scoops mind out of it. My point, however, is not to trace out the full extent of the skeptic's motivations; it is merely to deny that they, and what they lead him to, are senseless; or rather, to show that what he wants to know – namely, what it is we go on in the idea that behavior is expressive – is the right thing to want to know.

I take the philosophical problem of privacy, therefore, not to be one of finding (or denying) a "sense" of "same" in which two persons can (or cannot) have the same experience, but one of learning why it is that something which from one point of view looks like a common occurrence (that we frequently have the same experiences – say looking together at a view of mountains, or diving into the same cold lake, or hearing a car horn stuck; and that we frequently do not have the same experiences – say at a movie, or learning the results of an election, or hearing your child cry) from another point of view looks impossible, almost inexpressible (that I have your experiences, that I *be* you). What is it I cannot do? Since I have suggested that this question is a real one (i.e., that the sense of "cannot" here is real), and since nevertheless I have suggested that the question has no answer (on the ground that the words "cannot have his feeling" are "too weak" for the experience they wish to convey), I would need, in accounting for these facts, to provide a characterization of this sense of incapacity *and* provide the reason for our insistence upon putting it into words. I find that, at the start of this experience, I do not want to give voice to it (or do not see what voice to give it) but only to point (to others, or rather to the fact, or the being, of others) and to gesture towards my self. Only what is there to point to or gesture towards, since everything I know you know? It shows; everything in our world shows it. But I am filled with this feeling – of our separateness, let us say – and I want you to have it too. So I give voice to it. And then my powerlessness presents itself as ignorance – a metaphysical finitude as an intellectual lack. (Reverse Faust, I take the bargain of supernatural ignorance.)

Consider, finally, how *special* the use of "I know he is in pain" is as an expression of certainty. Almost as special as the use of "I know I'm in pain" as an expression of exasperation. (And of course "I know he's in pain" is very likely to *be* an expression of exasperation.) To bring out *how* special the expression of certainty is, consider the other non-first person always (so far as I know) neglected in these discussions, the second person: "I know you are in pain." I said that the reason "I know I am in pain" is not an expression of certainty is that it is an expression of pain – it is an exhibiting of the object about which someone (else) may be certain. I might say here that the reason "I know you are in pain" is not an expression of certainty is that it is a response to this exhibiting; it is an expression of *sympathy.* ("I know what you're going through"; "I've done all I can"; "The serum is being flown in by special plane.")

But why is sympathy expressed in this way? Because your suffering makes a *claim* upon me. It is not enough that I *know* (am certain) that you suffer – I must do or reveal something (whatever can be done). In a word, I must *acknowledge* it, otherwise I do not know what "(your or his) being in pain" means. Is. (This is "acknowledging it *to* you." There is also something to be called "acknowledging it *for* you"; for example, I know you want it known, and that you are determined not to make it known, so I tell. Of course I do not acknowledge it the way you do; I do not acknowledge it by *expressing pain*.) But obviously sympathy may not be forthcoming. So when I say that "We must acknowledge another's suffering, and we do that by responding to a claim upon our sympathy," I do not mean that we always in fact *have* sympathy, nor that we always ought to have it. The claim of suffering may go unanswered. We may feel lots of things – sympathy, *Schadenfreude*, nothing. If one says that this is a *failure* to acknowledge another's suffering, surely this would not mean that we fail, in such cases, to *know* that he is suffering? It may or may not. The point, however, is that the concept of acknowledgment is evidenced equally by its failure as by its success. It is not a description of a given response but a category in terms of which a given response is evaluated. (It is the sort of concept Heidegger calls an *existentiale*.) A "failure to know" might just mean a piece of ignorance, an absence of something, a blank. A "failure to acknowledge" is the presence of something, a confusion, an indifference, a callousness, an exhaustion, a coldness. Spiritual emptiness is not a blank. – Just as, to say that behavior is expressive is not to say that the man impaled upon his sensation must express it in his behavior; it is to say that in order not to express it he must *suppress* the behavior, or twist it. And if he twists it far or often enough, he may lose possession of the region of the mind which that behavior is expressing.

This may seem clearly false, for if I am in pain how could I lose possession of that knowledge, whatever I do to my behavior? The specialness in the example of pain, always a matter waiting to become problematic in these discussions, may be easiest to overlook here. Let me conclude, therefore, with a word about this, marking a direction investigation might take. Three features of the concept of pain seem immediately relevant: (1) It is a phenomenon fully transparent to consciousness. (2) It is expressed by more or less definite forms of behavior. (3) It presents a case in which the distinction between the inner and the outer seems easy to draw. It is obvious enough that such features are useful to the skeptic's line of thought. The first feature secures intuitiveness for his remark that "even though *I* can't know, *he* knows"; the second eases the idea that there is a *clear* lack which may prevent my knowing, namely the absence of that definite behavior, and simultaneously undermines any standing which his *words* might naturally have in my knowing him; the third enables whatever stability the skeptical conclusion has. (A phenomenon such as envy, or the sense of loss, or working on a jigsaw puzzle, or a ringing in the ears, would lack one or another of these features. But it would be hasty to conclude that the skeptic had chosen his example just in order to illustrate his prior conclusions. It may be, rather, that the example is produced by the problem he takes himself to see, forced upon him by intellectual honesty and phenomenological scrupulousness; and then he reads off his conclusions from that necessary example.) Elsewhere, the first feature is what Wittgenstein is going on in remarking that "It can't be said of me at all (except perhaps as a joke) that I *know* I am in pain"; the second encourages the idea that Wittgenstein criteria are exclusively behavioral; combined with this, the third creates the impression that he is a behaviorist. (He isn't a skeptic, so what else can he be?)

Of course Wittgenstein often denies that a particular feeling or experience is decisive for the application of a concept to others (or to oneself). Never, however, to deny the importance – much less deny the existence (whatever that would mean) – of the inner, but to bring to light false ideas of what is "inner." Similarly, he often speaks of criteria as consisting in what someone "says and does"; but rarely does he speak of someone's *behavior*. We are sometimes interested in an incongruence between feeling and its expression, but then we are perhaps interested in how someone *acts*; if his *behavior* (e.g., his deportment) is in question, that is not necessarily because his feeling is obscure – on the contrary, it may be obvious – but because it is incongruent with the place he is in. We are often interested in explaining someone's behavior; but we can hardly in general do this by appealing to *those* feelings (the ones expressed by the behavior in question), since what we may have been asking for is precisely an explanation for his feeling that way. We know (it is obvious) that dolls do not have feelings; but it should be no less obvious that dolls also do not exhibit behavior. Whether robots exhibit (creaturely) behavior (forms of *life*) is as much a problem – is perhaps the same problem – as whether they "have" "consciousness." – But if "behavior" and "consciousness" go together, in their presence and in their absence, how do "outer" and "inner" come apart?

We don't know whether the mind is best represented by the phenomenon of pain, or by that of envy, or by working on a jigsaw puzzle, or by a ringing in the ears. A natural fact underlying the philosophical problem of privacy is that the individual will take *certain* among his experiences to represent his *own* mind – certain particular sins or shames or surprises of joy – and then take his mind (his self) to be unknown so far as *those* experiences are unknown. (This is an inveterate tendency in adolescence, and in other troubles. But it is inherent at any time.) There is a natural problem of *making* such experiences known, not merely because behavior as a whole may seem irrelevant (or too dumb, or gross) at such times, but because one hasn't forms of words at one's command to release those feelings, and hasn't anyone else whose interest in helping to find the words one trusts. (Someone would have to *have* these feelings to know what I feel.) Here is a source of our gratitude to poetry. And this sense of unknownness is a competitor of the sense of childish fear as an explanation for our idea, and need, of God. – And why should the mind be less dense and empty and mazed and pocked and clotted – and why less a whole – than the world is? At least we can say that in the case of some mental phenomena, when you have twisted or covered your expressions far or long enough, or haven't yet found the words which give the phenomenon expression, I may know better than you how it is with you. I may respond even to the fact of your separateness from me (not to mention mine from you) more immediately than you.

To know you are in pain is to acknowledge it, or to withhold the acknowledgment. – I know your pain the way you do.

Notes

1 (1) Norman Malcolm, "The Privacy of Experience," in Avrum Stroll, ed. *Epistemology: New Essays in the Theory of Knowledge* (New York: Harper and Row, 1967), pp. 129–58. (2) John W. Cook, "Wittgenstein on Privacy," *The Philosophical Review*, Vol. LXXIV (1965), pp. 281–314; reprinted in G. Pitcher, ed. *Wittgenstein: The Philosophical Investigations* (New York: Doubleday Anchor Original, 1966). Page references to this article are according to its original occurrence.

2 The last of these diagnoses is Cook's (cf. pp. 294, 300). Because a number of my remarks – including the whole of the paragraph to which this note is attached – are prompted by reservations about specific diagnoses Cook elaborates (another central one concerns the "supposed literal sense" of sentences or statements – cf. pp. 296–7), I should say explicitly that I do not regard my remarks as overturning those diagnoses, and certainly not as exhausting their interest.

3

"The Frog and the Craftsman"

If the previous essay showed Cavell to be at home in the professional discourse of modern philosophy, this companion extract shows his prose to be equally capable of bearing up under the demands of more literary modes of composition. In this passage (taken from the fourth and final part of *The Claim of Reason*), he maintains his focus on the issue of skepticism about other minds, and his detailed recountings of more or less extraordinary or fairy-tale happenings are clearly related to the orthodox philosophical goal of clarifying one's intuitions by testing them against imaginary but imaginable circumstances. However, that orthodoxy has been given a Wittgensteinian inflection: for Cavell's method here is better described as returning words from their metaphysical to their everyday use – attempting to restore a fine-grained sense of the grammar of our concepts of mind and body by showing the projections that they can (and in particular, those that they cannot) sustain. In short, these imaginative exercises are as much a critique of the method of thought-experimentation as an exemplification of it; they remind us that the force of that method lies in its capacity to unearth and highlight the shared routes of interest and response that underlie the grammar of our words, not to outstrip or transcend them.

But this is not enough to account for the startling and idiosyncratic texture of these philosophical tales about human embodiment. References to philosophical texts from every phase of the history of modern philosophy, and from both sides of the divide between the "Anglo-American" and the "Continental" traditions, are interwoven with one another and with a variety of narrative fragments or compressed short stories, to compose a text that presents itself as holding open the question of what might count as writing philosophically in the late twentieth century. Just as a modernist painter aims to maintain a connection with past aesthetic achievements in her tradition, but can no longer rely upon employing shared conventions in order to do so, so Cavell attempts to inherit the Western philosophical tradition by testing which projections

Originally published in *The Claim of Reason: Wittgenstein, Skepticism, Morality, and Tragedy*, by Stanley Cavell (Oxford: Clarendon Press, 1979), pp. 395–411. Copyright © 1979 by Oxford University Press, Inc. Reprinted by permission.

it can (and which it cannot) sustain. For him, to repress the texts typically assigned to the "Continental" tradition is to lose touch with one half of the philosophical mind; but to undo that repression whilst maintaining a Wittgensteinian faith in the resources of ordinary language turns out to require reopening the question of the proper relation between philosophy and literature. Thus, in a manner prefigured by the logic of interpersonal acknowledgment, this attempt to question a prevailing division within the discipline of philosophy cannot be divorced from the task of questioning the prevailing division of labor between philosophy and other humanistic disciplines within our culture.

Animals other than humans have bodies more or less like the human body, homologous with it. Why do I think that if there are human souls the human body is the only fitting locale for them?

I do not wish to deny that the frog body is the best picture of the frog soul. Nor do I wish to deny that I can think this frog is a Prince – if, that is, I can think that a Prince has suffered enchantment, or anyway metamorphosis. What am I thinking? Not merely that he has been given a frog's body, fitted into one as it were. He *is* a frog – anyway he lives as a frog, says what frogs say, loves what frogs love. He has been changed into something *else*. Has he the soul of a frog? I might say he has the consciousness of a frog, though he has the self-consciousness of a Prince. But there are limits. No magic can change a frog into a Prince – a frog, that is, who had never been a Prince. He can be given a Prince's shape, that is all. He has the self-consciousness of a frog. Then the frog in him will, I imagine, keep trying to get out. There will be moments of embarrassment when he needs to speak, or when suddenly he tucks his legs under himself and leaps from the throne. But these moments can be covered over, either with royal explanations or with judicious applications to the court of mass hallucination or blindness – trivial magic by comparison. – I say they are both frogs, the charmed one on the pad in the pond for all the world a frog, and the charmed one on the throne in the hall for all the court a Prince. I also say there is a difference. But how shall I respond to this difference, how express my knowledge of it? If I care for both of them, I feed both of them flies. In each case I might, or might not, put the fly on a golden plate and lay it before its recipient with deference, perhaps at the table, perhaps on the ground. Others may from time to time not understand, or not appreciate, my behavior. Neither from time to time may I. Or rather, I may not understand my convictions, since they are expressed in what seem incompatible ways.

What really goes into caring for them, beyond the willingness to do them some service? Which of them could one love? One might have an erotic attachment to the one on the throne, but not, if one is normal, to the one on the pad. To which of them might I direct *agape*, my love not for him but for the humanity in him? – But where is this humanity? I cannot settle upon it. I might weep the fortunes of the Prince, and as I do a tear may fall upon the one in the pond. But is it for *him*, the one in the pond, that I am cast down? He may be all right, he may be content. If the Prince were otherwise intact but thought he was a frog then I might weep for him even though he was content. – But if I cannot settle upon saying of either the Prince who is a frog or the frog who is a Prince that he is a human being, I am also not content to say that I regard either of them *as* a human being. What would be the point of saying this, beyond expressing my caring about them? But I care about things other than human beings – animals, trees, statues. And I do not regard these as human beings. Though that might depend upon who I am. – Whoever you are you cannot care about these things the *way* you care about human beings. – But suppose I do not care about human beings. Must I? – If you do not then you can express care only where there is no mutuality. – But suppose I find greater mutuality, anyway sympathy, with a chipmunk. You may find that incredible. But I would like to ask you to consider the individual case.

In failing to settle upon the humanity of the charmed frogs, I perhaps failed to make life sufficiently difficult for myself. I avoided sufficiently individualizing either the one in the pond or the one in the court. If the one in the pond had been, say, the Princess my sister, and responds to me in ways that strike me as her ways – a certain tilt of the head when she rebuked my boorishness, a certain petulance in the way she sometimes turned from me, a certain stillness when she listened to music – then I might feel I had a secret, whose responsibility I could evade only at my peril. But what is my secret? That my sister is no longer a human being? And does this mean that my sister, in particular, is now a frog? Is anything any longer my sister? Where, for example, is she? If my sister, when intact, had been inside her body, then why am I so reluctant to say that she is inside the frog's body? If, on the other hand, my sister had been identical with her body, then why do I have any special attachment to *this* frog at all, whom I have just recently met?

And do these questions trace our genuine alternatives, that either I am inside my body or else I am my body? They seem made for our indecision about whether to say that a sensation, for example, is obviously either private or not private. They also suggest that the problem of others may not be fundamentally epistemological but fundamentally metaphysical. How can we know whether we know there are others until we know what we want to know, what there is to know? But how is this different in the case of the problem of the existence of the world? Are we no longer interested in that question because science is not interested in it in the way we were? Then would the establishment of a science of mind answer that question, or talk us out of it? (What is our interest in science?)

In the meantime, to get at our idea of the human being we will have to go through our ideas of the intactness of the human being, hence through our ideas of the losses of intactness, the ways in which a soul and a body can be lost to one another, in which my experience cannot move freely to the one through the other. We should not make life easy for ourselves here, because we are to test not merely the limits of our identity but the limits of our humanity. Being human is the power to grant being human. Something about flesh and blood elicits this grant from us, and something about flesh and blood can also repel it. How far can we maintain fellow-feeling, let alone love, in the face of a failure of intactness, of a deformation of the body or of the psyche? But perhaps such questions only test the degree of our saintliness. And is that necessary in order to test the degree of our humanity? Apparently, if humanity has degrees.

The idea we have of the human being is not, I assume, likely to be captured by a definition which specifies a genus. If we say that the human being is the rational animal, we have yet to specify the *connection*. (The philosophical usefulness of the genus *homo* is limited by the fact that all its species, with one exception, are extinct. If we had the others for comparison we might *see* what difference sapience makes and not wonder about the connection it must have with the body.) If mind-body dualism is true, then a preestablished harmony between them is easier to believe than a connection. It does not help enough for Descartes to say that the soul is not in the body as a pilot is in a ship, because he is left with the idea that there is some *place* in which they connect. – Right. The connection is *closer* than the image of a pilot suggests; more pervasive. – But closeness is not the issue. I expect that the relation between the stone and the statue is pervasive, but they are not close to one another, they do not touch at every place, or at any place. The smile is not close to the face. I would rather say that the statue is the epiphenomenon of the (worked) stone. But why "worked"? Why not say that the statue just *is* the stone? Because that is partial, or prejudicial; it suggests that any stone can be seen or treated as a statue. This entails a particular view of art and of experience. – Is Wittgenstein subject to this partialness, when he says that "My attitude towards him is my attitude towards a soul"? My attitude is a state of just this organism; it is a passage of just my history; a passage I might find myself in, or take, at any time, regardless of the circumstances. Suppose the attitude noted as "towards a soul" is one I find myself in, or take, towards a stone. Let my attitude be what it may, it cannot turn a stone into a human being. The lamp illuminates hands and gems indifferently. Say that the gem does something special with the light; it nevertheless does nothing to the lamp. – This proves merely that the lamp has no attitudes. The statue is not *in* the stone (except on a certain myth of the sculptor); the statue is not *on* the stone (except in the case of intaglio). The statue is stone.

I am not this piece of flesh (though perhaps Falstaff was his); I am not in this flesh (though perhaps Christ was in his, but then his body was also bread); nor am I my flesh and blood (though somebody else is); nor am I of my flesh (though I hope somebody is). I am flesh.

Kant, if I understand, in the *Groundwork of the Metaphysics of Morals*, reverses the Aristotelian field and thus redirects the problem of connection. He regards the human being as a species of the genus of rational beings, to wit, the species that has the distinction of being animal, i.e., being embodied: the human being is the animal rational. Hence the human being is no longer the highest among creatures but the lowest among hosts. The direction to the human is not animation but incarnation. (The former sets Frankenstein's limitation; the latter Pygmalion's. Pygmalion overcame his limitation through desire and prayer; Frankenstein through craft and theft.) This results from, and serves, Kant's purpose, which is not to explain the fact of our freedom but to show the possibility of it, i.e., to vindicate our inescapable conviction of it; one might say: our attitude toward ourselves and others as possessing it. Being human is aspiring to being human. Since it is not aspiring to being the only human, it is an aspiration on behalf of others as well. Then we might say that being human is aspiring to being seen as human. This is a possible interpretation of Frankenstein and of Pygmalion. Their shared limitation is then that they could accept being seen only by their own creation. This still sounds as if their aspiration was to be God. But how is this aspiration different from that toward the human? The confusion seems inherent in the reception of Christianity. The message of the words of Christ, that we share a common nature, that we are flesh, seems consistently overshadowed by the message of the fact of Christ, that only a God, or the son of God, could bear being human.

Kant's image of the animal rational, demanding of itself the acknowledgment of others (Kant thinks of it as respect), and aspiring to be worthy of it in return, never knowing whether it is truly embodied, in oneself or others, is his continuation of the ancient interpretation of human separateness as a message of human incompleteness. What will complete the human work is, however, not one other but only all others. So to have an idea of the human being is to have an ideal of the human being; and for Kant this ideal entails, and is entailed by, an ideal of the human community. According to this ideal, love must not absorb respect and respect does not require love. Genuine love and genuine respect will both know this.

In asking whether there is such a thing as soul-blindness, I do not mean to insist that there are such things as souls, nor that anybody believes there are. But I do, I expect, mean to insist that we may sincerely and sanely not know whether we believe in such a thing, as we may not know whether we believe in God, or in idols. I assume further that one may believe, or protest, that there are souls and yet not know that there are human beings; for that knowledge would require believing that there are embodied souls, something incarnate. And I assume that some people may not believe, or not know, that there are human beings. It may seem that you could believe that the human body is the best picture of the human soul and yet deny that anything corresponds to the picture. My intuition is that this is false, that not to believe there is such a thing as the human soul is not to know what the human body is, what it is of, heir to.

Call the belief in the soul psychism. Then a serious psychology must take the risk of apsychism. It can no more tolerate the idea of another (little) man inside, in here, than a serious theology can tolerate the idea of another (large) man outside, up there. Nor of small or large anythings, call them spirits. What would these be but points or stretches of etherealized matter, without doubt unverifiable? And idolatrous besides. The spirit of the wind is neither smaller nor larger than the wind; and to say it is *in* the wind is simply to say that it exists only where there is a wind. If I say the spirit of the wind is the wind, I wish to be understood as telling you something not about a spirit but about the wind. (I claim to know nothing about spirits that you do not know.) On that understanding, then: The spirit of the body is the body. – Wittgenstein takes the risk of apsychism, the risk that his understanding of the human body (as, for example, a picture) is unnecessary, or insincere, or dead. If this is behaviorism in disguise then a statue is a stone in disguise.

Suppose what you think is that the soul does not exist. Your problem may be to discover how to get rid of it. First you must discover what happened to it. Nietzsche's travails can be said to be directed to such a task. In asking what happened to God, Nietzsche turns over large amounts of fairly unacceptable material. One had hoped that for the achievement of sanity a little madness would go far enough. But Nietzsche persists in turning up such an image of God as that of a riddled, bloody corpse whose open wounds we attempt to fill, i.e., deny, with knots of religion, which is to say, with fragments of Christian suffering, especially guilt (*Zarathustra*, "On Priests"). (Our *via negativa* begins with the infliction of those holes, or lacks, our tributes of unlikeness from ourselves; and ends with the filling of those holes so as to deny their presence.) The path of the soul in this biography is no longer upward; but since it cannot but aspire, it aspires downward. The soul and the body no longer fit. You might say that the soul has become disembodied, loose;

but of course loose inside. It is a spirit, and not mine. For it to get outside I must be exorcised. You cannot see it, but you can hardly avoid noticing its effects. You can readily infer it. – I think I know persons for whom such issues really do not exist; pre-Christians as it were. But I know of almost no one who has *recovered* from them.

How could it happen that a statue and its stone no longer fit? You may ruin the statue by altering the stone slightly; you may not ruin the statue by altering the stone greatly. You cannot ruin the stone, except for certain purposes; you can also improve it for certain purposes. (Using it for a statue is not improving it.) If you destroy the stone, say pulverize it, you destroy the statue. You might just erase the statue, which was itself the erasing of the stone. You cannot hack a limb from a stone, except figuratively, or anthropomorphically; and if you hack something from a statue you may or may not produce a different statue. A statue in fragments – i.e., without intactness – may be poignant, but not horrifying. A statue may not (no longer) fit the place it is in. This compromises its intactness, imposes a false presence or animation upon it. But not everyone is to be expected to sense this. Surrealism depends upon a vigorous, even bourgeois, sense of appropriateness. This sense may be quite absent, as it were a thing of the past. At least one person in our culture rich enough to have at his disposal a museum's number of statues has them placed about his golf course. A wilderness of monies.

The statue has aspects. By walking around it, by the changing light, in your changing mood, the figure can be seen as vulnerable, as indomitable, as in repose, as if in readiness. A doll has occasions. I am thinking of a rag doll. It can be happy or sad, fed or punished. In repose it has aspects, for example it can be seen as sleeping or dead or sun-bathing. But only if you do not know which is true. – There is only one who knows which is true, the one whose doll it is. And that one cannot strictly be said to *know* it at all, except as a joke, or perhaps as a fiction. – Why not? Because he cannot be in doubt about his doll's (inner) state? Of course he can be in doubt. He might take her to a psychiatrist. You might think he could not be in doubt, or be mistaken, because anything *he* says about the doll *must* be true. But he might be lying about the doll's mood, either to test the genuineness of my interest, or to deprive me of a relationship with the doll. – No, but the point is that anything he *knows* about the doll must be true, whether he says what he knows or not, and whether he knows what he knows by observation or not. – But isn't that merely what it means to know? And the question remains whether he knows, or at all times must know.

There are criteria in terms of which I settle judgments about the (other's) doll. To know whether a concept applies I have to look – at the doll. I have to determine whether I can see it in this way, get that occasion for it to dawn for me. Otherwise I am only humoring the one whose doll it is. Perhaps I am tired, or have a headache; I cannot in any case experience the meaning of the words about the doll. The doll seems rags. I still know what a doll is; but at the moment I am doll-blind. Generally, if I care, I will have to justify my concept by continuing the doll's history: "I don't think she's really hungry. She got into the cookie jar earlier. See how sneaky she looks." I may scatter some crumbs on her dress to prove it, if there is something at hand I can use for crumbs. If I say "See. Now she's comfortable", something must have changed, or I must have done something, put a pillow under her head, or rearranged her so that she is no longer sitting on her foot. If the other, the one whose doll it is, tells me that she likes sitting on her foot – say because it makes her sit taller – and puts her back in her former attitude, then perhaps that is the end of this matter. At some point my say comes to an end. I defer to the one whose doll it is. If I do not, what then? Perhaps the doll becomes our scapegoat; cursed, and cast out.

When I defer to the one whose doll it is, do I defer to his greater power? Power to do what? I respect his relationship to the doll, its being his. This need not be a matter of recognizing his ownership of it. (I recognize his ownership by, for example, not taking the doll from him, not without due process.) I recognize his authority over the doll, his having the last word over it; hence I hold him responsible for it. The most this demands is that the doll be (regarded as) his to play with, for a while, in a particular place. Even if he owns it, his authority is not unlimited; there are still rules in this house. Whether it is better for him to own a doll, to have it for always rather than for a specified while, or until he decides to give it up, or whether it is better for him or for anyone to own anything for always, are empirical questions, or ought to be. (We seem to give children an idea that someone owns their bodies. How, otherwise, shall we explain their having the extraordinary idea of feeling guilty for hurting themselves, even when the game they were playing was not, apparently, forbidden; guilty even for becoming ill? It would then strike them as a declaration of their freedom to say that they own their *own* bodies. But this would merely be an escape from one conceptual cell; or from a dungeon into an enclosed yard. Some are told that their body is a temple. That seems to rule out ownership, except perhaps by a congregation. But it is otherwise a dangerously open idea, especially concerning the conditions for admission.)

Do I respect the doll? I may respect its feelings, lay it comfortably in a nice box before storing it for another generation. But it has no say, for example, about whether it *is* comfortable. It has no voice in its own history. It exists in limbo. – What is the doll? (I would like to answer that question because I feel I know absolutely everything there is to know about dolls. But I would like not to have to answer it since of course I know absolutely nothing about dolls that others do not know. So there is nothing to tell. But there may yet be something to say.) The doll is certainly not the form of the rags. Which form would it be? And if I say that the doll is the life of the rags, that must also be a remark about us, those of us who have a voice in its history. For me to be part of its life, I have to enter into its history, achieve the spirit in which concepts of life are applied to it.

Do I know more about dolls and statues than I know about human beings? That would be extraordinary, since after all I am a human being. Or perhaps not so extraordinary; dolls and statues are human products, so a human being could know everything that has gone into them. Nothing can look, feel, be broken and perhaps be mended like a doll that is not a doll. Nothing can look, feel, be broken and perhaps be restored like a statue that is not a statue. But presumably there can be something, or something can be imagined, that looks, feels, be broken and perhaps healed like a human being that is nevertheless not a human being. What are we imagining? It seems that we are back to the idea that something humanoid or anthropomorphic lacks something; that one could have all the characteristics of a human being *save one*.

What would fit this idea? How about a perfected automaton? They have been improved to such an extent that on more than one occasion their craftsman has had to force me to look inside one of them to convince me that it was not a real human being. – Am I imagining anything? If so, why this way? Why did I have to be forced? What did I see when I looked inside? (How) did that convince me?

Go back to a stage before perfection. I am strolling in the craftsman's garden with him and his friend. He is in his usual white laboratory coat, his friend is wearing gloves and a hat with its brim so low it almost covers his eyes. To make a long story short, the craftsman finally says, with no little air of pride: "We're making more progress than you think. Take my friend here. He's one." The craftsman offers his friend a seat on one of the wroughtiron benches and bids him relax. He leans back, crosses his legs, accepts a proffered cigarette with thanks. Then the craftsman raises his friend's left trouser leg and gives the leg a tap. It is undeniably metal. But so what? Then he asks his friend to remove his gloves. The hands turn out to be leathery or rubbery or something, anyway pretty obviously not real hands. But so what? So the friend has a metal leg and two prosthetic hands, and this is a terrible way to treat him; it is obscene; a striptease of misery. I do not wish to draw it out in much more detail. – It is clear enough that we may arrive at a conclusion that convinces me the friend is an automation. The craftsman knocks the friend's hat off to reveal a manikin's head (with, as a joke, a couple of glass buttons for eyes) which he rotates through 360 degrees; he rips open the friend's shirt to reveal a chest of hammered brass which, prompted by the craftsman's prying knife inserted into an all but invisible seam running straight down from the pit of the arm, snaps off to reveal something like clockwork.

It is less clear, but still clear enough, that we may not arrive at a convincing conclusion. As the years go on, I am invited for a walk with the craftsman and his friends in their garden whenever there is a new development. The routine is always the same. I have seen the leg and the hands get progressively more lifelike until I almost no longer marvel at them. Today is special however; I can tell from the craftsman's nervous gestures and the suppressed eagerness of his voice that there has been some new breakthrough. . . . The brass chest snaps off and, to my horror, I see no clockwork, but, for all the world, the insides of a human being. Recoiled, aghast, I can hardly attend to the craftsman's delighted words: "Of course, it's far from perfect, and most of it is superficial fakery, especially the bones. The digestive and circulatory systems are not bad, but we have to do more work on the blood, which doesn't congeal in the normal temperature range. The immediate problem with the nervous system has to do with the relative response rates of the fibre systems. That is crudely put, of course. It's really a problem of their interaction. As matters stand, the pain-responses are too – how shall I say? – on and off. Don't you agree?" (He demonstrates by prodding the friend's left hand. The response is quick but definitely mechanical.) "We could simulate better responses, by, for example, making the limbs slightly more sluggish. But the genuine issue is how to get the pain itself so that it gets better prepared and fades better."

I can hardly look, and when I look I hardly know what to look at, or look for. As a matter of fact, I throw an anxious glance at the manikin face, expecting – I'm not sure. But it is reassuringly rigid, its crude eyes reassuringly glazed. I confess the thought does occur to me that I should check that head; or not so much the thought as the impulse occurs to see whether the head might not be just a shell, and inside it – what? A real head, or the insides of a real head, or stuff that looks like the real insides? The impulse fades as my trust reasserts itself. And I feel not a little foolish. What would it prove to look inside when I have *already* looked inside? – Am I foolish not to ask the craftsman what he means by "the pain itself"? But I took myself to understand him well enough. He meant, roughly, everything that happens between cause and effect, I mean between what went in from outside and what comes out from inside. Well, he may want to be more sophisticated than that and call the pain itself just what happens at the change of direction, the point of transfer between going in and coming out. I might have objected to this as follows: "There cannot be anything happening *between* a cause and its effect." Presumably I do not want to conclude that therefore there is nothing that *is* the pain. Then I must conclude that there is something wrong with this picture of causation. If there are "points of transfer", they must occur at *each* point. And a stimulus cannot set up a causal network. This must be in effect all the time. So what pain is is a change in the rate of transfer, or a change in the rate of change of direction. But if so, then that must be a way of representing all psychological phenomena. They must form a system. – But why am I thinking of this in relation to the craftsman? Have his activities put him in any better position for investigating these matters than I am in? I am more interested in learning whether he really wanted my agreement about the pain-responses.

Time passes. One day the craftsman is quite beside himself with suppressed excitement. He insists that I pay special attention to each of our procedures. The leg and the hands are by now really astonishing. The movement of the legs crossing and of the cigarette being lit are simply amazing. I want to see it all again. And as for the voice, I would bet anything that no one could tell. So far I'm dazzled. Then the craftsman knocks off the hat to reveal what is for all the world a human head, intact. He rotates it through about 45 degrees and then stops himself with an embarrassed smile. The head turns back to its original position, but now its eyes turn toward mine. Then the knife is produced. As it approaches the friend's side, he suddenly leaps up, as if threatened, and starts grappling with the craftsman. They both grunt, and they are yelling. The friend is producing these words: "No more. It hurts. It hurts too much. I'm sick of being a human guinea pig, I mean a guinea pig human."

Do I intervene? On whose behalf? Let us *stipulate* that the friend is not a ringer, not someone drawn into these encounters from outside. – It is important to ask whether we *can* stipulate this. If we cannot, then it seems that the whole thing *must* simply be a science or a fairy tale. But if it were taken as science or fairy tale then we would not *have* to stipulate this. It would be accepted without question. – But only if it were a successful story. There are rules about these things. Suppose I had told my story leaving myself out and ending it with the friend yelling his words. Then I would have composed a primitive science fable whose moral has been drawn from a thousand better places: We are Frankensteins whose creations are meddlings with nature and will one day rise against us. No serious publication would take the story, but it is a complete one. If, however, I tell it as I have, with myself in it, and I add the question, "Do I intervene?", then the story is not complete. If I stop there, a sensible reader will be contemptuous at my incompetence; I do not know the rules. I have not given enough evidence to know whether, for example, the friend is a ringer, nor to make the sheer speculation an interesting one.

Let us try to complete it in such a way that the craftsman is shown to know that the friend is not a ringer. Then the friend is who, or what, the craftsman knows him to be. What does the craftsman know? Suppose, satisfied with the degree of my alarm, and my indecision about whether to intervene, the craftsman raises his arm and the friend thereupon ceases struggling, moves back to the bench, sits, crosses his legs, takes out a cigarette, lights and smokes it with evident pleasure, and is otherwise expressionless. (I may be having a little trouble with the rules of the fiction here. Could a being, for example a fictional being, evidence pleasure and be otherwise expressionless? How about otherwise impassive? That is prejudicial. A thing cannot be impassive unless that thing *can* have passions. Perhaps I should just omit "with evident pleasure".) The craftsman is happy: "We – I mean I – had you going, eh? Now you realize that the struggling – I mean the movements – and the words – I mean the vocables – of revolt were all built in. He is – I mean it is – meant – I mean designed – to do all that. Come, look here." He raises the knife again and moves toward the friend.

Do I intervene? That is, do I go on with the story? I can imagine only one interesting continuation (without adding more characters). It is one in which my interest shifts from the friend to the craftsman. I turn on him: "You fool! You've built in too much! You've built in the passions as well as the movements and the vocables of revolt! You've given this artificial body a real soul." (That is, a soul; there are no artificial souls – none, anyway, that are not real souls.) Then the end may consist in our realization that this had to be.

Or it may go on with our investigating why it had to be. But then our problem is a conceptual one, and we will have to start telling one another new stories, or vying with one another for our pictures of the passions. In any case, I have learned that if something humanoid differs *in some respect* from a human being – that it has all the characteristics of a human being save one – that respect will not be something going on just inside, or just outside. This is why my interest shifts away from the friend. I can learn no more from him, anyway, no more about him by looking inside him. I know what I will see if I look.

Isn't this just an assumption, a particular interpretation of the story? Maybe the imitation insides, in the former story, were just virtuosity for the sake of virtuosity. They have been cleaned up in the new model. There is nothing there but acceptable strata and zones of silk-like and sponge-like substances and golden spun wire thinner than spider's threads. This is what the craftsman knows and he just wants to show me where the micro-computers and energy sources are placed. – Then I will insist that he show me this by using X-rays or diagrams, not a knife. – So then you are interested, after all, in what is going on inside him. – But not in order to settle whether the friend is a human being. This could be settled by *stipulating* that if I am shown a micro-computer or energy source inside then I am to conclude that he is not one. But this is arbitrary. Why stop there? A human being could contain such devices. Why go that far? If the ideas of silk and sponge and wire have not convinced me, why would any of these further accompaniments? – But if looking inside *might not* settle the question whether the friend is a human being, why isn't this more interesting than ever, or, if you like, more amazing than ever? And doesn't this at least suggest that we cannot *know* that another is sentient? – It may suggest what state someone is in who takes it this way.

For it is not I, at this stage of the story, who refuses to press for a settlement; it is the teller of the story, with me in it, who refuses to see that the story is incomplete. If I, in the story, am unsettled about the humanity or automatonity of the friend, it is only my subservience to the craftsman's view that would prompt me to look inside. Whatever doubts I have about the friend's insides I equally have, or should be permitted to have, about his outsides as well. Why, for example, does he have just five fingers on each hand; and why hands; and why toes instead of rollers; and why not eyes in the back of his head; and why, if it is, is his "sense" of "hearing" restricted to the human – I mean, roughly to *my* – range? (What would count as his being hard of hearing, or deaf?) Isn't *this* all virtuosity just for virtuosity's sake? It corrupts the craftsman's craft. Form should picture function.

How far can my subservience to the craftsman extend? Suppose I have trained myself to think of the friend as having not feelings but "feelings". (Cp. Hilary Putnam, "Robots: Machines or . . . ?".) Which means that I have trained myself to show him, for example, not sympathy but "sympathy"; and perhaps learned not to be impatient with him if I think he is complaining too much – I mean of course "complaining" too much, and "impatient" with him ("him"). Then one day, my back turned, the friend grabs my arm ("grabs"?), wheels me around, and the craftsman approaches me with his knife. "So," he says, "you have accommodated yourself to the friend, have you? You have learned how to treat him. Your attitude towards him is your attitude towards a "soul", is it? You hedge his soul, do you?" Then he rips open my shirt and snaps off my chest to reveal (I glance down) some elegant clockwork. You cannot imagine my surprise. – Can I? I can imagine either of two conclusions the craftsman may wish me to draw from this demonstration that I am not, for all I know, in any better position, soul-wise or body-wise, than the friend.

One is: For all I know, all I have are, for example, "pains". The other is: For all I know, the friend has, for example, *pains*.

To accept the latter conclusion is to accept the friend as an other, a fellow sufferer, unhedged. In what would acceptance consist? The craftsman continues: "Does he have pain, is he subject to pain, or not? Decide!" But even with the knife pointed at me I cannot decide. Before, when the craftsman asked for my agreement, I was in a position to decide something, there was room for me to have a say, and there was the same room for the craftsman. But now I am being asked whether I do or do not share the life of suffering with this other, and at the same time I am shown that I do not know whether I am observing or leading that life. Has the craftsman given up *his* say, granted the friend autonomy? If he told me that he had, could I believe him? I understand him no better than I understand the friend. If what the craftsman says is that he has decided that the friend suffers, or decided to say so, then who is hedging?

To settle upon the former conclusion – that for all I know all I have are "pains" – I would presumably have to give up the idea that I am, and know that I am, a human being. Could I conceive of myself as something *less* than a human, on a par with whatever it was I was conceiving the friend to be? If this is what I am, and I know it, then this is doubtless my secret. Why did I not think that the friend might be harboring such a secret? Perhaps because I did not think of him as a *lapsed* human. If he has such a secret, he could never tell it to me, for I could understand it no better than I can understand him: he is private to me.

But this is ridiculous. He has no comparison at his disposal. Whatever painish thing he has, he thinks of it as *pain*. Then how am I different? Well, he may not have a painish thing at all, let alone think anything about its status. Whereas I certainly have, and do. I feel for example, abashed by the recent revelation concerning my body. And what *I* feel, when I feel abashed, *is* what feeling abashed is. That is not a very persuasive definition. But I do not mean it to preclude others from feeling it too. I just mean to assure myself that no one is in a better position to know what feeling abashed or feeling pain is than I am.

How would I know if another is in fact equally well placed? If I think my feeling is somehow connected to this machinery and other stuff under me, into whose works I happen to have fallen, then I might think that the friend's feeling would similarly be connected to his stuff, if he had the feeling. But of course I could not be sure. I am certain that my abashment comes from this body – not because it causes it (though it may) but because it is its object, it is that in the face of which I am abashed. But again the friend may not feel this way about his body; he may enjoy it, as Thoreau did his set of false teeth. Any inference from his body to him therefore amounts to a sheer guess. It is not that all I have to go on in making this inference is just one case (mine); it is that I cannot use even that case; I do not know if it enters in. (Of course what I know of myself and take myself for enters utterly into what I can know of another and take him for. Only the idea that the other is *analogous* to me fails to bring out how I enter in.)

Instead of settling for a guess, I may fix my attention on the body of the other as upon his or her entrails and find myself transfixed with the conviction that he or she is besouled. I have divined it; I have penetrated the veil of the other by taking his body as an omen, in this case a good omen, of a soul. If others credit my gift generally, I will be set up as a seer and soothsayer. Regarding a seer and soothsayer as "the one who knows" (i.e., sees and says) the state of another would be an intellectually more coherent response to skeptical doubt than regarding the other as the one who alone knows the state of himself. If the statement that the other has what I have, i.e., has sentience, is a hypothesis, then it may have either of two outcomes. If the one about whom the hypothesis is made is the only one who knows the outcome, this is not only uncheckable, but depends upon a *comparison* of what the other knows with what I know, and there *could* be nobody to make the comparison. Anyway *he* could not and *I* could not.

Here is a further alternative. I from time to time find that I have intuitions about the state of the friend. Usually I have an intuition of his pain when his body is contorted, sometimes not. He cannot *volunteer* news of his condition to me, because then I would have to believe him, and that I cannot do. (Or will not do, because I regard such beliefs as superstitions: they can never be checked.) Nor can he *show* me how it is with him, because all he could do to show me, for example that he is in pain, would be, for example, to contort his body, or point at it; and such things may or may not produce my intuition of his pain. (If someone were such that he constantly had intuitions about all the others he knew, he would go mad. Only God could bear to be God. An understanding of the first commandment.) Suppose the friend and I prove to be mutually intuitive, with a normally expected range of failures in our intuitions. The most plausible theory of ourselves would be that we are pure minds, unextended beings. (It would be nonsense to imagine that we might be one another, and hence "feel what the other feels". For I am characterized by nothing but being the one I am; and the same goes for him.) The bodies associated with each of us are enormously convenient to have; they make us visible and audible to one another. Well, strictly speaking *I* (and of course *he*) are not made visible and audible; but the bodies are necessary to prompt the intuitions we have of one another. (We might have philosophical disputes about whether we are immortal, whether we could survive unassociated with a body, hence without the possibility of being intuited by our own kind. But we may not be interested in the question. What happens to us at the death of the body is what happens to the music when the music concludes. There is a period of reverberation, and then nothing.)

Suppose one day I notice that my feelings have become uniformly associated with what is happening to my body, that, for example, I always have a pain when my body contorts and never otherwise, or almost never; or I may notice that my intuitions about the friend's pain come over me only when his body contorts, almost never otherwise, and he almost always confirms the intuition, i.e., I find I take his word. I may then no longer regard the body as something with which I and he are each associated, something we each "have", but something we each of us *have*. The most plausible theory about us now is that we are human beings. The analogy between us is now excellent. I can check on his feelings by expressing my intuitions (for his confirmation or disconfirmation); and it makes sense to check on the connection between his body and his feelings because it makes sense to check on the connection between mine and mine. One day it occurs to me that I no longer understand what it means to check this. If I have a pain, there *must* be a cause; if I do not, where I ought to have, then there must be a cause for *that*. Doubt about whether I have a body is out of the question. Doubt about whether he has a body is also out of the question, unless my intuitions about him cease. Then I may think that to say I *have* a body does not go deep enough in expressing my connection with it. I would prefer to say that I *am* my body, even though I am satisfied that I am not. I do not know that I am not my body, as though I know that it is false to say that I am. It is rather that to say so falsifies my convictions on the matter; my body is not what I take myself to be. – That is because one does not *take* oneself to *be* anything. – Then what is the point of telling me what I am? It is, analogously, not false to say that I *have* a body, unless that suggests, for example, that I might not have one, as I might not have a left arm. If I say that I necessarily have a body, I am leaving out my relation to *this* one. And if I say I necessarily have *this* body, then I am not sure I believe it, not at any rate as I believe that I do have this one.

It may be that the sense of falsification comes from the way I understand the phrase "have a body". It is really a mythological way of saying that I am flesh. But I am not satisfied with this myth, for it implies that I also have something other than a body, call it a soul. Now I have three things to put together: a body, a soul, and me. (So there are four things to be placed: I plus those three.) But I no more *have* a soul than I have a body. That is what I say here and now. People who say they have a soul sometimes militantly take its possession as a point of pride, for instance

William Ernest Henley and G. B. Shaw. Take the phrase "have a soul" as a mythological way of saying that I am spirit. If the body individuates flesh and spirit, singles me out, what does the soul do? It binds me to others.

4

The Avoidance of Love (External-World Skepticism)

Despite its extreme brevity and allusiveness, this short passage (extracted from the closing pages of Cavell's essay on *King Lear*) condenses much that is of importance in the initial orientation of Cavell's Wittgensteinian approach to skepticism. For the extracts relating to skepticism so far assembled have focused exclusively upon other minds; but modern skepticism also raises questions about our right to claim knowledge of anything external to the subject's present moment of consciousness, not just of other minds. Our picture of Cavell's understanding of the skeptical impulse would thus be importantly incomplete without some indication of his views about this more wide-ranging variant of skepticism. Those views are developed in great detail in Part Two of *The Claim of Reason*; but this early passage gives a particularly perspicuous sense of their overall shape. In particular, it underlines Cavell's sense of the human seriousness of modern skepticism. It need not be an intellectual game designed to introduce technical problems in epistemology; it can also give expression to the sense that modern scientific and cultural developments have put in question the authenticity of any human claim to make contact with a reality external to our subjectivity. And it also reveals that an inflection of the concept of acknowledgment can contribute to overcoming skeptical anxieties of this particular kind. For on Cavell's view, skepticism errs in thinking that, since the world's existence cannot be known with certainty, it may not be real; what this really shows is that the world's presentness to us is not a function of knowing, but of acceptance. The similarities and differences between the concepts of acknowledgment and acceptance later become the explicit focus of the final stretches of *The Claim of Reason*, and then of the Beckman lectures (in *In Quest of the Ordinary*).

The immediate context of this invocation of the concept of acceptance also has a wider significance. First, it suggests Cavell's sense of skepticism as a specifically modern and broadly cultural phenomenon.

Originally published in *Must We Mean What We Say? A Book of Essays*, by Stanley Cavell (Cambridge: Cambridge University Press, 1969), pp. 322–5. Reprinted by permission.

He explicitly relates the advent of modern skepticism to the rise of the
new science and the death of God; and his sense of the Shakespearian
corpus as a place in which various manifestations of the skeptical impulse
and its overcoming find literary rather than philosophical expression is
clearly not unrelated to the fact that Shakespeare was a contemporary of
Bacon, Galileo, and Descartes. In short, for Cavell, skepticism is anything but an exclusively or narrowly philosophical issue. Secondly, however, it shows that Cavell takes his interest in skepticism not only to
maintain a connection between his preoccupations and those of earlier
modern philosophers, but also to establish a bridge between the Anglo-
American and Continental traditions in philosophy. For what Cavell
means by acknowledgment and acceptance are importantly shaped by his
understanding of the early Heidegger's characterization of human existence as Being-with and Being-in-the-world, and by the latter's attempts
to show that skepticism errs not by making false claims but by raising a
question where none can intelligibly be asked. This sense of a connection
between Wittgensteinian and Heideggerian concerns is a constant theme
in Cavell's later writings.

Epistemology will demonstrate that we cannot know, cannot be certain of,
the future; but we don't believe it. We anticipate, and so we are always
wrong. Even when what we anticipate comes to pass we get the wrong idea
of our powers and of what our safety depends upon, for we imagine that
we *knew* this would happen, and take it either as an occasion for congra-
tulations or for punishments, of ourselves or others. Instead of acting as
we can and remaining equal to the consequences. (Here one might
consider the implication of the fact that you say "I knew it!" with sharp
relief or sudden anguish, and that of course it does not mean that in fact
you were fully apprized of a particular outcome. It means, roughly, that
"something told you," something you wish you had harkened to.
And while that is no doubt true, the frame of mind in which you express
it, by saying in that particular way that you *knew*, assures that you will
not harken. Because it reveals a frame of mind in which you had tried,
and are going on trying now, to alchemize a guess or a hope or a suspicion
into a certainty, a *pry* into the future rather than an intimation of conscience.)

Nietzsche thought the metaphysical consolation of tragedy was lost
when Socrates set *knowing* as the crown of human activity. And it is a
little alarming, from within the conviction that the medium of drama
which Shakespeare perfected also ended with him, to think again that
Bacon and Galileo and Descartes were contemporary with those events.
We will hardly say that it was *because* of the development of the new
science and the establishing of epistemology as the monitor of philosoph-

ical inquiry that Shakespeare's mode of tragedy disappeared. But it may be that the loss of presentness – which is what the disappearance of that mode of tragedy means – is what works us into the idea that we can save our lives by knowing them. This seems to be the message both of the new epistemology and of Shakespeare's tragedy themselves.

In the unbroken tradition of epistemology since Descartes and Locke (radically questioned from within itself only in our period), the concept of knowledge (of the world) disengages from its connections with matters of information and skill and learning, and becomes fixed to the concept of certainty alone, and in particular to a certainty provided by the (by my) senses. At some early point in epistemological investigations, the world normally present to us (the world in whose existence, as it is typically put, we "believe") is brought into question and vanishes, whereupon all connection with a world is found to hang upon what can be said to be "present to the senses"; and that turns out, shockingly, not to be the world. It is at this point that the doubter finds himself cast into skepticism, turning the existence of the external world into a problem. Kant called it a scandal to philosophy and committed his genius to putting a stop to it, but it remains active in the conflicts between traditional philosophers and their ordinary language critics, and it inhabits the void of comprehension between continental ontology and Anglo-American analysis as a whole. Its relevance to us at the moment is only this: The skeptic does not gleefully and mindlessly forgo the world we share, or thought we shared; he is neither the knave Austin took him to be, nor the fool the pragmatists took him for, nor the simpleton he seems to men of culture and of the world. He forgoes the world for just the reason that the world is important, that it is the scene and stage of connection with the present: he finds that it vanishes exactly with the effort to *make* it present. If this makes him unsuccessful, that is because the presentness achieved by certainty of the senses cannot compensate for the presentness which had been elaborated through our old absorption in the world. But the wish for genuine connection is there, and there was a time when the effort, however hysterical, to assure epistemological presentness was the best expression of seriousness about our relation to the world, the expression of an awareness that presentness was threatened, gone. If epistemology wished to make knowing a substitute for that fact, that is scarcely foolish or knavish, and scarcely some simple mistake. It is, in fact, one way to describe the tragedy *King Lear* records.

For its characters, having for whatever reason to forgo presentness to their worlds, extend that disruption in their knowing of it (Lear and Edmund knowing they cannot be loved, Regan knowing the destination of Gloucester, Edgar knowing he is contemned and has to win acceptance). But how do we stop? How do we learn that what we need is not more knowledge but the willingness to forgo knowing? For this sounds to us as though we are being asked to abandon reason for irrationality (for we know what these are and we know these are alternatives), or to trade knowledge for superstition (for we know when conviction is the one and when it is the other – the thing the superstitious always take for granted). This is why we think skepticism must mean that we cannot know the world exists, and hence that perhaps there isn't one (a conclusion some profess to admire and others to fear). Whereas what skepticism suggests is that since we cannot know the world exists, its presentness to us cannot be a function of knowing. The world is to be *accepted*; as the presentness of other minds is not to be known, but acknowledged. But what is this "acceptance," which caves in at a doubt? And where do we get the idea that there is something we cannot do (e.g., prove that the world exists)? For this is why we take Kant to have said that there are things we cannot know; whereas what he said is that something cannot be known – *and* cannot coherently be doubted either, for example, that there is a world and that we are free. When Luther said we cannot know God but must have faith, it is clear enough that the inability he speaks of is a logical one: there is not some comprehensible activity we cannot perform, and equally not some incomprehensible activity we cannot perform. Our relation to God is that of parties to a testament (or refusers of it); and Luther's logical point is that you do not accept a promise by knowing something about the promisor. How, if this is the case, we become confused about it clearly requires explanation, and the cure will be sufficiently drastic – crucifying the intellect. But perhaps no less explanation is required to understand why we have the idea that knowing the world exists is to be understood as an instance of knowing that a particular object exists (only, so to speak, an enormously large one, the largest). Yet this idea is shared by all traditional epistemologists.[1] (Its methodological expression is the investigation of our knowledge of the external world by an investigation of a claim that a particular object exists.) Nor is it surprising that it is the intellect which, still bloody from its victories, remains to be humbled if the truth here is to emerge. Reason seems able to overthrow the deification of everything but itself. To imagine that what is therefore required of us is a new rage of irrationality would be about as intelligent as to imagine that because heaven rejects the prideful man what it craves is a monkey. For the point of forgoing knowledge is, of course, to know.

Note

1 A particularly brilliant occurrence of it runs through Hume's *Dialogues on Natural Religion*: It is the essential assumption of Cleanthes (the new believer) which Philo (the new skeptic) does not question, and I suppose that one or other of them, or both

together, pretty well exhaust Hume's discoveries in this region. Freed from this assumption, the *experience* of design or purpose in the world (which Cleanthes always begins with and comes back to, and which Philo confirms) has a completely different force. It is no longer a modest surmise about a particular object, for which there is no good evidence (none against, but none for); but rather, being a natural and *inescapable* response, it has, in terms of Hume's own philosophizing, the same claim to reveal the world as our experience of causation (or of objecthood) has. – This is essentially the view of Hume's *Dialogues* that I have presented in my classes over a number of years. In the spring of 1967 I began studying and teaching the writings of Heidegger, and the discussion of the concepts of *world* and *worldhood* near the beginning of *Being and Time* seem to me not only intuitively clear against this background, but to represent the beginnings of a formidable phenomenological investigation of a phase of empiricism, indeed of traditional epistemology altogether. Part II of this essay bears marks of that reading, notably in the transition from the concept of being in someone's *presence* to that of being in his *present* (e.g., p. 337); but the ideas do not derive from that reading, and my understanding of Heidegger's work is still too raw for me to wish to claim support from it.

I am not unaware of the desperate obscurity of these remarks about traditional epistemology, both in this note and in the section of this essay from which it is suspended. That is the point at which my reliance on my doctoral thesis is most sustained.

5

Ending the Waiting Game

This extract is taken from the opening half of Cavell's early essay on Beckett's *Endgame*. On one level, it conveys the broad interpretative principles and context through which Cavell motivates a compelling reading of one of Beckett's most powerful and challenging texts. Once again, we can see the literary-critical consequences of the ordinary language philosopher's attempts to recontextualize words as uttered by recognizably human beings in recognizably human situations; and here, that attempt includes a heightened sensitivity to the psychological, spiritual, and aesthetic consequences of developments in late twentieth-century politics and science. The essay also constitutes one of Cavell's most sustained examinations of *literary or theatrical* modernism; his entire reading begins from a desire to understand Beckett as a modernist writer, to grasp how he is able to acknowledge the history, tradition, and resources of theatre and literature rather than simply taking them for granted or entirely rejecting them. And the pivot of this achievement turns out to be Beckett's ability to keep faith with language: on Cavell's reading, *Endgame* embodies a penetrating diagnosis of the prevailing physiognomies of ordinary language, both its impoverishments and its stubborn retentions of human significance – of the human inability not to mean what language gives us to mean.

This interpretation of the modes of meaning upon which Beckettian dialogue relies provides the basis for a critique of the reductiveness of certain philosophical pictures of ordinary language. On Cavell's view, Beckett's maddened but motivated characters dramatize the positivist assumption that meaningfulness can be exhaustively captured in systems of logical notation by engaging in repartée whose cutting edge depends upon its endless and specific contraventions of the endlessly specific conventions which structure ordinary language without being capturable in logical calculi. More generally, however, this Beckettian conception of ordinary language embodies an ambivalence that is rarely registered in philosophers' straightforwardly negative or positive deployments of the

Originally published in *Must We Mean What We Say? A Book of Essays*, by Stanley Cavell (Cambridge: Cambridge University Press, 1969), pp. 117–37. Reprinted by permission.

concept, but which is absolutely central to Cavell's use of it. He takes Beckett to confirm that nothing can be more human than to deny the conventional implications of ordinary language, that our uses of language – being woven into our forms of life – cannot be perfectly insulated from the superficialities, crazinesses, and forms of self-destructiveness that sometimes pervade our culture and its practices. *Endgame* presents us with a vision of ordinary language and life as both cause and cure of philosophical and spiritual confusions that guides Cavell throughout his career. His faith in the ordinary is never superstitious or untroubled.

I

Who are these people? Where are they, and how did they get there? What can illuminate their mood of bewilderment as well as their mood of appalling comprehension? What is the source of their ugly power over one another, and of their impotence? What gives to their conversation its sound, at once of madness and of plainness?

I begin with two convictions. The first is that the ground of the play's quality is the *ordinariness* of its events. It is true that what we are given to see are two old people sticking half up out of trash cans, and an extraordinarily garbed blind paraplegic who imposes bizarre demands on the only person who can carry them out, the only inhabitant of that world who has remaining to him the power of motion. But take a step back from the bizarrerie and they are simply a family. Not just any family perhaps, but then every unhappy family is unhappy in its own way – gets in its own way in its own way. The old father and mother with no useful functions any more are among the waste of society, dependent upon the generation they have bred, which in turn resents them for their uselessness and dependency. They do what they can best do: they bicker and reminisce about happier days. And they comfort one another as best they can, not necessarily out of love, nor even habit (this love and this habit may never have been formed) but out of the knowledge that they were both there, they have been through it together, like comrades in arms, or passengers on the same wrecked ship; and a life, like a disaster, seems to need going over and over in reminiscence, even if that is what makes it disastrous. One of their fondest memories seems to be the time their tandem bicycle crashed and they lost their legs: their past, their pain, has become their entertainment, their pastime. Comfort may seem too strong a term. One of them can, or could, scratch the other where the itch is out of reach, and Nagg will tolerate Nell's girlish re-rhapsodizing the beauties of Lake Como if she will bear his telling again his favorite funny story. None of this is very *much* comfort perhaps, but then there never is very *much* comfort.

The old are also good at heaping curses on their young and at controlling them through guilt, the traditional weapons of the weak and dependent. Nagg uses the most ancient of all parental devices, claiming that something is due him from his son for the mere fact of having begot him. Why that should ever have seemed, and still seem, something in itself to be grateful for is a question of world-consuming mystery – but Hamm ought to be the least likely candidate for its effect, wanting nothing more than to wrap up and send back the gift of life. (His problem, as with any child, is to find out where it came from.) Yet he keeps his father in his house, and lays on his adopted son Clov the same claim to gratitude ("It was I was a Father to you"). Like his father, powerless to walk, needing to tell stories, he masks his dependence with bullying – the most versatile of techniques, masking also the requirements of loyalty, charity, magnanimity. All the characters are bound in the circle of tyranny, the most familiar of family circles.

Take another step back and the relationship between Hamm and his son-servant-lover Clov shows its dominance. It is, again, an ordinary neurotic relationship, in which both partners wish nothing more than to end it, but in which each is incapable of taking final steps because its end presents itself to them as the end of the world. So they remain together, each helpless in everything save to punish the other for his own helplessness, and play the consuming game of manipulation, the object of which is to convince the other that you yourself do not need to play. But any relationship of absorbing importance will form a world, as the personality does. And a critical change in either will change the world. The world of the happy man is different from the world of the unhappy man, says Wittgenstein in the *Tractatus*. And the world of the child is different from the world of the grown-up, and that of the sick from that of the well, and the mad from the un-mad. This is why a profound change of consciousness presents itself as a revelation, why it is so difficult, why its anticipation will seem the destruction of the world: even where it is a happy change, a world is always lost. I do not insist upon its appearing a homosexual relationship, although the title of the play just possibly suggests a practice typical of male homosexuality, and although homosexuality figures in the play's obsessive goal of sterility – the non-consummation devoutly to be wished.

The language sounds as extraordinary as its people look, but it imitates, as Chekhov's does, the qualities of ordinary conversation among people whose world is shared – catching its abrupt shifts and sudden continuities; its shades of memory, regret, intimidation; its opacity to the outsider. It is an abstract imitation, where Chekhov's is objective. (I do not say "realistic," for that might describe Ibsen, or Hollywoodese, and in any case, as it is likely to be heard, would not emphasize the fact that art had gone into it.) But it is an achievement for the theater, to my mind, of the same magnitude. Not, of course, that the imitation of the ordinary is the only, or best, option for writing dialogue. Not every dramatist wants this quality; a writer like Shakespeare can get it whenever he wants it. But to insist upon the ordinary, keep its surface and its rhythm, sets a powerful device. An early movie director, René Clair I believe, remarked that if a person were shown a film of an ordinary whole day in his life, he would go mad. One thinks, perhaps, of Antonioni. At least he and Beckett have discovered new artistic resource in the fact of boredom; not as a topic merely, but as a dramatic technique. To miss the ordinariness of the lives in *Endgame* is to avoid the extraordinariness (and ordinariness) of our own.

II

I said there are two specific convictions from which my interpretation proceeds. The second also concerns, but more narrowly, the language Beckett has discovered or invented; not now its use in dialogue, but its grammar, its particular way of making sense, especially the quality it has of what I will call *hidden literality*. The words strew obscurities across our path and seem willfully to thwart comprehension; and then time after time we discover that their meaning has been missed only because it was so utterly bare – totally, therefore unnoticeably, in view. Such a discovery has the effect of showing us that it is *we* who had been willfully uncomprehending, misleading ourselves in demanding further, or other, meaning where the meaning was nearest. Many instances will come to light as we proceed, but an example or two may help at the outset.

At several points through the play the names God and Christ appear, typically in a form of words which conventionally expresses a curse. They are never, however, used (by the character saying them, of course) to curse, but rather in perfect literalness. Here are two instances: "What in God's name could there be on the horizon?" (p. 31); "Catch him [a flea] for the love of God" (p. 33). In context, the first instance shows Hamm really asking whether anything on the horizon is appearing in God's name, as his sign or at his bidding; and the second instance really means that if you love God, have compassion for him, you will catch and kill the flea. Whether one will be convinced by such readings will depend upon whether one is convinced by the interpretation to be offered of the play as a whole, but they immediately suggest one motive in Beckett's uncovering of the literal: it removes curses, the curses under which the world is held. One of our special curses is that we can use the name of God naturally only to curse, take it only in vain. Beckett removes this curse by converting the rhetoric of cursing; not, as traditionally, by using the name in prayer (*that* alternative, as is shown explicitly elsewhere in the play, is obviously no longer open to us) but by turning its formulas into declarative utterances, ones of pure denotation – using the sentences "cognitively," as the logical positivists used to put it. Beckett (along with other philosophers recognizable as existentialist) shares with positivism its wish to escape connotation, rhetoric, the noncognitive, the irrationality and awkward memories of ordinary language, in favor of the directly verifiable, the isolated and perfected present. Only Beckett sees how infinitely difficult this escape will be. Positivism said that statements about God are meaningless; Beckett shows that they mean too damned much.

To undo curses is just one service of literalization; another is to unfix clichés and idioms:

> HAMM. Did you ever think of one thing?
> CLOV. Never.
>
> (p. 39)

The expected response to Hamm's question would be, "What?"; but that answer would accept the question as the cliché conversational gambit it appears to be. Clov declines the move and brings the gesture to life by taking it literally. His answer means that he has always thought only of *many* things, and in this I hear a confession of failure in following Christ's injunction to take no thought for your life, what ye shall eat, or what ye shall drink; nor yet for your body, nor for tomorrow – the moral of which is that "thine eye be single." Perhaps I hallucinate. Yet the Sermon on the Mount makes explicit appearance in the course of the play, as will emerge. Our concerns with God have now become the greatest clichés of all, and here is another curse to be undone.

> CLOV. Do you believe in the life to come?
> HAMM. Mine was always that.
>
> (p. 49)

Hamm knows he's made a joke and, I suppose, knows that the joke is on us; but at least the joke momentarily disperses the "belief" in the cliché "life to come," promised on any Sunday radio. And it is a terribly sad joke – that the life we are living is not our life, or not alive. Or perhaps it's merely that the joke is old, itself a cliché. Christ told it to us, that this life is nothing. The punch line, the knock-out punch line, is that there is no other but this to come, that the life of waiting for life to come is all the life ever to come. We don't laugh; but if we could, or if we could stop finding it funny, then perhaps life would come to life, or anyway the life of life to come would end. (Clov, at one point, asks Hamm: "Don't we laugh?", not because he feels like it, but out of curiosity. In her longest speech (p. 19), Nell says: "Nothing is funnier than unhappiness . . . It's like the funny story we have heard too often, we still find it funny, but we don't laugh any more.") As it is, we've heard it all, seen it all too often, heard the promises, seen the suffering repeated in the same words and postures, and they are like any words which have been gone over so much that they are worn strange. We don't laugh, we don't cry; and we don't laugh that we don't cry, and we obviously can't cry about it. That's funny.

So far all that these examples have been meant to suggest is the sort of method I try to use consistently in reading the play, one in which I am always asking of a line either: What are the most ordinary circumstances under which such a line would be uttered? Or: What do the words literally say? I do not suggest that every line will yield to these questions, and I am sharply aware that I cannot provide answers to many cases for which I am convinced they are relevant. My exercise rests on the assumption that different artistic inventions demand different routes of critical discovery; and the justification for my particular procedures rests partly on an induction from the lines I feel I have understood, and partly on their faithfulness to the general direction I have found my understanding of the play as a whole to have taken. I have spoken of the effect of literalizing curses and clichés as one of "undoing" them, and this fits my sense, which I will specify as completely as I can, that the play itself is about an effort to undo, to end something by undoing it, and in particular to end a curse, and moreover the commonest, most ordinary curse of man – not so much that he was ever born and must die, but that he has to figure out the one and shape up to the other and justify what comes between, and that he is not a beast and not a god: in a word, that he is a man, and alone. All those, however, are the facts of life; the curse comes in the ways we try to deny them.

I should mention two further functions of the literal which seem to me operative in the play. It is, first, a mode which some forms of madness assume. A schizophrenic can suffer from ideas that he is literally empty or hollow or transparent or fragile or coming apart at the seams.[1] It is also a mode in which prophecies and wishes are fulfilled, surprising all measures to avoid them. Birnam Forest coming to Dunsinane and the overthrow by a man of no woman born are textbook cases. In the *Inferno*, Lucifer is granted his wish to become the triune deity by being fixed in the center of a kingdom and outfitted with three heads. *Endgame* is a play whose mood is characteristically one of madness and in which the characters are fixed by a prophecy, one which their actions can be understood as attempting both to fulfill and to reverse.

A central controversy in contemporary analytic philosophy relates immediately to this effort at literalizing. Positivism had hoped for the construction of an ideal language (culminating the hope, since Newton and Leibniz at the birth of modern science, for a *Characteristica Universalis*) in which everything which could be said at all would be said clearly, its relations to other statements formed purely logically, its notation perspicuous – the form of the statement *looking* like what it means. (For example, in their new transcription, the statements which mean "Daddy makes money" and "Mommy makes bread" and "Mommy makes friends" and "Daddy makes jokes" will no longer look alike; interpretation will no longer be required; thought will be as reliable as calculation, and agreement will be as surely achieved.) Post-positivists (the later Wittgenstein; "ordinary language philosophy") rallied to the insistence that ordinary language – being *speech*, and speech being more than the making of statements – contains implications necessary to communication, perfectly comprehensible to anyone who can speak, but not recordable in logical systems. If, for example, in ordinary circumstances I ask "Would you like to use my scooter?", I must not simply be *inquiring* into your state of mind; I must be *implying* my willingness that you use it, offering it to you. – I *must*? Must not? But no one has been able to explain the force of this *must*. Why mustn't I just be inquiring? A positivist is likely to answer: because it would be bad manners; or, it's a joke; in any case most people wouldn't. A post-positivist is likely to feel: That isn't what I meant. Of course it *may* be bad manners (even unforgivable manners), but it *may* not even be odd (e.g., in a context in which you have asked me to guess which of my possessions you would like to use). But suppose it isn't such contexts, but one in which, normally, people *would* be offering, and suppose I keep insisting, puzzled that others are upset, that I simply want to know what's on your mind. Then aren't you going to have to say something like: You don't know what you're saying, what those words mean – a feeling that I have tuned out, become incomprehensible. Anyway, why is the result a *joke* when the normal implications of language are defeated; what kind of joke?

Hamm and Clov's conversations sometimes work by defeating the implications of ordinary language in this way.

    HAMM.   I've made you suffer too much.
              (*Pause.*)
              Haven't I?
    CLOV.   It's not that.

HAMM. (*shocked*). I haven't made you suffer too much?
CLOV. Yes!
HAMM. (*relieved*). Ah you gave me a fright!
(*Pause. Coldly.*)
Forgive me.
(*Pause. Louder.*)
I said, Forgive me.
CLOV. I heard you.

(pp. 6–7)

Hamm's first line looks like a confession, an acknowledgment; but it is just a statement. This is shown by the question in his next speech, which is to determine whether what he said was true. His third speech looks like an appeal for forgiveness, but it turns out to be a command – a peculiar command, for it is, apparently, obeyed simply by someone's admitting that he heard it. How could a *command for forgiveness* be anything but peculiar, even preposterous? (Possibly in the way the Sermon on the Mount is preposterous.) An ordinary circumstance for its use would be one in which someone needs forgiveness but cannot *ask* for it. Preposterous, but hardly uncommon. (One of Hamm's lines is: "It appears the case is . . . was not so . . . so unusual" (p. 44); he is pretty clearly thinking of himself. He is *homme*. And "Ha-am" in Hebrew means "the people." Probably that is an accident, but I wouldn't put anything past the attentive friend and disciple of James Joyce.[2]) In Hamm's case, moreover, it would have been trivially preposterous, and less honest, had he really been *asking* for forgiveness "for having made you suffer too much": How much is just enough? We have the need, but no way of satisfying it; as we have words, but nothing to do with them; as we have hopes, but nothing to pin them on.

Sometimes the effect of defeating ordinary language is achieved not by thwarting its "implications" but by drawing purely logical ones.

HAMM. I'll give you nothing more to eat.
CLOV. Then we'll die.
HAMM. I'll give you just enough to keep you from dying. You'll be hungry all the time.
CLOV. Then we won't die.

(pp. 5–6)

Clov can hardly be meaning what his words, taken together and commonly, would suggest, namely "It makes no difference whether we live or die; I couldn't care less." First, in one sense that is *so trivial* a sentiment, at their stage, that it would get a laugh – at least from clear-headed Hamm. Second, it is not true. How could it make no difference when the point of the enterprise is to die to that world? (Though of course *that* kind of living and dying, the kind that depends on literal food, may make no difference.) And he *could* care less, because he's *trying* to leave (as he says, p. 7). If he were really empty of care, then maybe he could stop trying, and then maybe he could do it. The conventional reading takes Hamm's opening remark as a *threat*; but there are no more threats. It is a plain statement and Clov makes the inference; then Hamm negates the statement and Clov negates the conclusion. It is an exercise in pure logic; a spiritual exercise.

The logician's wish to translate out those messy, non-formal features of ordinary language is fully granted by Beckett, not by supposing that there is a way out of our language, but by fully accepting the fact that there is nowhere else to go. Only he is not going to call that rationality. Or perhaps he will: this is what rationality has brought us to. The strategy of literalization is: you say *only* what your words say. That's the game, and a way of winning out.

I refer to contemporary analytical philosophy, but Hamm presents a new image of what the mind, in one characteristic philosophical mood, has always felt like – crazed and paralyzed; this is part of the play's sensibility. One thinks of Socrates' interlocutors, complaining that his questions have numbed them; of Augustine faced with his question "What is Time?" (If you do not ask me, I know; if you ask me, I do not know). Every profound philosophical vision can have the shape of madness: The world is illusion; I can doubt everything, that I am awake, that there is an external world; the mind takes isolated bits of experience and associates them into a world; each thing and each person is a metaphysical enclosure, and no two ever communicate directly, or so much as perceive one another; time, space, relations between things, are unreal. . . . It sometimes looks as if philosophy had designs on us; or as if it alone is crazy, and wants company. Then why can't it simply be ignored? But it *is* ignored; perhaps not simply, but largely so. The question remains: What makes philosophy possible? Why can't men *always* escape it? Because, evidently, men have minds, and they think. (One mad philosophical question has long been, Does the mind *always* think? Even in sleep? It is a frightening thought.) And philosophy is what thought does to itself. Kant summarized it in the opening words of the *Critique of Pure Reason*: "Human reason has this peculiar fate that in one species of its knowledge it is burdened by questions which . . . it is not able to ignore, but which . . . it is also not able to answer." And Wittgenstein, saying in his *Investigations* that his later methods (he compared them to therapies) were to bring philosophy peace at last, seemed to find opportunity, and point, within such disaster: "The philosopher is the man who has to cure himself of many sicknesses of the understanding before he can arrive at the notions of the sound human understanding" (*Remarks on the Foundations of Mathematics*, p. 157) – as though there were no other philosophical path to sanity, save through madness. One will not have understood the opportunity if one is *eager* to seize it. Genuine philosophy may begin in wonder, but it continues in reluctance.

III

The medium of Beckett's dialogue is repartée, adjoining the genres of Restoration comedy, Shakespearean clowning, and the vaudeville gag, but also containing the sound of some philosophical argument and of minute theological debate. It is the sound in which victory or salvation consists (not exactly in proving a point or defending a position but) in coming up with the right answer – or rather, with the *next* answer, one which continues the dialogue, but whose point is to win a contest of wits by capping a gag or getting the last word. And within stringent conventions: for example, your entry must include an earlier bit of the dialogue, which it furthers or overturns, and it must be at least as witty as the entry it follows. The game is won by the one who gets off the last word, and no reply is a priori the last, hence best; no direction of reply the most likely; you never know, on hearing it, that a given reply will be the end; it is solely a matter of personal invention and resourcefulness. This is perhaps why defeat here can have its special pang of humiliation and why the knack of answering is so powerful a weapon. With it one can control not only cocktail parties and revolutionary movements, but relationships whose medium is an interminable, if frequently interrupted, discussion; and usually a discussion whose principal theme is the sickness of the relationship itself. What counts as insight or perceptiveness in such dialectic is the wit to come up with an answer, resulting in that special state of impotence in which the other knows he is not convinced but feels he hasn't the right not to be convinced. (A conclusion endemic in philosophical and theological exchange.) He may think of the right, and the right answer, in thirty minutes, or thirty years. And wittiness need not make you laugh. The device of aphorism depends upon the sound of wit, and its effect is of hilarity, but with all passion spent.

A necessary task of critical description in grasping Beckett would be to capture his particular force of wit, distinguishing it from its neighbors. One element in this description must be that literalizing of words I have taken as characteristic of his writing. One effect Beckett achieves with his dexterity of the curt, stunted line is that of the riddle posed, a situation in which you know that the correctness of the answer logically depends upon its being witty. (This effect, if it occurs, would express Hamm and Clov's constant air of strained puzzlement.) Not so much the sort of riddle which depends upon a play of words ("What snake is a mathematician?" "An adder"), nor on distracting clues ("What coat has no buttons and is put on wet?" "A coat of paint"), nor upon finding a verbal twist ("What is the difference between a schoolteacher and a railroad conductor?" "One trains the mind, the other minds the train"), but one whose difficulty lies in avoiding a conventional reading, seeing the syntax a new way, whose answer, therefore, is not recognized to be right immediately on being told it (you have first to go over and refigure the syntax), but which is suddenly seen to make perfect sense ("What can go up a chimney when it's down, but can't go down when it's up?" "An umbrella").

Another technique is harder for me to characterize, partly because I know of no literary form or figure with which to compare it. It is a phenomenon I have often encountered in conversation and in the experience of psychotherapy – the way an utterance which has entered naturally into the dialogue and continues it with obvious sense suddenly sends out an intense meaning, and one which seems to summarize or reveal the entire drift of mood or state of mind until then unnoticed or unexpressed. I am remembering a conversation in which a beautiful and somewhat cold young lady had entered a long monologue about her brother, describing what it was like to live for the summer with him alone in their step-mother's New York apartment, telling of her fears that he was becoming more and more unhappy, more than once mentioning suicide; a beautiful young man like that. And then she said: "When I was in the shower, I was afraid of what my brother might do." The line came at us; I seemed to know that she had not been talking about her fears for her brother, but her fears of him. "What might your brother do?" But she had become perplexed, we were both rather anxious, the subject got lost; the line, however, stayed said. It would not be quite right to say that something was revealed; but there was as it were an air of revelation among us.

There are several examples of this effect in *Endgame*; two or three achieve the spiritual climaxes of the play, letting its meaning swell out suddenly, like a child playing with the volume control of a radio. Twice (p. 53, p. 68) Hamm comes out with: "Use your head can't you, use your head, you're on earth, there's no cure for that!". The natural, or conventional, reading will emphasize the word *that*, and this way makes a stunning enough effect. But another reading becomes possible, emphasizing the word *cure*; and with that I have the feeling of revelation stirring. No *cure* for that, but perhaps there is something else for it – if we could give up our emphasis upon cure. There is faith, for example.

Other instances must wait for more context, but after convincing myself of several of them, I am able, perhaps too willing, to hear it happening in Hamm's early, very innocuous line: "Quiet, quiet, you're keeping me awake" (p. 18) – said to his parents shortly after they have popped up. What is keeping him awake? His parents talking, obviously; but they are not talking loudly. It seems Hamm is curious, cannot not listen. What are they talking about, what does Hamm hear? Some moments earlier Hamm had said, "It's the end of the day like any other day," and dismissed Clov. A few lines earlier still his father Nagg had lifted the lid of his bin and stared listening to Hamm and Clov. When Clov leaves and Hamm quiets down, Nagg knocks on the lid of Nell his wife. She comes up with:

> What is it my pet?
> (*Pause.*)
> Time for love?
> NAGG. Were you asleep?
> NELL. Oh no!
> NAGG. Kiss me.
>
> (p. 14)

The husband of an old married couple nudges his dozing wife and she turns to him with encouragement. That is what Hamm may be hearing to keep him awake. This idea would naturally explain Hamm's silence, save for his complaint at being kept awake and for one later brief speculation, throughout the long intercourse which now ensues between his parents. They have meant not to disturb him, but he is disturbed, and powerless to intervene. If this is accepted, something definite follows about the way the scene is to be played. Hamm will not then say "Quiet, quiet . . ." *to* his parents, as a straight request; rather he will say it to them as if in reverie, remembering something, not seeing them here and now but as characters of his imagination. An imagination stuffed with jealousy, competition, disgust, murderousness, guilt – states in which little boys begin their lives. Some are paralyzed in them, never stand on their own feet. His parents certainly do not think he has spoken to them. Nagg says – and the stage direction is (*Soft*) – "Do you hear him?". They are over-hearing him, as he is over-hearing them, and soon they go back to over-looking him. They will play most of the scene in bed-whispers.

The sudden turning of an obvious line into a cry of anxiety is something one expects of Chekhov, who is, I suppose, the closest classical equivalent to Beckett's glazing of calm onto terror. But in Chekhov the lines implode a different way: first, they characterize their speakers; second, their effect, like the effect of gestures, depends upon when and to whom they are made; third, they shape the silence which surrounds them so that what is unsaid leads a life of its own, sapping the life of the speakers and cursing what is left. His characters speak in order that they not have to hear themselves: that is the drama of his plays. Beckett has no such resources. Chekhov, in a word, is the greater dramatist, but Beckett is the superior showman, or raconteur; and like any strong performer he exploits his limitations. His lines do not individuate his characters nor further the action of the play; their interest is intrinsic. Words, we feel as we hear them, *can* mean in these combinations, and we want them to, they speak something in us. But what do they mean, and what in us, who in us, do they speak for? Nothing is left unsaid, but the speakers are anonymous, the words lead a life of their own. To own them, to find out who says them, who can mean them when, is the drama of the play.

Our relationship to the characters, accordingly, is different. About Vershinin we can say: He cannot bear not to dream; the future which he can be no part of is more precious to him than any present, *is* his present. About Irina we can say: She says she wants to go to Moscow, but there is no Moscow, and she cannot survive that knowledge. It is not that our relationship to Beckett's characters is more intimate, but that there is no distance at all or no recognizable distance between them and us. After Chekhov we know that each of us has his Moscow and that each has his way of foregoing reality. From Beckett no such statements emerge, or not this way. We cannot see ourselves *in* his characters, because they are no more characters than cubist portraits are particular people. They have the abstraction, and the intimacy, of figures and words and objects in a dream. Not that what we see is supposed to be our dream, or any dream. It is not surrealism, and its conventions are not those of fantasy. If this were a movie its director would not be Cocteau but Hitchcock.

There is no world just the other side of this one, opened onto through mirrors; escapes, if they come, will be narrower than this. There is only this world, unenchanted, unsponsored, but more fantastic than we can tell. The unbelievable, the plain truth which you cannot tell, that others will think you mad when you try to tell, is one of Hitchcock's patented themes. Take two people as pointedly ordinary as Robert Cummings and Priscilla Lane, have them discover, during the war, a plot to blow up a ship in the Brooklyn Navy Yard, have them momentarily elude the plotters only to find themselves in the midst of a private charity ball, the house owned by a colleague of the enemies, the immaculately proper servants guarding each exit, their only hope of escape lying in convincing the unknowing among the well-dressed mob of dancers and patrons under the crystal chandeliers and the spell of society dance music that their socially prominent and conscientious hostess is a Nazi sympathizer sheltering a gang of saboteurs – why anyone present would have to be mad to believe such a tale.

Beckett's characters have such a tale to tell, but their problem is not to distinguish friends from foes under the tuxedos, for there are neither friends nor foes any more; nor to prevent a disaster from happening or a culprit from escaping justice, for no one in particular is the culprit and all disasters have taken place. Their problem is not to become believable, but to turn off the power of belief altogether since it has become, because useless, the source of unappeasable, unbelievable pain. Suspense is for Hitchcock what faith is for the Christian, an ultimate metaphysical category, directing life's journey and making the universe come clear, and clean at the end. The overwhelming question for both is: How will the truth come out at last? Beckett's couples have discovered the final plot: that there is no plot, that the truth has come out, that *this* is the end. But they would be mad to believe it and they cannot, being human, fully give up suspense. So they wait. Not *for* something, for they know there is nothing to wait for. So they try not to wait, but they do not know how to end.

But why should ending it be a problem, and why should the problem be an intellectual one, going beyond assembling the stamina for suicide? Because, evidently, suicide is not the end. I do not mean what Hamlet seems to mean (and perhaps he didn't either) that such an end has consequences, and hence is not the end. I mean it is not the *right* end, not the right solution to some particular problem. This has two implications: (1) Man is the animal for whom to be or not to be is a *question*: its resolution therefore must have the form of an *answer*. (2) It must form the answer to a *particular* reason for ending. Hamlet shuns suicide not because of the divine canon against self-slaughter; there is ample canon against other-slaughter as well, which he does not often hesitate to break. His real hesitations are over the right of vengeance and the belief in ghosts,[3] hesitations which have survived the God-slaughter of the succeeding centuries. He shuns suicide just because it makes no sense for his unhappiness. His problem is not one of radical failure or dishonor or abandonment. (I take it that suicide can solve these unhappiness: in the first case because it serves as punishment, in the second because it serves as sacrifice, in the third because it vengefully turns the tables, turning the abandoner into the abandoned. All convert suffering into action; in all, impotence has become unbearable; in all, the act is toward silence, toward a shelter from a torment of accusation.) Hamlet's problem, on the contrary, is that he alone has the success of knowledge, the honor of succession, and the presence of motive to doctor the time. It makes no sense to run from that conjunction through use of suicide, though the thought of running from it may move him closer to suicide.

Why do men stay alive in the face of the preponderance of pain over pleasure, of meaninglessness over sense? Camus" answer is, in effect, that suicide, as a response to the general condition of human life, is a contradiction, because the condition to which it would be a response is life's absurdity, and suicide does not *respond* to this absurdity, but removes it. That seems a very academic way of putting the problem. Camus is right that this is *the* philosophical problem, because until it is answered one's chance for moral existence has not begun – or ended; one has not taken one's life into one's own hands. And after it is answered the supposed need for a philosophical "foundation" for morality vanishes, which is the reason all such foundations – metaphysical, epistemological, political or religious – strike one as conceived in bad faith.

It is true that Hamm wants death, at least there is no life he wants, and one can say that his entire project is to achieve his death. Why will suicide not answer? Because he cannot imagine his death apart from imagining the death of the world. *That* is what he wants, and his death is wanted as a necessary, and welcome, entailment of that. If the imagination of death requires the imagination of *leaving*, of farewells, then Hamm is not imagining his death. (Perhaps this means he cannot imagine his life either. In the eighth *Duino Elegy*: ". . . so leben wir und nehmen immer Abschied.") He wants to end, but without taking leave. But where does the motive come from to destroy the whole world?

It is as if personal escape, individual non-existence, private relief, are insufficient to neutralize the pain which would motivate suicide; as long as *anyone* can remember, the memory which is to die has not died; as long as anything breathes, I am not at rest. But how can anyone take in, or even conceive, an ambition or obligation large enough to encompass the death of the world? Perhaps, however, largeness is not at issue. If we are to speak of ambition or obligation, the question is: How does this *specific* obligation come to be shouldered?

Merely the connection between the death of personal existence and the death of the world is not new. Hamlet and Lear both crave death, and knowing they must be the *last* to die, crave the death of their worlds. Certainly Hamm, for all his efforts, cannot surpass them in their *disgust* with the world, especially with its fruitfulness. But their worlds were limited to the coherent state; the universe outside that was not their responsibility. Christ had wished the death of all, but in order for the re-birth of all. What is new is to wish for unlimited surcease, and without the plan of redemption.

It must be some widening knowledge of such a wish – heard by Nietzsche before this century turned on us the news now reaching our ears – which functions in our awareness of the Bomb. I would scarcely deny its objective threat, but one senses reactions to it that are not reactions to an objective threat. Sometimes they are hysterically fearful ("Better Red than dead," as though the *others* are willing to send them over at any moment), sometimes hysterically repressive and rational (the mode of all official rhetoric employing concepts of deterrence, over-kill, etc. – language breaking down in front of our ears, denoting nothing we know or imagine). I do not suggest that there is some *right* reaction waiting to be had. The situation *is* in fact mad. We know, sort of, that the world may end in twenty minutes (and to qualify this by calculating whether 30,000,000 or 50,000,000 persons will survive, or to speculate whether plant life will continue, is merely tragic relief). And we know there is nothing we can do to stop it which is not absurdly disproportionate to the event. So we treat it, or improvise around it, using the reactions we know: forgetfulness, habit, hope against hope, humor, hysteria, fantasy. The Three Sisters are no more out of touch with their world than we are with ours. We are a billion times three sisters.

One thinks of *Dr Strangelove*. The film has been criticized because it presents superficial explanations of our final difficulties (it's all due to mad Generals, boy scout Generals, German rocket designers, bullies and dupes in high places) and childish solutions to them (get the bastards out, we want anarchy). Perhaps these are motives of the film, and doubtless some of its ardent fans have been fans of those explanations and solutions. But the issue is a false one. The clearest fact about the film is its continuous brilliance, and any understanding of it must understand that. It is not, for example, the result of brilliant movie-making, at which it is quite routine; nor the result of brilliant ideas, for it has no ideas (which is perhaps sufficient reason not to defend it, as has been tried, as satire). Its brilliance is that of farce, with its stringent rhythm of entrances and concealments; and of silent comedy, with its sight gags. Only it is abstract. The figure displaced under the bed or into the closet is not a person but a turn of mind; the object that drops on the head is not a loose chandelier but a tight loyalty; the inappropriate get-up is not a feather boa or a spittoon on the foot from which you cannot extricate yourself, but a habit of response. It is a collage whose bits are as common as sand: Who has never endowed a pop tune with Proustian power of recall and summary; or straightened out an awkward moment with a piece of pop seriousness ("Of course it's not just physical; I respect you as a person"); or thrilled when, at Saturday matinees, the tight-faced soldier nudges the door open with one hand and in the other holds a sub-machine gun upright in world-preserving coolness? If these fantasies are worthless, we are worthless. And nothing in all of Beckett's sadness is sadder than the scene in which Slim Pickens encourages his crew of doom by reminding them that the folks back home are counting on them. Inappropriate no doubt now; but the Second World War – and it is from movies about that

War that this scene is taken – depended upon scenes like that, and it is not clear that without such scenes the outcome of the War would have been the same. What is so sad is that it is something good in us that has turned out to be so inappropriate. What is the solution? To see to it that our minds are no longer composed of trivial tunes, adolescent longings and movie clips? No doubt. Exactly what would one have in mind?

Dr Strangelove's strategies of sacrifice are singly clear to laugh at; but they amount to that mood of hilarity which does not produce laughter. It also suggests, what I take *Endgame* to be about, that we think it is right that the world end. Not perhaps morally right, but inevitable; tragically right. In a world of unrelieved helplessness, where Fate is not a notable Goddess but an inconspicuous chain of command, it would be a relief to stop worrying and start loving the Bomb (the extent to which these are accepted as our fixed alternatives is a measure of our madness.) A love too precious for this world, no doubt; but God will witness how powerful and true to itself. (I can hear the lyrics for the new *Liebestod*. They begin: "Extremism in the defense of liberty is no vice. I regret that I have but three billion lives to give for my country.") The official rhetoric is rational, but it bears to ordinary consciousness the same relation as advanced theology to the words and the audience of a revivalist. What *does* an ordinary Christian think when he says, or hears, that Christ died to save sinners? What does an ordinary citizen think when he says, or hears, that our defence systems provide such and such a margin of warning, or sees a sign saying "Fallout Shelter'? We speak about the dangers of "accidental war," but what does this mean? Not that the *whole* war will be an accident, but that it will *start* accidentally. From then on it will be planned. We are imagining that, if ordered to, men will "push buttons" which they *know* will mean the destruction of their world. Why do we imagine they will do this? Because they are soldiers and will be following orders and thereby doing a soldier's duty? That seems no more satisfactory an explanation here than its use to explain the behavior of extermination squads. In both cases, what is suppressed is the fact that the content of an act is essentially related to that action's counting as a duty. (Kant, I believe, is still thought to have denied this, and thus, I suppose, to have contributed to the moral destruction of Germany. What Kant denies, however, is only that anything *other* than the content of an act – in particular, its being performed from a particular motive (other than duty itself) or its having certain consequences – can make the act morally right.) For an action even to seem to be a duty it must be taken as on the whole good, or to lead to good; or at the least a regrettable necessity – and necessary on grounds other than the mere fact that it has been commanded: it is necessary in order that a greater good may supervene.

Someday, if there is someday, we will have to learn that evil thinks of itself as good, that it could not have made such progress in the world unless people planned and performed it in all conscience. Nietzsche was not crazy when he blamed morality for the worst evils, though he may have become too crazy about the idea. This is also why goodness, in trying to get born, will sometimes look like the destruction of morality. I am scarcely to be taken as presenting a theory of Nazism, any more than of the acquiescence to world destruction, so it would be irrelevant to point to other considerations which help explain human involvement in events of such catastrophe, for example to ways in which one denies to oneself the name and meaning and consequence of one's actions, to ways in which one merely hopes, out of a helplessness to see or to take any alternative, that one will be justified, and so on. What I am suggesting is that one dimension of our plight can only be discovered in a phenomenology of the Bomb.[4] For it has invaded our dreams and given the brain, already wrinkled with worry, a new cut. And it has finally provided our dreams of vengeance, our despair of happiness, our hatreds of self and world, with an instrument adequate to convey their destructiveness, and satisfaction.

Notes

1 On this topic see Stanley R. Palombo and Hilde Bruch, "Falling Apart: The Verbalization of Ego Failure," *Psychiatry*, vol. 27, no. 3, August, 1964. But the issue is philosophically complex. Drs Palombo and Bruch emphasize the *spatial* and *physical* basis of such terms, whereas I was led to speak of it as the *literal*. I do not, however, wish to pre-judge the possible identity of spatiality (or physicality) with literality, and in particular I do not mean to suggest that when one is not meaning one's words with purely spatial or physical reference one is then using them metaphorically. For two sorts of reasons: The metaphorical statement "Juliet is the sun" refers to two physical objects, grammatically equating them, and it would not work as a metaphor unless one knew what those two objects were. Contrariwise, a statement like "It will take a long time" is not metaphorical even though time does not come in (spatial) lengths. There are two grounds for denying that it is metaphorical: (1) There are good reasons (one could say, there are facts which explain) why the concept of length is applied to the measurement of time; in particular the facts of our world which make it normal for longer distances to take longer to traverse than shorter distances. There are not comparable facts which explain why Juliet is equated with the sun, though the metaphor depends upon one's knowing facts about the sun (e.g., that the day begins with it, that it is the source of life) and it summarizes many things Romeo takes to be facts about Juliet. (2) What Empson calls the "pregnancy" of metaphor – the fact that its paraphrase is indefinitely long and elaborate – is essential to it. Whereas in statements about the length of time it is not up to each of us to determine how much of the concept of length, or which facts about measuring lengths, apply to the measurement of time. This is related to the fact that no one could have *invented* the normal application of length to time. But the topic is enormous, and needs investigation.

2 Though it is hard to be reasonable. I am thinking of the syllable "Om," holy in Eastern mysticism. Rudolf Otto, in *The Idea of the Holy* (New York: Oxford University Press, 1958; first published in 1923) says this about it: ". . . no word, nor even a complete syllable, for the *m* in which it ends is not an ordinary 'm,' but simply the long-pro-tracted nasal continuation of the deep 'o' sound. It is really simply a sort of growl or groan, sounding up from within as the quasi-reflex expression of profound emotion in circumstances of a numinous-magical nature, and serving to relieve consciousness of a felt burden, almost physical in its constraining force" (p. 193). A conjunction of three intimations lead me to look up, and constrain me to quote, that passage: (1) Wondering, and skeptical, about the Hebrew word, I noted that the "a" is not doubled in Hamm's name, but that the "m" is, and I looked for significance in that. (2) Hamm is not called by name by any of the other characters, though each of the others is. He does say his own name once, however (in a line in which it is followed by a word clearly echoing it): "But for me, no father. But for Hamm, no home" (p. 38). (". . . but the Son of man hath not where to lay his head.") (3) A critical moment at the end of the play concerns the sudden appearance of a young boy outside the shelter: in a passage omitted from the English version, he is said to be looking at his navel.

  The succeeding paragraph in Otto further encourages, or discourages, speculation: "This *Om* is exactly parallel to the similar sound in Sanskrit, *Hum* . . .". Hm.

3 In *The Question of Hamlet* (New York: Oxford University Press, 1959), Harry Levin points to these as Hamlet's "double dilemma" (p. 24).

4 An instance of what I have in mind is Resnais'' film *Hiroshima Mon Amour*. It has been called an anti-war film, on the ground, I suppose, of its display of the evil of the Bomb. But while it doubtless contains such an awareness (that evil is, after all, pretty obvious) its real subject is the evil of using the Bomb as an excuse – or, which is perhaps the same, a symbol – for inner horror, and thence about the oblique and ironic relations between inner and outer worlds generally. This suggests both a political and aesthetic problem. (1) While one does not expect, and does not want, politicians to become phenomenologists, nor to give up the most practical worries they can find, one of their biggest worries, and perhaps a new one, is this new importance, and power, of phenomenological awareness, making realistic appraisal and accommodation difficult in a new way. (2) The aesthetic problem concerns what limits there may be to subjects of art. Is, for example, the Bomb too practically engulfing to fit requirements of artistic treatment?

6

Music Discomposed

This passage from the first of a pair of early essays examining contemporary writings in music journals and journals of philosophical aesthetics is
perhaps the most brutally detached from its surroundings of all the
extracts included in this volume. I have, in effect, attempted to isolate
those places where Cavell's patient and detailed examination of specific
disputes between advocates of rival methods of musical composition and
performance give rise to more general reflections upon the problems
faced both by musicians and by artists more generally in so far as they
confront the condition of modernism. In his analysis of the ways in which
concepts of composition and improvisation are variously modified, re-
pressed, or reaffirmed by contemporary musicians and musical theorists,
Cavell explores what might be involved in questioning the conventions of
an artistic tradition without entirely losing touch with its concerns. In
effect, he raises the question of what counts as an acknowledgment of the
conditions of possibility of musical composition, and what as their denial. And he further clarifies his understanding of modernism by discussing the aesthetic consequences of a modernist artist's loss of a guaranteed
audience and an unquestioned history, of the new centrality of issues of
sincerity and fraudulence, and of the altered role played by critics in
establishing agreement in aesthetic judgments.

Two other aspects of this extract may be worth emphasizing here.
First, by clarifying what Cavell takes to be the condition of modernism in
the arts, it provides essential background for grasping what he might
mean by claiming that serious philosophy in the late twentieth century is
in the same condition (Essay 3 in this collection illustrates what the
consequences of this claim for philosophical composition might be). And
second, this essay's focus upon music provides a rare acknowledgment in
his writing of an interest that has been central to his life; encouraged by
his musically gifted mother, Cavell learnt to play a variety of musical
instruments at an early age, studied composition at the Juilliard conser-

Originally published as 'Music Discomposed' by Stanley Cavell in *Art, Mind, and Religion*,
eds W. H. Capitan and D. D. Merrill; published in 1967 by the University of Pittsburgh
Press. Reprinted by permission of the publisher.

vatory, and turned decisively from music to philosophy only in his late twenties. Only in his later autobiographical writing and his related work on opera (cf. chapters 1 and 3 of *A Pitch of Philosophy*) has this aspect of the life of his mind become once again an explicit focus of his philosophical reflections.

What these journals suggest is that the possibility of fraudulence, and the experience of fraudulence, is endemic in the experience of contemporary music; that its full impact, even its immediate relevance, depends upon a willingness to trust the object, knowing that the time spent with its difficulties may be betrayed. I do not see how anyone who has experienced modern art can have avoided such experiences, and not just in the case of music. Is Pop Art art? Are canvases with a few stripes or chevrons on them art? Are the novels of Raymond Roussel or Alain Robbe-Grillet? Are art movies? A familiar answer is that time will tell. But my question is: *What* will time tell? That certain departures in art-like pursuits have become established (among certain audiences, in textbooks, on walls, in college courses); that *someone* is treating them with the respect due, we feel, to art; that one no longer has the right to question their status? But in waiting for time to tell that, we miss what the present tells – that the dangers of fraudulence, and of trust, are essential to the experience of art. If anything in this paper should count as a thesis, that is my thesis. And it is meant quite generally. Contemporary music is only the clearest case of something common to modernism as a whole, and modernism only makes explicit and bare what has always been true of art. (That is almost a definition of modernism, not to say its purpose.) Aesthetics has so far been the aesthetics of the classics, which is as if we investigated the problem of other minds by using as examples our experience of *great* men or *dead* men. In emphasizing the experiences of fraudulence and trust as essential to the experience of art, I am in effect claiming that the answer to the question "What is art?" will in part be an answer which explains why it is we treat certain objects, or how we *can* treat certain objects, in ways normally reserved for treating persons.

Both Tolstoy's *What Is Art?* and Nietzsche's *Birth of Tragedy* begin from an experience of the fraudulence of the art of their time. However obscure Nietzsche's invocation of Apollo and Dionysus and however simplistic Tolstoy's appeal to the artist's sincerity and the audience's "infection," their use of these concepts is to specify the genuine in art in opposition to specific modes of fraudulence, and their meaning is a function of that opposition. Moreover, they agree closely on what those modes of fraudulence are: in particular, a debased Naturalism's heaping up of random realistic detail, and a debased Romanticism's substitution of the stimulation and exacerbation of feeling in place of its artistic control and release; and in both, the constant search for "effects.'

*   *   *   *   *

How can fraudulent art be exposed? Not, as in the case of a forgery or counterfeit, by comparing it with the genuine article, for there *is* no genuine article of the right kind. Perhaps it helps to say: If we call it a matter of comparing something with the genuine article, we have to add (1) that what counts as the genuine article is not *given*, but itself requires critical determination; and (2) that what needs to be exposed is not that a work is a *copy*. (That of course *may* be an issue, and that *may* be an issue of forgery. Showing fraudulence is more like showing something is imitation – not: *an* imitation. The emphasis is not on copying a *particular* object, as in forgery and counterfeit, but on producing *the effect* of the genuine, or having some of its properties.) Again, unlike the cases of forgery and counterfeit, there is no one feature, or definite set of features, which may be described in technical handbooks, and no specific tests by which its fraudulence can be detected and exposed. Other frauds and imposters, like forgers and counterfeiters, admit *clear* outcomes, conclude in dramatic discoveries – the imposter is unmasked at the ball, you find the counterfeiters working over their press, the forger is caught signing another man's name, or he confesses. There are no such proofs possible for the assertion that the art accepted by a public is fraudulent; the artist himself may not know; and the critic may be shown up, not merely as incompetent, nor unjust in accusing the wrong man, but as taking others in (or out); that is, as an imposter.

The only exposure of false art lies in recognizing something about the object itself, but something whose recognition requires exactly the same capacity as recognizing the genuine article. It is a capacity not insured by understanding the language in which it is composed, and yet we may not understand what is said; nor insured by the healthy functioning of the senses, though we may be told we do not *see* or that we fail to *hear* something; nor insured by the aptness of our logical powers, though what we may have missed was the object's consistency or the way one thing followed from another. We may have missed its tone, or neglected an allusion or a cross current, or failed to see its point altogether; or the object may not have established its tone, or buried the allusion too far, or be confused in its point. You often do not know which is on trial, the object or the viewer: modern art did not invent this dilemma, it merely insists upon it. The critic will have to *get* us to see, or hear or realize or notice; help us to appreciate the tone; convey the current; point to a connection; show how to take the thing in . . . What this getting, helping, conveying, and pointing consist in will be shown in the specific ways the critic accomplishes them, or fails to accomplish them. Sometimes you can say he is exposing an object to us (in its fraudulence, or genuineness); sometimes you can say he is exposing us to the object. (The latter is, one should add, not always a matter of noticing fine differences by exercising taste; sometimes it is a matter of admitting the lowest common emotion.) Accordingly, the critic's anger is sometimes directed at an object, sometimes at its audience, often at both. But sometimes, one supposes, it is produced by the frustrations inherent in his profession. He is part detective, part lawyer, part judge, in a country in which crimes and deeds of glory look alike, and in which the public not only, therefore, confuses one with the other, but does not know that one or the other has been committed; not because the news has not got out, but because what counts as the one or the other cannot be defined until it happens; and when it has happened there is no sure way he can get the news out; and no way at all without risking something like a glory or a crime of his own.

One line of investigation here would be to ask: Why does the assertion "You have to *hear* it!" mean what it does? Why is its sense conveyed with a word which emphasizes the function of a sense organ, and in the form of an imperative? The combination is itself striking. One cannot be commanded to hear a sound, though one can be commanded to listen to it, or for it. Perhaps the question is: How does it happen that the *achievement* or *result* of using a sense organ comes to be thought of as the *activity* of that organ – as though the aesthetic experience had the form not merely of a continuous effort (e.g., listening) but of a continuous achievement (e.g., hearing).

Why – on pain of what – must I hear it; what consequence befalls me if I don't? One answer might be: Well, then I wouldn't hear it – which at least says that there is no point to the hearing beyond itself; it is worth doing in itself. Another answer might be: Then I wouldn't *know* it (what it is about, what it is, what's happening, what is *there*). And what that seems to say is that works of art are objects of the sort that can only be *known in sensing*. It is not, as in the case of ordinary material objects, that I know *because* I see, or that seeing is *how* I know (as opposed, for example, to being told, or figuring it out). It is rather, one may wish to say, that *what* I know is what I see; or even: seeing *feels* like knowing. ("Seeing the point" conveys this sense, but in ordinary cases of seeing the point, once it's seen it's known, or understood; about works of art one may wish to say that they require a continuous seeing of the point.) Or one may even say: In such cases, knowing functions like an organ of sense. (The religious, or mystical, resonance of this phrase, while not deliberate, is welcome. For religious experience is subject to distrust on the same grounds as aesthetic experience is: by those to whom it is foreign, on the ground that its claims must be false; by those to whom it is familiar, on the ground that its quality must be tested.)

Another way one might try to capture the idea is by saying: Such objects are only *known by feeling*, or *in* feeling. This is not the same as saying that the object expresses feeling, or that the aesthetic response consists in a feeling of some sort. Those are, or may be, bits of a theory about the aesthetic experience and its object; whereas what I am trying to describe, or the descriptions I am trying to hit on, would at best serve as data for a theory. What the expression "known by feeling" suggests are facts (or experiences) such as these: (1) What I know, when I've *seen* or *heard* something is, one may wish to say, not a matter of *merely* knowing it. But what more is it? Well, as the words say, it is a matter of *seeing* it. But one could also say that it is not a matter of *merely* seeing it. But what more is it? Perhaps "merely knowing" should be compared with "not really knowing": "You don't really know what it's like to be a Negro"; "You don't really know how your remark made her feel"; "You don't really know what I mean when I say that Schnabel's slow movements give the impression not of slowness but of infinite length." You merely say the words. The issue in each case is: What would *express* this knowledge? It is not that my knowledge will be real, or more than *mere* knowledge, when I acquire a particular feeling, or come to see something. For the issue can also be said to be: What would express the acquisition of that feeling, or show that you have seen the thing? And the answer might be that I now *know* something I didn't know before. (2) "Knowing by feeling" is not like "knowing by touching"; that is, it is not a case of providing the *basis* for a claim to know. But one could say that feeling functions as a touchstone: the mark left on the stone is out of the sight of others, but the result is one of knowledge, or has the form of knowledge – it is directed to an object, the object has been tested, the result is one of conviction. This seems to me to suggest why one is anxious to communicate the experience of such objects. It is not merely that I want to tell you how it is with me, how I feel, in order to find sympathy or to be left alone, or for any other of the reasons for which one reveals one's feelings. It's rather that I want to tell you something I've seen, or heard, or realized, or come to understand, for the reasons for which *such* things are communicated (because it is news, about a world we share, or could). Only I find that I can't *tell* you; and that makes it all the more urgent to tell you. I want to tell you because the knowledge, unshared, is a burden – not, perhaps, the way having a secret can be a burden, or being misunderstood; a little more like the way, perhaps, not being believed is a burden, or not being trusted. It matters that others know what I see, in a way it does not matter whether they know my tastes. It matters, there is a burden, because unless I can tell what I know, there is a suggestion (and to myself as well) that I do *not* know. But I *do* – what I see is *that* (pointing to the object). But for that to communicate, you have to see it too. Describing one's experience of art is itself a form of art; the burden of describing it is like the burden of producing it. Art is often praised because it brings men together. But it also separates them.

The list of figures whose art Tolstoy dismisses as fraudulent or irrelevant or bad, is, of course, unacceptably crazy: most of Beethoven, all of Brahms and Wagner; Michelangelo, Renoir; the Greek dramatists, Dante, Shakespeare, Milton, Goethe, Ibsen, Tolstoy. . . . But the sanity of his procedure is this: it confronts the fact that we often do not find, and have never found, works we would include in a canon of works of art to be of importance or revelance to us. And the implication is that apart from this we cannot know that they are art, or what makes them art. One could say: objects so canonized do not exist for us. This strikes Tolstoy as crazy – as though we were to say we know that there are other minds because other people have told us there are.

*   *   *   *   *

But I was discussing some writing now current about the new music. Perhaps I can say more clearly why it leads, or has led me, to these various considerations by looking at three concepts which recur in it over and over – the concepts of composition, improvisation, and chance.

The reason for their currency can be put, roughly, this way. The innovations of Schoenberg (and Bartok and Stravinsky) were necessitated by a crisis of composition growing out of the increasing chromaticism of the nineteenth century which finally overwhelmed efforts to organize music within the established assumptions of tonality. Schoenberg's solution was the development of the twelve-tone system which, in effect, sought to overcome this destructiveness of chromaticism by accepting it totally, searching for ways to organize a rigidly recurring total chromatic in its own terms. History aside, what is essential is that no assumption is any longer to be made about how compositional centers or junctures could be established – e.g., by establishing the "dominant" of a key – and the problem was one of discovering what, in such a situation, could be heard as serving the structural functions tonality used to provide. Schoenberg's twelve-tone "rows" and the operations upon them which constitute his system, were orderings and operations upon pitches (or, more exactly, upon the familiar twelve classes of pitches). About 1950, composers were led to consider that variables of musical material other than its pitches could also be subjected to serial ordering and its

Schoenbergian transformations – variables of rhythm, duration, density, timbre, dynamics, and so on. But now, given initial series of pitches, rhythms, timbres, dynamics, etc., together with a plot of the transformations each is to undergo, and a piece is written or, rather, determined; it is, so it is said, totally organized. What remains is simply to translate the rules into the notes and values they determine and see what we've got. Whether what such procedures produce is music or not, they certainly produced philosophy. And it is characteristic of this philosophy to appeal to the concepts of composition, chance, and improvisation.

The motives or necessities for these concepts are not always the same. In the writing of John Cage, chance is explicitly meant to *replace* traditional notions of art and composition; the radical ceding of the composer's control of his material is seen to provide a profounder freedom and perception than mere art, for all its searches, had found. In the defense of "total organization," on the contrary, chance and improvisation are meant to *preserve* the concepts of art and composition for music; to explain how, although the composer exercises choice only over the initial conditions of his work, the determinism to which he then yields his power itself creates the spontaneity and surprise associated with the experience of art; and either (a) because it produces combinations which are unforeseen, or (b) because it includes directions which leave the performer free to choose, i.e., to improvise. It is scarcely unusual for an awareness of determinism to stir philosophical speculation about the possibilities of freedom and choice and responsibility. But whereas the more usual motivation has been to preserve responsibility in the face of determinism, these new views wish to preserve choice by foregoing responsibility (for everything but the act of "choosing").

Let us listen to one such view, from Ernst Krenek, who was for years a faithful disciple of Schoenberg and who has emerged as an important spokesman for total organization.

Generally and traditionally "inspiration" is held in great respect as the most distinguished source of the creative process in art. It should be remembered that inspiration by definition is closely related to chance, for it is the very thing that cannot be controlled, manufactured or premeditated in any way. It is what falls into the mind (according to the German term *Einfall*) unsolicited, unprepared, unrehearsed, coming from nowhere. This obviously answers the definition of chance as "the absence of any known reason why an event should turn out one way rather than another." Actually the composer has come to distrust his inspiration because it is not really as innocent as it was supposed to be, but rather conditioned by a tremendous body of recollection, tradition, training, and experience. In order to avoid the dictations of such ghosts, he prefers to set up an impersonal mechanism which will furnish, according to premeditated patterns, unpredictable situations . . . the creative act takes place in an area in which it has so far been entirely unsuspected, namely in setting up the serial statements. . . . What happens afterwards is predetermined by the selection of the mechanism, but not premeditated except as an unconscious result of the predetermined operations. The unexpected happens by necessity. The surprise is built in. ("Extents and Limits of Serial Techniques," *Musical Quarterly*, XLVI, 1960, pp. 228–9)

This is not serious, but it is meant; and it is symptomatic – the way it is symptomatic that early in Krenek's paper he suggests that the twelve-tone technique "appears to be a special, or limiting, case of serial music, similar to an interpretation of Newtonian mechanics as a limiting expression of the Special Theory of Relativity, which in turn has been explained as a limiting expression of that General Theory." (Note the scientific caution of "appears to be.") The vision of our entire body of recollection, tradition, training, and experience as so many ghosts *could* be serious. It was serious, in their various ways, for Kierkegaard, Marx, Nietzsche, Emerson, Ibsen, Freud, and for most of the major poets and novelists of the past hundred years. It is not merely a modern problem; it is, one could say, the problem of modernism, the attempt in every work to do what has never been done, because what is known is known to be insufficient, or worse. It is an old theme of tragedy that we will be responsible for our actions beyond anything we bargain for, and it is the prudence of morality to have provided us with excuses and virtues against that time. Krenek turns this theme into the comedy of making choices whose consequences we accept as the very embodiment of our will and sensibility although we cannot, in principle, see our responsibility in them. He says that "the composer has come to distrust his inspiration," but he obviously does not mean what those words convey – that the composer (like, say, Luther or Lincoln) is gripped by an idea which is causing him an agony of doubt. What in fact Krenek has come to distrust is the composer's capacity to feel any idea as his own. In denying tradition, Krenek is a Romantic, but with no respect or hope for the individual's resources; and in the reliance on rules, he is a Classicist, but with no respect or hope for his culture's inventory of conventions.

It is less my wish here to detail the failings or to trace the symptoms in such philosophizing as Krenek's, than it is to note simply that theorizing of this kind is characteristic of the writing about new music – alternating, as was suggested, with purely technical accounts of the procedures used in producing the work. For this fact in itself suggests (1) that such works cannot be *criticized*, as traditional art is criticized, but must be defended, or rejected, as art altogether; and (2) that such work would not exist but for the philosophy. That, in turn, suggests that the activity going into the production, or consumption, of such products cannot be satisfied by the art it yields, but only in a philosophy which seems to give justification and importance to the activity of producing it. I am not suggesting that such activity is in fact unimportant, nor that it can in no way be justified, but only that such philosophizing as Krenek's does not justify it and must not be used to protect it against aesthetic assessment. (Cage's theorizing, which I find often quite charming, is exempt from such strictures, because he clearly believes that the work it produces is no more important than the theory is, and that it is not justified by the theory, but, as it were, illustrates the theory. That his work is performed as music – rather than a kind of paratheater or parareligious exercise – is only another sign of the confusions of the age. I do not speak of his music explicitly meant to accompany the dance.)

I have suggested that it is significant not only *that* philosophy should occur in these ways, but also that it should take the content it has. I want now to ask why it is that the concepts of chance and improvisation should occur at all in discussing composition; what might they be used to explain?

* * * * *

What is composition, what is it to compose? It seems all right to say, "It is to make something, an object of a particular sort." The question then is, "What sort?" One direction of reply would be, "An object of art." And what we need to know is just what an object of art is. Suppose we give a minimal answer: "It is an object in which human beings will or can take an interest, one which will or can absorb or involve them." But we can be absorbed by lots of things people make: toys, puzzles, riddles, scandals. . . . Still, something is said, because not *everything* people make is an object of this sort. It is a problem, an artistic problem – an experimental problem, one could say – to discover what will have the capacity to absorb us the way art does. Could someone be interested and become absorbed in a pin, or a crumpled handkerchief? Suppose someone did. Shall we say, "It's a matter of taste"? We might dismiss him as mad (or suppose he is pretending), or, alternatively, ask ourselves what he can possibly be *seeing in* it. That these *are* our alternatives is what I wish to emphasize. The situation demands an explanation, the way watching someone listening intently to Mozart, or working a puzzle, or, for that matter, watching a game of baseball, does not. The forced choice between the two responses – "He's mad" (or pretending, or on some drug, etc.) or else "What's in it?" – are the imperative choices we have when confronted with a new development in art. (A revolutionary development in science is different: not because the new move can initially be proved to be valid – perhaps it can't, in the way we suppose that happens – but because it is easier, for the professional community, to spot cranks and frauds in science than in art; and because if what the innovator does is valid, then it is *eo ipso* valid for the rest of the professional community, *in their own work*, and as it stands, as well.) But objects of art not merely interest and absorb, they move us; we are not merely involved with them, but concerned with them, and care about them; we treat them in special ways, invest them with a value which normal people otherwise reserve only for other people – *and* with the same kind of scorn and outrage. They *mean* something to us, not just the way statements do, but the way people do. People devote their lives, sometimes sacrifice them, to producing such objects just in order that they will have such consequences; and we do not think they are mad for doing so. We approach such objects not merely because they are interesting in themselves, but because they are felt as made by someone – and so we use such categories as intention, personal style, feeling, dishonesty, authority, inventiveness, profundity, meretriciousness, etc., in speaking of them. The category of intention is as inescapable (or escapable with the same consequences) in speaking of objects of art as in speaking of what human beings say and do: without it, we would not understand what they are. They are, in a word, not works of nature but of *art* (i.e., of act, talent, skill). Only the concept of intention does not function, as elsewhere, as a term of excuse or justification. We follow the progress of a piece the way we follow what someone is saying or doing. Not, however, to see how it will come out, nor to learn something specific, but to see what *it* says, to see what someone has been able to make out of these materials. A work of art does not express some particular intention (as statements do), nor achieve particular goals (the way technological skill and moral action do), but, one may say, celebrates the fact that men can intend their lives at all (if you like, that they are free to choose), and that their actions are coherent and effective at all in the scene of indifferent nature and determined society. This is what I understand Kant to have seen when he said of works of art that they embody "purposiveness without purpose.'

Such remarks are what occur to me in speaking of compositions as objects *composed*. The concepts of chance and of improvision have natural roles in such a view: the capacities for improvising and for taking and seizing chances are virtues common to the activity leading to a composition. It suggests itself, in fact, that these are two of the virtues necessary to act coherently and successfully at all. I use "virtue" in what I take to be Plato's and Aristotle's sense: a capacity by virtue of which one is able to act successfully, to follow the distance from an impulse and intention through to its realization. Courage and temperance are virtues because human actions move precariously from desire and intention into the world, and one's course of action will meet dangers or distractions which, apart from courage and temperance, will thwart their realization. A world in which you could get what you want merely by wishing would not only contain no beggars, but no human activity. The success of an action is threatened in other familiar ways: by the lack of preparation or foresight; by the failure of the most convenient resources, natural or social, for implementing the action (a weapon, a bridge, a shelter, an extra pair of hands); and by a lack of knowledge about the best course to take, or way to proceed. To survive the former threats will require ingenuity and resourcefulness, the capacity for improvisation; to overcome the last will demand the willingness and capacity to take and to seize chances.

Within the world of art one makes one's own dangers, takes one's own chances – and one speaks of its objects at such moments in terms of tension, problem, imbalance, necessity, shock, surprise. . . . And within this world one takes and exploits these chances, finding, through danger, an unsuspected security – and so one speaks of fulfillment, calm, release, sublimity, vision. . . . Within it, also, the means of achieving one's purposes cannot lie at hand, ready-made. The means themselves have inevitably to be fashioned for *that* danger, and for *that* release – and so one speaks of inventiveness, resourcefulness, or else of imitativeness, obviousness, academicism. The *way* one escapes or succeeds is, in art, as important as the success itself; indeed, the way constitutes the success – and so the means that are fashioned are spoken of as masterful, elegant, subtle, profound. . . .

I said: in art, the chances you take are your own. But of course you are inviting others to take them with you. And since they are, nevertheless, your own, and your invitation is based not on power or authority, but on attraction and promise, your invitation incurs the most exacting of obligations: that *every* risk must be shown worthwhile, and every infliction of tension lead to a resolution, and every demand on attention and passion be satisfied – that risks those who trust you can't have known they would take, will be found to yield value they can't have known existed. The creation of art, being human conduct which affects others, has the commitments any conduct has. It escapes morality; not, however, in escaping commitment, but in being free to choose only those commitments it wishes to incur. In this way art plays with one of man's fates, the fate of being accountable for everything you do and are, intended or not. It frees us to sing and dance, gives us actions to perform whose consequences, commitments, and liabilities are discharged in the act itself.

The price for freedom in this choice of commitment and accountability is that of an exactitude in meeting those commitments and discharging those accounts which no mere morality can impose. You cede the possibilities of excuse, explanation, or justification for your failures; and the cost of failure is not remorse and recompense, but the loss of coherence altogether.

The concept of improvisation, unlike the concept of chance, is one which has established and familiar uses in the practice of music theorists and historians. An ethnomusicologist will have recourse to the concept as a way of accounting for the creation-cum-performance of the music of cultures, or classes, which have no functionaries we would think of as composers, and no objects we would think of as embodying the intention to art; and within the realm of composed (written) music, improvisation is, until recent times, recognized as explicitly called for at certain sharply marked incidents of a performance – in the awarding of cadenzas, in the opportunities of ornamentation, in the realization of figured bass. In such uses, the concept has little explanatory power, but seems merely to name events which one knows, as matters of historical fact (that is, as facts independent of anything a critic would have to discover by an analysis or interpretation of the musical material as an aesthetic phenomenon), not to have been composed.

My use of the concept is far more general. I mean it to refer to certain qualities of music generally. Perhaps what I am getting at can be brought out this way. In listening to a great deal of music, particularly to the time of Beethoven, it would, I want to suggest, be possible to imagine that it was being improvised. Its mere complexity, or a certain kind of complexity, would be no obstacle. (Bach, we are told, was capable of improvising double fugues on any given subjects.) I do not suggest that a chorus or a symphony orchestra can be imagined to be improvising its music; on the contrary, a group improvisation itself has a particular *sound*. On the other hand I do not wish to restrict the sense of improvisation to the performance of one player either. It may help to say: One can hear, in the music in question, how the composition is *related* to, or could grow in familiar ways, from a process of improvisation; as though the parts meted out by the composer were re-enactments, or dramatizations, of successes his improvisations had discovered – given the finish and permanence the occasion deserves and the public demands, but containing essentially only such discoveries. If this could be granted, a further suggestion becomes possible. Somewhere in the development of Beethoven, this ceases to be imaginable. (I do not include *all* music after Beethoven. Chopin and Liszt clearly seem improvisatory, in the sense intended; so do Brahms Intermezzi, but not

Brahms Symphonies; early Stravinsky, perhaps, but not recent Stravinsky.)

Why might such a phenomenon occur? It is, obviously enough, within contexts fully defined by shared formulas that the possibility of full, explicit improvisation traditionally exists – whether one thinks of the great epics of literature (whose "oral-formulaic" character is established), or of ancient Chinese painting, or of Eastern music, or of the theater of the Commedia dell'Arte, or jazz. If it seems a paradox that the reliance on formula should allow the fullest release of spontaneity, that must have less to do with the relation of these phenomena than with recent revolutions in our aesthetic requirements. The suggestion, however, is this. The context in which we can hear music as improvisatory is one in which the language it employs, its conventions, are familiar or obvious enough (whether because simple or because they permit of a total mastery or perspicuity) that at no point are we or the performer in doubt about our location or goal; there are solutions to every problem, permitting the exercise of familiar forms of resourcefulness; a mistake is clearly recognizable as such, and may even present a chance to be seized; and just as the general range of chances is circumscribed, so there is a preparation for every chance, and if not an inspired one, then a formula for one. But in the late experience of Beethoven, it is as if our freedom to act no longer depends on the possibility of spontaneity; improvising to fit a *given* lack or need is no longer enough. The entire enterprise of action and of communication has become problematic. The problem is no longer how to do what you want, but to know what would satisfy you. We could also say: Convention as a whole is now looked upon not as a firm inheritance from the past, but as a continuing improvisation in the face of problems we no longer understand. Nothing we now have to say, no *personal* utterance, has its meaning conveyed in the conventions and formulas we now share. In a time of slogans, sponsored messages, ideologies, psychological warfare, mass projects, where words have lost touch with their sources or objects, and in a phonographic culture where music is for dreaming, or for kissing, or for taking a shower, or for having your teeth drilled, our choices seem to be those of silence, or nihilism (the denial of the value of shared meaning altogether), or statements so personal as to form the possibility of communication without the support of convention – perhaps to become the source of new convention. And then, of course, they are most likely to fail even to seem to communicate. Such, at any rate, are the choices which the modern works of art I know seem to me to have made. I should say that the attempt to re-invent convention is the alternative I take Schoenberg and Stravinsky and Bartok to have taken; whereas in their total organization, Krenek and Stockhausen have chosen nihilism.

* * * * *

The sketches I have given of possible roles of improvisation and chance in describing composition obviously do not fit their use in the ideology of the new music; they may, however, help understand what that ideology is. When a contemporary theorist appeals to *chance*, he obviously is not appealing to its associations with taking and seizing chances, with risks and opportunities. The point of the appeal is not to call attention to the act of composition, but to deny that act; to deny that what he offers is composed. His concept is singular, with no existing plural; it functions not as an explanation for particular actions but as a metaphysical principle which supervises his life and work as a whole. The invocation of chance is like an earlier artist's invocation of the muse, and serves the same purpose: to indicate that his work comes not from *him*, but *through* him – its validity or authority is not a function of his own powers or intentions. Speaking for the muse, however, was to give voice to what all men share, or all would hear; speaking through chance forgoes a voice altogether – there is nothing to say. (That is, of course, by now a cliché of popular modernism.) This way of forgoing composition may perhaps usefully be compared with the way it is forgone in modernist painting. The contemporary English sculptor Anthony Caro is reported to have said: "I do not compose." Whatever he meant by that, it seems to have clear relevance to the painting of abstract expressionism and what comes after.[1] If you look at a Pollock drip painting or at a canvas consisting of eight parallel stripes of paint, and what you are looking for is *composition* (matters of balance, form, reference among the parts, etc.), the result is absurdly trivial: a child could do it; I could do it. The question, therefore, if it is art, must be: How is this to be seen? What is the painter doing? The problem, one could say, is not one of escaping inspiration, but of determining how a man could be inspired to do *this*, why he feels *this* necessary or satisfactory, how he can *mean* this. Suppose you conclude that he cannot. Then that will mean, I am suggesting, that you conclude that this is not art, and this man is not an artist; that in failing to mean what he's done, he is fraudulent. But how do you know?

Note

1 Reported by Michael Fried (who showed me its significance) in an article on Caro in *The Lugano Review*, 1965. See, in addition, his *Three American Painters*, the catalog essay for an exhibition of the work of Noland, Olitski, and Stella, at the Fogg Museum, in the spring of 1965; and his "Jules Olitski's New Paintings," *Artforum*, November 1965.

7

Kierkegaard's *On Authority and Revelation*

This essay is probably one of the most neglected of those in *Must We Mean What We Say?*; and this neglect is unjustified for many reasons. First, as a reading of one of Kierkegaard's less well-known but typically provocative writings, it shows Cavell's ability to trace the logical rigor of texts whose designs upon their reader are often taken to be "merely" rhetorical or literary, or else devoted to spiritual special pleading. Second, in its concluding discussion of the ways in which the artist has come to occupy the position allotted by Kierkegaard to the apostle, Cavell gives a glancing sense of the depth of significance he was inclined to attribute to modernist art at this stage of his career. Perhaps most importantly, however, the portrait it paints of Kierkegaard's general approach to the task of writing on religious matters reveals a striking family resemblance between it and Wittgenstein's later philosophical methods; in effect, it presents Kierkegaard's pseudonymous authorship as aiming to criticize the religious culture of Europe by reminding both believers and non-believers of the distinctive grammar of religious concepts. Consequently, it also constitutes a step in Cavell's distinctively modern and modernist concern to clarify the defining conditions of his own cultural practice by clarifying its relations with neighboring modes of thought and life; for Kierkegaard's writings at once clarify the nature of a religious form of life, exemplify a grammatical investigation of religious concepts, and demonstrate affinities between explicitly religiously motivated intellectual projects and those which appear to be resolutely distinct from such concerns.

With the benefit of hindsight, this last point allows us to see this essay as one of the earliest indications of Cavell's sense that modernist philosophy must be thought of as inheriting or laying claim to a species of spiritual fervor standardly associated with religious convictions. We have already seen (in Essay 4) that Cavell takes the death of God to be one of the defining conditions of modern culture; but in more recent years, he

Originally published in *Must We Mean What We Say? A Book of Essays*, by Stanley Cavell (Cambridge: Cambridge University Press, 1969), pp. 163–79. Reprinted by permission.

has explicitly associated the philosophers and writers to whom he is most committed – Wittgenstein, Heidegger, Emerson, and Thoreau – with a tradition of moral (often shading into and shadowed by religious) thinking that he calls Emersonian or Moral Perfectionism. The five concluding extracts in this volume chart the main lines of this development in Cavell's thought; but this early essay – together with the insistent surfacing of religious texts in the concluding part of *The Claim of Reason* as very often articulating "the truth in foul disguise," as Nietzsche has it (cf. Essay 3) – should make it clear that Cavell's acknowledgment of a perfectionist impulse was long in preparation.

"I myself perceive only too well," Kierkegaard says in beginning a second Preface to his Cycle of Ethico-Religious Essays, "how obvious is the objection and how much there is in it, against writing such a big book dealing in a certain sense with Magister Adler." His first answer to this objection is just that the book is "about" Adler only in a certain sense, the sense, namely, in which he is a Phenomenon, a transparence through which the age is caught. But that is scarcely a serious answer, because what the objection must mean is: Why use the man Adler in this way? And Kierkegaard has an answer to this as well: it enabled him to accomplish something which "perhaps it was important for our age that [I] should accomplish and which could be accomplished in no other way." This is not a moral defense for his treatment; it does not, for example, undertake to show that an action which on the surface, or viewed one way, appears callous or wanton, is nevertheless justified or anyway excusable. Kierkegaard goes on to offer what looks like an aesthetic defense of his treatment of Adler – "without him [I] could not have given my presentation the liveliness and the ironical tension it now has." This moral shock is succeeded by another as we realize that the presentation in question is not offered for its literary merit, but for its value as a case study; it is the justification of a surgeon, whose right to cut into people is based on his skill and credentials and whose right to present his cases to others is based on his office and on the obligation to transmit his knowledge to his peers.

Why, on this ground, is the Adler case of profit? Of what is he a typical, and until now undiagnosed, case? He is a case of a particular and prevalent and virulent confusion, and an initial diagnosis is broached: "Disobedience is the secret of the religious confusion of our age" (xviii). But what is the secret? Isn't this just what the case was widely known to be all about? Adler's claim to have had a revelation was certainly a case for the Church, and in particular a case of confusion; he was suspended on the ground that his mind was deranged (Lowrie's Preface, p. ix) and finally deposed after replying evasively to the ecclesiastical interrogatories. This seems patently a case of trying unsuccessfully to evade the Church's authority. But it seems Kierkegaard's view of the case is different: ". . . the whole book is essentially . . . about the confusion from which the concept of revelation suffers in our confused age. Or . . . about the confusion involved in the fact that the concept of authority has been entirely forgotten in our confused age" (p. xvi). The concept is *entirely forgotten*. This suggests not merely that Adler, for instance, was disobedient in this particular case; it suggests that Adler would not have known what obedience consisted in. And it implies that no one else would have known either, in particular not the Church. The concept of revelation, on the other hand, is not forgotten; it is confused. Adler suffers from this, but so do all men in our age, in particular men of the Church. When Bishop Mynster appealed to Adler's mental derangement as the ground for suspending him, he was evading the same thing Adler would come to evade, the claim to a revelation; and in this evasion the Church is disobedient to its divine command to preach and clarify, to hold open, the word of God.

So the case deepens. For it is not merely that the situations of the extraordinary preacher and the ecclesiastical authority are morally analogous, each suffering his own confusion and each falling into his own disobedience. The third Preface Kierkegaard composed seems to me to go farther, almost saying that they suffer identical consequences, the same confusion of mind, that they are both, as the age is, spiritually deranged. The political events of 1848, which called out this final Preface, are interpreted by Kierkegaard as an attempt to solve a religious problem in political terms, an attempt which will go on, and with increasing confusion and fury, until men turn back to themselves:

> Though all travel in Europe must stop because one must wade in blood, and though all ministers were to remain sleepless for ruminating [about constitutional amendments, votes, equality, etc.] and though every day ten ministers were to lose their reason, and every next day ten new ministers were to begin where the others left off, only to lose their reason in turn – with all this not one step forward is made, an obstacle to it is sternly fixed, and the bounds set by eternity deride all human efforts. . . . Ah, but to get the conflagration quenched, the spontaneous combustion brought about by the friction of worldliness, i.e., to get eternity again – bloodshed may be needed and bombardments, *item* that many ministers shall lose their reason. (p. xxi)

The book on Adler is about a minister who has lost his reason, and the flat ambiguity of Kierkegard's "many ministers" registers exactly the ambiguity of concepts, the confusion of realms, which he finds the cause, and the content, of our sickness. Both political and religious ministers madly try to solve religious problems with political means, the one by "levelling" worldly differences into a horrible parody of what is, Christianly, already a fact; the other by trying to approach by reason what is always grasped by faith, or by trying to make a shift of emotion do what only a change of heart can do. This points to a second ambiguity in Kierkegaard's prediction, recorded in the phrase "shall lose their reason." To lose their reason, religiously understood as "[letting] the understanding go" (p. xxii) is precisely what the ministers, what we all, should do; it is precisely because we are incapable of that "leap into the religious" (but equally incapable of letting go of religious categories, of "Christianity of a sort") that we are confused. This is one way Adler is seen by Kierkegaard as a Satire upon the Present Age, and one prompting, throughout the book, for Kierkegaard's recourse to his categories of the comic and ironic. Adler performed the one saving act, he lost his reason; only he did it the way he does everything else, the way things normally are done in our reflective age: he did it literally, not religiously. He went crazy. But just in this lies the real defense of Adler, the *moral* answer to the question "Why expose Adler?" The derangement of this minister is shared by all ministers. Of course in his case the derangement may have got out of hand, he went too far; but this, as Kierkegaard says in the concluding sections of his book, is to his "advantage" as a Christian, because it came from a real spiritual movement toward inner self-concern. Religiously considered, other ministers are in the same, or in a worse, state; so it is unjust that Adler should be singled out for deposition on the ground of derangement. And the Bishop should have considered it religiously. For the Church, Adler is not a transparent medium, but an opaque glass, a mirror. Perhaps this is a way of seeing why, while Kierkegaard calls Adler a satire on the present *age*, he calls him an epigram on the Christendom of our age – a terse and ingenious expression of it.

Of course this does not mean that there are no valid religious grounds on which to question and perhaps depose Adler. What it means is that providing these religious grounds, in our age, for our age, will require *overcoming the specific confusion* which has deprived us of religious ground altogether; hence the form of activity will be one of *regaining clarity*. (In this book, Kierkegaard characterizes our age in a few, very specific, and often repeated, ways; his task is to provide correctives specific to them. For example, he finds that we are absent-minded, so his task is to provide presence of mind; he finds us lightminded (lightheaded?), so his task is to inject seriousness and balance; he finds us *distrait*, so his task is to attract our attention.) In his first Preface Kierkegaard says he uses the

Adler case "to defend dogmatic concepts," and in the second Preface he claims that from the book one will "get a clarity about certain dogmatic concepts and an ability to use them" ·(p. xv). By "defend dogmatic concepts" he does not mean "provide a dogmatic backing for them," but rather something like "defend them as themselves dogmatic"; as, so to speak, carrying their own specific religious weight – something, it is implied, theology now fails to do – and this is a matter of coming to see clearly what they mean. So his task is one of providing, or re-providing, their meaning; in a certain sense, giving each its definition. This definition is not to provide some new sense to be attached to a word, with the purpose of better classifying information or outfitting a new theory; it is to clarify what the word does mean, as we use it in our lives – what it means, that is, to anyone with the ability to use it. Now an activity which has the form of taking us from confusion to clarity by means of defining concepts in such a way has, from Socrates to Wittgenstein, signalled philosophical activity.

As I do not insist that philosophy is exhausted in this activity, so I do not insist that Kierkegaard is, in this book, exclusively philosophical. The question I want to turn to is, rather: How far is the book on Adler to be considered a book of philosophy? There are several reasons for pressing this question:

1. It recognizes that the *kind* of writing before us is problematic, and so keeps faith with Kierkegaard's own efforts, as an author and as a Christian, to write distinct kinds of works.

2. This book is itself about writing, about the differences between real and fake authors: our amnesia of the concept of authority is expressed by an amnesia of genuine writing and reading: speech, never easy, has now fully become talk. Adler's confused disobedience to religious authority is not merely analogous to, but is instanced by his disobedience, as an author, to the requirements of art. Adler's books are not only fake religion, they are fake books – and the one because of the other.

3. The emphasis on philosophy distinguishes Kierkegaard's effort here from other efforts with which it may be confused:

(*a*) If one says he writes to defend Christianity and to reform Christendom, then one must know his differences from (say) Luther. "[Luther's] . . . day is over," Kierkegaard said in a work composed during the period in which he was reading and writing about Adler; "No longer can the individual . . . turn to the great for help when he grows confused."[1] Luther saw the Church in bondage, Kierkegaard sees it in a position of false mastery and false freedom; Luther's problem was to combat a foreign institution motivated politically and economically, but Kierkegaard's problem is that the mind itself has become political and economic; Luther's success was to break the hold of an external authority and put it back into the individual soul, but what happens when *that* authority is broken? Luther's problem was to combat false definitions of religious categories, but Kierkegaard has to provide definition for them from the beginning; Luther could say, "The mass is not a sacrifice, but a promise," and now Kierkegaard's problem is that no one remembers what a promise is, nor has the authority to accept one.

(*b*) The emphasis on philosophy serves as a corrective to calling it psychology. Kierkegaard is often praised in our age as a "profound psychologist," and while I do not wish to deny him that, it seems to me attractively misleading praise, especially about such efforts as the present book; because what is profound psychology in Kierkegaard's work is Christianity itself, or the way in which Kierkegaard is able to activate its concepts; and because the way he activates them, wherever else it is, is through philosophy, through attention to the distinct applicability of concepts – perhaps one could say, attention to the a priori possibility of applying the concepts in general: it is what Kant called Transcendental Logic, what Hegel called Logic, why Oxford philosophers are moved to speak of their attention to words as a question of logic; Wittgenstein called it "grammar." Take the originating concern of the book on Adler: "How far a man in our age may be justified in asserting that he had a revelation" (p. 91). This is the question the Church ought to have confronted – in order to confront itself, as it stands, with the fact that it cannot answer it. Because this question of being "justified in asserting" is not a matter of determining how likely it is, given a certain man's psychological make-up and given a particular historical condition, that he had or will have a revelation (it is always unlikely); nor a matter of determining whether one is religiously prepared to receive a revelation (for, religiously speaking, there is no human preparation possible); nor a matter of determining psychological variation and nuance in different instances of the experience of a revelation and tracing its antecedents and consequences in a particular man's worldly existence. The question is whether, no matter *what* occurs in a man's life, we are conceptually prepared to call it a revelation, whether we have the power any longer to recognize an occurrence as a revelation, whether anything any longer could conceivably count for us as a revelation – could, so to speak, *force us to assert* that what has taken place is a revelation. Of course, anyone can, and occasionally will, *use the word* "revelation," to refer perhaps to a striking or unexpected experience – this, as emerged in the interrogation of Adler, is what happened in his case. And quite generally: ". . . every Christian term, which remaining in its own sphere is a qualitative category, now, in reduced circumstances, can do service as a clever expression which may signify pretty much everything" (p. 103). The serious issue, which is simultaneously the logico-philosophical and the Christian issue, remains: for a Christian church to be in a position in which it has to say that God is hidden or distant or silent, is one thing; for it to be in a position in which it would not find it conceivable that God should speak to us, is something else. In the latter case, the implication is, one should stop referring to such a thing as Christianity altogether.

Let me, then, call attention to two procedures characteristic of Kierkegaard's writing which I think of as philosophical, and philosophically correct:

1. He frequently wishes to show that a question which appears to need settling by empirical means or through presenting a formal argument is really a conceptual question, a question of grammar. (This is one way of putting the whole effort of the book on Adler.) Take the question John Stuart Mill raises in his essay on Revelation (Part IV of *Theism*): "Can any evidence suffice to prove a divine revelation?" Mill's answer, after careful consideration and reasoning is that "miracles have no claim whatever to the character of historical facts and are wholly invalid as evidences of any revelation"; but he adds to this the concession that if a certain sort of man ". . . openly proclaimed that [a precious gift we have from him] did not come from him but from God through him, then we are entitled to say that there is nothing so inherently impossible or absolutely incredible in this supposition as to preclude anyone from hoping that it may perhaps be true. I say from hoping; I go no further. . . ." From a Kierkegaardian perspective, Mill has gone nowhere at all, and indeed there is nowhere to go along those lines. For the answer to his question is just, No. The statement "A revelation cannot be proven by evidence" is not an empirical discovery, nor a sensible topic for an argument; it is a grammatical remark. (Religiously speaking, such a thing *is* "absolutely incredible.") One factor of Mill's hope is that there is a God through whom the gift can have come; and he regards someone as "entitled" to this hope because there is some evidence for his existence. For Kierkegaard, to hope for such a thing on such a ground is not an act of piety and intellectual caution; it is a hope for nothing: *hoping it* is as incoherent as *believing it firmly*. Other grammatical remarks in, or to be elicited from, the book on Adler are, for example, "Religion only conquers without force"; "One must *become* a Christian"; "Christianity is not plausible.'

2. The other philosophical procedure to be mentioned is what Kierkegaard calls "qualitative dialectic." Very generally, a dialectical examination of a concept will show how the meaning of that concept changes, and how the subject of which it is the concept changes, as the context in which it is used changes: the dialectical meaning is the history or confrontation of these differences. For example, an examination of the concept of *silence* will show that the word means different things – that silence is different things – depending on whether the context is the

silence of nature, the silence of shyness, the silence of the liar or hypocrite, the short silence of the man who cannot hold his tongue, the long silence of the hero or the apostle, or the eternal silence of the Knight of Faith. And the specific meaning of the word in each of those contexts is determined by tracing its specific contrasts with the others – the way its use in one context "negates" its use in another, so to speak.

There is one dialectical shift which is of critical importance for Kierkegaard, that which moves from "immanent" to "transcendent" contexts. It is, I believe, when he is speaking of this shift that he characteristically speaks of a *qualitative* (sometimes he adds, decisive) difference in meaning. (This is the point at which his insistence on God as "wholly other" finds its methodological expression.) The procedure is this: he will begin with an immanent context, appealing to ordinary contexts in which a concept is used, for example, ordinary cases of silence, or of authority, or of coming to oneself, or of being shaken, or of living in the present, or of offense . . ."; and then abruptly and sternly he will say that these concepts are decisively or qualitatively different when used in a transcendental sense, when used, that is, to characterize our relationship to God. ("The situation is quite otherwise . . ."; "It is quite another matter with . . .") Sometimes he is *merely* abrupt and stern, and offers us no further help in understanding; as if to say, You know perfectly well what I mean; as if to rebuke us for having forgotten, or for refusing to· acknowledge, something of the clearest importance. Sometimes, of course, he does go further; then he will describe what the life of a man will look like which calls for description, which can only be understood in terms of – which (he sometimes puts it) *is lived in* – Christian categories. A man's life; not a striking experience here and there, or a pervasive mood or a particular feeling or set of feelings. As if to say: in that life, and for that life, the Christian categories have their full, mutually implicating meaning, and apart from it they may have any or none (pp. 103, 104, 115, 165). And contrariwise, a life which does not invite, require description in terms of (is not lived within) the mutual implications of these categories – no matter how religious it is in some sense, and however full it may be of sublime and intricate emotion – is not a Christian life.

When I said that I thought this procedure was philosophically correct, I did not mean to suggest that I found it philosophically clear. As an *account* of "qualitative differences of meaning" (in terms of "immanence," "transcendence," "qualitative," etc.), I find it all but useless. But it begins and ends in the right place, with the description of a human existence; and each difference in each existence makes what seems intuitively the right kind of difference. And it seems to me right that Kierkegaard should suggest that we *do* or could know, without explanation,

what it means to say that a man "stands before God" or that "This night
shall thy sould be required of thee"; know what they mean not just in
some sense, but know what they mean in a sense which we may wish to
call *heightened*. That we may not know this all the time is no proof against
our knowing; this may only indicate what kind of knowledge it is – the
kind of knowledge which can go dead, or become inaccessible. Nor
would the fact that we cannot *explain* the (heightened) meaning of such
utterances prove that we do not understand them, both because it is not
clear what an explanation would consist in, and because knowing where
and when to use an utterance seems proof that one knows what it means,
and knowing where and when to use it is not the same as being able to
give an explanation of it. It is true that in the religious case an explanation
seems *called for*; but this may only mean, one might say, that we are
perplexed about *how* we know its meaning, not whether we do; and even
that not all the time. And, again, this particular situation may be characteristic of a particular kind of meaning rather than a situation in which
meaning is absent. There might even be an explanation for the sense, as
I wish to put it, that we are balancing on the edge of a meaning. And
Kierkegaard's explanations, however obscure, are not obviously wrong.
He does not, for example, say that religious utterances are metaphorical.

While Kierkegaard's account sometimes refuses explanations of
meaning, sometimes seems to rebuke us for being confused about a
meaning which should be clear with a qualitatively decisive clarity,
sometimes seems to suggest a mode of explanation for that sense of
"balancing on the edge of a meaning," he would nevertheless not be
surprised at Positivism's claim, or perception, that religious utterances
have *no* cognitive meaning. Indeed, he might welcome this fact. It indicates that the crisis of our age has deepened, that we are no longer
confused, and that we have a chance, at last, to learn what our lives really
depend upon. Utterances we have shared about our infinite interests no
longer carry any cognitive meaning. Well and good; we have now completely forgotten it. Then it is up to each man to find his own.

"To imagine a language," says Wittgenstein in one of his best mottoes,
"is to imagine a form of life." When a form of life can no longer be
imagined, its language can no longer be understood. "Speaking metaphorically" is a matter of speaking in certain ways using a definite form
of language for some purpose; "speaking religiously" is not accomplished
by using a given form, or set of forms, of words, and is not done for any
further purpose: it is to speak from a particular perspective, as it were to
mean anything you say in a special way. To understand a metaphor you
must be able to interpret it; to understand an utterance religiously
you have to be able to share its perspective. (In these ways, speaking
religiously is like telling a dream.) The religious is a Kierkegaardian Stage

of life; and I suggest it should be thought of as a Wittgensteinian form of life. There seems no reason not to believe that, as a given person may never occupy this stage, so a given age, and all future ages, may as a whole not occupy it – that the form will be lost from men's lives altogether. (It would be a phenomenon like everyone stopping having dreams.)

It is Kierkegaard's view that this has happened to the lives of the present age. Wittgenstein, late in the *Investigations*, remarks that "One human being can be a complete enigma to another. We learn this when we come into a strange country with entirely strange traditions; and, what is more, even given a mastery of the country's language. We do not *understand* the people. (And not because of not knowing what they are saying to themselves.) We cannot find our feet with them." Toward the end of the book on Adler, Kierkegaard has this:

> Most men live in relation to their own self as if they were constantly out, never at home. . . . The admirable quality in Magister A. consists in the fact that in a serious and strict sense one may say that he was fetched home by a higher power; for before that he was certainly in a great sense "out" or in a foreign land . . . spiritually and religiously understood, perdition consists in journeying into a foreign land, in being "out" . . . (pp. 154–5)

One may want to say: A human being can be a complete enigma to himself; he cannot find his feet with himself. Not because a particular thing he does puzzles him – his problem may be that many of the puzzling things he does do *not* puzzle him – but because he does not know why he lives as he does, what the point of his activity is; he understands his words, but he is foreign to his life.

Other major writers of the 19th century share the sense of foreignness, of alienation, Kierkegaard describes; and not merely their own alienation from their societies, but of self-alienation as characteristic of the lives common to their time; which is perhaps the same as seeing their time as alienated from its past. They can be understood as posing the underlying concern of Kierkegaard's book: ". . . how it comes about that a new point of departure is created in relation to the established order" (p. 192; cf. p. xxi). Kierkegaard's answer is that it comes "from ABOVE, from God," but the test of this answer depends on confronting it with the major answers given it by (say) Marx, and Freud, and Nietzsche (both the Nietzsche of the *Birth of Tragedy* and the Nietzsche of *Zarathustra*). This should forcibly remind one how little of the complexity of Kierkegaard's book I have brought out; for politics, psychology, art, and the final break with God are all themes of the dialectical situation within which *The Book on Adler*, like Adler himself, is produced. I began by indicating some lines through which the religious plane intersects the psychological; let me end with a word or two about its intersection in this book with the political and with the aesthetic.

The Introduction, written one year before the *Communist Manifesto*, starts the imagery of the newspaper which recurs throughout the book – the image of its gossip, of its volatilization of concepts, the universal (no-man's) intelligence it wishes to be, the fourth estate which undermines the idea of *estates* altogether with their recognized authority and responsibilities, pulverizes them into a gritty mixture called the public, from whom nothing but violence and distraction can be expected. Four years earlier Marx had written some articles for his newspaper[2] against a rival editor who had raised the question: "Should philosophy discuss religious matters in newspaper articles?" Marx despises the mind which could frame this question as passionately as Kierkegaard would, and Marx responds to it by criticizing it, as Kierkegaard would; that is to say, he responds dialectically. The point of application of his criticism is evidently different, not to say opposite from Kierkegaard's, but it clarifies for me a particular lack in Kierkegaard's "ethico-religious investigation" of his age and of the way that determines its possibilities for a new departure. He was deeply responsive with the "criticism of religion" which Marx said is now (in 1844) complete in Germany (*Critique of Hegel's Philosophy of Right*). Kierkegaard can be seen as attempting to carry its completion to the North, while at the same time one of his dominating motives would be to criticize religion's criticizers. Nothing an outsider can say about religion has the rooted violence of things the religious have themselves had it at heart to say: no brilliant attack by an outsider against (say) obscurantism will seem to go far enough to a brilliant insider faced with the real obscurity of God; and attacks against religious institutions in the name of reason will not go far enough in a man who is attacking them in the name of faith. The criticism of religion, like the criticism of politics which Marx invented, is inescapably dialectical (which is, I take it, a reason Marx said it provided the origin for his criticism), because everything said on both sides is conditioned by the position (e.g., inside or outside) from which it is said. (This emerges in so differently conceived a work as Hume's *Dialogues*, in its outbreaks of irony.) Kierkegaard is fully dialectical where religious questions are concerned, as is displayed not merely in his long attention to different Stages of life, but in the many particular examples in which the same sentence is imagined to be said by men in different positions and thereby to mean differently. (On the recognition that they mean differently depends salvation, for the Gospel saves not because of what it says but because of who it is who has said it.) But his dialectical grasp is loosened

when he comes to politics, where his violence does not see its own
position and where the object he attacks is left uncriticized. He attacks
newspapers and gossip and the public, as no doubt they deserve (on
religious and on every other ground); but he does not consider, as it is
Marx's business to consider, that what is wrong with them is itself a
function of the age (not the other way around), and that a press which
really belonged to the public (a public which belonged to itself) would
reflect its audience otherwise than in gossip, and that its information
would become, thereby, personal – existential in the relevant sense. We
now know that this has not happened, but we should not therefore know
that it is inevitable that it has not happened. I do not suggest that if it did
happen Kierkegaard's problems would become solved, or irrelevant. But
to the extent such a question is neglected, Kierkegaard's damning of
society to perdition and his recourse to the individual, is suspect – it may
be that a fear of the public is only the other side of a fearful privacy, which
on his own ground would create the wrong silence and the wrong
communication and provide no point for a new departure.

* * * * *

In our age, as yet an unknown distance from that of Kierkegaard, we are
likely to read his books as aesthetic works, thus apparently denying his
fervent claims that they are religious (even, with the present book,
ignoring his claim that it can be understood essentially only by theologians – a remark I choose to interpret ironically or aesthetically, as a rebuke
to theologians for not attending to their job of defending the faith, in the
categories of the faith, but instead help deliver it bound and gagged into
the hands of philosophy). We read him running the risk, and feeling the
pinch, of his damning outbursts against the merely curious, who translate
the real terrors of the religious life into sublime spectacles of suffering
with which to beguile their hours of spiritual leisure (cf. pp. 158–9). I
take heart from the realization that both his and our concepts of aesthetics are historically conditioned; that the concepts of beauty and sublimity which he had in mind (in deploring the confusion between art and
religion) are ones which our art either repudiates or is determined to win
in new ways; that, in particular, our serious art is produced under
conditions which Kierkegaard announces as those of apostleship, not
those of genius. I do not insist that for us art has become religion (which
may or may not describe the situation, and which as it stands describes
phenomena other than those I have in mind) but that the activity of
modern art, both in production and reception, is to be understood in
categories which are, or were, religious.

The remarkable Introduction is, in effect, an essay in aesthetics – or is something I wish aesthetics would become. Its distinction between "premise-authors" and "genuine authors" is drawn in a vital place – the place at which one must criticize a given work, perhaps the work of a given period, not as deficient in this or that respect, but dismiss it as art altogether. This kind of occasion is characteristic of the modern in the field of art. It does not arise as a problem until some point in the 19th century. I might call the problem "the threat of fraudulence," something I take to be endemic to modern art. One cannot imagine an audience of new music before Beethoven, or viewers of the paintings or spectators of the theater of that period, as wondering, or having the occasion to wonder, whether the thing in front of them was a piece of genuine art or not. But sometime thereafter audiences did begin to wonder, until by now we grow up learning and cherishing stories of the outrage and rioting which accompanied the appearance of new works, works *we* know to be masterpieces. At the same time, the advanced critics of the period in which this is becoming manifest (e.g., Matthew Arnold, Tolstoy, Nietzsche) were finding that it was precisely the work acceptable to the public which was the real source of fraudulence. It is characteristic of our artistic confusion today that we no longer know, and cannot find or trust ourselves to find occasion to know, which is which, whether it is the art or its audience which is on trial. Kierkegaard, who knew one when he saw one, defines the genuine author in terms of his moral relation to his work and to his audience: having a position of his own, the real author can give to the age what the age needs, not what it demands, whereas the fraudulent artist will "make use of the sickness of our age" (p. 5) by satisfying its demands; the genuine author "needs to communicate himself" (p. 8) whereas the false author is simply in need (of praise, of being in demand, of being told whether he means anything or not); the genuine is a physician who provides remedies, the false is a sick man, and contagious (p. 11). Kierkegaard has other ways of capturing the experience of this difference (which he calls a qualitative difference), and when we find him saying that

> . . . it is a suspicious circumstance when a man, instead of getting out of a tension by resolution and action, becomes literarily productive about his situation in the tension. Then no work is done to get out of the situation, but the reflection fixes the situation before the eyes of reflection, and thereby fixes (in a different sense of the word) the man . . . (p. 173)

we recognize that writers in our time, such as Georg Lukács and Sartre, have not deepened this definition of the problem of modernism. Adler is, of course, a premise-author, and Kierkegaard goes on in the body of his book to use the out-throw of imagery and contrasts which emerge in this Introduction to mark the features by which one knows that Adler is no better an apostle than he is an author; in both fields he lacks, in a word, the authority. I do not suppose Kierkegaard meant to suggest that a genuine author has to have, or claim, God's authority for his work, but his description of the apostle's position characterizes in detail the position I take the genuine modern artist to find himself in: he is pulled out of the ranks by a message which he must, on pain of loss of self, communicate; he is silent for a long period, until he finds his way to saying what it is he has to say (artistically speaking, this could be expressed by saying that while he may, as artists in former times have, begin and for a long time continue imitating the work of others, he knows that this is merely time-marking – if it is preparation, it is not artistic preparation – for he knows that there are no techniques at anyone's disposal for saying what he has to say); he has no proof of his authority, or genuineness, other than his own work (cf. p. 117) (artistically speaking, this is expressed by the absence of conventions within which to compose); he makes his work repulsive, not, as in the case of the apostle, because of the danger he is to others (p. 46) but because mere attraction is not what he wants (artistically, this has to do with the various ways in which art has today withdrawn from, or is required to defeat, its audience); he must deny his personal or worldly authority in accomplishing what he has to do (artistically, this means that he cannot rely on his past achievements as securing the relevance of his new impulse; each work requires, spiritually speaking, a new step); art is no longer a profession to which, for example, a man can become apprenticed (religiously speaking, it is a "call," but there is no recognized calling in which it can be exercised); finally, the burden of being called to produce it is matched by the risk of accepting it (religiously speaking, in accepting or rejecting it, the heart is revealed). Art produced under such spiritual conditions will be expected to have a strange, unheard of *appearance*. Kierkegaard puts it this way:

> That a man in our age might receive a revelation cannot be absolutely denied [i.e., I take it, denying it would suffer the same confusion as affirming it], but the whole phenomenal demeanor of such an elect individual will be essentially different from that of all earlier examples . . . (p. 46)

All this does not mean (it is not summarized by saying) that the artist *is* an apostle; because the concept of an apostle is, as (because) the concept of revelation is, forgotten, inapplicable. So, almost, is the concept of art.

To the extent that one finds such considerations an accurate expression of one's convictions about the modern enjambment of the impulse to
art and to religion, one will want to re-examine the whole question of
Kierkegaard's own authorship – a task which could take a form related to
Kierkegaard's book on Adler: for Kierkegaard is a "case" with the same
dimensions, and no less a phenomenon than Adler, if harder to see
through. In particular, in the light of our un-aestheticizing of aesthetics,
what shall we make of Kierkegaard's famous claim for himself that he
was, from the beginning, a *religious* author, that the Pseudonymous works
were part of a larger design which, at the appropriate moment, emerged
in directness?[3] Since, presumably, he denied being an apostle, his claim
says nothing about any special spiritual position he occupies as a Christian; he, like many others – like Adler – is a writer about religious matters.
What the claim means, to our position, is that he is a *genuine* author, that
he shares *that* fate. One fate of the genuine modern author is exactly his
indirectness; his inability, somehow just because of his genuineness, to
confront his audience directly with what he must say. Kierkegaard's claim
to religious authorship sounds too much as though the Pseudonymous
works were a strategy he employed for the benefit of others; whereas
those works ought to be seen as a function of his inner strategy, as a
genuine writer, to find ways of saying what he has it at heart to say. For
it is very peculiar to us – in an age of Rilke, Kafka, Joyce, Mann, Beckett,
non-objective painting, twelve-tone music – to hear an artist *praising* the
strategy of indirectness, thinking to encompass its significance by acknowledging its usefulness as a medium of communication. What else
have we had, in major art of the past hundred years, but indirectness:
irony, theatricality, yearning, broken forms, denials of art, anti-heroes,
withdrawals from nature, from men, from the future, from the past. . . .
What is admirable in a work like *Fear and Trembling* is not its indirectness
(which, so far as this is secured by the Pseudonym, is a more or less
external device) nor its rather pat theory about why Abraham must be
silent. What is admirable, exemplary, is its continuous awareness of the
pain, and the danger, of that silence – of the fear of the false word, and
the deep wish that the right word be found for doing what one must:
what, to my mind, Kierkegaard's portrait of Abraham shows is not the
inevitability of his silence, but the completeness of his wish for directness, his refusal of anything less. Exemplary, because while we are
stripped of Abraham's faith and of his clarity, it is still his position we
find ourselves in. For certainly we cannot see ourselves in Kierkegaard's
alternative, we are not Tragic Heroes: our sacrifices will not save the
State. Yet we are sacrificed, and we sacrifice. Exemplary, because in our
age, which not only does not know what it needs, but which no longer
even demands anything, but takes what it gets, and so perhaps deserves

it; where every indirectness is dime-a-dozen, and any weirdness can be
assembled and imitated on demand – the thing we must look for, in each
case, is the man who, contrary to appearance, and in spite of all, speaks.

Notes

This book, *On Authority and Revelation: The Book on Adler, or a Cycle of Ethico-Religious
Essays*, was translated, with an Introduction and Notes, by Walter Lowrie (Princeton:
Princeton University Press, 1955). All references are to this edition.

1 Søren Kierkegaard, *The Present Age* (New York: Harper & Row, 1962, Torchbook),
pp. 58, 81.
2 These pieces are collected under the title "The Leading Article of No. 179 of *Kölnische
Zeitung*," in a volume of selected writings of Marx and Engels entitled *On Religion*
(Moscow: Foreign Languages Publishing House, n.d.).
3 See Søren Kierkegaard, *The Point of View for My Work as an Author* (New York:
Harper & Row, 1962, Torchbook).

8

The Avoidance of Love (Theater)

In this third and final extract from Cavell's early essay on *King Lear,* his sense of what drives the events of the play has inexorably generated questions about the nature of Shakespearian drama, and about the nature of theater as such. For if his reading of the play is correct, the evidence in its favor is perfectly obvious – no high degree of learning or discrimination is required to perceive it; so the question arises – why had critics overlooked it? Cavell's general answer is: the often-underestimated difficulty of seeing the obvious – a difficulty that ordinary language philosophers take to be at the heart of the confusions of skepticism, with its distortions of the familiar grammar of ordinary words. But more specifically, he claims that, in so far as critics or readers or viewers of this play overlook the specific and all-too-familiar straits of mind that motivate its characters (shame, fear of love, and so on), they participate in the very responses that dominate its events: just as the characters variously fail to acknowledge one another, so the critics have failed to acknowledge the characters. But how is it possible for a concept whose home is in the characterization of relations between human beings be applicable to the relations between human beings and fictional characters? How might one (fail to) acknowledge a character in a play? This extract provides Cavell's answers to these questions.

Such a detailed analysis of our concept of a "character in a play" amounts to a grammatical investigation of a concept that is central to our understanding of theater, and so of the role played by that art form in our culture. This extract therefore adds another piece to the general portrait that Cavell attempts to provide (in *Must We Mean What We Say?* and elsewhere) of the determining conditions of each of a number of strands of modern Western culture – a portrait that subserves his modernist project of exploring the present conditions of possibility of the various human practices that border on philosophy, and thereby of clarifying the determining conditions of the practice of philosophy in modernity.

Originally published in *Must We Mean What We Say? A Book of Essays,* by Stanley Cavell (Cambridge: Cambridge University Press, 1969), pp. 326–40. Reprinted by permission.

But it is also part of Cavell's interpretation of *King Lear* that Shakespeare deliberately works to create the experience of overlooking the obvious in his audience, and thereby brings them to participate in the failures of acknowledgment – the enactments of skepticism – under examination in the play itself. So Cavell's identification of a role for concepts of acknowledgment in the relation between audience and characters is also meant to ground the distinctive claim that Shakespeare is attempting to create a mode of theater in which the structures of skepticism and its overcoming are not just studied on stage, but woven into the experience of theatrical performance. For Cavell, Shakespearian tragedy attempts to utilize the resources of theater to create a space in which failures of acknowledgment (in relation to fictional characters) can be recognized and overcome, so that members of the audience might thereby be empowered to acknowledge and overcome parallel enactments of skepticism in their relations to other human beings outside the theater. Shakespearian drama thus offers itself as a weapon in the cultural battle between skepticism and its overcoming that Cavell sees as fundamental to modernity.

In each case the first task of the dramatist is to gather us and then to silence and immobilize us. Or say that it is the poster which has gathered us and the dimming house-lights which silence us. Then the first task of the dramatist is to reward this disruption, to show that this very extraordinary behavior, sitting in a crowd in the dark, is very sane. It is here that we step past the carry of Dr Johnson's words. He is right in dismissing – anyway, in denying – the idea that we need to have what happens in a theater made credible, and right to find that such a demand proceeds from a false idea that otherwise what happens in a theater is incredible, and right to say that our response to the events on a stage is neither to credit nor to discredit them: we know we are in a theater. But then he does not stop to ask, What is it that we then know? What is a theater? Why are we there? – anyway, not for longer than it takes to answer, ". . . the spectators . . . come to hear a certain number of lines recited with just gesture and elegant modulation." It is not clear to me how seriously this straight-faced remark is meant. Its rhetoric may be that of the academic's put-down of the enthusiast. (Listeners come to an opera to hear a certain number of tunes sung with just pitch and elegant phrasing. Spectators at a football game go to see a certain number of gigantic men attack one another for the possession of a bag of air.) Or it may be that *Garrick's* gestures and modulations were worth assembling for. Or it may be that the London theaters of that time typically provided an experience of expert recitation. What seems clear enough is that the theater was not important to Johnson; that a certain provision of inside entertainment was sufficient to justify the expense of an evening there. But if the point is entertainment, then his difficult acquaintance Hume had re-raised a question which needs attention: Why should such matters provide entertainment? Hume's even more difficult acquaintance Rousseau, for whom the theater was important, re-raised the next question: What is the good of such entertainment?

What is the state of mind in which we find the events in a theater neither credible nor incredible? The usual joke is about the Southern yokel who rushes to the stage to save Desdemona from the black man. What is the joke? That he doesn't know how to behave in a theater? That would be plausible here, in a way it would not be plausible in accounting for, or dealing with, the child screaming at Red Riding Hood, or the man lighting a cigarette in church. It treats him like the visitor who drinks from the finger bowl. That fun depends upon the anxious giggle at seeing our customs from a distance, letting them show for a moment in their arbitrariness. We have no trouble understanding what his mistake has been, and the glimpse of arbitrariness is beneficial because the custom justifies itself again: we see the point of having the finger bowl and so (apart from threats to symbol and caste) it doesn't matter that there are other ways of keeping clean, it is enough that this is our way. But what mistake has the yokel in the theater made, and what is *our* way? He thinks someone is strangling someone. – But that is true; Othello is strangling Desdemona. – Come on, come on; you know, he thinks that very man is putting out the light of that very woman right now. – Yes, and that is exactly what is happening. – You're not amusing. The point is that he thinks something is really happening, whereas nothing is really happening. It's play acting. The woman will rise again to die another night. – That is what I thought was meant, what I was impatiently being asked to accede to. The trouble is that I really do not understand what I am being asked, and of course I am suggesting that you do not know either. You tell me that that woman will rise again, but I know that she will not, that she is dead and has died and will again die, die dead, die with a lie on her lips, damned with love. You can say there are two women, Mrs Siddons and Desdemona, both of whom are mortal, but only one of whom is dying in front of our eyes. But what you have produced is two names. Not all the pointing in the world to *that* woman will distinguish the one woman from the other. The trouble can be put two ways; or, there are two troubles and they pull opposite ways: you can't point to one without pointing to the other; and you can't point to both at the same time. Which just means that *pointing* here has become an incoherent activity. Do you wish to say that Mrs Siddons has not died, or does not die? These are not incomprehensible remarks, but the first implies that she had been in danger and the second suggests that she is not scheduled for death. At least our positions would then be distinguishable, if incomprehensible. I mean, the intentions with which we go to the theater are equally incomprehensible. You go, according to what has so far come out, in order to find that Mrs Siddons is not dead; I go to watch Desdemona die. I don't particularly enjoy the comparison, for while I do not share your tastes they seem harmless enough, where mine are very suspect.

The case of the yokel has its anxieties. How do we imagine we might correct him? – that is, *what* mistake do we suppose him to have made? If we grant him the concept of play-acting, then we will tell him that this is an instance of it: "They are only acting; it isn't real." But we may not be perfectly happy to have had to say that. Not that we doubt that it is true. If the thing *were* real. . . . But somehow we had *accepted* its non-factuality, it made it possible for there to have been a play. When we say it, in assurance, it comes out as an empirical assertion. Doubtless it has a very high degree of probability, anyway there is no reason to think that Mrs Siddons is in danger; though of course it is not logically absurd to suppose otherwise. – But now our philosophical repressions are getting out of control. This isn't at all what we meant to be saying. Beforehand, her danger was absolutely out of the question, we did not have to rule it out in order to go on enjoying the proceedings. We do not *have* to now either, and yet the empirical and the transcendental are not as clearly separate as, so to speak, we thought they were. "They are only pretending" is something we typically say to children, in reassurance; and it is no happier a thing to say in that context, and no truer. The point of saying it there is not to focus them on the play, but to help bring them out of it. It is not an instructive remark, but an emergency measure. If the child cannot be brought out of the play by working through the content of the play itself, he should not have been subjected to it in the first place.

Neither credible nor incredible: that ought to mean that the concept of credibility is inappropriate altogether. The trouble is, it is inappropriate to real conduct as well, most of the time. That couple over there, drinking coffee, talking, laughing. Do I believe they are just passing the time of day, or testing out the field for a flirtation, or something else? In usual cases, not one thing or another; I neither believe nor disbelieve. Suppose the man suddenly puts his hands to the throat of the woman. Do I believe or disbelieve that he is going to throttle her? The time for that question, as soon as it comes to the point, is already passed. The question is: What, if anything, do I do? What I believe hangs on what I do or do not do and on how I react to what I do or do not do. And whether something or nothing, there will be consequences. At the opening of the play it is fully true that I neither believe nor disbelieve. But I am something, perplexed, anxious. . . . Much later, the warrior asks his wife if she has said her prayers. Do I believe he will go through with it? I know he will, it is a certainty fixed forever; but I hope against hope he will come to his senses; I appeal to him, in silent shouts. Then he puts his hands on her throat. The question is: What, if anything, do I do? I do nothing; that is a certainty fixed forever. And it has its consequences. *Why* do I do nothing? Because they are only pretending? That would be a reason not to do anything if it were true of the couple over there, who just a moment ago were drinking coffee, laughing. There it is a reason because it tells me something I did not know. Here, in the theater, what does it tell me? It is an excuse, whistling in the dark; and it is false. Othello is not pretending. Garrick is not pretending, any more than a puppet in that part would be pretending. I know everything, and yet the question arises: Why do I sit there? And the honest answer has to be: There is nothing I can do. Why not?

If the yokel is not granted the concept of play-acting, you will not be able to correct him, and that has its own anxiety; not just that of recognizing that people may be wholly different from oneself, but in making us question the inevitability of our own concept of acting, its lucidity to ourselves. You may then have to restrain him and remove him from the theater; you may even have to go so far as to stop the play. *That* is something we can do; and its very extremity shows how little is in our power. For that farthest extremity has not touched Othello, he has vanished; it has merely interrupted an evening's work. Quiet the house, pick up the thread again, and Othello will reappear, as near and as deaf to us as ever. – The transcendental and the empirical crossing; possibilities shudder from it.

The little joke on the yokel is familiar enough of its kind. The big joke, and not just on the yokel, is his idea that *if* the thing were in fact happening he would be able to stop it, be equal to his chivalry. It is fun to contemplate his choices. Will he reason with Othello? (After Iago has destroyed his reason.) Tell him the truth? (Which the person who loves him has been doing over and over.) Threaten him, cross swords with him? (That, one would like to see.) – There is nothing and we know there is nothing we can do. Tragedy is meant to make sense of that condition.

It is said by Dr Johnson, and felt by Tom Jones' friend Partridge, that what we credit in a tragedy is a possibility, a recognition that if we were in such circumstances we would feel and act as those characters do. But I do not consider it a very live possibility that I will find myself an exotic warrior, having won the heart of a young high-born girl by the power of my past and my capacity for poetry, then learning that she is faithless. And if I did find myself in that position I haven't any idea what I would feel or do. – That is not what is meant? Then what is? That I sense the possibility that I will feel impotent to prevent the object I have set my soul on, and won, from breaking it; that it is possible that I will trust someone who wishes me harm; that I can become murderous with jealousy and know chaos when my imagination has been fired and then gutted and the sense of all possibility has come to an end? But I know, more or less, these things now; and if I did not, I would not know what possibility I am to envision as presented by this play.

*   *   *   *   *

It may seem perverse or superficial or plain false to insist that we *confront* the figures on a stage. It may seem perverse: because it is so obvious what is meant in saying we do *not* confront them, namely, that they are characters in a play. The trouble with this objection is its assumption that it is obvious what kind of existence characters in a play have, and obvious what our relation to them is, obvious why we are present. Either what I have been saying makes these assumptions less comfortable, or I have failed to do what I wished to do. It may seem superficial: because saying that we "confront" them seems just a fancy way of saying that we *see* them, and nobody would care to deny that. The trouble is that we no more merely see these characters than we merely see people involved elsewhere in our lives – or, if we do merely see them that shows a specific response to the claim they make upon us, a specific form of acknowledgment; for example, rejection. It may seem plain false: because we can no more confront a character in a play than we can confront any fictitious being.

The trouble is, there they are. The plain fact, the only plain fact, is that we do not *go up* to them, even that we cannot. – "Obviously not. Their existence is fictional." – Meaning what? That they are not real? Meaning what? That they are not to be met with in space and time? This means they are not in nature. (That is, as Leibniz puts it, they are not objects to which one of *every* pair of opposite predicates truly applies – e.g., that one or the other of them has children or has not, ate breakfast or did not. But no such pair can be ruled out in advance of coming to know a character; and more is true of him than we take in at a glance, or in a generation of glances. And more that we are responsible for knowing. Call him our creation, but then say that creation is an exhausting business. It would not be creation from nothing, but from everything – that is, from a totality, the world of the words.) And neither is God in nature, neither are square roots, neither is the spirit of the age or the correct tempo of the Great Fugue. But if these things do not exist, that is not because they are not in nature. And there have so far always been certain people who have known how to find each of them. Calling the existence of Lear and others "fictional" is incoherent (if understandable) when used as an explanation of their existence, or as a denial of their existence. It is, rather, the name of a problem: *What* is the existence of a character on the stage, what kind of (grammatical) entity is this? We know several of its features:

1. A character is not, and cannot become, aware of us. Darkened, indoor theaters dramatize the fact that the audience is invisible. A theater whose house lights were left on (a possibility suggested, for other reasons, by Brecht) might dramatize the equally significant fact that we are also inaudible to them, and immovable (that is, at a *fixed* distance from them). I will say: We are not in their presence.

2. They are in our presence. This means, again, not simply that we are seeing and hearing them, but that we are acknowledging them (or specifically failing to). Whether or not we acknowledge others is not a matter of choice, any more than accepting the presence of the world is a matter of choosing to see or not to see it. Some persons sometimes are capable of certain blindnesses or deafnesses toward others; but, for example, avoidance of the presence of others is not blindness or deafness to their claim upon us; it is as conclusive an acknowledgment that they are present as murdering them would be. Tragedy shows that we are responsible for the death of others even when we have not murdered them, and even when we have not manslaughtered them innocently. As though what we have come to regard as our normal existence is itself poisoning.

But doesn't the fact that we do not or cannot go up to them just mean that we do not or cannot acknowledge them? One may feel like saying here: The acknowledgment cannot be *completed*. But this does not mean that acknowledging is impossible in a theater. Rather it shows what acknowledging, in a theater, is. And acknowledging in a theater shows what acknowledgment in actuality is. For what is the difference between tragedy in a theater and tragedy in actuality? In both, people in pain are in our presence. But in actuality acknowledgment *is* incomplete, in actuality there is no acknowledgment, unless we put ourselves in their presence, reveal ourselves to them. We may find that the point of tragedy in a theater is exactly relief from this necessity, a respite within which to prepare for this necessity, to clean out the pity and terror which stand in the way of acknowledgment outside. ("Outside of here it is death" – maybe Hamm the actor has the theater in mind.)

3. How is acknowledgment expressed; that is, how do we put ourselves in another's presence? In terms which have so far come out, we can say: By revealing ourselves, by allowing ourselves to be seen. When we do not, when we keep ourselves in the dark, the consequence is that we convert the other into a character and make the world a stage for him. There is fictional existence with a vengeance, and there is the theatricality which theater such as *King Lear* must overcome, is meant to

overcome, shows the tragedy in failing to overcome.[1] The conditions of
theater literalize the conditions we exact for existence outside – hiddenness, silence, isolation – hence make that existence plain. Theater does
not expect us simply to stop theatricalizing; it knows that we can theatricalize its conditions as we can theatricalize any others. But in giving us a
place within which our hiddenness and silence and separation are accounted for, it gives us a chance to stop.

When we had the idea that acknowledgment must be incomplete in a
theater, it was as if we felt *prevented* from approaching the figures to
whom we respond. But we are not prevented; we merely in fact, or in
convention, do not. Acknowledgment is complete without that; that is
the beauty of theater. It is right to think that in a theater *something* is
omitted which must be made good outside. But what is omitted is not the
claim upon us, and what would make good the omission is not necessarily approaching the other. For approaching him outside does not satisfy
the claim, apart from making ourselves present. (Works without faith.)
Then what expresses acknowledgment in a theater? What plays the role
there that revealing ourselves plays outside? That is, what counts as
putting ourselves into a character's presence? I take this to be the same
as the question I asked at the beginning of this discussion: What is the
mechanism of our identification with a character? We know we cannot
approach him, and not because it is not done but because nothing would
count as doing it. Put another way, they and we do not occupy the same
space; there is no path from my location to his. (We could also say: there
is no distance between us, as there is none between me and a figure in my
dream, and none, or no one, between me and my image in a mirror.) We
do, however, occupy the same time.

And the time is always now; time is measured solely by what is now
happening to them, for what they are doing now is all that is happening.
The time is of course not necessarily *the* present – that is up to the
playwright. But the time presented, whether the present or the past, is
this moment, at which an arrival is awaited, in which a decision is made
or left unmade, at which the past erupts into the present, in which reason
or emotion fail. . . . The novel also comprises these moments, but only as
having happened – not necessarily *in* the past; that is up to the novelist.
– But doesn't this amount only to saying that novels are narrated and that
the natural sound of narration is the past tense? Whereas plays have no
narrator. – What does it mean to say they "have no narrator," as though
having one is the normal state of affairs? One may feel: the lack of a
narrator means that we confront the characters more directly, without
interposed descriptions or explanations. But then couldn't it equally be
said that, free of the necessity to describe or explain, the dramatist is free
to leave his characters more opaque?

Here I want to emphasize that no character in a play *could* (is, logically, in a position from which to) narrate its events. This can be seen various ways:

1. No mere character, no mere human being, commands the absolute credibility of a narrator. When he (who?) writes: "He lay flat on the brown, pine-needled floor of the forest, his chin on his folded arms, and high overhead the wind blew in the tops of the pine trees," there is no doubt possible that there is a forest here and that its floor is pine-needled and brown, and that a man is lying flat on it. No character commands this credibility of assertion, not because he may not be as honest as a man can be, but because he is an actor; that is, what he is doing or suffering is part of what is happening; he is fixed in the present. The problem is not so much that he cannot, so to speak, see *over* the present, but that he cannot insert a break in it; if he narrates, then *that* is what he is doing, that has become what is now happening. But a narrator cannot, I feel like saying, make anything happen; that is one source of his credibility. (The use of so-called "first person narrative" cedes absolute credibility, but then *this* narrator is not so much a character of the events he describes as he is the antagonist of the reader. We will have to return to this.)

2. This comes out if we notice the two points in *King Lear* at which Shakespeare provides a character with a narration: the Gentleman's account to Kent concerning Cordelia's reception of his letters (*IV; iii*, 12–33) and Edgar's late account of his father's death (*V, iii*, 181–218). As one would expect of any narration by one character to another, these speeches have the effect of interrupting the action, but the difference is that the Gentleman speaks when Shakespeare has interrupted the action for him (or when the events are themselves paused, as for breath); whereas Edgar takes it upon himself to interrupt the action, and as with every other action in this play, Shakespeare tallies its cost. This act of narration occurs within the same continuity of causation and freedom and responsibility as every other act of the play. For it emerges that this long tale has provided the time within which Edmund's writ on the life of Lear and on Cordelia could be executed. Edgar's choice to narrate then and there is as significant as the content of his narration, and his responsibility for this choice is expressed by the fact that his narration (unlike the Gentleman's) is first person. This further suggests why one may feel that a "first person narrative" is not a narrative; or rather, why the more a first person account takes on the formal properties of a narrative, a tale, the more suspicious the account becomes. For a first person account is, after all, a confession; and the man who has something to confess has something to conceal. And the man who has the word "I" at his disposal has the quickest device for concealing himself. And the man who makes a tale with this word is either distracted from the necessity of authenticating his use of it, or he is admitting that he cannot provide its authentica-

tion by himself, and so appealing for relief. We have had occasion to notice moments in Edgar's narration which show that he remains concealed to himself throughout his revelations. The third person narrator, being deprived of self-reference, cannot conceal himself; that is to say, he has no self, and therefore nothing, to conceal. This is another source of his credibility. Then what is the motive for telling us these things? Which really means: What is ours in listening to it?

Philosophy which proceeds from ordinary language is proceeding from the fact *that* a thing is said; that it is (or can be) said (in certain circumstances) is as significant as what it says; its being said then and there is as determinative of what it says as the meanings of its individual words are. This thought can sometimes bring to attention the extraordinary *look* of philosophical writing. The form of say, Descartes' *Meditations* is that of a first person narrative: "Nevertheless, I must remember that I am a man, and that consequently I am accustomed to sleep and in my dreams to imagine the same things that lunatics imagine when awake, or sometimes things which are even less plausible." But one realizes that there is no particular person the narrative is about (if, that is, one had realized that it looks as if there were some particular person it is about and that if there is not there ought to be some good reason why it sets out to look as if there were), and that its motive, like the motive of a lyric poem, is absolute veracity. And someone whose motive is absolute veracity is likely to be very hard to understand.

3. Accounts which are simultaneous with the events they describe – which are written or spoken in the present tense – are, for instance, reports or announcements; reporters and announcers are people who tell you what *is* happening. There is room, so to speak, for their activity because they are in a position to know something *we* do not know. But here, in a theater, there is no such position. We are present at what is happening.

* * * * *

I will say: We are not in, and cannot put ourselves in, the presence of the characters; but we are in, or can put ourselves in, their *present*. It is in making their present ours, their moments as they occur, that we complete our acknowledgment of them. But this requires making their present *theirs*. And that requires us to face not only the porousness of our knowledge (of, for example, the motives of their actions and the consequences they care about) but the repudiation of our perception altogether. This is what a historian has to face in knowing the past: the epistemology of other minds is the same as the metaphysics of other times and places. Those who have felt that the past has to be *made* relevant to the present fall into the typical error of parents and children – taking difference from each other to threaten, or promise, severance from one another. But we are severed; in denying that, one gives up not only knowledge of the position of others but the means of locating one's own. In failing to find the character's present we fail to make *him* present. Then he is indeed a fictitious creature, a figment of my imagination, like all the other people in my life whom I find I have failed to know, have known wrong. How terribly difficult this is to stop doing is indexed by the all but inescapable temptation to think of the past in terms of theater. (For a while I kept a list of the times I read that some past war or revolution was a great drama or that some historical figure was a tragic character on the stage of history. But the list got too long.) As if we were spectators of the past. But from what position are we imagining that we can see it? One there, or one here? The problem is sometimes said to be that we have our own perspective, and hence that we see only from an angle. But that is the same impulse to theatricality, now speaking with a scientific accent. (If bias or prejudice is the issue, then a man has his ordinary moral obligation to get over it.) For there is no *place* from which we can see the past. Our position is to be discovered, and this is done in the painful way it is always done, in piecing it out totally. That the self, to be known truly, must be known in its totality, and that this is practical, is the teaching, in their various ways, of Hegel, of Nietzsche, and of Freud.

If the suggestion is right that the "completion of acknowledgment" requires self-revelation, then making the characters present must be a form of, or require, self-revelation. Then what is revealed? Not something about me personally. Who my Gloucester is, and where my Dover is, what my shame attaches to, and what love I have exiled in order to remain in control of my shrinking kingdom – these are still my secrets. But perhaps I am better prepared for the necessity to give them up, freed of pity for myself and terror at myself. What I reveal is what I share with everyone else present with me at what is happening: that I am hidden and silent and fixed. In a word, that there is a point at which I am helpless before the acting and the suffering of others. But I know the true point of my helplessness only if I have acknowledged totally the fact and the true cause of their suffering. Otherwise I am not emptied of help, but withholding of it. Tragedy arises from the confusion of these states. Catharsis, if that is the question, is a matter of purging attachment from everything but the present, from pity for the past and terror of the future. My immobility, my transfixing, rightly attained, is expressed by that sense of awe, always recognized as the response to tragedy.[2] In another word, what is revealed is my separateness from what is happening to them; that I am I, and here. It is only in this perception of them as separate from me that I make them present. That I make them *other*, and face them.

And the point of my presence at these events is to join in confirming this separateness. Confirming it as neither a blessing nor a curse, but a fact, the fact of having one life – not one rather than two, but this one rather than any other. I cannot confirm it alone. Rather, it is the nature of this tragedy that its actors have to confirm their separateness alone, through isolation, the denial of others. What is purged is my difference from others, in everything but separateness.

Their fate, up there, out there, is that they must act, they are in the arena in which action is ineluctable. My freedom is that I am not now in the arena. Everything which can be done is being done. The present in which action is alone possible is fully occupied. It is not that my space is different from theirs but that I have no space within which I can move. It is not that my time is different from theirs but that I have no present apart from theirs. The time in which that hint is laid, in which that knowledge is fixed, in which those fingers grip that throat, is all the time I have. There is no time in which to stop it. At his play, Claudius knows this; which makes him an ideal auditor of serious drama. Only he was unlucky enough to have seen the play after he had actually acted out the consequences of its, and of his, condition: so it caught his conscience instead of scouring it.

Now I can give one answer to the question: Why do I do nothing, faced with tragic events? If I do nothing because I am distracted by the pleasures of witnessing this folly, or out of my knowledge of the proprieties of the place I am in, or because I think there will be some more appropriate time in which to act, or because I feel helpless to un-do events of such proportion, then I continue my sponsorship of evil in the world, its sway waiting upon these forms of inaction. I exit running. But if I do nothing because there is nothing to do, where that means that I have given over the time and space in which action is mine and consequently that I am in awe before the fact that I cannot do and suffer what it is another's to do and suffer, then I confirm the final fact of our separateness. And that is the unity of our condition.

The only essential difference between them and me is that they are there and I am not. And to empty ourselves of all other difference can be confirmed in the presence of an audience, of the community, because every difference established between us, other than separateness, is established by the community – that is, by us, in obedience to the community. It is by responding to this knowledge that the community keeps itself in touch with nature. (With Being, I would say, if I knew how.) If C. L. Barber is right (in *Shakespeare's Festive Comedy*) in finding that the point of comedy is to put society back in touch with nature, then this is one ground on which comedy and tragedy stand together. Comedy is fun because it can purge us of the unnatural and of the merely natural by laughing at us and singing to us and dancing for us, and by making us laugh and sing and dance. The tragedy is that comedy has its limits. This is part of the sadness within comedy; the emptiness after a long laugh. Join hands here as we may, one of the hands is mine and the other is yours.

Notes

1 That the place of art is now pervasively threatened by the production of objects whose hold upon us is theatrical, and that serious modernist art survives only in its ability to defeat theater, are companion subjects of Michael Fried's "Art and Objecthood" (*Artforum*, vol. V, no. 10, June, 1967, pp. 12–23). It is, among other things, the most useful and enlightening explanation of the tastes and ambitions of the fashionable modern sensibility I know of. Its conjunction with what I am saying in this essay (even to the point of specific concepts, most notably that of "presentness") is more exact than can be made clear in a summary, and will be obvious to anyone reading it. I take this opportunity to list other of Fried's recent writings which develop the notions and connections of modernism and seriousness and theatricality, but which I have not had occasion to cite specifically: "Shape as Form: Frank Stella's New Paintings," *Artforum*, vol. V, no. 3, November, 1966, pp. 18–27; "The Achievement of Morris Louis," *Artforum*, Vol. v, no. 6, February, 1967, pp. 34–40 (the material of this essay is incorporated in Fried's forthcoming book on Louis, to be published by Harry N. Abrams, Inc.); "New Work by Anthony Caro," *Artforum*, vol. V, no. 6, February, 1967, pp. 46–7; "Jules Olitski," introductory essay to the catalogue of an exhibition of Olitski's work at the Corcoran Gallery, Washington, D.C., April–June, 1967; "Two Sculptures by Anthony Caro," *Artforum*, vol. VI, no. 6, February 1968, pp. 24–5. Because Fried's work is an instance of what I call "philosophical criticism," let me make explicit the fact that this title is not confined to such pieces as "Art and Objecthood" nor to those on Stella and on Olitski, all of which are intensely theoretical or speculative; it applies equally to the two short pieces on Caro, each of which just consists of uninterrupted descriptions (in the first case of four, in the second case of two) of Caro's sculptures. Moreover, this writing would not be "philosophical" in the relevant sense if it did not essentially contain, or imply, descriptions of that sort. Not, of course, that I suppose my having spoken of "bringing the world of a particular work to consciousness of itself" (ibid.), will convey what sorts of descriptions these are, to anyone who has not felt them. To characterize them further would involve investigations of such phenomena as "attending to the words themselves" and "faithfulness to a text.'

2 Here I may mention J. V. Cunningham's *Woe or Wonder: The Emotional Effect of Shakespearean Tragedy* (Denver: University of Denver Press, 1951), a work I have more than once had on my mind in thinking of these topics, less for particular detail than for its continuous sense that the effect of tragedy is specific to it, hence part of its logic.

9

"Photograph, Screen, and Star"

These three early chapters from *The World Viewed* form a companion piece to the previous extract. There, Cavell argued that the difference between fictional existence and real existence is not to be understood in terms of the idea that a given (set of) predicates is applicable to real people and not to characters in a play or vice versa; it lies rather in differences in the relations that are possible between two real people and between a person and a character in a play. In these chapters, Cavell explores the nature of film by exploring its material basis – photography; and he does so by posing the question of how best to characterize the relation between an object in the flesh (as it were) and the same object in a photograph. He argues that the difference between the two resides not in some (set of) predicates that apply to the one and not to the other, but in differences in the relations that are possible between a person and an object, on the one hand, and a person and a photograph of that object, on the other. Of course, these relational differences are not the same in the two cases of theater and moving pictures: the audience cannot relate to characters in a film as it can to characters in a play, and the relation between actor and character in films is very different from that between actor and character in the theater.

This grammatical investigation of photographs does not just clarify the differences and similarities between film and theater; it also involves specifying the differences between paintings and photographs, with a view to untangling their troubled relations, and so further contributes to clarifying the distinctive characteristics of the various visual arts, and thus of the aesthetic sphere more generally. But this distinctively modernist project of exploring what is specific to each facet of modern culture co-exists with Cavell's inclination to see these different domains as linked by common preoccupations. His understanding of the relation between an audience and the characters in a play allowed him to characterize it in terms of the concept of acknowledgment, and so to attribute to Shake-

Originally published in *The World Viewed: Reflections on the Ontology of Film*, by Stanley Cavell (Cambridge, MA: Harvard University Press, copyright © 1971, 1974, 1979 by Stanley Cavell), pp. 16–29. Reprinted by permission of the publisher.

spearian drama a social role in combating outbreaks of skepticism in Western culture; and in the same way, his understanding of an audience's relation to the world of a movie, determined as it is by the camera's capacity to record reality, ensures that film is a moving image of skepticism, but one that can also be employed to overcome the skeptical impulse.

Sights and Sounds

There are two continuously intelligent, interesting, and to me useful theorists I have read on the subject of the material basis of film. Erwin Panofsky puts it this way: "The medium of the movies is physical reality as such."[1] André Bazin emphasizes essentially this idea many times and many ways: at one point he says, "Cinema is committed to communicate only by way of what is real"; and then, "The cinema [is] of its essence a dramaturgy of Nature."[2] "Physical reality as such," taken literally, is not correct: that phrase better fits the specialized pleasures of *tableaux vivants*, or formal gardens, or Minimal Art. What Panofsky and Bazin have in mind is that the basis of the medium of movies is photographic, and that a photograph is *of* reality or nature. If to this we add that the medium is one in which the photographic image is projected and gathered on a screen, our question becomes: What happens to reality when it is projected and screened?

That it is reality that we have to deal with, or some mode of depicting it, finds surprising confirmation in the way movies are remembered, and misremembered. It is tempting to suppose that movies are hard to remember the way dreams are, and that is not a bad analogy. As with dreams, you do sometimes *find* yourself remembering moments in a film, and a procedure in *trying* to remember is to find your way back to a characteristic mood the thing has left you with. But, unlike dreams, other people can help you remember, indeed are often indispensable to the enterprise of remembering. Movies are hard to remember, the way the actual events of yesterday are. And yet, again like dreams, *certain* moments from films viewed decades ago will nag as vividly as moments of childhood. It is as if you had to remember what happened *before* you slept. Which suggests that film awakens as much as it enfolds you.

It may seem that this starting point – the projection of reality – begs the question of the medium of film, because movies, and writing about movies, have from their beginnings also recognized that film can depict the fantastic as readily as the natural.[3] What is true about that idea is not denied in speaking of movies as "communicating by way of what is real": the displacement of objects and persons from their natural sequences and locales is itself an acknowledgment of the physicality of their existence. It is as if, for all their insistence on the newness of the medium, the antirealist theorists could not shake the idea that it was essentially a form of painting, for it was painting which had visually repudiated – anyway, forgone – the representation of reality. This would have helped them neglect the differences between representation and projection. But an immediate fact about the medium of the photograph (still or in motion) is that it is not painting. (An immediate fact about the *history* of photography is that this was not at first obvious.)

What does this mean – not painting? A photograph does not present us with "likenesses" of things; it presents us, we want to say, with the things themselves. But wanting to say that may well make us ontologically restless. "Photographs present us with things themselves" sounds, and ought to sound, false or paradoxical. Obviously a photograph of an earthquake, or of Garbo, is not an earthquake happening (fortunately), or Garbo in the flesh (unfortunately). But this is not very informative. And, moreover, it is no less paradoxical or false to hold up a photograph of Garbo and say, "That is not Garbo," if all you mean is that the object you are holding up is not a human creature. Such troubles in notating so obvious a fact suggest that we do not know what a photograph is; we do not know how to place it ontologically. We might say that we don't know how to think of the *connection* between a photograph and what it is a photograph of. The image is not a likeness; it is not exactly a replica, or a relic, or a shadow, or an apparition either, though all of these natural candidates share a striking feature with photographs – an aura or history of magic surrounding them.

One might wonder that similar questions do not arise about recordings of sound. I mean, on the whole we would be hard put to find it false or paradoxical to say, listening to a record, "That's an English horn"; there is no trace of temptation to add (as it were, to oneself), "But I know it's really only a recording." Why? A child might be very puzzled by the remark, said in the presence of a phonograph, "That's an English horn," if something else had already been pointed out to him as an English horn. Similarly, he might be very puzzled by the remark, said of a photograph, "That's your grandmother." Very early, children are *no longer* puzzled by such remarks, luckily. But that doesn't mean we know why they were puzzled, or why they no longer are. And I am suggesting that we don't know either of these things about ourselves.

Is the difference between auditory and visual transcription a function of the fact that we are fully accustomed to hearing things that are invisible, not present to us, not present with us? We would be in trouble if we weren't so accustomed, because it is the nature of hearing that what is heard comes *from* someplace, whereas what you can see you can look *at*. It is why sounds are warnings, or calls; it is why our access to another world is normally through voices from it; and why a man can be spoken to by God and survive, but not if he sees God, in which case he is no longer in *this* world. Whereas we are not accustomed to seeing things that are invisible, or not present to us, not present with us; or we are not accustomed to acknowledging that we do (except for dreams). Yet this seems, ontologically, to be what is happening when we look at a photograph: we see things that are not present.

Someone will object: "That is playing with words. We're not seeing something not present; we are looking at something perfectly present, namely, a *photograph*." But that is affirming something I have not denied. On the contrary, I am precisely describing, or wishing to describe, what it means to say that there is this photograph here. It may be felt that I make too great a mystery of these objects. My feeling is rather that we have forgotten how mysterious these things are, and in general how *different* different things are from one another, as though we had forgotten how to value them. This is in fact something movies teach us.

Suppose one tried accounting for the familiarity of recordings by saying, "When I say, listening to a record, 'That's an English horn,' what I really mean is, 'That's the *sound* of an English horn'; moreover, when I am in the presence of an English horn playing, I still don't literally hear the horn, I hear the sound of the horn. So I don't worry about hearing a horn when the horn is not present, because *what* I hear is exactly the same (ontologically the same, and if my equipment is good enough, empirically the same) whether the thing is present or not." What this rigmarole calls attention to is that sounds can be perfectly copied, and that we have various interests in copying them. (For example, if they couldn't be copied, people would never learn to talk.) It is interesting that there is no comparable rigmarole about visual transcriptions. The problem is not that photographs are not visual copies of objects, or that objects can't be visually copied. The problem is that even if a photograph were a copy of an object, so to speak, it would not bear the relation to its object that a recording bears to the sound it copies. We said that the record reproduces its sound, but we cannot say that a photograph reproduces a sight (or a look, or an appearance). It can seem that language is missing a word at this place. Well, you can always invent a word. But one doesn't know what to pin the word *on* here. It isn't that there aren't sights to see, nor even that a sight has by definition to be especially *worth* seeing (hence could not be the sort of thing we are *always* seeing), whereas sounds are being thought of here, not unplausibly, as what we always hear. A sight *is* an object (usually a very large object, like the Grand Canyon or Versailles, although small southern children are frequently held, by the person in charge of them, to be sights) or an extraordinary happening, like the aurora borealis; and what you see, when you sight something, is an object – anyway, not the sight of an object. Nor will the epistemologist's "sense-data" or "surfaces" provide correct descriptions here. For we are not going to say that photographs provide us with the sense-data of the objects they contain, because if the sense-data of photographs were the same as the sense-data of the objects they contain, we couldn't tell a photograph of an object from the object itself. To say that a photograph is of the surfaces of objects suggests that it emphasizes texture. What is missing is not a word, but, so to speak, something in nature – the fact that objects don't *make* sights, or *have* sights. I feel like saying: Objects are too *close* to their sights to give them up for reproducing; in order to reproduce the sights they (as it were) make, you have to reproduce *them* – make a mold, or take an impression. Is that what a photograph does? We might, as Bazin does on occasion, try thinking of a photograph as a visual mold or a visual impression. My dissatisfaction with that idea is, I think, that physical molds and impressions and imprints have clear procedures for getting *rid* of their originals, whereas in a photograph, the original is still as present as it ever was. Not present as it once was to the camera; but that is only a mold-machine, not the mold itself.

Photographs are not *hand*-made; they are manufactured. And what is manufactured is an image of the world. The inescapable fact of mechanism or automatism in the making of these images is the feature Bazin points to as "[satisfying], once and for all and in its very essence, our obsession with realism."[4]

It is essential to get to the right depth of this fact of automatism. It is, for example, misleading to say, as Bazin does, that "photography has freed the plastic arts from their obsession with likeness,"[5] for this makes it seem (and it does often look) as if photography and painting were in competition, or that painting had wanted something that photography broke in and satisfied. So far as photography satisfied a wish, it satisfied a wish not confined to painters, but the human wish, intensifying in the West since the Reformation, to escape subjectivity and metaphysical isolation – a wish for the power to reach this world, having for so long tried, at last hopelessly, to manifest fidelity to another. And painting was not "freed" – and not by photography – from its obsession with likeness. Painting, in Manet, was *forced* to forgo likeness exactly because of its own obsession with reality, because the illusions it had learned to create did not provide the conviction in reality, the connection with reality, that it craved.[6] One might even say that in withdrawing from likeness, painting freed photography to be invented.

And if what is meant is that photography freed painting from the idea that a painting had to be a picture (that is, *of* or *about* something else), that is also not true. Painting did not free itself, did not force itself to maintain itself apart, from *all* objective reference until long after the establishment of photography; and then not because it finally dawned on painters that paintings were not pictures, but because that was the way to maintain connection with (the history of) the art of painting, to maintain conviction in its powers to create paintings, meaningful objects in paint.

And are we sure that the final denial of objective reference amounts to a complete yielding of connection with reality – once, that is, we have given up the idea that "connection with reality" is to be understood as "provision of likeness"? We can be sure that the view of painting as dead without reality, and the view of painting as dead with it, are both in need of development in the views each takes of reality and of painting. We can say, painting and reality no longer *assure* one another.

It could be said further that what painting wanted, in wanting connection with reality, was a sense of *presentness*[7] – not exactly a conviction of the world's presence to us, but of our presence to it. At some point the unhinging of our consciousness from the world interposed our subjectivity between us and our presentness to the world. Then our subjectivity became what is present to us, individuality became isolation. The route to conviction in reality was through the acknowledgment of that endless presence of self. What is called expressionism is one possibility of representing this acknowledgment. But it would, I think, be truer to think of expressionism as a representation of our *response* to this new fact of our condition – our terror of ourselves in isolation – rather than as a representation of the world from within the condition of isolation itself. It would, to that extent, not be a new mastery of fate by creating selfhood against no matter what odds; it would be the sealing of the self's fate by theatricalizing it. Apart from the wish for selfhood (hence the always simultaneous granting of otherness as well), I do not understand the value of art. Apart from this wish and its achievement, art is exhibition.

To speak of our subjectivity as the route back to our conviction in reality is to speak of romanticism. Perhaps romanticism can be understood as the natural struggle between the representation and the acknowledgment of our subjectivity (between the acting out and the facing off of ourselves, as psychoanalysts would more or less say). Hence Kant, and Hegel; hence Blake secreting the world he believes in; hence Wordsworth competing with the history of poetry by writing out himself, writing himself back into the world. A century later Heidegger is investigating Being by investigating *Dasein* (because it is in *Dasein* that Being shows up best, namely as questionable), and Wittgenstein investigates the world ("the possibilities of phenomena") by investigating what we say, what we are inclined to say, what our pictures of phenomena are, in order to wrest the world from our possessions so that we may possess it again. Then the recent major painting which Fried describes as objects of *presentness* would be painting's latest effort to maintain its conviction in its own power to establish connection with reality – by permitting us presentness to ourselves, apart from which there is no hope for a world.

Photography overcame subjectivity in a way undreamed of by painting, a way that could not satisfy painting, one which does not so much defeat the act of painting as escape it altogether: by *automatism*, by removing the human agent from the task of reproduction.

One could accordingly say that photography was never in competition with painting. What happened was that at some point the quest for visual reality, or the "memory of the present" (as Baudelaire put it), split apart. To maintain conviction in our connection with reality, to maintain our presentness, painting accepts the recession of the world. Photography maintains the presentness of the world by accepting our absence from it. The reality in a photograph is present to me while I am not present to it; and a world I know, and see, but to which I am nevertheless not present (through no fault of my subjectivity), is a world past.

Photograph and Screen

Let us notice the specific sense in which photographs are of the world, of reality as a whole. You can always ask, pointing to an object in a photograph – a building, say – what lies behind it, totally obscured by it. This only accidentally makes sense when asked of an object in a painting. You can always ask, of an area photographed, what lies adjacent to that area, beyond the frame. This generally makes no sense asked of a painting. You can ask these questions of objects in photographs because they have answers in reality. The world of a painting is not continuous with the world of its frame; at its frame, a world finds its limits. We might say: A painting *is* a world; a photograph is *of* the world. What happens in a photograph is that *it* comes to an end. A photograph is cropped, not necessarily by a paper cutter or by masking but by the camera itself. The camera crops it by predetermining the amount of view it will accept; cutting, masking, enlarging, predetermine the amount after the fact. (Something like this phenomenon shows up in recent painting. In this respect, these paintings have found, at the extremest negation of the photographic, media that achieve the condition of photographs.) The camera, being finite, crops a portion from an indefinitely larger field; continuous portions of that field could be included in the photograph in fact taken; in principle, it could all be taken. Hence objects in photographs that run past the edge do not feel cut; they are aimed at, shot, stopped live. When a photograph is cropped, the rest of the world is cut *out.* The implied presence of the rest of the world, and its explicit rejection, are as essential in the experience of a photograph as what it explicitly presents. A camera is an opening in a box: that is the best emblem of the fact that a camera holding on an object is holding the rest of the world away. The camera has been praised for extending the senses; it may, as the world goes, deserve more praise for confining them, leaving room for thought.

The world of a moving picture is screened. The screen is not a support, not like a canvas; there is nothing to support, that way. It holds a projection, as light as light. A screen is a barrier. What does the silver screen screen? It screens me from the world it holds – that is, makes me invisible. And it screens that world from me – that is, screens its existence from me. That the projected world does not exist (now) is its only difference from reality. (There is no feature, or set of features, in which it differs. Existence is not a predicate.) Because it is the field of a photograph, the screen has no frame; that is to say, no border. Its limits are not so much the edges of a given shape as they are the limitations, or capacity, of a container. The screen *is* a frame; the frame is the whole field of the screen – as a frame of film is the whole field of a photograph, like the frame of a loom or a house. In this sense, the screen-frame is a mold, or form.[8]

The fact that in a moving picture successive film frames are fit flush into the fixed screen frame results in a phenomenological frame that is indefinitely extendible and contractible, limited in the smallness of the object it can grasp only by the state of its technology, and in largeness only by the span of the world. Drawing the camera back, and panning it, are two ways of extending the frame; a close-up is of a part of the body, or of one object or small set of objects, supported by and reverberating the whole frame of nature. The altering frame is the image of perfect attention. Early in its history the cinema discovered the possibility of *calling* attention to persons and parts of persons and objects; but it is equally a possibility of the medium not to call attention to them but, rather, to let the world happen, to let its parts draw attention to themselves according to their natural weight. This possibility is less explored than its opposite. Dreyer, Flaherty, Vigo, Renoir, and Antonioni are masters of it.

Audience, Actor, and Star

The depth of the automatism of photography is to be read not alone in its mechanical production of an image of reality, but in its mechanical defeat of our presence to that reality. The audience in a theater can be defined as those to whom the actors are present while they are not present to the actors.[9] But movies allow the audience to be mechanically absent. The fact that I am invisible and inaudible to the actors, and fixed in position, no longer needs accounting for; it is not part of a convention I have to comply with; the proceedings do not have to make good the fact that I do nothing in the face of tragedy, or that I laugh at the follies of others. In viewing a movie my helplessness is mechanically assured: I am present not at something happening, which I must confirm, but at something that has happened, which I absorb (like a memory). In this, movies resemble novels, a fact mirrored in the sound of narration itself, whose tense is the past.

It might be said: "But surely there is the obvious difference between a movie house and a theater that is not recorded by what has so far been said and that outweighs all this fiddle of differences. The obvious difference is that in a theater we are in the presence of an actor, in a movie house we are not. You have said that in both places the actor is in our presence and in neither are we in his, the difference lying in the mode of our absence. But there is also the plain fact that in a theater a real man is *there*, and in a movie no real man is there. That is obviously essential to the differences between our responses to a play and to a film." What that means must not be denied; but the fact remains to be understood. Bazin meets it head on by simply denying that "the screen is incapable of putting us 'in the presence of' the actor"; it, so to speak, relays his presence to us, as by mirrors.[10] Bazin's idea here really fits the facts of live television, in which the thing we are presented with is happening simultaneously with its presentation. But in live television, what is present to us while it is happening is not the world, but an event standing out from the world. Its point is not to reveal, but to cover (as with a gun), to keep something on view.

It is an incontestable fact that in a motion picture no live human being is up there. But a human *something* is, and something unlike anything else we know. We can stick to our plain description of that human something as "in our presence while we are not in his" (present *at* him, because looking at him, but not present *to* him) and still account for the difference between his live presence and his photographed presence to us. We need to consider what is present or, rather, since the topic is the human being, *who* is present.

One's first impulse may be to say that in a play the character is present, whereas in a film the actor is. That sounds phony or false: one wants to say that both are present in both. But there is more to it, ontologically more. Here I think of a fine passage of Panofsky's:

> Othello or Nora are definite, substantial figures created by the playwright. They can be played well or badly, and they can be "interpreted" in one way or another; but they most definitely exist,

no matter who plays them or even whether they are played at all. The character in a film, however, lives and dies with the actor. It is not the entity "Othello" interpreted by Robeson or the entity "Nora" interpreted by Duse, it is the entity "Greta Garbo" incarnate in a figure called Anna Christie or the entity "Robert Montgomery" incarnate in a murderer who, for all we know or care to know, may forever remain anonymous but will never cease to haunt our memories.[11]

If the character lives and dies with the actor, that ought to mean that the actor lives and dies with the character. I think that is correct, but it needs clarification. Let us develop it slightly.

For the stage, an actor works himself into a role; for the screen, a performer takes the role onto himself. The stage actor explores his potentialities and the possibilities of his role simultaneously; in performance these meet at a point in spiritual space – the better the performance, the deeper the point. In this respect, a role in a play is like a position in a game, say, third base: various people can play it, but the great third baseman is a man who has accepted and trained his skills and instincts most perfectly and matches them most intimately with his discoveries of the possibilities and necessities of third base. The screen performer explores his role like an attic and takes stock of his physical and temperamental endowment; he lends his being to the role and accepts only what fits; the rest is nonexistent. On the stage there are two beings, and the being of the character assaults the being of the actor; the actor survives only by yielding. A screen performance requires not so much training as planning. Of course, both the actor and the performer require, or can make use of, experience. The actor's role is his subject for study, and there is no end to it. But the screen performer is essentially not an actor at all: he *is* the subject of study, and a study not his own. (That is what the content of a photograph is – its subject.) On a screen the study is projected; on a stage the actor is the projector. An exemplary stage performance is one which, for a time, most fully creates a character. After Paul Scofield's performance in *King Lear*, we know who King Lear is, we have seen him in flesh. An exemplary screen performance is one in which, at a time, a star is born. After *The Maltese Falcon* we know a new star, only distantly a person. "Bogart" *means* "the figure created in a given set of films." His presence in those films is who he is, not merely in the sense in which a photograph of an event is that event; but in the sense that if those films did not exist, Bogart would not exist, the name "Bogart" would not mean what it does. The figure it names is not only in our presence, we are in his, in the only sense we could ever be. That is all the "presence" he has.

But it is complicated. A full development of all this would require us to place such facts as these: Humphrey Bogart was a man, and he appeared in movies both before and after the ones that created "Bogart." Some of them did not create a new star (say, the stable groom in *Dark Victory*), some of them defined stars – anyway meteors – that may be incompatible with Bogart (e.g., Duke Mantee and Fred C. Dobbs) but that are related to that figure and may enter into our later experience of it. And Humphrey Bogart was both an accomplished actor and a vivid subject for a camera. Some people are, just as some people are both good pitchers and good hitters; but there are so few that it is surprising that the word "actor' keeps on being used in place of the more beautiful and more accurate word "star"; the stars are only to gaze at, after the fact, and their actions divine our projects. Finally, we must note the sense in which the creation of a (screen) performer is also the creation of a character – not the kind of character an author creates, but the kind that certain real people are: a type.

Notes

1 Erwin Panofsky, "Style and Medium in the Moving Pictures," in Daniel Talbot, ed., *Film* (New York: Simon and Schuster, 1959), p. 31.

2 André Bazin, *What Is Cinema?*, trans. Hugh Gray (Berkeley: University of California Press, 1967), p. 110.

3 Certainly I am not concerned to deny that there may be, through film, what Paul Rotha in his *The Film Till Now* (first published in 1930) refers to as "possibilities . . . open for the great sound and visual [i.e., non-dialogue sound, and perhaps non-photographically visual] cinema of the future." But in the meantime the movies have been what they have been.

4 Bazin, *op. cit.*, p. 12.

5 *Loc. cit.*

6 See Michael Fried, *Three American Painters* (Cambridge, Mass.: Fogg Art Museum, Harvard University, 1965), n. 3; and "Manet's Sources," *Artforum*, March 1969, pp. 28–79.

7 See Michael Fried, "Art and Objecthood," *Artforum*, June 1967; reprinted in Gregory Battcock, ed., *Minimal Art* (New York: E. P. Dutton, 1968), pp. 116–47.

8 When painting found out how to acknowledge the fact that paintings had shapes, shapes became forms, not in the sense of patterns, but in the sense of containers. A form then could *give* its shape to what it contained. And content could transfer its significance as painting to what contains it. Then shape *pervades*, like gravity, or energy, or air. (See Michael Fried, "Shape as Form," *Artforum*, November 1966; reprinted in Henry Geldzahler's catalogue, *New York Painting and Sculpture: 1940–1970* [New York: E. P. Dutton, 1969].)

9 This idea is developed to some extent in my essays on *Endgame* and *King Lear* in *Must We Mean What We Say?* (New York: Scribner's, 1969). [In summarizing it here, Cavell erroneously conflates "actor" and "character": Ed.]

10 Bazin, *op. cit.*, p. 97.

11 Panofsky, *op. cit.*, p. 28.

10

The Same and Different: *The Awful Truth*

This essay – which forms the concluding chapter in *Pursuits of Happiness* – is a reading of one of the films in a genre that Cavell entitled "The Hollywood Comedy of Remarriage;" and in his examination of that genre, two main lines of Cavell's thought intersect. As their title suggests, the plots of remarriage comedies are devoted to bringing a not-so-young romantic couple back together, together again; they chart their capacity to overcome threats internal to their marriage, various versions of the threat of divorce, and so depict marriage as constituted by a continuously renewed willingness to remarry. On one level, therefore, these couples represent variants of the pairs at the centre of Shakespearian drama. Their struggles to maintain their relationship represent studies in acknowledgment, and so show how skepticism about other minds might be enacted and overcome. And – in classic Romantic style – Cavell presents their capacity for acknowledgment as a trope for the human capacity to accept the world; their willingness to remain married to one another figures the human willingness to remain wedded to the world. At the same time, however, Cavell's earlier examination of the ontology of film (in *The World Viewed* – see Essay 9) prepares the ground for aspects of his treatment of these movies. In particular, he sees part of their achievement as lying in their capacity to acknowledge the conditions of their own possibility as movies – in their containing scenes which in various ways register and evaluate their capacity to transcribe reality, their reliance upon actors or stars who have priority over the characters they play, and so on.

This reading of *The Awful Truth* has, however, many more specific points of interest, ones which derive from the film's distinctive inflections of the basic conditions of its genre, rather than from their reiteration. For example, it interrogates the generally active or educative role assigned to

Originally published in *Pursuits of Happiness: The Hollywood Comedy of Remarriage*, by Stanley Cavell (Cambridge, MA: Harvard University Press, 1981, copyright © 1981 by the President and Fellows of Harvard College), pp. 229–63. Reprinted by permission of the publisher.

the principal male in its companion comedies by giving Irene Dunne a strikingly active role in the film's closing third (only that of Katharine Hepburn in *Bringing Up Baby* is comparable); and its dialogue explicitly studies the questions of identity through change that are posed by any genre that stakes the reality of marriage upon the ability of the partners to maintain their connection to one another in and through the events of every new scene. In addition, Cavell takes the film's lack of any knock-out comic scene to show that it takes the roots of the comedic to lie in the everyday; and he takes its focus upon alternations of night and day in the city (rather than changes of season, or shifts from city to country – as its companion comedies prefer) to indicate a sense that marriage requires the achievement of a mode of diurnality – an attitude to one's experience such that the ordinary events of each and every day can elicit interest enough to maintain a relationship from one day to the next. In short, this movie not only connects the question of marriage to that of achieving a new inhabitation of time; it also thereby studies the preconditions of that relationship to the ordinary or the everyday for which Cavell's Wittgensteinian philosophy strives – one through which skepticism might be overcome.

On certain screenings I have felt *The Awful Truth* (1937) to be the best, or the deepest, of the comedies of remarriage. This feeling may be found eccentric on any number of grounds. That I expect little initial agreement with it is registered in the qualification "on certain screenings." By the qualification I mean not only that there have been screenings on which I have not felt this way; I mean also to suggest that the experience of this film is more dependent on the quality of the individual session of screening than its companion films are. Specifically, my connection with the film, even my understanding of it, has been especially dependent, it seems to me, on the presence with me of an appreciative audience. This could mean either that my responses are less free than in other cases, requiring infectiousness and a socially inspired willingness to be pleased, to be sociable; or that my responses are more free, participating or not as they require, the film not forcing its attention upon me. Is the latter possibility really credible? It proposes an achievement of this film – that is, an achievement of its director, Leo McCarey – that transcends the comparable achievements of Frank Capra, Howard Hawks, and George Cukor. The transcendence is not, no doubt, by very much, but the surprise is that Leo McCarey should be setting the example at all for his more famous, or more prominent, colleagues. To get past what may be hardly more than prejudice here, it may help to note Jean Renoir's remark that "Leo McCarey understood people better than any other Hollywood director."[1] There could hardly be, from that source, higher praise.

Nor would McCarey's colleagues in the genre of remarriage themselves have been surprised at his presence. You may not find that Cukor is remembering McCarey when near the beginning of *The Philadelphia Story* Dinah says, "Nothing possibly in the least ever happens around here," three years after Aunt Patsy had said, near the beginning of *The Awful Truth*, "Nothing unusual ever happens around here." Since Dinah's line occurs in the play *The Philadelphia Story*, maybe it was just Philip Barry who was remembering Aunt Patsy a year or two later and Cukor didn't care one way or the other whether the line was retained for the film script. Or maybe the writers and directors in question were all remembering, or each work discovering for itself, a way of warning its audience, taking it by the hand as if to say, that a narrative is about to begin. ("What's happening?" asks Beckett's blind Hamm, trapped between beginning and ending.) But can it be doubted that Howard Hawks is paying homage to McCarey in all but taking over the content of the great restaurant sequence in *His Girl Friday* from the great restaurant or nightclub sequence in *The Awful Truth*? In both sequences, Cary Grant, as a group awkwardly settles itself around a table, opens a conversation with his estranged wife and with Ralph Bellamy by saying, "So you two are going to get married." Grant then quizzes them about where they will live, and elaborately pictures his wife's pleasure in getting away from the big city with its rigors of elegant shops and theaters to the peace and quiet and adventure of the West (Oklahoma City in the present film, Albany in the later). In both the woman tries to protect her new man against the onslaughts of the old and in both the conversation turns, with some relief, to a business proposition. There is also in both a moment (in *The Awful Truth* this comes not within the restaurant sequence but in the sequence that follows it in Bellamy's apartment) at which Grant, breaking up laughing as he begins reciting an intimate memory, has to be signaled off the subject by the woman. And we should note that the last night, at Grant's prospective in-laws" house, as Irene Dunne puts on her sister act, she says, in greeting the father of the family, "I never would have recognized you from his description," thus preparing the way for Walter's initial words to Bruce, "Hildy, you led me to expect a much older man.'

If *The Awful Truth* does have a certain specialness, perhaps this is to be attributed less to its director than to some special place it occupies in the genre of remarriage. It is the only member of the genre in which the topic of divorce and the location in Connecticut are undisplaced, that is, in what one is most likely to take as their natural places; in which the pair's story both opens with the former and closes at the latter. But how do we know that this kind of natural or straight account is so important, more important, say, than the fact that in this film the woman's father is

not present but is replaced by someone called the woman's "Aunt'?
Besides, if genre itself were decisive, Hitchcock's *Mr. and Mrs. Smith*
(1941), which works brilliant variations within the genre, would have
more life for us than is to be derived from its somewhat cold comforts.
Any answer having to do with the depth of participation in the genre
must invoke a director's authority with the genre, his nativeness or
subjection to it, the director and the genre knowing how to get the best
from one another.

And this must mean, according to our understanding of this genre,
knowing how to take a woman most deeply into the forces that constitute
the genre, which in turn means finding a woman, and finding those
qualities in a woman, in whom and in which those forces can most fully
be given play. Here is a place we come unprotectedly upon the limitation
of criticism by the fact of something that is called personal taste. About
It Happened One Night I said that its appreciation depended on a certain
acceptance of Claudette Colbert; but my sense of *The Awful Truth* is that
if one is not willing to yield to Irene Dunne's temperament, her talents,
her reactions, following their detail almost to the loss of one's own
identity, one will not know, and will not care, what the film is about.
Pauline Kael, for instance, in her Profile of Cary Grant has this to say
about Irene Dunne in *The Awful Truth*: "though she is often funny, she
overdoes the coy gurgles, and that bright toothy smile of hers – she shows
both rows of teeth, prettily held together – can make one want to slug
her."[2] Whatever the causes of this curious response, it disqualifies whatever
she has to say as a response to *The Awful Truth*.

It is, I believe, particularly hard to recall the sequence of events that
constitute the film; and since I am going to take something like this
difficulty to be internal to McCarey's achievement in it, it will help to
summarize its main segments. (1) In a prologue, at the Gotham Athletic
Club, Jerry Warriner (Cary Grant) is about to get a sun-lamp treatment
sufficient to make it appear that he's spent the last two weeks in Florida,
"even if it takes all afternoon." He is speaking to a passing acquaintance
with a squash racket: "What wives don't know won't hurt them." And he
adds, "And what you don't know won't hurt you." He invites the acquaintance to come home with him later on for protection, I mean for
drinks. (2) Entering the house with this, and other acquaintances, Jerry
discovers that his wife is not at home. He invents the explanation that
she's at her Aunt Patsy's place in Connecticut, an explanation which
collapses when Aunt Patsy walks in looking for her. Lucy Warriner (Irene
Dunne) enters, in evening dress, followed by Armand Duvall, her singing
teacher, it emerges, with a story about chaperoning a dance and then on
the road back having the car break down miles from nowhere, and

spending the night at a very inconvenient inn. Jerry mockingly pretends to believe the story and is complimented by Armand for having "a continental mind." The guests take the cue to leave, Jerry says his faith is destroyed, Lucy says she knows what he means and tosses him a California orange that he had brought her as from Florida. She says he's returned to catch her in a truth, to which he responds by calling her a philosopher. He gives a speech which includes the lines: "Marriage is based on faith. When that's gone everything's gone." She asks if he really means that and upon his affirming it she telephones for a divorce. (3) Her lawyer, on the phone, repeatedly tells Lucy not to be hasty, that marriage is a beautiful thing; he is repeatedly interrupted by his wife asking him why they have to be interrupted, whom he repeatedly invites, each time covering the phone, to shut her mouth. (4) In divorce court, Mr Smith (the dog Asta) is tricked by Lucy into choosing to live with her. Jerry asks for visiting rights. (5) Aunt Patsy wants to get out of the apartment she and Lucy have taken and have some fun tonight for a change. Lucy objects that they haven't an escort. Aunt Patsy stalks out and comes back with their neighbor from across the hall, Dan Leeson (Ralph Bellamy). Jerry appears for his visiting time with Mr Smith, whom he accompanies at the piano. The others leave. (6a) Dan's mother warns him in general about women and in particular about that kind of woman; (6b) Aunt Patsy warns Lucy against acting on the rebound, pointing out to her that her toast is burning; (6c) 6a continued; (6d) 6b continued. (7) In a nightclub Jerry's friend Dixie Belle sings and enacts "My Dreams are Gone with the Wind." On each recurrence of the title line air jets from the floor blow Dixie Belle's flowing skirt up higher and higher – she finally gives up trying to hold it down. On meeting Dixie Belle, Lucy had said, with some surprise (presumably given her view of Jerry's taste in women), that she seems like a nice girl. When Jerry corrects Dan's impression that Lucy dislikes dancing, Dan, from whom we learn that he is a champion dancer, takes her onto the floor. The music changes and Dan is moved to take over the floor with his champion jitterbugging. Jerry so thoroughly enjoys Lucy's taste of country life that he tips the orchestra to repeat the same number. Jerry pulls up a chair to the edge of the dance floor, sits legs crossed, his arms draped before him carelessly, perfectly, fronting the dancers and the camera, looking directly at the world with as handsome a smile as Cary Grant has it in him to give, in as full an emblem of the viewer-viewed, the film turned explicitly to its audience, to ask who is scrutinizing whom, as I know in film. I think of it as a hieratic image of the human, the human transfigured on film. This man, in words of Emerson's, carries the holiday in his eye; he is fit to stand the gaze of millions. Call this the end of Act One. (8a) Lucy and Dan at the piano in his apartment make a duet of "Home on the Range";

(8b) Jerry enters to discuss their business deal about a mine; (8c) Dan's
mother comes in with gossip about Lucy; Jerry sort of clears her name
with a speech of mock gallantry, exiting on the line, "Our marriage was
one of those tragedies you read about in the newspapers," but Maw is
still not satisfied, whereupon Lucy retreats to let her and Dan sort the
matter out alone. (9) Lucy returns to her apartment to find Jerry there,
rewarding himself with a drink for having, he says, given her that swell
reference; she haughtily refuses an offer of financial help from him, and
laughs heartily as the piano top falls on his hand. As they walk toward the
door for Jerry to leave, Dan knocks. She opens the door, concealing
Jerry behind it. Dan apologizes for his mother's suspicions and insists on
reading Lucy a poem of love he has written for her. As he embarks on it
Jerry from behind the door prods Lucy to laughter with surreptitious
pencil jabs in her ribs. The phone rings, just the other side of Jerry.
Lucy answers; we are shown by an insert that it is Armand; Lucy asks
whoever it is to wait and puts down the phone; as she crosses back past
Jerry to complete her exchange with Dan, behind her back Jerry picks up
the phone and learns who is on the other end. Lucy gets rid of Dan by
giving him a kiss; he departs noisily. Lucy makes an appointment into
the waiting phone, handed to her by Jerry, for three o'clock the next
afternoon, explaining to Jerry after she hangs up that it was her mass-
euse. Jerry finally leaves, saying he's just seen a three-ring circus. The
situation prepares for the juggling of farce. (10) At three o'clock, evidently the next afternoon, Jerry forces his way into Armand's apartment only
to discover Lucy singing for a musicale. (11) The farce erupts as Mr
Smith fetches Armand's hat for Jerry, whom it doesn't fit, try as he will.
The two men find themselves in the same bedroom, Armand to avoid
Jerry, Jerry to avoid Dan and Maw who have come together this time to
apologize again. From the bedroom the two men dash across the living room past the assembled others and out the door. Lucy had written
a letter to Dan telling him that she was still in love with Jerry and had
asked Aunt Patsy to deliver it. Dan says, a moroser if wiser man, "I've
learned a lot about women from you, Lucy; I've learned that a man's best
friend is his mother." As he and his best friend start their exist, Aunt
Patsy takes Lucy's letter from the mantle and delivers it: "Here's your
diploma." Call this the end of Act Two. (12a) Mr Smith barks at the
society page of the newspaper Lucy is reading; it says that Jerry and
Barbara Vance are to be married as soon as his divorce is final, which
incidentally is today; (12b) The newspaper comes alive in a montage of
Jerry and Barbara's whirlwind romance, which mostly consists of their
attending or participating in society sports events; a sequence that reads
like the society segment of, say, a *Movietone News.* (13) In Jerry's apartment, to say goodbye on the eve of their final decree, Lucy recites a

poem written in another time for her by Jerry. She introduces it by saying, "This will hand you a laugh," but neither of them is tickled in the ribs. They sample some champagne that the life has gone out of; evidently they are unable to celebrate either divorce or marriage. To account for Lucy's presence when she answers a phone call from Barbara Vance, Jerry invents the tale that his sister is visiting from Europe, then after a pause explains that she can't come over with him tonight because she's busy and anyway is returning to Europe almost immediately. Lucy says he's slipping. (14) That night, at the Vance house, Lucy interrupts a flagging family occasion with a vulgar display as his low-down sister. She claims to be a nightclub performer and shows them how with Dixie Belle's "Gone with the Wind" ("There's a wind effect right here but you will just have to use your imagination"). Jerry joins her on her exit from the song and dance, and (15) they drive to their conclusion in Connecticut.

That there is not a dull scene in the film is less important a fact, or less surprising given its company, than that there is no knock-out scene, nothing you might call a winning scene, until perhaps the end of the two-men-in-a-bedroom farce, which in my outline I figured as the end of Act Two; but possibly the preceding recital sequence can be taken so, or perhaps the sequence preceding the recital, as Jerry pokes Lucy in the ribs to laugh at Dan's poem. Even if you consider what my outline figured as the end of Act One as a winning scene, this night club sequence takes place much later in its film than, say, the restaurant sequence of *His Girl Friday* in its film, which already followed several instances of knock-out business. We have in this absence of a certain kind of scene the beginning of an explanation of the particular achievement of this film – *if*, that is to say, one regards this film as a serious achievement. Speaking of an absence in this regard is putting negatively a virtue that, put positively, empowers the presenting of an unbroken line of comic development, a continuous unfolding of thought and of emotion, over a longer span than is imagined in the companions among the genre of comedy in which we are placing the film. I understand the point of the achievement to be the tracking of the comedic to its roots in the everyday, to show the festival to which its events aspire to be a crossroads to which and from which a normal life, an unended diurnal cycle, may sensibly proceed. I want to spell out this perception a little further now, if more or less abstractly, as a kind of gauge of this film's role in the genre of remarriage.

The diurnal succession of light and dark takes the place in these films of the annual succession of the seasons in locating the experience of classical comedy. The point is to show that the diurnal, the alternation of day and night, and in the city, mostly sheltered from the natural seasons (as in a film studio), is itself nevertheless interesting enough to inspire life, interesting enough to be lived happily; lived without, one may say, outbreaks of the comic, as if there is no longer a credible place from which our world can be broken into; that is, no communal place, no place we have agreed upon ahead of time. An answer is being given to an ancient question concerning whether the comic resides fundamentally in events or in an attitude toward events. In claiming these films to enlist on the side of attitude here, I am assuming that sanity requires the recognition of our dependence upon events, or happenstance. The suggestion is that happiness requires us not to suppose that we know ahead of time how far, or where, our dependence on happenstance begins and ends. I have had occasion in speaking of the career of Othello to invoke Montaigne's horrified fascination by the human being's horror of itself, as if to say: life is hard, but then let us not burden it further by choosing tragically to call it tragic where we are free to choose otherwise. I understand Montaigne's alternative to horror to be the achievement of what he calls at the end a gay and sociable wisdom. I take this gaiety as the attitude on which what I am calling diurnal comedy depends, an attitude toward human life that I learn mostly from Thoreau, and partly from Kierkegaard, to call taking an interest in it. Tragedy is the necessity of having your own experience and learning from it; comedy is the possibility of having it in good time.

(Should someone take the ideas of attitude and of perspective here as being matters of some known element of psychology, say of some particular feeling or matter of will, it may help to say that attitude and perspective enter as well into the constitution of knowledge, the constitution of the world. The difference between taking a statement as true a posteriori or as true a priori can be said to be a difference in the attitude you take toward it. When the hero of *Breathless* says "There is no unhappy love," he is not, as some may be, leaving the matter open to question, to evidence; for him it is knowledge a priori; you may say a definition. One wants to say here: it is a truth not necessary in all imaginable worlds but necessary in *this* – I mean in *my* – world: "When I love thee not, chaos is come again" – at that moment there will be no world, things will have gone back to before there is a world. And attitude and perspective, and I suppose something like the same division of attitude and perspective, are at play in the distinction between the factual and the fictional. The question is again how a matter gets *opened to experience, and how it is determined* by language or, let us say, by narration. The truths of arithmetic cannot be more certain than that Hamlet had a doublet and wore it all unbraced. Ophelia's word for it *cannot* be doubted. Some who concern themselves with the problem of fiction may be making too little of the problem of fact.)

"The tracking of the comedic to its roots in the everyday." This is my formulation of the further interpretation of the genre of remarriage worked out in *The Awful Truth*. I intend it to account for several features of the genre that differentiate it from other comic forms.

For example, the stability of the conclusion is not suggested by the formula "they lived happily ever after" but rather requires words to the effect that *this* is the way they lived, where "this" covers of course whatever one is prepared to call the conclusion of the work but covers it as itself a summary or epitome of the work as a whole. (In an earlier chapter I express this density of the conclusion by speaking of its aphoristic quality.) There is no other life for them, and this one suffices. It is a happy thought; it is this comedy's thought of happiness.

Again, I have pointed several times to the absence, or the compromise, of the festival with which classical comedy may be expected to conclude, say a wedding; I have accounted for this compromise or subversion by saying variously that this comedy expects the pair to find happiness alone, unsponsored, in one another, out of their capacities for improvising a world, beyond ceremony. Now I add that this is not to be understood exactly or merely as something true of modern society but as something true about the conversation of marriage that modern society comes to lay bare. The courage, the powers, required for happiness are not something a festival can reward, or perhaps so much as recognize, any longer. Or rather, whatever festival and ceremony can do has already been done. And wasn't this always true? In attacking the magical or mechanical view of the sacraments, Luther says, "All our life should be baptism." I once took this as a motto for romantic poetry.[3] I might take a variation of it as a motto for the romance of marriage: all our life should be festival. When Lucy acknowledges to Aunt Patsy her love for Jerry after all, what she says is, "We had some grand laughs." Not one laugh at life – that would be a laugh of cynicism. But a run of laughs, within life; finding occasions in the way we are together. He is the one with whom that is possible for me, crazy as he is; that is the awful truth.

"Some grand laughs" is this comedy's lingo for marriage as festive existence. The question, accordingly, is what this comedy means by laughter. Whatever it means it will not be something caused and prevented by what we mostly call errors. This is a further feature in which the comedy of remarriage differs from other comedy.[4] The obstacles it poses to happiness are not complications unknown to the characters that a conclusion can sort out. They have something to learn but it cannot come as news from others. (Nor is our position as audience better in this regard than that of the characters. To the extent that the effect of classical comedy depends on a sense of our superiority to comic characters, the comedy of remarriage undermines that effect. We are no more superior to these characters than we are to the heroes and heroines of any adventure.) It is not a matter of the reception of new experience but a matter of a new reception of your own experience, an acceptance of its authority as your own. Kierkegaard wrote a book about our having lost the authority, hence so much as the possibility, of claiming to have received a revelation.[5] If this means, as Kierkegaard sometimes seems to take it to mean, the end of Christianity, then if what is to succeed Christianity is a redemptive politics or a redemptive psychology, these will require a new burden of faith in the authority of one's everyday experience, one's experience of the everyday, of earth not of heaven (if you get the distinction). I understand this to be the burden undertaken in the writing of Emerson and of Thoreau; doubtless this is a reason it is hard to place them in a given field. One might take the new burden of one's experience to amount to the claim to be one's own apostle, to forerun oneself, to be capable of deliverances of oneself. This would amount to an overcoming of what, in *The Claim of Reason*, I call the fear of inexpressiveness.[6] Here is a form in which art is asked to do the work of religion. Naturally this situation makes for new possibilities of fraudulence, among both those who give themselves out as apostles and those who think of themselves as skeptics.

It is centrally as a title for these three features of diurnal comedy, the comedy of dailiness – its conclusion not in a future, a beyond, an ever after, but in a present continuity of before and after; its transformation of a festival into a festivity; its correction not of error but of experience, or of a perspective on experience – that I retain the concept of remarriage as the title for the genre of films in question. The title registers, to my mind, the two most impressive affirmations known to me of the task of human experience, the acceptance of human relatedness, as the acceptance of repetition. Kierkegaard's study called *Repetition*, which is a study of the possibility of marriage; and Nietzsche's Eternal Return, the call for which he puts by saying it is high time, a heightening or ascension of time; this is literally *Hochzeit*, German for marriage, with time itself as the ring. As redemption by suffering does not depend on something that has already happened, so redemption by happiness does not depend on something that has yet to happen; both depend on a faith in something that is always happening, day by day.

Thus does the fantasy of marriage being traced out in these chapters project a metaphysic, or a vision of the world that succeeds the credibility of metaphysics. It was only a matter of time, because as the fantasy becomes fuller and clearer to itself it poses for itself the following kinds of question. What must marriage be for the value of marriage to retain its eminence, its authority, among human relations? And what must the world be like for such marriage to be possible? Since these are questions about the concept as well as about the fact of marriage, they are questions about marriage as it is and as it may be, and they are meant as questions about weddedness as a mode of human intimacy generally, intimacy in its aspect of *devotedness*.

This recent conjunction of ideas of the diurnal, of weddedness as a mode of intimacy, and of the projection of a metaphysics of repetition, sets me musing on an old suggestion I took away from reading in Gertrude Stein's *The Making of Americans*. She speaks, I seem to recall, to the effect that the knowledge of others depends upon an appreciation of their repeatings (which is what we are, which is what we have to offer). This knowing of others as knowing what they are always saying and believing and doing would, naturally, be Stein's description of, or direction for, how her reader is to know her own most famous manner of writing, the hallmark of which is its repeatings. The application of this thought here is the suggestion that marriage is an emblem of the knowledge of others not solely because of its implication of reciprocity but because it implies a devotion in repetition, to dailiness. "The little life of the everyday" is the wife's description of marriage in *The Children of Paradise*, as she wonders how marriage can be a match for the romantic glamour of distance and drama. A relationship "grown sick with obligations" is the way Amanda Bonner describes a marriage that cannot maintain reciprocity – what she calls mutuality in everything. (This is a promissory remark to myself to go back to Stein's work. But the gratitude I feel to it now should be expressed now, before looking it up, because it comes from a memory of the work as providing one of those nightsounds or daydrifts of mood whose orientation has more than once prevented a good intuition from getting lost. This is not unlike a characteristic indebtedness one acquires to films. It is just such a precious help that is easiest to take from a writer without saying thanks – and not, perhaps, because one grudges the thanks but because one awaits an occasion for giving it which never quite seems to name itself.)

As the technical, or artistic, problem of the conclusion of the members of the genre of remarriage is that of providing them with epitomizing density, the artistic problem of the beginning of *The Awful Truth* is to preserve its diurnal surface, to present comic events whose dailiness is not interrupted by comic outbreaks but whose drift is toward a massive breakthrough to the comic itself as the redemption of dailiness, a day's creation beyond itself. The risk of such a structure is dullness; it must open an accepting tameness, domesticity, as one pole of the comic (as Mr Pettibone does). The reward of the structure is scope, the distance it gets in discovering its conclusion. One might picture the narrative structure as preparations followed by surprises (like a chess game); or perhaps as sowing followed by reaping. This would leave out the fact that the sowing is a sequence of reapings (or of surprises too mild individually to be noticed as such), increases of interest, of a willingness to be pleased, say to be civilized; and the reapings a sequence of discoveries whose originality cannot be thought of as sown, unless perhaps as dragon's teeth.

What I called the abstractness of these claims has its own interest, but it is useful here to the extent that the claims alert us to points of the film's concreteness that we might otherwise slip past. This should become assessible as we now go on to follow certain lines of force through the film.

The Awful Truth is the only principal member of the genre of remarriage in which we see the central pair literally take their own marriage to court (sequence 4). The point of the sequence is to dramatize the dog's role as the child of the marriage (though really he is its muse, since a squabble over who was to buy him was the thing that, according to Lucy's sworn testimony, precipitated their marriage). How funny is it when the dog is asked to choose which of the pair he wants to live with, and when Lucy tricks him with Jerry's home-coming present of a rubber mouse into "choosing" her? About as funny as the idea that these people do not know what it means that they happened to get married as if to make a home for a dog, and that a court of law is no more capable of telling them whether their marriage has taken, or is worth the taking, or else the leaving, than it is of determining reasonably the custody of a dog.

You learn to look, in a McCarey scene, for the disturbing current under an agreeable surface. He has the power to walk a scene right to that verge at which the comic is no longer comic, without either losing the humor or letting the humor deny the humanity of its victims. (Not for nothing is he the director of the Marx brothers as well as of *Love Affair*, 1939, also with Irene Dunne.) Chaplin and Keaton cross the verge into pathos or anxiety, as if dissecting the animal who laughs, demonstrating the condition of laughter. Hawks crosses the verge without letting you stop laughing; as he does in his adventures. What do people imagine when they call certain film comedies "madcap"? Do they imagine that a virgin's burning brain is in itself wildly comic, or particularly so if she is free enough, that is, if her father is rich enough, that no magic can stop her from laughing, that is, from thinking and trying not to think? Aunt Patsy will call Barbara Vance a "madcap heiress." This seems a tip from McCarey that calling his comedy "madcap" would be about as useful as taking the humorless', conventional, all but nonexistent Barbara Vance to be the heroine of his film. (A tip reinforced the next year by Hawks, or one of his sources, in naming the heroine of *Bringing Up Baby* Susan Vance.) This is, in any case, not exactly our problem since the women we are following are on the whole to be understood as married. Now for the last time: What is comic about that?

(Before proceeding, I note a further point about the occurrence of the epithet "madcap heiress" in this film. It is what sets off the thing I called in my outline of the film's sequences, at sequence 12b, the transformation of the newspaper photo into an installment of *Movietone News*. The implication is that the invention of stories about madcap heiresses is the work of scandalmongers, of gossip columnists or of movie reviewers, not the business of serious comic films. Accordingly when Jerry describes, for the benefit of Dan's mother, his and Lucy's marriage as "one of those tragedies you read about in the newspapers," he may be taken to mean that something newspapers call a tragedy is as likely as not to be what newspapers would make of it, unless perhaps they made of it a madcap comedy. These are further moments in the vicissitudes of the image of the newspaper that constitutes a feature of the genre of remarriage. While I have noted major occurrences of this feature, or its equivalent, in all but one of the films of our genre [I have not looked for an explanation of its absence in *Bringing Up Baby*], I have not given the attention it deserves to formulating the significance of their interrelations.)

In the opening sequence, what does Jerry mean by "what wives don't know" and by "and what you don't know'? It is definite that he has been away from home for two weeks and that he has told his wife he was to be in Florida. But nothing else is definite. For all we know what doesn't hurt his acquaintance because he doesn't know it is that there is nothing to know, of the kind the acquaintance suspects. Maybe for some reason Jerry is less interested in the fact of philandering than in the possibility of it, that what is important to him is not the cultivating of dalliances but the cultivating of a reputation for them. It seems only mildly awkward for him when his wife shows him, in the following sequence, that she knows he hasn't been in Florida. Anyway why was Florida safer than New York? His being caught in a lie is less relevant to their ensuing agreement to divorce than her being, as she puts it, caught in a truth. Why? What is so awful about the truth that nothing happened? And why would a married man find it more important to seem unfaithful than to be so? Perhaps it is his way of dramatizing his repeated philosophy that "Marriage is based on faith. If you've lost that you've lost everything"; his way of testing her faith, a test he himself seems miserably to fail. Is he projecting his guilt upon her? Is he withholding his innocence from her? What we know is that he is hiding something and that he is blaming her for something.

I have noted that divorce is asked for by asking to be free. If what Jerry is trying to establish is what we might call the freedom of marriage, then his complex wish for reputation is logical. All that freedom requires is, so to speak, its own possibility. As long as he *can* choose he *is* free – free for example to choose faithfulness. This would be creating a logical space within marriage in which to choose to be married, a way in which not to feel trapped in it. But it turns out that this space will have to be explored by Jerry in the way our genre dictates, by his choosing to remarry, to begin again.

An effort at freedom is mocked in the ensuing scene (sequence 2) when continental Armand repeatedly praises Jerry for having a continental mind. That he hasn't any such thing where his wife is concerned is evident enough; but it is a way of describing the reputation we have surmised him to want to establish for himself. Lucy picks up on this theme when she says to Armand, who offers to stay to protect her from Jerry's accusations, "It's all right. American women are not accustomed to gallantry." The film is announcing itself to be both in and out of a tradition that includes French farce and Restoration comedy, which means declaring its territory to be America and to be cinema. Freedom in marriage is not to be discovered in the possibility of adultery, which thus becomes unusable for comedy; it becomes either irrelevant or else the stuff of melodrama. But Jerry could not be imagined to be, however obscurely, declaring his freedom in marriage apart from imagining him to be responding to some sexual contention between himself and Lucy. That sexuality is under contention means both that sexual satisfaction is a reasonable aspiration between them, and that divorce is a reasonable, civilized alternative. (It is, for example, made explicitly clear that divorce is economically feasible for the woman.) But what this contention covers, what this dragon's tooth will produce, only time can tell.

McCarey is in a position to declare a distance from French farce because he shows himself, in what Jerry calls "that two-men-in-a-bedroom farce," expert, where required, in putting farce on the stage – or rather, in staging it for the screen. That McCarey's farce is made not for the stage but for film is in effect stated by giving the dog a pivotal, independent role in its choreography, with trickier and more irreversible business (for example, a mirror worked by the dog away from a wall to crash at a farcically timed moment) than you could count on for each performance of a play. Mr Smith, the muse of the marriage, seems here to be preventing its putting itself back together. But he is really saying only what the film is saying, that the marriage will not go back together until it goes further, until, that is to say, the pair's conversation stops putting an innocent bystander into the woman's bedroom. There are always bystanders, one as innocent as the next. Here farce is the name of that condition of a life whose day and night must be kept from touching, which apprehends the approach of truth as awful. Not being tragic, irreversible, it is here a condition of which the right laugh would be the right cure.

In comparison with the brilliance of the farce sequence (sequence 11), the little sequence of Lucy and Dan singing "Home on the Range" (7a), with which Act Two opens (according to my figures), can seem so tame, or thin, as to give no support to thought at all, or for that current of disturbance that I have said McCarey keeps in circulation. But I find the little sequence equal to the farce – not equal in the virtuosity of its business, which is next to nothing, but in its compression of concepts.

The woman accompanies herself and her suitor as together they sing a colossally familiar tune, one no American could fail to know, not something folk but something folksy, a favorite butt of sophisticated society. Dan Leeson has virtually stepped out of its shell. It is on this note that these Americans can meet, that any American can meet any other; they cannot therefore merely despise it. The woman does not despise it, the man might just mean it, as it stands; this would be for a woman of her gallantry sufficient reason not to despise it. She even perceives the genuine longing, a moment of originality, in the song's variation of its opening five note pattern at the words "Home, home on the range"; the intensity in this variation, both in the words and in the music, is the occasion for her departure into harmonizing – a departure Dan cannot bear up under. (To check the rightness of her departure, say the words without the tune. To gauge the song's originality, or passion, compare it with "The Man on the Flying Trapeze," the song of *It Happened One Night*, which opens with the identical configuration of five notes, which then repeat on each recurrence without variation.) When she compliments them on their performance he replies, "Never had a lesson in muh life. Have you?" These sentences pretty well seal the man's fate, whatever she and Jerry will be able to work out. This man does not know who this woman is, he does not appreciate her; these things follow from his not appreciating her voice and her attitude toward her voice. That exchange about lessons is a gag based on the knowledge that Irene Dunne is a singer, a piece of knowledge no one who knew anything about her could have failed to know. The initial point of the gag is its satisfaction of the demand of the genre that each member of it declare the identity of the flesh and blood actress who plays its central female character. The consequent point of the gag is to establish that in the fiction of this film as well the identity of the character played by this woman, the one called Lucy Warriner, is also of someone identified with and by her voice. This becomes increasingly pertinent.

In the scene preceding the duet, in the nightclub, Dan's hesitation in recognizing Dixie Belle's self-evidently southern accent as a southern

accent need not be taken to show his unrelieved stupidity. He is intelligent enough to have made and preserved a lot of money and intelligent
enough to have fallen in love with this particular woman and to have
asked her, as they and Aunt Patsy leave Jerry and Mr Smith alone in her
apartment that first night, whether she still cares for that fellow, applying
a parable from his experience with perfect accuracy: "Down on my ranch
I've got a red rooster and a little brown hen. They fight a lot too. But
every once in a while they stop fighting and then they can get right
friendly." His hesitation over Dixie Belle's accent is directly a proof
solely that he has no ear. His reaction after his duet with Lucy just goes
to show that in the world of these films this lack of ear is fatal.

And what is that terrible American pride in never having had a lesson?
Is it different from taking pride in any other handicap? I suppose it is no
worse than taking pride in having had a lot of lessons, or in being free of
handicaps. Dan has an American mind. His ideology of naturalness with
respect to human or artistic gifts is to be assessed against a continental
ideology of cultivation (call it pride in lessons), attitudes made for one
another; and assessed along with his ideology of exploitation of the gifts
of nature (expressed in the next scene by his declared experience and
hence training in making the mineral contents of his land holdings pay
off). His pride in his empty mediocrity with art serves to underscore his
deafness to the fact that the woman is accomplished and, moreover, that
her attitude toward her accomplishments has a particular humor about
it, not making too much of her natural extension of a capacity most
people have, secure in the knowledge that it can – for many a normal
person, ones without handicaps of the ear – provide pleasures. Her
attitude, the pleasure she takes in her gifts, is as internal to the pleasures they give as Fred Astaire's acceptance of his own virtuosity is to
the pleasure it gives, not making too little of his supernatural extension
of a capacity most people have. Dunne and Astaire share this signal
mark – making neither too much nor too little of something – of sophistication.

"Home on the Range" is, finally, and not altogether surprisingly, about
home, or rather about a yearning to have a home. One might have
doubted whether this is pertinent to its presence in a genre which is so
centrally about the finding, or refinding, of a home; but I assume this
doubt is allayed in recognizing that the other featured song in *The Awful
Truth*, "My Dreams are Gone With the Wind," is also about this yearning, or dream: "I used to dream about a cottage small, a cottage small by
a waterfall. But now I have no home at all; my dreams are gone with the
wind." (Not surprisingly the man's idea of home invokes open spaces,
the woman's invokes closed. But it really is a home on the range Dan
Leeson has made for himself, not sheerly taken the range itself as home,

however much the American male's inheritance of Huck Finn may fantasize this possibility, this way of taking the song.) As said, the singing of the male song, or rather the man's responses to the singing of it, places irrecoverable distance between the two who sing it; the singing of the female song has the opposite effect.

Before considering that effect let us loop back and collect the instances of singing throughout the films of remarriage we have been reading. It seems a firm commitment of the genre to make room for singing, for something to sing about and a world to sing in.

His Girl Friday is the only exception to this rule; it is part of its blackness to lack music almost entirely. I recall only a few bars of Hollywood up-sweep during its last seconds, startlingly breaking the musical silence, as if to help measure the abnormality of this depicted world one last time before helping to clear the theater. Most recently, concerning *Adam's Rib*, we spoke of a man using a song as his capping claim upon a woman. In *Bringing Up Baby* the pair sing "I Can't Give You Anything but Love, Baby" to soothe the savage breast of a leopard (whatever that is). In *The Lady Eve* it is the man's father who sings and whose song helps lend him the authority he will require to affect the conclusion. It happens, however, that his son, our hero, is whistling his father's tune about filling the bowl until it doth run over as he awaits his heroine on the deck the morning after the night of their first encounter. Since the father's song occurs in the film much later than the son's whistling it is virtually impossible to note the coincidence on a single viewing.

"The Man on the Flying Trapeze" is variously a good song for *It Happened One Night*. Its folk song alternation of verse and refrain allows Capra to get from it not only a general occasion for an expression of social solidarity, but a specification of this solidarity as one in which individual (taking the verse) and society (giving the refrain) exchange celebratory words with one another in harmony and with pleasure. It is also to the point that the song is about the spoiling of innocence and domesticity by male glamour and villainy. It is further to the point that Shapely's seedy, unsocial villainy is expressed as his leaving himself out of the song. It is while the society of the bus is cheerfully affirming its solidarity that Shapely discovers Ellie's photograph in a newspaper and looks back knowingly over his seat at her and Peter singing. (That the value of singing, for Capra, lies in its moral or social power and not in its isolated aesthetic power, that is to say, in what Capra understands as isolated, is emphasized by the figure of the road thief, who will sing more or less incessantly and whose singing is not without a certain aesthetic standing. But his is a narcissistic kind of vocalizing, not a way of casting

his lot with others; it is a form of emotional theft.) Then why is it just
when the bus driver is himself drawn into the song and lifts his hands
from the wheel momentarily to begin the "Oh-h-h" of the refrain, that
the bus of state skids off the road (into a depression)? What happens next
is that the mother is discovered to have fainted from hunger. Is the idea
that society has skidded *because* it, or its leadership, was blindly drawn
away from attending to business? (The great binge of the twenties followed by the morning after of the thirties – a view of the Depression
presented, perhaps itself mocked, in a New Yorker cartoon of the period
which shows a society party in full swing on an airplane which is about to
crash, into a mountain.) Or is it that the solidarity is compromised by
those who are left outside the song of society – ones too poor to sing,
whom private good will must pause to succor, and ones too cowardly and
self-centered to join in song, spectators of society, not participants in it,
who will have to be scared off? (Peter gives the child of the mother who
has fainted his last ten bucks, or rather Ellie gives it, assuming that there
is more where that came from; still she gives it. And Peter scares off
Shapely with another yarn.)

One might speak of this singing as over-determined. A reason not to
speak so may seem to be that Freud's concept of over-determination
describes the formation of mental phenomena, for example of symptoms
or of images in a dream, where the point is that just *this* symptom or
image has occurred and not something else. Whereas what? The song in
this film might have been different and differently sung and differently
placed? But the fact that just *it* is here, where and as it is here, is what I
wish to account for. Over-determination seems a good name for the
formation of its appearance since the concept does not prejudge how
much in the appearance is the result of intention and how much of the
genre, how much is the result of specific function and how much of
general structure.

Still, among the determinants of singing throughout our genre, I emphasize singing's special relation to the man, as though the man's willingness to sing, or readiness to subject himself to song, is a criterion of his
fitness for the woman. And I emphasize the characteristic sound shared
by "The Man on the Flying Trapeze" and "Home on the Range" with
other songs in three-quarter time that invoke the social pleasures of the
out-of-doors or of popular entertainments, songs such as "Bicycle Built
for Two" and "Take Me Out to the Ball Game." In coming from an era
essentially earlier than the time of these films, in constituting perhaps the
first sound of the universally and persistently popular American song,
these songs establish what Americans are apt to think of as the popular in
song: the ground, I was saying, on which any American can meet any
other. This force is most surprisingly confirmed when in *The Philadelphia*

Story Dexter is finally moved to sing. That he must sing, enter his claim that way, is explicitly and locally established by his having to claim Tracy at the hands of Mike, who has already established his claim by singing. Dexter is moved to song by the ecstasy of seeing George depart. He rushes to a decorated wedding table and lifts its candles out of their arrangement one by one to shake them as if ringing tuned bells. Thus accompanying himself, invoking peals of bells, he sings the opening phrase and a half of "The Loveliest Night of the Year," another three-quarter time tune in the major mode associated with the circus. That it is this sound of the popular and the association with a popular form of entertainment that is what is pertinent is registered in Dexter's singing not with words but with universal dah-dah-dah's. Whether his ecstasy is that of a child going to the circus or of a man getting rid of a clown, it is unimportant to decide; and surely it heralds some tightrope walking. The imaginary ringing of bells seems to be what then sets off the wedding music to begin the closing festival. That Dexter's tune is popular where Mike's ("Over the Rainbow") had been sophisticated plays into the hands of the American or national aspirations I was pressing toward the end of the discussion of *The Philadelphia Story*, both by having the heroes from different classes equal in song, even possibly reversed in their allegiances to sophistication, and by suggesting that film is the mode of modern entertainment in which the distinction between the popular and the learned or the serious breaks down, incorporating both.

Only in *The Awful Truth* among the members of our genre does the woman sing for the man, for his pleasure and for his commitment. (Marlene Dietrich and Mae West have sung for these reasons, but then the singing was not for former husbands, and probably not for prospective ones either. This is part of the point of Irene Dunne's song to her man, as will emerge. In "More of *The World Viewed*" I speak of Dietrich and West, along with Garbo, as "courtesan figures" who seem "to triangulate the classical possibilities outside of marriage"; p. 206.) Hence only here can the man show his inhabitation with the woman of the realm of music not by himself singing but by listening, by appreciating what is sung to him, for him.

What the woman sings for him is that other featured song of the film, Dixie Belle's "My Dreams are Gone With the Wind." Earlier I described her performance here, posing as his sister, as her claiming to have known him intimately forever, which is her way of constructing their past together, a generic obligation. Her song and dance are meant one way for Barbara Vance and her family and another way, a private way, for Jerry. It is essential to her plot not merely that Jerry come to be forced to leave this house but that he rejoice in his having a way out, or anyway that he want to leave with her more than he wants anything else. Her solution is to create her identity so that the very thing that repels the proper Vances is what attracts Jerry, that he has a hidden, improper sister.[7] He is of course impressed by the sheer daring of Lucy's performance, by the fact of it as well as by its content. His intimate, lucid smiles of appreciation acknowledge her emotional virtuosity, and they redeem, that is, incorporate, his earlier, hieratic, exalted smile at her discomfiture dancing with Dan in the nightclub.

But she wants and gets more than a spiritual victory, or more than revenge. The suggestion of sexual depth between them, and so also of sexual problems, is registered in her displaying the incestuous basis of their past. But her therapeutic move, let me say, is to demonstrate that what is his sister in her is not her ladylike accomplishments, as for example her trained voice and her ability to dance; his sister in her is what she shares with Dixie Belle, her willingness to lend her talents and her training to the expression of what Dixie Belle expresses, her recognition of their capacity to incorporate those improprieties. Her incorporation of familiarity and eroticism redeems both. And I would like to say further that she thereby redeems the fact of incorporation itself, that we live off one another, that we are cannibals. Thus she uses her sophistication, her civilization, to break through civilization to its conditions.

So it is not, to my mind, too much to say that on the way Irene Dunne plays this song and dance the recognition of her and her fictive husband's mystery, hence of the mystery of the film, depends. It requires the perfect deployment of her self-containment, her amused but accepting attitude toward the necessity for complication, for the pleasures of civilization; one could say it requires her respect for the doubleness (at the least) of human consciousness, for the comedy of being human, neither angel nor beast, awkward as between heaven and earth. For it is essential to its effect that her performance remain outside the song and its routine but at the same time show her awareness of its inner worth, to show both her difference from and her solidarity with Dixie Belle and Dixie Belle's performance. You might call this the redemption of vulgarity by commonness.

I have been putting these responses to the song and dance of incorporation as from its sister's side. Put from its Dixie Belle side Lucy is declaring herself, to Jerry alone of course, as the woman he strays from the house to keep company with. She proposes herself as a field on which he may weave passion and tenderness, so that he might desire where he loves; or she reminds him of this possibility by reminding him who she is. Her proposal of herself as this kind of object is at once an offer and a challenge. It is not certain that either of them is really up to it. But her daring proposal is irreversible, and his exit with her means that he is taking her up on it.

This calls for Connecticut, a chance for perspective and reconciliation, emotional and intellectual, say poetic or say philosophical. And again there is a problem about getting there. In *Adam's Rib* (as in *The Lady Eve*) you don't see the pair traveling there; it seems a place that exists mostly through the ambiguously projected extensions of a home movie, that is, it exists for movies. In *Bringing Up Baby* the road to Connecticut is paved with accidents, feathers, a sheriff directly descended from Dogberry, and a stolen car. In *The Awful Truth* the road also requires the infringement of the law and the abandoning of the everyday car in which you began the journey. Evidently the world elsewhere has its own laws and its entry demands a new mode, or new vehicle, of transport.

On the road to Aunt Patsy's place in Connecticut, Jerry asks Lucy if he can use her car to drive himself back to town after he drops her off. They are stopped either for speeding or for playing the car radio too loud, anyway for some species of joyriding. During the ensuing discussion Lucy sees to it (by releasing the brakes of her car and letting it roll into a ditch) that her car is not fit for further use that night – for example, not for a return trip. She is thus recreating a version of the scene she described for Jerry (and us) as she returned home with Armand that first afternoon. They are miles from nowhere but, unlike that earlier night when Armand's car broke down a million miles from nowhere and they had to find an inn, she and Jerry attract the help of two motorcycle policemen. When each of the pair is then shown being given a ride the rest of the way to Aunt Patsy's on the handlebars of a motorcycle, one realizes that these vehicles are no less mythological than, say, the motorcycles in Cocteau's *Orphée*. Continuing their ride through the Connecticut countryside Lucy continues her drunk act. Bouncing up and down on the handlebars she sets off an exciting siren. She encourages Jerry to have fun too but his bounce produces only a choric raspberry. They are being driven back into the land of childhood, in this moment through the region in which little boys are disdainful of little girls. If Jerry does not know, on internal grounds, that this is different from anything that *could* have happened between Lucy and Armand, then he doesn't deserve to be here. The awful truth is that the truth of such matters can only be known on internal grounds.

(Again, for the last time, you can take the presence of these policemen not as messengers who transport those brave enough to demand happiness across the border from dailiness to comic enchantment, but as

lackeys of the rich who make themselves available for the private purposes of those who are irresponsible because they own the law. My
question is whether one of these views is less mythological than the other.
Each is a total view, hence each is capable of accounting for the other.
My conviction is that our lives depend on neither of them, as they stand,
winning out completely over the other.)

They arrive at their destination less than an hour before midnight is to
end their marriage, as a cuckoo clock will show that has not one door but
a pair of doors and a pair of skipping persons appearing out of them
every quarter hour, instead of a cuckoo or two or in place of gargoyles
and virgins and knights and a scythed figure of time as death. It is another
mythological object, a cinematic object, producible only on film. As Aunt
Patsy has provided the locale for their conclusion she will provide Lucy's
costume for it, a silk nightgown that Lucy is shown to tuck and tie up
somehow so that it fits her. Evidently she needs not only encouragement and authority but instruction and preparation of a kind that a
woman is fitter than a man to give. This would be why her "Aunt" appears
instead of her father – or rather why, when it is this woman, at her phase of
the story we are unearthing, whose Aunt appears, it is Aunt Patsy
(Cecil Cunningham) and not the woman's aunt of *Bringing Up Baby*
(May Robson), who when her friend Major Applegate suggests she might
be capable of emitting erotic signals resembling a leopard's, responds
"Now don't be rude, Horace." Aunt Patsy would have accepted the
compliment.

Here is what happens in Connecticut. Lucy feigns first surprise that
Aunt Patsy is not at the cabin and then a vast fatigue that sends
her bounding light-heartedly upstairs to bed. Jerry is quite aware that her
expressions of surprise and of fatigue are put on. Is his apparent resigna-
tion a sign merely that since he can't leave anyway (there won't be a car
until tomorrow) he might as well see where this will all lead, putting
himself in her hands, even if somewhat skeptically? Does he by now
realize that she was not drunk during her act at the Vances'? And does
he realize that this would have no bearing at all on whether she meant
her incorporation of the familial and the erotic by one another, though it
would have a bearing on how clear her memory of it is? His resig-
ning himself, skeptically, into her hands is a continuation or confirmation
of his taking her up on her exit from the Vances'. He does not see how the
thing is to be managed, what the road is that will lead back to their life
together, but after her recent performance who knows what she is capable
of?

Mr Smith is not present, but after adjusting Aunt Patsy's nightgown to
herself Lucy notices a black cat on the bed. Apparently their remarriage
is to be dogged by a different muse, or totem, from that of their original

marriage, or an additional one. Lucy shoos it off. I take it for granted that the black cat is a traditional symbol for female sexuality. Then does Lucy shoo the cat away because of what it stands for or because it merely stands for it? – as if to say: no more symbols of marriage, the real thing is about to take over. A rattling door comes open and in the adjoining room we see, through the open doorway, Jerry dressed in a nightshirt lent him by the caretaker. (This is, as far as I know, the original time that Cary Grant's sophistication and the kind of attractiveness he exhibits are tested by the mild indignity of a quasi-feminine get-up. A year later, in *Bringing Up Baby*, Howard Hawks will take this possibility to one of its extremes.) The cuckoo clock strikes for the first time in our presence, in close-up, to show 11:15 – the marriage has forty-five minutes left to run, that is, the divorce has forty-five minutes in which to be headed off. The two child-like figurines, somewhere between live figurines and automatons, perhaps like animated figures of celluloid, appear from adjacent doorways in the clock and in parallel skip mechanically a few steps out, then turn and skip back in, the two doors closing with the last chimes. The house clock seems to be modeled on a Swiss chalet, and for all we know it is a replica of the country house our pair are now in.

In their respective beds, in adjacent rooms, as if their lives were parallel, not touching, and the skipping they had done together now seems mechanical, each looks at his and at her side of the same rattling door, silently urging it to open again. It does, upon which the pair mumble things about this oddity to one another. Jerry gets out of bed to, it turns out, examine and close the door, Lucy stays in her bed. He is still not able to see how to carry himself across the threshold. The clock strikes 11:30 and the figurines duly appear to celebrate the fact. Back in bed, Jerry notices that the source of the current that is causing the door to rattle and to open is coming from his partly raised window. He thereupon throws caution to the winds and raises the window all the way. For some reason, though the door rattles mightily it does not open. Can it be that their hopes are really gone with the wind – that unlike Dixie Belle's wind ex nightclub machina, Jerry's wind ex studio machina is going to fail, like just so much air? Lucy has to help some more. We are shown that it is the black cat that is stopping the door from opening, at first by lying in front of it, then when Jerry turns up the wind, by pushing desperately against the door with an outstretched paw, in a human gesture of, I find, unending hilarity. That cat knows that its hopes for an undisturbed life are due any second to be gone with the wind. After another moment Lucy notices the cat and shoos it out of the way again, as she had shooed it off the bed. With cooperation now from both Jerry and Lucy the door opens once again, this time discovering Jerry down on all fours, presumably from having been looking through the keyhole, presumably to discover what the barrier is to his dreams' opening up. That this discovers him to want the door open, while Lucy is left hidden in bed, is only fair: the invitation, the possibility of renewal, has been fully extended in her song and dance. But how can renewal come about? – the perennial question of reformers and revolutionaries, of anyone who wants to start over, who wants another chance. Even in America, the land of the second chance, and of transcendentalist redeemers, the paradox inevitably arises: you cannot change the world (for example, a state of marriage) until the people in it change, and the people cannot change until the world changes. The way back to their marriage is the way forward, as if to a honeymoon even more mysterious than their first. Taking a leaf from Plato's *Parmenides* they discuss their human plight in some metaphysical dialogue, the longest stretch of philosophical dialogue among the films of remarriage, the amplest obedience to the demand of the genre for philosophical speculation, for the perception that remarriage, hence marriage, is, whatever else it is, an intellectual undertaking, in the present instance, an undertaking that concerns, whatever else it concerns, change.

The relevant dialogue of this final sequence I find impossible to remember accurately, and it deserves preserving:

(The door opens for the second time.)
JERRY: In half an hour we'll no longer be Mr and Mrs. – Funny, isn't it?
LUCY: Yes, it's funny that everything's the way it is on account of the way you feel.
JERRY: Huh?
LUCY: Well, I mean if you didn't feel the way you feel, things wouldn't be the way they are, would they?
JERRY: But things are the way you made them.
LUCY: Oh no. They're the way you think I made them. I didn't make them that way at all. Things are just the same as they always were, only you're just the same, too, so I guess things will never be the same again. Ah-h. Good night.
. . .
(The door has opened for the third and last time.)
LUCY: You're all confused, aren't you?
JERRY: Uh-huh. Aren't you?
LUCY: No.
JERRY: Well you should be, because you're wrong about things being different because they're not the same. Things are different, except in a different way. You're still the same,

only I've been a fool. Well, I'm not now. So, as long as I'm different, don't you think things could be the same again? Only a little different.

LUCY: You mean that, Jerry? No more doubts?

(Jerry doesn't answer her in so many words but says he's worried about the darn lock, the one on the door. Taking a cure from her glance he props a chair under the knob of the door but then seems surprised to find that he's locked them together in the same room. She lies back laughing.)

What I had in mind in referring to Plato's *Parmenides* was such a passage as this:

PARMENIDES: Then, that which becomes older than itself, also becomes at the same time younger than itself, if it is to have something to become older than.

ARISTOTLES: What do you mean?

PARMENIDES: I mean this. – A thing does not need to become different from another thing which is already different; it is different, and if its different has become, it has become different; if its different will be, it will be different; but of that which is becoming different, there cannot have been, or be about to be, or yet be, a different – the only different possible is one which is becoming.

ARISTOTLES: That is inevitable.

Philosophy, which may begin in wonder (thus showing its relation to tragedy), may continue in argument (thus showing its kinship with comedy). Human thinking, falling upon itself in time, is not required of beings exempt from tragedy and comedy.

Having invited Jerry to Connecticut to think again, Lucy prompts him to think by her all but open sexual arousal, under the bedsheet, over the threshold, as the minutes edge away. ("All but": he's still got to make a move.) The beginnings of philosophy in sexual attraction is how Plato sees the matter in *The Symposium*. Having once mentioned this vision in connection with Godard's films,[8] I am moved to mention here that the image in *Breathless* in which the couple climb together under a bedsheet, which then moves in patterns too abstract to read but unmistakable in erotic significance, has a precedent in the quite fantastic line of abstract impressions Irene Dunne invests her covering bedsheet with to signal Lucy's mounting arousal accompanying the tides of philosophy.

These signals of desire, and I suppose anxiety, are picked up from the opening mysteries of Jerry's absence from both home and Florida. If his cause was genuinely unrequited desire, or some dissatisfaction that adventures can make good, Lucy's new creation of herself is giving him a chance to right the balance. The price he will have to pay is, in his turn, that of change as well; he requires a move that will leave him different and, therefore, not different (because otherwise what would he be different *from?*). He must come to stand to himself in, say, the relation that remarriage stands to marriage, succeeding himself. (Can human beings change? The humor, and the sadness, of remarriage comedies can be said to result from the fact that we have no good answer to that question.) I spoke of Jerry's having to change as a price he must pay to right the balance of his marriage. I think of it as the price I ended up with in calculating Jerry's motive for his absences as the establishing of the possibility of freedom in marriage: he is going to have to find this freedom through remarriage. What this turns out to mean, at the conclusion of *The Awful Truth*, is that he can no longer regard a sexual imbalance in the marriage as the woman's fault.

I get there this way. I assume to begin with that there is a sexual brief each is holding against the other at the opening of what we know of their story. Jerry's "what wives don't know" mystery suggests this right off; it is confirmed by their never touching one another, after their homecoming embrace is interrupted (except, as mentioned, at the end of the sister routine, and then as a brief theatrical walkaway); then their shared difficulties at the end with the door fit in with this line of thought. I assume further that Lucy's sister routine is not only triggered by Jerry's having made up the explanation or excuse for Barbara Vance's benefit that the woman in his apartment is his sister, but that the routine constitutes an answer to that explanation or excuse, a prophetic realization of it. These assumptions add up for me as follows.

Lucy's routine takes up Jerry's casting her as his sister as if it had been an explanation or excuse for *her* benefit, a statement of the cause of their loss of faith, of their faith in faithfulness, a loss in their sexual conversation. Then her song and dance for him that puts together kinship and desire is her reply to this excuse. I might translate her reply in something like these terms: Very well, I see the point. We do have this problem of having known one another forever, from the first, of being the first to show one another what equality and reciprocity might be. If this means being brother and sister, that cannot, to that extent, be bad. What is necessary now is not to estrange ourselves but to recognize, without denying our natural intimacy, that we are also strangers, separate, different; to keep our incestuousness symbolic, tropic, so that it joins us, not letting it lapse into literality, which will enjoin us. I'll show you that to be your sister, thus understood, will be to be stranger to you than you have yet known me to be. I am changed before your eyes, different so to speak from myself, hence not different. To see this you will have correspondingly to suffer metamorphosis. There is a wind effect here but you will just have to use your imagination.

So she gives rise to herself, recreates herself; and, it can be said, creates herself in his image, though it is an image he did not know he had or know was possible in this form. "The trouble with most marriages," Jerry announces in the second sequence of the film, preparing his sentences about faith, "is that people are always imagining things." It turns out that what is wrong is not with imagination as such but with the way most people use their imaginations, running it mechanically along ruts of suspicion. This causes, at best, farce, the negation of faith.

"You're all confused, aren't you?" she asks him, inviting him to work through the philosophy for himself. "Uh-huh. Aren't you?" His honesty deserves one further invitation, one last chance. "No," she offers him. It is the explicitness he needed. He was confused because he felt she was confused and he felt impotent to provide clarity for them. But if after all she is clear, that is another story. He casts his confusion about changing, becoming different, into words, thus making himself vulnerable to the therapy of love.

It is midnight. The figurine children skip out in their parallel paths to celebrate this hour of comedy. After they turn to skip back the boy is drawn to an escapement from the mechanism of time and accompanies the girl into her side of the habitation. The wind, an action of nature, that effects the closing of the door of marriage, is the work of no machine. We will have to imagine it for ourselves.

We are asked by this ending to imagine specifically how what we are shown adds up to the state of forgiveness the pair have achieved. In Connecticut the road back is to be found from what Jerry had called the road to Reno, which he characterizes as paved with suspicions. In *The Lady Eve* and in *Bringing Up Baby* and in *Adam's Rib*, as said, the discovery of the road back from divorce is explicitly entitled forgiveness; in *His Girl Friday* the place of forgiveness is taken by what the film calls a reprieve. Tracy's way of accepting George's suggestion in *The Philadelphia Story* that they "let bygones be bygones" is an acceptance of an interpretation of forgiveness as putting the past into the past and clearing the future for a new start, from the same or from a different starting place. I have at various junctures characterized this forgiving, the condition of remarriage, as the forgoing of revenge. When Tracy forgoes revenge toward George she finds nothing left for him. I take the experience of the end of a romantic comedy as a matter of a kind of forgetting, one that requires the passage, as it were, from one world (of imagination) to another, as from dreaming to waking, something that suggests itself as a natural way to describe the recovery from the viewing of a film as such. My adducing of *A Midsummer Night's Dream* in thinking about *The Philadelphia Story* offers an example of what this forgetting can look like. Emerson and Thoreau call the passage to this experience, I take it, dawn. The winning of a new beginning, a new creation, an innocence, by changes that effect or constitute the overcoming of revenge, extends a concatenation of ideas from Nietzsche's *Zarathustra*. In a related moment in "On Makavejev On Bergman" I quote the following from the section "Three Metamorphoses": "I name you three metamorphoses of the spirit: how the spirit shall become a camel, and the camel a lion, and the lion at last a child. There are many heavy things for the spirit, for the strong weight-bearing spirit in which dwells respect and awe: its strength longs for the heavy, for the heaviest . . . To create freedom for itself and a sacred No even to duty: the lion is needed for that, my brother . . . Why must the preying lion still become a child? The child is innocence and forgetfulness, a new beginning, a sport, a self-propelling wheel, a first motion, a sacred Yes." Camels of heavy marriages we know; and lions who can disdain them. A comic No to marriage is farce. I am taking our films to be proposing a comic Yes.

Nietzsche's vision of becoming a child and overcoming revenge is tied up with the achievement of a new vision of time, or a new stance toward it, an acceptance of Eternal Recurrence. And here we are, at the concluding image of *The Awful Truth*, watching two childlike figures returning, and meant to return as long as they exist, into a clock-house, a home of time, to inhabit time anew. How can my linking of Friedrich Nietzsche and Leo McCarey not be chance? How *can* it be chance?

All you need to accept in order to accept the connection are two propositions: that Nietzsche and McCarey are each originals, or anyway that each works on native ground, within which each knows and can mean what he does; and that there are certain truths to these matters which discover where the concepts come together of time and of childhood and of forgiveness and of overcoming revenge and of an acceptance of the repetitive needs of the body and the soul – of one's motions and one's motives, one's ecstacies and routines, one's sexuality and one's loves – as the truths of oneself. They will, whatever we discover, be awful truths, since otherwise why do truths about ourselves take such pains to find and to say?

On the way to these closed doors of marriage we have been given a moment that I recur to in my experience as to an epitome of the life of marriage that the films of our genre ask us to imagine, an image I take as epitomizing their aspiration to what I called a while ago life as festival, not something at the conclusion of a comedy but something of its character from beginning to end. I have in mind the conclusion of the sequence of the musicale (sequence 10), in which Jerry goes to interfere with an assignation and finds himself in the midst of a decorous recital. We know enough by this time of the practice of this kind of film to consider the sudden discovery of Lucy in front of the piano as the door flings open not as the surprising revelation that she is not after all engaged in an erotic form of life but that after all she is. Then it is her singing (whatever that is) that has been primarily felt by Jerry to be something beyond him, out of his control; not her singing teacher, who (whatever he is) is patently a secondary fiddle. Jerry, at any rate, is knocked to the ground by her performance here. His aplomb everywhere else is perfect. Lucy's strategy in her sister routine will require that he make the connection between her publicly singing a proper recital piece in a ladylike manner and her privately singing an improper piece in its appropriate manner. The epitome I say we are given of the life of marriage behind doors, for us to imagine, of marriage as romance, as adventure – of the dailiness of life, its diurnal repetitiveness, as its own possibility of festivity – is the moment of Lucy's response to Jerry's discomfiture as he tries to make himself inconspicuous at the unanticipated recital and winds up on the floor in a tableau with chair, table, and lamp. The spectacle he makes of himself starts a laugh in her which she cannot hold back until after she finishes her song but which pushes into her song to finish with it, its closing cadence turning to laughter. The moment of laughter and song becoming one another is the voice in which I imagine the conversation of marriage aspired to in these comedies to be conducted. We heard Lucy speaking to Aunt Patsy of the grand laughs she and Jerry have had. (All she will tell him, or warn him of, visiting him at his apartment, before becoming his sister, is that his ancient poem to her, which she is about to recite, will hand him a laugh.) At the musicale we are privileged to witness one of the grand laughs. This princess is evidently neither unwilling nor unable to laugh, indeed she generally seems on the brink of laughing. The truth is that only this man can bring her laughter on, even if he is sometimes reduced to poking her ribs with a pencil. This may not be worth half a father's kingdom, but she finds it, since he asks, worth giving herself for.

Notes

1 Reported by Andrew Sarris in *The American Cinema* (New York: E. P. Dutton and Co., 1968), p. 100.
2 *The New Yorker*, July 14, 1975. Reprinted in *When the Lights Go Down* (New York: Holt, Rinehart and Winston, 1980), p. 7.
3 "A Matter of Meaning It," in *Must We Mean What We Say?*, p. 229.

4 I call attention here to Harry Levin's rich Introduction to the Signet edition of *The Comedy of Errors*.

5 An essay of mine about that book, "Kierkegaard's *On Authority and Revelation*," appears in *Must We Mean What We Say?*

6 See, for example, pp. 351, 473.

7 In another Leo McCarey film, *Once upon a Honeymoon* (1942), another woman's (Ginger Rogers's) identity is established for Cary Grant by the fact that she is revealed as someone surprisingly (given our introduction to her) capable of burlesque dancing. Here I recommend Robin Wood's valuable essay, "Democracy and Shpontanuity: Leo McCarey and the Hollywood Tradition," *Film Comment*, vol. 12 no. 1, January–February 1976. In *Together Again* (Charles Vidor, 1944), a fascinating, sometimes brilliant, but unsuccessful member of the genre of remarriage, an eminently honorable Irene Dunne, mayor of a New England town (in Vermont, not Connecticut), is briefly, scandalously, mistaken for a stripper.

8 *The World Viewed*, p. 100.

11

Macbeth Appalled

This reading of a Shakespeare play indicates how Cavell's general approach to Shakespeare, founded as it was upon a perception of his drama as being in combat with the modern skeptical impulse, is likely to be continued when that perception is less systematically emphasized than it was in the earlier readings collected in *Disowning Knowledge*. The interpretation of *Antony and Cleopatra* with which Cavell concluded his introduction to that collection already offered some hints pertaining to this question. Without ever losing contact with his general assumption that the relationship between the two main protagonists exemplified the human significance of skepticism about other minds and about the external world, Cavell there emphasized three other aspects of this play: its stress upon the interpenetration of the political and the erotic, its highly specific sense of history and in particular of a period in which a certain promise of religion has been missed or otherwise gone unfulfilled, and its fascination with the female capacity to deploy essentially theatrical resources in order to enact one's own existence and keep faith with the truth of a marriage.

This reading of *Macbeth* maintains a focus upon all three of those themes; it thereby connects Cavell's interest in Shakespeare with certain other aspects of his intellectual project – in particular, with his interest in Thoreau and Emerson, and their conviction that human existence can be maintained in the face of skepticism only by enacting it, by the human individual exercising her capacity to realize her own individuality (cf. Essays 14 and 15). However, it does so by studying what is, in effect, a failed or corrupted version of the marriages that Cavell examined in the remarriage comedies; in *Macbeth*, marriage appears as a form of spiritual vampirism, in which the man and woman reinforce one another's nightmarish visions of the inconsequentiality of human action and identity rather than providing a way of overcoming them. In this respect, the essay forms an appropriate transition to Cavell's work on the film genre he calls "Melodramas of the Unknown Woman," which he understands

Reprinted by permission from *Raritan: A Quarterly Review*, vol. 12, no. 2 (Fall 1993). Copyright © 1993 by *Raritan*, 31 Mine Street, New Brunswick, NJ 08903.

as related to the remarriage comedies by systematic negation, and so as constituting studies of standing threats to marriage that cannot be overcome in the ways the comedies illustrate.

Other matters of general significance for understanding Cavell's intellectual project also emerge in this essay. It opens by sketching in Cavell's sense of the positive and negative significances inherent in recent developments in Shakespeare studies – particularly the new historicism, in which Cavell detects traces of metaphysical impulses, attempts to deny things that are not obviously capable of being asserted. Its general, bipartite structure derives from Cavell's sense of Shakespeare's sensitivity to two of the conditions of the possibility of language as such – the recurrence and the commonality of words. And the play's resulting interest in prophecy or foretelling allows Cavell to further develop his understanding of the nature of interpretation; this reflexive strand in the essay reinforces and refines his belief that skepticism is a threat to the practice of literary criticism, and not just one topic in the texts that critics study.

When a given text is claimed to work in the light, or in the shadow, of another – taking obvious extremes, as one of a given work's sources or as one of its commentaries – a measure of the responsibility of such a linking is the degree to which each is found responsive to the other, to tap the other, as for its closer attention. *Macbeth* is a likely work to turn to in these terms on a number of counts. Being Shakespearean melodrama, it takes up the question of responsiveness, the question, we might say, of the truth of response, of whether an action or reaction is – or can be – sensually or emotionally adequate to its cause, neither withholding nor excessive (Macbeth's to news of his wife's death, or Macduff's to his wife's and his childrens', or Macbeth's to Banquo's reappearance, or Lady Macbeth's to Macbeth's return from the wars). More than any other Shakespearean tragedy, *Macbeth* thematically shows melodramatic responsiveness as a contest over interpretations, hence over whether an understanding is – or can be – intellectually adequate to its question, neither denying what is there, nor affirming what is not there (a deed, a dagger). As if what is at stake is the intelligibility of the human to itself.

The question of human intelligibility takes the form, in what I want to begin to work through in *Macbeth*, of a question of the intelligibility of human history, a question whether we can see what we make happen and tell its difference from what happens to us, as in the difference between human action and human suffering. I conceive of *Macbeth* as belonging as much with Shakespearean histories as with the tragedies, but not as a history that takes for granted the importance of the political and of what constitutes a pertinent representation of its present condition. It raises, rather, the question of what history is a history of, hence the question of how its present is to be thought of. This continues the direction I was taking the last time I was caught up in a text of Shakespeare's, in thinking about *Antony and Cleopatra*. There, accepting as uncontroversial the ideas that a Shakespeare history play forms some precedent or parable for its own political present, and that the playing of Antony and Cleopatra and their company is a setting for world catastrophe, I proposed thinking through the play as a representation of the catastrophe of the modern advent of skepticism (hence also of the advent of the new science, a new form of knowing), taken as an individual and a historical process. (This is recorded in the introduction to my *Disowning Knowledge*.) But while certain contemporary historical events are accepted as sources for *Macbeth* – accounts of the Gowrie Conspiracy and of the Gunpowder Plot – there is not, to my knowledge, an uncontroversial sense of the play as unfolding, in its claustrophobic setting, its own sense of its present politics and of human history. On the reading of the play proposed here this lack of clarity itself becomes a certain confirmation of the play's invocation of its sense of its own matrix, specifically a sense of the political as itself changing, as itself a scene of obscurity, even, one might say, of the occult.

I might describe the drift of this reading as following out my sense that the texts of *Macbeth* and of *Antony and Cleopatra* – I am glad to accept them as dating within a year or so of one another – are opposite faces of a study of the interpenetration of the erotic and the political. Here is a way I described the changeover of worlds envisioned in *Antony and Cleopatra*: "Hegel says that with the birth of Christianity a new subjectivity enters the world. I want to say that with the birth of skepticism, hence of modern philosophy, a new intimacy, or wish for it, enters the world; call it privacy shared (not shared with the public, but from it)." *Macbeth*, I conjecture, secretes its own environment of a new intimacy, of privacy shared, a setting not exactly of world catastrophe but of a catastrophe of privacy, hence of a certain politics. This privacy is expressed in philosophy as a catastrophe of knowledge. It may be thought of as the skeptical isolation of the mind from the body, simultaneously a sense that everything is closed to, occluded in, human knowledge (in philosophy?) and at the same time that everything is open to human knowledge (in science? in magic?). The aspiration and eroticization of the new science invoked at the opening of *Antony and Cleopatra* ("Then must you needs find out new heaven, new earth") marks its relation to and distance from the closing of the world of *Macbeth* within magic, science's origin and shadow.

It matters to me, in ways some of which will become explicit, to mention in passing another sort of unfinished or continuing business of mine determining my interest in history in *Macbeth* – my attention in recent years to the work of Emerson, in which narrative history, let us say, is under incessant attack. It is clear enough that Emerson's mission as a writer of the philosophical constitution of a new nation is in part to free its potential members from an enslaving worship of the past and its institutions, in religion, in politics, in literature, in philosophy. But the anticipation is quite uncanny, in his "History," the first essay of his First Series of Essays, of the spirit of the Annales historians' disdain for great events, their pursuit of the uneventful, a pursuit requiring an altered sense of time and of change, an interpretation of what I call the ordinary or the everyday. I had thought that Emerson's formulations concerning history would play a more extensive role in this text – or in some unwritten one of which the present text is perhaps a fragment – than has so far proven the case. At present I will be content with four citations from "History":

I have no expectation that any man will read history aright, who thinks that what was done in a remote age, by men whose names have resounded far, has any deeper sense than what he is doing to-day.

But along with the civil and metaphysical history of man, another history goes daily forward – that of the external world, – in which he is not less strictly implicated.

I am ashamed to see what a shallow village tale our so-called History is. . . . What does Rome know of rat and lizard? What are Olympiads and Consulates to these neighboring systems of being? Nay, what food or experience or succor have they for the Esquimaux seal-hunter, for the Kanaka in his canoe, for the fisherman, the stevedore, the porter?

When a thought of Plato becomes a thought to me, – when a truth that fired the soul of Pindar fires mine, time is no more.

The immediate background for what follows formed itself in an unpredicted interaction of two seminars I was teaching two springs ago. The more elaborate of these was a large seminar on recent trends in Shakespearean criticism that my colleague Marjorie Garber and I were offering on an experimental basis to a group of students divided between the study of literature and of philosophy. The division itself is one that various trends in contemporary literary theory have promised to move beyond, but which, in my part of the academic forest, is kept in place by all but immovable institutional forces. The trends in criticism we proposed to consider fell, not surprisingly, into the more or less recognizable categories of feminist, psychoanalytic, and new historicist work; but while as an outsider to the institutions of Shakespeare study I was happy for the instruction in recontextualizing this material, and while the feminist and the psychoanalytic continued to seem to me about what I expected criticism to be, the new historicist, for all its evident attractions, kept presenting itself to me as combating something that I kept failing to grasp steadily or clearly. Put otherwise, in reading the feminist and/or the psychoanalytic critics I did not feel that I had *in advance* to answer the questions, What does Shakespeare think women are, or think psychology is?, but that I could read these pieces as part of thinking about these questions; whereas I found myself, in reading the new historicist critics, somehow required to have an independent answer to the question, What does Shakespeare think history is?

The form the question took for me more particularly was, How does Shakespeare think things happen? – is it in the way science thinks, in the way magic thinks, or religion, or politics, or perhaps in the way works of art, for example, works of poetic drama think? It is not clear that these questions make good sense. You may even feel in them a certain unstable frame of mind, as if there is already palpable in them a response to *Macbeth*.

This form of the question of history was shaped for me by the other seminar I was offering that spring, on Romanticism and skepticism, in which the romantic fantasy of a union between philosophy and poetry was a recurrent topic, particularized in the question to what extent Emerson is to be thought of as a philosopher and the question of the extent to which, or sense in which, Wittgenstein's thinking is a function of his writing. An important theoretical statement of the questions of philosophy and writing for the seminar was Heidegger's "On the Origin of the Work of Art," taking up its formulation according to which the *work* of the work of art is that of letting truth happen; and taking up Heidegger's relating, as the German does, of the idea of happening to the idea of history; so that the implied notion is that truth becomes historical in art. This can be seen as a contesting of Hegel's finding that the belief in art as the highest expression of truth is a thing of the past. Behind both Heidegger and Emerson we read Friedrich Schlegel, the great translator and follower of Shakespeare, who had called for the union of philosophy and poetry, who had said that what happens in poetry happens in a given work always or never, whose concept of *poesis*, or poetic making or work, evidently inspires Heidegger's idea of the particular, irreplaceable work art does, and who in his extraordinary essay "On Incomprehensibility" cites Shakespeare's "infinitely many depths, subterfuges, and intentions" as an example of the conscious artist enabled to carry on "ironically, hundreds of years after their deaths, with their most faithful followers and admirers," and who also in that essay on incomprehensibility had said, "I absolutely detest incomprehension, not only the incomprehension of the uncomprehending but even more the incomprehension of the comprehending" – the moral of which I take to concern the present human intellectual task as one of undoing our present understanding of understanding, a task I find continued with startling faithfulness to Schlegel's terms in Emerson's "Self-Reliance," understanding this essay to be, as it quite explicitly declares itself to be, an essay on human understanding.

In the reading we assigned ourselves for our Shakespeare seminar, I found *Macbeth* to be the text of Shakespeare's about which the most interesting concentration of current critical intelligence had been brought to bear. Both Marjorie Garber and Janet Adelman have recently published major discussions of the play, as has Steven Mullaney, whose work cites its affiliation with, and is cited in the work of, Stephen Greenblatt. While *Macbeth* is not given special attention in Greenblatt's *Shakespearean Negotiations*, certain sentences from that book's introduction – entitled "The Circulation of Social Energy" – rather haunt the preoccupations that will guide my remarks here. Greenblatt's introduction concludes with the sentence, "The speech of the dead, like my own speech, is not private property," about which I feel both that I agree with the intuition or impulse being expressed, and at the same time, that this expression invites me to deny something – something about the privacy of language – that I have never affirmed, that no one can simply have affirmed. I must try, even briefly, to articulate this double feeling.

I am not alone in finding the most significant work of this century on the idea of the privacy of language to be Wittgenstein's *Philosophical Investigations*. Wittgenstein rather cultivates the impression – which the prevailing view of him takes as his thesis – that he denies language is private; whereas his teaching is that the assertion or the denial either of the publicness or of the privateness of my language is empty. Philosophers, typically modern philosophers, do chronically seem to be denying something, typically that we can know there is a world and others and we in it, and then denying that they are denying it. Wittgenstein is distinguished by *asking* (as it were nonrhetorically), "What gives the impression that I want to deny anything?" His answer has to do with his efforts to destroy philosophical illusions (ones he takes apparently as endemic in Western philosophical thought): denial is in the effect of a presiding, locked philosophical struggle between, let us say, skepticism and metaphysics. To understand this effect or impression is part of Wittgenstein's philosophical mission. For him simply to *deny* that he is *denying* privacy, say by asserting publicness, would accordingly amount to no intellectual advance. It would merely constitute a private assertion of publicness, as though publicness itself had become private property. Something of the sort is a way of putting my intuition of what *Macbeth* is about; one might call it the privatization of politics or think of it as a discovery of the state of nature.

Because at the moment I see my contribution to the study of *Macbeth* to lie perhaps in addressing certain features of its language that I find peculiar to it, I shall mostly forgo discussion of recent important work, and its conflicts, on the question of gender in *Macbeth*, as for instance Janet Adelman's proposal (in "Born of Woman") that the play embodies at once fantasies of absolute maternal domination and of absolute escape from that domination (a discussion, besides, whose generosity in the notation of the critical literature goes beyond my scholarship); and as Marjorie Garber's rather conflicting proposal (in "Macbeth: The Male Medusa") that the play studies gender indeterminacy. I mark this elision here and at the same time give a little warm-up, out-of-context exercise in the way I read Shakespeare's lines, by taking a certain exception to Garber's interpretation in that piece of a familiar exchange in *Macbeth*, one that can be taken as involving a discourse of gender.

When Macbeth says, "I dare do all that may become a man. / Who dares do more is none," Lady Macbeth replies, "What beast was't then / That made you break this enterprise to me? / When you durst do it, then you were a man" (I, vii, 46–49). Garber reads this as an all-too-familiar sexual taunt, a questioning of her partner's masculinity. Without denying the taunt in Lady Macbeth's question, I find myself struck by her taunting interpretation of Macbeth's idea of excessive daring as meaning that to strike beyond certain human limits is to be a beast. If we take it – something that will come back – that Lady Macbeth shares with Macbeth, as they share every other idea, something like the idea of men as beasts, then this tells another way to hear her puzzling continuation: "To be more than what you were, you would / Be so much more the man" (I, vii, 50–51). That is: To be more beast *is* to be more man. On this way of thinking, her sexual taunt is something more than, or is prejudicially confined in being called, an "attack upon his masculinity, his male identity." It is as much an attack on human sexuality as such, as it has revealed itself; surely including an attack on its presence in her.

My fastening on to the species reading of the sexual taunt – its expression of an anxiety about *human* identity – has been prepared by the way I have over the years addressed the issue of philosophical skepticism as an expression of the human wish to escape the bounds or bonds of the human, if not from above then from below. I call it the human craving for, and horror of, the inhuman, of limitlessness, of monstrousness. (Besides being a beast, another specieslike contrast with being human is being a monster. It may be that Macbeth and Lady Macbeth have reason to suppress this possibility while they can, to cover it with a somewhat different horror.) There is in me, accordingly, a standing possibility that I use the more general, or less historical (is it? and is it more metaphysical?) species anxiety to cover a wish to avoid thinking through the anxiety of gender. If there is a good reason to run this risk it is that the reverse covering is also a risk, since knowing what is to be thought about the human is part of knowing what is to be thought about gender.

The risks of confining interpretation – to move now further into the play – are exemplified in the much-considered announcement of Macduff's that he was untimely ripped from the womb. Macbeth's response is to denounce, or pray for, or command disbelief in, the "fiends / That palter with us in a double sense; / That keep the word of promise to our ear, / And break it to our hope" (III, viii, 19–22). The picture here is that to wish to rule out equivocation, the work of witches, is the prayer of tyranny. The picture is itself equivocal, however, since it must be asked why Macbeth believes Macduff. That means both: Why does he believe this man? and Why does he believe what this man says? Here I can merely assert something. In turning against Macduff (to "try the last against him"), Macbeth is contesting not simply a man (whatever that is) but an interpretation; or really a double interpretation. The first interpretation, I believe uncontested, is that being of no woman born just means being untimely ripped from the womb. Some critics have expressed puzzlement and dissatisfaction over this interpretation, feeling that a fateful moment is made to depend on a quibble, as if Shakespeare is being superficial or sloppy; yet they feel forced to accept it, presumably because Macbeth accepts it. But I do not know that any have expressed a sense that Macbeth may himself (though he has suggested other possibilities – that Macduff derives from a girl, or from witches) have felt forced.

This is the burden of what I suggest as the second interpretation Macbeth contests in his fatal encounter with Macduff, one that associates with the name of Caesar the procedure of delivering a child by an incision through the abdominal wall and uterus. Macbeth had identified Banquo as the one "under [whom] / My genius is rebuk'd; as, it is said, / Mark Antony's was by Caesar" (III, i, 53–55). It is congenial to my sense of things that this fact of Caesar's rebuke cited by Macbeth about Mark Antony is notable in *Antony and Cleopatra*; beyond this, my suggestion that Macbeth silently associates Macduff's origin as partaking of Caesar's and so transfers to the antagonist before him the power to rebuke or subdue his spirit (for example the power to force his acceptance of that other's interpretation of what is between them), is a reading which reveals Macbeth to be afraid of domination by a masculine as much as by a feminine figure. I say he is contesting an interpretation (or fantasy), and it is one to which, this being tragedy, he succumbs, having (always) already accepted an interpretation (that of witchery) – as if the other face of tyranny (or a redescription of its fear of equivocation) is fixation, say superstition. (Of course my second interpretation depends on granting that Shakespeare knew the surgical procedure in question under the Caesarean interpretation.)

Since (what proves to be) the equivocation of "no woman born" is a construction of the witches, and since fixating its meaning as being ripped untimely is Macbeth's response to Macduff's fixing of himself as rebuker and subduer, I am taking the play to characterize interpretation as a kind of inner or private contest between witchcraft and tyranny, which it almost identifies as a war between the feminine and the masculine. This formulation contests, while to an unassessed extent it agrees with, the perception of the play in Steven Mullaney's "Lying Like Truth." I agree particularly with Mullaney's sense that the play virtually announces its topic as, whatever else, equivocation, and that standing interpretations of equivocation, or ambiguity, do not account for the extraordinary language of this play. But, putting aside here Mullaney's elegant presentation of the play as a presentation of treasonous language (which nevertheless seems to me a confined interpretation), he cites too few of the actual words of the play to clarify his claim of their specialness. For example, he claims that the "language [Macbeth] would use [to lie] instead masters him." How shall we assess whether Mullaney's idea of being mastered comes to more than an assertion of one of the common facts of words, that they have associations beyond their use on a particular occasion? Certainly we must not deny it: A word's reach exceeds a speaker's grasp, or what's language for?

This is to say: words recur, in unforetellable contexts; there would be no words otherwise; and no intentions otherwise, none beyond the, let me say, natural expression of instinct; nothing would be the expression of desire, or ambition, or the making of a promise, or the acceptance of a prophecy. Unpredictable recurrence is not a sign of language's ambiguity but is a fact of language as such, that there are words.

I strew my reservation concerning Mullaney's description of *Macbeth*'s language with references to various of the play's famous topics – ambition, prophecy, promise – to register my awareness that in claiming, despite my reservation, to share a sense of the play's specialness of language, the weight of this reservation depends on proposing an alternative account. I shall sketch two elements of such a proposal, isolating two common features or conditions of the medium of the play – its language to begin with – that the text of *Macbeth* particularly acknowledges, or interprets. One can think of the idea of a text's uniqueness, or difference, as the theory of language the text holds of itself, as Friedrich Schlegel more or less puts it. I will call these features of language language as prophecy and as magic or mind-reading.

These features interpret conditions of what can be called the possibility of language as such. Prophecy, or foretelling, takes up the condition of words as recurrent; mind-reading takes up words as shared. Philosophy has wished to explain the recurrence of words (which may present itself as their evanescence) by a theory of what it calls universals; and similarly (taking universals as concepts or as rules) to explain their sharing or mutuality, so far as this is seen to be a separate question. Wittgenstein's *Investigations* questions precisely the necessity and possibility of these places of philosophical explanation. In this light, *Macbeth* represents the world whose existence philosophy is horrified by, and created by – the possibility that there is no end to our irrationalities, to our will to intellectual emptiness.

My idea of the first of the conditions of language acknowledged by this play – language as prophecy – is that a kind of foretelling is effected by the way the play, at what prove to be charged moments, will bond a small group of generally small words so that they may then at any time fall upon one another and discharge or expel meaning. The play dramatizes the fact that a word does not exist until it is understood as repeated. Examples I specify a bit here are the foretelling of the words *face*, *hand*, *do* and *done*, *success* and *succession*, *time*, *sleep*, and *walk*. That the acknowledgment of words as foretelling is a specific strain within the Shakespearean virtuosity is indicated in contrasting it with words as telling or counting in *The Winter's Tale* (as recounted in *Disowning Knowledge*). Foretelling emphasizes the unpredictable *time* of telling, unguarded as it were from the time of understanding. Take the case of *do* and *done*. The word leaps from a witch's "I'll do, I'll do, and I'll do," to Lady Macbeth's "What's done cannot be undone," and Macbeth's "[I] wish the estate o'th' world were now undone." I take up the word from what is perhaps its most intricate instance: "If it were done, when 'tis done, then 'twere well / It were done quickly" (I, vii, 1–2).

As a statement is grammatically what can prove to be true or false, and be verified or modified, so a human action is what can prove to succeed or fail, and be justified or excused – words and deeds carry within themselves the terms, or intentions, of their satisfaction. With recurrence on my mind, and having said that without the recurrence of words there are no words (hence no expression beyond that of organic need, no expression, we might say, that *contains* desire), I hear Macbeth's speculation of deeds done in the doing, without consequence, when surcease is success, to be a wish for there to be no human action, no separation of consequence from intention, no gratification of desire, no showing of one's hand in what happens. It is a wish to escape a condition of the human which, while developing terms of Emerson's essay "Fate," I have described as the human fatedness to significance, ourselves as victims of intelligibility. And I have claimed that it is this perception that Wittgenstein captures in identifying the human form of life as that of language. Something of the sort is, I believe, meant in recent years when it is said that language speaks us, or that the self is created by language. The implication in these formulations seems often to be that we are not exactly or fully responsible for what we say, or that we do not have selves. And yet the only point of such assertions – cast in a skeptical tone – is to deny a prior stance or tone of metaphysics, a metaphysical "picture" of what it is to "be" responsible or to "have" a self (a picture no doubt at the service of politics, but what is not?). Such skeptical assertions would deny that the self is everything by asserting that it is nothing, or deny that we are in control of a present plenum of meaning by denying that we have so much as a single human hand in what we say. These assertions and denials of metaphysics are the victories of tyranny over witchcraft, Macbeth's occupation. Whose story is it that the self is self-presence, that meaning is the fullness of a word? It is not truer than it is false.

A famous registration of what I am calling the fatedness to significance is Freud's idea of the overdetermination of meaning in human action and passion. If we follow Jean Laplanche (in *Life and Death in Psychoanalysis*) in watching the origins of human significance in the emergence of human sexuality, tracing the transfiguration of psychic drives out of biological instincts, then may we not further recognize in this origin of desire the origin of time, say of the delay or interval or containment in human satisfaction; hence the origin of the end of time, say of the repetitiveness of desire's wants and satisfactions; hence the origin of reality, say of something "beyond" me in which my satisfaction is provided, or not? Then we have a way of thinking about why Macbeth, in wishing for the success of his act to be a surcease of the need of action, for a deed that undoes doing, must (logically) wish for an end to time. For to destroy time is what he would, with paralyzing paradox, risk the future for: "that but this blow / Might be the be-all and the end-all – here, / But here, upon this bank and shoal of time" (I, vii, 4–6). This is what "We'd jump the life to come" in favor of (whether the life to come is taken to mean the rest of his time, or the rest of time). Why? (And suppose the life to come suggests the life to come *from* him. He says that the worth of his kingship is bound up for him with the question of his succession. But we have just heard him say in effect that success would consist for him in surcease, in remaining, with respect to the act which is the type of the consequential – producing progeny – "unlineal," "unfruitful." Well, does he want babies or not? Is this undecidable? If we say so, then Macbeth is the picture of undecidability.)

Both he and Lady Macbeth associate doing, in addition to time, with thinking: "I am afraid to think what I have done," he says (II, ii, 50); and a few lines earlier she had said, "These deeds must not be thought / After these ways; so, it will make us mad" (II, ii, 32–33). If there were nothing done or to do there would be nothing to think about. Before we come to ponder what it is they have to think about, I note that the opposite of thinking in Macbeth's mind is sleep ("sore labour's bath, / Balm of hurt minds" (II, ii, 37–38), and that in acting to kill action and end time Macbeth "does murther Sleep" (II, ii, 35); so that in acting metaphysically to end thought he consigns himself absolutely to thinking, to unending watchfulness. Lady Macbeth at last finds a solution to the problem of thinking how not to think, when there is no obvious way not to think, in sleepwalking, which her witness describes as a version of watchfulness.

Before moving from language as foretelling to the second of the conditions of language which I hypothesize the play particularly to acknowledge – language as magic or mind-reading – I simply note two foretellings or occurrences of the idea of walking (or walking as sleeping) that bond with the ambiguity or reciprocity, real or imagined, of action without consequence, say of the active and the passive becoming one another. First, the witnessing Doctor's description of Lady Macbeth's sleepwalking – "to receive at once the benefit of sleep, and do the effects of watching" – seems most literally a description of the conditions of a play's audience, and play-watching becomes, along with (or as an interpretation of) sleepwalking, exemplary of human action as such, as conceived in this play – yet another of Shakespeare's apparently unending figurations, or explorations, of theater; here, theater as the scene, and as the perception or witnessing of the scene, that is, of human existence, as sleepwalking. Macbeth's all but literal equivalent of sleepwalking is his walking, striding, pacing (all words of his), to his appointment to murder, led by "a dagger of the mind, a false creation" (II, i, 38), moving like a ghost (II, i, 56).

Another bonding of the idea of walking with that of acting without acting is Macbeth's description of life as "but a walking shadow; a poor player" (V, v, 24). While in this inaudibly familiar speech about all our tomorrows I remark that Macbeth has a use for something like the idea that life, construed as a tale, signifies nothing – he has, as said, been trying to achieve the condition of insignificance ever since his speech about ending time, and before that. That life's but a walking shadow, a poor player, like both mad Lady Macbeth and sad Macbeth and like the perhaps sane players playing them, is a tremendous thought, but not something Macbeth learned just now, upon hearing of his wife's death. Perhaps it is something he can *say* now, say for himself, now that she is dead – that human life does not, any more than a human player, signify its course for and beyond itself; it is instead the scene or medium in which significance is found, or not. She is apt to have found this idea unmanly, anyway as diverging from her point of view. To speak of a player who "struts and frets" is simply, minus the melodramatic mode, to speak of someone who walks and cares, hence signifies acting and suffering and talking about both in view of others, which pretty well covers the human territory. And what is wrong with strutting and fretting for an "hour on the stage" that is not wrong with time altogether? Is "signifying nothing" the decay of their having been "promised greatness" (favorite words of both Macbeth and Lady Macbeth in their opening speeches)? And is this announcement of greatness taken as a hint of pregnancy and issue, or is it perhaps the promise of exemption from time (if that is different); or is it, given the hints of religious contestation in the play, a charge against the promise of eternity, against something Macbeth calls, thinking of the Witches, the "metaphysical'? It is imaginable that Macbeth is taking revenge against any and all of these promises of consequence, perhaps against the idea of history as fulfilling promises.

Of course this speech about insignificance, or say inexpressiveness, is an expression of limitlessly painful melancholy; but again, that pain is not new to Macbeth, not caused by the news of his wife's death. His response to that news I find in full – before the metaphysics of time and meaning, so to speak, take over – to be: "She should have died hereafter; / There would have been a time for such a word." That is all. Is it so little? He says that like everything else that happens her death is untimely, as if not hers: nothing is on or in time when nothing is desired, when desire is nothing, is not yours. And he says that he is incapable of mourning now; and if not capable now, then when not? The wrong time for death is an ultimately missed appointment; no time for mourning death sets an ultimate stake in disappointment. Here is a view of human history, history as unmournable disappointment. Macbeth's speech goes on to explore it. Perhaps it is a perception Lady Macbeth perished in trying to protect her husband from. This is something he can say now, no longer protecting her from her failure to protect him. If so, then the play's study of history is a study of their relationship, this marriage. What is this marriage?

In arriving at [this] question . . . I open what is for myself the encompassing question of why, in thinking about Shakespearean tragedy, I have previously avoided turning to this play. Two questions have, it seems forever, dogged me about *Macbeth*. What is the source of the attractiveness of this terrible pair? And why have I always felt intimate yet unengaged with their famous moments? As if I have and have not wanted to consider that this pair, representing the most extensive description the Shakespearean corpus devotes to an undoubted marriage (that of Cleopatra's with Antony is not undoubted), represents, to some as yet unmeasured extent, an always standing possibility of marriage itself.

Masculine disappointment together with feminine deflection of that disappointment indicates a more or less familiarly cursed marriage; and I was suggesting that the mood of "Tomorrow and tomorrow and tomorrow" is informed by knowledge Macbeth brings onto the stage from the beginning. If that is so, then the events of the play, the ambition for and against greatness and exemption, are in defense against this knowledge. In asking what this marriage is we have crossed to the second of the conditions of language that I have been claiming this play particularly to acknowledge: the first was language as prophesy, as foretelling; the second is language as mind-reading, a particular sharing of words, as if by magic.

As foretelling in *Macbeth* may be contrasted with telling or counting in *The Winter's Tale*, so sharing words in *Macbeth* may be compared with sharing words in *Coriolanus*, namely with words figured as food; in *Macbeth* words may rather, it seems, be something like potions: "Hie thee hither, / That I may pour my spirits in thine ear" (I, v, 25–26). There recurrently seems to me a phantasm glancing in these words of Lady Macbeth, beyond the idea of her wishing to inspire her husband, or give him courage, through her words; some more literal or imagined posture in which she invades him with her essence. Anyone might note that the play associates the production of words with the production and reception of blood: "We but teach / Bloody instructions, which, being taught, return / To plague th" inventor. This even-handed justice / Commends th" ingredience of our poison'd chalice / To our own lips" (I, vii, 8–12); "My gashes cry for help' / "So well thy words become thee, as they wounds" (I, ii, 43–44), as if in a tragedy of blood – and in this one, as the Arden editor reports, blood is mentioned over one hundred times – words are wounds, and the causes of wounds. I am drawn to test for the phantasm I allude to because of my sense of the pairs of certain cursed marriages, as in a relation of a sort I have elsewhere called spiritual vampirism.

The idea of words as mind-reading is a conception of reading as such – or play-watching – reading the text of another as being read by the other. Uttering words as mind-reading is represented in the language of this marriage, in which each of the pair says what the other already knows or has already said; or does not say something the other does not say, either assuming the other knows, or keeping a pledge of silence. They exemplify exchanges of words that are not exchanges, that represent a kind of negation of conversation. For example: Macbeth prays to "let

that be, / Which the eye fears, when it is done, to see" (I, iv, 52–53), and
Lady Macbeth is soon incanting "That my keen knife see not the wound
it makes" (I, v, 52); again, she fears that he is "without / The illness that
should attend" ambition (I, v, 19–20), and later he says to her, "Things
bad begun make strong themselves by ill" (III, iii, 55); and earlier,
Macbeth's letter tells Lady Macbeth that greatness is promised her, and
she repeats this in her ensuing soliloquy as something promised him. And
let us add that before she reads, while sleepwalking, the letter she has in
that condition written herself, as a kind of script of the play (a suggestion
of Marjorie Garber's), Macbeth at the opposite end of the play had
already written a letter which forms a script for her words; the first words
we hear her say are his. But my hypothesis is that the play's sense of
mind-reading, of being trapped in one another's mind, in false, draining
intimacies (the idea of vampirism), is expressed preeminently in what the
pair of the marriage do not, or not in good time, say to, or say for, one
another. I note three topics about which they are silent: the plan to kill
Duncan, their childlessness, and the relation of Lady Macbeth to the
witches. I imagine there are different causes for silence in the three cases.

The pair's initial implicitness to one another over the plan to kill
Duncan means to me not that each had the idea independently but that
each thinks it is the other's idea, that each does the deed somehow for the
other. It is an omen that neither knows why it is done. This will come
back.

The compulsively repeated critical sneer expressed in the question
"how many children had Lady Macbeth?" expresses anxiety over the
question of the marriage's sexuality and childlessness, as if critics are
spooked by the marriage. But I speak for myself. Is there any good
reason, otherwise, to deny or to slight the one break in Lady Macbeth's
silence on the subject of her childlessness, her assertion that she has
suckled a (male) child? There may be good reason for her husband to
deny or doubt it, in his considering whose it might be. If we do not deny
her assertion, then the question how many children she had is of no
interest that I can see; the interesting question is what happened, in fact
or in fantasy, to the child she remembers. (David Willbern, as I recall, in
a fine essay suggests in passing that her suckling is a fantasy. If so, then
what is the fantasy of remembering a (fantasied) child?) And if we do not
deny or slight her assertion then the fate of the child is *their* question, a
fact or issue for them of a magnitude to cause the magnitude and
intimacy of guilt and melancholy Macbeth begins with and Lady Macbeth ends with. Its massive unspokenness is registered by the reverse of
the procedure of the recurrence of words, namely by the dispersal or
dissemination of words for birth throughout the play – *deliver, issue, breed,
labour, hatch'd, birthdom, bring forth*. I would like to include the punning

use of *borne*, repeated by Lenox in his nervously ironic "Men must not walk too late" speech (a nice instance of the prophetic or foretelling use of "walk," especially of Lady Macbeth's last appearance). This listing of terms for child-bearing perhaps tells us nothing about early references in the play to becoming great or to "the swelling act / Of the imperial theme" (I, iii, 128–29). But when one is caught by the power – it will not happen predictably – of the vanished child, one may wonder even over Lady Macbeth's response upon the initial entrance to her of Macbeth, "I feel now / The future in the present," which in turn is, and is not, Macbeth's perception of history. (A sense of pregnancy, but without assurance of reproduction, may suggest the monstrous as much as it does the sterile.)

Anticipating for some reason an especially negative reaction to the last instance of deflected birth and death I am about to adduce, I emphasize that I am not undertaking to persuade anyone of unspoken presence. I am testifying to something guiding me that I cannot distinguish from a valid intuition. If I do not eventually discover a satisfying tuition for it, I will have to give it up as a guide. Perhaps it is not an intuition of free interpretation but a dagger of the mind, precisely not to be followed. But if one could know this in advance, or settle it, there would be no spiritual danger of the kind criticism runs, no such acts and thoughts to be responsible for or to; one would be either a witch or a tyrant. I would like to say: The great responsibility of philosophy is responsiveness – to be awake after all the others have fallen asleep.

The instance I am thinking of is the opening human question of the play, I mean the first words spoken after the witches have delivered themselves of their opening questions and answers about their meeting again. Duncan enters and encounters something that brings forth his response, "What bloody man is that?" If we take it to heart that in this tragedy, or say medium, of blood, blood is associated both with death and with birth, and that bloody figures and figures of children originate or appear from, as it were, the witches' cauldron, then this appearance of the questionable bloody man – as from the cauldron – may be seen to begin the play. It figures beginnings – of plays, of human actions – as consequences, as conclusions manifested, synthesized, conjured. The witches'' cauldron accordingly appears as the origin of theater, as the scene of apparitions or appearances, and as the source or representation of the human as that which identifies and denies itself – or, as Hamlet virtually says, as that which imitates itself so "abominably," in the form of abominations, objects of horror to themselves.

That a first-night, or a first-day, audience may not at first recognize a connection between the bloody man and the cauldron is true enough, but not obviously more surprising than anything else not recognized, on the first, or on the hundred-and-first, encounter. I assume that any complexity the average mortal finds in a play of Shakespeare's is something Shakespeare is capable of having placed there. The critical question is: How? By what means? The question whether an author intends any or all of what happens is a convenient defense against this critical question. Recent attacks on intentionality share the (metaphysical) picture of intention that they would criticize, one that makes its importance absolute, as if, if intention counts for anything in meaning, it counts for everything. (We have seen the pattern before.) Metaphysics, so described, here concerning intention, might be called magic thinking. So let us say: Intention is merely of the last importance. Everything (else) has first to be in place for it to do what it does – as in putting a flame to a fuse. And of course accidents can happen. Would one like to imagine that the man of blood follows the witches' incantations by accident? Magicless, impotent witches are no easier to imagine than the other kind.

But I cannot stop the intuition here, the intuition of the magic of theater and its voices and its other apparitions, of the declaration of theater as the power of making things appear, along of course with the powers of equivocation and of casting spells. (Are only witches and warlocks so empowered? Or are they only convenient paranoid projections of what we accept as humdrum human power? Glendower's metaphysical claim to call up monsters, together with Hotspur's skeptical question as to whether they will come when he calls them, forms another instance of fixated philosophical sides that Shakespeare may be taken as bringing to confusion. Is this the accomplishment of philosophy, or its cue?) What has happened to Macbeth? What is the element of difference to his consciousness that brings forth his guilt and private violence and melancholy, as if settling something? This question draws me to imagine the bloody man – a poor player whom we never see again, who in Shakespeare's source was killed – against the question I impute to Macbeth (granted as it were that Lady Macbeth knows the answer) about what happened at the death and birth of his child. (Macbeth is not the only Shakespearean male to find birth mysterious and unnatural, who might believe anything about it and about those to whom and from whom it happens. This is cardinal in the essay of Janet Adelman's that I cited earlier.) I do not look for a stable answer to be found by Macbeth: he protests his acceptance and his doubt of the witches throughout. But that there are witches and that they bring forth children may provide him with a glance of explanation, perhaps of hope, perhaps of despair; an explanation at once of *the presence of the absence* of his child and of the *absence in the presence* of his wife.

I ask here only that we allow Macbeth to have posed for himself the issue that so many critics now so readily take as answered – that there is some inner connection between Lady Macbeth and witchery. Some approve the idea that in her opening scene she is casting a spell on herself ("unsex me here . . . fill me, from the crown to the toe, top-full / Of direst cruelty" (I, v, 41–43) – though here I seem to have heard every interpretation of these frightening words except the one that seems unforced to me; that it expresses rage, human as can be, at the violence and obligation of sexual intercourse, at what Laplanche calls, in *Life and Death in Psychoanalysis*, the traumatic nature of human sexuality: her husband is returning any moment from the wars. And none fail to remark that she is presenting herself as a mother, in her fashion ("Take my milk for gall, you murth'ring ministers" ([I, v, 48]). If she is a witch it follows both that witches are mothers and presumably that she is capable of destroying their child with her own hands. (Is there a difference supposed in the pronunciation of "murth'ring" and "mothering'? Or is this identity a critical commonplace?)

We are, of course, in the middle of the third of the three topics I said the pair are silent about; the first two were their plan of Duncan's murder and their vanished child; the third is the topic and the logic of monstrousness. What is there for them to discuss about this? Others may speculate with detachment over the belief in witches, but it is the likes of Macbeth who, finding themselves confronted with witches, have to ask how you tell who is a witch (the commonest question there could be about witches); and have to carry through the logic that if anyone is a witch then his wife may be one; that hence he may be the master and the minister of a witch, figures named in the play (and he has perhaps tasted his wife's milk or gall and had her pour her spirits in his ear and felt chastised by the valor of her tongue, but I will not speculate here); hence that he has had a child with a witch, produced something monstrous that has to die, as if he were a devil, not a man (he is called "Hell-hound" by Macduff [V, viii, 3]). There is nothing to discuss: No individual human knows more than any other what the difference is between the human and the monstrous, as no human is exempt from the wish for exemption from the human. I mean no one is in a position to tell another that there are or are not witches, any more than to tell another that there are or are not humans.

Here is a way of considering this play's contribution to the continuing European discussion of witches contemporary with it – its sense of metaphysical denial (say denial of our fundamental metaphysical ignorance of difference between the human and the monstrous) projected through human society by legalizing the identification of witches. It seems to me just like Shakespeare to have already infiltrated this discussion (as noted in *Disowning Knowledge*) by coloring Othello's psychological torture of Desdemona (who, on the pattern of Lady Macbeth, is anything but a witch) as a witch trial – a sense of the erotic denial introduced into one's human identity by the projection of one's sense of bewitchment. (Another of Shakespeare's indirections with his sources is his hedging of Mark Antony, who, on the pattern of Coriolanus, is anything but a Christ, with signs of Christ.)

By the time of Macbeth's last encounter with the witches, at the opening of Act IV, he seems to have accepted his participation in their realm, undertaking, successfully, to "conjure" them (IV, i, 50). In the ensuing appearances or apparitions from the cauldron to Macbeth (and to us) of the armed head and of the bloody child and of the child crowned, we have the pattest declaration by the play of its theory of the work of theater as the conjuring of apparitions; and I am taking it, if you like in deferred action, to figure for us (and for Macbeth, whoever, in identification with us, he is), what we see (saw) when at the beginning we encounter(ed) the bloody man, the origin and destiny of his child, hence of himself. Now one may feel that all this takes Macbeth's sense of bewitchment or exemption to be a function of an incredible capacity for literalization on his part. But is it really more than is shown by his sense that he is to be dominated by a man who exists from no woman? Moreover, literalization is perhaps not so uncommon, but is an ordinary part of magic thinking, like imagining that to claim that an author means what he or she says is to claim that his or her intention has created all the conditions in conjunction with which intention does what it does, as if the striking match creates the fuse it lights, together with the anger and the enemy and the opportunity in and for and from which it is struck. (In a sense, no doubt, it does. What sense?)

To work toward a close of these remarks, one that takes them back to my opening intuitions of *Macbeth* as a history play that questions whether anything can be known – or known to be made – to happen, I come back to the murder of Duncan. What I have said or implied about this so far is that Macbeth walks to it in a sleep and that each of the pair acts it out as for the other, assuming its origination in the other, so that the desire for the deed and the time of the deed can never be appropriate, never quite intelligible. To raise the question of what it is that is thus done on borrowed time, with stolen words, let us take it that it is performed with that dagger of the mind Macbeth speculates might be the instrument of murder and ask what wound in the mind it makes, one that each of the pair asks not to see – which we now understand as impossibly asking the other not to see.

I pause to remark that it is probably the sense of their silence to one another about unsilenceable topics that has above all prompted critics to suggest that scenes are missing from the play. I am in effect claiming that what is missing is not absent but is present in the play's specific ways of saying nothing, say of showing the unspeakable. A methodological point of interest thus arises concerning the subject of what you might call critical responsibility. My claim is that readers/watchers of the play are meant to read its silences; that, in effect, the speculation about a missing scene is a cover for the speculator's missing response to scenes that *are* present. This implies that should, as it were, a missing scene show up for this play, it could prove neither the truth nor the falsity of what I claim the silence is about. To accept such a scene is to be willing to rethink the play; perhaps it would contain further silences. There is, by my definition, no scene missing from the play I mean to be considering here, the one constituted in the Arden edition I cite from. (How many plays have the Macbeths?)

My account of the pair's silence about the plan to kill Duncan depends here mostly on three elements that indicate that they each imagine Macbeth's deathblow to direct itself to Lady Macbeth.

The first element is Macbeth's speech as he reenters from having gone, after the discovery of Duncan's body, to see his handiwork: "From this instant, / There's nothing serious in mortality; / All is but toys" (II, iii, 90–92). Good readers have characteristically felt that something is horrifyingly disproportionate in these words of Macbeth's, disagreeing about Macbeth's sincerity or degree of consciousness in saying them. My sense is that these words cannot take their direction from the figure of Duncan, however they may recognize his disfigurement; but that the only object whose loss for Macbeth could amount to the radical devaluation of the human world is Lady Macbeth, together with some phantasm in the idea of "toys," as of some existence left behind. (A measure of the disproportion in Macbeth's speech on Duncan's death – "nothing serious in mortality" – is to set it with Cleopatra's on Antony's death – "nothing left remarkable / Beneath the visiting moon" (IV, xv) – where I assume no sense of disproportion. How far this connection verifies my general sense of these plays as history plays about a break in history, as turns in the history of privacy, or say skepticism, hence in the history of marriage, hence in the history of legitimacy and succession, I do not guess now.)

That Lady Macbeth shares this knowledge of herself as the object of the killing is how I take the second element I cite in this connection, that of her fainting upon Macbeth's words that recount in vivid and livid detail his killing of Duncan's grooms: "Who could refrain / That had a heart to love, and in that heart / Courage, to make's love known?" (II, iii, 114–16). It is she alone who knows what Macbeth loves, to whom whatever he does makes his love known. (But the sincerity or reality of her fainting is a matter of controversy. Am I simply assuming it? I might say I have provided an argument in favor of its reality. But I would rather say that it is still perfectly possible to insist that the fainting is insincere, put on by her to divert the attention of the company, only this will now have to include her knowledge of what Macbeth's deed was in killing his love; and then the idea of her insincerity will perhaps seem less attractive.) After Lady Macbeth is helped to exit from this scene, she is never an active presence in the play's events. This is why the fact of her death comes to Macbeth as no shock.

The third element in defining the object of Macbeth's killing is Lady Macbeth's entrance to him upon his words, "I have no spur / To prick the sides of my intent, but only / Vaulting ambition, which o'erleaps itself / And falls on th' other" (I, vii, 25–26). By now I will take no one by surprise in expressing my sense that the line should be left alone (I mean, to begin with, that it should not be taken to be incomplete) to nominate Lady Macbeth as the other. (This at the same time leaves the line to mark this entrance as a cardinal declaration in this play that its study or acknowledgment of theatrical entrances is of their quality as appearances or apparitions, called forth, conjured.) Critics have wished to see in Macbeth's image of "overleaping" here an image of himself as the rider of a horse, mounting it or jumping it, overeagerly. I do not say this is wrong; but since Macbeth's words are that it is *his* intent whose sides are, or are not, to be pricked, there is a suggestion that he is identifying himself also as the horse (as earlier he associates himself with a wolf and later identifies himself as a baited bear); a horse by whom or by what ridden is unclear, ambiguous: perhaps it is by his ambition, perhaps by the ambition of another, so that "falling on the other" means falling to the other, to be responsible for it, but perhaps it means falling upon the other, as its casualty. Then the falling is not overeager, but an inevitable self-projection of human promise. (If one insists that not he but strictly his intent is the horse, he remaining strictly the rider, then again his intent outruns his control not because of overeagerness but because of the separate lives of intention and of the world, we riding, as best we can, between.)

If we take it as ambiguous whether Macbeth is imagining himself as the rider or as the horse, the ambiguity is then an expression of the pair's mutual mind-reading, their being as it were over-literally of one mind: whatever occurs to one occurs to the other; whatever one does the other does; in striking at her he strikes at himself; his action is something he suffers. Sleepwalking seems a fair instance of a condition ambiguous as between doing something and having something happen to you. Other actions pertinent to this play, exemplary of the ambiguity or reciprocity of acting and suffering, or in Emerson's words, between getting and having, are giving birth and the play of sexual gratification. The reciprocity presents itself to Macbeth as requiring an assassination that trammels up consequence, all consequence, an act of metaphysics whose consequence is of being assassinated; as if acts of realizing your world, acts of self-empowerment, are acts of self-assassination, the openest case

in which doing a deed and suffering the deed are inseparable. The logic
is that of narcissism, and the sense is that there is a narcissism under a
negative sign, with love replaced by hatred. You need not think that
masculinity and femininity are determined by a prior determination of
activity and passivity in order to think that prior to the individuation that
begins individuating others – to the formation of the human self that is
subject to others and subjects others, that knows passion and that knows
action, that is bewitchable and tyrannical – there is nothing either decid-
able or undecidable about the self's gender. And if "being" a gender (one
rather than another) is a mode like, or is part of, "having" a self (this one
rather than another), is individuation ever over? There are always others
to tell you so and others to tell you otherwise. Are they others?

A psychological account of the state in which punishment of an object
(or former object) of love is a state of self-punishment is given by Freud
in his statement of the etiology of melancholia. I shall quote some
sentences from Freud's "Mourning and Melancholia" and then close
with a few sentences about why I find their association with *Macbeth*,
through Nietzsche, significant, I mean why I want to follow them on.

> An object-choice, an attachment of the libido to a particular person,
> had at one time existed; then, owing to a real slight or disappoint-
> ment coming from this loved person, the object-relationship was
> shattered. The result was not the normal one of a withdrawal of the
> libido from this object and a displacement of it onto a new one, but
> something different. . . . It was withdrawn into the ego . . . [where]
> it served to establish an identification of the ego with the aban-
> doned object. Thus the shadow of the object fell upon the ego, so
> that the [ego] could henceforth be criticized by a special mental
> faculty, the forsaken object. . . . The melancholic displays . . . an
> impoverishment of his ego on a grand scale. In mourning it is the
> world which has become poor and empty; in the melancholic, it is
> the ego itself.

"Impoverishment of his ego on a grand scale" – it seems a move in an
auction of nothingness, self-punishment as for the murder, finally, of the
world. Guilt as melancholia seems a reasonable formulation of Macbeth's frame of mind. It is a suggestion from which to reenter the texts
from which I reported that I have begun asking tuition for my intuitions
about this play.

The passages from "Mourning and Melancholia" just quoted were
adduced a few years ago in Timothy Gould's study of Nietzsche's Pale
Criminal (a figure in an early section of *Thus Spoke Zarathustra*), which
appeared in the Summer, 1986 issue of *Soundings*. In readducing the

passages here I am in effect claiming that Nietzsche's Pale Criminal, whatever else, is a study of *Macbeth*. That section of *Zarathustra* speaks of guilt that expresses itself in madness after the deed and madness before the deed, and it proposes a problematic of blood and of human action in which performing a deed is taken over by an image of the performance of the deed, an image which functions to fixate or exhaust the doer's identity so that he becomes nothing but the doer of this deed, suffering subjective extinction as it were in the doing of what he does. It speaks, accordingly, to why Macbeth thinks of himself (thinking shared, as it must be, by Lady Macbeth) as in a sea of blood of his own giving, so as pale. (Macbeth once asks "seeling Night," with its "bloody and invisible hand" to release him from that "which keeps me pale" [III, ii, 46–50] and in her sleepwalking Lady Macbeth will say, or say again, "Look not so pale . . . give me your hand" [V, i, 59, 63].) In a world of blood, to be pale, exceptional, exempt, without kin, without kind, is to want there to be no world, none outside of you, nothing to be or not to be yours, neither from nor not from your hand; but to be pale is to be drained and to demand blood, to absorb what is absorbing you.

And the bearing of Macbeth as Nietzsche's Pale Criminal is significant for me, to be followed on, because of Nietzsche's response (so I claim) to Emerson's "Experience," a centerpiece of the seminar on romanticism and skepticism I mentioned at the outset of Part I of this essay. (Emerson's essay opens with the question, "Where do we find ourselves?" The introduction to Nietzsche's *Genealogy of Morals* opens with the two sentences: "We are unknown to ourselves, we knowers. How should we have found ourselves when we have never looked for ourselves?") Emerson's "Experience" is about the inability, and the ability, to mourn the death of his five-year-old son; the essay works toward the discovery of the social, call it America, toward the discovery of succession, imaged by Emerson as coming to walk, to take steps, beginning in what is quite explicitly described as walking in your sleep. Emerson here responds to, takes responsibility for, Shakespeare's and Kant's and America's ideas of success and succession: in effect, he is claiming to enter history by becoming their successor. It is an essay, as I have put it in the first chapter of *This New Yet Unapproachable America*, where the image of the human hand emblematizes the question of how deeds enter and work in the world, the question of how, as Emerson phrases it, you "realize your world," something Emerson's critics, as he reports in his essay, keep complaining that he has himself failed to do. But realizing his world is of course precisely what Emerson takes himself to be doing, in his writing, in the way only humans can; non-magically, as it were; by letting something happen, the reversal of denial. This is more or less, not for unrelated reasons, how Heidegger and Wittgenstein also think, so that what is most active is what is most passive, or receptive. This suggests that we do not know whether knowing – for example, knowing whether one is human or inhuman – is a masculine or a feminine affair.

I am citing bits of what might, in another world, be called the history of the reception of *Macbeth*, or part of its historical circulation or exchange or energy, say of its money or blood of the mind, as a way of saying that if Shakespeare's play is a distinctive event in the history it remembers and enacts – if it is to continue to happen to its culture, to the extent that it, or anything, has ever happened to its culture as art happens, as truth happens in art, not alone as conclusion but as premise, not alone as document but as event – that is because events happen as this work shows them to happen, contains them, no more nor less clearly. In emphasizing, rather than Shakespeare's sources, Shakespeare's writing as a source variously open to appropriation, I may find my own provocation in it, without claiming to speak for it – as for example fixing its own mode of appropriating sources. Then I am in effect claiming that the Shakespearean play here claims a power to challenge authority that is based on birth and inheritance; that the political as realm of royal blood never recovers from this portrait which locates its causes in unsayable privacy (as in this marriage), in royal authority's sleek imitability (as in Malcolm's apparent libeling of himself, and in Macbeth's bloody hand as the imitation and inheritor of the king's healing touch); nor recovers from its support by treasonableness in expansive masculinity (as in Macduff); nor from its vanity (as in Banquo's narcissistic mirror).

So I am in effect verifying the familiar idea that a Shakespeare history play develops from the morality tradition, but taking its moral direction to put a kink in the old history – taking it not as directed to teach the proper conduct of king and subject, but instead to constitute a moral about what history is, or has become – that what happens is not what is news, not a tale of a world, real or fictional; that such things are accounts merely of trivial horrors, consequences of old deeds, revenge returning, as Macbeth learns, as kings typically learn, too late; that learning what has happened is exemplified by the learning of what is happening now, or as Emerson more or less puts the matter, that history is not of the past, but for example is in our sleep-watching of this play; so that you need not become a horror-dealing, horror-dealt tyrant in order to recognize what is worth doing and worth having. And might you learn how not to become the victim of a tyrant? But what if, after the passing of tyrants, you yourself play the confiner?

12

Psychoanalysis and Cinema: The Melodrama of the Unknown Woman

This essay – originally delivered as the 1985 Edith Weigert Lecture – inaugurated Cavell's examination of a film genre he labelled "The Melodrama of the Unknown Woman;" this genre is derived from remarriage comedy by the systematic negation of the latter's themes and structures, and shows the threats that dog the happiness for which those comedies hold out hope. Thus, the women of the melodramas attempt to achieve their own existence by metamorphosis apart from the educative satisfactions of marriage, in the presence of their mother and children, and through the medium of essentially ironic modes of language. For these women, neither society nor their male acquaintance can help them to transform their haunting of their world into an inhabitation of it; on the contrary, their world enforces that dematerialization, and so their refusal of its demands is at once a condemnation of that world and its inhabitants as they stand, and a call for their transformation. Here again, Cavell's interest in Emerson and Thoreau shows its influence (cf. Essays 14 and 15). These women's attempts to attain a further, more realized state figures the general human need to enact one's existence in the face of skepticism; and their role as standing critics of society in the name of a further, attainable state of social justice indicates the political significance of these seemingly personal or erotic matters. As Essay 17 will demonstrate, these aspects of the melodramas in effect prefigure the structures of Emersonian or Moral Perfectionism.

However, this essay also constitutes a further, and highly influential, step in Cavell's engagement with psychoanalysis. Freudian concepts have, of course, guided many of his readings of texts from the outset; and – as his 1981 essay on "The Politics of Interpretation" (collected in *Themes Out of School*) first made clear in highly condensed form – the model of the relationship between reader and author that he has found in

Originally published in *Images in Our Souls: Cavell, Psychoanalysis and Cinema*, eds J. H. Smith and W. Kerrigan (Baltimore: Johns Hopkins University Press, 1987), pp. 11–43. Reprinted by permission.

the texts which mean most to him is psychoanalytic in character (its distinctive feature being that the text analyzes the reader, utilizing structures of transference and counter-transference to seduce her desire from its fixations). But in this essay, a third connection opens up – and one that derives from Cavell's perception of skepticism as gender-inflected; for if it is right to think of the mode of active passivity required for skepticism's overcoming as distinctively feminine in character, it becomes striking that the case-histories at the core of psychoanalysis involve Freud questioning women, to whom he attributes a distinctive capacity for bodily expressiveness (or active passivity). Cavell is thereby brought to ask two key questions. First, do psychoanalytic procedures involve the victimization of women by male interrogation, or do they rather provide a space within which the distinctively but not exclusively female capacity to own one's body of expressions can be exercised? Second, can psychoanalysis itself accordingly be thought of as the last place in modern culture in which the human psyche receives proof of its own existence (as unknown to itself, as unconscious)? The answers to these questions deeply affect the future trajectory of Cavell's project.

When the man in Max Ophuls's film *Letter from an Unknown Woman* reaches the final words of the letter addressed to him by the, or by some, unknown woman, he is shown – according to well-established routines of montage – to be assaulted by a sequence of images from earlier moments in the film. This assault of images proves to be death-dealing. His response to finishing the reading of the letter is to stare out past it, as if calling up the film's images; and his response to the assault of the ensuing repeated images is to cover his eyes with the outstretched fingers of both hands in a melodramatic gesture of horror and exhaustion. Yet he sees nothing we have not seen, and the images themselves (as it were) are quite banal – his pulling the veil up over the woman's hat, the two of them at the Prater amusement park in winter, her taking a candied apple, their dancing, his playing a waltz for her on the piano in an empty ballroom. An apparently excessive response to apparently banal images – it seems a characterization of a response to film generally, at least to certain kinds of film, perhaps above all to classical Hollywood films. But since Max Ophuls is a director, and this is a film, of major ambition, the implication may be that this man's response to the returning images of the film and of his past – his horror and exhaustion – somehow underlies our response to any film of this kind, perhaps to major film as such, or ought to. It seems a particular mode of horror that these hands would ward off, since we may equally think of the images looming at this man not as what he has seen but as what he has *not* seen, has refused to see. Then are we sure that we have seen what it is up to us to see? What motivates these images? Why does their knowledge constitute an assault? If *Letter from an Unknown Woman* were merely the high-class so-called woman's film, or tearjerker, it is commonly taken to be – as the bulk of the melodramas I will refer to here are taken to be – it and they could not justify and satisfy the imposition of such questions of criticism. The only proof that any of them can do so is, of course, to provide a convincing reading in which one or another of them does so. That is not what I want to attempt here, but instead to do less and more than that. Less, because the passages of reading I provide here concern only certain isolated moments of any film. But more, because I will adduce moments from two groups of films designed at once to suggest the range and detail of their relations as a whole and to sketch the intellectual palette that convincing readings will, for my taste, have to support. Here I am looking for a sense of the ground on which any reading I would be moved to offer will succeed or fail.

In accepting the assignment to give this year's Weigert lecture on the topic of psychoanalysis and cinema, I knew that I would want to use the occasion to take further the work represented in my book *Pursuits of Happiness*. That book defines a genre of film – a genre I name the comedy of remarriage – on the basis of what I call reading the individual members of a set of films, which is meant to prove them to constitute a genre, where proving this constitution turns in part on showing the group as a whole to enact, and, I hope, to illuminate, Freud's early vision (in *Three Essays on the Theory of Sexuality*) that "the finding of the object is in fact the refinding of it," together with a surprising conjunction of preconceptions in what can be called philosophy. In remarriage comedy, unlike classical comedy, happiness, such as it is, is arrived at not by a young pair's overcoming social obstacles to their love, but instead by a somewhat older pair's overcoming obstacles that are between, or within, themselves (facing divorce, being brought *back* together, and finding one another *again*). A remarkable sequence of consequences flows from this shift of emphasis, segments of which will be rehearsed in what follows.

Remarriage comedy, in effect enacting what Freud calls the diphasic character of human sexuality, displays the nostalgic structure of human experience. Since these films, being major achievements of the art of film, thus reveal some internal affinity of the phenomenon of nostalgia with the phenomenon of film, the popular nostalgia now associated with movies stands to be understood as a parody, or avoidance, of an inherent, treacherous property of the medium of film as such. The drama of the remarriage genre, the argument that brings into play the intellectual and emotional bravery of the beautiful, lucid pairs whose interactions or conversations form the interest of the genre – Irene Dunne and Cary Grant, Barbara Stanwyck and Henry Fonda, Katharine Hepburn and Spencer Tracy – turns on their efforts to transform an intimacy as

between brother and sister into an erotic friendship capable of withstand-
ing, and returning, the gaze of legitimate civilization. They conduct, in
short, the argument of marriage. In *The Philadelphia Story* (directed by
George Cukor in 1940) this ancient intimacy – here between Katharine
Hepburn and Cary Grant – is called, twice, having grown up together. In
The Awful Truth (directed by Leo McCarey in 1937) the woman (Irene
Dunne) actually, climactically, enacts a role as her husband's sister (the
husband is again Cary Grant), in which this high-minded society lady
blatantly displays her capacity for low-down sexiness.

The transformation of incestuous knowledge into erotic exchange is a
function of something I call the achievement of the daily, of the diurnal,
the putting together of night and day (as classical comedy puts together
the seasons of the year), a process of willing repetition whose concept is
the domestic, or marriage, however surprising the images of marriage
become in these films. "Repetition" is the title Kierkegaard gives to his
thoughts about the faith required in achieving marriage (*Repetition*); and
repetition, or rather eternal recurrence, is the recipe Nietzsche discovered
as the antidote for our otherwise fated future of nihilism, the thing
Nietzsche calls "the revenge against time and its 'It was' " – a revenge
itself constituting a last effort not to die of nostalgia. Nietzsche explicitly
invokes the concept of marriage in his prophetic cry (in *Thus Spoke
Zarathustra*) for this redemption or reconception of time. He says it is
"high time" for this, and in German the literal translation of "high time"
is *Hochzeit* (wedding); moreover, his symbol of eternal recurrence is the
(wedding) ring. These ideas of repetition may be said to require of our
lives the perpetual invention of the present from the past, out of the past.
This seems to be the vision of Freud's *Beyond the Pleasure Principle*, in
which death – I take it to be psychological death – comes either through
the success of this invention, that is, the discovery of one's own death
(hence, surely, of one's own life, say, of one's willingness to live), or else
through the relapse of the psychological into the biological and beyond
into the inorganic, which may be viewed as counter modes of repetition.

In writing *Pursuits of Happiness* I incurred a number of intellectual
debts that I propose here not to settle but somewhat to identify and
organize – in effect, to rewrite certain of my outstanding promissory
notes. My initial business will be to confirm a prediction of *Pursuits of
Happiness* to the effect that there must exist a genre of film, in particular
some form of melodrama, adjacent to, or derived from, that of remarriage comedy, in which the themes and structure of the comedy are
modified or negated in such a way as to reveal systematically the threats
(of misunderstanding, of violence) that in each of the remarriage
comedies dog its happiness. I am calling the new genre the melodrama of
the unknown woman. My next main business will be to say how I cloak

my debt to the writing of Freud, which means to say what I conceive certain relations of psychoanalysis and philosophy to consist in. My concluding piece of business, as a kind of extended epilogue, will be to produce a reading of the moment I invoked in opening these remarks, a man's melodramatic covering of his eyes, from the Ophuls film from which I have adapted the title of the new genre.

The prediction that some form of melodrama awaited definition was based on various moments from each of the comedies of remarriage. In the earliest of the definitive remarriage structures, *It Happened One Night* (directed by Frank Capra in 1934, with Clark Gable and Claudette Colbert), the pair work through episodes of poverty, theft, blackmail, and sordid images of marriage; in *The Awful Truth* the pair face distrust, jealousy, scandal, and the mindless rumoring of a prospective mother-in-law; in *His Girl Friday* (from 1940, directed by Howard Hawks, with Cary Grant and Rosalind Russell) the pair deal with political corruption, brutal moralism, and wasting cynicism; in *The Lady Eve* (from 1941, directed by Preston Sturges, with Fonda and Stanwyck), with duplicity and the intractableness of the past; in *The Philadelphia Story*, with pretentiousness, perverseness, alcoholism, and frigidity.

But it is in the last of the remarriage comedies, *Adam's Rib* (from 1949, directed by George Cukor, with Hepburn and Tracy), that melodrama threatens on several occasions almost to take the comedy over. The movie opens with a sequence, in effect a long prologue, in which a wife and mother tracks her husband to the apartment of another woman and shoots him. Played by the virtuoso Judy Holliday, the part is continuously hilarious, touching, and frightening, so that one never rests content with one's response to her. An early sequence of the film proper (so to speak) consists of the screening of a film-within-a-film, a home movie that depicts the principal pair's coming into possession of their country house in Connecticut, in which Spencer Tracy twice takes on comically the postures and grimaces of an expansive, classical villain, threatening, with a twirl of his imaginary mustache, to dispossess Katharine Hepburn of something more precious than country houses. These passing comic glimpses of the man's villainous powers recur more disturbingly toward the end of the film, when he in turn tracks his spouse and confronts her in what he might conceivably take to be a compromising situation, and for all the world threatens to shoot her and her companion (David Wayne). What he is threatening them with soon proves to be a pistol made of licorice, but not too soon for us to have confronted unmistakably a quality of violence in this character that is as genuine – such is the power of Spencer Tracy as an actor on film – as his tenderness and playfulness. I say in the chapter on *Adam's Rib* in *Pursuits of Happiness* that

Tracy's character as qualified in this film declares one subject of the genre as a whole to be the idea of maleness itself as villainous, say sadistic. (Having made his legal point, Tracy turns the candy gun on himself, into his mouth, and proceeds to eat it – a gesture that creates its comic effect but that also smacks of madness and of a further capacity for violence and horror hardly less frightening on reflection than the simple capacity for shooting people in anger.) The suggestion I drew is that if the male gender as such, so far in the development of our culture, and in so beautifully developed a specimen of it as Spencer Tracy, is tainted with villainy, then the happiness in even these immensely privileged marriages exists only so far as the pair together locate and contain this taint – you may say domesticate it, make a home for it – as if the task of marriage is to overcome the villainy in marriage itself. Remarriage comedies show the task to be unending and the interest in the task to be unending.

The taint of villainy leaves a moral cloud, some will say a political one, over these films, a cloud that my book does not try, or wish, to disperse. It can be pictured by taking the intelligent, vivid women in these films to be descendants of Nora in Ibsen's *A Doll's House*, who leaves her husband and children in search of what she calls, something her husband has said she required, an education. She leaves saying that he is not the man to provide her with one, implying both that the education she requires is in the hands of men and that only a man capable of providing it, from whom it would be acceptable, could count for her as a husband. Thinking of the woman of remarriage comedy as lucky to have found such a man, remarriage comedy studies, among other matters, what has made him, inescapably bearing the masculine taint, acceptable. That she can, with him, have what the woman in *The Awful Truth* calls "some grand laughs" is indispensable, but not an answer; the question becomes how this happens with him.

This prompts two further questions, with which we are entered into the melodrama of unknownness. What of the women who have not found, and could not manage or relish a relationship with such a man, Nora's other, surely more numerous, descendants? And what, more particularly, of the women of the same era on film who are at least the spiritual equals of the women of remarriage comedy but whom no man can be thought to educate – I mean the women we might take as achieving the highest reaches of stardom, of female independence so far as film can manifest it – Greta Garbo and Marlene Dietrich and, at her best, Bette Davis?

The price of the woman's happiness in the genre of remarriage comedy is the absence of her mother (underscored by the attractive and signal presence, whenever he is present, of the woman's father) together with the strict absence of children for her, the denial of her as a mother – as if the woman has been abandoned, so far, to the world of men. Could remarriage comedies achieve their happiness in good faith if they denied the possibility of another path to education and feminine integrity? It would amount to denying that the happiness of these women indeed exacts a price, if of their own choice, affordable out of their own talents and tastes, suggesting instead that women without these talents and tastes are simply out of luck. Such an idea is false to the feeling shown by these women toward women unlike themselves – as, for example, Rosalind Russell's toward the outcast woman in *His Girl Friday*, or Irene Dunne's toward the nightclub singer whose identity she takes on in *The Awful Truth*, or Claudette Colbert's toward the mother who faints on the bus in *It Happened One Night*. It is as if these moments signal that such films do not stand in generic insulation from films in which another way of education and integrity is taken.

With one further feature of the way of education sought by Nora's comedic progeny, I can formulate the character I seek in a melodrama derived from the comedy of remarriage that concerns those spiritually equal women (equal in their imagination of happiness and their demand for it) among those I am calling Nora's other progeny.

The demand for education in the comedies presents itself as a matter of becoming created, as if the women's lives heretofore have been non-existent, as if they have haunted the world, as if their materialization will constitute a creation of the new woman and hence a creation, or a further step in the creation, of the human. This idea has various sources and plays various roles as the theory of remarriage develops in *Pursuits of Happiness*. Theologically, it alludes to the creation of the woman from Adam in *Genesis*, specifically its use by Protestant thinkers, impressive among them John Milton, to ratify marriage and to justify divorce. Cinematically, it emphasizes the role of the camera in transforming human figures of flesh and blood into psychic shadows of themselves, in particular in transforming the woman, of whose body more than is conventional is on some occasion found to be revealed (today such exposure would perhaps be pointless), so that Katharine Hepburn will be shown pointedly doing her own diving in *The Philadelphia Story*, or awkwardly crawling through the woods in a wet, clinging dress, or having her skirt torn off accidentally on purpose by the man in *Bringing Up Baby*, or being given a massage in *Adam's Rib*. The most famous of all such exposures, I guess, is that of Claudette Colbert showing some leg to hitch a ride in *It Happened One Night*. Dramatically, the idea of creation refers to a structure Northrop Frye calls Old Comedy – he is, however, thinking primarily of Shakespearean drama – in which the woman holds the key to the happy outcome of the plot and suffers something like death and resurrection: *All's Well That Ends Well* and *The Winter's Tale* would be signal examples. I take Hermione in *The Winter's Tale* to be the other primary source (along with Ibsen's Nora) of the woman in remarriage comedy, understanding that play as a whole, in the light of the film genre, as the greatest of the structures of remarriage. *The Winter's Tale* also proves (along with *A Doll's House*) to underlie the women of the derived melodrama of unknownness, since while Hermione's resurrection at the close of the play (which I interpret as a kind of marriage ceremony) is a function of Leontes's faith and love, it is before that a function of Paulina's constancy and effectiveness, and the ceremony provides Hermione not just with her husband again (to whom she does not at the end speak) but as well with her daughter again (to whom she does speak).

In remarriage comedy the transformation of the woman is accomplished in a mode of exchange or conversation that is surely among the glories of dialogue in the history of the art of talking pictures. The way these pairs talk together I propose as one perfect manifestation of what Milton calls that "meet and cheerful conversation" (by which he means talk as well as more than talk), which he, most emphatically among the Protestant thinkers so far as I have seen, took to constitute God's purpose in instituting sexual difference, hence marriage. But now if deriving a genre of melodrama from remarriage comedy requires, as I assume, the retaining of the woman's search for metamorphosis and existence, it nevertheless cannot take place through such ecstatic exchanges as earmark the comedies; which is to say that the woman of melodrama, as shown to us, will not find herself in what the comedies teach us marriage is, but accordingly in something less or conceivably more than that.

Then the sense of the character (or underlying myth) of film I was to look for in establishing a genre of melodrama may be formulated in the following way: a woman achieves existence (of fails to), or establishes her right to existence in the form of a metamorphosis (or fails to), apart from or beyond satisfaction by marriage (of a certain kind) and with the presence of her mother and of her children, where something in her language must be as traumatic in her case as the conversation of marriage is for her comedic sisters – perhaps it will be an aria of divorce, from husband, lover, mother, or child. (A vast, related matter, which I simply mention here, is that what is normally called adultery is not to be expected in these structures, since normally it plays no role in remarriage comedies – something that distinguishes them from Restoration comedy and from French farce. Thus, structures such as *Anna Karenina* and *Madame Bovary* are not members of what I am calling the melodrama of the unknown woman. In this genre it will not be the threat of social scandal that comes between a woman and a man, and no man could recover from participation in the special villainy that exercises the law to separate a woman irrevocably from her child.)

The films I begin from that seem to obey these intuitive requirements, together with guesses as to their salient roles within the genre, are, in summary, these seven or eight: *Blonde Venus*, with Marlene Dietrich, directed by Josef von Sternberg in 1932, which particularly emphasizes that the woman has nothing to learn from the men there are; *Stella Dallas*, directed by King Vidor in 1937, with Barbara Stanwyck and John Boles, which emphasizes the woman's business as a search for the mother, perhaps carrying a shame of the mother; *Showboat*, the Oscar Hammerstein–Jerome Kern operetta (literally a melodrama), directed by James Whale in 1936, which, as it were, mythically prepares Irene Dunne, because of the supporting or grounding presence in it of Helen Morgan and Paul Robeson, for her lead in the *The Awful Truth*, thus establishing an inner connection between this comedy and this melodrama; *Random Harvest*, with Ronald Colman and Greer Garson, directed by Mervyn LeRoy, in 1942, which most purely underscores the persistence of the feature in this genre of melodrama of the goal of remarriage itself; *Now Voyager*, also from 1942, which elaborates most completely the feature of metamorphosis as Bette Davis is transformed from Aunt Charlotte into the mysterious, magnetic Camille Vale, unforgettably helped by Paul Henreid and Claude Rains; *Mildred Pierce*, directed by Michael Curtiz in 1945, in which Joan Crawford emphasizes the theatricality in this melodrama, although one may decide that the feel of this feature in the film is too crazy to link it to the other members, so that it becomes rather a link to some further genre; *Gaslight*, directed by George Cukor in 1944, with Ingrid Bergman and Charles Boyer, which portrays in full length, no doubt with melodramatic or operatic exaggeration, the villainous, mind-destroying mode of marriage that both the comedy and the derived melodrama of remarriage set themselves against; *Letter from an Unknown Woman*, 1948, which emphasizes, by failure, fantasies of metamorphosis and fantasies of perfect communication and of the transcendence of marriage. I add to the list Eric Rohmer's *The Marquise of O*, made in 1977 with startling faithfulness to the Heinrich von Kleist tale of 1805. The odd dates of origin and cinematic transcription are not the only respects in which Kleist's tale plays a special role in relation to the genre of unknownness. This tale most hideously expresses the villainy of the husband of the genre (he has, under the signs of impeccable honor, raped the woman he wants to marry while she is in a drugged sleep), and it also finds an ending of the most secure conjugal happiness, of the comedy of existence truly achieved, of any member of the genre. It is as if this tale undertakes all by itself to redeem the violence and ugliness that will cling to sexual hunger and satisfaction at their best – as if to prepare the soul for what Jacques Laplanche, in his *Life and Death in Psychoanalysis*, calls the traumatic nature of human sexuality, thus harking all the way back to Breuer and Freud's *Studies on Hysteria*.

This list of candidates for membership in this genre of melodrama that I propose to derive from remarriage comedy is bound to seem less perspicuous than the list of films from which I began in defining the comic genre. While the melodramas were all made in Hollywood and all within the same two decades as the comedies (except for *The Marquise of O*), they lack the overlapping of directors, actors and actresses, and of that critical sound – of high and embattled wit – that gives a sensuous coherence to the group of comedies. And, of course, individually the melodramas are less ingratiating and, perhaps partly for that reason, less famous, or rather less beloved, than the comedies. (This difference in coherence may go to show, after all, something Tolstoy did not exactly say: that only happy remarriages are alike.) But if I am right that the melodramas belong together as I say they do, that will serve to justify my concept of the genre, which is used not primarily to establish a classification of objects but to articulate, let me say, the arguments among them. This is a significant matter, which I pass here with two remarks: (1) The list of members is in principle never closed, membership always being determined experimentally, which is to say, in specific acts of criticism, on the basis of a work's participation in the genre's argument; (2) if the case for the genre is good enough, it ought itself to suggest some understanding of its films' relative unknownness, or lack of love.

But what is all this about unknownness? What does it mean to say that it motivates an argument? And what has the argument to do with nihilism and diurnal recurrence? And why is it particularly about a woman that the argument takes place? What is the mystery about her lack of creation? And why should melodrama be expected to "derive" from comedy? And what is it that makes the absence of a woman's mother a scene of comedy and the presence of her mother a scene of melodrama? And – perhaps above all – what kinds of questions are these? Philosophical? Psychoanalytic? Historical? Aesthetic? If, as I hope, one would like to answer "All of these!" then one will want to say how it is that the same questions can belong to various fields that typically, in our culture, refuse to listen to one another.

The questions express further regions of what I called the intellectual debts incurred in writing *Pursuits of Happiness*, ones I had the luxury then of mostly leaving implicit. The debt I have worked on most explicitly in the past several years concerns the ideas of the diurnal, and of eternal repetition, and of the uneventful, as interpretations of the ordinary or everyday.

The concept of the ordinary reaches back to the earliest of my debts in philosophy. The first essay I published that I still use – "Must We Mean What We Say?" (1958) – is a defense of so-called ordinary language philosophy as represented by the work a generation ago at Oxford of J. L. Austin and at Cambridge of the later Wittgenstein. Their work is commonly thought to represent an effort to refute philosophical skepticism, as expressed most famously in Descartes and in Hume, and an essential drive of my book *The Claim of Reason* (1979) is to show that, at least in the case of Wittgenstein, this is a fateful distortion, that Wittgenstein's teaching is on the contrary that skepticism is (not exactly true, but not exactly false either; it is) a standing threat to the human mind, that our ordinary language and its representation of the world *can* be philosophically repudiated and that it is essential to our inheritance and mutual possession of language, as well as to what inspires philosophy, that this should be so. But *The Claim of Reason*, for all its length, does not say, any more than Austin and Wittgenstein do very much to say, what the ordinary is, why natural language is ordinary, beyond saying that ordinary or everyday language is exactly not a special philosophical language and that any special philosophical language is answerable to the ordinary, and beyond suggesting that the ordinary is precisely what it is that skepticism attacks – as if the ordinary is best to be discovered, or say that in philosophy it is only discovered, in its loss. Toward the end of *The Claim of Reason*, the effort to overcome skepticism begins to present itself as the motivation of Romanticism, especially its versions in Coleridge and Wordsworth and in their American inheritors Emerson and Thoreau. In recent years I have been following up the idea that what philosophy in Wittgenstein and Austin means by the ordinary or everyday is figured in what Wordsworth means by the rustic and common and what Emerson and Thoreau mean by the today, the common, the low, the near.

But then *Pursuits of Happiness* can be seen as beginning to pay its philosophical debts even as it incurs them. I have linked its films' portrait of marriage, formed through the concepts of repetition and devotion, with what, in an essay that compares the projects of Emerson and of Thoreau with – on an opposite side of the American mind – those of Edgar Allan Poe and of Nathaniel Hawthorne, I called their opposite efforts at the interpretation of domestication, call it marriage. From this further interpretation of the ordinary (the ordinary as the domestic) the thought arises that, as in the case of literature, the threat to the ordinary that philosophy names skepticism should show up in film's favorite threat to forms of marriage, namely in forms of melodrama. This thought suggests that, since melodramas together with tragedy classically tell stories of revenge, philosophical skepticism will in return be readable as such a story, a kind of violence the human mind performs in response to its discovery of its limitation or exclusion, its rebuff by truth.

The problem of the existence of other minds is the formulation given in the Anglo-American tradition of philosophy to the skeptical question whether I can know of the existence (not, as in Descartes and in Hume, of myself and of God and of the external world, but) of human creatures other than myself, know them to be, as it were, like myself, and not, as we are accustomed to asking recently with more or less seriousness, some species of automation or alien. In *Pursuits of Happiness*, I say explicitly of only two of the comedies that they are studies of the problem of the existence of the other, but the overcoming of skeptical doubt can be found in all remarriage comedy: in *It Happened One Night* the famous blanket that empirically conceals the woman and thereby magnifies her metaphysical presence dramatizes the problem of unknownness as one of splitting the other, as between outside and inside, say between perception and imagination (and since the blanket is a figure for a film screen, film as such is opened up in the split); in *The Lady Eve* the man's not knowing the recurrence of the same woman is shown as the cause of his more or less comic, hence more or less forgivable, idiocy; in *The Awful Truth* the woman shows the all-knowing man what he does not know about her and helps him find words for it that take back the divorce; in *Adam's Rib* the famously sophisticated and devoted couple demonstrate in simple words and shows and in surrealistic ordinariness (they climb into bed with their hats on) that precisely what neither of them knows, and what their marriage is the happy struggle to formulate, is the difference between them; in *The Philadelphia Story* the man's idea of marriage, of the teaching that the woman has chosen to learn, is his willingness to know her as unknown (as he expresses it, "I'll risk it, will you?").

Other of my intellectual debts remain fully outstanding, to Freud's work before all. A beholdenness to Sigmund Freud's intervention in Western culture is hardly something for concealment, but I have until now on the whole left my commitment to it fairly implicit. This has happened not merely out of intellectual terror at Freud's achievement but in service of an idea and in compensation for a dissatisfaction I might formulate as follows: psychoanalytic interpretations of the arts in American culture have, until quite recently, on the whole been content to permit the texts under analysis not to challenge the concepts of analysis being applied to them, and this seemed to me to do injustice both to psychoanalysis and to literature (the art that has attracted most psychoanalytic criticism). My response was to make a virtue of this defect by trying, in my reading of film as well as of literature and of philosophy, to recapitulate what I understood by Freud's saying that he had been preceded in his insights by the creative writers of his tradition – that is, to arrive at a sense (it was my private touchstone for when an interpretation had gone far enough) for each text I encountered that psychoanalysis had become called for, as if called for in the history of knowledge, as if each psychoanalytic reading were charged with rediscovering the reality of psychoanalysis. This still does not seem to me an irrelevant ambition but also no longer a sufficient response in our altered environment, in which some of the most interesting and useful criticism and literary theory being produced is in decisive part psychoanalytic in inspiration, an alteration initiated for us most prominently by the past two or so decades of work in Paris and represented in this country by – to pick examples from which I have profited in recent months – Neil Hertz on the Dora case and on Freud's "The Uncanny," Shoshana Felman on Poe and on Henry James's *The Turn of the Screw*, and Eve Kosovsky Sedgwick on homophobia in *Bleak House*.[1] And now my problem has become that I am unsure whether I understand the constitution of the discourses in which this material is presented in relation to what I take philosophy to be, a constitution to which, such as it is, I am also committed. So some siting of this relation is no longer mine to postpone.

I content myself here with saying that Freud's lifelong series of dissociations of his work from the work of philosophy seems to me to protest too much and to have done harm (however necessary, and to whatever good) whose extent is only now beginning to reveal itself. I call attention to one of these dissociations in which Freud's ambivalence on the matter bleeds through. It comes in chapter 4 of *The Interpretation of Dreams*, just as he has distinguished "the operations of two psychical forces (or we may describe them as currents or systems)" (*S.E.* 4:144). Freud goes on to say: "These considerations may lead us to feel that the interpretation of dreams may enable us to draw conclusions as to the structure of our mental apparatus which we have hoped for in vain from philosophy" (145). Given that this feeling is followed up by Freud in the extraordinary chapter 7, which ends the book, a piece of theoretical speculation continuous with the early, posthumously published "Project for a Scientific Psychology," the ambiguity of the remark seems plain: it can be taken – and always is, so far as I know – to mean that our vain waiting for *philosophy* is now to be replaced by the positive work of something else, call it psychoanalysis (which may or may not be a "scientific" psychology); but the remark can equally be taken to mean that our *waiting* for philosophy is at last no longer vain, that philosophy has been fulfilled in the form of psychoanalysis. That this form may destroy earlier forms of philosophizing is no bar to conceiving of psychoanalysis as a philosophy. On the contrary, the two thinkers more indisputably recognized as philosophers who have opened for me what philosophy in our age may look like, such as could interest me – Wittgenstein in his *Philosophical Investigations* and Martin Heidegger in such a work as *What Is Called Thinking?* – have both written in declared opposition to philosophy as they received it. Heidegger has called philosophy the deepest enemy of thinking, and Wittgenstein has said that what he does replaces philosophy.

The idea of "replacing" here has its own ambiguity. It could mean what the logical positivists roughly meant, that philosophy, so far as it remains intelligible, is to become logic or science. Or it could mean what I take Wittgenstein to mean, that the impulse to philosophy and the consequences of it are to be achieved by replacing, or reconceiving, the ground or the place of the (thus preserved) activity of philosophizing. And something like this could be said to be what every original philosopher since at least Descartes and Bacon and Locke has illustrated. It is as if in Wittgenstein and in Heidegger the fate to philosophize and the fate to undo philosophizing are located as radical, twin features of the human as such. I am not choosing one sense of replacement over the other for Freud's relation to philosophy. On the contrary, my sense remains that the relation is so far ambiguous or ambivalent. Such matters are apt to be discussed nowadays in terms of Freud's preoccupation with what is called priority or originality – issues differently associated with the names of Harold Bloom and of Jacques Derrida. So it may be worth my saying that Bloom, in "Freud's Concepts of Defense and the Poetic Will," the essay of his that constituted the annual lecture to the Forum on Psychiatry and the Humanities for 1978 (published 1980), strikes me as unduly leveling matters to speak of Freud's crisis in *Beyond the Pleasure Principle* as obeying the structure of a poet's demand, against his precursors, for equal immortality. Freud's problem there was less to establish his originality or uniqueness than to determine whether the cost or curse of that *obvious* uniqueness might not itself be the loss of immortality. I find that I agree here with what I understand to be Derrida's view (of chapter 2 anyway) of *Beyond the Pleasure Principle*, that in it, and in anticipation of his own death, Freud is asking himself whether his achievement, uniquely among the sciences (or, for that matter, the arts) in being bound to the uniqueness of one man's name, is inheritable: this is the question enacted by the scenes of Freud the father and grandfather circling the *Fort/Da* game of repetition and domination, looking so much like the inheritance of language itself, of selfhood itself. What is at stake is whether psychoanalysis is inheritable – one may say repeatable – as science is inheritable, our modern paradigm for the teachable. If psychoanalysis is not thus inheritable, it follows that it is not exactly a science. But the matter goes beyond this question. If psychoanalysis is not exactly (what we mean by) a science, then its intellectual achievement may be lost to humankind. But if this expresses Freud's preoccupation in *Beyond the Pleasure Principle* and elsewhere, then the preoccupation links his work with philosophy, for it is in philosophy that the question of the loss of itself is internal to its faithfulness to itself.

This claim reveals me as one of those for whom the question whether philosophy exists sometimes seems the only question philosophy is bound to, that to cease caring what philosophy is and whether it exists – amid whatever tasks and in whatever forms philosophy may appear in a given historical moment – is to abandon philosophy, to cede it to logic or to science or to poetry or to politics or to religion. That the question of philosophy is the only business of philosophy is the teaching I take from the works of Wittgenstein and of Heidegger that I have claimed the inheritance of. The question of inheritance, of continued existence, appears in their work as the question whether philosophy can be taught, or, say, the question how thinking is learned, the form the question takes in *Beyond the Pleasure Principle*. It is perhaps primarily for this reason that my philosophical colleagues in the Anglo-American profession of philosophy still, on the whole (of course, there are exceptions), hold Wittgenstein or Heidegger at a distance, at varying distances from their conceptions of themselves.

What would be lost if philosophy, or psychoanalysis, were lost to us? One can take the question of philosophy as the question whether the life of reason is (any longer) attractive and recognizable, or as the question whether by my life I can and do affirm my existence in a world among others, or whether I deny this – of myself, of others, and of the world. It is some such question that Nietzsche took as the issue of what he called nihilism, a matter in which he had taken decisive instruction from Ralph Waldo Emerson. I persist, as indicated, in calling the issue by its, or its ancestor's, older name of skepticism, as I persist in thinking that to lose knowledge of the human possibility of skepticism means to lose knowledge of the human, a possibility I envision in *The Claim of Reason*, extending a problematic of Wittgenstein's, under the title of soul-blindness.

It is from a perspective in which our culture appears as having entered on a path of radical skepticism (hence on a path to deny this path) from the time of, say, Descartes and Shakespeare – or, say, from the time of the fall of Kings and the rise of the new science and the death of God – that I see, late in this history, the advent of psychoanalysis as the place, perhaps the last place, in which the human psyche as such (the idea that there is a life of the mind, hence a death) receives its proof. And it receives proof of its existence in the only form in which that psyche can (any longer) believe it – namely, as essentially unknown to itself, say unconscious. As Freud puts it in the closing pages of *The Interpretation of*

Dreams: "The unconscious is the true psychical reality" (*S.E.* 5:613). This can seem a piece of mere rhetoric on Freud's part, arbitrarily underrating the reality of consciousness and promoting the unconscious out of something like a prejudice that promotes the reality of atomic particles over the reality of flesh and blood and its opposable things – and certainly on less, or no, compelling intellectual grounds. Whereas, seen in its relation to, or as a displacement of, philosophy, Freud's assertion declares that for the mind to lose the psychoanalytic intuition of itself as unconscious would be for it to lose the knowledge that it exists. (One may feel here the need for a dialectical qualification or limitation: this loss of proof, hence of human existence, is specific to the historical and political development in which the individual requires such a proof before, as it were, his or her own eyes, a private proof. The question may then be open whether, in a further development, the proof might be otherwise possible, say, performed before the answering heart of a community. But in that case, would such a proof be necessary? Would philosophy?)

How easy this intuition is to lose (the mind's [psychoanalytic] intuition of its existence as unconscious), how hard the place of this intuition is to find – the place of the proof of existence constituted in the origin of psychoanalysis as a fulfillment of a philosophy – is emblematized by how obscure this or any relation of philosophy and psychoanalysis is to us, an obscurity our institutions of learning serve to enforce. (I do not just mean that psychoanalysis is on the whole not a university subject and only questionably should become one; I mean as well that philosophy is, or should become, only questionably such a subject.)

The tale to be told here is as yet perhaps untellable by us and for us in America – the tale of Freud's inheritance (inescapable for an ambitious student of German culture of Freud's time) of the outburst of thinking initiated by Kant and then developed continuously by Fichte, Schelling, Hegel, Schopenhauer, and Nietzsche. One possible opening passage of this story is from the same closing pages I was just citing from *The Interpretation of Dreams:* "What I . . . describe is not the same as the unconscious of the philosophers" (*S.E.* 5:614). "In its innermost nature it [i.e., psychical reality, the unconscious] is as much unknown to us as the reality of the external world, and it is as incompletely presented by the data of consciousness as is the external world by the communications of our sense organs" (*S.E.* 5:613). Freud allows himself to dismiss what he calls "the unconscious of the philosophers" (no doubt referring to what some philosophers have referred to with the word "unconscious") without allowing himself to recognize that his connecting in the same sentence the innermost nature of psychic reality and the innermost nature of external reality as equally, and hence apparently for the same reasons, unknown, is pure Kant, as Freud links the unknown ground of both inner and outer to a realm of an unconditioned thing-in-itself, which Kant virtually calls the It (he spells it X) (cf. *Critique of Pure Reason*, A109).[2]

Kant's linking of the inner and the outer sounds like this: "The conditions of the *possibility of experience* in general are at the same time the *possibility of the objects of experience*" (A158, B197). Heidegger, in *What Is Called Thinking?*, quotes this passage from Kant and from it in effect rapidly derives the tradition of German so-called Idealism. He adduces some words of Schelling, in which the pivot of inner and outer sounds this way: "In the final and highest instance, there is no being other than willing. Willing is primal being and to [willing] alone belong all [primal being's] predicates: being unconditioned, eternity, independence of time, self-affirmation. All philosophy strives only to find this highest expression" (90–1). The predicates of being unconditioned and of independence of time will remind us of Freud's predicates of the unconscious. Schelling's lectures in Berlin in 1841 were, as noted in Karl Lowith's *From Hegel to Nietzsche*, attended by Engels, Bakunin, Kierkegaard, and Burckhardt. And 1841 is also the year of Emerson's first volume of essays. It sounds this way: "Permanence is a word of degrees. Every thing is medial" (404). "It is the highest power of divine moments that they abolish our contritions also . . . for these moments confer a sort of omnipresence and omnipotence, which asks nothing of duration, but sees that the energy of the mind is commensurate with the work to be done, without time. . . . I unsettle all things . . . I simply experiment" ("Circles," 411–12).

Compared with the philosophical culture of Schelling's audience, Emerson's mostly had none; yet his philosophizing was more advanced than Schelling's – if Nietzsche's is (since Emerson's transcendental realm is not fixed, the direction or height of the will is in principle open). Heidegger claims for his quotation from Schelling that it is the classic formulation of the appearance of metaphysics in the modern era, an appearance that is essential "to understand[ing] that – and how – Nietzsche from the very start thinks of revenge [the basis of nihilism] and the deliverance from revenge in metaphysical terms, that is, in the light of Being which determines all beings" (90). However remote the fate of such a claim may seem to us here and now, it will, if nothing else, at any time stand between us and our desire, however intermittent, yet persistent, for an exchange with contemporary French thought; since Heidegger's interpretation of Nietzsche is one determinant of the Paris of, say, Derrida's Plato and Rousseau and of Lacan's Freud. (It may be pertinent to cite the effort in recent decades to bring Freud within the orbit of German philosophizing, in particular within that of Heidegger's thought, an effort made by the existential-analytic movement [*Daseinsanalyse*]. This is not the time to try to assess that effort, but I may just note that my emphasis on Freud as, so to speak, an immediate heir of German classical philosophy implies that establishing his relation to philosophy does not require mediation [or absorption] by Heidegger. The point of this emphasis is that Freud's is to be understood as an alternative inheritance, a competing inheritance, to that of Heidegger's. Otherwise, Freud's *breaking* with philosophy, his [continued] subjection to it and its subjection to him, will not get clear. Then Wittgenstein's is a third inheritance, or path, from Kant.)[3]

In these paths of inheritance, Freud's distinction is to have broken through to a practice in which the Idealist philosophy, the reigning philosophy of German culture, becomes concrete (which is roughly what Marx said socialism was to accomplish). In Freud's practice, one human being represents to another all that that other has conceived of humanity in his or her life and moves with that other toward an expression of the conditions that condition that utterly specific life. It is a vision and an achievement quite worthy of the most heroic attributes Freud assigned himself. (And it is perhaps the vision that most intuitively backs my thought that Freud's claim to philosophy lies not [directly] in his sympathy with science and its philosophy but in his struggle with, or against, German Idealism.) But psychoanalysis has not surmounted the obscurities of the philosophical problematic it inherits of representation and reality. Until it stops shrinking from philosophy (from its own past), it will continue to shrink before the derivative question, for example, of whether the stories of its patients are fantasy merely or (also?) of reality, and it will continue to waver between regarding the question as irrelevant to its work and as of the essence of it.

It is hardly enough to appeal here to conviction in reality, because the most untutored enemy of the psychological, as eagerly as the most sophisticated enemy, will inform you that conviction is one thing, reality another. The matter is to express the intuition that fantasy shadows anything we can understand reality to be. As Wittgenstein more or less puts an analogous matter: the issue is not to explain how grammar and criteria allow us to relate language to the world but to determine what language relates the world to be. This is not well expressed as the priority of mind over reality or of self over world (as, among others, Bloom expresses it [1980, 7]. It is better put as the priority of grammar – the thing Kant calls conditions of possibility (of experience and of objects), the thing Wittgenstein calls possibilities of phenomena – over both what we call mind and what we call the world. If we call grammar the Logos, we will more readily sense the shadow of fantasy in this picture.

From the reassociation of psychoanalysis with philosophy in its appearance on the stage of skepticism, as the last discoverer of psychic reality (the latest discoverer, its discoverer late in the recession of that reality), I need just two leaps in order to get to the interpretation I envision of the moment I began with from *Letter from an Unknown Woman*. The two leaps I can represent as questions that together have haunted the thoughts I am reporting on here. The first is: Why (granted the fact) does psychic reality first present itself to psychoanalysis – or, why does psycho-analysis first realize itself – through the agency (that is, through the suffering) of women, as reported in the *Studies on Hysteria* and in the case of Dora, the earliest of the longer case histories? The second question is: How, if at all, is this circumstance related to the fact (again, granted the fact) that film – another invention of the last years of the nienteenth century, developing its first masterpieces within the first decades of the twentieth century – is from first to last more interested in the study of individual women than of individual men? Men are, one could say, of interest to it in crowds and in mutual conflict, but it is women that bequeath psychic depth to film's interests. (It is to my mind a question whether certain apparently obvious exceptions [Chaplin, Keaton, Gary Cooper, for example] are exceptions to the contrast with the masculine.) My conviction in the significance of these questions is a function, not surprisingly, of my speculations concerning skepticism, two junctures of it especially. The one is a result of my study of Shakespeare's tragedies and romances as elaborations of the skeptical problematic; the other concerns the role of the human body in the skeptical so-called problem of other minds. I will say something about each of these junctures.

Since we are about to move into speculations concerning differences in the knowing of women from that of the knowing of men, I just note in passing that I am not leaping to but skipping over the immensely import-ant matter of determining how it is that the question of sexual difference turns into a question of some property that men are said to have that women lack, or perhaps vice versa – a development that helps to keep us locked into a compulsive uncertainty about whether we wish to affirm or to deny difference between men and women. As *Adam's Rib* ends, Tracy and Hepburn are joking about this vulgar error of looking for a *thing* that differentiates men and women. (It is my claim that they are joking; it is commoner, I believe, to assume – or imagine, or think, or opine – that they are perpetuating this common error. Here is a neat touchstone for assessing the reception of these comedies; perhaps their endings form the neatest set of such touchstones.)

In Lacan, the idea of the phallus as signifier is not exactly a laughing matter. The reification, let me put it, of sexual difference is registered, in the case of knowledge, by finding the question of a difference in mas-culine and feminine knowing to turn into a question of some fixed way women know that men do not know, and vice versa. Since in ordinary, nonmetaphysical exchanges we do not conceive there to be some fact one gender knows that the other does not know, any more than we conceive there to be some fact the skeptic knows that the ordinary human being does not know, the metaphysical exchanges concerning their differences are apt to veer toward irony, a sense of incessant false position, as if one cannot know what difference a world of difference makes. No one exactly denies that human knowledge is imperfect; but then how does that become the skeptic's outrageous removal of the world as such? No one exactly denies that there are differences between men and women; but then how does that become an entire history of outrage? It is from this region that one must expect an explanation for climactic passages of irony that characterize the melodrama of the unknown woman.

When in *Blonde Venus* Marlene Dietrich hands a derelict old woman the cash her husband has handed her, repeating to the woman, in raging mockery, the self-pitying words her husband had used to her in paying her back, to be quits with her, the money she had earlier given him to save his life, the meanness of the man's gesture is branded on his character. When toward the end of *Letter from an Unknown Woman* the man calls out smoothly to the woman, whose visit he interprets as a willingness for another among his endless dalliances, having disappeared to get some champagne, "Are you lonely out there?" and she, whose voice-over tells that she came to offer her life to him, replies, mostly to the camera, that is, to us, "Yes. Very lonely," she has taken his charming words as her cue for general death.

The state of irony is the negation, hence the equivalent in general consequence, of the state of conversation in remarriage comedy. Some feminists imagine that women have always spoken their own language, undetected by men; others argue that women ought to develop a language of their own. The irony in the melodrama of unknownness develops the picture, or figuration, for what it means idiomatically to say that men and women, in denying one another, do not speak the same language. I am not the only male of my acquaintance who knows the victimization in this experience, of having conversation negated, say, by the male in others. The finest description known to me of ironic, systematic incomprehension is Emerson's, from "Self-Reliance": "Well, most men have bound their eyes with one or another handkerchief and attached themselves to some one of these communities of opinion. This conformity makes them not false in a few particulars, authors of a few lies, but false in all particulars. Their every truth is not quite true. Their two is not the real two [as in the idea of two genders? or of just two Testaments?]; their four is not the real four [as in the idea of four corners of the earth? or of just four Gospels?]: so that every word they say chagrins us, and we know not where to begin to set them right" (264).

The first of my concluding leaps or questions about the origination of psychoanalysis and of film in the sufferings of women concerns the most theoretically elaborated of the studies I have so far produced of Shakespeare, on *The Winter's Tale*. It has raised unforgettably for me, I might say traumatically, the possibility that philosophical skepticism is inflected, if not altogether determined, by gender, by whether one sets oneself aside as male or female. And if philosophical skepticism is thus inflected then, according to me, philosophy as such will be. The issue arises as follows: Leontes obeys the structure of the skeptical problematic in the first half of *The Winter's Tale* as perfectly as his forebear Othello had done, but in the later play jealousy, as an interpretation of skeptical, world-removing doubt, is a cover story not for the man's fear of female desire (as Othello's story is) but for his fear of female fecundity, represented in Leontes's doubt that his children are his. Leontes's story has figured in various talks of mine in the past two or three years, and more than once a woman has afterward said to me in effect: If what Cartesian skepticism requires is the doubt that my children are mine, count me out. It is not the only time the surmise has crossed my mind that philosophical skepticism, and a certain denial of its reality, is a male business; but from the dawning of *The Winter's Tale* on me the business seems to me to be playing a role I know I do not fathom in every philosophical move I make. (It is the kind of answer I can contribute to the question who or what Shakespeare is to say that it is commonly in texts associated with this name that the bearing of a philosophical issue, or rather the issue of modern philosophy, is established.)

From the gender asymmetry here it should not be taken to follow that women do not get into the way of skepticism, but only that the passion of doubt may not express a woman's sense of separation from others or that the object of doubt is not representable as a doubt as to whether your children are yours. The passion is perhaps another form of fanaticism, as in part Leontes's is. (*Letter from an Unknown Woman* suggests that the fanaticism is of what you might call love.) And the object of doubt might be representable as one directed not toward the question of one's children but toward the question of the father of one's children.

(This is the pertinence of Kleist's *The Marquise of O*, the main reason in its content for what I called its specialness in relation to the melodrama of unknownness.) But how can one know and show that this other passion and this other object create equivalents or alternatives to masculine skepticism?

It is at this juncture of the skeptical development that psychoanalysis and cinema can be taken as asking of the woman: How is it that you escape doubt? What certainty encloses you, whatever your other insecurities, from just this torture? At an early point in my tracking of the skeptic, I found myself asking: Why does my search for certainty in knowing the existence of the other, in countering the skeptic's suspicion concerning other minds, come to turn upon whether I can know what the other *knows?* So the formulation of what we want from the woman as an access to her knowledge would record the skeptical provenance of the woman's presence at the origin of psychoanalytic and of cinematic discovery. But then we must allow the question: But *who* is it who wants to know? A natural answer will be: The man wants the knowledge. This answer cannot be wrong; it is the answer feminists may well give to Freud's handling of the case of the woman he called Dora. But the answer might be incomplete.

This is the point at which two sources of material bearing on psychoanalysis and feminism warrant being prominently brought into play, which I can now barely name. The first is represented in two texts of Jacques Lacan's entitled "God and the *Jouissance* of the Woman" and "A Love Letter," which when I came upon them twelve months ago struck me at several points as having uncanny pertinence to the considerations that arise here. When Lacan announces, "There is no such thing as The woman" (144) (sometimes paraphrased or translated as "The woman does not exist" [137]) I was bound to ask myself whether this crossed the intuition I have expressed as the task of the creation of the woman. I find that some of Lacan's followers react to the remark as obvious and as on the side of what women think about themselves, while others deny this reaction. I take it to heart that Lacan warns that more than one of his pupils have "got into a mess" (144) about the doctrines of his in which his view of the woman is embedded; clearly I do not feel that I can negotiate these doctrines apart from the painful positions I am unfolding here.

My hesitations over two further moments in Lacan's texts – moments whose apparent pertinence to what I am working on strikes me too strongly to ignore – are hesitations directed less to my intellectual difficulties with what is said than to the attitude with which it is said. When Lacan says, "I believe in the *jouissance* of the woman in so far as it is something more" (147), he is casting his view of women as a creed or credo ("I believe"), as an article of faith in the existence and the difference of the woman's satisfaction. So he may be taken as saying: What there is (any longer?) of God, or of the concept of the beyond, takes place in relation to the woman. It matters to me that I cannot assess the extent or direction (outward or inward) of Lacan's mock heroism, or mock apostlehood here, since something like this belief is in effect what I say works itself out, with gruesome eloquence, in the case of Othello, who enacts Descartes's efforts to prove that he is not alone in the universe by placing a finite, feminine other in the position assigned by Descartes to God. Moreover, letting the brunt of conviction in existence, the desire of the skeptical state, be represented by the question of the woman's orgasm, is an interpretation of Leontes's representation of the state of skepticism by the question of the woman's child (following a familiar equation in Freud's thinking of the production of the child with the form of female sexual satisfaction, an equation present in Shakespeare's play). So skeptical grief would be represented for the man not directly by the question "Were her children caused by me?" but by the double question "Is her satisfaction real and is it caused by me?'

The other source of material (still within my first leap) that I can do little more than name here is the excellent collection of essays, subtitled *Freud-Hysteria-Feminism* (C. Bernheimes and C. Kahane, eds, *In Dora's Case*; New York: Columbia University Press, 1985), on the Dora case. Here I lift up one consideration that speaks to both of the leaps or questions at hand: How does the problem of knowing the existence of the other come to present itself as knowing what the other knows? And: Who is it who wants to know of the woman's existence? The former seems – in the light of the Dora collection – a way of asking what the point is of the "talking cure" (the name of psychoanalytic therapy that Anna O., the woman whose case was reported by Breuer in *Studies on Hysteria*, was the first to use); and the answer to the latter seems routinely assumed to be Freud the man. The contributors to the volume are about equally divided between men and women, and it seems to me that while the men from time to time are amazed or appalled by Freud's assaults upon Dora's recitations, the women, while from time to time admiring, are uniformly impatient with Freud the man. The discussions are particularly laced with dirty talk, prompted generally by Freud's material and drawn particularly by a remark of Lacan's on the case in which, in an ostentatious show of civilization, he coolly questions the position of the partners in Freud's fantasy of Dora's fantasy of oral intercourse. It is in their repetition of Lacan's question, not now coolly but accusingly, that the women's impatience is clearest; it is a kind of structural impatience. To talk to Freud about his talking cure is to be caught up in the logic expressed by Lacan (in "A Love Letter") in the formula: "Speaking of love is in itself a *jouissance*." Feeling the unfairness in thus being forced to talk love to Freud, a woman may well accuse him of ignorance in his designs upon Dora, upon her knowledge, not granting him the knowledge that his subject is the nature of ignorance of exactly what cannot be ignored. She may well be right.

The consideration I said I would lift from the discussions of Dora takes on the detail of Freud's choice of the fictitious name Dora in presenting his case. Freud traces his choice to the paradigm of a change of name his sister had required of, and chosen for, her maidservant. The women represented in this collection on the whole use this information to accuse

Freud of treating the woman he called Dora like a servant, of thus taking revenge on her for having treated him in this way. It is an angry interpretation, which seeks to turn the tables on the particular brilliance Freud had shown in calling Dora's attention to her angry treatment of him in announcing her termination of treatment by giving him two weeks' notice. A less impatient interpretation would have turned Freud's act of naming around again, taking it not as, or not alone as, a wish to dominate a woman, but as a confession that he is thinking of himself in the case through an identification with his sister. As if the knowledge of the existence of a woman is to be made on the basis of already enlisting oneself on that side.

This takes me to the other of my concluding leaps or questions, now concerning not generally the genderedness of the skeptical problematic, but specifically concerning the role of the body in the problem of other minds. To counter the skeptical emphasis on knowing what the other doubts and knows, I have formulated my intuition that the philosophical recovery of the other depends on determining the sense that the human body is expressive of mind, for *this* seems to be what the skeptic of other minds directly denies, a denial prepared by the behaviorist sensibility in general. Wittgenstein is formulating what behaviorism shuns – and so doubtless inviting its shunning of him – in his marvelous remark: "The human body is the best picture of the human soul" (178). One can find some such idea expressed in the accents of other thinkers – for example, in Hegel's *Philosophy of Fine Art*: "The Human shape is the sole sensuous phenomenon that is appropriate to mind" (186); or again in Emerson's essay "Behavior": "Nature tells every secret once. Yes, but in man she tells it all the time, by form, attitude, gesture, mien, face and parts of the face, and by the whole action of the machine" (1039). Freud is expressing the idea in one of his reasonably measured, yet elated, Hamlet-like recognitions of his penetration of the secrets of humanity. In the middle of his writing of the Dora case he turns aside to say: "He that has eyes to see and ears to hear may convince himself that no mortal can keep a secret. If his lips are silent, he chatters with his finger-tips; betrayal oozes out of him at every pore" (*S.E.* 7:77–8). Freud's twist on the philosophers here is registered in his idea of our expressions as betraying ourselves, giving ourselves (and meaning to give ourselves) away – as if, let us say, the inheritance of language, of the possibility of communication, inherently involves disappointment with it and (hence) subversion of it.

Expression as betrayal comes out particularly in Freud's phrase from his preceding paragraph, in which he describes one of what he calls Dora's "symptomatic acts" as a "pantomimic announcement" (specifically in this case, an announcement of masturbation). Freud and Breuer had earlier spoken of the more general sense of human behavior as pantomimic – capable of playing or replaying the totality of the scenes of hidden life – in terms of the hysteric's "capacity for conversion," "a psycho-physical aptitude for transposing very large sums of excitation into the somatic innervation" ("The Neuro-Psychoses of Defence," *S.E.* 3:50), which is roughly to say, a capacity for modifying the body as such rather than allowing the excitation to transpose into consciousness or to discharge into practice. While this capacity is something possessed by every psycho-physical being – that is, primarily human beings – a particular aptitude for it is required for a given sufferer to avail herself or himself of hysteria over other modes of symptom formation, as in obsessions or phobias. The aptitude demands, for example, what Freud calls "somatic compliance," together with high intelligence, a plastic imagination, and hallucinatory "absences," which Anna O. (in *Studies on Hysteria*) taught Breuer to think of as her "private theater."

It seems to me that Freud describes the aptitude for hysterical conversion with special fascination – as if, for example, the alternative choice of obsession were, though no less difficult to fathom, psychologically rather undistinguished. (See, for example, "The Neuro-Psychoses of Defence," *S.E.* 3:51.) Breuer and Freud's most famous statement of the matter, in their "Preliminary Communication" of 1893, is: "Hysterics suffer mainly from reminiscences," a statement to be taken in the light of the insistence that hysterical motor symptoms "can be shown to have an original or long-standing connection with traumas, and stand as symbols for them in the activities of the memory" ("Frau Emmy von N.," *S.E.* 2:95). Hysterical symptoms are "mnemonic symbols," where this means that they bear some mimetic allegiance to their origins. Freud will say fifteen years later, in the "Rat Man" case, that "the leap from a mental process to a somatic innervation – hysterical conversion . . . can never be fully comprehensible to us" (*S.E.* 10: 157), a claim I find suspicious coming from him, as though he wishes sometimes to appear to know less than he does, or feels he does, about the powers of women.

In place of an argument for this, I offer as an emblem for future argument the figure of the woman who on film may be understood to have raised "the psycho-physical aptitude for transposing . . . large sums of excitation into the somatic innervation" to its highest art; I mean Greta Garbo, I suppose the greatest, or the most fascinating, cinematic image on film of the unknown woman. (Perhaps I should reassure you of my intentions here by noting that Freud's sentence following the one I just repeated about the psycho-physical aptitude in question begins: "This aptitude does not, in itself, exclude psychical health" [*S.E.* 3:50].) It is as if Garbo has generalized this aptitude beyond human doubting – call this aptitude a talent for, and will to, communicate – generalized it to a point of absolute expressiveness, so that the sense of failure to know her, of her being beyond us (say visibly absent) is itself the proof of her existence. (The idea of absolute expressiveness locates the moment in the history of skepticism at which such a figure appears as the moment I characterize in *The Claim of Reason* as the anxiety of inexpressiveness.)

This talent and will for communication accordingly should call upon the argument of hysteria for terms in which to understand it. In Garbo's most famous postures in conjunction with a man, she looks away or beyond or through him, as if in an absence (a distance from him, from the present), hence as if to declare that this man, while the occasion of her passion, is surely not its cause. I find (thinking specifically of a widely reprinted photograph in which she has inflected her face from that of John Gilbert's, her eyes slightly raised, seeing elsewhere) that I see her *jouissance* as remembering something, but, let me say, remembering it from the future, within a private theater, not dissociating herself from the present moment, but knowing it forever, in its transience, as finite, from her finitude, or separateness, as from the perspective of her death. As if she were herself transformed into a mnemonic symbol, a monument of memory. (This would make her the opposite of the femme fatale she is typically said – surely in defense against her knowledge – to be.) What the monument means to me is that a joyful passion for one's life contains the ability to mourn, the acceptance of transience, of the world as beyond one – say, one's other.

Such in my philosophy is the proof of human existence that, on its feminine side, as conceived in the appearance of psychoanalysis, it is the perfection of the motion picture camera to provide.

Here I come upon my epilogue, and a man's hands over his eyes, perhaps to ward off a woman's returning images. *Letter from an Unknown Woman* is the only film in our genre of melodrama that ends with the woman's apparent failure; but as in *Gaslight*, her failure perfectly shadows what the woman's success in this genre of human perplexity has to overcome: the failure here is of a woman's unknownness to prove her existence to a man, to become created by a man; a tale the outcome of which is not the transcendence of marriage but the collapse of a fantasy of remarriage (or of perpetual marriage), perhaps in favor of a further fantasy, of revenge, of which the one we see best is a screen; a tale in which the woman remains mute about her story, refusing it both to the man and to the world of woman; and a tale in which the characters' perspective of death is not to know forever the happiness of one's own life but finally to disown it, to live the death of another (as they have lived the other's life). (For some this will establish the necessity of psychology; for others, the necessity of politics; for others, the need of art.)

A reading of the film, in the context I have supplied here, might directly begin with the marks of these fantasies, of their negations of the reality, as it were, of remarriage as established in the genre that explores remarriage. For example, the woman in Ophuls's film is shown to be created through metamorphosis, not, however, by or with the man, but for him, privately – as her voice-over tells him (and us) posthumously: "From that moment on I was in love with you. Quite consciously I began to prepare myself for you. I kept my clothes neater so that you wouldn't be ashamed of me. I took dancing lessons; I wanted to become more graceful, and learn good manners – for you. So that I would know more about you and your world, I went to the library and studied the lives of the great musicians." What is causing this vortex of ironies, the fact of change or the privacy of it? The idea that woman's work is not to converse with men but to allure them is hardly news, and it is laid out for observation in Ophuls's work, in his participation in the world of fashion and glamour. That the intimacy of allure exactly defeats the intimacy of conversation is a way to put the cause of irony in the film, not alone its incessance in its closing sequences ("Are you lonely out there?") but also at the beginning of their reencounter, as the woman tracks the man back in Vienna until he notices her. He says, "I ought to introduce myself" and she interrupts with, "No. I know who you are" – a remark that could not be truer or more false.

Privacy and irony are in turn bound up in the film with the theme and structure of repetitions. Again this feature here negates its definitive occurrences in remarriage comedy, where repetitiveness is the field of inventiveness, improvisation, of the recurrence of time, open to the second chance; in (this) melodrama time is transient, closed, and repetition signals death – whether the repetition is of its camera movements (for example, the famous ironic repetition of the girl's waiting and watching on the stairs) or its words ("I'll see you in two weeks, two weeks") or its imagery (the woman's denial of chance and her weddedness to fate is given heavy symbolization in the film's endless iteration of iterated iron bars, which become less barriers against this woman's desire than the medium of it). Passing these essential matters, the moment I close with is also one of ironic repetition, and I ask of the woman's returning images: Why are they death-dealing?

Of course, they must make the man feel guilt and loss; but the question is why, for a man whose traffic has been the sentiments of remorse and loss, the feeling this time is fatal. Surely it has to do with the letter itself, beginning as from the region of death ("By the time you read this I may be dead") and ending in the theme of nostalgia ("If only . . . if only . . ."). And, of course, it has to do with the fact that there is a double letter, the depicted one that ends in a broken sentence, and the one that depicts this one, the one bearing the title *Letter from an Unknown Woman*, this film that ends soon but distinctly after, narrated from the beginning, it emerges, by the voice of a dead woman, ghost-written. The implication is somehow that it is the (ghost) woman who writes and sends the film. What can this mean? That the author of the film is a question for the film is suggested when the man says to his mute servant, who enters as the man has finished reading the letter, "You knew her," and the servant nods and writes a name on a page on the desk on which the letter lies, by the feeling that the servant is signing the letter, and hence the film. No doubt Ophuls is showing his hand here, breaching and so declaring, as it were, his muteness as a director, as if declaring that directing (perhaps composing of any kind) is constantly a work of breaching muteness (how fully, and how well timed, are further questions). But this cannot deny that it is a woman's letter he signs, assigns to himself as a writer, a letter explicitly breaching, hence revealing, muteness.

Moreover, the letter already contained a signature, on the letterhead of the religious order in whose hospital the unknown woman died, of someone styled "Sister-in-charge." Whether or not we are to assume that this is the same locale to which the unknown woman had gone to be delivered anonymously of her and the man's child, her connection with the religious order happens in front of our eyes, as she leaves the train platform after rushing to see the man off for a hastily remembered concert tour. Walking directly away from us, she gradually disappears into blackness at the center of the vacant screen, upon which, at what we might project as her vanishing point, there is a rematerialization, and the figure of the woman is replaced by, or transformed into, walking at the same pace toward us, what turns out as it comes into readable view to be a nun. So the woman is part of the world of religion, of a place apart inhabited, for all we see of it, solely by women, a world Ophuls accordingly also assigns himself, I mean his art, in signing the woman's letter. (Whether in claiming the mazed position of the feminine the actual director is manifesting sympathy with actual women or getting even with them; and whether in competing with the feminine other the director is silencing the woman's voice in order to steal it and sport its power as his (?) own; and whether positive [or negative] personal intentions could overtake the political opportunism [or political insight] of any such gesture; these are questions that I hope are open, for my own good.)

Granted that forces both lethal and vital are gathered here, and granted that the film is the medium of visible absence, I ask again how these forces, in the form of returning images, deal death. Since I mostly am not considering here the narrative conditions of the woman depicted as writing the letter, I leave aside the question whether the vengeance in this act is to be understood as endorsed or reversed in the director's counter-signing of it. I concentrate now on the sheer fact that the images return as exact moments we and the man have witnessed, or perhaps imagined, together. The present instants are mechanically identical with the past, and this form of repetition elicits its own amalgam of the strange and the familiar. I take it as a repetition that Freud cites as causing the sense of the uncanny in his essay to which he gives that title. Then this is also a title Ophuls's film suggests for the aesthetic working of film as such, an idea of some vision of horror as its basis. Freud's essay includes a reading of E. T. A. Hoffmann's romantic tale "The Sand-Man," a tale that features a beautiful automation, something not untypical of Hoffman or more generally of the romantic tale of the fantastic. Freud begins his reading by denying, against a predecessor's reading, that the uncanniness of the tale is traceable to the point in the story of "uncertainty whether an object is living or inanimate" (*S.E.* 17:230). Now that point is precisely recognizable as an issue of philosophical skepticism concerning our knowledge of the existence of other minds. But Freud insists that instead the uncanny in Hoffmann's tale is directly attached to the idea of being robbed of one's eyes, and hence, given his earlier findings, to the castration complex.

I find this flat denial of Freud's itself uncanny, oddly mechanical, since no denial is called for, no incompatible alternative is proposed: one would have expected Sigmund Freud in this context to invoke the castration complex precisely as a new explanation or interpretation of the particular uncertainty in question, to suggest it as Hoffmann's pre-psychoanalytic insight that one does not see others as other, acknowledge their (animate) human existence, until the oedipal drama is resolved under the threat of castration. (This is a step, I believe, that Jacques Lacan has taken; I do not know on what ground.) Instead Freud's, as it were, denial that the acknowledgment of the existence of others is at stake amounts, to my mind, to the denial that philosophy persists within psychoanalysis, that the psychoanalytic tracing of traumatically induced exchanges or metamorphoses of objects of love and subjects of love into and out of one another remains rooted in philosophy.

And I think we can say that when the man covers his eyes – an ambiguous gesture, between avoiding the horror of knowing the existence of others and avoiding the horror of not knowing it, between avoiding the threat of castration that makes the knowledge accessible and avoiding the threat of outcastness should that threat fail – he is in that gesture both warding off his seeing something and warding off at the same time his being seen by something, which is to say, his own existence being known, being seen by the woman of the letter, by the mute director and his camera – say, seen by the power of art – and seen by us, which accordingly identifies us, the audience of film, as assigning ourselves the position, in its passiveness and its activeness, of the source of the letter and of the film; which is to say, the position of the feminine. Then it is the man's horror of us that horrifies us – the revelation, or avoidance, of ourselves in a certain way of being feminine, a way of being human, a mutual and reflexive state, let us say, of victimization. The implications of this structure as a response to film, to art, to others, for better and for worse, is accordingly a good question. I guess it is the question Freud raises in speaking, in "Analysis Terminable and Interminable," of "the repudiation of the feminine" – which he named as the bedrock beyond which psychoanalysis cannot go. My thought is that film, in dramatizing Freud's finding, oddly opens the question for further thought.

I leave you with a present of some words from the closing paragraphs of Henry James's "The Beast in the Jungle."

The creature beneath the sod [the buried woman companion] *knew* of his rare experience, so that, strangely now, the place had lost for him its mere blankness of expression. . . . (T)his garden of death gave him the few square feet of earth on which he could still most live . . . by clear right of the register that he could scan like an open page. The open page was the tomb of his friend. . . . He had before him in sharper incision than ever the open page of his story. . . .

The name on the table smote him . . . and what it said to him, full in the face, was that *she* was what he had missed. . . . Everything fell together . . .; leaving him most of all stupefied at the blindness he had cherished. The fate he had been marked for he had met with a vengeance . . .; he had been the man of his time, *the* man, to whom nothing on earth was to have happened. . . . This horror of waking – *this* was knowledge.

James's tale in theme and quality better measures Ophuls's film than the story of Stefan Zweig's from which its screenplay was, excellently, adapted. Such is the peculiar distribution of powers among the arts.

Notes

This paper is a revised version of the Edith Weigert Lecture, sponsored by the Forum on Psychiatry and the Humanities, Washington School of Psychiatry, October 18, 1985.

1 In this connection I want to reaffirm my continuing indebtedness to the work and friendship of Michael Fried. His extraordinary book, *Realism, Writing, Disfiguration: On Thomas Eakins and Stephen Crane* (Chicago, 1987), also more explicitly relates itself to Freudian concepts than his past writing has done. I cannot forbear noting specifically, for those who will appreciate the kind of confirmation or ratification one may derive from simultaneous or crossing discoveries in writing that one admires, the

light thrown by Fried's breakthrough discussion of Stephen Crane on the passage from James's "The Beast in the Jungle" on which the present essay closes.

2 In a set of editorial notes prepared for my use, Joseph H. Smith, in responding to my claim that Freud here takes on Kant's views exactly at a point at which he wishes to distinguish the psychoanalytic idea of the unconscious from "the unconscious of the philosophers," finds that "it is inconceivable to me that Freud was unaware of being Kantian here." I am grateful, first of all, for the confirmation that the Kantian provenance of Freud's thought seems so patent. But further, as to whether Freud could in that case have been "unaware" of the provenance, I would like to propose the following: if Freud was aware of it, then his omitting of Kant's name just here, where he is explicitly dissociating himself from philosophy, is motivated, deliberate, showing an awareness that his claim to dissociation is from the beginning compromised, say ambivalent; but if, on the contrary, Freud was not aware of his Kantianism just here, say unconscious of it, then he was repressing this fact of his origin. Either of these possibilities, suppression or repression, I am regarding as fateful to the development of psychoanalysis as a field of investigation (supposing this more distinct from psychoanalysis as a therapy than it perhaps can be) and rather in support of my claim that Freud's self-interpretation of his relation to philosophy is suspicious and, contrary to what I know of its reception by later psychoanalysts, ought to be treated.

I cite one piece of positive evidence here to indicate Freud's ambivalent awareness of resistant understanding of the depth of his intellectual debt to Kant (one may press this evidence to the point of suppression or repression). Of the dozen or so references to Kant listed in the general index of the *Standard Edition*, one bears directly on whether Freud saw the Kantianism of his view of the proof and the place of the unconscious. At the end of the first section of "The Unconscious" Freud says this:

> The psycho-analytic assumption of unconscious mental activity appears to us . . . as an extension of the corrections undertaken by Kant of our views on external perception. Just as Kant warned us not to overlook the fact that our perceptions are subjectively conditioned and must not be regarded as identical with what is perceived though unknowable, so psycho-analysis warns us not to equate perceptions by means of consciousness with the unconscious mental processes which are their object. Like the physical, the psychical is not necessarily in reality what it appears to us to be. [*S. E.* 14: 171]

This expression of indebtedness to Kant precisely discounts the debt, since Kant equally "warned us" not to equate the appearance of the psychic with the reality of it, the warning Freud arrogates to psychoanalysis as an "extension" of Kant's philosophical contribution to the study of knowledge. It is the *connection* of the study of inner and outer that my paper claims is "pure Kant."

Now Freud might have meant something further in his arrogation. He might have been compressing, in his discounting of the debt to Kant, a claim to the effect that Kant did not lay out the conditions of the appearance of the inner world with the systematicness with which he laid out the conditions of the appearance of the outer world, the world of objects; in short, that Kant lacked the tools with which to elicit a system of categories of the understanding for the psyche, or the subjective, comparable to the one he elicited for the external, or the objective, world. These tools, unlike those of Aristotle that Kant deployed, came into the possession of Western thought only with psychoanalysis. Something of this sort seems to me correct. But if Freud had claimed this explicitly, hence taken on the obligation to say whether, for example, his "categories" had the same status as Kant's, then the awareness would have been inevitable that his quarrel with philosophy was necessary, was philosophy. Unawareness of his inheritance of Kant would then indeed have been inconceivable.

3 After a conversation with Professor Kurt Fischer, now at the University of Vienna, I realize that I should, even in this opening sketch of the problem of inheriting philosophy, be more cautious, or specific, in speaking of Freud's "inheritance" of classical German philosophy. I do not mean that an Austrian student in the later nineteenth century would have had just the same philosophical education as a German student of the period; nor does my claim require that Freud read so much as a page in one of Kant's works. It would have been enough for my (or Freud's) purposes for him to have received his Kant from the quotations of Kant he would have encountered in his reading of Schopenhauer. My focus – that is, in speaking here of Freud's inheritance of the German outburst – is on who Freud is, on what becomes of ideas in that mind, rather than on what, apart from a mind of that resourcefulness, German philosophy is thought to be. I assume that more or less the same ought to be said of the inheritance of German thought by that other Austrian student, Wittgenstein.

13

The Ordinary as the Uneventful

This short paper (reprinted in *Themes Out of School*) was delivered in reply to an address given by Paul Ricoeur in 1980 entitled "The Eclipse of Event in Modern French Historiography." In that address, Ricoeur equates the *Annales* historians' turning away from a history of "short-term" and high-political events (battles, successions, deaths, and marriages) with a turning away from the lives of individual human beings in favor of that of more or less anonymous collectivities. Cavell's reply contests this interpretation, suggesting that these historians are rather turning to a different conception of individual lives, and in so doing contesting an assumption about what is the most fateful influence upon such lives – events or the uneventful.

This paper exemplifies the way in which Cavell's writing can be dense with implication. In this handful of pages, he crystallizes a fundamental set of issues in the philosophy of history, and so contributes to a clarification of the grammar of a set of concepts – history, narrative, time – that are important both within that discipline and outside it. He also identifies an important parallel between the methods of the *Annales* historians and those of ordinary language philosophers, thereby establishing a sense in which yet another humanities discipline might be seen to share in the distinctively modern and modernist preoccupations of his own. And he further establishes an equation between the concept of the ordinary and that of the uneventful that brings his interests in Wittgenstein and Austin into fruitful alignment with those of Emerson and Thoreau. This brief reply to Ricoeur accordingly exemplifies Cavell's general sense that philosophy's fruitfulness lies not in its advancing theories, but in its responsiveness to the theorizing of others; philosophy progresses by holding itself open to the words and deeds of others, and returning those

About most of Professor Ricoeur's resourceful and instructive paper I will have little to say directly. Reading it has intensified my guilt in

Originally published in *Themes Out of School: Effects and Causes* (San Francisco: North Point Press, 1984), pp. 188–94. Reprinted by permission of the author.

reminding me of the years I have failed to meet summer resolutions to read more of the French historians of the *Annales* school. I console myself for my ignorance tonight with the thought that my presence here is justified by my wish first of all to participate in honoring the name of Lionel Trilling, whose work has been so nourishing to me, from the time I began searching for my way into the world of the mind; and then to salute the remarkable and growing accomplishments of Paul Ricoeur, not only for the daunting extent of them but for an inspiration in them that lends profit to professional American philosophy every day, I mean his ability to write philosophy as though the fiction that the Continental and the Anglo-American traditions of philosophy have not entered upon their lamentable course of mutual shunning. His paper tonight clearly exemplifies this ability, and on the odd ground of the philosophy of history – odd because while Anglo-American analytical philosophy has worked in the theory of history, that tradition refuses history, whether as a mode of knowledge or as a repository of knowledge, as a source of inspiration or of commitment in the remainder of philosophy. For an analyst, philosophy of science is philosophy, philosophy of language is philosophy, but philosophy of history – like philosophy of literature or philosophy of religion – is at most an application of philosophy. It is pertinent to what I will be saying to add that in recent years my anguish over the rift between the traditions of philosophy has been succeeded or joined by an anguish over the inability of American philosophy to inherit the writing of Emerson and Thoreau – which means that a rift between cultures has been succeeded or joined in my mind by a sense of rift within one culture – hence within culture itself, as I have inherited it.

Ricoeur apparently does not quarrel with the craft of history as practiced by historians associated with *Annales*, but only with their self-understanding of their craft, especially with their antipathy toward something they refer to as events, their understanding of themselves in opposition to a traditional history characterized as, or so far as it can justly be characterized as, a history of events. Ricoeur seeks to show that there is a way to understand or to extend the concept of event so that the *Annales* historians can be seen themselves to be talking about events. His argument here, in outline, is that the writing of history cannot fully escape narrative discourse, and that since this discourse requires the concept of an event, the writing of history – if even of long time spans – cannot escape the thought of the subjects of those time spans as events.

Ricoeur cautions against taking him to be pleading for a more narrative kind of history. His idea is rather of what he calls an indirect relation of history to story. Here he follows Fernand Braudel's articulation of history into three temporal layers and then proposes that what characterizes the history of long durations as history is its relation to the history of short durations, a relation he calls "emergence." But how does Ricoeur know that the level of long durations *requires* such a provision of what he calls historical intentionality? Why does he assume that this level has no way of justifying itself as history autonomously? In his closing pages he seems to speak of his conception of the historical as related to a conception of the human being, of what it is to know a human existence. But then isn't it plausible to assume that the rival conception of history has its rival grasp of human existence? I take it that it has, and that this is something Braudel means when he speaks in his inaugural lecture to the Collège de France of narrative history as "an authentic philosophy of history,"[1] for he goes on to say: "To the narrative historians, the life of men is dominated by dramatic accidents, by the actions of those exceptional beings who occasionally emerge, and who often are the masters of their own fate and even more of ours." Braudel calls this a "first stage of history" and declares it the task of history to get beyond it – away from the "monotonous game" of intercrossing and singular destinies, toward the tackling of "the social realities in themselves and for themselves." Surely this alternative history, however briefly and polemically stated, extends its own, competing philosophy of history, a competing conception of the human being and of the knowledge of human existence. And if so then whether the levels of long span and short span are to be seen to emerge or to derive from one another, or whether each is to be understood as autonomous, depends upon confronting those philosophies of history with one another. How you conceive of history will then determine how you conceive of an event, not the other way around. Braudel's opposition is evidently to a concept of event one of whose negative features is that it theatricalizes human existence. Is the force of Ricoeur's *tu quoque* that the *Annales* historians likewise theatricalize human existence, that this is an inevitability of history's grounding in narration? If not, what assurance have we that he is speaking of the same concept?

While I have already implied that I am not in a position to elicit and assess what may be the actual contours of the *Annales* historians' self-understanding, I can still go on to do something philosophers typically do in the absence of a command of the facts: I can ask what such a self-understanding might look like, and I can do that in the guise of asking myself what I would mean if I claimed that there is a history of the human being to which we are blinded by the traditional histories of flashing, dramatic events. I can do this, moreover, by taking the opening three criteria of an event Ricoeur articulates – that it is of something past, something done by or done to human beings, and something unrepeatable – and then instead of going on to appeal with Ricoeur to the idea of narrative as placing, hence maintaining, the concept, I shall appeal to a fourth criterion of what I understand our ordinary concept of an event to be – at any rate, our concept of something we are likely to regard as an historical (as opposed say to a meteorological) event.

My fourth criterion is that an event is something to which some fairly definite public already attaches some fairly definite importance. Obvious examples are the things high schools in my day used to call current events, the things newspapers call news (as opposed, say, to human interest stories), the things that appear on calendars of events (and that will vary specifically according as the institution the calendar serves is a church, a university, or a court). (The phrase "a blessed event" is hyperbolical not because a private moment is being called blessed but because it is being called an event.)

This criterion about attaching importance seems, I believe, to note a trivial or weak feature of the concept of an event, all but negligible. If so then if it serves to elicit the self-understanding I seek, the result will be strong, since I will not have imported a prejudicial element into the concept. The self-understanding suggested by an attempt to escape or to depose events so construed would then be an attempt to escape the dictation of what it is interesting or important to think about and write history about, a dictation by the precept and example of what a fairly definite public already attaches a fairly definite importance to; a demand to let one's own discourse determine its interest for itself.

But escaping dictation seems a negative goal, saying only what these writers will try not to do. Does the idea of escaping the event contain in itself some hint as to a positive goal, saying something about what these writers are trying to do? Immediately, the turning away from events as made by exceptional individuals proposes that history turn to an interest in a different set or class of people, call them the unexceptional. Beyond this, it suggests that history, that the human being thinking historically, is *to interest itself differently* in human existence, whatever individual or class it turns its attention to.

To say how I would express this difference of interest I must make a little detour and indicate that the refusal of the dictation of importance, the wish for one's discourse to establish its own interest, points to a philosophical site which, to my mind, locates perhaps the most fruitful point of intersection of Anglo-American with Continental philosophizing. I mean the point concerning the issue of what it is worth saying, the discovery that much of what is said, especially by philosophers, i.e., by the human being philosophizing, is empty, say bankrupt, the result of speaking not meaninglessly, as the positivists used to like to say, as if words themselves had insufficient sense, but rather speaking pointlessly, as if we had nothing in mind, or nothing at heart to say. I have described this state as a mild and intermittent form of madness, of self-stupefaction. In Heidegger this is sometimes raised as a matter of what it is worth questioning (and it is worth noting in the present context that one of the guiding terms he questions in questioning Being is that of *Ereignis*, one of whose meanings is *event*); in Wittgenstein the issue is sometimes put as a matter of finding the home language game for an expression, a way of understanding its role in everyday language. For Heidegger our stupefaction results from an insufficient capacity to leave the ordinary language of everyday or average talk; for Wittgenstein – and on this point he and J. L. Austin are at one – our stupefaction results from an insufficient capacity to cleave to the everyday, which in this context may be thought of as holding on to comprehensible reasons for questioning ourselves.

It was always being said, and I believe it is still felt, that Wittgenstein's and Austin's return to ordinary language constitutes an anti-intellectual or unscientific defense of ordinary beliefs. While this is a significantly wrong idea it is hard to say what is wrong with it. I think it takes Wittgenstein's whole philosophy, at least, to say what is wrong with it, which really comes to presenting the right alternative. I will simply assert, for present purposes, that Wittgenstein's and Austin's return to ordinary or everyday language is, before anything else, a formidable attack on skepticism, epitomized by the difficult thought that it is not quite right to say that we believe the world exists (though certainly we should not conclude that we do not believe this, that we fail to believe its existence), and wrong even to say we know it exists (while of course it is equally wrong to say we fail to know this). And if one convinces oneself of the truth of such observations, it is then at issue, and much harder, to determine *what* it is right to say here, what truly expresses our convictions in our relation to the world. The idea is less to defend our ordinary beliefs than to wean us from expressing our thoughts in ways that do not genuinely satisfy us, to stop forcing ourselves to say things that we cannot fully mean. What the ordinary language philosopher is sensing – but I mean to speak just for myself in this – is that our natural relation to the world's existence is – as I sometimes wish to express it – closer, or more intimate, than the ideas of believing and knowing are made to convey. And I am for myself convinced that the thinkers who best convey this experience, or aspiration, of closeness, convey it most directly and most practically, are not such as Austin and Wittgenstein but such as Emerson and Thoreau. This sense of, let me say, my natural relation to existence is what Thoreau means by our being *next* to the laws of nature, by our *neighbouring* the world, by our being *beside* ourselves. Emerson's idea of the *near* is one of the inflections he gives to the common, the low, as in the passage from *Nature* beginning: "I ask not for the great, the remote, the romantic; what is doing in Italy or Arabia; what is Greek art, or Provençal minstrelsy; I embrace the common, I explore and sit at the feet of the familiar, the low. Give me insight into today, and you may have the antique and future worlds.'

That was my detour, meant to afford me a formulation of what I called the positive interest that a history may have whose self-understanding proposes an escape from events. Now I will say that such a history is interested not in what Ricoeur calls the *eventless*, as though it seeks, as it were, what is not happening; such a history is interested rather in the *uneventful*, seeking, so to speak, what is not out of the ordinary.

The uneventful, so conceived, is an interpretation of the everyday, the common, the low, the near; you may call it an empirical interpretation, still pre-philosophical. What is uneventful at one date and place is not the same as what is uneventful at another date and place, so that the translations of one to another may be knowable only to something we will call history. One might still maintain that there is a sense of the concept of event in which the *Annales* historians write about events indirectly; what I have wished to indicate is that there is a sense of the concept of event – apparently the sense they care about, a sense I find in what I permit myself to call our concept of event – in which they definitively do not write about events. While Ricoeur does not deny that the craft of the *Annales* historians is one that produces history, while indeed his effort can be taken as one of showing why it is history, still the most he has shown is that their craft *can* be looked at as he proposes, not that it must be. So *can* you look at human beings through the concept (perhaps extended) of a machine; that does not show that human beings are machines.

Braudel writes, in the lecture I cited a few moments ago: "There is . . . a history slower still than the history of civilizations, a history which almost stands still, a history of man in his intimate relationship to the earth which bears and feeds him; it is a dialogue which never stops repeating itself, which repeats itself in order to persist, which may and does change superficially, but which goes on, tenaciously, as though it were somehow beyond time's reach and ravages." It is not for me to say whether such a vision inspires good history, but it strikes me as expressing the thought of an ambitious philosophy. In confessing that it sounds to me like a thought of Emerson's or Thoreau's I mean to register that while the opening essay of Emerson's first volume of *Essays* is entitled "History", the position of it is an indictment of what we know as history, of what this history takes the human creature to be; and the indictment carries the implication that what *he* writes is what should be known as history: "I am ashamed to see what a shallow village tale our so-called History is. How *many* times we must say Rome, and Paris, and Constantinople! What does Rome know of rat and lizard? What are Olympiads and Consulates to these neighboring systems of being? Nay, what food or experience or succor have they for the Esquimaux seal-hunter, for the Kanàka in his canoe, for the fisherman, the stevedore, the porter?" But now we may consider that when and where Emerson was writing, under the influence of what he knew of Kant and Hegel as much as of anything else, there was little possibility of understanding history as an autonomous discourse that might investigate empirically, in its own way, those very features of the human adventure Emerson spent his life getting what he sometimes calls the meaning of; little possibility of imagining a new rapprochement between the ambitions of history and of philosophy. This is where we came in.

Note

1 In *On History*, essays of Braudel's translated by Sarah Matthews (Chicago, 1980), p. 11.

14

Words and Sentences

With this extract (which contains the whole of the first and a portion of the second chapter of *The Senses of Walden*), we begin to explore Cavell's attempts to find, in American Transcendentalism, the beginnings of an indigenous tradition of thought that is worthy of the title "philosophy." The book from which this extract is taken was Cavell's first venture in this direction; published in 1972, it has remained relatively little known – in part because its defense of Thoreau participates in the very repression of Emerson as a thinker which Cavell later repudiates, identifying it as the prime cause of the tradition's failure to get beyond its beginnings. Since, however, Cavell now takes Thoreau to be Emerson's best reader, grasping the structures of thought that he identified in this early reading of *Walden* is the best possible preparation for his later interpretations of Emerson's own essays.

The passages in this extract make it clear that Thoreau's project as a writer is essentially prophetic: he identifies his fellow-citizens as spiritually destitute, living lives of quiet desperation, and he offers his own writing as an exemplification of what will be required of them if they are to reorient themselves and become once more capable of acknowledging their experience and their lives as their own. Since Thoreau is a writer, his call to overcome skepticism takes the form of writing in ways which acknowledge the conditions of possibility of the enterprise of writing. This means composing a text that acknowledges language as shared and systematically meaningful, the supra-individual and transgenerational repository of words that can be meant by human beings; and since, as a text, it is written to be read, it must also acknowledge the position of its readers. As we will see (cf. Essay 17), the general form of this structure of diagnosis and exemplification prefigures a more detailed blueprint that Cavell sees as internal to Moral Perfectionism. In addition, Cavell's opening emphasis upon the explicitly and continuously religious register of Thoreau's prose makes it clear that he sees Moral Perfectionism as in competition with religion; it is motivated by a spiritual fervor that makes

Originally published in *The Senses of Walden* (New York: Viking Press, 1972), pp. 3–35, 46–69. Reprinted by permission of the author.

use of religious concepts, but sees traditional religious uses of those concepts as its most intimate enemy. In this sense, Moral Perfectionism is necessarily a revision or recounting of religion.

The very greatest masterpieces, when one is fresh from them, are apt to seem neglected. At such a time one knows, without stint, how unspeakably better they are than anything that can be said about them. An essential portion of the teaching of *Walden* is a full account of its all but inevitable neglect.

I assume that however else one understands Thoreau's topics and projects it is as a writer that he is finally to be known. But the easier that has become to accept, the more difficult it becomes to understand why his words about writing in *Walden* are not (so far as I know) systematically used in making out what kind of book he had undertaken to write, and achieved. It may be that the presence of his mysterious journals has too often attracted his serious critics to canvass there for the interpretation of *Walden*'s mysteries. My opening hypothesis is that this book is perfectly complete, that it means in every word it says, and that it is fully sensible of its mysteries and fully open about them.

Let us begin to read in an obvious place, taking our first bearings, and setting some standards, by looking at his explicit directions in the early chapter entitled "Reading." "The heroic books, even if printed in the character of our mother tongue, will always be in a language dead to degenerate times; and we must laboriously seek the meaning of each word and line, conjecturing a larger sense than common use permits out of what wisdom and valor and generosity we have" (III, 3).[1] This may sound like a pious sentiment, one of those sentences that old-fashioned critics or book clubs like to cite to express their high-mindedness. But it is the first step in entertaining Thoreau's intentions and ambitions to understand that he is there describing the pages he has himself readied for our hands. This may not be obvious at first, because the very extremity of his praise for what he calls "classics" and for "reading, in a high sense," together with his devotion to the "ancients," seems to imply that the making of such a book, a heroic book, in the America he depicts and in "this restless, nervous, bustling, trivial nineteenth century" (XVIII, 14), is not a feasible enterprise. But it is axiomatic in *Walden* that its author praises nothing that he has not experienced and calls nothing impossible that he has not tried. More specifically, what is read in a high sense is "what we have to stand on tiptoe to read and devote our most alert and wakeful hours to" (III, 7); and again, "There are probably words addressed to our condition exactly, which, if we could really hear and understand, would be more salutary than the morning or the spring to our lives" (III, 11). Given the appearance of morning and spring in this book, what words could be *more* salutary than these? But then, given such words in the book as, "Morning is when I am awake and there is dawn in me" (II, 14), we recognize that morning may not be caused by sunrise, and may not happen at all. To discover how to earn and spend our most wakeful hours – whatever we are doing – is the task of *Walden* as a whole; it follows that its task, for us who are reading, is epitomized in discovering what reading in a high sense is and, in particular, if *Walden* is a heroic book, what reading *Walden* is. For the writer of *Walden*, its task is epitomized in discovering what writing is and, in particular, what writing *Walden* is.

It is hard to keep in mind that the hero of this book is its writer. I do not mean that it is about Henry David Thoreau, a writer, who lies buried in Concord, Massachusetts – though that is true enough. I mean that the "I" of the book declares himself to be a writer. This is hard to keep in mind because we seem to be shown this hero doing everything under the sun but, except very infrequently, writing. It takes a while to recognize that each of his actions is the act of a writer, that every word in which he identifies himself or describes his work and his world is the identification and description of what he understands his literary enterprise to require. If this seems to reduce the stature of what he calls his experiment, that is perhaps because we have a reduced view of what such an enterprise may be.

The obvious meaning of the phrase "heroic book," supported by the mention of Homer and Virgil (III, 6), is "a book about a hero," an epic. The writer is aligning himself with the major tradition of English poetry, whose most ambitious progeny, at least since Milton, had been haunted by the call for a modern epic, for a heroic book which was at once a renewed instruction of the nation in its ideals, and a standing proof of its resources of poetry. For the first generation of Romantics, the parent generation to Thoreau's, the immediate epic event whose power their literary epic would have to absorb, was the French Revolution – the whole hope of it in their adolescence, and the scattered hopes in their maturity. The writer of *Walden* alludes to the three revolutions most resonant for his time. Of the Puritan revolution he says that it was "almost the last significant scrap of news" from England (II, 19). Why almost? We don't really need a key for this, but Thoreau provides one in an essay on Carlyle which he wrote while living at Walden: "What . . . has been English news for so long a season? What . . . of late years, has been England to us – to us who read books, we mean? Unless we remembered it as the scene where the age of Wordsworth was spending itself, and a few younger muses were trying their wings . . . Carlyle alone, since the death of Coleridge, has kept the promise of England." As against the usual views about Thoreau's hatred of society and his fancied private declaration of independence from it, it is worth hearing him from the outset publicly accept a nation's promise, identify the significant news of a nation with the state of its promise, and place the keeping of that promise in the hands of a few writers.

Of the events which keep burning on the Continent, the writer of *Walden* is apparently dismissive: "If one may judge who rarely looks into the newspapers, nothing new does ever happen in foreign parts, a French revolution not excepted" (II, 19). Marx, at about the same time, puts the point a little differently in his *Eighteenth Brumaire*, suggesting that it is only if you think like a newspaper that you will take the events of 1848 (or 1830) as front-page history; they belong on the theater page, or in the obituaries. But in *Walden*'s way of speaking, its remark also means that *the* French Revolution was not new. For example, the revolution we had here at home happened first, the one that began "two miles south" of where the writer is now sitting, on "our only field known to fame, Concord Battle Ground" (II, 10). For an American poet, placed in that historical locale, the American Revolution is more apt to constitute the absorbing epic event. Only it has two drawbacks: first, it is overshadowed by the epic event of America itself; second, America's revolution never happened. The colonists fought a war against England all right, and they won it. But it was not a war of independence that was won, because we are not free; nor was even secession the outcome, because we have not departed from the conditions England lives under, either in our literature or in our political and economic lives.

I understand the writer of *Walden* to be saying at least these things, in his way, when he announces for the second time the beginning of his "experiment": "When first I took up my abode in the woods, that is, began to spend my nights as well as days there, which, by accident, was on Independence Day, or the Fourth of July, 1845, my house was not finished for winter" (II, 8). Good and learned readers, since at least Parrington, will have such a passage behind them when they describe Thoreau as having written a "transcendental declaration of independence." But why does the writer say "by accident'? Merely to mock America's idea of what independence comes to, and at the same time ruefully admit that he is, after all, one of us? But he has been insisting on these things from the beginning. From *what* is he supposed to have declared his independence? Clearly not from society as such; the book is riddled with the doings of society. From society's beliefs and values, then? In a sense – at least independence from the way society practices those beliefs and values. But that was what America was for; it is what the original colonists had in mind.

Earlier, as an introduction to the first time we see the hero at his experiment, about to describe the building of his house, he quotes at

some length from two accounts, one contemporary and one nearly contemporary, of the first shelters the colonists made for themselves to get
them through the first winter in the world which for them was new (I, 57).
We know the specific day in the specific year on which all the ancestors of
New England took up their abode in the woods. That moment of origin is
the national event reenacted in the events of *Walden*, in order this time to
do it right, or to prove that it is impossible; to discover and settle this land,
or the question of this land, once for all. This is one reason that taking up
the abode on the Fourth of July is an accident.

Any American writer, any American, is apt to respond to that event in
one way or another; to the knowledge that America exists only in its
discovery and its discovery was always an accident; and to the obsession
with freedom, and with building new structures and forming new human
beings with new minds to inhabit them; and to the presentiment that this
unparalleled opportunity has been lost forever. The distinction of
Walden's writer on this point (shared, I suppose, by the singer of *Leaves
of Grass* and by the survivor in *Moby Dick*) lies in the constancy of this
mood upon him, his incarnation, one may call it, of this mood at once of
absolute hope and yet of absolute defeat, his own and his nation's. His
prose must admit this pressure and at every moment resolutely withstand
it. It must live, if it can, pressed between history and heaven:

> In any weather, at any hour of the day or night, I have been anxious
> to improve the nick of time, and notch it on my stick too; to stand
> on the meeting of two eternities, the past and the future, which is
> precisely the present moment; to toe that line. (I, 23)

This open acknowledgment of his mysticism, or rather of the path to it,
is also a dedication of his prose to that path. This is what "and notch it
on my stick too" means – that he is writing it down, that his writing and
his living manifest each other. The editor of *The Variorum Walden*,
Walter Harding, is surely right to refer here to Robinson Crusoe's
method of telling time; but that reference alone does not account for the
methods of *Walden*'s writer, for what he would mean by telling time, in
particular for what he means in claiming to notch not merely the passing
of time but his improvement of it. It is when the writer has just gone over
the succession of farms he had bought in imagination, and comes to his
abode in the woods, that he says, "The present was my next experiment
of this kind, which I purpose to describe more at length" (II, 7). Of
course he means that the building of his habitation (which is to say, the
writing of his book) is his present experiment. He also means what his
words say: that the present is his experiment, the discovery of the
present, the meeting of two eternities. ("God himself culminates in the

present moment" [II, 21].) The most extended moment of the book which puts together the ideas of art and of the presentness which admits eternity, is the closing parable about the artist from Kouroo, the surface of which relates those ideas to the notching of a stick.

To say that the writer reenacts the Great Migration and the inhabitation of this continent by its first settlers is not to suggest that we are to read him for literal alignments between the history of the events in his woods and in theirs. That would miss the significance of both, because the literal events of the Puritan colonization were from the beginning overshadowed by their meaning: it was itself a transcendental act, an attempt to live the idea; you could call it a transcendental declaration of freedom. (In his "Plea for Captain John Brown," Thoreau praised this man once as a Puritan and once as a Transcendentalist.) This means that the writer's claims to privacy, secrecy, and isolation are as problematic, in the achievement and in the depiction of them, as any other of his claims. The more deeply he searches for independence from the Puritans, the more deeply, in every step and every word, he identifies with them – not only in their wild hopes, but in their wild denunciations of their betrayals of those hopes, in what has come to be called their jeremiads. (This is a standing difficulty for America's critics, as for Christianity's; Americans and Christians are prepared to say worse things about their own behavior than an outsider can readily imagine.) His identification extends even to the further meaning of the migration: to perform an experiment, a public demonstration of a truth; to become an example to those from whom they departed; to build, as they said to themselves, "a city on a hill."

This is one way I understand the writer's placing himself "one mile from any neighbor." It was just far enough to be seen clearly. However closely Thoreau's own "literary withdrawal" resembles those of the Romantics, in its need for solitude and for nature, the withdrawal he depicts in *Walden* creates a version of what the Puritan Congregationalists called a member of the church's congregation: a visible saint. On this ground, the audience for the writer's words and acts is the community at large, congregated. His problem, initially and finally, is not to learn what to say to them; that could not be clearer. The problem is to establish his right to declare it.

I have come to trust *Walden* and to trust its accuracy to its intentions when it says: "If you stand right fronting and face to face to a fact, you will see the sun glimmer on both its surfaces, as if it were a cimeter, and feel its sweet edge dividing you through the heart and marrow, and so you will happily conclude your mortal career" (II, 22). I cannot say that this writing always and everywhere brings me to this conclusion. But it often does, often enough so that when it does not I am not quick to determine whether it is failing me, or I it. My subject is nothing apart from sensing the specific weight of these words as they sink; and that means knowing the specific identities of the writer through his metamorphoses, and defining the audiences in me which those identities address, and so create; and hence understanding who I am that I should be called upon in these ways, and who this writer is that he takes his presumption of intimacy and station upon himself. For someone who cannot yield to Thoreau's words, or does not find them to warrant this power to divide him through, my subject will seem empty, even grotesque. Emerson did not quite share this enthusiasm, and yet he knew as well as anyone has known how good a writer Thoreau was, as he proved in his speech at Thoreau's funeral by the sentences he chose to read from the unpublished manuscripts. But in the large of it, the writing made him, as he said to his journal, "nervous and wretched" to read. I find this response also to be accurate and essential to the reading of *Walden* – just not final. (The writer of *Walden* knows how trying his trials can be: "I sometimes try my acquaintances by such tests" [I, 35].)

How far off a final reading is, is something I hope I have already suggested. Every major term I have used or will use in describing *Walden* is a term that is itself in play within the book, part of its subject – e.g., migration, settling, distance, neighborhood, improvement, departure, news, obscurity, clearing, writing, reading, etc. And the next terms we will need in order to explain the first ones will in turn be found subjected to examination in Thoreau's experiment. The book's power of dialectic, of self-comment and self-placement, in the portion and in the whole of it, is as instilled as in Marx or Kierkegaard or Nietzsche, with an equally vertiginous spiraling of idea, irony, wrath, and revulsion. Once in it, there seems no end; as soon as you have one word to cling to, it fractions or expands into others. This is one reason that he says, "There are more secrets in my trade than in most men's . . . inseparable from its very nature" (I, 23). But we do not yet know much else about that trade.

We started thinking along one line about what the writer of *Walden* calls "heroic books"; and while I take him there to be claiming an epic ambition, the terms in which he might project such an enterprise could not be those of Milton or Blake or Wordsworth. His talent for making a poem could not withstand such terms, and the nation as a whole to which he must speak had yet to acquire it. (He knows from the beginning, for example, that his book will not come in twelve or twenty-four parts.) In Thoreau's adolescence, the call for the creation of an American literature was still at a height: it was to be the final proof of the nation's maturity, proof that its errand among nations had been accomplished, that its specialness had permitted and in turn been proved by an original intelligence. In these circumstances, an epic ambition would be the ambition to compose the nation's *first* epic, so it must represent the bringing of language to the nation, words of its own in which to receive instruction, to assess its faithfulness to its ideal. The call for a new literature came, compounding difficulties, at an inconvenient moment in English literature generally, when it was all a writer like Carlyle could do to keep alive his faith in it. John Stuart Mill, three years younger than Emerson, says in his autobiography that a Romantic poem had helped him recover from the critical depression that preceded his maturity; but once he was recovered, it was Bentham's vision, not Coleridge's, say, that elicited the devotions of a model intellectual. Matthew Arnold, five years younger than Thoreau, spent a life accommodating to his nation's loss of poetry.

According to the assumption that the chapter on reading is meant as a description of the book before us, the one the writer in it went into the woods to write, it is explicitly said to be a scripture, and the language it is written in is what its writer calls the "father tongue."

> Those who have not learned to read the ancient classics in the language in which they were written must have a very imperfect knowledge of the history of the human race; for it is remarkable that no transcript of them has ever been made into any modern tongue, unless our civilization itself may be regarded as such a transcript. Homer has never yet been printed in English, nor Aeschylus, nor Virgil even, works as refined, as solidly done, and as beautiful almost as the morning itself; for later writers, say what we will of their genius, have rarely, if ever, equaled the elaborate beauty and finish and the lifelong and heroic literary labors of the ancients. . . . That age will be rich indeed when those relics which we call Classics, and the still older and more than classic but even less known Scriptures of the nations, shall have still further accumulated, when the Vaticans shall be filled with Vedas and Zendavestas and Bibles, with Homers and Dantes and Shakespeares, and all the centuries to come shall have successively deposited their trophies in the forum of the world. By such a pile we may hope to scale heaven at last. (III, 6)

The hardest thing to understand or believe about this is that the word "scripture" is fully meant. This writer is writing a sacred text. This commits him, from a religious point of view, to the claim that its words are revealed, received, and not merely mused. It commits him, from a literary point of view, to a form that comprehends creation, fall, judgment, and redemption; within it, he will have discretion over how much poetry to include, and the extent of the moral code he prescribes; and there is room in it for an indefinite amount of history and for a small epic or two. From a critical point of view, he must be readable on various, distinct levels. *Walden* acknowledges this in a characteristic way: " 'They pretend,' as I hear, 'that the verses of Kabir have four different senses; illusion, spirit, intellect, and the exoteric doctrine of the Vedas'; but in this part of the world it is considered a ground for complaint if a man's writings admit of more than one interpretation" (XVIII, 7). (This is characteristic in its orientalizing of the mundane. There is just one text in the culture for which he writes that is known to require interpretation on four distinct levels.)

Ways in which these commitments are to be realized in *Walden* are made specific in the meaning of "father tongue."

> Books must be read as deliberately and reservedly as they were written. It is not enough even to be able to speak the language of that nation by which they are written, for there is a memorable interval between the spoken and the written language, the language heard and the language read. The one is commonly transitory, a sound, a tongue, a dialect merely, almost brutish, and we learn it unconsciously, like the brutes, of our mothers. The other is the maturity and experience of that; if that is our mother tongue, this is our father tongue, a reserved and select expression, too significant to be heard by the ear, which we must be born again in order to speak. (III, 3)

Were it not for certain current fantasies according to which human beings in our time have such things to say to one another that they must invent something beyond the words we know in order to convey them, it would be unnecessary to emphasize that "father tongue" is not a new lexicon or syntax at our disposal, but precisely a rededication to the inescapable and utterly specific syllables upon which we are already disposed. Every word the writer uses will be written so as to acknowledge its own maturity, so as to let it speak for itself; and in a way that holds out its experience to us, allows us to experience it, and allows it to tell us all it knows. "There are probably words addressed to our condition exactly, which, if we could really hear and understand, would be more salutary than the morning. . . ." There are words with our names on them – that is to say, every word in our nomenclature – but their existence is only probable to us, because we are not in a position to bring them home. In loyalty both to the rules of interpreting scripture and to the mother tongue, which is part of our condition, the writer's words must on the first level make literal or historical sense, present the brutest of fact. It is that condition from which, if we are to hear significantly, "we must be born again." A son of man is born of woman; but rebirth, according to our Bible, is the business of the father. So *Walden*'s puns and paradoxes, its fracturing of idiom and twisting of quotation, its drones of fact and flights of impersonation – all are to keep faith at once with the mother and the father, to unite them, and to have the word born in us.

Canonical forms of rebirth are circumcision and baptism. True circumcision is of the heart. It has never been very clear how that is to happen; but of course one ought not to expect otherwise: understanding such circumcision requires that you have undergone it; it is a secret inseparable from its very nature. Perhaps it will happen by a line of words so matured and experienced that you will see the sun glimmer on both its surfaces, as if it were a scimitar, and feel its sweet edge dividing you through the heart. Christ is to come with a sword, and in Revelation the sword is in his mouth, i.e., the sword is words. Of baptism, two moments are called for. The water of Walden Pond is unique, but so is every other body of water, or drop, or place; and as universal. John could have used that water in the wilderness as well as any other. The baptism of water is only a promise of another which is to come, of the spirit, by the word of words. This is immersion not in the water but in the book of Walden.

There is a more direct sense in which scripture is written in the father language: it is the language of the father, the word of God; most particularly it is spoken, or expressed, by prophets.

Then the word of the Lord came unto me, saying, Before I formed thee in the belly I knew thee; and before thou camest forth out of the womb I sanctified thee, and I ordained thee a prophet unto the nations. Then said I, Ah, Lord God! behold, I cannot speak: for I am a child.

But the Lord said unto me, Say not, I am a child: for thou shalt go to all that I send thee, and whatsoever I command thee, thou shalt speak. . . . Then the Lord put forth his hand, and touched my mouth. And the Lord said unto me, Behold, I have put my words in thy mouth. (Jeremiah 1:4–9)

It is Ezekiel who anticipates most specifically the condition of prophecy in *Walden*:

And he said unto me, Son of man, go, get thee unto the house of Israel, and speak with my words unto them. For thou art not sent to a people of a strange speech and of an hard language, but to the house of Israel; Not to many people of a strange speech and of an hard language, whose words thou canst not understand. Surely, had I sent thee to them, they would have hearkened unto thee. But the house of Israel will not hearken unto thee; for they will not hearken

unto me: for all the house of Israel are impudent and hardhearted.
(Ezekiel 3: 4–7)

The world of Ezekiel shares other particular features with the world of
Walden: its writer received his inspiration "by waters"; it is written in
captivity (what constitutes our captivity in *Walden* has yet to be out-
lined); it ends with elaborate specifications for the building of a house.

Milton, in *The Reason of Church Government*, trusted himself to identify
with the vocation of Jeremiah and of the author of Revelation in justifying
his right and his requirement to write as he did, "to claim . . . with good
men and saints" his "right of lamenting"; and he further attested to his
sincerity by announcing that in undertaking this task he was postponing
the use of his particular talent, to compose the nation's epic: " . . . to fix
all the industry and art I could unite to the adorning of my native tongue;
not to make verbal curiosities the end . . . but to be an interpreter and
relater of the best and sagest things among mine own citizens throughout
this island in the mother dialect. ["For what are the classics but the
noblest recorded thoughts of man?" (III, 3)]. That what the greatest and
choicest wits of Athens, Rome, or modern Italy, and those Hebrews of
old did for their country, I in my proportion, with this over and above of
being a Christian, might do for mine."

Do we really believe, even when it comes from John Milton, in the
seriousness of such an identification and ambition? Or do we believe it,
or tolerate it, just because it comes from Milton, who twenty-five years
later made good with *Paradise Lost* on some highest promise or other?
And if we cannot believe it, is that a skepticism about religion or about
literature? And if we may believe it about Milton, would we find it
credible that any later writer, and an American to boot, could justly, or
sanely, so aspire? Blake's placing of himself on this ground is (though
with apparently increasing exceptions) not credited. And by the time
Wordsworth finds the seer in the child, the idea of the poet-prophet can
conveniently seem to us the sheerest of Romantic conceits.

The writer of *Walden* is not counting on being believed; on the contrary, he converts the problem or condition of belief into a dominant
subject of his experiment. As I was suggesting, his very familiarity with
the fact that he will not be hearkened to, and his interpretation of it, are
immediate identifications with Jeremiah and Ezekiel. His difference from
them on this point, religiously speaking, is that the time of prophecy is
past; the law has been fulfilled. So for both unbelievers and believers it is
a stumbling block that a man should show himself subject to further
prophecy. Yet this is New England, whose case rests upon the covenant.
It ought to remain accessible to specific identifications with the prophets
of the covenant.

The writer of *Walden* establishes his claim upon the prophetic writings of our Scripture by taking upon his work four of their most general features: (1) their wild mood-swings between lamentation and hope (because the position from which they are written is an absolute knowledge of faithlessness and failure, together with the absolute knowledge that this is not necessary, not from God, but self-imposed; and because God's prophets are auditors of the wild mood-swings of God himself); (2) the periodic confusions of their authors' identities with God's – stuck with the words in their mouths and not always able to remember how they got there; (3) their mandate to create wretchedness and nervousness (because they are "to judge the bloody city" and "show her all her abominations" [Ezekiel 22:2]); (4) their immense repetitiveness. It cannot, I think, be denied that *Walden* sometimes seems an enormously long and boring book. (Again, its writer knows this; again it is part of his subject. "An old-fashioned man would have lost his senses or died of ennui before this" [IV, 22]. He is speaking of the lack of domestic sounds to comfort one in the woods, and he is also speaking of his book. In particular, he is acknowledging that it is not a novel, with its domestic sounds.) I understand this response to *Walden* to be a boredom not of emptiness but of prolonged urgency. Whether you take this as high praise of a high literary discovery, or as an excuse of literary lapse, will obviously depend on how high you place the book's value.

Chapter VII, called "The Bean Field," contains the writer's most open versions of his scriptural procedures or, as he puts it later, his revisions of mythology (XIV, 22), because he says there explicitly that he is growing his beans not to eat but solely in order to get their message, so to speak: "I was determined to know beans . . . perchance, as some must work in fields if only for the sake of tropes and expression, to serve a parable-maker one day" (VII, 10, 11). He acknowledges that he is himself the parable-maker whom his work in the field will serve one day by composing an explicit parable in which his weeding of the field becomes the actions of Achilles before Troy:

> A long war, not with cranes, but with weeds, those Trojans who had sun and rain and dews on their side. Daily the beans saw me come to their rescue armed with a hoe, and thin the ranks of their enemies, filling up the trenches with weedy dead. Many a lusty crest-waving Hector, that towered a whole foot above his crowding comrades, fell before my weapon and rolled in the dust. (VII, 10)

It is an uncommonly obvious moment; it gives no further significance either to his or to Achilles' behavior. It has nothing of the force and resonance he can bring to fable or to the mock-heroic when he wants to

– e.g., in the comparison of his townsmen with Hercules (I, 3), in the battle of the ants (XII, 12–13), or in the new myth of the locomotive (IV, 8–10). What the writer is mocking in the obviousness of this parable is parable-making itself, those moralizings over nature that had become during the past century a literary pastime, and with which his writing would be confused. With good reason: whatever else *Walden* is, it certainly depends on the tradition of topographical poetry – nothing can outdo its obsession with the seasons of a real place. The writer acknowledges this, too, in allowing the mockery – it is filially gentle – to point at himself and, hence, at Transcendentalism generally. This comes out pointedly in the following paragraph, when, after quoting Sir John Evelyn's "philosophical discourse of earth" and another piece of scientific-pious prose about " "lay fields which enjoy their sabbath," " he breaks off abruptly with, "I harvested twelve bushels of beans" (VII, 11).

Less obviously, hoeing serves the writer as a trope – in particular, a metaphor – for writing. In the sentences preceding his little parable of the hoer-hero, the writer has linked these two labors of the hand: "– it will bear some iteration in the account, for there was no little iteration in the labor –" (VII, 10). So the first value of the metaphorical equation of writing and hoeing is that his writing must bear up under repetitiveness. He takes the metaphor further: "making . . . invidious distinctions with [my] hoe, leveling whole ranks of one species, and sedulously cultivating another." That is, the writer's power of definition, of dividing, will be death to some, to others birth.

As elsewhere in *Walden*, an explicit fable from a foreign classic signals that another parable is under foot. The over-arching parable of the chapter on "The Bean Field" is one that describes the writer-hoer most literally, one which itself takes harrowing to be (a metaphor of) the effect of words:

> See, I have this day set thee over the nations and over the kingdoms,
> to root out, and to pull down, and to destroy, and to throw down,
> to build, and to plant. (Jeremiah 1:10)

Here is the parable-maker he is serving *this* day, whether hoeing or writing. The tropes and expressions for the sake of which he works in his field had already been employed; to perform "for the sake of them" is to perform because of them, in order that it shall be fulfilled as it is written. So of course he can only be serving "perchance." It is only through chance that he has been singled out for this service; the ordination is not his to confer, though it is his to establish. And only perchance will his service have its effect; there is a good chance that it will not.

If it does not work, he will not know why – whether it is his people's immovability, or God's, or his own. He keeps saying he doesn't much like hoeing, or the way he is hoeing; he is as irritated by it as he is by other men's devotion to nothing else but. And in fact the second half of this chapter feels thin and irritable; a bad mood is in it. The writer's assertions of hope or of rebuke do not flex upon themselves and soar, but remain mere assertions, moralizings; it has been a bad harvest for him. He manifests nothing like the equanimity in his later knowledge of harvesting: "The true harvest of my daily life is somewhat as intangible and indescribable as the tints of morning or evening. It is a little star-dust caught, a segment of the rainbow which I have clutched" (XI, 7). In the first part of "The Bean Field" the sun is lighting him to hoe his beans (VII, 4), and it comes back at the end ("We are wont to forget that the sun looks on our cultivated fields and on the prairies and forests without distinction" [VII, 16]). But at the center of the chapter the light of nature had gone bad: " . . . I have sometimes had a vague sense all the day of some sort of itching and disease in the horizon" (VII, 7). This happens "when there was a military turnout of which I was ignorant"; American militarism's conception of patriotism infects even the sky; its present manifestation is the Mexican War. This is not the only time he associates despair with a corrupted idea of patriotism: "I sometimes despair of getting anything quite simple and honest done in this world by the help of men. They would have to be passed through a powerful press first, to squeeze their old notions out of them" (I, 38). But "the great winepress of the wrath of God" (Revelation 14: 19) is not perfectly effective. The writer continues: " . . . and there would be someone in the company with a maggot in his head." In *Walden*'s "Conclusion" the "maggot in their heads" is patriotism (XVIII, 2).

The writer's next paragraph is uncharacteristically flat in its irony, totally exempting himself from it. "I felt proud to know that the liberties of Massachusetts and of our fatherland were in such safe keeping; and as I turned to my hoeing again I was filled with an inexpressible confidence, and pursued my labor cheerfully with a calm trust in the future" (VII, 8). His mood of mock vainglory persists, and it produces perhaps the most revolting image in the book: "But sometimes it was a really noble and inspiring strain that reached these woods, and the trumpet that sings of fame, and I felt as if I could spit a Mexican with a good relish" (VII, 9). That is, our bayonets in Mexico are the utensils of cannibals.

He acknowledges this despairing, revolted mood a page or so later when he again picks up the tilling theme from Jeremiah, this time with a didactically explicit acceptance of that identity:

> I said to myself, I will not plant beans and corn with so much industry another summer, but such seeds, if the seed is not lost, as sincerity, truth, simplicity, faith, innocence, and the like, and see if they will not grow in this soil, even with less toil and manurance, and sustain me, for surely it has not been exhausted for these crops. Alas! I said this to myself; but now another summer is gone, and another, and another, and I am obliged to say to you, Reader, that the seeds which I planted, if indeed they *were* seeds of those virtues, were wormeaten or had lost their vitality, and so did not come up. (VII, 15)

It is when Jeremiah is momentarily free of God's voice, and hence of the ordainment to speak to kingdoms and nations, that he says, and hence says to himself:

> When I would comfort myself against sorrow, my heart is faint in me. Behold the voice of the cry of the daughter of my people because of them that dwell in a far country: Is not the Lord in Zion? is not her king in her? Why have they provoked me to anger with their graven images, and with strange vanities? The harvest is past, the summer is ended, and we are not saved. (Jeremiah 8: 18–20)

"Alas! I said this to myself": What he said to himself was, Alas! – and alas, that I can say it only to myself. The writer knows that "he that ploweth should plow in hope" (I Corinthians 9: 10). But he has also known, from the beginning, that he is unable to follow that injunction faithfully: " . . . the same sun which ripens my beans illumines at once a system of earths like ours. If I had remembered this it would have prevented some mistakes. This was not the light in which I hoed them" (I, 13).

Hoeing is identified not just with the content and effect of words; it is also an emblem of the physical act of writing, as though the sheer fact that a thing is written is as important as what is said. For the writer's hoe, the earth is a page; with it, the tiller "[makes] the yellow soil express its summer thought in bean leaves and blossoms rather than in wormwood and piper and millet grass, making the earth say beans instead of grass" (VII, 4). This is figured when the artist from Kouroo writes a name in the sand with the point of his stick. The underlying idea of nature as a book is familiar enough; in Bacon, it justifies the scientific study of nature; in Deism, it might be used to ornament a teleological argument for the existence of God. But for an Ezekiel, let us say, these are hardly the issues. In what we call spring, and what the writer of *Walden* shows to be an Apocalypse, bringing his life in the woods to an end, the vision of blood and excrement is transformed into a vision of the earth and its dependents in a crisis of foliation; these leaves in turn produce a vision of the world as an open book (XVII, 7–9). The idea is literalized when he speaks of "the fine print, the small type, of a meadow mouse" (XIV, 18); or speaks of the snow as reprinting old footsteps "in clear white type alto-relievo" (IX, 9).

But heroic books are themselves a part of nature; "the noblest written words are as commonly as far behind or above the fleeting spoken language as the firmament with its stars is behind the clouds. *There* are the stars, and they who can may read them" (III, 4). It may seem that the writer is placing his idea of the meaning of nature in a different category altogether from the meaning of words when he turns from the chapter called "Reading" to that called "Sounds" and remarks, "Much is published, but little printed" (IV, 1). We know he means that nature is at every instant openly confiding in us, in its largest arrangements and in its smallest sounds, and that it is mostly lost on our writers. But the remark also describes the ontological condition of words: the occurrence of a word is the occurrence of an object whose placement always has a point, and whose point always lies before and beyond it. "The volatile truth of our words should continually betray the inadequacy of the residual statement. Their truth is instantly *translated*; its literal monument alone remains" (XVIII, 6). (Wittgenstein in the *Investigations* (section 432) records a related perception: "Every sign *by itself* seems dead.")

This theme is declared as the book opens, in its flat first sentence: "When I wrote the following pages, or rather the bulk of them, I lived alone, in the woods, a mile from any neighbor, in a house which I had built by myself, on the shore of Walden Pond, in Concord, Massachusetts, and earned my living by the labor of my hands only." On a second perusal, this sentence raises more questions than it answers – about where Concord is, and what a pond is, and how far a mile is, and who the neighbor is, and what earning a living is. Now what is "the bulk" of the pages he wrote? We know that Thoreau wrote about half of *Walden* during the years in which his hut was his abode; but *every* page the writer writes, wherever he is and whatever writing is, is merely, or ontologically, the bulk of writing: the mass or matter of it, the body or looming of it, its physical presence. Writing is a labor of the hands. We know from the third paragraph of the book that labor which is not the labor of slaves has a finish; and we know, from what is said about hoeing, that labor ·at its best "[yields] an instant and immeasurable crop" (VII, 6). Writing, at its best, will come to a finish in each mark of meaning, in each portion and sentence and word. That is why in reading it "we must laboriously seek the meaning of every word and line; conjecturing a larger sense. . . ."

We are apt to take this to mean that writing, in a high sense, writing which is worth heroic reading, is meant to provide occasions for our conjecturing. That is not wrong, but it is likely to be lukewarm, a suggestion that the puns and paradoxes, etc., are tips or goads to us to read with subtlety and activity, and that we are free to conjecture the writer's meaning. But in *Walden*, reading is not merely the other side of writing, its eventual fate; it is another metaphor of writing itself. The writer cannot invent words as "perpetual suggestions and provocations"; the written word is already "the choicest of relics" (III, 3, 5). His calling depends upon his acceptance of this fact about words, his letting them come to him from their own region, and then taking that occasion for inflecting them one way instead of another then and there, or for refraining from them then and there; as one may inflect the earth toward beans instead of grass, or let it alone, as it is before you are there. The words that the writer raises "out of the trivialness of the street" (III, 3) are the very words or phrases or lines used there, by the people there, in whatever lives they have. This writer's raising of them to us, by writing them down, is only literally, or etymologically, a matter of style, scratching them in. Raising them up, to the light, so to speak, is the whole thing he does, not the adornment of it. The manner is nothing in comparison with the act. And the labor of raising them up is itself one of seeking "the meaning of each word and line," of "conjecturing a larger sense . . . out of what wisdom and valor and generosity" the writer has (III, 3). Conjecturing is not for the writer, and hence not for the reader, what we think of as guesswork. It is casting words together and deriving the conclusions of each. This is how his labor of the hands earned his living, whatever it was.

Why is the isolation of the written from the spoken word his understanding of the father tongue? Why is it his realization of the faith of the prophets? That is, how does his understanding of his position – in Concord, Massachusetts, "in the Presidency of Polk, five years before the passage of Webster's Fugitive-Slave Bill" (XII, 14) – take him beyond the knowledge prophets have always had of the ineffectiveness of God's words in their mouths; or take him to a different resolution of his ordainment?

I understand his strategy as an absolute acceptance of Saint Paul's interpretation of Christ's giving "gifts unto men" (Ephesians 4): "I therefore, the prisoner of the Lord, beseech you that ye walk worthy of the vocation wherewith ye are called." According to Paul, the gifts for "the perfecting of the saints, for the work of the ministry, for the edifying of the body of Christ" are divided – among apostles, prophets, evangelists, pastors, and teachers. For the writer of *Walden*, in declaring writing to be such a gift, in such a service, the problem of walking worthy of it is different from, anyway later than, Milton's view of his talent: he must learn not merely what to write, in order that his trust not be buried; he must undertake to write absolutely, to exercise his faith in the very act of marking the word. He puts his hand upon his own mouth.

This fulfillment of his call to prophecy overthrows the mode of the old and the new prophecies of the word – their voicing of it. It directly disobeys the cardinal motivation of Puritan preaching – that the word be spoken and confessed aloud. The time for such prophesying is absolutely over. We have heard it said, "We shall all stand before the judgment seat of Christ. . . . every tongue shall confess to God. So then, every one shall give account of himself to God" (Romans 14: 10–12). But *Walden* shows that we *are* there; every tongue has confessed what it can; we have heard everything there is to hear. There were prophets, but there is no Zion; knowing that, Jesus fulfilled them, but the kingdom of heaven is not entered into; knowing that, the Founding Fathers brought both testaments to this soil, and there is no America; knowing that, Jonathan Edwards helped bring forth a Great Awakening, and we are not awake. The experiment of man ("We are the subjects of an experiment" [V, 10]) has failed. Not that any of man's dreams may not come to pass. But there is absolutely no more to be *said* about them. What is left to us is the accounting. Not a recounting, of tales or news; but a document, with each word a warning and a teaching; a deed, with each word an act.

This is what those lists of numbers, calibrated to the half cent, mean in *Walden*. They of course are parodies of America's methods of evaluation; and they are emblems of what the writer wants from writing, as he keeps insisting in calling his book an *account*. As everywhere else, he undertakes to make the word good. A true mathematical reckoning of the sort he shows requires that every line be a mark of honesty, that the lines be complete, omitting no expense or income, and that there be no mistake in the computation. Spoken words are calculated to deceive. How are written words different? The mathematical emblem embodies two ways. First, it is part of a language which exists *primarily* as notation; its point is not the fixing of a spoken language, which had preceded it, but the fixing of steps, which can thereby be remarked. Second, the notation works only when every mark within it means something, in its look and its sequence. Among written works of art, only of poetry had we expected a commitment to total and transparent meaning, every mark bearing its brunt. The literary ambition of *Walden* is to shoulder the commitment in prose.

This ambition, directed toward the establishing of American literature, had to overcome two standing literary achievements with speech: Wordsworth's attempted redemption of the human voice and of poetry by one another; and America's peculiar exaltation of the oration and the sermon. The task of literature is to rescue the word from both politics and religion. "God is only the president of the day, and Webster is his orator" (XVIII, 14). Even Emerson, in his literature of the sermon, has made a false start. However wonderful, it is not a beginning but an end of something. His voice consoles; it is not of warning, and so not of hope.

I will not insist upon it, but I understand the allusion to Emerson in *Walden* to acknowledge this relation to him.

> There was one other with whom I had "solid seasons," long to be remembered, at his house in the village, and who looked in upon me from time to time; but I had no more for society there. (XIV, 23)

It may be the most unremarkable paragraph of the book; not just because it is one of the shortest, but because it contributes nothing to the account of the visitors the writer received. What is it there for? "I had no more for society there," beyond saying that no one else visited him, can be taken as saying that he could give no more time or take no more interest in Emerson's social position, which is all he offered. But this writer knows who Emerson is, his necessity as a presence and as a writer. Why would he take a crack at him? Nor can the paragraph be there merely to make the account complete, for the notching must mark not simply the occurrence of time but the improvement of it. So in this case the act of marking must itself be the improvement. There is an earlier notice of a visitor whose name the writer is "sorry I cannot print . . . here" (VI, 8). For me, these curiosities come together in Ezekiel's vision which contains the myth of the writer:

> And [God] called to the man clothed with linen, which had the writer's inkhorn by his side; And the Lord said unto him, Go through the midst of the city, through the midst of Jerusalem, and set a mark upon the foreheads of the men that sigh and that cry for all the abominations that be done in the midst thereof.
> And to the others he said in mine hearing, Go ye after him through the city, and smite: let not your eye spare, neither have ye pity: . . . but come not near any man upon whom is the mark. . . .
> (Ezekiel 9: 3–6)

The writer's nameless marking of Emerson is done in order to preserve him and, simultaneously, to declare that his own writing has the power of life and death in it. America's best writers have offered one another the shock of recognition but not the faith of friendship, not daily belief. Perhaps this is why, or it is because, their voices seem to destroy one another. So they destroy one another for us. How is a tradition to come out of that?

Study of *Walden* would perhaps not have become such an obsession with me had it not presented itself as a response to questions with which I was already obsessed: Why has America never expressed itself philosophically? Or has it – in the metaphysical riot of its greatest literature?

Has the impulse to philosophical speculation been absorbed, or exhausted, by speculation in territory, as in such thoughts as Manifest Destiny? Or are such questions not really intelligible? They are, at any rate, disturbingly like the questions that were asked about American literature before it established itself. In rereading *Walden*, twenty years after first reading it, I seemed to find a book of sufficient intellectual scope and consistency to have established or inspired a tradition of thinking. One reason it did not is that American culture has never really believed in its capacity to produce anything of permanent value – except itself. So it forever overpraises and undervalues its achievements.

How is one to write so as to receive the power of life and death? Shelley's "unacknowledged legislators of the world" still had to be poets; Carlyle saw modern heroes in mere men of letters. For Thoreau these are not answers, but more questions. How is writing to declare its faithfulness to itself, in that power? How is it to rescue language?

My discussion suggests the following direction of answer. Writing – heroic writing, the writing of a nation's scripture – must assume the conditions of language as such; re-experience, as it were, the fact that there is such a thing as language at all and assume responsibility for it – find a way to acknowledge it – until the nation is capable of serious speech again. Writing must assume responsibility, in particular, for three of the features of the language it lives upon: (1) that every mark of a language means something in the language, one thing rather than another; that a language is totally, systematically meaningful; (2) that words and their orderings are meant by human beings, that they contain (or conceal) their beliefs, express (or deny) their convictions; and (3) that the saying of something when and as it is said is as significant as the meaning and ordering of the words said.

Until we are capable of serious speech again – i.e., are reborn, are men "[speaking] in a waking moment, to men in their waking moments" (XVIII, 6) – our words do not carry our conviction, we cannot fully back them, because either we are careless of our convictions, or think we haven't any, or imagine they are inexpressible. They are merely unutterable. ("The at present unutterable things we may find somewhere uttered" [III, 11]. Perhaps in the words he is now writing.) The written word, on a page, will have to show that a particular man set it there, inscribed it, chose, and made the mark. Set on its page, "carved out of the breath of life itself" (III, 5), the word must stand for silence and permanence; that is to say, for conviction. Until we can speak again, our lives and our language betray one another; we can grant to neither of them their full range and autonomy; they mistake their definitions of one another. A written word, as it recurs page after page, changing its company and modifying its occasions, must show its integrity under these pressures – as though the fact that all of its occurrences in the book of pages are simultaneously there, awaiting one another, demonstrates that our words need not haunt us. If we learn how to entrust our meaning to a word, the weight it carries through all its computations will yet prove to be just the weight we will find we wish to give it.

How is a writer to show, or acknowledge, something true of language as such? I have begun in this chapter to answer that question for the writer of *Walden* – according to my reading of him. So another question has arisen: What will it mean to be the reader of such a writer?

* * * * *

> I should not obtrude my affairs so much on the notice of my readers if very particular inquiries had not been made by my townsmen concerning my mode of life, which some would call impertinent, though they do not appear to me at all impertinent, but, considering the circumstances, very natural and pertinent. Some have asked what I got to eat; if I did not feel lonesome; if I was not afraid; and the like. Others have been curious to learn what portion of my income I devoted to charitable purposes; and some, who have large families, how many poor children I maintained. I will therefore ask those of my readers who feel no particular interest in me to pardon me if I undertake to answer some of these questions in this book. (I, 2)

We know the first joke: those questions, and ones like them, *are* the book. The underlying joke is the way in which we know that. The writer shows an initial air of fun by modifying the inquiries concerning his life with "which some would call impertinent" – leaving it open whether that refers to the inquiries or the townsmen or the life. His townsmen are not impertinent, because they have no idea what they are asking: they do not know, for example, that in a sense the first paragraph contains a full answer, or enough of an account for someone to find out the rest if he really wants to know; and, in a sense, the answer requires the whole book; and then after that, one will still have to find out for oneself.

His problem – at once philosophical, religious, literary, and, I will argue, political – is to get us to ask the questions, and then to show us that we do not know what we are asking, and then to show us that we have the answer. The fiction is that some unknown people have asked him these prompting questions. Underlying the fiction is the question: Where does the book begin, the bulk of whose pages he wrote in the woods? That is, at what point do we realize that the "I" of the first paragraph, the second word of the book, has merged with the "I" the book is about? Whenever we realize it, what we will realize is that we were from the first *already* reading it, i.e., that is the form the phenomenological appearance of this knowledge will take. The only book we are to be given is this one, and it is now passing in front of us, *being* written as it were.

To get us to ask the questions. That means to fox us into opening our mouths. It is not only Socrates who is characteristically prompted to philosophize when a townsman opens his mouth. And for the same reason as in this book: because, like the loon, and like Chanticleer, and like the fox, we thereby betray ourselves; or, like the writer of this book, we "thus unblushingly publish [our] guilt" (I, 79). Under the circumstances, this is the pertinent first step to knowledge: a good book is one that elicits our conviction, one by whose wisdom we are "convicted" (III, 8).

The writer discovered that to make a book like his, to collect evidence in the experiment, "You only need sit still long enough in some attractive spot in the woods that all its inhabitants may exhibit themselves to you by turns" (XII, 11) – i.e., in succession, and by turning, and perhaps as vaudeville routines, for your pleasure and profit. Whom does he examine at that spot? Who is the neighbor for whom he is crowing? The chapter on "Reading" identifies his readers as students – and himself, consequently, as teacher. Eventually, students will be anyone whose "education is sadly neglected" (III, 12); and one day we might all "become essentially students" (III, 1) – that is, one day we might find out what essential studying is. Before that day, he speaks of his readers in various ways, e.g., as those "who are said to live in New England" (I, 3) and as "the mass of men who are discontented" (I, 21). But who knows where or who these people are? The first fact the writer knows about his readers, and acts on, is that they are reading his pages now: the repetitions of "pages" are capped by his emphasis on those who "have come to this page" (I, 7), who are present at the very word the writer has printed there: then that is where you are living now, and what you are working at, and "[you] know whether [you] are well employed or not" (I, 21).

As the surface of his words challenges us to conjecture and calculate with them, their plain content challenges our right to go on reading them. "Adventure on life now" (I, 20), he tells us. So let's drop the book. But then it is "the adventurous *student*" who is promised something more salutary than the morning or the spring to our lives. So let's stay on the track of this book. But am I well employed *here*? ("A man sits as many risks as he runs" [VI, 17].) And won't that same question recur no matter where I present myself? Does it matter whether I read, say, *Walden*, or go, say, to Walden? And then I realize that I am in no position to answer that question; yet I cannot shake it. The choice to go on reading or not is left absolutely up to me – whether I am to invest interest here or not. Nothing *holds* my interest, no suspense of plot or development of character; the words seem continuously at an end. The writer keeps writing things I know I ought not to have stopped trying to say for myself; and shows me a life there is no reason I do not live. An old-fashioned man would have lost his senses.

The writer keeps my choices in front of me, the ones I am not making and the ones I am. This makes me wretched and nervous. My choices appear as curiosities, and to be getting the better of me. Curiosity grows with every new conjecture we find confirmed in the words. It seems all but an accident that we should discover what they mean. This becomes a mood of our acts of reading altogether: it is an accident, utterly contingent, that we should be present at these words at all. We feel this as the writer's withdrawal from the words on which he had staked his presence; and we feel this as the words' indifference to us, their disinterest in whether we choose to stay with them or not. Every new clarity makes the writer's existence obscurer to us – that is, his willingness to remain obscure. How can he apparently so completely not care, or have made up his mind, that we may not understand? This feeling may begin our almost unbearable sense of his isolation. Did he not feel lonesome? We are asking now. And then we find ourselves, perhaps, alone with a book in our hands, words on a page, at a distance.

Of course, alone is where he wants us. That was his point of origin, and it is to be our point of departure for this experiment, this book of travels, this adventure "to explore the private sea, the Atlantic and Pacific Ocean of one's being alone" (XVIII, 2): he attracts us so that we put ourselves on this spot, and then turns us around, and so loses us. "Not till we are lost, in other words, not till we have lost the world [here he provides a little object lesson in reading] do we begin to find ourselves, and realize where we are and the infinite extent of our relations." And, "not till we are completely lost, or turned around – for a man needs only to be turned around once with his eyes shut in this world to be lost – do we appreciate the vastness and strangeness of Nature" (VIII, 2). The difficulty in keeping us at the point of departure, and on our own, is one reason he says, "I do not suppose that I have attained to obscurity" (XVIII, 8). That is, I do not know whether I have finally been able to leave you sufficiently alone, to make you go far enough to find us both; I cannot assume that I have kept still long enough in my "attractive spot," so I may have frightened some of its inhabitants away. I may have brought them to "feel [some] particular interest in me" (I, 2), without getting them to be interested in themselves. He is facing out the problem of writing altogether. His writing has not attained itself until it has completely absorbed the responsibility for its existence, i.e., for calling upon his neighbors; in the present case, until it is absolutely still, without assertion, without saying anything that requires his reader to take *his* word for what he says. (The words of *Walden* are no more his than the water of Walden.) "I have not attained to obscurity" means that the I, the ego, has not disappeared; and also that he has not reached the secrets of his trade.

Let us go back to those secrets, for he identifies them with his losses, in perhaps his most famously cryptic passage.

> I long ago lost a hound, a bay horse, and a turtledove, and am still on their trail. Many are the travelers I have spoken to concerning them, describing their tracks and what calls they answered to. I have met one or two who had heard the hound, and the tramp of the horse, and even seen the dove disappear behind a cloud, and they seemed as anxious to recover them as if they had lost them themselves. (I, 24)

I have no new proposal to offer about the literary or biographical sources of those symbols. But the very obviousness of the fact that they are symbols, and function within a little myth, seems to me to tell us what we need to know. The writer comes to us from a sense of loss; the myth does not contain more than symbols because it is no set of desired things he has lost, but a connection with things, the track of desire itself. Everything he can list he is putting in his book; it is a record of losses. Not that he has failed to make some gains and have his finds; but they are gone now. He is not present to them now. Or, he is trying to put them behind him, to complete the crisis by writing his way out of it. It is a gain to grow, but humanly it is always a loss of something, a departure. Like any grownup, he has lost childhood; like any American, he has lost a nation and with it the God of the fathers. He has lost Walden; call it Paradise; it is everything there is to lose. The object of faith hides itself from him. Not that he has given it up, and the hope for it; he is on the track. He knows where it is to be found, in the true acceptance of loss, the refusal of any substitute for true recovery. (The logic, if not quite the message, is the same as Pascal's: "Shall he who alone knows nature know it only to his undoing? Shall he who alone knows it live in solitary misery? He must not see nothing at all; nor must he see enough to believe that he possesses it; he must see enough to know that he has lost it; for, to know his loss, he must see and not see; and that is precisely his natural condition. Whichever side he takes I shall not leave him at rest.")

He is not fully recovered. He has come back, "a sojourner in civilized life again" (I, 1). He was a sojourner there before, and now again he sojourns there instead of at Walden. This is a likely place to see the need for *Walden*'s paradoxes. It is natural to take the words "sojourner in civilized life again" to suggest that the writer will be returning to Walden, where he was not sojourning, but at home. That is not false; for one thing, he is returning in his writing. But in the terms of his book, the sense in which it is true that he was at home in Walden is that he learned there how to sojourn, i.e., spend his day. That life on earth is a test and a sojourn is hardly news. We merely sometimes forget what a land of pilgrims means, or forget to discover it. It is not the writer's invention that to be peregrine is to be a stranger, any more than it is his fancy that perdition is the loss of something. He keeps emphasizing that he is back "in civilized life again" by explicitly going back within the book to visit Walden – e.g., to measure its height on the shore or to record the day in successive years on which its ice breaks up – as though testing his condition now with conditions there, and with his condition when he abode there.

The little myth of the hound, horse, and turtledove refers to "one or two" – viz., travelers, hence strangers – who had heard and seen what he has lost, and seemed as anxious to recover them as if the losses were theirs. Here the writer fully identifies his audience as those who realize that they have lost the world, i.e., are lost to it. The fate of having a self – of being human – is one in which the self is always to be found; fated to be sought, or not; recognized, or not. My self is something, apparently, toward which I can stand in various relations, ones in which I can stand to other selves, named by the same terms, e.g., love, hate, disgust, acceptance, knowledge, ignorance, faith, pride, shame. In the passage in question, *Walden*'s phenomenological description of finding the self, or the faith of it, is one of trailing and recovery; elsewhere it is voyaging and discovery. This is the writer's interpretation of the injunction to know thyself. His descriptions emphasize that this is a continuous *activity*, not something we may think of as an intellectual preoccupation. It is *placing* ourselves in the world. That you do not know beforehand what you will find is the reason the quest is an experiment or an exploration. The most characteristic of the writer's reflexive descriptions is that of finding himself in some attitude or locale: "I found myself suddenly neighbor to the birds" (II, 9); "I found myself suddenly in the shadow of a cloud" (X, 3); "I found repeatedly, of late years, that I cannot fish without falling a little in self-respect" (XI, 5); "I find myself beginning with the letters *gl*" (IV, 19). The place you will come to may be black (XVIII, 2), something you would disown; but if you have found yourself there, that is so far home; you will either domesticate that, naturalize yourself there, or you will recover nothing.

It is to those who accept this condition of human existence that the writer accords the title of traveler or stranger. It is the first title he accords himself (after writer). Those to whom he addresses his account are therefore his "kindred from a distant land" (I, 2). Here is another underlying perception, or paradox, of *Walden* as a whole – that what is most intimate is what is furthest away; the realization of "our infinite relations," our kinships, is an endless realization of our separateness. The simple and sincere account the writer requires of "every writer, first or last" will come from a distance because "if he has lived sincerely, it must have been in a distant land to me." Why take this merely as a complacent or academic disclaimer of his own sincerity? Of course he will not *claim* to be sincere – what would be the point? – especially not on the first page of his voyage; for sincerity is the end, and he only requires it "first or last." It will turn out that to be sincere, pure – he will centrally call it chastity – is to find God (XI, 11); and "How shall a man know if he is chaste? He shall not know it" (XI, 12). In particular, nothing he can do, or not do, will prove it. To say that a man who has lived sincerely "must have been in a distant land to me" is just an opening definition of sincerity as the capacity to live in one's own separateness, to sail the Atlantic and Pacific Ocean of one's being alone.

These thoughts are dramatized in the next paragraph, the book's third: "I would fain say something, not so much concerning the Chinese and Sandwich Islanders as you who read these pages, who are said to live in New England; something about your condition, especially your outward condition or circumstances in this world. . . . I have traveled a good deal in Concord"; and then he goes on to compare his townsmen with Hercules and with Brahmins performing "conscious penance." The surface is clear enough: Concord is stranger to him, and he to it, than the ends of the earth. But why does this watchman of the private sea insist especially on his readers' *outward* condition or circumstances in this world? Because the outward position or circumstance in this world is precisely the position of outwardness, outsideness to the world, distance from it, the position of stranger. The first step in attending to our education is to observe the strangeness of our lives, our estrangement from ourselves, the lack of necessity in what we profess to be necessary. The second step is to grasp the true necessity of human strangeness as such, the opportunity of outwardness.

The writer modulates the theme of outsideness throughout the book. One good summary of his idea occurs in a model of the Ode to Dejection he does not propose to write: ". . . from outward forms to win / The passion and the life, whose fountains are within." Coleridge despairs of victory; Thoreau's proposal is to brag from just that perch of possibility. If only to wake his neighbors up – and not succeed in awakening them to the passion and the life; and not succeed in awakening himself. What he knows is that "The morning wind forever blows, the poem of creation is uninterrupted; but few are the ears that hear it. Olympus is but the outside of the earth everywhere" (II, 8). The abode of the gods is to be entered not merely at the outermost point of the earth or at the top of the highest mountain, and maybe not at all; but anywhere, only at the point of the present.

But just this endless occasion is the constant possibility of dejection, which, in the words of Coleridge, is to gaze upon beauty, but with a blank eye; to see, and not to feel it. This is the characteristic threat of prophecy, and of the knowledge of the gospel: since you have seen and heard, there is no further sacrifice for you, the blood will be on your own head. If Thoreau's words merely show us promises we can never accept, then his beauty mocks us; he has realized the fear in his epigraph and written an ode to dejection. I take those words to mean that dejection is the obvious subject to treat of, the metaphysical condition shared by writer and reader, here and now, where we live. It is the condition, as Coleridge shows it, of "grief without a pang," grief "Which finds no natural outlet, no relief, / In wood, or sign, or tear –." It is without expression.

This is the vision in *Walden*'s paragraph with the famous opening line: "The mass of men lead lives of quiet desperation" (I, 9); the short paragraph harps on the word "despair," or an inflection of it, six times. Thoreau proposes not to keep quiet about the despair any longer. But the bragging, while it will not praise dejection or melancholy, will recognize how formidable a foe it is, and hence acknowledge and absorb the Romantic poets' bravery in facing it with their odes. The bragging and the wild laughter will have to take place *over* despair, and perhaps will express only that shrill sound. Then it may at least wake his neighbors up to their actual condition.

In the writer's words, as they take on more life, this condition is explicitly described as a want of expression.

> While such a sun holds out to burn, the vilest sinner may return. Through our own recovered innocence we discern the innocence of our neighbors. You may have known your neighbor yesterday for a thief, a drunkard, or a sensualist, and merely pitied or despised him, and despaired of the world; but the sun shines bright and warm this first spring morning, re-creating the world. . . . There is not only an atmosphere of good will about him, but even a savor of holiness groping for expression. (XVII, 19)

So the secrets of his trade are the ones his neighbors keep: that they are in despair, which is quiet; and that there is holiness in them, which gropes, like a blind man, or a child.

The hymn-form in the first line of this excerpt – not the book's only activation of the old pun on sun/son – completes the identification of despair with sin, and affords the writer his confession of that sin. This acknowledgement validates his discernment of his neighbors' condition. "I never dreamed of any enormity greater than I have committed. I never knew, and never shall know, a worse man than myself" (I, 107). These are not presumptuous modesties. They are acceptances of epistemological fact, necessary limits of knowledge.

The writer will give this double condition (of sin and innocence, his neighbors" and his own) expression in the book, if he can. But there are further secrets about what expression requires:

> Sometimes I heard the foxes as they ranged over the snow crust, in moonlight nights, in search of a partridge or other game, barking raggedly and demoniacally like forest dogs, as if laboring with some anxiety, or seeking expression, struggling for light. . . . They seemed to me to be rudimental, burrowing men, still standing on their defence, awaiting their transformation. Sometimes one came near to my window, attracted by my light, barked a vulpine curse at me, and then retreated. (XV, 4)

There is a lot in this, a crossroads and summary of many conceptions. The fox, Chanticleer's adversary, is related to men by its cursing ("Our hymn books resound with a melodious cursing of God and enduring him forever" [I, 109]), and related to the man writing his story by burrowing ("My instinct tells me that my head is an organ for burrowing" [II, 23]). It is also to the point that the fox's bark is demonic; that the foxes are curiously attracted to this writer by his light; and that it is winter. But for the moment we are looking at its interpretation of seeking expression, viz., as laboring with anxiety (the travelers were anxious to recover the bay horse, hound, and turtledove) and, in particular, as awaiting transformation; moulting.

We have noticed that awaiting the word of the father tongue requires rebirth; and the writer associates the volatile truth of words, instantly translated from their graves, with his effort to "lay the foundation of a true expression" (XVIII, 6). Our emphasis here is on the writer's association of finding expression with a moment of imminent hope and imminent despair. He enacts this association in a passage that shows him reading. At the opening of "Brute Neighbors," the Hermit, accepting an invitation from the Poet to go fishing, sends him off to dig bait while he comes to the conclusion of a meditation:

> Let me see; where was I? Methinks I was nearly in this frame of mind; the world lay about at this angle. Shall I go to heaven or a-fishing? If I should soon bring this meditation to an end, would

another so sweet occasion be likely to offer? I was as near being resolved into the essence of things as ever I was in my life. . . . My thoughts have left no track, and I cannot find the path again. . . . I will just try these three sentences of Con-fut-see; they may fetch that state about again. I know not whether it was the dumps or a budding ecstasy. Mem. There never is but one opportunity of a kind. (XII, 5)

This is the condition of serious reading. You need to be prepared to find either state.

A writer in meditation is literally a human being awaiting expression. The writer in *Walden* assumes a larger burden of this waiting than other men may: partly because it is his subject that the word and the reader can only be awakened together; partly because, as once before, there is an unprecedented din of prophecy in the world. Everyone is saying, and anyone can hear, that this is the new world; that we are the new men; that the earth is to be born again; that the past is to be cast off like a skin; that we must learn from children to see again; that every day is the first day of the world; that America is Eden. So how can a word get through whose burden is that we do not understand a word of all this? Or rather, that the way in which we understand it is insane, and we are trying again to buy and bully our way into heaven; that we have failed; that the present is a task and a discovery, not a period of America's privileged history; that we are not free, not whole, and not new, and we know this and are on a downward path of despair because of it; and that for the child to grow he requires family and familiarity, but for a grownup to grow he requires strangeness and transformation, i.e., birth? One of the writer's trades is that of "reporter to a journal, of no very wide circulation" (1, 27). Merely to say that Thoreau refers here to his private journal leaves his devotion to it as mysterious as ever, and fails to compute the pun. The writer is a reporter because what he is writing is news, about the world we have made; in particular, that infinitely more is changing than is realized, and infinitely less.

His immediate problem is not that his account has never been "audited" ("I have not set my heart on that" [I, 30]). His problem is that every line of his account is cause for despair, because each is an expression he has waited for, and yet with each he is not transformed. Within his book, the placement of the epigraph sentence declares that fact:

The present was my next experiment of this kind, which I purpose to describe more at length, for convenience, putting the experience of two years into one. As I have said, I do not propose to write an ode to dejection but to brag as lustily as chanticleer in the morning, standing on his roost, if only to wake my neighbors up. (II, 7)

Since "experiment of this kind" directly refers to the possessing of a house, and since that has just before been shown to be, rightly understood, a poetic exercise, the present experiment is the book at hand. "I do not propose to write an ode to dejection" parallels "I purpose to describe more at length": his plan "for convenience, [to] put the experience of two years into one," widely praised as his artistic achievement, is so far a cause for his despair as a man and as a writer of the kind he wishes to be. Why is one year better than two? "The phenomena of the year take place every day in a pond on a small scale" (XVII, 2). And what is sacred about a day? The experiment is the present – to make himself present to each circumstance, at every eventuality; since he is writing, in each significant mark. The very awareness of time compromises presentness; the succession of words is itself a rebuke. There never is but one opportunity of a kind. That is the threat, but also the promise. To go on, untransformed, unchaste so far as you know, means that you have not been divided by the fact and concluded your mortal career. But to learn to await, in the way you write, and therewith in every action, is to learn not to despair of opportunity unforeseen. That was always the knack of faith. Crowing, if it is not followed by the last day, will at any rate express acceptance of that promise; if there is not dawn in him, the crower is at any rate studying "an infinite expectation of the dawn" (II, 15). He will then simply glory, if only to reject, to disperse, despair; if only to remind his neighbors, who themselves are glorying, that there is a less foolish cause for doing so.

To realize where we are and what we are living for, the conditions of our present, the angle at which we stand to the world, the writer calls "improving the time," using a preacher's phrase and giving his kind of turn to it. No one's occasions are exactly those of another, but our conditions of improvement are the same, especially our outsideness and, hence, the world's presence to us. And our conditions are to be realized within each calling, whatever that happens to be. Each calling – what the writer means (and what anyone means, more or less) by a "field" of action or labor – is isomorphic with every other. This is why building a house and hoeing and writing and reading (and we could add, walking and preparing food and receiving visitors and giving charity and hammering a nail and surveying the ice) are allegories and measures of one another. All and only true building is edifying. All and only edifying actions are fit for human habitation. Otherwise they do not earn life. If your action, in its field, cannot stand such measurement, it is a sign that the field is not yours. This is the writer's assurance that his writing is not a substitute for his life, but his way of prosecuting it. He writes because he is a writer. This is why we can have the sense, at once, that he is attaching absolute value to his words, and that they do not matter. What matters is that he show in the way he writes his faithfulness to the specific conditions and acts of writing as such.

Faithfulness to writing as such, as it is given to him to write, I have characterized as faithfulness to conditions of language as such. If we now include among these conditions the fact that the writing is to be read, this will establish a different set of occasions for acknowledging those conditions, a different position with respect to them, a different field of action. As the writer must establish or create his mode of presence to the word, he must admit or create the reader's mode of presence to it. It is the ground upon which they will meet.

The reader's position has been specified as that of the stranger. To write to him is to acknowledge that he is outside the words, at a bent arm's length, and alone with the book; that his presence to these words is perfectly contingent, and the choice to stay with them continuously his own; that they are his points of departure and origin. The conditions of meeting upon the word are that we – writer and reader – learn how to depart from them, leave them where they are; and then return to them, find ourselves there again. We have to learn to admit the successiveness of words, their occurrence one after the other; and their permanence in the face of our successions.

The endless computations of the words of *Walden* are part of its rescue of language, its return of it to us, its effort to free us and our language of one another, to discover the autonomy of each. For the word to return, what is necessary is not that we compute complexities around it, and also not exactly that we surround it with simplicities, but that we see the complexities *it* has and the simplicity it may have on a given occasion if we let it. Immediately, this means that we recognize that we have a choice over our words, but not over their meaning. Their meaning is in their language; and our possession of the language is the way we live in it, what we ask of it. ("To imagine a language is to imagine a form of life.") That our meaning a word is our return to it and its return to us – our occurring to one another – is expressed by the word's literality, its being just these letters, just here, rather than any others.

In religion and politics, literality is defeated because we allow our choices to be made for us. In religion our hymn books resound with a cursing of God because the words are used in vain. We are given to say that man's chief end is to glorify God and to enjoy him forever. But we do not let the words assess our lives, we do not mean what they could mean, so what we *do* when we repeat those words becomes the whole meaning of "man," and "chief end," and "glorify," and "God," etc., in our lives; and that is a curse. In politics we allow ourselves to say, e.g., that a man is a fugitive who is merely running from enslavement. That is an attempted choice of meaning, not an autonomous choice of words.

Beyond the bondage to institutions, we have put nature in bondage, bound it to our uses and to our hurried capacities for sensing, rather than learning of its autonomy. And this means that an object named does not exist for us in its name. We do not know what the bottom of a pond is if we do not know, e.g., what it is to sound the bottom, vaguely imagining that it is abysmally deep. We do not literally mean that we are searching for "the evening robin, at the end of a New England summer day" where he sings on his twig, unless we mean *him* and *the* twig (XVII, 15). We do not know what "Walden" means unless we know what Walden is. The return of a word requires the recovery of its object for us. This was one quest of Romantic poetry, and of the Kantian project to answer skepticism. In *Walden*, both of the tasks are accepted.

Words come to us from a distance; they were there before we were; we are born into them. Meaning them is accepting that fact of their condition. To discover what is being said to us, as to discover what we are saying, is to discover the precise location from which it is said; to understand why it is said from just there, and at that time. The art of fiction is to teach us distance – that the sources of what is said, the character of whomever says it, is for us to discover. ("Speech is for the convenience of those who are hard of hearing" [VI, 3]. This is not an injunction against speaking, but a definition of speakers, i.e., of mankind.) Speaking together face to face can seem to deny that distance, to deny that facing one another requires acknowledging the presence of the other, revealing our positions, betraying them if need be. But to deny such things is to deny our separateness. And that makes us fictions of one another.

A text which is an account has no audience, or one could say that its audience consists of isolated auditors. To read the text accurately is to assess its computations, to check its sentences against our convictions, to prove the derivation of its words. Since every mark counts, the task is to arrive in turn at each of them, as at conclusions. A deep reading is not one in which you sink away from the surface of the words. Words already engulf us. It is one in which you depart from a given word as from a point of origin; you go deep as into woods. Understanding is a matter of orientation, of bearings, of the ability to keep to a course and to move in natural paths from any point to any other. The depths of the book are nothing apart from its surfaces. Figurations of language can be thought of as ways of reflecting the surfaces and depths of a word onto one another.

I mention two of the writer's characteristic procedures meant to enforce our distance from the words and our presentness to them – to show our hand in accepting or arriving at them. First, there is his insistence on the idea of what we *call* something, or what something is said by us to be. In the opening fifty pages of *Walden* there are a dozen instances of modifications like "so-called" or "what is called." For example: "By a seeming fate, commonly called necessity . . ." (I, 5); "None can be an impartial or wise observer of human life but from the vantage ground of what *we* should call voluntary poverty" (I, 19); "The cost of a thing is the amount of what I will call life which is required to be exchanged for it" (I, 45); "The religion and civilization which are barbaric and heathenish build splendid temples; but what you might call Christianity does not" (I, 78). The meaning of the modification is clear in each context, and hardly surprising: what is called necessary is commonly a myth; what we call voluntary poverty may in fact be "simplicity, independence, magnanimity, and trust"; I will call your labor life, for the sake of argument and so as not to raise too many questions at once; what you might call Christianity, if you were accurate to its own criteria, does not exist or is in any case not what you do call Christianity. The point of modification is to suggest that our words are our calls or claims upon the objects and contexts of our world; they show how we count phenomena, what counts for us. The point is to get us to withhold a word, to hold ourselves before it, so that we may assess our allegiance to it, to the criteria in terms of which we apply it. Our faithlessness to our language repeats our faithlessness to all our shared commitments.

A second characteristic procedure by which the writer of *Walden* enforces the distance and presentness of words is his construction of sentences whose meaning, in context, requires an emphasis other than, or in addition to, the one their surface grammar suggests. I will give some examples of these constructions, without comment, supplying the emphasis I take the context to require, and assuming that it will be obvious how each would otherwise habitually be emphasized: "The *present* was my next experiment of this kind"; "I sometimes *try* my acquaintances by such tests"; "It is a ridiculous demand which England and America make, that you shall speak so that *they* can understand you"; "I am a sojourner in *civilized* life again"; "I would fain say something concerning you who are said to *live* in New England"; "I think that we may safely trust a good *deal* more than we do" (I, 15); "the gross but somewhat foreign form of servitude called *Negro* Slavery" (I, 8); "In eternity there is indeed *something* true and sublime" (II, 21); "I do not propose to write an *ode* to dejection"; "I do not *propose* to write an ode to dejection." The fact that different emphases eclipse one another shows our hand in what we choose to say. This mode of controlling ambiguity shows that our mind is chanced, but not forced, by language. The point is to get us to assess our orientation or position toward what we say.

The assessments of our commitment and orientation, the idea of our distance from words and others and of their presence to us, are matters the writer often registers by his extraordinary placements of the word "interest." For example: "It was easy to see that they could not long be companions. . . . They would part at the first interesting crisis in their adventures" (I, 100); "A young man tried for a fortnight to live on hard, raw corn on the ear. . . . The human race is interested in these experiments" (I, 87); "How much more interesting an event is that man's supper who has just been forth in the snow to hunt, nay, you might say, steal, the fuel to cook it with! His bread and meat are sweet" (XIII, 12). It would be a fair summary of the book's motive to say that it invites us to take an interest in our lives, and teaches us how.

If *Walden* is a scripture it must contain a doctrine. (I take its writer to be acknowledging this in saying "I too had woven a kind of basket of a delicate texture" [I, 31]. A set of canonical Buddhist scriptures is called the "Three Baskets.") I have wished to suggest, or predict, a movement from more or less formal questions about the kind of book *Walden* is to matters more or less concerning its doctrine. Before going on to say more consecutively what I can about that, I pause to rehearse what I think of as the book's low myth of the reader. It may be thought of as a one-sentence fable: The writer has been describing the early spring days in which he went down to the woods to cut down timber for his intended house; he depicts himself carrying along his dinner of bread and butter wrapped in a newspaper which, while he was resting, he read. A little later he says:

> In those days, when my hands were much employed, I read but little, but the least scraps of paper which lay on the ground, my holder, or tablecloth, afforded me as much entertainment, in fact answered the same purpose as the Iliad. (I, 65)

If you do not know what reading can be, you might as well use the pages of the *Iliad* for the purpose for which newspaper is used after a meal in the woods. If, however, you are prepared to read, then a fragment of newspaper, discovered words, are sufficient promptings, bespeaking distant and kindred lives and deaths. The events in a newspaper, our current lives, are epic, and point morals, if we know how to interpret them. The words of the *Iliad* should come to us as immediately as election results or rumors of war.

> I kept Homer's Iliad on my table through the summer, though I looked at his page only now and then. Incessant labor with my hands, at first, for I had my house to finish and my beans to hoe at the same time, made more study impossible. (III, 2)

More study than what? More than looking at Homer's page now and then or more than hoeing his beans? ("I did not read books the first summer;

I hoed beans" [IV, 2].) From his description, I picture the book lying open on the table. Could looking at a page now and then, under any circumstances, constitute study? If not, how would turning the pages help?

Note

1 To make my references to *Walden* independent of any particular edition, I shall give citations by chapter and paragraph, roman numerals for the former, arabic for the latter. References to "Civil Disobedience" are also according to paragraph, preceded by "CD.'

15

Being Odd, Getting Even

This essay (reprinted in *In Quest of the Ordinary*) is one of a sequence in which Cavell makes amends for his initial dismissal of Emerson as a thinker. The sequence as a whole constitutes Cavell's attempt to inherit an intellectual project that ended with Thoreau – the establishment and maintenance of an American difference in philosophy, of a tradition in thought that is responsive to both the English and the Franco-German halves of the European mind, but which opens paths into a new philosophical world.

In this essay, the European tradition is represented by Descartes and his conception of the *cogito*, unsuccessfully thrown into the fight against skepticism; Cavell argues that Emerson's notion of self-reliance is an attempt to revive that conception by revising it in ways which amount to the claim that human beings exist only in so far as they acknowledge their existence – claim it, stake it, enact it (a relation here to Heidegger's early conception of distinctively human being is noted but not developed). This claim leads on to an examination of the ways in which Emerson's essays exemplify such anti-skeptical enactments of his own existence, and thence to an analysis of the model of writing and reading that his essays embody (the previous Essay, with its laying-out of Thoreau's model of these matters, is most directly relevant here – as is Essay 17, which makes it clear how these matters relate to the tradition of Moral Perfectionism). The essay ends by working out a set of connections between Emerson's conception of human existence and that of Poe. This allows Cavell to explore the varying significance of different invocations of madness in the work of philosophers aiming to oppose skepticism, and to develop his increasingly distinctive sense of the structures of ordinary language (his recounting of the grammar of the word "word" leading to the emergence of the notion of word-imps). It also produces a set of closing remarks which strikingly weave together his interests in Shakes-

Reprinted from *Reconstructing Individualism: Autonomy, Individuality, and the Self in Western Thought*, eds Thomas C. Heller, Morton Sosna, and David E. Wellbery, with the permission of the publishers, Stanford University Press. Copyright © 1986 by the Board of Trustees of the Leland Stanford Junior University.

peare and film comedies and melodramas with new inflections of the concepts of madness, revenge, theatricalization, and – perhaps most important – the ordinary understood as the domestic (Essay 13 is relevant here). But most generally, this ending to the essay implies that the American difference in philosophy ineluctably shifts our sense of the difference between philosophy and literature; once again, revising our conception of a discipline entails revising our conception of the economy of the culture that frames it.

In the lobby of William James Hall at Harvard, across the story-tall expanse of concrete above the bank of elevators facing you as you enter, brass letters spell out the following pair of sentences, attributed by further such letters to William James:

> THE COMMUNITY STAGNATES WITHOUT THE IMPULSE
> OF THE INDIVIDUAL
> THE IMPULSE DIES AWAY WITHOUT THE SYMPATHY
> OF THE COMMUNITY

The message may be taken as empirically directed to whoever stands beneath and reads it, and thence either as a warning, or an exhortation, or a description of a state of current affairs – or else it may be taken as claiming a transcendental relation among the concepts of community and individual as they have so far shown themselves. Does this multiplicity produce what certain literary theorists now speak of as the undecidable? Or is the brass indifference of this writing on the wall an apt expression of our avoidance of decision, a refusal to apply our words to ourselves, to take them on?

This lecture is a kind of progress report on my philosophical journey to locate an inheritance of Wittgenstein and Heidegger, and of Emerson and Thoreau before them, for all of whom there seems to be some question whether the individual or the community as yet, or any longer, exists. This question (or, you may say, this fantasy) gives ground equally for despair and for hope in the human as it now stands. It is also the question or fantasy in which I have been seeking instruction from certain Hollywood comedies of remarriage and, before them, from Shakespearean romance and tragedy. In this mood I do not wish to propose a solution to the riddle of whether society is the bane or the blessing of the individual, or to offer advice about whether a better state of the world must begin with a reformation of institutions or of persons, advice that would of course require me to define institutions and individuals and their modes of interpenetration. So I will pick up the twist in the story of the discovery of the individual where Descartes placed it in his *Meditations* – before, so to speak, either individual or institutional differences come into play. This twist is Descartes's discovery that my existence requires, hence permits, proof (you might say authentication) – more particularly, requires that if I am to exist I must name my existence, acknowledge it. This imperative entails that I am a thing with two foci, or in Emerson's image, two magnetic poles – say a positive and a negative, or an active and a passive.

Such a depiction may not seem to you right off to capture Descartes's cogito argument. But that something like it does capture that argument is what I understand the drift of Emerson's perhaps inaudibly familiar words in "Self-Reliance" to claim. My first task here will be to establish this about Emerson's essay; my second will be to say why I think Emerson is right, as right in his interpretation and inheritance of Descartes as any other philosophical descendant I know of. Following that, as a third principal task, I will take up a pair of tales by Edgar Allan Poe, primarily "The Imp of the Perverse" and subordinately "The Black Cat." These stories, I find, engage with the same imperative of human existence: that it must prove or declare itself. And since Poe's "The Imp of the Perverse" alludes more than once to *Hamlet*, it will bring us to my title, the idea of thinking about individuality (or the loss of it) under the spell of revenge, of getting even for oddness.

Emerson's incorporation of Descartes into "Self-Reliance" is anything but veiled. At the center of the essay is a paragraph that begins: "Man is timid and apologetic; he is no longer upright; he dares not say 'I think,' 'I am,' but quotes some saint or sage." It is my impression that readers of Emerson have not been impressed by this allusion, or repetition, perhaps because they have fallen into an old habit of condescending to Emerson (as if to pay for a love of his writing by conceding that he was hardly capable of consecutive thought, let alone capable of taking on Descartes), perhaps because they remember or assume the cogito always to be expressed in words that translate as "I think, *therefore* I am." But in Descartes's Second Meditation, where I suppose it is most often actually encountered, the insight is expressed: "*I am, I exist*, is necessarily true every time that I pronounce it or conceive it in my mind." Emerson's emphasis on the *saying* of "I" is precisely faithful to this expression of Descartes's insight.

It is this feature of the cogito that is emphasized in some of the most productive thinking about Descartes in recent analytical philosophy, where the issue, associated with the names of Jaakko Hintikka and Bernard Williams, is phrased as the question whether the certainty of existence required and claimed by the cogito results from taking the claim "I think" as the basis (i.e., premise) for an inference, or as the expression of some kind of performance. Williams does not quite rest with saying, with Hintikka, that the cogito just is not an inference, and just is a performance of some kind, but Williams does insist that it is not an ordinary, or syllogistic, inference, as he insists, at the end of his intricate discussion, that the performance in play is no less peculiar of its kind, demanding further reflection. The cogito's peculiarity can be summarized as follows, according to Williams. On the one hand, the force of the first person pronoun is that it cannot fail to refer to the one using it, hence one who says "I exist" must exist; or, put negatively, "I exist" is undeniable, which is to say, "I do not exist" cannot coherently be said. On the other hand, to be said sensibly, "I" must distinguish the one saying it, to whom it cannot fail to refer, from others to whom it does not, at that saying, refer. But Descartes's use of it arises exactly in a context in which there are no others to distinguish himself (so to speak) from. So the force of the pronoun is in apparent conflict with its sense.

Compared with such considerations, Emerson's remark about our not daring to say "I think," "I am," seems somewhat literary. But why? Emerson is picking up a question, or a side of the question, that succeeds the inferential or performance aspect of the cogito – namely, the question of what happens if I do *not* say (and of course do not say the negation of) "I am, I exist" or "conceive it in my mind." An analytical philosopher will hardly take much interest in this side of the question, since it will hardly seem worth arguing for or against the inference that if I do not say or perform the words "I am" or their equivalent (aloud or silently), therefore I perhaps do not exist. Surely the saying or thinking of some words may be taken to bear on whether the sayer or thinker of them exists at most in the sense of determining whether he or she *knows* of his or her existence, but surely not in the sense that the saying or thinking may create that existence.

But this assurance seems contrary to Descartes's findings. He speculates a few paragraphs after announcing the cogito: "I am, I exist – that is certain; but for how long do I exist? For as long as I think; for it might perhaps happen, if I totally ceased thinking, that I would at the same time completely cease to be." This does not quite say that my ceasing to think would cause, or would be, my ceasing to exist. It may amount to saying so if I must think of myself as having a creator (hence, according to Descartes, a preserver) and if all candidates for this role other than myself dropped out. These assumptions seem faithful to Descartes's text, so that I am prepared to take it that the cogito is only half the battle concerning the relation of my thinking to my existing, or perhaps "I think, therefore I am" expresses only half the battle of the cogito: Descartes establishes to his satisfaction that I exist only while, or if *and only if*, I think. It is this, it seems, that leads him to claim that the mind always thinks, an idea Nietzsche and Freud will put to further use.

Emerson goes the whole way with Descartes's insight – that I exist only if I think – but he thereupon denies that I (mostly) do think, that the "I" mostly gets into my thinking, as it were. From this it follows that the skeptical possibility is realized – that I do not exist, that I as it were haunt the world, a realization perhaps expressed by saying that the life I live is the life of skepticism. Just before the end of the Second Meditation, Descartes observes that "if I judge that [anything, say the external world] exists because I see it, certainly it follows much more evidently that I exist myself because I see it." Since the existence of the world is more doubtful than my own existence, if I do not know that I exist, I so to speak even more evidently do not know that the things of the world exist. If, accordingly, Emerson is to be understood as describing the life left to me under skepticism – implying that I do not exist among the things of the world, that I haunt the world – and if for this reason he is to be called literary and not philosophical, we might well conclude, So much the worse for philosophy. Philosophy shrinks before a description of the very possibility it undertakes to refute, so it can never know of itself whether it has turned its nemesis aside.

But it seems to me that one can see how Emerson arrives at his conclusion by a continuing faithfulness to Descartes's own procedures, to the fact, as one might put it, that Descartes's procedures are themselves as essentially literary as they are philosophical and that it may even have become essential to philosophy to show as much. After arriving at the cogito, Descartes immediately raises the question of his metaphysical identity: "But I do not yet know sufficiently clearly what I am, I who am sure that I exist." He raises this question six or seven times over the ensuing seven or eight paragraphs, rejecting along the way such answers as that he is a rational animal, or that he is a body, or that his soul is "something very rarefied and subtle, such as a wind, a flame, or a very much expanded air . . . infused throughout my grosser components," before he settles on the answer that he is essentially a thing that thinks. There is nothing in these considerations to call argument or inference; indeed, the most obvious description of these passages is to say that they constitute an autobiographical narrative of some kind. If Descartes is philosophizing, and if these passages are essential to his philosophizing, it follows that philosophy is not exhausted in argumentation. And if the power of these passages is literary, then the literary is essential to the power of philosophy; at some stage the philosophical becomes, or turns into, the literary.

Now I think one can describe Emerson's progress as his having posed Descartes's question for himself and provided a fresh line of answer, one you might call a grammatical answer: I am a being who to exist must say I exist, or must acknowledge my existence – claim it, stake it, enact it.

The beauty of the answer lies in its weakness (you may say its emptiness) – indeed, in two weaknesses. First, it does not prejudge what the I or self or mind or soul may turn out to be, but only specifies a condition that whatever it is must meet. Second, the proof only works in the moment of its giving, for what I prove is the existence only of a creature who *can* enact its existence, as exemplified in actually giving the proof, not one who at all times does in fact enact it. The transience of the existence it proves and the transience of its manner of proof seem in the spirit of the *Meditations*, including Descartes's proofs for God; this transience would be the moral of Descartes's insistence on the presence of clear and distinct ideas as essential to, let me say, philosophical knowledge. Only in the vanishing presence of such ideas does proof take effect – as if there were nothing to rely on but reliance itself. This is perhaps why Emerson will say, "To talk of reliance is a poor external way of speaking."

That what I am is one who to exist enacts his existence is an answer Descartes might almost have given himself, since it is scarcely more than a literal transcript of what I set up as the further half of the cogito's battle. It is a way of envisioning roughly the view of so-called human existence taken by Heidegger in *Being and Time:* that Dasein's being is such that its being is an issue for it (p. 68). But for Descartes to have given such an answer would have threatened the first declared purpose of his *Meditations*, which was to offer proof of God's existence. If I am one who can enact my existence, God's role in the enactment is compromised. Descartes's word for what I call "enacting" – or "claiming" or "staking" or "acknowledging" – is "authoring." In the Third Meditation:

> I wish to pass on now to consider whether I myself, who have the idea of God, could exist if there had been no God. And I ask, from what source would I have derived my existence? Possibly from myself, or from my parents . . . But if I were . . . the author of my own being, I would doubt nothing, I would experience no desires, and finally I would lack no perfection . . . I would be God (himself) . . . Even if I could suppose that possibly I have always been as I am now . . . it would not follow that no author of my existence need then be sought and I would still have to recognize that it is necessary that God is the author of my existence.

Apparently it is the very sense of my need for a human proof of my human existence – some authentication – that is the source of the idea that I need an author. ("Need for proof" will be what becomes of my intuition of my transience, or dependence, or incompleteness, or unfinishedness, or unsponsoredness – of the intuition that I am unauthorized.)

But surely the idea of self-authorizing is merely metaphorical, the merest exploitation of the coincidence that the Latin word for author is also the word for creating, nothing more than the by now fully discredited romantic picture of the author or artist as incomprehensibly original, as a world-creating and self-creating genius. It is true that the problematic of enacting one's existence skirts the edge of metaphysical nonsense. It asks us, in effect, to move from the consideration that we may sensibly disclaim certain actions as ours (ones done, as we may say, against our wills), and hence from the consideration that we may disclaim certain of our thoughts as ours (ones, it may be, we would not dream of acting on, though the terrain here gets philosophically and psychologically more dangerous), to the possibility that none of my actions and thoughts are mine – as if, if I am not a ghost, I am, I would like to say, *worked*, from inside or outside. This move to the metaphysical is like saying that since it makes sense to suppose that I might lack any or all of my limbs I might lack a body altogether, or that since I never see all of any object and hence may not know that a given object exists I may not know that the external world as such exists. Ordinary language philosophy, most notably in the teaching of Austin and of Wittgenstein, has discredited such moves to the metaphysical, as a way of discrediting the conclusions of skepticism. But in my interpretation of Wittgenstein, what is discredited is not the appeal or the threat of skepticism as such, but only skepticism's own pictures of its accomplishments. Similarly, what is discredited in the romantic's knowledge about self-authoring is only a partial picture of authoring and of creation, a picture of human creation as a literalized anthropomorphism of God's creation – as if to create myself I were required to begin with the dust of the ground and magic breath, rather than with, say, an uncreated human being and the power of thinking.

That human clay and the human capacity for thought are enough to inspire the authoring of myself is, at any rate, what I take Emerson's "Self-Reliance," as a reading of Descartes's cogito argument, to claim. I take his underlying turning of Descartes to be something like this: there is a sense of being the author of oneself that does not require me to imagine myself God (that may just be the name of the particular picture of the self as a self-present substance), a sense in which the absence of doubt and desire of which Descartes speaks in proving that God, not he, is the author of himself is a continuing task, not a property, a task in which the goal, or the product of the process, is not a state of being but a moment of change, say of becoming – a transience of being, a being of transience. (Emerson notes: "This one fact the world hates; that the soul *becomes*.") To make sense of this turn, Emerson needs a view of the world, a perspective on its fallenness, in which the *uncreatedness* of the individual manifests itself, in which human life appears as the individual's failure at self-creation, as a continuous loss of individual possibility in the face of some overpowering competitor. This is to say that, if my gloss of Emerson's reading of Descartes is right, the cogito's need arises at particular historical moments in the life of the individual and in the life of the culture.

Emerson calls the mode of uncreated life "conformity." But each of the modern prophets seems to have been driven to find some way of characterizing the threat to individual existence, to individuation, posed by the life to which their society is bringing itself. John Stuart Mill (in *On Liberty*) called it the despotism of opinion, and he characterized being human in his period in terms of deformity; he speaks of us as withered and starved, and as dwarfs (pp. 58–9). Nietzsche called the threat: the world of the last man ("Zarathustra's Prologue," §5), the world of the murderers of God (*Gay Science*, §125). Marx thinks of it rather as the preexistence of the human. Freud's discovery of the uncomprehended meaningfulness of human expression belongs in the line of such prophecy. Emerson's philosophical distinction here lies in his diagnosis of this moment and in his recommended therapy.

It is as a diagnosis of this state of the world that Emerson announces that Descartes's proof of self-existence (the foundation, Descartes named it, of the edifice of his former opinions, the fixed and immovable fulcrum on which to reposition the earth) cannot, or can no longer, be given, thus asking us to conclude (such is the nature of this peculiar proof) that man, the human, does not, or does no longer, exist. Here is Emerson's sentence again, together with the sentence and a half following it: "Man is timid and apologetic; he is no longer upright; he dares not say 'I think,' 'I am,' but quotes some saint or sage. He is ashamed before the blade of grass or the blowing rose . . . they are for what they are; they exist with God today." We can locate Emerson's proposed therapy in this vision of so-called man's loss of existence if we take the successive notations of this vision as in apposition, as interpretations of one another: being apologetic; being no longer upright; daring not to say, but only quoting; being ashamed, as if for not existing today. There are, as Wittgenstein is once moved to express himself (§525), a multitude of familiar paths leading off from these words in all directions. Let us take, or at least point down, two or three such paths.

To begin with, the idea that something about our mode of existence removes us from nature, and that this has to do with being ashamed, of course alludes to the romantic problematic of self-consciousness (or the post-Kantian interpretation of that problematic), a particular interpretation of the Fall of Man. But put Emerson's invocation of shame in apposition to his invocation of our loss of uprightness, and he may be taken as challenging, not passing on, the romantic interpretation of the Fall as self-consciousness, refusing to regard our shame as a metaphysically irrecoverable loss of innocence but seeing it instead as an unnecessary acquiescence (or necessary only as history is necessary) in, let me say, poor posture, a posture he calls timidity and apologeticness. I will simply claim, without citing textual evidence (preeminently the contexts in which the word "shame" and its inflections are deployed throughout Emerson's essay), that the proposed therapy is to become ashamed of our shame, to find our ashamed posture more shameful than anything it could be reacting to. One might say that he calls for more, not less, self-consciousness; but it would be better to say that he shows self-consciousness not to be the issue it seems. It, or our view of it, is itself a function of poor posture.

But really everything so far said about existence, preexistence, and so forth may be some function of poor posture – including, of course, our view of what poor posture may be. Bad posture Emerson variously names, in one passage, as peeping or stealing or skulking up and down "with the air of a charity-boy, a bastard, or an interloper in the world which exists for him"; in another, he finds men behaving as if their acts were fines they paid "in expiation of daily non-appearance on parade," done "as an apology or extenuation of their living in the world – as invalids and the insane pay a high board. Their virtues are penances." This vision of human beings as in postures of perpetual penance or self-mortification will remind readers of *Walden* of that book's opening pages (not to mention Nietzsche's *Genealogy of Morals*).

Good posture has two principal names or modes in "Self-Reliance": standing and sitting. The idea behind both modes is that of finding and taking and staying in a place. What is good in these postures is whatever makes them necessary to the acknowledgment, or the assumption, of individual existence, to the capacity to say "I." That this takes daring is what standing (up) pictures; that it takes claiming what belongs to you and disclaiming what does not belong to you is what sitting pictures. Sitting is thus the posture of being at home in the world (not peeping, stealing, skulking, or, as he also says, leaning), of owning or taking possession. This portrayal of the posture of sitting is, again, drawn out in *Walden*, at the opening of the second chapter ("Where I Lived, and What I Lived For") where what Thoreau calls acquiring property is what most people would consider passing it by. Resisting the temptation to follow the turnings of these paths, I put them at once in apposition to the notation that in not daring to say something what we do instead is to quote.

There is a gag here that especially appeals to contemporary sensibilities. Emerson writes, "Man dares not say . . . but quotes." But since at that moment he quotes Descartes, isn't he confessing that he too cannot say but can only quote? Then should we conclude that he is taking back or dismantling (or something) the entire guiding idea of "Self-Reliance"? Or is he rather suggesting that we are to overcome the binary opposition between saying and quoting, recognizing that each is always both, or that the difference is undecidable? That difference seems to me roughly the difference between what Thoreau calls the mother tongue and the father tongue, hence perhaps makes the difference between language and literariness. And since I am taking the difference between saying and quoting as one of posture, the proposal of undecidability strikes me as the taking of a posture, and a poor one. I imagine being told that the difference in posture partakes of the same undecidability. My reply is that you can decide to say so. My decision is otherwise. (It is helped by my intuition that a guiding remark of Freud's is conceivable this way: Where thought takes place in me, there shall I take myself.)

Emerson's gag, suggesting that saying is quoting, condenses a number of ideas. First, language is an inheritance. Words are before I am; they are common. Second, the question whether I am saying them or quoting them – saying them firsthand or secondhand, as it were – which means whether I am thinking or imitating, is the same as the question whether I do or do not exist as a human being and is a matter demanding proof. Third, the writing, of which the gag is part, is an expression of the proof of saying "I," hence of the claim that writing is a matter, say the decision, of life and death, and that what this comes to is the inheriting of language, an owning of words, which does not remove them from circulation but rather returns them, as to life.

That the claim to existence requires returning words to language, as if making them common to us, is suggested by the fourth sentence of "Self-Reliance": "To believe your own thought, to believe that what is true for you in your private heart is true for all men, – that is genius." (One path from these words leads to the transformation of the romantics' idea of genius: Genius is not a special endowment, like virtuosity, but a stance toward whatever endowment you discover is yours, as if life itself were a gift, and remarkable.) Genius is accordingly the name of the promise that the private and the social will be achieved together, hence of the perception that our lives now take place in the absence of either.

So Emerson is dedicating his writing to that promise when he says: "I shun father and mother and wife and brother when my genius calls me. I would write on the lintels of the door-post, *Whim.*" (I will not repeat what I have said elsewhere concerning Emerson's marking of Whim in the place of God and thus staking his writing as a whole as having the power to turn aside the angel of death.) The point I emphasize here is only that the life-giving power of words, of saying "I," is your readiness to subject your desire to words (call it Whim), to become intelligible, with no assurance that you will be taken up. ("I hope it may be better than Whim at last, but we cannot spend the day in explanation.") Emerson's dedication is a fantasy of finding your own voice, so that others, among them mothers and fathers, may shun you. This dedication enacts a posture toward, or response to, language as such, as if most men's words as a whole cried out for redemption: "Conformity makes them not false in a few particulars, authors of a few lies, but false in all particulars . . . so that every word they say chagrins us and we know not where to begin to set them right."

Citing authorship as the office of all users of language, a thing as commonly distributed as genius, is the plainest justification for seeing the enactment or acknowledgment of one's existence as the authoring of it and in particular for what we may take as Emerson's dominating claims for his writing: first, that it proves his human existence (i.e., establishes his right to say "I," to tell himself from and to others); second, that what he has proven on his behalf, others are capable of proving on theirs.

These claims come together in such a statement as "I will stand for humanity," which we will recognize as marking a number of paths: that Emerson's writing is in an upright posture; that what it says represents the human, meaning both that his portrait of himself is accurate only in so far as it portrays his fellows and that he is writing on their behalf (both as they stand, and as they stand for the eventual, what humanity may become); that he will for the time being stand humanity, bear it, as it is; and that he will stand up for it, protect it, guard it, presumably against itself. But to protect and guard someone by writing to and for that same one means to provide them instruction, or tuition.

The path I am not taking at this point leads from Emerson's speaking of "primary wisdom as Intuition," to which he adds, "All later teachings are tuitions." I note this path to commemorate my annoyance at having to stand the repeated, conforming description of Emerson as a philosopher of intuition, a description that uniformly fails to add that he is simultaneously the teacher of tuition, as though his speaking of all later teachings as tuitions were a devaluing of the teachings rather than a direction for deriving their necessary value. Take the calling of his genius as a name for intuition. Marking *Whim* on his doorpost was intuition's tuition; an enactment of the obligation to remark the calling, or access, of genius; to run the risk (or, as Thoreau puts it, to sit the risk) of noting what happens to you, of making this happenstance notable, remarkable, thinkable – of subjecting yourself, as said, to intelligibility.

How could we test the claim Emerson's writing makes to be such enactment, its claim to enact or acknowledge itself, to take on its existence, or, in Nietzsche's words, or rather Zarathustra's (which I imagine are more or less quoting Emerson's), to show that Emerson "does not say 'I' but performs 'I'" ("On the Despisers of the Body," p. 34)? (The mere complication of self-reference, the stock-in-trade of certain modernizers, may amount to nothing more than the rumor of my existence.) How else but by letting the writing teach us how to test it, word by word?

"Self-Reliance" as a whole presents a theory – I wish we knew how to call it an aesthetics – of reading. Its opening words are "I read the other day," and four paragraphs before Emerson cites the cogito he remarks, "Our reading is mendicant and sycophantic," which is to say that he finds us reading the way he finds us doing everything else. How can we read his theory of reading in order to learn how to read him? We would already have to understand it in order to understand it. I have elsewhere called this the (apparent) paradox of reading; it might just as well be called the paradox of writing, since of writing meant with such ambitions we can say that only after it has done its work of creating a writer (which may amount to sloughing or shaking off voices) can one know what it is to write. But you never know. I mean, you never know when someone will learn the posture, as for themselves, that will make sense of a field of movement, it may be writing, or dancing, or passing a ball, or sitting at a keyboard, or free associating. So the sense of paradox expresses our not understanding how such learning happens. What we wish to learn here is nothing less than whether Emerson exists, hence could exist for us; whether, to begin with, his writing performs the cogito he preaches.

He explicitly claims that it does, as he must. But before noting that, let me pause a little longer before this new major path, or branching of paths: the essay's theory of reading, hence of writing or speaking, hence of seeing and hearing. The theory, not surprisingly, is a theory of communication, hence of expression, hence of character – character conceived, as Emerson always conceives it, as naming at once, as faces of one another, the human individual and human language. The writing side of the theory is epitomized in the remark: "Character teaches above our wills. Men imagine that they communicate their virtue or vice only by overt actions, and do not see that virtue or vice emit a breath every moment." The reading side of the theory is epitomized in: "To talk of reliance is a poor external way of speaking. Who has more obedience than I masters me, though he should not raise his finger."

On the reading side, the idea of mastering Emerson is not that of controlling him, exactly (though it will be related to monitoring him), but rather that of coming into command of him, as of a difficult text, or instrument, or practice. That this mastery happens by obedience, which is to say, by a mode of listening, relates the process to his dedicating of his writing as heeding the call of his genius, which to begin with he is able to note as Whim. It follows that mastering his text is a matter of discerning the whim from which at each word it follows. On the writing side, the idea of communicating as emitting a breath every moment (as if a natural risk of writing were transmitting disease) means that with every word you utter you say more than you know you say (here genteel Emerson's idea is that you cannot smell your own breath), which means in part that you do not know in the moment the extent to which your saying is quoting.

(Let me attract attention to another untaken path here, on which one becomes exquisitely sensible of the causes of Nietzsche's love of Emerson's writing. I am thinking now of Nietzsche's *Ecce Homo*, a book about writing that bears the subtitle *How One Becomes What One Is*. Its preface opens with the declaration that the author finds it indispensable to say who he is because in his conversations with the educated he becomes convinced that he is not alive; the preface continues by claiming or warning that to read him is to breathe a strong air. This book's opening part, "Why I Am So Wise," closes by saying that one of its author's traits that causes difficulty in his contacts with others is the uncanny sensitivity of his instinct for cleanliness: the innermost parts, the entrails, of every soul are *smelled* by him [pp. 233–4].)

So the question Emerson's theory of reading and writing is designed to answer is not "What does a text mean?" (and one may accordingly not wish to call it a theory of interpretation) but rather "How is it that a text we care about in a certain way (expressed perhaps as our being drawn to read it with the obedience that masters) invariably says more than its writer knows, so that writers and readers write and read beyond themselves?" This might be summarized as "What does a text know?" or, in Emerson's term, "What is the genius of the text?"

Here I note what strikes me as a congenial and fruitful conjunction with what I feel I have understood so far of the practices of Derrida and of Lacan. Others may find my conjunction with these practices uncongenial if, for example, they take it to imply that what I termed the genius of the text, perhaps I should say its engendering, is fatal to or incompatible with the idea of an author and of an author's intention. This incompatibility ought to seem unlikely since both genius and intending have to do with inclination, hence with caring about something and with posture. Austin, in a seminar discussion at Harvard in 1955, once compared the role of intending with the role of headlights (on a miner's helmet? on an automobile?). (This material is published under the title "Three Ways of Spilling Ink.") An implication he may have had in mind is that driving somewhere (getting something done intentionally) does not on the whole happen by hanging a pair of headlights from your shoulders, sitting in an armchair, picking up an unattached steering wheel, and imagining a destination. (Though this is not unlike situations in which W. C. Fields has found himself.) Much else has to be in place – further mechanisms and systems (transmission, fuel, electrical), roads, the industries that produce and are produced by each, and so on – in order for headlights and a steering mechanism to do their work, even to be what they are. Even if some theorists speak as though intention were everything there is to meaning, is that a sensible reason for opposite theorists to assert that intention is nothing, counts for nothing in meaning? Is W. C. Fields our only alternative to Humpty Dumpty?[1]

But I was about to locate Emerson's explicit statement, or performance, of his cogito. In his eighth paragraph he writes: "Few and mean as my gifts may be, I actually am, and do not need for my own assurance or the assurance of my fellows any secondary testimony." Earlier in the paragraph he had said: "My life is for itself and not for a spectacle. . . . I ask primary evidence that you are a man, and refuse this appeal from the man to his actions." And two paragraphs later he will promise: "But do your work, and I shall know you."

In refusing the evidence of actions, or say behavior, Emerson is refusing, as it were before the fact, the thrashing of empiricist philosophy to prove the existence of other minds by analogy with one's own case, which essentially involves an appeal to others' behavior (and its similarity to our own) as all we can know of them with certainty. But how does Emerson evade and counter the picture on which such a philosophical drift repeatedly comes to grief, namely the picture according to which we cannot literally or directly have the experiences of others, cannot have what it is he apparently calls "primary evidence" of their existence? Emerson's counter is contained in the idea of what I called his promise: "But do your work, and I shall know you." Your work, what is yours to do, is exemplified, when you are confronted with Emerson's words, by reading those words – which means mastering them, obeying and hence following them, subjecting yourself to them as the writer has by undertaking to enact his existence in saying them. The test of following them is, according to Emerson's promise, that you will find yourself known by them, that you will take yourself on in them. It is what Thoreau calls conviction, calls being convicted by his words, read by them, sentenced. To acknowledge that I am known by what this text knows does not amount to agreeing with it, in the sense of believing it, as if it were a bunch of assertions or as if it contained a doctrine. To be known by it is to find thinking in it that confronts you. That would prove that a human existence is authored in it. But how will you prove thinking? How will you show your conviction?

One possibility Emerson presents as follows: "The virtue in most request is conformity. Self-reliance is its aversion." This almost says, and nearly means, that you find your existence in conversion, by converting to it, that thinking is a kind of turning oneself around. But what it directly says is that the world of conformity must turn from what Emerson says as he must turn from it and that since the process is never over while we live – since, that is, we are never finally free of one another – his reader's life with him will be a turning from, and returning from, his words, a moving on from them, by them. In "Fate," Emerson will call this aversion "antagonism": "Man is a stupendous antagonism," he says there. I can testify that when you stop struggling with Emerson's words they become insupportable.

But why does self-reliance insist that it will know its other, even create its other, meaning authorize the other's self-authorization, or auto-creation? Because it turns out that to gain the assurance, as Descartes had put it, that I am not alone in the world has turned out to require that I allow myself to be known. (I have called this requirement subjecting myself to intelligibility, or, say, legibility.) But doesn't this beg the question whether there *are* others there to do this knowing?

I would say rather that it orders the question. The fantasy of aloneness in the world may be read as saying that the step out of aloneness, or self-absorption, has to come without the assurance of others. (Not, perhaps, without their help.) "No one comes" is a tragedy for a child. For a grown-up it means the time has come to be the one who goes first (to offer oneself, allow oneself, to be, let us say, known). To this way of thinking, politics ought to have provided conditions for companionship, call it fraternity; but the price of companionship has been the suppression, not the affirmation, of otherness, that is to say, of difference and sameness, call these liberty and equality. A mission of Emerson's thinking is never to let politics forget this.

In declaring that his life is not for a spectacle but for itself, Emerson is not denying that it is a spectacle, and he thus inflects and recrosses his running themes of being seen, of shame, and of consciousness. A last citation on this subject will join "Self-Reliance" with Poe's "Imp of the Perverse."

In his fifth paragraph, Emerson says: "The man is as it were clapped into jail by his consciousness. As soon as he has once acted or spoken with *éclat* he is a committed person, watched by the sympathy or the hatred of hundreds, whose affections must now enter into his account. There is no Lethe for this." The idea is that we have become permanently and unforgettably visible to one another, in a state of perpetual theater. To turn aside consciousness, supposing that were possible, would accordingly only serve to distract us from this fact of our mutual confinement under one another's guard. The solution must then be to alter what it is we show, which requires turning even more watchfully to what it is we are conscious of and altering our posture toward it.

For example: "A man should learn to detect and watch that gleam of light which flashes across his mind from within, more than the lustre of the firmament of bards and sages. Yet he dismisses without notice his own thought, because it is his. In every work of genius we recognize our own rejected thoughts; they come back to us with a certain alienated majesty." Here I find a specification of finding myself known in this text; in it certain rejected thoughts of mine do seem to come back with what I am prepared to call alienated majesty (including the thought itself of my rejected thoughts). Then presumably this writer has managed not to dismiss his own thoughts but to call them together, to keep them on parade, at attention. ("Tuition" speaks differently of being guarded; and unguarded.)

Yet he speaks from the condition of being a grown-up within the circumstances of civil (or uncivil) obedience he describes, so he says all he says clapped into jail by his consciousness – a decade before Thoreau was clapped into jail, and for the same reason, for obeying rejected things. How is he released? If, going on with Emerson's words, there were Lethe for our bondage to the attention of others, to their sympathy or hatred, we would utter opinions that would be "seen to be not private but necessary, would sink like darts into the ear of men and put them in fear" – that is, my visibility would then frighten my watchers, not the other way around, and my privacy would no longer present confinement but instead the conditions necessary for freedom. But as long as these conditions are not known to be achieved, the writer cannot know that I am known in his utterances, hence that he and I have each assumed our separate existences. So he cannot know but that in taking assurance from the promise of knowing my existence he is only assuming my existence and his role in its affirmation, hence perhaps shifting the burden of proof from himself and still awaiting me to release him from his jail of consciousness, the consciousness of the consciousness of others. When is writing *done*?

That "Self-Reliance" may accordingly be understood to show writing as a message from prison forms its inner connection with Poe's "Imp of the Perverse." (The thought of such a message, of course, forms other connections as well – for example, with Rousseau's *Social Contract*, whose early line, "Man is born free and everywhere he is in chains," names a condition from which the writer cannot be exempting his writing, especially if his interpretation of his writing's enchainment is to afford a step toward the freedom it is compelled, by its intuition of chains, to imagine.) I can hardly do more here than give some directions for how I think Poe's tale should, or anyway can, be read. This is just as well, because the validation of the reading requires from first to last that one take the time to try the claims on oneself. The claims have generally to do with the sound of Poe's prose, with what Emerson and Nietzsche would call its air or its smell. Poe's tale is essentially about the breath it gives off.

The sound of Poe's prose, of its incessant and perverse brilliance, is uncannily like the sound of philosophy as established in Descartes, as if Poe's prose were a parody of philosophy's. It strikes me that in Poe's tales the thought is being worked out that, now anyway, philosophy exists only as a parody of philosophy, or rather as something indistinguishable from the perversion of philosophy, as if to overthrow the reign of reason, the reason that philosophy was born to establish, is not alone the task of, let us say, poetry but is now openly the genius or mission of philosophy itself. As if the task of disestablishing reason were the task of reconceiving it, of exacting a transformation or reversal of what we think of as thinking and so of what we think of as establishing the reign of thinking. A natural effect of reading such writing is to be unsure whether the writer is perfectly serious. I dare say that the writer may himself or herself be unsure, and that this may be a good sign that the writing is doing its work, taking its course. Then Poe's peculiar brilliance is to have discovered a sound, or the condition, of intelligence in which neither the reader nor the writer knows whether he or she is philosophizing, is thinking to some end. This is an insight, a philosophical insight, about philosophy: namely, that it is as difficult to stop philosophizing as it is to start. (As difficult, in Wittgenstein's words, as to bring philosophy peace [§133]. Most people I know who care about philosophy either do not see this as a philosophical problem or do not believe that it has a solution.)

A convenient way of establishing the sound of Poe's tales is to juxtapose the opening sentences of "The Black Cat" with some early sentences from Descartes's *Meditations*. Here is Descartes:

> There is no novelty to me in the reflection that, from my earliest years, I have accepted many false opinions as true, and that what I have concluded from such badly assured premises could not but be highly doubtful and uncertain. . . . I have found a serene retreat in peaceful solitude. I will therefore make a serious and unimpeded effort to destroy generally all my former opinions. . . . Everything which I have thus far accepted as entirely true and assured has been acquired from the senses or by means of the senses. But I have learned by experience that these senses sometimes mislead me, and it is prudent never to trust wholly those things which have once deceived us. . . . But it is possible that, even though the senses occasionally deceive us . . . there are many other things which we cannot reasonably doubt . . . – as, for example, that I am here, seated by the fire, wearing a winter dressing gown, holding this

paper in my hands, and other things of this nature. And how could
I deny that these hands and this body are mine, unless I am to
compare myself with certain lunatics . . . [who] imagine that their
head is made of clay, or that they are gourds, or that their body is
glass? . . . Nevertheless, I must remember that I am a man, and that
consequently I am accustomed to sleep and in my dreams to imagine the same things that lunatics imagine when awake. . . . I
realize so clearly that there are no conclusive indications by which
waking life can be distinguished from sleep that I am quite
astonished, and my bewilderment is such that it is almost able to
convince me that I am sleeping.

Now listen to Poe:

For the most wild, yet almost homely narrative which I am about to
pen, I neither expect nor solicit belief. Mad indeed would I be to
expect it, in a case where my very senses reject their own evidence.
Yet, mad am I not – and very surely do I not dream. But to-morrow
I die, and today I would unburthen my soul. My immediate purpose
is to place before the world, plainly, succinctly, and without comment, a series of mere household events. In their consequences,
these events have terrified – have tortured – have destroyed me. Yet
I will not attempt to expound them.

The juxtaposition works both ways: to bring out at once Poe's brilliance
(and what is more, his argumentative soundness) and Descartes's creepy,
perverse calm (given the subjects his light of reason rakes across), his air
of a mad diarist.

Moreover, the *Meditations* appear within the content of "The Imp of
the Perverse," as indelibly, to my mind, as in "Self-Reliance." Before
noting how, let me briefly describe this lesser-known tale. It is divided
into two parts, each more or less eight paragraphs in length. The first half
is, as Poe says about certain of Hawthorne's tales, not a tale at all but an
essay. The essay argues for the existence of perverseness as a radical,
primitive, irreducible faculty or sentiment of the soul, the propensity to
do wrong for the wrong's sake, promptings to act for the reason that we
should not – something it finds overlooked by phrenologists, moralists,
and in great measure "all metaphysicianism," through "the pure arrogance of the reason." This phrase "the pure arrogance of the reason," to
my ear, signals that Poe is writing a *Critique* of the arrogance of pure
reason – as if the task, even after Kant, were essentially incomplete, even
unbegun. (This characterization is not incompatible with the appreciation of Poe as a psychologist, but only with a certain idea of what

psychology may be.) The second half of "The Imp of the Perverse," which tells the tale proper, begins:

> I have said thus much, that in some measure I may answer your question – that I may explain to you why I am here – that I may assign to you something that shall have at least the faint aspect of a cause for my wearing these fetters, and for my tenanting this cell of the condemned. Had I not been thus prolix, you might either have misunderstood me altogether, or, with the rabble, have fancied me mad. As it is, you will easily perceive that I am one of the many uncounted victims of the Imp of the Perverse.

Since we have not been depicted as asking, or having, a question, the narrator's explanation insinuates that we ought to have one about his presence; thus it raises more questions than it formulates.

The tale turns out to be a Poe-ish matter about the deliberately wrought murder of someone for the apparent motive of inheriting his estate, a deed that goes undetected until some years later the writer perversely gives himself away. As for the means of the murder: "I knew my victim's habit of reading in bed. . . . I substituted, in his bed-room candlestand, a [poisoned] wax-light of my own making, for the one which I there found." The self-betrayal comes about when, as he puts it, "I arrested myself in the act." That act is murmuring, half-aloud, "I am safe," and then adding, "yes, if I be not fool enough to make open confession." But "I felt a maddening desire to shriek aloud. . . . Alas! I well, too well understand that, to *think*, in my situation, was to be lost. . . . I bounded like a madman through the crowded thoroughfare. At length, the populace took the alarm, and pursued me."

To the first of my directions for reading "The Imp" I expect nowadays little resistance: both the fiction of the writer's arresting himself and wearing fetters and tenanting the cell of the condemned and the fiction of providing a poisonous wax light for reading are descriptions or fantasies of writing, modeled by the writing before us. There is, or at least we need imagine, no actual imprisoning and no crime but the act of the writing itself. What does it mean to fantasize that words are fetters and cells and that to read them, to be awake to their meaning, or effect, is to be poisoned? Are we being told that writer and reader are one another's victims? Or is the suggestion that to arrive at the truth something in the reader as well as something in the writer must die? Does writing ward off or invite in the angel of death?

I expect more resistance to, or puzzlement at, the further proposal that the fiction of words that are in themselves unremarkable ("I am safe"), but whose saying annihilates the sayer, specifies the claim that "I well, too well understand that, to *think*, in my situation, was to be lost" – which is a kind of negation or perversion of the cogito. Rather than proving and preserving me, as in Descartes, thinking precipitates my destruction. A little earlier Poe's narrator makes this even clearer: "There is no passion in nature so demoniacally impatient, as that of him, who shuddering on the edge of a precipice, thus meditates a plunge. To indulge for a moment, in any attempt at *thought*, is to be inevitably lost; for reflection but urges us to forbear, and *therefore* it is, I say, that we *cannot* . . . we plunge, and are destroyed." If the Whim drawing on Emerson's "Self-Reliance" is to say "I do not think, therefore I do not exist," that of Poe's Imp is to say, "I think, therefore I am destroyed." This connection is reinforced, in this brief passage, by the words "meditates" and "demoniacally." Poe's undetected, poisoned wax light may even substitute for, or allude to, Descartes's most famous example (of materiality) in the *Meditations*, the piece of melting wax whose identity cannot be determined empirically, but only by an innate conception in the understanding. (That in Poe's tale the act of thinking destroys by alarming the populace and turning them against the thinker and that perverseness is noted as the confessing of a crime, not the committing of it – as if the confessing and the committing were figurations of one another – mark paths of parody and perverseness I cannot trace here. That thinking will out, that it inherently betrays the thinker – [th]inker – is a grounding theme of *Walden*. Its writer declares in the opening chapter, "Economy," that what he prints must in each character "thus unblushingly publish my guilt." He says this upon listing the costs of what he ate for the year. It is as if his guilt consists exactly in keeping himself alive ("getting a living," he says) in his existing, as he exists, and his preserving himself, for example, by writing.)

My third suggestion for reading Poe's tale is that the presiding image collecting the ideas I have cited and setting them in play is given in its title. The title names and illustrates a common fact about language, even invokes what one might think of as an Emersonian theory of language: the possession of language as the subjection of oneself to the intelligible. The fact of language it illustrates is registered in the series of imp words that pop up throughout the sixteen paragraphs of the tale: *impulse* (several times), *impels* (several times), *impatient* (twice), *important, impertinent, imperceptible, impossible, unimpressive, imprisoned*, and, of course, *Imp*. Moreover, *imp.* is an abbreviation in English for *imperative, imperfect, imperial, import, imprimatur, impersonal, implement, improper*, and *improvement*. And *Imp*. is an abbreviation for *Emperor* and *Empress*. Now if to speak of the imp of the perverse is to name the imp in English, namely as the initial sounds of a number of characteristically Poe-ish terms, then to speak of something called the perverse as containing this imp is to speak of language itself, specifically of English, as the perverse. But what is it about the imp of English that is perverse, hence presumably helps to produce, as users of language, us imps?

It may well be the prefix *im-* that is initially felt to be perverse, since, like the prefix *in-*, it has opposite meanings. With adjectives it is a negation or privative, as in *immediate, immaculate, imperfect, imprecise, improper, implacable, impious, impecunious*; with verbs it is an affirmation or intensive, as in *imprison, impinge, imbue, implant, impulse, implicate, impersonate*. (It is not impossible that *per-verse*, applied to language, should be followed out as meaning poetic through and through.) In plain air we keep the privative and the intensive well enough apart, but in certain circumstances (say in dreams, in which, according to Freud, logical operations like negation cannot be registered or pictured but must be supplied later by the dreamer's interpretation) we might grow confused about whether, for example, *immuring* means putting something into a wall or letting something out of one, or whether *impotence* means powerlessness or a special power directed to something special, or whether *implanting* is the giving or the removing of life, or whether *impersonate* means putting on another personality or being without personhood.

But the fact or idea of imp words is not a function of just that sequence of three letters. "Word imps" could name any of the recurrent combinations of letters of which the words of a language are composed. They are part of the way words have their familiar looks and sounds, and their familiarity depends upon our mostly not noticing the particles (or cells) and their laws, which constitute words and their imps – on our not noticing their necessary recurrences, which is perhaps only to say that recurrence constitutes familiarity. This necessity, the most familiar property of language there could be – that if there is to be language, words and their cells must recur, as if fettered in their orbits, that language is grammatical (to say the least) – insures the self-referentiality of language. When we do note these cells or molecules, these little moles of language (perhaps in thinking, perhaps in derangement), what we discover are word imps – the initial, or it may be medial or final, movements, the implanted origins or constituents of words, leading lives of their own, staring back at us, calling upon one another, giving us away, alarming – because to note them is to see that they live in front of our eyes, within earshot, at every moment.

But the perverseness of language, working without, even against, our thought and its autonomy, is a function not just of necessarily recurring imps of words but of the necessity for us speakers of language (us authors of it, or imps, or Emperors and Empresses of it) to mean something in and by our words, to desire to say something, certain things rather than others, in certain ways rather than in others, or else to work to avoid meaning them. Call these necessities the impulses and the implications of the saying of our words. There is – as in saying "I am safe," which destroyed safety and defeats what is said – a question whether in speaking one is affirming something or negating it. In particular, in such writing as Poe's has the impulse to self-destruction, to giving oneself away or betraying oneself, become the only way of preserving the individual? And does it succeed? Is authoring the obliteration or the apotheosis of the writer?

In the passage I cited earlier from "The Black Cat," the writer does not speak of being in fetters and in a cell, but he does name his activity as penning; since the activity at hand is autobiography, he is penning himself. Is this release or incarceration? He enforces the question by going on to say that he will not expound – that is, will not remove something (presumably himself) from a pound, or pen. But this may mean that he awaits expounding by the reader. Would this be shifting the burden of his existence onto some other? And who might we be to bear such a burden? Mustn't we also seek to shift it? Granted that we need one another's acknowledgment, isn't there in this very necessity a mutual victimization, one that our powers of mutual redemption cannot overcome? Is this undecidable? Or is deciding this question exactly as urgent as deciding to exist?

I will draw to a close by forming three questions invited by the texts I have put together.

First, what does it betoken about the relation of philosophy and literature that a piece of writing can be seen to consist of what is for all the world a philosophical essay preceding, even turning into, a fictional tale – as it happens, a fictional confession from a prison cell? To answer this would require a meditation on the paragraph, cited earlier, in which Poe pivots from the essay to the tale, insinuating that we are failing to ask a question about the origin of the writing and claiming that without the philosophical preface – which means without the hinging of essay and tale, philosophy and fiction – the reader might, "with the rabble, have fancied me mad," not perceiving that he is "one of the many uncounted victims of the Imp of the Perverse." The meditation would thus enter, or center, on the idea of counting, and it is one I have in fact undertaken, under somewhat different circumstances, as part 1 of *The Claim of Reason*.

There I interpret Wittgenstein's *Philosophical Investigations*, or its guiding idea of a criterion, hence of grammar, as providing in its responsiveness to skepticism the means by which the concepts of our language are *of* anything, as showing what it means to have concepts, how it is that we are able to word the world together. The idea of a criterion I emphasize is that of a way of counting something as something, and I put this together with accounting and recounting, hence projecting a connection between telling as numbering or computing and telling as relating or narrating. Poe's (or, if you insist, Poe's narrator's) speaking pivotally of being an uncounted victim accordingly suggests to me that philosophy and literature have come together (for him, but who is he?) at the need for recounting, for counting again, and first at counting the human beings there are, for reconceiving them – a recounting beginning from the circumstances that it is I, some I or other, who counts, who is able to do the thing of counting, of conceiving a world, that it is I who, taking others into account, establish criteria for what is worth saying, hence for the intelligible. But this is only on the condition that I count, that I matter, that it matters that I count in my agreement or attunement with those with whom I maintain my language, from whom this inheritance – language as the condition of counting – comes, so that it matters not only what some I or other says but that it is some particular I who desires in some specific place to say it. If my counting fails to matter, I am mad. It is being uncounted – being left out, as if my story were untellable – that makes what I say (seem) perverse, that makes me odd. The surmise that we have become unable to count one another, to count for one another, is philosophically a surmise that we have lost the capacity to think, that we are stupefied.[2] I call this condition living our skepticism.

Second, what does it betoken about fact and fiction that Poe's writing of the Imp simultaneously tells two tales of imprisonment – in one of which he is absent, in the other present – as if they are fables of one another? Can we know whether one is the more fundamental? Here is the relevance I see in Poe's tale's invoking the situation of Hamlet, the figure of our culture who most famously enacts a question of undecidability, in particular, an undecidability over the question whether to believe a tale of poisoning. (By the way, Hamlet at the end, like his father's ghost at the beginning, claims to have a tale that is untellable – it is what makes both of them ghosts.) In Poe's tale, the invocation of *Hamlet* is heard, for example, in the two appearances of a ghost, who the first time disappears upon the crowing of a cock. And it is fully marked in the second of the three philosophical examples of perversity that Poe's narrator offers in order to convince any reader, in his words, "who trustingly consults and thoroughly questions his own soul" of "the entire radicalness of the propensity in question":

The most important crisis of our life calls, trumpet-tongued, for immediate energy and action. We glow, we are consumed with eagerness to commence the work. . . . It must, it shall be under-taken today, and yet we put it off until to-morrow; and why? There is no answer, except that we feel *perverse*, using the word with no

comprehension of the principle. To-morrow arrives, and with it a
more impatient anxiety to do our duty, but with this very increase
of anxiety arrives, also, a nameless, a positively fearful because
unfathomable, craving for delay.

These words invoke Hamlet along lines suspiciously like those in which
I have recently been thinking about what I call Hamlet's burden of proof
– but no more suspiciously, surely, than my beginning to study Poe while
thinking about Hamlet.

Hamlet studies the impulse to take revenge, usurping thought as a
response to being asked to assume the burden of another's existence, as
if that were the burden, or price, of assuming one's own, a burden that
denies one's own. Hamlet is asked to make a father's life work out
successfully, to come out even, by taking his revenge for him. The
emphasis in the question "to be or not" seems not on whether to die but
on whether to be born, on whether to affirm or deny the fact of natality,
as a way of enacting, or not, one's existence. To accept birth is to
participate in a world of revenge, of mutual victimization, of shifting and
substitution. But to refuse to partake in it is to poison everyone who
touches you, as if taking your own revenge. This is why if the choice is
unacceptable the cause is not metaphysics but history – say, a posture
toward the discovery that there is no getting even for the oddity of being
born, hence of being and becoming the one poor creature it is given to
you to be. The alternative to affirming this condition is, as Descartes's
Meditations shows, world-consuming doubt, which is hence a standing
threat to, or say condition of, human existence. (I imagine that the
appearance of the cogito at its historical moment is a sign that some
conditions were becoming ones for which getting even, or anyway overcoming, was coming to seem in order: for example, the belief in God and
the rule of kings.) That there is something like a choice or decision about
our natality is what I take Freud's idea of the diphasic structure of human
sexual development (in "Three Essays") to show – a provision of, so to
speak, the condition of the possibility of such a decision. The condition
is that of adolescence, considered as the period in which, in preparation
for becoming an adult, one recapitulates, as sufering rebirth, one's
knowledge of satisfactions. This is why, it seems to me, one speculates
about Hamlet's age but thinks of him as adolescent. These matters are
represented in political thought under the heading of consent, about
which, understandably, there has from the outset been a question of
proof.

Finally, what does it betoken about American philosophy that Emerson
and Poe may be seen as taking upon themselves the problematic of the
cogito (Emerson by denying or negating it, Poe by perverting or subvert-

ing it) and as sharing the perception that authoring – philosophical writing, anyway, writing as thinking – is such that to exist it must assume, or acknowledge, the proof of its own existence? I have in effect said that to my mind this betokens their claim to be discovering or rediscovering the origin of modern philosophy, as sketched in Descartes's *Meditations*, as if literature in America were forgiving philosophy, not without punishing it, for having thought that it could live only in the banishing of literature. What does it mean that such apparent opposites as Emerson and Poe enter such a claim within half a dozen years of one another?

Let us ask what the connection is between Emerson's ecstasies (together with Thoreau's) and Poe's horrors (together with Hawthorne's). The connection must be some function of the fact that Poe's and Hawthorne's worlds, or houses and rooms, have other people in them, typically marriages, and typically show these people's violent shunning, whereas Emerson's and Thoreau's worlds begin with or after the shunning of others ("I shun father and mother and wife and brother when my genius calls me") and typically depict the "I" just beside itself. The interest of the connection is that all undertake to imagine domestication, or inhabitation – as well, being Americans, they might. For Emerson and Thoreau you must learn to sit at home or to sit still in some attractive spot in the woods, as if to marry the world, before, if ever, you take on the burden of others; for Poe and Hawthorne even America came too late, or perhaps too close, for that priority.

A more particular interest I have in the connection among these American writers is a function of taking their concepts or portrayals of domestication and inhabitation (with their air of ecstasy and of horror turned just out of sight) to be developments called for by the concepts of the ordinary and the everyday as these enter into the ordinary language philosopher's undertaking to turn aside skepticism, in the pains Austin and Wittgenstein take to lay out what it is that skepticism threatens. In the work of these philosophers, in their stubborn, accurate superficiality, perhaps for the first time in recognizable philosophy this threat of world-consuming doubt is interpreted in all its uncanny homeliness, not merely in isolated examples but, in Poe's words, as "a series of mere household events."

I end with the following prospect. If some image of marriage, as an interpretation of domestication, in these writers is the fictional equivalent of what these philosophers understand to be the ordinary, or the everyday, then the threat to the ordinary named skepticism should show up in fiction's favorite threat to forms of marriage, namely, in forms of melodrama. Accordingly, melodrama may be seen as an interpretation of Descartes's cogito, and, contrariwise, the cogito can be seen as an interpretation of the advent of melodrama – of the moment (private and public) at which the theatricalization of the self becomes the sole proof of its freedom and its existence. This is said on tiptoe.

Notes

1 In linking W. C. Fields's suffering of convention with Humpty Dumpty's claim to be master, by his very wishes, of what words shall mean (and thinking of his fate), I find I have not forgotten a passage during the discussions of "Must We Mean What We Say?" the day I delivered it in 1957 (at Stanford, it happens). Against a certain claim in my paper, one philosopher cited Humpty Dumpty's view of meaning (by name) as obviously, in all solemnity, the correct one. This was, I think, the first time I realized the possibility that parody is no longer a distinguishable intellectual tone since nothing can any longer be counted on to strike us in common as outrageous.
2 I find it hard not to imagine that this surmise has to do with the history of the frantic collection of statistical tables cited in Ian Hacking's "Making Up People," and "Prussian Statistics." Emerson's essay "Fate" self-consciously invokes the new science of statistics as a new image of human fate – a new way in which others are finding us captured by knowledge and which Emerson finds a further occasion for ignorance.

16

Declining Decline

The subtitle of this essay (the first of the pair of essays comprising *This New Yet Unapproachable America*) is "Wittgenstein as a Philosopher of Culture," which admirably encapsulates its concerns. Most immediately, Cavell aims to develop a conception of Wittgenstein's philosophy in which his concern with culture is not restricted to the content of the remarks on various cultural matters which have been collected in *Culture and Value*. It is rather focused upon culture understood as an aspect of or synecdoche for forms of life, and so inevitably leads to a deeper and more detailed exploration of Wittgenstein's key assumption that "to imagine a language is to imagine a form of life." In this context, Cavell's early ideas on the topic (addressed in Essay 1) are expanded to allow for a dual-aspect interpretation of "forms of life" – these aspects being labelled as the "biological" and the "ethnological" senses of the term. The complex interplay between these two senses opens a space in which Cavell can identify the sources of his intuition that there is a perfectionist moment in Wittgenstein's thought – that the latter's commitment to philosophy leaving everything as it is might none the less be compatible with a vision of the grammar of ordinary words as embodying the resources for a critique of existing forms of human culture in the name of an unattained but attainable further state of society and self. Essay 17 provides a wider conceptual framework in terms of which to locate this strand of Wittgenstein's thought.

This same conceptual space also allows Cavell to give a detailed reading of the opening remarks of the *Philosophical Investigations* – a reading which manifests his distinctive sense of the way in which Augustine's remarks about the child acquiring language from its elders guide the development of the whole of the book (an issue further explored in the concluding essay of *Philosophical Passages*). This reading reiterates and deepens his early sense that the question of how and whether language is passed on is inseparable from the question of how and

Originally published in *This New Yet Unapproachable America: Lectures after Emerson after Wittgenstein* (Albuquerque, NM: Living Batch Press/Chicago: University of Chicago Press, 1989), pp. 32–75. Reprinted by permission.

whether culture can be inherited, and that both have a moral or ethical dimension – they are questions of acknowledgment. It is from this perspective that Cavell is able to explain with particular clarity his sense of the multiple connections between the air of spiritual fervor that pervades Wittgenstein's philosophy and the fundamental orientations of Heidegger's and Emerson's paths of thinking; for all three, morality or ethics or spirituality is not a separate branch of philosophy but its abiding core. And as a consequence, these perfectionist philosophers can neither simply dismiss nor simply appropriate the concerns and concepts of Christian texts and traditions. The culture of which Wittgenstein is a philosopher is a culture of the Book.

Everydayness as Home

The *Investigations* lends itself to, perhaps it calls out for, competing emphases in its consideration of human discourse – an emphasis on its distrust of language or an emphasis on its trust of ordinary human speech. The competition is the emblem of philosophy's struggle with itself. Every student of the book will have some reaction to both sides, or voices.

Those who emphasize Wittgenstein's distrust of language take most to heart the side of Wittgenstein's thought that speaks variously of "problems arising through a misinterpretation of our forms of language" (*Philosophical Investigations*, §111). Coming to the *Investigations* not from the *Tractatus* but as it were for itself, what strikes me is rather the side of Wittgenstein that trusts ordinary speech, that finds what peace there is from the "deep disquietudes" (ibid.) of our philosophical misinterpretation in the appeal of the everyday. I do not mean that in the *Tractatus* Wittgenstein distrusts everyday language (for everyday interests?). There he had famously said at 5.5563, "In fact, all the propositions of our everyday language, just as they stand, are in perfect logical order." But that order is exactly not, as I would like to say it is for the *Investigations*, recognized as the medium of philosophical thinking. The power of this recognition of the ordinary for philosophy is bound up with the recognition that refusing or forcing the order of the ordinary is a cause of philosophical emptiness (say avoidance) and violence. Whatever the distance between what in the passage just quoted from the *Tractatus* is called *unserer Umgangssprache* (translated by Pears and McGuinness as "our everyday language," and may, no less dangerously, be translated as "our colloquial speech"; C. K. Ogden's earlier translation has "our colloquial language") and what in the *Investigations* is called *unserer alltäglichen Sprache* (§134) (translated by Anscombe as "our everyday language"), their continuity in Wittgenstein's thought is secured by his sense of them both as *ours*; the distance is measured by his later sense of the ordinary in connection with an idea of home. What I had in mind in alluding to some "danger" in translating *Umgangssprache* as colloquial speech is that it may make words appear as fashions of speech, dictates of sociability, manners of putting something that are more or less evanescent or arbitrary and are always to be passed beyond philosophically into something more permanent and precise. The danger in translating *Umgangssprache* as colloquial speech is that it leaves out the German word's extraordinary representation of everyday language as a form of circulation, communication as exchange; it makes the word too, let us say, colloquial. I do not say that the informality of the colloquial is insignificant, merely that it is no more significant than the formality of the colloquy. Yet philosophers find it their intellectual birthright to distrust the everyday, as in Descartes's second meditation: ". . . words impede me, and I am nearly deceived by the terms of ordinary language. For we say that we see the same wax. . . ." And I know of no respectable philosopher since the time of Descartes who entrusts the health of the human spirit to ordinary language with Wittgenstein's completeness. (I am not here considering Austin and the areas of conjunction between him and Wittgenstein. I merely say that my old teacher seems to me (except in certain notable cases) fantastically underrated in the circles I mostly move in – either scientized or else accepted as the superficial sensibility he liked to portray himself, with profound deviousness, to be.) Philosophers before Wittgenstein had found that our lives are distorted or waylaid by illusion. But what other philosopher has found the antidote to illusion in the particular and repeated humility of remembering and tracking the uses of humble words, looking philosophically as it were beneath our feet rather than over our heads?

Inquiring that way (into entrusting the health of the human spirit) I am in fact armed with names, before all with those of Emerson and of Thoreau, whose emphasis on what they call the common, the everyday, the near, the low, I have in recent years repeatedly claimed as underwriting the ordinariness sought in the ordinary language methods of Wittgenstein and of Austin. I will come back more than once to Emerson and to Thoreau, but I have at once to acknowledge a commitment, given my stake in the method of the recovery of the ordinary, to find a measure of Wittgenstein's originality in the originality of his approach to the everyday.

I continue to be caught by Wittgenstein's description of his itinerary as asking oneself: "Is the word ever actually used this way in the language game which is its original home?" (§116). It expresses a sense that in philosophy (wherever that is) words are somehow "away," as if in exile, since Wittgenstein's word seeks its *Heimat*. The image or sense of our words as out, as absent, or truant, casts a certain light on Wittgenstein's speaking of language in philosophy as "idle" (cf. §132): it presents that condition as caused, not as it were by something in language, but, since these are our words, caused by us; or at least it is a condition for which we, each of us philosophers, is responsible, or say answerable, not perhaps as if we personally banish our words but as if it is up to us to seek their return. Wittgenstein says in the sentence following that containing *Heimat*: "What *we* do is to bring words back from their metaphysical to their everyday use." *Wir* führen die Wörter . . . We as opposed to "philosophers" (to that side of ourselves); and, I think, the *way* we "bring" them as opposed to the way philosophers "use" them. (From which point of view is the idea of "use" seen here, from that of philosophy or that of the everyday? *Is* the everyday a point of view? Is thinking so itself a philosophical distortion? Then perhaps there is a suggestion that to think of the daily round of exchange as "using" words is already to surmise that we misuse them, mistreat them, even everyday. As if the very identifying of the everyday may take too much philosophy.) It would a little better express my sense of Wittgenstein's practice if we translate the idea of bringing words back as *leading* them back, shepherding them; which suggests not only that we have to find them, to go to where they have wandered, but that they will return only if we attract and command them, which will require listening to them. But the translation is only a little better, because the behavior of words is not something separate from our lives, those of us who are native to them, in mastery of them. The lives themselves have to return.

But now, even if someone agreed that such intuitions are from time to time expressed in Wittgenstein's writing, doesn't the fancifulness or melodrama of the way I have expressed them show at once that they present a psychological problem (mine, not Wittgenstein's), to be treated at best as aesthetic matters? I might reply that my expressions are no more melodramatic than such moments in Wittgenstein as his describing us as "captive" and "bewitched" in relation to language. But this might only mean that Wittgenstein occasionally yields to a flair for melodrama. That aside for the moment, Wittgenstein's sense of the loss or exile of words is much more extreme than the couple of images I have cited.

The sense of words as "away," as having to be guided "back," pervades the *Investigations*, to the extent, say, that the sense of speaking "outside a language-game" (§47) is something that pervades the *Investigations*. I pick here a phrase about outsideness whose entrance is quite casual, without drama, both to indicate the pervasiveness of the sense I wish to describe and to recognize that it may be shared only if it describes one's sense of one's own practice in thinking as derived from Wittgenstein's. That he inspires *various* practices is sufficiently notorious that I need hardly apologize for wishing to follow my own, so long as it genuinely traces back to his text, to however limited a region. My feeling, however, is that the threat or fact of exile in Wittgenstein's philosophizing – I mean of course the exile of words – is not limited.

Exile is under interpretation in Wittgenstein's general characterization: "A philosophical problem has the form: 'I don't know my way about' " (§123). That characterization is just made for Wittgenstein's idea of a "perspicuous (re)presentation" (cf. §122) as marking the end or disappearance of a philosophical problem. What Wittgenstein means by a grammatical investigation and its eliciting of our criteria is precisely the philosophical path to this end or disappearance of a philosophical problem. Then one can take the idea of not knowing one's way about, of being lost, as the form specifically of the *beginning* or *appearance* of a philosophical problem. I am naturally attracted by the implication of the German here – *Ich kenne mich nicht aus* – that the issue is one of a loss of self-knowledge; of being, so to speak, at a loss. If there is melodrama here, it is everywhere in the *Investigations*.

Doubtless I bear the marks of reading in Thoreau and in texts of related writers. I think of the eighth chapter of *Walden*, entitled "The Village": "Not till we are lost [or turned around], in other words, not till we have lost the world, do we begin to find ourselves, and realize where we are and the infinite extent of our relations." Lost and found and turning are founding concepts of Thoreau's *Walden*, which takes up into itself various scriptural traditions of the identification of spiritual darkness as loss, of requiring a turn, of the search for a path; as for instance in what is I suppose the greatest opening moment in Western literature specifically to picture this state: "In the middle of the journey of our life I came to myself within a dark wood where the straight way was lost. Ah, how hard a thing it is to tell of that wood. . . ." Of course I cite Dante to associate Wittgenstein's text with another greatness, but equally to remember the commonness of a certain dimension of the *Investigations*' preoccupations, including the stress on difficulty. (The opening short paragraph of *Walden* does not contain the word *journey* but instead *sojourner*.)

But even if some connection were granted here, Wittgenstein's form of philosophical problem does not speak of *a* middle of a journey, but of many journeys, many middles, of repeated losses and recoveries of oneself; the comparison is therefore after all exaggerated, melodramatically excessive. – In a sense I agree with this and in a sense I disagree. Disagree, in that the *Investigations* exhibits, as purely as any work of philosophy I know, philosophizing as a spiritual struggle, specifically a struggle with the contrary depths of oneself, which in the modern world will present themselves in touches of madness. "Of course, if water boils in a pot, steam comes out of the pot and also pictured steam comes out of the pictured pot. But what if one insisted on saying that there must also be something boiling in the picture of the pot?" (§297). Here Wittgenstein seems deliberately to ask whether this insistence – this excess, this little scene of melodrama – comes from him or from his interlocutor (whoever or whatever that is, and supposing there is just one). Suppose that Descartes discovered for philosophy that to confront the threat of or temptation to skepticism is to risk madness. Then since according to me the *Investigations* at every point confronts this temptation and finds its victory exactly in never claiming a final philosophical victory over (the temptation to) skepticism, which would mean a victory over the human, its philosopher has to learn to place and to replace madness, to deny nothing, at every point.

But I also agree with the objection that I exaggerate, because Wittgenstein notably does not sound the note of excess; on the contrary, some are able to read him to question or to deny that we so much as ordinarily suffer, unavoidably exhibit, for example, pain. If his *Investigations* is a work of continuous spiritual struggle, then a certain proportion in tone, this psychological balance, is the mark of its particular sublimity, the measure of his achievement for philosophy. In speaking of this struggle I take for granted that Wittgenstein is the name of both sides in it, both voices (for my purposes now I need only invoke two), which I have called the voice of temptation and the voice of correctness. So that the exile of words in the interlocutor's desperations and yearnings – "But surely another person cannot have THIS pain!" (§253) – is, one might say, exile from oneself. But I do not say that the struggle is entirely with oneself; it will be necessary in philosophy to take on the madness, or disproportion, in others.

In characterizing the assertion containing the hyperbolic "THIS pain" (said, in Wittgenstein's narrative, as one strikes oneself on the breast) as expressing desperation and yearning, I mean to invite attention to Wittgenstein's response to that outcry: "The answer to this is that one does not define a criterion of identity by emphatic stressing of the word 'this.'" How is this an "answer"? And why isn't the better, more direct response to say "Oh yes I can!" and strike oneself in the same way in the same place? That would not exactly be false. It might even be effective (as a joke). But what it displays is that the effort to deny skepticism is itself an expression of skepticism. That "more direct" response denies the other's expression of desperation and yearning while, so to speak, expressing them on its own behalf. Then the question is how Wittgenstein's answer admits the expression, answers to it.

Another measure of Wittgenstein's achievement in these regions, another common intellectual guise against which to take his scale, is to see the affinity of what I call his narrations of exile from oneself with what from the nineteenth century we learn to call alienation. Here I adduce a passage from Kierkegaard's volume *The Book on Adler, or A Cycle of Ethico-Religious Essays*, a volume also entitled *The Religious Confusion of the Present Age*. Kierkegaard writes:

> Most men live in relation to their own self as if they were constantly out, never at home. . . . The admirable quality in Magister A. consists in the fact that in a serious and strict sense one may say that he was fetched home by a higher power; for before that he was certainly in a great sense "out" or in a foreign land. . . . Spiritually and religiously understood, perdition consists in journeying into a foreign land, in being "out." (pp. 154–5)

Perdition of course is a way of saying: lost. And this is the Kierkegaard whose Knight of Faith alone achieves not exactly the everyday, but "the sublime in the pedestrian" (*Fear and Trembling*, p. 52). I do not quite wish to imply that Kierkegaard's (melodramatic) sense of the pedestrian here, with its transfigurative interpretation of the human gait of walking, is matched in Wittgenstein's idea of the ordinary. Yet it seems to me that I can understand Kierkegaard's perception as a religious interpretation of Wittgenstein's. In that case an intuitive sense is afforded that the everyday, say the temporal, is an achievement, that its tasks can be shrunk from as the present age shrinks from the tasks of eternity; a sense, I would like to say, that in both tasks one's humanity, or finitude, is to be, always is to be, accepted, suffered. What challenges one's humanity in philosophy, tempts one to excessive despair or to false hope, is named skepticism. It is the scene of a struggle of philosophy with itself, for itself. Then why can't it be ignored? For Wittgenstein that would amount to ignoring philosophy, and surely nothing could be more easily ignored – unless false hope and excessive despair are signs or effects of unobserved philosophy.

Life Forms

In speaking just now of a possible religious interpretation of Wittgenstein's idea of the ordinary, I was remembering the phrase used by Wittgenstein's friend Dr Drury when he reports asking himself whether he can see – as Wittgenstein had suggested to him that it may be seen – "that the problems discussed in the *Investigations* are being seen from a religious point of view" (*Recollections of Wittgenstein*, R. Rhees, ed.; Totowa, NJ, 1981, p. 79). But although what Kierkegaard called his cycle of "Ethico-Religious" essays is about "the present age" in a way one perhaps expects a philosophy or critique of culture to be, its relation *to itself*, as it were, is not what one demands of a work of philosophy, certainly not what the *Investigations* expects of its relation to itself, of its incessant turnings upon itself. What the ·association does suggest is significance in the fact that, granted the intuitive pervasiveness of something that may express itself as a moral or religious demand in the *Investigations*, the demand is not the subject of a *separate* study within it, call it Ethics. It is as if the necessities of life and culture depicted in the *Investigations* are beyond the reach of what we think of as moral judgment. (It isn't that skepticism is good or bad, right or wrong, prudent or rash; I do not wish – do you think otherwise? – to say that you *ought* to lead words back to their everyday use.) To say something about what such a spiritual struggle may be I need to go back to the second of what I called my differences of emphasis from other views of the *Investigations*, namely to Wittgenstein's idea of forms of life.

The idea is, I believe, typically taken to emphasize the social nature of human language and conduct, as if Wittgenstein's mission is to rebuke philosophy for concentrating too much on isolated individuals, or for emphasizing the inner at the expense of the outer, in accounting for such matters as meaning, or states of consciousness, or following a rule, etc.; an idea of Wittgenstein's mission as essentially a business of what he calls practices or conventions. Surely this idea of the idea is not wrong, and nothing is more important. But the typical emphasis on the social eclipses the twin preoccupation of the *Investigations*, call this the natural, in the form of "natural reactions" (§185), or in that of "fictitious natural history" (p. 230), or that of "the common behavior of mankind" (§206). The partial eclipse of the natural makes the teaching of the *Investigations* much too, let me say, conventionalist, as if when Wittgenstein says that human beings "agree in the language they use" he imagines that we have between us some kind of contract or an implicitly or explicitly agreed upon set of rules (which someone else may imagine we lack). Wittgenstein continues by saying: "That [agreement in language] is not an agreement in opinions but in form of life" (§241). A conventionalized sense of form of life will support a conventionalized, or contractual, sense of agreement. But there is another sense of form of life that contests this.

Call the former the ethnological sense, or horizontal sense. Contesting that there is the biological or vertical sense. Here what is at issue are not alone differences between promising and fully intending, or between coronations and inaugurations, or between barter and a credit system, or between transferring your money or sword from one hand to another and giving your money or sword into the hands of another; these are differences within the plane, the horizon, of the social, of human society. The biological or vertical sense of form of life recalls differences between the human and so-called "lower" or "higher" forms of life, between, say, poking at your food, perhaps with a fork, and pawing at it, or pecking at it. Here the romance of the hand and its apposable thumb comes into play, and of the upright posture and of the eyes set for heaven; but also the specific strength and scale of the human body and of the human senses and of the human voice.

Sometimes Wittgenstein seems to court a confusion over the emphasis as between the social and the natural. For example: "What has to be accepted, the given, is – so one could say – forms of life" (p. 226). Both friendly and unfriendly commentators on Wittgenstein seem to have taken this as proposing a refutation of skepticism with respect to the existence of other minds. Taken in its social direction this would mean that the very existence of, say, the sacrament of marriage, or of the history of private property, or of the ceremony of shaking hands, or I guess ultimately the existence of language, constitutes proof of the existence of others. This is not in itself exactly wrong. It may be taken as a vision, classically expressed, of the social as natural to the human. But if, as more recently, it is taken as a refutation of skepticism, then it begs the skeptical question. Because if what we "accept" as human beings "turn out to be" automata or aliens, then can't we take it that automata or aliens marry and own private property and shake hands and possess language? You may reply that once it turns out who these things are we (who?) will no longer fully say that they (or no longer let them?) marry, own, shake, speak. Perhaps not, but then this shows that from the fact of their exhibiting or "participating in" social forms it does not follow that they are human.

In *The Claim of Reason* (p. 83) I give the formulation about forms of life having to be accepted, being the given, its biological direction – emphasizing not *forms* of life, but forms of *life* – and I take it thus to mark the limit and give the conditions of the use of criteria as applied to others. The criteria of pain, say, do not apply to what does not exhibit a form of life, so not to the realm of the inorganic, and more specifically in the context of the *Investigations*, not to the realm of machines; and there is no criterion for what does exhibit a form of life. This interpretation is part of my argument that criteria do not and are not meant to assure the existence of, for example, states of consciousness; that they do not provide refutations of skepticism. Then the question becomes: Why do we expect otherwise? Why are we disappointed in criteria, how do we become disappointed as it were with language as such?

Wittgenstein's formulation about having to accept the given plays its part, I feel sure, in conveying a political or social sense of the *Investiga-*

tions as conservative. This was the earliest of the political or social descriptions, or accusations, I recall entered against the *Investigations*. Writers as different as Bertrand Russell and Ernest Gellner greeted the book's appeal to the ordinary or everyday as the expression of a so to speak *petit bourgeois* fear of change, whether of individual inventiveness or of social revolution. Now I think that Wittgenstein must leave himself open to something like this charge, because a certain distrust, even horror, of change – change that comes in certain forms – is part of the sensibility of the *Investigations*. But simply to say so neglects the equally palpable call in the book for transfiguration, which one may think of in terms of revolution or of conversion. ("Our examination must be turned around . . . but about the fixed point of our real need" (§108).) Wittgenstein does not harp on the word "need," or the word "necessity", any more than on the word "turn," but the weight of an idea of true need in opposition to false need seems to me no less in the *Investigations* than in those philosophical texts that more famously and elaborately contain early considerations of artificial necessities, such as the *Republic* and *The Social Contract* and *Walden*.

I have suggested that the biological interpretation of form of life is not merely another available interpretation to that of the ethnological, but contests its sense of political or social conservatism. My idea is that this mutual absorption of the natural and the social is a consequence of Wittgenstein's envisioning of what we may as well call the human form of life. In being asked to accept this, or suffer it, as given for ourselves, we are not asked to accept, let us say, private property, but separateness; not a particular fact of power but the fact that I am a man, therefore of *this* (range or scale of) capacity for work, for pleasure, for endurance, for appeal, for command, for understanding, for wish, for will, for teaching, for suffering. The precise range or scale is not knowable a priori, any more than the precise range or scale of a word is to be known a priori. Of course you can *fix* the range; so can you confine a man or a woman, and not all the ways or senses of confinement are knowable a priori. The rhetoric of humanity as a form of life, or a level of life, standing in need of something like transfiguration – some radical change, but as it were from inside, not *by* anything; some say in another birth, symbolizing a different order of natural reactions – is typical of a line of apparently contradictory sensibilities, ones that may appear as radically innovative (in action or in feeling) or radically conservative: Luther was such a sensibility; so were Rousseau and Thoreau. Thoreau calls himself disobedient, but what he means is not that he refuses to listen but that he insists on listening differently while still comprehensibly. He calls what he does revising (mythology). Sensibilities in this line seem better called revisors than reformers or revolutionaries.

They can seem to make themselves willfully difficult to understand. Take Emerson's remark in the third paragraph of "Self-Reliance": "Accept the place the divine providence has found for you, the society of your contemporaries, the connection of events." Every reader of Emerson's remark I have encountered takes that sentence as if it preached conservatism, as if it said: Accept the place society has found for you. What it says is something like the reverse, since the place divine providence has found for you might require that you depart from the society of your contemporaries, say exile yourself; then accepting the society of your contemporaries means acknowledging that it is from exactly them that you seek exile, so to them in yourself that you will have to justify it. Then why does Emerson give the impression (I assume deliberately) of political conservatism in this very sentence? It is a question to my mind of the same rank as Wittgenstein's question: "What gives the impression that we want to deny anything?" (§305). Something *is* under attack in Wittgenstein, *ways* of arriving at the certainty of our lives, pictures of closeness and connection, that themselves deny the conditions of human closeness. In the Emerson remark what is under attack is, one might say, a way of arriving at the future (a way of discovering America), pictures of progress and of piety that deny that the conditions of a society of undenied human beings remain to be realized.

Here I take to heart another similarly posed remark of Wittgenstein's, giving the distinct impression of political conservatism: "[Philosophy] leaves everything as it is" (§124). To my ear the remark is also distinctly radical, since leaving the world as it is – to itself, as it were – may require the most forbearing act of thinking (this may mean the most thoughtful), to let true need, say desire, be manifest and be obeyed; call this acknowledgment of separateness. Should this possibility be dismissed as the function of a philosopher's innocence? Dismissed, perhaps, in favor of a politician's experience? What do we imagine – if we do – the connection to be between violent thinking (the most unforbearing) and violent action, either for change at any cost, or at all costs for permanence? – clutching at difference, denying separateness. (Emerson will enter this region again when we follow out, in the following lecture, his detection of clutching in human thinking and practice.) I am of course proposing here a connection between Wittgenstein's idea of philosophy's leaving everything as it is and Heidegger's idea of thinking as "letting-lie-before-us" (as in his elaboration of a saying of Parmenides in the last chapters of *What is Called Thinking?*). Some readers of Wittgenstein and some of Heidegger will, I know, find the proposal of a connection here to be forced, even somewhat offensive. I think it is worth wondering why. The proposal would, for example, be *pointless* apart from an interest in Wittgenstein's proposal that "grammar tells what kind of object anything is"

(§373) together with the conviction that grammar, through its schematism in criteria, is given in the ordinary.

Wittgenstein's appeal or "approach" to the everyday finds the (actual) everyday to be as pervasive a scene of illusion and trance and artificiality (of need) as Plato or Rousseau or Marx or Thoreau had found. His philosophy of the (eventual) everyday is the proposal of a practice that takes on, takes upon itself, precisely (I do not say exclusively) that scene of illusion and of loss; approaches it, or let me say reproaches it, intimately enough to turn it, or deliver it; as if the actual is the womb, contains the terms, of the eventual. The direction out from illusion is not up, at any rate not up to one fixed morning star; but down, at any rate along each chain of a day's denial. Philosophy (as descent) can thus be said to leave everything as it is because it is a refusal of, say disobedient to, (a false) ascent, or transcendence. Philosophy (as ascent) shows the violence that is to be refused (disobeyed), that has left everything not as it is, indifferent to me, as if there are things in themselves. Plato's sun has shown us the fact of our chains; but that sun was produced by these chains. Sharing the intuition that human existence stands in need not of reform but of reformation, of a change that has the structure of a transfiguration, Wittgenstein's insight is that the ordinary has, and alone has, the power to move the ordinary, to leave the human habitat habitable, the same transfigured. The practice of the ordinary may be thought of as the overcoming of iteration or replication or imitation by repetition, of counting by recounting, of calling by recalling. It is the familiar invaded by another familiar. Hence ordinary language procedures, like the procedures of psychoanalysis, inherently partake of the uncanny. (Such a passage, posting concepts together that point in so many untaken directions, may, I know, be distracting. I post them, beyond orientation for myself, for readers who have a certain taste for signs, and especially for any who have, or may, come upon essays of mine entitled "Recounting Gains, Showing Losses: Reading *The Winter's Tale*" (in *Disowning Knowledge: In Six Plays of Shakespeare*); or "Being Odd, Getting Even: Descartes, Emerson, Poe" or "The Uncanniness of the Ordinary" (both in *In Quest of the Ordinary*).)

In what appears as the first section of Part II of the *Investigations* Wittgenstein gives a name for something to call the human form of life; he calls it, more or less, talking.

One can imagine an animal angry, frightened, unhappy, happy, startled. But hopeful? And why not?

Can only those hope who can talk? Only those who have mastered the use of a language. That is to say, the phenomena of hope are modes [Modificationen] of this complicated form of life.

"Grief" describes a pattern [Muster] which recurs with different variations, in the weave of our life. If a man's bodily expression of sorrow and of joy alternated, say with the ticking of a clock, here we should not have the characteristic formation of the pattern of sorrow or of the pattern of joy. (p. 174)

What does it mean to say that talking, that is, the possession of language, is a complicated form of life? I suppose Wittgenstein's meaning is not obvious, partakes of his peculiar difficulty. I note three strands: (1) It perceives the human as irreducibly social and natural, say mental and physical. This may seem an empty piety in the absence of the specification of this doubleness, I mean unity. But what would count as its (further) specification? (2) It is a perception that matches Freud's (and perhaps Hegel's and Marx's and Nietzsche's) of the universal determination of meaning, or the meaningful (or "Reason") in human life, the perception that human conduct is to be read. (3) It perceives that everything humans do and suffer is as specific to them as are hoping or promising or calculating or smiling or waving hello or strolling or running in place or being naked or torturing. This listing is to recall patterns in the weave of our life, modifications of the life of us talkers, that are specific and confined to us, to the human life form, like running in place or hoping, as well as patterns we share with other life forms but whose human variations are still specific, like eating or sniffing or screaming with fear.

Then is a culture as a whole to be thought of as a system of modifications of our lives as talkers? And would this imply that there is something unmodified in human life, pre-cultural as it were? We might perhaps be ready to say that culture as a whole is the work of our life of language, it goes with language, it is language's manifestation or picture or externalization. These are themselves of course pictures. They may be ones common at a certain stage in the history of culture. To imagine *a* language means to imagine a modified form of talking life.

I do not see a direct way to alleviate the obscurity of this moment, but indirectly it may help to try to say why the obscurity is so awful just here. It seems to me another function of the obscurity – if unavoidable then perhaps valuable – of Wittgenstein's idea of a criterion, hence of grammar. Suppose that philosophical sensibilities are all but bound to differ in their feel for the basis of language, some inclining toward looking for it in its exchange between talkers, some in its relation to the things of the world. If you are sufficiently satisfied with a relativist or behaviorist account of these faces of language, you may be satisfied with a contingent explanation of their connection. But if your intuition is of something a priori, of some necessity, both in the exchange of language in culture and in the relation of language with the world, you will be perplexed at the possibility of a connection between these necessities (as if things of the world had to care what human beings must go through in order to know them!). It is as if such a perplexed sensibility shared Kant's sense of the a priori as the possibility of language but then could not tolerate two of Kant's intellectual costs: (1) the thing in itself as a remainder or excess beyond the categories of the understanding; and (2) the Aristotelian table of judgments as the key to the completeness of those categories. The lack of tolerance of just these costs seems to me an understandable motivation for Heidegger's reconception of the idea of the *thing* that is fundamental to his later philosophy. His reconception implies that the recuperation or recoupment or redemption of the thing (in itself) – a process essential to the redemption of the human – will come about only by a shift of Western culture; a shift, now only in preparation, that will alter Western man's process of judgment.

However opposite in other respects Wittgenstein's intellectual taste is from Heidegger's, in linking the comprehension of the objective and the cultural they are closer together than each is to any other major philosopher of their age. For Wittgenstein's idea of a criterion – if the account of his idea in *The Claim of Reason* is right, as far as it goes – is as if a pivot between the necessity of the relation among human beings Wittgenstein calls "agreement in form of life" (§241) and the necessity in the relation between grammar and world that Wittgenstein characterizes as telling what kind of object anything is (§373), where this telling expresses essence (§375) and is accomplished by a process he calls "asking for our criteria." If, for example, you know what in the life of everyday language counts as – what our criteria are for – arriving at an opinion, and for holding firmly to an opinion, and for suddenly wavering in your opinion, and trying to change someone's (perhaps a friend's, perhaps an enemy's) opinion of someone or something (of a friend, an enemy, an option), and for having no or a low opinion of something, and for being opinionated, and being indifferent to opinion (that of the public or that of a private group), and similar things; then you know what an opinion *is*. And you will presumably understand why Wittgenstein will say: "I am not of the *opinion* that he has a soul" (p. 178). And he could have said: I am not of the opinion that there is a God, or that the world exists. It is part of Wittgenstein's vision that our very sense of arbitrariness in our language, a certain recurrent suspicion or a certain reactive insistence on the conventionality of language (an inevitable suspicion from time to time (in the modern period?)) is itself a manifestation of skepticism as to the existence of the world and of myself and others in it (in the modern period?).

I do not suppose these thoughts (about a Wittgensteinian criterion as the pivot between two necessities) are anything but controversial; indeed my wish to locate so generally the intuitions in play is only to indicate that the matter must be controversial, I mean it is not to be settled apart from settling one's view of Wittgenstein's procedures and goals in philosophy altogether. Relating Heidegger's later problematic of the *thing* to Kant's legacy, as at the outset of my philosophical writing I related the theme in the *Investigations* of "possibilities of phenomena" (§90) (that is, telling what kind of object anything is) to the theme of possibility in the *Critique of Pure Reason*, I am now accounting for Heidegger's and Wittgenstein's closeness as a function of their moving in structurally similar recoils away from Kant's settlement with the thing in itself, a recoil toward linking two "directions" of language – that outward, toward objects, and that inward, toward culture and the individual. (Accordingly my general response, for example, to Kripke's influential interpretation of Wittgenstein on rules is that since the solution Kripke proposes for what he calls Wittgenstein's skepticism with respect to rules continues a conventionalist view of agreement, agreement about ordinary usage, the way he interprets Wittgenstein's skepticism must be equally conventionalist, or rather it must have a hook of arbitrariness already in it. That Wittgenstein *can* be taken so is important; no less important is that he need not be so taken. Then the philosophical task is to uncover the forces in this alternative, to discover whether for example one side takes undue credit from the denial of the other.)

I may formulate the difficulty of settlement here as follows: You cannot understand what a Wittgensteinian criterion is without understanding the force of his appeal to the everyday (why or how it tells what kind of object anything is, for example); and you cannot understand what the force of Wittgenstein's appeal to the everyday is without understanding what his criteria are. This is not a paradox; what it means is that what philosophically constitutes the everyday *is* "our criteria" (and the possibility of repudiating them). The paradoxical sound registers that here one reaches a limit in Wittgenstein's teachability. It is another way of saying that skepticism underlies and joins the concept of a criterion and that of the everyday, since skepticism exactly repudiates the ordinary as constituted by (or by the repudiation of) our criteria. So the appeal to criteria against skepticism cannot overcome skepticism but merely beg its question.

If someone has come (by a skeptical process) to the philosophical conviction that being of or changing an opinion is something like having or losing or modifying an inclination or a disposition, and (hence) that nothing another does can insure with certainty that he is in such a state, it will do no intellectual good to assure such a one that we do after all share criteria for being of an opinion. The skeptical conviction precisely escapes that assurance; it would be as if I were to take another's word that he exists. Of course people can confirm for me that the world exists and I in it, but only on condition that I let them, that I find I take their word. Their confirmation is thus "conditional," or derivative; but this does not mean that taking their word is inessential.

The *Investigations* as a Depiction of Our Times

Let us see whether we can now sketch what I called a perspective from which the writer of the *Investigations* is a philosopher – even a critic – of culture. I start here from a variation on a question Professor von Wright poses in his paper "Wittgenstein in Relation to His Times" (in *Wittgenstein and His Times*, edited by B. McGuinness; Chicago, 1982). Von Wright asks whether "Wittgenstein's attitude to his times," while naturally essential to understanding Wittgenstein's intellectual personality, is also essential in understanding Wittgenstein's philosophy. Von Wright describes the attitude in question, for good reason, as Spenglerian, and he sees the link between the attitude and the conceptual development of the philosophy in "Wittgenstein's peculiar view of the nature of philosophy."

> Because of the interlocking of language and ways of life, a disorder in the former reflects disorder in the latter. If philosophical problems are symptomatic of language producing malignant outgrowths which obscure our thinking, then there must be a cancer in the *Lebensweise*, in the way of life itself.

Given my sense of two directions in the idea of a form of life, von Wright's appeal here to "a cancer in the way of life" makes me uneasy. "Way of life" again to me sounds too exclusively social, horizontal, to be allied so directly with human language as such, the life form of talkers. And the idea of a cancer in a culture's way of life does not strike me as a Spenglerian thought. "Cancer" says that a way of life is threatened with an invasive, abnormal death, but Spengler's "decline" is about the normal, say the internal, death and life of cultures. I quote three passages from the Introduction to *The Decline of the West*:

> I see, in place of that empty figment of *one* linear history . . . the drama of a *number* of mighty Cultures, each springing with primitive strength from the soil of a mother-region to which it remains firmly bound throughout its own life-cycle; each stamping its material, its mankind, in *its own* image; each having *its own* idea, *its own* passions, *its own* life, will and feeling, *its own* death. . . .

. . . every Culture has *its own* Civilization. In this work, for the first time the two words, hitherto used to express an indefinite, more or less ethical, distinction, are used in a periodic sense, to express a strict and necessary *organic succession*. The Civilization is the inevitable *destiny* of the Culture. . . . The "Decline of the West" comprises nothing less than the problem of Civilization.

These cultures, sublimated life-essences, grow with the same superb aimlessness as the flowers of the field. They belong . . . to the living Nature of Goethe, and not to the dead Nature of Newton. I see world-history as a picture of endless formations and transformations, of the marvelous waxing and waning of organic forms.

I am not in a position to claim that Wittgenstein derived his inflection of the idea of forms of life from Spengler's idea of cultures as organic forms (or for that matter from Goethe's living Nature), but Spengler's vision of Culture as a kind of Nature (as opposed, let us say, to a set of conventions) seems to me shared, if modified, in the *Investigations*.

Nor, similarly, as I have implied, do I think that the *Investigations* finds disorder in language itself. If those are right who insist that Wittgenstein thought this in the *Tractatus*, then in his progression to the *Investigations* he became more Spenglerian. Or perhaps he remained ambivalent about it. Then take what I am here reporting as my impression of his Spenglerian valence. This means that I think the griefs to which language repeatedly comes in the *Investigations* should be seen as normal to it, as natural to human natural language as skepticism is. (Hume calls skepticism an incurable malady; but here we see the poorness of that figure. Skepticism, or rather the threat of it, is no more *incurable* than the capacities to think and to talk, though these capacities too, chronically, cause us sorrow.) The philosophically pertinent griefs to which language comes are not disorders, if that means they hinder its working; but are essential to what we know as the learning or sharing of language, to our attachment to our language; they are functions of its *order*.

When Wittgenstein finds that "philosophy is a battle against the bewitchment of our intelligence by means of language" (§109) he is not as I understand him there naming language simply (perhaps not at all) as the efficient cause of philosophical grief, but as the medium of its dispelling. One may perhaps speak of language and its form of life – the human – as a standing opportunity for the grief (as if we are spoiling for grief) for which language is the relief. The weapon is put into our hands, but we *need* not turn it upon ourselves. What turns it upon us is philosophy, the desire for thought, running out of control. That has become an inescapable fate for us, apparently accompanying the fate of having human language. It is a kind of fascination exercised by the promise of philosophy. But philosophy can also call for itself, come to itself. The aim of philosophy's battle, being a dispelling – of bewitchment, of fascination – is, we could say, freedom of consciousness, the beginning of freedom. The aim may be said to be a freedom of language, having the run of it, as if successfully claimed from it, as of a birthright. Why intellectual bewitchment takes the forms it takes in the *Investigations* we have not said – Wittgenstein speaks of pictures holding us captive, of unsatisfiable cravings, of disabling sublimizings. He does not, I think, say very much about why we are victims of these fortunes, as if his mission is not to explain why we sin but to show us that we do, and its places.

I assume this is not exactly how others read the passage about the battle against bewitchment. But how close it is to, and distant from, a more familiar strain of reading may be measured by a small retranslation of a sentence from a passage two sections earlier (§107): "We have got on to slippery ice where there is not friction and so in a certain sense the conditions are ideal, but also, just because of that, we are unable to walk." It is important to me – speaking of closeness and distance – to recall here Kierkegaard's stress on walking as the gait of finitude; and to note that for a similar cause walking is a great topic of Thoreau's. Wittgenstein's passage continues in German as follows: *Wir wollen gehen; dann brauchen wir die* Reibung. Professor Anscombe translates: "We want to walk; so we need *friction*." This takes our wanting to walk as a given. But suppose, as in Kierkegaard and in Thoreau, walking is specifically a human achievement, a task in philosophy. I change the connective: "We want to walk; then we need friction." I would like this to suggest that our wanting to walk is as conditional – I might almost say as questionable – as our need for friction: If we want to walk, or when we find we are unable to keep our feet, then we will see our need for friction. The philosopher portrayed in the *Investigations*, confronted by unsatisfied interlocutors, has to show them their dissatisfactions, their loss of progress. This is not, to be sure, *making* someone want; it is at most helping them to allow themselves to want, but turned around the point of genuine need. May not such a role be one occupied by a philosopher of culture?

"When is a cylinder C said to fit into a hollow cylinder H? Only while C is stuck into H?" (§182). Compare: When do we want to speak of absolute simples? (§47); when do we feel that if I "experience the because" (§176), sense myself guided or influenced by a word or gesture, there must be a single feeling that *is* everywhere this experience?; when do we feel that if we say our steps are determined by a rule we must foresee every step the rule will ever determine?; when do we feel that if we see a thing we must see all of it, as if the literal things we see are as if membranes? Every reader of the *Investigations* will have some way of

addressing this pattern of self-defeat, say self-bewitchment, some accounting of it, even if it is to say no more than that in philosophy we
"misuse words." Wittgenstein provides, as said, a number of such addresses, perhaps the most elaborated of which is his attributing to philosophers a wish to find super-strong connections between consciousness
and its objects (§197), a super-order between super-concepts (§97), in
short "to sublime the logic of our language" (§38). In the slippery ice
passage the consequence of this requirement of sublimity is a conflict
with actual language that becomes "intolerable; the requirement is in
danger of becoming empty." Since a principal claim of *The Claim of
Reason* is that Wittgenstein's *Investigations* is endlessly in struggle with
skepticism, my various interpretations of skepticism can be taken as
indications of how what Wittgenstein calls "ideal conditions in a sense,"
this frozen emptiness of sublimity, is in turn to be interpreted.

In a word I find the motive to skepticism in this emptiness itself.
Anything short of the ideal is arbitrary, artificial, language at its most
mediocre. I must empty out *my* contribution to words, so that language
itself, as if beyond me, exclusively takes over the responsibility for
meaning. I say this struggle with skepticism, with its threat or temptation, is endless; I mean to say that it is human, it is the human drive to
transcend itself, make itself inhuman, which should not end until, as in
Nietzsche, the human is over. In letting such ideas, by way of interpreting
or picturing skepticism, leap out when they wish, I am also taking it that
philosophy has no monopoly on responses to the threat of skepticism. An
important competitor is what you may call romanticism in the arts. A
particularly pertinent instance is provided by a reading I recently prepared of Coleridge's *The Rime of the Ancient Mariner* which takes the
poem as an enactment, in its drift to a frozen sea below what the poet
calls "the line," of skepticism's casual step to the path of intellectual
numbness, and then of the voyage back to (or toward) life, pictured as
the domestic. But while philosophy has no monopoly, I of course think
the fate of skepticism is peculiarly tied to the fate of philosophy, and that
only in that tie are they both to be decided.

The connection between romanticism and skepticism takes one of its
ways from Kant, who for example would have helped Nietzsche to his
problem of overcoming the human, since Kant pictures human reason as
endlessly desiring to transcend, transgress, the limits of its human conditions. Wittgenstein's appearance at this intersection of romanticism and
skepticism and Kant is, so it seems to me, encoded in his use of the
concept of *subliming*. A pertinent formula of Kant's for the sublime is as
"the straining of the imagination to use nature as a schema for ideas [as
it were to picture the unconditioned] . . . [which is] forbidding [or ter-
rible] to sensibility, but which, for all that, has an attraction for us,

arising from the fact of its being a dominion which reason exercises over sensibility with a view to extending it to the requirements of its own realm (the practical) and letting it look out beyond itself into that infinite, which for it is an abyss." Of course these days we will be more alert to certain connections that Kant may have had no use for, and rather than saying that the terrible vision is for all that (i.e., despite that) attractive to us, we will know that it is attractive *because* terrible. What is this to know? In the previous section, on the Mathematically Sublime, Kant uses a different formula: "The point of excess for the imagination (toward which it is driven in the apprehension of the intuition) is like an abyss in which it fears to lose itself." Kant's conjunction of excess and abyss seems to me to match Wittgenstein's sense of the conjunction of the hyperbolic (super-connections, super-concepts, etc.) with the groundless as the ideal which philosophy finds at once forbidding or terrible, and attractive. (Here is bewitchment. If you say fascination, a psychoanalytic study should seem called for.) But whereas in Kant the psychic strain is between intellect and sensibility, in Wittgenstein the straining is of language against itself, against the commonality of criteria which are its conditions, turning as it were against its origins. – Thus a derivative romantic aesthetic problem-atic concerning the sublime moves to the center of the problematic of knowledge, or say of wording the world; quite as if aesthetics itself claims a new position in the economy of philosophy.

I was prompted to adduce Kant here, and Coleridge in passing, to indicate further my conviction (as in the cases of being lost, and turning, and walking) that the images Wittgenstein produces in his lyrical, or let me say sublime, descriptions of philosophy, are structurally motivated, imaginative necessities, not momentary or random flights of fancy. This derivation of the sublime will play a further role as I now go on, having accepted and a little specified Spengler's pertinence to Wittgenstein, to specify a certain difference between them that shows in that pertinence.

Noting that both Wittgenstein and Spengler write of a loss of human orientation and spirit that is internal to human language and culture, not an invasion of them, I cannot use an idea of the distortion of language and culture as what von Wright calls a "link" between Wittgenstein's writing and Spengler's. But von Wright's sense of a link from Wittgen-stein's philosophy to a Spenglerian attitude to his times still needs accounting for. I understand such a sense in two stages. It takes it as essential for a philosophy of culture to present its attitude to its times, the attitude that motivates the philosophy; and it takes Wittgenstein's atti-tude to be difficult to articulate, or difficult to assume. Since I have in effect claimed that there is a perspective from which the *Philosophical Investigations* may be seen as presenting a philosophy of culture, I have implied that its attitude to its time is directly presented in it, as directly as, say, in Spengler, or as in Freud or Nietzsche or Emerson. Then the difficulty in articulating the difficulty of Wittgenstein's attitude is the difficulty of finding this perspective.

Yet – so I will claim – the perspective is the one that will sound impossibly direct. My claim is that the *Investigations* can be seen, as it stands, as a portrait, or say as a sequence of sketches (Wittgenstein calls his text an album) of our civilization, of the details of what Spengler phrases as our "spiritual history" (p. 10), the image of "*our own* inner life" (p. 12). Then how shall we describe the details of the *Investigations* so that they may be seen to express "an attitude" – that is, so that the sequence of sketches appear as *details*, details as it were of one depiction, a depiction of *a* culture? (My question here is meant to invite comparing, eventually, the logic of the detail with that of the romantic fragment.)

I have meant various of my accounts of the events in the *Investigations* as instances of such descriptions. Ways I note the book's recurrence to ideas of disorientation and loss and turning are such instances; another is of its scene of ice as posing the choice between purity and walking; another is of its characterization of philosophy as the bearer of fascination (bewitchment) which it itself must challenge. (I believe I can be trusted to know that there are those who will take such considerations to be merely literary. Perhaps I should say explicitly that I can speak only for those who take Wittgenstein's work to be the work of a major (meaning what?) writer, and sense that his philosophy demanded this writing of itself. The merely literary is as impertinent to such writing (call it literature) as it is to anything (else) you may call philosophy.) Let us fill in some more details.

The *Investigations* is a work that begins with a scene of inheritance, the child's inheritance of language; it is an image of a culture as an inheritance, one that takes place, as is fundamental to Freud, in the conflict of voices and generations. The figure of the child is present in this portrait of civilization more prominently and decisively than in any other work of philosophy I think of (with the exception, if you grant that it is philosophy, of *Émile*). It discovers or rediscovers childhood for philosophy (the child in us) as Emerson and Nietzsche and Kierkegaard discover youth, the student, say adolescence, the philosophical audience conscious that its culture demands consent; youth may never forgive the cost of granting it, or of withholding it. The child demands consent of its culture, attention from it; it may never forgive the cost of exacting it, or of failing to.

The pervasiveness and decisiveness of the figure of the child in the *Investigations* is determined by Wittgenstein's heading his book with Augustine's paragraph that sets the scene of inheritance and instruction and of witnessing or fascination. Augustine's words precisely set the topics of Wittgenstein's book as a whole, so the scene of his words pervades the book. I recite them: when, my, elders, name, some object, accordingly, move, toward, I, saw, this, grasped, called, sound, uttered, meant, point, intention, shown, bodily movements, natural language of all peoples, expression, face, eyes, voice, state of mind, seeking, having, rejecting, words, repeated, used, proper places, various sentences, learnt, understood, signified, trained, signs, express my own desires. Abstracting the topics this way, the final one seems to stand out oddly against the rest – language as the expression of desire – since it is never separately questioned and since it must be assumed in all the events and adventures of language to follow. It is assumed in the opening example of the book, the presentation of the primitive, somewhat surrealist but perhaps otherwise unobjectionable "Five red apples," as well as in the definitely objectionable "When I say "I am in pain" I am at any rate justified before myself" (§289), in which, in reaching to speak outside language games I can I think be described as desiring to make my desire inconsequential, as it were to extinguish the relentless play of my desire, which Freud takes as the goal of desire altogether (in his idea of the death instinct in *Beyond the Pleasure Principle*). The *Investigations* closes, roughly, with an investigation of interpretation (seeing as) in which the possibility is envisioned that we lose our attachment to, our desire in, our words, which again means losing a dimension of one's attachment to the human form of life, the life form of talkers.

Along the way there are parables and allegories of language and of philosophy, as for example in the scene, following that of the apples, of the builders. Since the scene of the builders exemplifies a language more primitive than ours and is also part of a primitive idea of the way language functions, it is one enactment of what happens to the mind in the straits of philosophy. It is essential that we can, or can seem to, follow Wittgenstein's directive to "conceive" what he has described there "as a complete primitive language."

> Let us imagine a language for which the description given by Augustine is right. The language is meant to serve for communication between a builder A and an assistant B. A is building with building-stones; there are blocks, pillars, slabs and beams. B has to pass the stones, and that in the order in which A needs them. For this purpose they use a language consisting of the words "block," "pillar," "slab," "beam." A calls them out; – B brings the stone which he has learnt to bring at such-and-such a call. – Conceive this as a complete primitive language. (§2)

One may well sometimes feel that it is not language at all under description here since the words of the language (consisting of "block," "pillar," "slab," "beam") seem not to convey understanding, not to be *words*. (The feeling is expressed in R. Rhees's "Wittgenstein's Builders," *Discussions of Wittgenstein*; New York, 1970.) But while this feeling is surely conveyed by the scene, and must be accounted for, we need not take it as final, or unchallenged, for at least three lines of reason: (1) There are to begin with a pair of competing ways to take the scene, either as presenting something most remarkable or as something quite unremarkable, say as hyperbolic or as ordinary; as there are of taking Augustine's words themselves. (Spelling out this doubleness of reaction was for years my way of beginning the teaching of the *Investigations*. Certain of its consequences are recorded and developed in the first half of Warren Goldfarb's "I Want You To Bring Me A Slab," *Synthese*, 56 (1983), pp. 265–82.) One way of taking the scene pictures the builders as early humans, Neanderthalish, moving sluggishly, groaning out their calls; the other as men like us, but in an environment in which we can as it were realistically account for the "truncating" of the calls, say an environment full of noise and activity (as a realistic building site will be; Wittgenstein does not *say* there are no others around and no equipment). In the former case you may not *just* want to say that understanding is exhibited, but why should we not say, what the idea of describing a primitive language must itself be designed to exhibit, that there is understanding exhibited of a primitive kind? Is this empty? But isn't it what shows up in imagining the movements and voices as sluggish, as "early"? – the language, the behavior, the understanding are all of a piece, are of a primitive form of (human) life. (A child can be said to have just four words, but then imagine that stage of life with those words, imagine the happy repetitions, the improvised shrieks and coos, the experimental extensions of application, etc. The child has a future with its language; the builders have next to none.) Instead of the feeling that the builders lack understanding, I find I feel that they lack imagination, or rather lack freedom, or perhaps that they are on the threshold of these together. (2) Something *is* understood by the builders, that desire is expressed, *that* this object is called for. (This is a claim that one can, for example, readily imagine certain kinds of confusion and correction between the builders.) Therewith an essential of speech is present, a condition of it, and not something that can, as new words are taught, be taught. ("Therewith"? There I am taking the builders also as illustrating Augustine's scene as of an advent of language (challenging a picture of the accumulative "learning" of language), something that comes "with" an advent of the realm of desire, say of fantasy, "beyond" the realm of (biological) need. (I have been instructed, here particularly concerning Freud's concept of *trieb*, spanning the "relation" between biological instinct and psychological drive, by the exceptional study of Freudian concepts in Jean Laplanche's

Life and Death in Psychoanalysis.) Here it may help to ask whether Wittgenstein's builder has in mind a particular building. What would show that he is not merely improvising? Or not merely testing the assistant's obedience, or competence? Is this to be the first building, or to take its place within a realm of building?) (3) A further, non-competing interpretation of the builders is as an allegory of the ways many people, in more developed surroundings, in fact speak, forced as it were by circumstances to speak, with more or less primitive, unvaried expressions of more or less incompletely educated desires – here the generalized equipment and noise and the routines of generalized others, are perhaps no longer specifiable in simple descriptions. (Is it theory that is wanted?) This may be seen as a kind of political parody of the repetition (or say the grammar) without which there is no language. (I take the workers as political allegory in terms that allude to Heidegger's description of the everyday ("generalized equipment," "noise") in order to indicate a possible site of meeting, or passing, of Wittgenstein and Heidegger on the topos of the everyday – a place from which it can be seen both why Heidegger finds authenticity to demand departure and why Wittgenstein finds sense or sanity to demand return. It might help to say: Heidegger finds everyday life a mimetic expression of, exhaustive of the value of, everyday language; whereas Wittgenstein finds moments or crossings in everyday life and the language that imitates it to be broken shadows or frozen slides of the motion of our ordinary words, becoming the language of no one, unspeakable; moments which refuse the value of the experience of ordinary words, their shared memories, disappointed in them. Then we are evidently in touch with these words, but our touch is numbed or burned. I assume Wittgenstein has no diagnosis to offer of the anonymous, burned everyday, beyond his discovery of its invasion by, or production of, philosophy unconscious of itself. And I assume, further, that no one knows the extent of this invasion and unconscious production.)

Now take all this, the events of the *Investigations* – from the scene and consequences of inheritance and instruction and fascination, and the request for an apple, and the building of what might seem the first building, to the possibility of the loss of attachment as such to the inheritance; and these moments as tracked by the struggle of philosophy with itself, with the losing and turning of one's way, and the chronic outbreaks of madness – and conceive it as a complete sophisticated culture, or say a way of life, ours. (I assume it is not certain that one can do this, or is doing it. But I do, I guess, assume that it is not essentially less certain than that one can imagine the case of the builders as a complete primitive culture.) Then I will suggest, without argument, that what Wittgenstein means by speaking outside language games, which is to say, repudiating our shared criteria, is a kind of interpretation of, or a homologous form of, what Spengler means in picturing the decline of culture as a process of externalization.

> Civilization is the inevitable *destiny* of the Culture. . . . Civilizations are the most external and artificial states of which a species of developed humanity is capable. They are a conclusion . . . death following life, rigidity following expansion, petrifying world-city following mother-earth. They are . . . irrevocable, yet by inward necessity reached again and again . . . a progressive exhaustion of forms. . . . This is a very great stride toward the inorganic . . . – what does it signify?
> The world-city means cosmopolitanism in place of "home." . . . To the world-city belongs [a new sort of nomad], not a folk but a mob.

(In a footnote here Spengler declares "home" to be a profound word "which obtains its significance as soon as the barbarian becomes a culture-man and loses it again [with] the civilization-man . . .".) I note in passing as of interest for me for the future that this passage bears pertinently and differently also on Freud (with the progress to the inorganic) and on Heidegger (with the externalization and the loss of the concept of home). These figures would all alike, I believe, like to deny that they are romantics. If they are right about this then their nostalgia is even more virulent than it appears to be.

Granted a certain depth of accuracy in citing an aspect of Spengler as an enactment of an aspect of Wittgenstein's thought, then Wittgenstein's difference from Spengler should have that depth. I will characterize a difference by saying that in the *Investigations* Wittgenstein *diurnalizes* Spengler's vision of the destiny toward exhausted forms, toward nomadism, toward the loss of culture, or say of home, or say community: he depicts our everyday encounters with philosophy, say with our ideals, as brushes with skepticism, wherein the ancient task of philosophy, to awaken us, or say bring us to our senses, takes the form of returning us to the everyday, the ordinary, every day, diurnally. Since we are not returning to anything we have known, the task is really one, as seen before, of turning. The issue then is to say why the task presents itself as returning – which should show us why it presents itself as directed to the ordinary.

(Re)turning creates in the *Investigations*, I keep insisting, a quite fantastic practice ("to bring words back from their metaphysical to their everyday use"), and I have done nothing here to describe the way of the practice, but only to indicate what the stake in it is and why it is difficult to describe. Wittgenstein directs us at one point to the ordinary by demanding: Don't say "must," but *look and see* (cp. $66). Since he is there speaking about our insistence on an explanation of how a word refers, he is in effect asking us at the same time *to listen, to hear* the word – as if he is prescribing philosophy in the face of a mismatch between the eye and the ear, causing a spiritual nausea. This way of placing his prescription is meant to register why the stake is one from which morality – or say morality in isolation from philosophy, from the demand to turn around our needs, not merely redistribute their satisfactions, deep as *that* need is – cannot command and will not deliver us. This as it were pre-moral, philosophically chronic demand (this stand against destiny) is a piece of the intellectual fervor in the *Investigations* for which we started out seeking an account.

Contrariwise, the claim of this intellectual fervor is such that a practice unmotivated by it, one that does not stand to effect the deliverance from spiritual nausea, which is to say, to produce this turning/returning to the ordinary, will not count for it as philosophy. One may of course affect the fervor without following the practice, as one may affect psychoanalytic interpretations of others without attending to the procedures of psychoanalysis (the recognition of transference, the eliciting of association, the listening for fantasy, etc.). The fervor, or call it philosophical interest, may be modest and well commanded by the commitment to philosophical practice; it need not be lodged with a charisma of the magnitude of Wittgenstein's. Nevertheless I think it is true that the Wittgensteinian fervor is peculiarly vulnerable to a charlatanry (there are others) that philosophy should of all disciplines want most perfectly to free itself from. This vulnerability, I believe, causes grave distrust among those who have not felt the power of Wittgenstein's thought. It seems to me that Austin felt something of this distrust, call it a distrust of the need for the profound (which may imply that he did not credit, or not sufficiently, Wittgenstein's own distrust of it). I realize, as elsewhere, that speculation about matters such as these will offend certain philosophical sensibilities.

But this speculation seems to me called on by the incessant assaults of the *Investigations* not only on our beliefs, call them, and on our fantasies or pictures of how things must be, on our illusions as to our needs; as well as by the sense exhibited in the text of its own uniqueness, its isolated encounters with unnamed voices, without appeal to other writers for intellectual companionship.

It is in connection with this sense of uniqueness that I understand the book's attention to childhood and its inheritance, for I take its pervasive theme of the inheritance of language, the question, the anxiety, whether one will convey sufficient instruction in order that the other can go on (alone), as an allegory of the inheritability of philosophy – which is after all what the isolated, all but unnoticed child in Augustine's description of his past, did also inherit. (Of course philosophically the allegory would be worthless if it is not unallegorically right about inheriting language.) Inheritance of a discipline which is associated with the name of an isolated man, and which is allegorized by the inheritance of language, and specifically language as epitomized in fateful games, is also fair description of the famous scene in the second chapter of *Beyond the Pleasure Principle* of the game of *Fort* and *Da*. (I am indebted here to Derrida's memorable treatment of the scene in "Coming into One's Own.") And indeed the fit of this description for both Wittgenstein and for Freud is a cause of my sense of the mutual reflection of their temperaments and their intellectual fates. How far the shadows of conviction reach here will be evident if I confess that I see an affinity between Freud's use of the game with the exclamations *"Fort!"* and *"Da!"* and Wittgenstein's listing, near the beginning of the *Investigations* (§27), the exclamation *"Fort!"* among the half-dozen exclamations that epitomize differences among the differences in ways words function, to wean us from an arresting picture of unity.

Certain misgivings about Wittgenstein will arise from just that air of uniqueness and isolation, for some will read in it a vanity that mars his later work, a vanity only heightened by the insistence that he speaks for the common. Something of the sort may be felt (and the feeling may in particular cases be justified) about a certain entire line of thinkers, ones who declare themselves (or signal themselves by denying themselves to be) sages. Emerson is in this line, so it is not likely to enhance Wittgenstein's reputation, where it needs it, to say that Emerson hits off a characteristic experience of intellectual isolation in the *Investigations*. In "Self-Reliance" Emerson says:

> This conformity makes them [most men] not false in a few particulars, authors of a few lies, but false in all particulars. Their every truth is not quite true. Their two is not the real two, their four not the real four; so that every word they say chagrins us and we know not where to begin to set them right.

It is an expression of a specific experience of embarrassment and disappointment directed to one's culture as a whole (hence to oneself as compromised in the culture), to its inability to listen to itself; which of course will from time to time present itself as its inability or refusal to listen to *you*. So that when you preach, for instance, disobedience to it you are asking it to obey itself differently, better (recalling, recounting). Emerson's sign for disobedience is aversion ("Self-reliance is the aversion of conformity"). Aversion is Emerson's way of saying conversion. It names a comparable spiritual territory, together with an explicit disgust.

In giving us the means to conceive completely of our sophisticated culture (completely: without end) the *Investigations* does not paint mimetically the circumstances of our way of life, though it conveys the unmistakable impression that our patterns or modifications of the human form of life are undermining that life, deforming it. (If we say that the human life form is the life of the mind, then we have to ask what it sees in itself that drives it to cast itself under.) Here I propose that we take the famous description in the Preface to the *Investigations* – "this work, in its poverty and in the darkness of this time" – to be naming the time in question as what is conceived and depicted by and in the work as a whole, in its apparent empty-handedness ("Isn't my knowledge completely expressed in the explanations I could give?" (cp. §75)); its apparent denials, its embarrassments ("Explanations come to an end somewhere," "This is simply what I do" (cp. §1,217)); and madness. Its declaration of its poverty is not a simple expression of humility but a stern message: the therapy prescribed to bring light into the darkness of the time will present itself as, will in a sense be, starvation; as if our philosophical spirit is indulged, farced to the point of death. And Wittgenstein is fully clear in showing his awareness that his reader will (should) feel deprived by his teaching ("What gives the impression we want to deny anything?" "What we are destroying is nothing but structures of air" (cp. §118, 305)).

Poverty as a condition of philosophy is hardly a new idea. Emerson deploys it as an idea specifically of America's deprivations, its bleakness and distance from Europe's achievements, as constituting America's necessity, and its opportunity, for finding itself. (Toward the end of "Experience" there is a characteristic call for resolve: "And we cannot say too little of our constitutional necessity of seeing things under private aspects, or saturated with our humors. And yet is the God the native of these bleak rocks. That need makes in morals the capital virtue of self-trust. We must hold hard to this poverty. . . ." I read: The poverty that, morally speaking, is pleasing to the God and affords us access to the humanity of others – it is its poverty, not its riches, that constitutes America's claim upon others – is, philosophically speaking, our access to necessity, our route out of privacy.) Others take Emerson to advise America to ignore Europe; to me his practice means that part of the task of discovering philosophy in America is discovering terms in which it is given to us to inherit the philosophy of Europe. Its legacy may hardly look like philosophy at all, but perhaps rather like an odd development of literature. By European patterns, Americans will seem, in Thoreau's phrase, "*poor* students," the phrase by which Thoreau identifies the unaccommodated who are his rightful readers. It might well prove of peculiar interest to an American that what Wittgenstein in the *Investiga-tions* means by the ordinary should strike certain philosophical readers as an impoverished idea of philosophy in its own systematic shunning, its radical discounting, or recounting, of philosophical terms and arguments and results, its relentless project to, perhaps we can say, de-sublimize thought.

So I am understandably haunted by a reaction Wittgenstein in 1931 is reported by Waismann to have expressed concerning Schlick's teaching in an American university: "What can we give the Americans? Our half-decayed culture? The Americans have as yet no culture. But from us they have nothing to learn . . . *Russia*. The passion does promise some-thing. Whereas our talk hasn't the force to move anything" (*Recollections of Wittgenstein*, edited by Rhees, p. 205). Of the various matters raised in those sentiments I mention here just this strand, that in questioning whether Europe's central thought is inheritable further West and further East Wittgenstein is expressing an anxiety over whether Europe itself will go on inheriting philosophy; whether he, who represents a present of philosophy, can hand on his thoughts to another generation. If philos-ophy is to continue it must continue to be inherited; if it is to be inherited then *this*, say the *Investigations*, must be. (Thoreau's slanting of the word "poor" to name the students he writes for – specifying Emerson's search for "my poor" in "Self-Reliance" – reminds me to say that Wittgenstein's word for the indigence of his work is *Dürftigkeit*, not *Armut*. It goes without saying that Wittgenstein is not claiming that what constitutes philosophy's necessary material stripping is obvious. And he would have known, as well as Heidegger knew, the question in Hölderlin's Elegy "Bread and Wine": ". . . *wozu Dichter in dürftiger Zeit?*" It may be worth pausing sometime, caught by the attractions and repulsions between Wittgenstein and Heidegger, to consider what it signifies that when Heidegger is in the field of force of Hölderlin's words – say about the point of a poet in a time without – he writes philosophical essays about him, as if to get him into his system, contain him; whereas to imagine a comparable moment of recognition in Wittgenstein is to imagine a cer-tain identification in a moment in his Preface to his late work, in which he gives over the work and refuses it exemption from its times.)

How many candidates are there in a generation for the role of repre-senting a present of philosophy? It can come to seem that the inheritance of philosophy is philosophy's only necessary business. For those for whom this cannot present itself as a structural necessity of philosophy now, it is bound to present itself as insufferable in its arrogance. It might even then still be seen in its humility. What it claims for itself is no more than poverty, not Platonic or Augustinian or Cartesian or Kantian or Hegelian or Heideggerean lavishness. It is because this poverty claims itself as the continuation of philosophy (a different lavishness might afford not to care about this), as of a path that is wholly more significant than one's position along the path, that I take the anxiety, or fervor, of the *Investigations* not as a concern over its originality but over its intelligibility to another generation – call this its historical power to go on – apart from which the path may be lost. (I said that a lavishness different from the ones of the great philosophers might afford not to care whether the path of philosophy may be lost, and whether it may be taken in any way other than in poverty. This is how I would place the proposal not infrequently pressed upon me of Richard Rorty's idea of a general post-philosophical cultural conversation. Much as I may aspire to something in that proposal, I suffer from the generalized, conventionalized, use of words and thoughts that are presently suited, or armored, for such conversation, words such as "philosophy" and "ordinary" and "theory" and "conversation." What can I say?)

I have said in effect that the *Investigations can* be seen as a philosophy of culture, one that relates itself to its time as a time in which the continuation of philosophy is at stake. Now, in closing, I ask whether there is reason to insist that the book *is* to be taken so, that it so to speak seeks this perspective on itself.

For an answer I go back to another remark of Professor von Wright's: "[I think that] Wittgenstein's attitude to his time [a Spenglerian attitude of censure and disgust] makes him unique among the great philosophers." The philosophers von Wright compares Wittgenstein with are Plato and Descartes and Kant and Hegel. (The case of Heidegger would be a tricky one here, since in *What is Called Thinking?* Heidegger is at pains to distinguish his perception from that of what he calls Spengler's pessimism, hence to measure himself against it, in such a way as pertinently to raise the question whether the phenomenon under question here is exactly what we mean by an *attitude*. Still, Heidegger too obviously cannot be used in the present context as constituting for Wittgenstein a standard of the seriousness of philosophy, so I leave this issue aside for the present.) A Spenglerian attitude – say a question directed to the drift of one's culture as a whole that evinces radical dissent from the remaining advanced thought of that culture – would not make Wittgenstein unique among writers such as Montaigne and Pascal and Rousseau and Emerson and Nietzsche and Freud. So it is worth considering that the sense of Wittgenstein's uniqueness, which I share, comes from the sense that he is joining the fate of philosophy as such with that of the philosophy or criticism of culture, thus displacing both – endlessly forgoing, rebuking, parodying philosophy's claim to a privileged perspective on its culture, call it the perspective of reason (perhaps shared with science); anyway forgoing for philosophy any claim to perspective that goes beyond its perspective on itself. This is its poverty of perspective. But what makes this poverty philosophy?

I say that this philosophy lies in the practice, the commitment to go on in a certain way, call this discontinuously, which is to say, not in an endless deferring of claim that might as well be a gesture toward infinity, say transcendence; it lies rather in a particular refusal of endlessness, in an unguardedness, an openness. (A gesture toward an endlessness of deferral, an infinite, so toward some transcendent, occurs in the writing of Derrida and of Lacan; but then they are exactly questioning an older philosophical gesture of transcendence. I have to think about this remembering a complaint Austin made more than once about philosophers who insist that there are infinite uses of language – doubtless he would have had in mind Wittgenstein's saying, early in the *Investigations* (§23) that there are "countless" kinds of use – or that the "context" of a use is infinitely complex, as a way to defer getting down to the business of counting them. My love for Austin's gesture here did not stop me from asking myself – wasn't I supposed to? – what philosophy's business then is.) It is the practice that constitutes diurnalization, a way or weave of life to challenge the way or weave that exhausts the form of life of talkers. This is how I understand Wittgenstein's claim to give philosophy peace (§133). It is not that philosophy ought to be brought as such to an end, but that in each case of its being called for, it brings itself to an end.

In conceiving of the *Investigations* as the portrait of a complete sophisticated culture, two features bear on the conception of philosophy's poverty. First, in beginning with the words of someone else – in choosing to stop there, in hearing philosophy called upon in these unstriking words – the writer of the *Investigations* declares that philosophy does not speak first. Philosophy's virtue is responsiveness. What makes it philosophy is not that its response will be total, but that it will be tireless, awake when the others have all fallen asleep. Its commitment is to hear itself called on, and when called on – but only then, and only so far as it has an interest – to speak. *Any* word my elders have bequeathed to me as they moved obscurely about me toward the objects of their desires, may come to chagrin me. All my words are someone else's. What but philosophy, of a certain kind, would tolerate the thought? The second feature of the *Investigations* bearing on its poverty is that, in the culture it depicts, nothing is happening all at once, there is no single narrative for it to tell. What is of philosophical importance, or interest – what there is for philosophy to say – is happening repeatedly, unmelodramatically, uneventfully.

But the claim that a philosophical practice of the ordinary, not a morality or a religion apart from that practice, is what Wittgenstein throws into the balance against the externalization or nomadism of culture – a practice that he knows must only doubtfully be listened to – places him structurally in the position of a prophet. Is this becoming to philosophy?

What is true is: In the culture depicted in the *Investigations* we are all teachers and all students – talkers, hearers, overhearers, hearsayers, believers, explainers; we learn and teach incessantly, indiscriminately; we are all elders and all children, wanting a hearing, for our injustices, for our justices. Now imagine a world in which the voices of the interlocutors of the *Investigations* continue on, but in which there is no Wittgensteinian voice as their other. It is a world in which our danger to one another grows faster than our help for one another.

17

Moral Perfectionism

This essay forms the introduction to Cavell's 1988 Carus Lectures, published as *Conditions Handsome and Unhandsome*; it prepares the ground for his most explicit and systematic attempt to establish the continuing pertinence of his intellectual project to those of his colleagues in American philosophy, particularly those of Rawls and Kripke. But it also provides the clearest account Cavell has yet given of his conception of the tradition of Moral Perfectionism – a tradition with which he now identifies not only the writings of Wittgenstein, Heidegger, Nietzsche, Emerson, and Thoreau, but also the work of certain Shakespearian plays, the remarriage comedies and their companion melodramas, and even Beckett's *Endgame*. In effect, then, this essay attempts to delineate a conceptual space within which virtually all of Cavell's work hitherto appears as part of a larger whole; it therefore forms an appropriate concluding moment in this selection of readings.

Its first concern is to develop a conception of perfectionism that is not elitist, and so can be thought of as compatible with democratic moral and political impulses; its second is to show that this perfectionism is in fact an essential component or presupposition of any adequate democracy. This latter, more controversial enterprise rests upon making plausible the split or doubled conception of the self that is central to Moral Perfectionism – a conception that Cavell first identified in Thoreau (see Essay 14) and his teacher Emerson (see Essay 15), and which can also be seen as an inflection of the early Heidegger's perception of human individuals as necessarily either lost in inauthenticity or struggling to overcome that lostness. Since what is here at stake is whether an individual can be said to own her own experience, to have a life to lead, and so whether she can be said to have a genuine or authentic self, Cavell argues that these issues must be determined before questions of the self's duties to others can intelligibly be raised; after all, if a moral agent must (in Kantian terms)

Originally published in *Conditions Handsome and Unhandsome: The Constitution of Emersonian Perfectionism*, by Stanley Cavell (Chicago: University of Chicago Press, 1990), pp. 1–17. Copyright © 1990 by The University of Chicago. Reprinted by permission of the publisher.

live in accordance with a self-originating and self-given law, she must first have a self from which that law can emerge and to which it can apply.

This essay also spells out the intimacy of the connection Moral Perfectionism forges between attaining genuine selfhood and maintaining a relationship to an exemplary other. It is this connection that explains the incessant self-awareness of perfectionist texts; such authors cannot separate their sense of their culture's decline from their concern to manage their relationship with their readers in ways that might contribute to staying or reversing that decline. Here, Cavell's psychoanalytic model of reading (summarized in the Introduction, and in the preface to Essay 12) all but explicitly merges with the model he finds in Emerson and Thoreau; the goal of the perfectionist author is to seduce her reader from the present fixations of her desires, and to free her for a further, unattained but attainable state of self and society. Here is Cavell's most fundamental reason for thinking that the content and the form of his favored texts cannot be separated – that the concerns of such writing cannot be separated from the ways they work upon their readers.

Is Moral Perfectionism inherently elitist? Some idea of being true to oneself – or to the humanity in oneself, or of the soul as on a journey (upward or onward) that begins by finding oneself lost to the world, and requires a refusal of society, perhaps above all of democratic, leveling society, in the name of something often called culture – is familiar from Plato's *Republic* to works so different from one another as Heidegger's *Being and Time* and G. B. Shaw's *Pygmalion*. What the question means, and what I will mean in proposing that there is a perfectionism that happily consents to democracy, and whose criticism it is the honor of democracy not only to tolerate but to honor, called for by the democratic aspiration, it is a principal task of these Carus Lectures to clarify.

Because I have for some years seemed to myself to know, against the untiring public denials of the fact, that Emerson is a thinker with the accuracy and consequentiality one expects of the major mind, one worth following with that attention necessary to decipher one's own, I have found myself under increasing pressure to understand what makes the fact incredible, and not just to current academic philosophical and literary sensibilities. An obvious cause is Emerson's manner of writing, to justify which as philosophy would seem to require both justifying it as (the expression of) a mode of thinking and explaining why what it accomplishes is not to be accomplished in more canonical forms of argumentation. Beyond or behind this source of incredibility, or let me say resistance, another resistance has unscreened itself as separately thematizable, that Emerson's prose is in service of, or formed (however else) in view of, a moral outlook that has largely lived in the disfavor of academic moral philosophy, when, that is, that philosophy has taken notice of it at all. In the history of modern moral philosophy, a development that has been fairly orderly along a course set by the writings of Hume and of Kant, the reigning theories in contention, with exceptions perhaps more numerous and persuasive in recent decades than in the past, have been those of Utilitarianism (the favored teleological theory, founding itself on a concept of the good) and Kantianism (the favored deontological theory, founding itself on an independent concept of the right). From the perspective of these theories, Moral Perfectionism, seeming to found itself, let us say, on a concept of truth to oneself, may appear not to have arrived at the idea, or to disdain it, of other persons as counting in moral judgment with the same weight as oneself, hence to lack the concept of morality altogether.

Perfectionism, as I think of it, is not a competing theory of the moral life, but something like a dimension or tradition of the moral life that spans the course of Western thought and concerns what used to be called the state of one's soul, a dimension that places tremendous burdens on personal relationships and on the possibility or necessity of the transforming of oneself and of one's society – strains of which run from Plato and Aristotle to Emerson and Nietzsche, and pass through moments of opposites such as Kant and Mill, include such various figures as Kleist and Ibsen and Matthew Arnold and Oscar Wilde and Bernard Shaw, and end at my doorstep with Heidegger and Wittgenstein. (That Heidegger and Wittgenstein are instances of what I see as perfectionism is more important in my motivation to begin thinking through the subject – particularly, of course, given the course of Heidegger's biography – than their appearances in what follows here will make clear. In the case of Heidegger I take for granted that his emphasis in *Being and Time* on "authenticity" and his protesting that his writing is not to be comprehended within the separate discourse of ethics, intuitively attest to his belonging to the subject of perfectionism. How useful the subject will prove to be in coming to terms with Heidegger's history remains to be seen. In the case of Wittgenstein what I say here leaves his relation to perfectionism quite indirect, so I mention that I am extending the view of his *Investigations* that I propose in "Declining Decline: Wittgenstein as a Philosopher of Culture.")

Even before going on, in a moment, to amplify and specify perfectionist texts, the absence of women's names on this list of names might, should, at once raise the question, Where is the voice of the woman in this view of things: nowhere or everywhere? My intellectual access to this question lies most immediately or systematically in the thinking I have done about film, where certain comedies (remarriage comedies) exemplify relationships that make moral sense – to the extent that they are credibly happy – not in terms of Utilitarian or of Kantian lines of thought, but in terms, I am learning to say, of Emersonian Perfectionism. Certain melodramas derived from these comedies, or from which the comedies derive, accordingly exemplify relationships, and the end of them, that negate moral sense. Both genres essentially concern the status of the woman's voice, say her consent.

Since Emerson's thinking and Emerson's perfectionism are companion matters, I broach each of them as halves of my first lecture, and then in the second lecture I elaborate the thinking half by taking up the instance of Kripke's discussion of Wittgenstein's ideas of rules and privacy, and in the third lecture I elaborate the perfectionist half by taking up instances of its appearance in examples from film and from theater. The question of perfectionism needs initially more discussion since it goes counter to the particular account of perfectionism to be found in John Rawls's *A Theory of Justice*, which has, more than any other book of the past two decades, established the horizon of moral philosophy for the Anglo-American version or tradition of philosophy (at least). My admiration for Rawls's work is, among other reasons, for its accomplishment in establishing a systematic framework for a criticism of constitutional democracy from within. Is there a more serious and pressing political issue than the articulation of such a criticism? What I have to say concerning the issue in these lectures builds from my sense of rightness and relief in Rawls's having articulated a concept of justice accounting for the intuition that a democracy must know itself to maintain a state of (because human, imperfect, but), let me say, good enough justice. Apart from this state there are perfectionisms, but their role cannot, by hypothesis, be that of criticizing democracy from within.

My direct quarrel with *A Theory of Justice* concerns its implied dismissal of what I am calling Emersonian Perfectionism as inherently undemocratic, or elitist, whereas I find Emerson's version of perfectionism to be essential to the criticism of democracy from within. It should follow from this that Emersonian Perfectionism does not imply perfectibility – nothing in Emerson is more constant than his scorn of the idea that any given state of what he calls the self is the last. Yet I keep the old-fashioned word "perfection" in play for a number of reasons. An important reason, for me, is to register Emerson's sense – and Freud's, not to mention Plato's – that *each* state of the self is, so to speak, final: each state constitutes a world (a circle, Emerson says) and it is one each one also desires (barring inner or outer catastrophes). On such a picture of the self one could say both that significance is always deferred and *equally* that it is never deferred (there is no later circle until it is *drawn*). The section on perfectionism in *A Theory of Justice* (sec. 50) takes Nietzsche as epitomizing what Rawls calls the strong version of perfectionism; Rawls then dismisses the view as a serious contender in the arena of a democratic theory of justice on the basis, as I spell out in some detail in the first lecture, of what I find to be a misreading, or overfixed reading, of a set of Nietzschean sentences. My particular fascination with this dismissal is that the passage from Nietzsche is a virtual transcription of Emersonian passages, so that at a certain juncture of Rawls's book there occurs a continuation of American philosophy's repeated dismissal, I sometimes say repression, of the thought of Emerson. To what extent is this gesture necessary to philosophy?

A definition of what I mean by perfectionism, Emersonian or otherwise, is not in view in what follows. Not only have I no complete list of necessary and sufficient conditions for using the term, but I have no theory in which a definition of perfectionism would play a useful role. I emphasize accordingly that an open-ended thematics, let me call it, of perfectionism, which I shall adumbrate in a moment, is not to my mind a mere or poor substitute for some imaginary, essential definition of the idea that transcends the project of reading and thematization I am undertaking here. This project, in its possible continuations, itself expresses the interest I have in the idea. That there is no closed list of features that constitute perfectionism follows from conceiving of perfectionism as an outlook or dimension of thought embodied and developed in a set of texts spanning the range of Western culture, a conception that is odd in linking texts that may otherwise not be thought of together and open in two directions: as to whether a text belongs in the set and what feature or features in the text constitute its belonging.

Suppose that there is an outlook intuitively sketched out (sometimes negatively) in some imaginary interplay among the following texts. (I ask almost nothing from the idea of this interplay. It is not meant to do more than momentarily activate the fantasy, perhaps it vanishes early, that there is a place in the mind where the good books are in conversation, among themselves and with other sources of thought and pleasure; what they often talk about, in my hearing, is how they can be, or sound, so much better than the people who compose them, and why, in their goodness, they are not more powerful.) I begin by specifying texts, most of which are mentioned or alluded to in the pages to follow: Plato's *Republic*, Aristotle's *Nichomachean Ethics*, the Gospel according to St Matthew, Augustine's *Confessions*, Shakespeare's *Hamlet* and *Coriolanus* and *The Tempest*, Pascal's *Pensées*, Kant's *Foundations of the Metaphysics of Morals*, Friedrich Schlegel's *Athenaeum Fragments* and "On Incomprehensibility," Kleist's *The Marquise of O —*, Mill's *On Liberty* and *On the Subjection of Women*, Ibsen's *Hedda Gabler* and *A Doll's House*, Matthew Arnold's *Culture and Anarchy* and "Dover Beach," Emerson's "The American Scholar" and "Self-Reliance" and "Experience," Nietzsche's third *Untimely Meditation* entitled *Schopenhauer as Educator*, Marx's *Intro-*

duction to the Critique of Hegel's Philosophy of Right, Thoreau's *Walden*,
the critical writings of Oscar Wilde, certainly including his review of a
book about Confucius, Freud's *The Interpretation of Dreams, Civilization
and Its Discontents*, and "Delusions and Dreams in Jensen's *Gradiva*,"
Shaw's *Pygmalion*, W. C. Williams, *Selected Essays*, John Dewey's *Experience and Nature*, Heidegger's *Being and Time*, and "On the Origin of the
Work of Art," and *What is Called Thinking?*, Wittgenstein's *Philosophical Investigations*, Beckett's *Endgame*, and (the film) *The Philadelphia
Story*. Others might have been mentioned here, most of which appear
in related writings of mine: Ovid's *Metamorphoses*, Dante's *Divine Com-
edy*, Montaigne's *Essays*, Spinoza's *Ethics*, Milton's *Paradise Lost*,
Moliere's *Misanthrope, The Unborn: The Life and Teaching of Zen Master
Bankei*, Schiller's *On the Aesthetic Education of Man*, Rousseau's *The
Reveries of a Solitary Walker*, Goethe's *Faust* and *Wilhelm Meister*, Hegel's
Phenomenology of Spirit, Wordsworth's *Prelude*, Coleridge's *Biographia
Literaria*, Kierkegaard's *Repetition* and *Concluding Unscientific Postscript*,
Whitman's *Leaves of Grass*, Melville's *Pierre*, Dickens's *Hard Times* and
Great Expectations, Pater's *The Renaissance*, Dostoevsky's *The Idiot*,
Twain's *Huckleberry Finn*, William James's *Varieties of Religious Experi-
ence*, Henry James's "The Beast in the Jungle," Veblen's *Theory of the
Leisure Class*, D. H. Lawrence's *Women in Love*, and (the film) *Now
Voyager*.

Why bother making explicit what is for the most part so deliberately
obvious a list, particularly when sometimes only a fragment of these
works may be pertinent to the issue of perfectionism? I want, of course,
at once for it to call to mind a fraction of the play of voices left out
("forgotten?") in characteristic philosophical discussions about how we
might live, voices that will enter other conversations, more urgent ones
to my mind, about how we do live. Then is philosophy's omitting of texts
a sign of the fragility of their interplay? On the contrary, it seems to me,
to the extent it is something like forgetting, a sign of how massive the
resistance to it is. And while I mean the lists to contest the sense of
arbitrariness or exclusiveness in the perfectionist's characteristic call for
a conversion to "culture," I merely indicate, mostly by the inclusion of
two films, that the door is open to works of so-called popular culture; I
am playing it safe, or obvious, interested in asking philosophers whether
they imagine that they are able to speak more authoritatively for the
uncultivated than (other) works of high culture do. The presence or
absence of any text on the list is open to argument – or say subject to the
continuing conversation of the texts – none is safe because sacred, others
must, if the conversation is to continue, have a hearing. The process of
listing is less like hedging a word with a definition for a theoretical
purpose than it is like opening a genre for definition. (In the background

here are various efforts of mine, for example in the Introduction to *This New Yet Unapproachable America*, to characterize philosophy's anxiety about reading, expressed in its wish either to read everything or to read nothing. In the background too is a wish for an homage to Emerson's characteristic gesture of listing our models, the meaning of whose "greatness" is not to be taken for granted in Emersonian Perfectionism, precisely the contrary. In an old culture a list of obvious books might seem pretentious or ridiculous – like a gentleman's calling himself a gentleman. In a new culture it should be a reminder not so much of the sublimity of the human – Whitman's perception is not so much of the *works* of humankind – as of the humanness of the sublime.)

Given that a work is accepted as definitive for perfectionism, the issue of the features it contributes to the concept of perfectionism, or confirms, or modifies, also remains open. Take, for example, Plato's *Republic*. Obvious candidate features are its ideas of (1) a mode of conversation, (2) between (older and younger) friends, (3) one of whom is intellectually authoritative because (4) his life is somehow exemplary or representative of a life the other(s) are attracted to, and (5) in the attraction of which the self recognizes itself as enchained, fixated, and (6) feels itself removed from reality, whereupon (7) the self finds that it can turn (convert, revolutionize itself) and (8) a process of education is undertaken, in part through (9) a discussion of education, in which (10) each self is drawn on a journey of ascent to (11) a further state of that self, where (12) the higher is determined not by natural talent but by seeking to know what you are made of and cultivating the thing you are meant to do; it is a transformation of the self which finds expression in (13) the imagination of a transformation of society into (14) something like an aristocracy where (15) what is best for society is a model for and is modeled on what is best for the individual soul, a best arrived at in (16) the view of a new reality, a realm beyond, the true world, that of the Good, sustainer of (17) the good city, of Utopia. The soul's exploration by (imitating, participating in) Socrates' imitation (narration) of philosophical exchange (18) produces an imagination of the devolution of society and rebukes the institutions of current societies in terms of (19) what they regard as the necessities of life, or economy, and (20) what they conceive marriage to be good for (21) in relation to sexuality and to bearing children, the next generation; and (22) rebukes society's indiscriminate satisfactions in debased forms of culture, to begin with, (23) forms of debased philosophy; arriving at the knowledge that (24) the philosophical life is the most just and happy human life, knowledge whose demonstration depends on seeing, something precisely antithetical to academic philosophy, that (25) morality is not the subject of a separate philosophical study or field, separate from an imagination of the good city in which morality imposes itself; (26) the alternative is moralism; so that (27) the burdens placed on writing in composing this conversation may be said to be the achieving of an expression public enough to show its disdain for, its refusal to participate fully in, the shameful state of current society, or rather to participate by showing society its shame, and at the same time the achieving of a promise of expression that can attract the good stranger to enter the precincts of its city of words, and accordingly (28) philosophical writing, say the field of prose, enters into competition with the field of poetry, not – though it feels otherwise – to banish all poetry from the just city but to claim for itself the privilege of the work poetry does in making things happen to the soul, so far as that work has its rights.

Socrates speaks of his ideal state as "our city of words" at the end of book 9 of the *Republic*, and the question may well arise as to whether this city should appear as a further feature of perfectionist writing generally. Is this description of the city as words merely an artifact of the medium of Plato's philosophizing in the form of dialogue, calling special attention to the distance between our ability to inspire one another with dreams of a world of goodness and our (in)ability as citizens "to realize that world," as Emerson puts it at the close of "Experience"?

But suppose the noting of "our city" is a standing gesture toward the reader, or overhearer, to enter into the discussion, to determine his or her own position with respect to what is said – assenting, puzzled, bullied, granting for the sake of argument, and so on. Then the city has, in each such case of reading, one more member than the members depicted in a Platonic (or Wittgensteinian, or Emersonian) dialogue. (That Emerson's prose exists as a kind of conversation with itself, as a dialogue, is a burden of my first essay on that prose, "Thinking of Emerson.") And while Socrates goes on to say that "it makes no difference whether it [the ideal city, of words] exists anywhere or will exist," the reader's participation roots the idea that the Utopian vision participating in this presented city of words is one I am – or I am invited to be – already, reading, participating in. This implies that I am already participating in that transformation of myself of which the transformed city, the good city, is the expression. As Thoreau sees the matter in the fifth chapter ("Solitude") of *Walden*, a grand world of laws is working itself out *next* to ours, as if ours is flush with it. Then it may be a feature of any perfectionist work that it sets up this relation to its reader's world. What is next to me is, among other things, what I listen to, perhaps before me, for example, reading Thoreau's text, *Walden*; it is nearer than Walden may be, ever, and presents an attraction to its reader to find a Walden by not knowing in advance where it is and what it looks like. And what is next to me may be that any or all of this is dead.

Emerson discusses and depicts relations of his writing to its reading in countless ways, surely no fewer than Thoreau's ways, for example in such a remark as this: "So all that is said of the wise man by stoic or oriental or modern essayist, describes to each man his own idea, describes his unattained but attainable self" ("History," para. 5). It is Emerson's way to mean by "idea" here both our idea of the wise and our idea that it applies to us, neither of which we, before his words, may have known we harbored. I take for granted that Emerson is identifying himself as "the modern essayist," hence that he is claiming to be a path to one's unattained self. I will call it the next self, as claiming that Emerson is invoking what Thoreau invokes, a few paragraphs after his passage about what we are next to, in his observation that "with thinking we may be beside ourselves in a sane sense," thus identifying thinking as a kind of ecstasy. The implication is that the self is such that it is always beside itself, only mostly in an insane sense. (Thinking does not start from scratch; it, as it were, sides against and with the self there is, and so constitutes it. The question is, What must that be in order to be sided, to be capable of asides, to require parentheses?) Thoreau's interpretation of nextness contains a parody of what detractors of Transcendentalism understand its interest to amount to in a world beyond this one, an afterworld, available for the musing. (Something of the sort is parodied along the same lines in the third section of the first part of *Zarathustra*, in Nietzsche's punning title *Von den Hinterweltlern*, meaning afterworldsmen, sounding like backwoodsmen, suggesting that only hicks believe there is some other *place*.) What is in Thoreauvian nextness to us is part of this world, a way of being in it, a curb of it we forever chafe against.

I might at once declare that the path from the *Republic*'s picture of the soul's journey (perfectible to the pitch of philosophy by only a few, forming an aristocratic class) to the democratic need for perfection, is a path from the idea of there being one (call him Socrates) who represents for each of us the height of the journey, to the idea of each of us being representative for each of us – an idea that is a threat as much as an opportunity. Emerson's study is of this (democratic, universal) representativeness – it comes up in my first lecture under the head of "standing for" ("I stand here for humanity") – as a relation we bear at once to others and to ourselves: if we were not representative of what we might be (or what we were, in some Platonic or Wordsworthian past of our lives), we would not recognize ourselves presented in one another's possibilities; we would have no "potential." But there is little point in such a declaration now since, to begin with, we do not know whether the distance between, for example, Plato and Emerson, or between any minds finding themselves in one another, is well thought of as a path. The distance is measured by the difference between Plato's progress of conversation in the form of argumentative exchange and dialectical progression eventuating in the stratum of mythology, and Emerson's preparation of the "American Scholar" for a long period of stammering, poverty, and solitude eventuating perhaps in a text in which "we recognize our own rejected thoughts . . . come back to us with a certain alienated majesty" (words from the opening paragraph of "Self-Reliance" that will recur in the lectures to follow).

I will be speaking in the first lecture of Emerson's manner of thinking as characterized by what he calls transfiguration, which I take there as transfigurations of Kantian terms, a process whose extent is barely suggested; and already now, before the beginning, we see that we must think of the transfiguration in Emerson's prose of an unknown number of Platonic terms and images: for example, of chains (Emerson speaks of clapping ourselves into prison, from shamefully being ashamed of the eyes of others); of a sense of unreality (Emerson in effect claims that we do not exist, we are afraid to say "I am," and so haunt the world); of what the soul's "attraction" is to its journey (Kant reads it as an imperative, expressed by an "ought," a point of decisive difference in Emerson); of how to picture what constitutes such journeying (Emerson's word for it is taking steps, say walking, a kind of success(ion), in which the direction is not up but on, and in which the goal is decided not by anything picturable as the sun, by nothing beyond the way of the journey itself – this is the subject of Emerson's "Experience" as seen in my "Finding as Founding"); and of how Emerson sees "culture" (in his "Circles": "A new degree of culture would instantly revolutionize the entire system of human pursuits," quoted by Nietzsche near the close of *Schopenhauer as Educator*). Emerson is not suggesting that we add more books and concerts and galleries to our lives, nor speaking of any thing open only to persons possessing certain gifts or talents unequally distributed across the general population, nor of an extra degree of work asking to be rewarded for its public benefits, but of an attitude to our pursuits that is precisely unimposable and unrewardable, one that we would all instantly see the worth of could we but turn, revolutionize ourselves. Emerson's problem of representativeness, or exemplification ("imitation"), or perfection, thus begins earlier than Plato's, both in lacking a sun and in having no standing representative of the path to it. Emerson elects himself to be our representative man (anyone is entitled, and no one is, to stand for this election) and he warns that we have to – that we do – elect our (private) representative(s). In a sense his teaching is that we are to see beyond representativeness, or rather see it as a process of individuation. His praise of "the infinitude of the private man" (from the *Journals*, April 1840, as quoted in *Selections from Ralph Waldo Emerson*, ed. S. E. Whicher; Boston, 1957, p. 139) is not a praise of any existing man or men but an announcement of the process of individuation (an interpretation of perfectionism) before which there are no individuals, hence no humanity, hence no society. When in the seventh paragraph of "Self-Reliance" Emerson remarks of his sometimes succumbing to calls for philanthropy, "It is a wicked dollar, which by and by I shall have the manhood to withhold," we need not, we should not, take him to imagine himself as achieving a further state of humanity in himself alone.

These experiments with or transfigurations of the terms "representation" and "election" in Emerson's teaching suggest the reason he characteristically speaks of "my constitution," meaning for him simultaneously the condition of his body, his personal health (a figure for the body or system of his prose), and more particularly his writing (or amending) of the nation's constitution. The idea of his constitution accordingly encodes and transfigures Plato's picture of justice in the state as justice in the soul writ large. Such is philosophical writing, or authorship, early and late. Not, of course, always or everywhere. It may be, perhaps it should be, over; that too is an Emersonian question.

What exemplification (or "imitation") is in *The Republic* is a more famous, no doubt in part a more metaphysical, instance of the questions raised in Emersonian representativeness. (Emerson's transfiguration of illustrativeness into illustriousness is the region of his view of representativeness that I emphasize in my first lecture.) But the question or questions are no more important in the ancient economy of perfectionism than they are in the modern. Emerson's incessant attention to representation, to his own presentation of himself, of his authorship, of his constitution of words, together with his reader, as one another's illustrious other, might serve to caution against the impression of Plato's theory of art and poetry as something in which Plato's authorship is only inadvertently or unconsciously implicated. As if our superior perspective on Plato's artfulness permits us to place it better than he. As if the "banishing" of "poetry" from his republic – but not from his *Republic*, the city of words, the one of philosophical participation or exemplification – meant that Plato mistakenly took himself to have put behind him, outside his work, the problematic of originality, imitation, and corruption in conducting the life of philosophy, rather than philosophically to have staked out the problematic, to be staking it out, with or without the reader's responsiveness to it, election of it, there.

In my way of reading Emerson, his passage naming the unattained but attainable self suggests two ways of reading (reading him, to begin with), in one of which we are brought to recognize our own idea in his text (reading with our unattained self), in the other not (reading with our attained self, appreciating our given opinions, learning nothing new). To recognize the unattained self is, I gather, a step in attaining it. (Such reading is given a fuller description in my first lecture.) I do not read Emerson as saying (I assume this is my unattained self asserting itself) that there is one unattained/attainable self we repetitively never arrive at, but rather that "having" "a" self is a process of moving to, and from, nexts. It is, using a romantic term, the "work" of (Emerson's) writing to present nextness, a city of words to participate in. A further implication, hinted at a moment ago in passing, is that our position is always (already) that of an attained self; we are from the beginning, that is from the time we can be described as having a self, a next, knotted. An Emersonian sally at this idea is to say that we are (our thinking is) partial. (This idea will come back to stay in the first lecture.) That the self is always attained, as well as *to be* attained, creates the problem in Emerson's concept of self-reliance – he insists on it, though not in the following terms exactly – that unless you manage the reliance of the attained on the unattained/attainable (that is, unless you side that way), you are left in precisely the negation of the position he calls for, left in conformity. That one way or the other a side of the self is in negation – either the attainable negates the attained or vice versa – is the implication I drew earlier in saying that *each* state of the self is final, one we have desired, in this sense perfect, kept, however painful, in perfect place by us. In this dire sense, as said – but only in this sense – Perfectionism implies Perfectibility. (If Heidegger's distinction between the ontological and the ontic shows the pervasive draw or claim of one upon the other, so for instance shows how it happens that "Authentic Being-One's-Self . . . is . . . an existentiell modification of the 'they' – of the 'they' as an essential existentiale" (*Being and Time*, p. 168), then Emerson's idea of the unattained but attainable self may be thought of as replacing Heidegger's distinction, or vice versa.)

But again here the question may arise: Even if the intuitions I have been thematizing are true of *something*, why do I call it perfectionism, incurring or toying with metaphysical suggestions I say I want no part of? Most significant is the suggestion of a state, the same for all, at which the self is to arrive, a fixed place at which it is destined to come home to itself. Is it worth this risk of suggestion to be able to say, as if blocking the metaphysical with a paradox, that each state of the self is final? Why not call the view Attainabilism or the Ethics of Representation or of Excellence or of Virtue? I might answer this by saying that it is a mission of Emersonian Perfectionism precisely to struggle against false or debased perfectionisms and that it is a sufficient reason to keep the name Perfectionism to mark this mission. This is part of Emersonian Perfectionism's struggle against the moralistic, here the form of moralism that fixates on the presence of ideals in one's culture and promotes them to distract one from the presence of otherwise intolerable injustice. (Ideological criticism is a form, accordingly, of antimoralism; too often, in my experience, it is an unphilosophical form, one with an insufficiently ideological form of ideology, which is to say, an insufficient study of (its own) ideas.) The other pressing form of moralism for Emersonianism is the enforcement of morality, or a moral code, by immoral means, represented in the theocratic state, but still present in reforming states (as at the best they are).

It is to John Dewey's eternal credit to have combated, unrelentingly, both forms of moralism, the idealistic and the unreforming – if, as it strikes me, with inadequate philosophical and literary means. On such an occasion as the Carus lectures, prompting for me old memories, I remember, when first beginning to read what other people called philosophy, my growing feeling about Dewey's work, as I went through what seemed countless of his books, that Dewey was remembering something philosophy should be, but that the world he was responding to and responding from missed the worlds I seemed mostly to live in, missing the heights of modernism in the arts, the depths of psychoanalytic discovery, the ravages of the century's politics, the wild intelligence of American popular culture. Above all, missing the question, and the irony in philosophy's questioning, whether philosophy, however reconstructed, was any longer possible, and necessary, in this world. Positivism's answer, the reigning answer in the professional philosophy of the America in which I was beginning to read philosophy, shared pragmatism's lack of irony in raising the question of philosophy – in the idea that philosophy is to be brought to an end by philosophy, which in a sense is all that can preserve philosophy; and in the fact that the major modern philosophers, from Descartes and Locke and Hume to Nietzsche and Heidegger and Wittgenstein, have wished to overcome philosophy philosophically. (The irony of self-overcoming, call it the irony of "having" a self, say an identity, being the one you are rather than another, with its overcomings, is enacted in philosophy, no less perfectly when philosophy claims to be final and to be possessed by an individual.) But then positivism harbored no particular longing for a cultural or intellectual role for philosophy apart from its relation to logic and science.

I could not trust my reactions very far, and I could do nothing whatever sensible about them; but it seemed to me that the young teachers I was close to in those years, Henry Aiken, Abraham Kaplan, Morton White, all of whom took Dewey seriously, felt the lack of his work's power as well as the importance of its claims for philosophy – and, I trust, felt the thrill of certain moments of Dewey's writing. It was not until the force of Wittgenstein's *Philosophical Investigations* came over me, in my own reluctant beginnings as a teacher of philosophy, that I found the details of the philosophizing I seemed to imagine must exist, a beginning, deferred inventory of what I felt missing in Dewey, whose signature concepts are, to my ear, characteristically eclipsed by their very similarity to, yet incommensurability with, Wittgenstein's problematizings of "privacy," "thinking," "knowledge," "use," "practice," "context," "language," and "philosophy." And in coming to Heidegger's work a few years later, recognizing further items and transfigurations of the inventory I fancied for philosophy, leading or encouraging me to Emerson and to Shakespeare and what not, I would from time to time remember and cite a moment from Dewey that seemed part of what was moving me, but I was not moved to look again at what Dewey had actually said. When in the past decade Richard Rorty's *Philosophy and the Mirror of Nature* (Princeton, NJ, 1979) and *Consequences of Pragmatism* (Minneapolis, 1982) appeared, not even this work, which, among other matters, more than any other forced a reassessment of Dewey's contribution to our intellectual life, has enabled me to find my way back to Dewey's writing. I think the reason, if there is a reason, has to do with the fact that Rorty's placement of Dewey in the company of Wittgenstein and of Heidegger, whose voices have seemed to me to eclipse Dewey's, has been achieved, so I might put the matter, at the expense of giving up the question of the question of philosophy, of what it is, if anything, that calls for philosophy now, in favor of an idea that we are, or should be, past interest in the distinctions between philosophy and other modes of thought or of the presentation of thought. (An expense too high for me; for Rorty a gift.) Nevertheless, I am aware that it is because of my encounters with Rorty's work that I am moved now to go a little beyond the invocations of Dewey that have entered my writing from the earliest of the work I have published that I still use (in the essay "Must We Mean What We Say?", where the reference in note 31 to "American pragmatism" pretty much means Dewey) and for a moment to place my sense of what I found and what I missed in Dewey as that bears on what I have been saying about Emerson and perfectionism.

I found myself just now thinking of Dewey in connection with his tireless combating of two forms of moralism. So important is the feature of antimoralism that this alone constitutes Dewey as some sort of perfectionist – though surely not an Emersonian one. Tocqueville captures the sense of Deweyan perfectionism (in pt. 1, chap. 18 of *Democracy in America*: ed. P. Bradley, New York, 1945): "[The Americans] have all a lively faith in the perfectibility of man, they judge that the diffusion of knowledge must necessarily be advantageous, and the consequences of ignorance fatal; they all consider society as a body in a state of improvement, humanity as a changing scene, in which nothing is, or ought to be, permanent; and they admit that what appears to them today to be good, may be superseded by something better tomorrow." Taken one way this description can almost seem to fit Emerson as well as Dewey. To see how close and far they are to and from one another, consider just the difference in what each will call "knowledge" and "ignorance" and how each pictures this "difference." For Dewey, representing the international view, knowledge is given in science and in the prescientific practices of the everyday, that is, the learning of problem solving. For Emerson, the success of science is as much a problem for thought as, say, the failure of religion is. Again these words might be true, in a different spirit, of Dewey as well. Then it may help to say: for Dewey the relation between science and technology is unproblematic, even definitive, whereas for Emerson the power manifested in technology and its attendant concepts of intelligence and power and change and improvement are in contest with the work, and the concept of the work, of realizing the world each human is empowered to think. For an Emersonian, the Deweyan is apt to seem an enlightened child, toying with the means of destruction, stinting the means of instruction, of provoking the self to work; for the Deweyan the Emersonian is apt to look, at best, like a Deweyan. (In part Dewey's fine essay on Emerson reads this way; but in part it also reads like a poignant wish to find something in Emerson's achievement that he could put to use in his own work.) For Dewey the texture of the philosophical text barely exists, except as superstition and resistance to social change. For Emerson it is a question whether the problem sufficiently exists for philosophy, both the urgency of the need for transformative social change and the resistance to internal change, to transformative nextness. That we must have both is a sufficient reason for my siding with the endangered Emersonian.

False or debased perfectionisms seem everywhere these days, from bestselling books with titles like *Love Yourself* to the television advertisement on behalf of Army recruitment with the slogan, "Be all that you can be." Someone is apt to find these slogans difficult to tell from a remark of Emerson's in which he lists, among the "few great points" whose recurrence is "the secret of culture," what he words as "courage to be what we are." (This is from the concluding paragraph of "Considerations by the Way." Nietzsche gives *Ecce Homo* the subtitle: *How One Becomes What One Is*.) Then let us note, anticipating a cardinal theme of the lectures to follow, that Emersonian Perfectionism requires that we become ashamed in a particular way of ourselves, of our present stance, and that the Emersonian Nietzsche requires, as a sign of consecration to the next self, that we hate ourselves, as it were impersonally (bored with ourselves might be enough to say); and that in the television promise to be all you can be, the offer is to *tell* you what all you can be, most importantly, a mercenary. (I do not deny that it is better than certain alternatives.) Whatever the confusions in store for philosophical and moral thinking, ought we to let the fact of debased or parodistic versions of a possibility deprive us of the good of the possibility? The inevitability of debased claims to Christianity, or to philosophy, or to democracy, are, so one might put it, not the defeat, not even the bane, of the existence of the genuine article, but part of its inescapable circumstance and motivation. So that the mission of Perfectionism generally, in a world of false (and false calls for) democracy, is the discovery of the possibility of democracy, which to exist has recurrently to be (re)discovered (as with philosophy, and religion, and, I have to add, psychoanalysis).

Epilogue: The *Investigations'* Everyday Aesthetics of Itself

If the previous extract helps us to obtain a perspicuous surview of Cavell's life-long intellectual project, then the present one may serve to give some indication of its future horizons. Since it is introduced by Cavell's own reflections upon the connection between philosophy and modernity, as those issues are refracted in the writing of the *Philosophical Investigations*, it requires no further prefatory remarks from me.

Introduction

When, a couple of years after beginning to teach for a living, I found myself floored by Wittgenstein's *Investigations*, it took a further year for me to feel sufficient familiarity with the strangeness of the appearance of the ordinary in that text to offer a course of lectures on it, at Berkeley in 1960. That first time around, I presented it as what I called a modernist work, meaning to say that its incessant and explicit self-reflection struck me as unlike the self-consciousness of any other undoubted work of philosophy I knew. I did not then take the cue to ask whether, or how, or to what extent, philosophy on the whole can escape issues of modernity.

I suppose I imagined the answer to be more or less, and more or less obvious, that modern philosophy, in our tradition at any rate, sides with science; that is, it associates intellectual seriousness with the image of science, hence takes staple features of the concept of the modern, so far as it happens to ponder the matter at all – features, for example, such as rationalization, secularization, industrialization, the externalization or urbanization of human association, democratization, anti-democratization, the spread of the new science itself, the rise of romantic anti-rationalization, perhaps the fact of the academization of intellectual life at large – as natural accompaniments of the conditions and (perhaps checkered) progress of intellectual seriousness, accompaniments good or bad depending on your private point of view. That these developments might somehow, as with the arts, have made philosophy, in certain of its guises, difficult in a new way, difficult to identify as a continuation of its own past and difficult to value in something like a continuing way, mostly would not arise; or if it did arise – as with the philosophical revolution brought on by logical positivism – the break with the past, or forgetting of the past, was no more problematic than in the case of the development of the exact sciences; it is what you should expect, and is essentially for the good.

Even one inclined to side the work of philosophy with the work of the arts must recognize that such a work as Wittgenstein's *Investigations* would have – to be taken with philosophical seriousness in our professional philosophical culture – to be shown to bear up as part of the development of analytical philosophy; so the idea of its modernism rather dropped out, as an explicit issue, as my lectures on it developed in the next two decades. Those lectures effectively ended in 1979, with the publication of my *Claim of Reason*, which incorporated much of them; they made, heavily altered, a last appearance in 1984, but it was not until the spring of 1993 that I worked out new lectures on the *Investigations*, and found myself recurring to my earliest thoughts about that text, including what I can still call its modernism. The occasion for those new lectures was a course Hilary Putnam and I offered jointly, the dynamics of which, importantly because I could count on Putnam's demanding of our students the most exacting attention to Wittgenstein's position in contemporary debates concerning the philosophy of language and the philosophy of mind, allowed me, even encouraged me, in my half of the weeks of lecturing, to move more systematically toward an articulation of Wittgenstein's manner, the sheer sense of the deliberateness and beauty of his writing, as internal to the sense of his philosophical aims, than I had ever tried before.

Two main lines of reason prepared the way for this departure. Generally, I have in recent years increasingly wished to respond to developments in German and French post-metaphysical anti-metaphysical philosophy, especially as in Heidegger and in Derrida, one aspect of which has meant taking up an issue Heidegger and Derrida raise incessantly for themselves, their broken relation to the past of philosophy, what I am calling the modernist issue. (It may be that a philosophy does not wonder what to make of the modern unless it is has to ask itself what to do about it. This would then be a decisive issue over which the German-French and the English-American philosophical traditions are split.) Specifically, I completed last year a fairly extended discussion of certain dimensions of Derrida's "Signature Event Context," the second half of which Derrida devotes to J. L. Austin's theory of performative utterances. In my essay, two features of modern philosophy make themselves increasingly felt – the question of philosophy's seriousness and the sense of it as occurring in some aftermath of culture. I found that my essay had become something like a study of seriousness, while on the way it quotes four scenes or phantasms of intellectual destruction – one each from Emerson, Nietzsche, Wittgenstein, and Derrida – within which philosophy, if it is to continue (a matter that is not assured), is to recover itself. Now a year later, I realize that Nietzsche's *Genealogy of Morals* can be said to have raised the issue of the seriousness of philosophy explicitly together with that of philosophy's destruction, or self-destruction, portraying an enterprise of reflection whose claim to seriousness was its ideal of the search for truth, and whose conviction ended by turning the search upon its own motives and finding them fatal to its ideal. If philosophy is to find itself again it must be in the fact and the concept of the future: when Nietzsche calls, in the subtitle of *Beyond Good and Evil*, for "a philosophy of the future," he evidently means both that the philosopher whose words now will last is yet to come, and that such a one must come as a thinker about the future. Which seems to mean that serious philosophy must in future present itself as a form of originality, recounting origins, saying something new about the new.

This claim would provide a further degree of illumination for me in several guiding ideas I have counted on in my work: (1) A sense of Wittgenstein and Heidegger each harping on their differences from their predecessors or intellectual competitors that has not seemed to me sheer arrogance on their part, but also not just the arrogance native to philosophy, yet something internal to their sense of what they have to say – as if they each harbor a sense of something left unexpressed in their writing and hence leaving them pervasively exposed to misunderstanding, to being taken wrongly, taken less radically than they take themselves. A structural requirement of originality promises some help in articulating this sense, and forms a further point of resemblance between these massively different thinkers. (2) A sense of Wittgenstein and Austin, taken as the definitive, also decisively different, representatives of ordinary language practice in philosophy, as underwritten in their orientation toward or search for the ordinary in the writing of Emerson (and of Thoreau). I have not hitherto emphasized their point of intersection on the demand for the new, for a promised future still denied us. Here the fact of what Emerson means by genius, and most famously calls self-reliance – defined as the aversion to conformity, that is, a turning away from (but since it is continuous it is also a turning again toward) society as it stands (it is a capacity shared by every functioning human being, like the capacity to exercise the moral law) – is to be understood as characterizing Emerson's own prose. It is the mark of that prose to philosophize by means of ordinary words (which often means identifying words that have been enclosed by philosophy – such as understanding, reason, accident, necessity, idea, impression – and retrieving their ordinariness)

in such a way as to demand an originality of expression, a negation of
unoriginal conformity, in every particular. (Heidegger's attempt to re-
trieve the primordial Greek words from their decline in (or as) the history
of Western metaphysics seems to be working imaginatively at the re-
motest distance from Emerson's, or from Wittgenstein's, ideas of philosophical originality. But the shared aversion to metaphysics in the name
of a new, or perhaps old, experience of originality, suggests that the
distance may at certain junctures not exactly be remote.) Emerson's call
for the "new" is specified – but so obviously as to be made all but
unremarkable – in the call for a new language for a new nation, a New
World for an Old World, something both Emerson and Thoreau fear has
not happened, and hence cannot under known, or given, circumstances
be made to happen. (3) A sense of Wittgenstein's philosophical challenge
to the old ("History now has a kink in it") as like and as unlike analogous
challenges in modernist art.

I want to expand on this third idea or intuition a little, the idea I cited
as coloring my first attempts at lecturing on *Philosophical Investigations*,
which developed as I moved back to Harvard in 1963. Shortly thereafter
I began publishing material relating to certain developments in the arts
and in philosophy (much of it gathered into my first book, *Must We Mean
What We Say?*) that gave me impressions such as the following: Ambitious or new art, that which recognizes a break with what seems a
continuous, developing history of artistic traditions and practice, now
exists in two states, one I called the modernist (in which the present
wishes to maintain the artistic quality, say the greatness, of the past,
despite the differences the look and sound of the art, as it were, must
discover precisely to preserve its status), and the other, doubtless showing my prejudices, or commitments, I called the modernizing (in which
the present would forget the past by, so to speak, embracing the fact of
the present, in its transience, its fashionableness, its distrust of, even
contempt for, greatness); apparently ungrounded, the modern in the arts,
in both its states, courts the charge of fraudulence; both states cause what
may be called philosophy, the modernist by embodying its theory of itself
(an origin of romanticism), the modernizing by inviting as a response to
it an outpouring of theory and manifesto; and since I spoke of modernist
art as assuming the condition of philosophy, bearing absolute responsibility for itself ("seriousness"), I was bound to ask what effect this
assumption had on what is called philosophy, whether philosophy contained a counter-move toward assuming the condition of art, a wish to
bear some new responsibility for its own literary conditions, something
encouraged by my growing fascination with the writing of Wittgenstein
and of Heidegger, and later with that of Emerson and of Thoreau, given
their difference in sound and look from what most of my profession of

philosophy acknowledged as philosophy; and it seemed to me that the power of that profession to discourage this move to the literary, let's call it, came not alone from its formidable institutional power (unlike the arts and the sciences, philosophy essentially now finds its *sole* support in the university), but equally from its quality as philosophy: academic painting or music need not be recognized as a competitor of advanced art, but modern academic philosophy, in its power genuinely, all but exclusively, to represent the present of the history of philosophy, is the scourge of the non-academic, let us say, the literary, in philosophical ambition; a way of putting this asymmetry between art and philosophy is to say that philosophy's struggle against what it perceives as fraudulence or charlatanry (it knows its debasement under the name of sophistry) is as ancient as the establishing of philosophy in Plato, whereas the struggle of the arts against their debasement is definitively new, say modern – a further mark, evidently, of the arts assuming the condition of philosophy; it is part of Wittgenstein's originality to have internalized the issue of philosophy's enmity toward a kind of charlantry (a test of its seriousness) by including forced or fixated or otherwise inauthentic responses to philosophical perplexity as an essential part of the investigation of those perplexities (through the medium of what is called his "interlocutor," voicing his or her insistences or disappointments or cravings in the face of Wittgenstein's corrections), as if we are, in striving to become the philosopher it is in us to become, meant to overcome the sophist it is equally in us to remain.

Two encounters, now thirty years later, have helped confirm my decision to introduce the essay to follow on Wittgenstein's aesthetics of itself with these reminiscences of the modern. The first encounter was finding that Jurgen Habermas, in *The Philosophical Discourse of Modernity*, takes up the Derrida–Austin debate as a proposed effort at "levelling the genre distinction between philosophy and literature," hence, according to Habermas, as one proposal of the modern. Now my identification of *Philosophical Investigations* as essentially proposing an aesthetics of itself may be seen as challenging any given distinction between supposed genres of philosophy and of literature that I am aware of. The rigor of its self-descriptions is meant as evidently philosophical; but it is a rigor that – puzzling as this may at first sound – essentially and explicitly claims something like beauty for certain of its characteristic passages. Notwithstanding, it does not follow that the distinction between philosophy and literature is thereby meant to be levelled, but rather that the genres occur simultaneously, and perhaps work to deepen their differences, even to bring them to a crisis. Is this new?

It is evidently related to the romantic call, as in the Schlegels' two sets of *Fragments*, for the union of philosophy and poetry. This call is interpreted by Lacoue-Labarthes and Nancy in their *The Literary Absolute* as realized in the production of poetry that realizes the demand to contain its own theory. In Wittgenstein's *Investigations*, so I claim, we have philosophizing that demands of itself the periodic expression of its aims in something like the realm of the poetic; one might equally find it to be in something like the realm of the mythic. As important to my mind as the importance Wittgenstein attaches to this condition of his work is the fact that this condition is essentially dismissed by the profession of philosophy which is, nevertheless, this work's chief, or only, institutional protection. The question of the essay following this Introduction may be put as asking whether this price is necessary to this protection. This again bears comparison, in its differences, with Heidegger's later work, which characteristically philosophizes off of the reading of certain poetry, thus "containing" it, but not by competing with it, anyway not by composing something like poetry of its own.

Having alluded to my own discussion of Derrida in relation to Austin, I should perhaps note that I find Habermas's discussion of their encounter to be hampered by his having used, instead of the primary text of Derrida's in question, Jonathan Culler's recounting of it (which, whatever its own merits, does not reproduce the texture of intersections traced by Derrida's attractions to and withdrawals from Austin) and thus been helped to take certain of Derrida's presentations of the issue between his thought and Austin's too much at face value. For example, Habermas summarizes Derrida, not perhaps incorrectly, as asserting that Austin's theory of speech acts demands or implies that intention determines whether such an act is in effect, and that Austin's theory of language in general requires excluding theoretical attention from nonstandard, non-serious, etiolated, parasitic, poetic, comic, theatrical linguistic performances – a view of Austin that Habermas apparently accepts, whatever his other reservations about Derrida.

But this is not Austin. Derrida has significant responses to offer of Austin's work, permanently significant, in my view, for example on the subject of the relation of voice and writing in Austin's conception; but the topics Habermas summarizes are not the place to find them, while they do seem to summarize, regrettably, the received views of Austin on those topics. This helps to cause or continue an intellectual environment in which Austin's original work, however indirectly influential, goes largely unread, characteristically replaced, mostly I guess in literary studies, by the interpretation of it given in John Searle's prominent account of it.

I said that there were two recent encounters that reassured me of the pertinence of the essay to follow. The second was learning of the work of Peter Galison which documents convincingly – something variously and more or less sensed over the years – the implication, or shared intellectual and cultural aspirations, of the great Bauhaus movement in modern architecture in Rudolf Carnap's epochal *Logische Aufbau der Welt*, and which cites the architect Adolf Loos's resonance for Wittgenstein (the Wittgenstein of the *Tractatus*, so influential for Carnap and the other founders of logical positivism). Galison emphasizes the shared feature of that philosophy's and that architecture's each, and perhaps together, craving a new beginning, constructing from the ground up a lucid world in which and from which to live and to think. He sees the end of this joint vision with the rise of Nazism and the mass emigration of European intellectuals to America, most particularly the end of the goal of affecting their society's everyday life. The vision was more fundamental, understandably, to the aspirations of the Bauhaus than to those of the philosophers, but it was important personally to Otto Neurath among the positivists, while less so, or only abstractly, to Wittgenstein, and it became more or less irrelevant to established professors trying to rebuild their private and professional lives in an alien land.

But the concept of everyday life, and I think an idea of philosophy's having an effect on it, becomes of the most decisive importance in Wittgenstein's later philosophy, and still introduced in connection with an image of architecture, or anyway with an image of the cooperative act of building. I have in mind, of course, the most elaborated early example, I might call it the entering example, of *Philosophical Investigations*, in which a builder calls out one of the four "words" to his name to his assistant as a sign for him to bring one of the four building-blocks at his disposal. I have rehearsed various of the interpretations I have placed upon this example over the years in a long essay entitled "Notes on the Opening of Wittgenstein's *Investigations*" which records and comments on the opening weeks of the lectures, mentioned earlier, that I used to give on that work. Here I add, about to propose a new path through the *Investigations*, two further features of its entering example of the builders. First, there is its simple invoking of philosophy's ancient sense, if not often thematized, of intimacy between its aspirations and those of architecture, whether in Plato's descriptions of public spaces for philosophical encounter, or in Descartes's and Hume's specification of private spaces for it; or in the pride Kant takes in what he calls his architectonic, or in today's most intimate challenge to that pride, in deconstruction; or in Heidegger's identification, in his late essays, of thinking as a kind of building and dwelling, a matter in which he had been anticipated, and to my mind surpassed, in Thoreau's sometimes uncannily close project called *Walden*. Second, there is in Wittgenstein's example of the builders, in its explicit primitiveness, and in the consequent question whether anything we can call understanding is happening between the figures as described, a question, so one might put the matter, of whether we can recognize their humanness, what it is they desire of one another, their relatedness to our desires. The impression Wittgenstein's opening narrative now gives me is as of philosophy's beginning in a scene of aftermath, amid the destruction he will later confess his readers might sense in his refiguring of what human beings call important and interesting; as if in thus declaring of his work that it seeks to begin again, newly, for a future, he reveals his consequent knowledge that this means he may not be understood, and not because he is failing to employ all the means for understanding at his disposal, but because his readers will not feel a relatedness toward it of the kind they desire, not know what response its words and scenes may desire.

*　*　*　*　*

The *Investigations*' Everyday Aesthetics of Itself

We have all, I assume, heard it said that Wittgenstein is a writer of unusual powers. Perhaps that is worth saying just because the powers are so unusual, anyway in a philosopher, and of his time and place. But why is this worth repeating – I assume we have all heard it repeated – since as far as I know no one has denied it? Evidently the repetition expresses an uncertainty about whether Wittgenstein's writing is essential to his philosophizing; whether, or to what extent, the work of the one coincides with the work of the other. If you conceive the work of philosophy as, let's say, argumentation, then it will be as easy to admire as to dismiss the writing – to admire it, perhaps, as a kind of ornament of the contemporary, or near contemporary, scene of professional philosophy, hence as something that lodges no philosophical demand for an accounting. But if you cannot shake an intuition, or illusion, that more is at issue than ornamentation (not that that issue is itself clear), and you do not wish to deny argumentation, or something of the sort, as internal to philosophy, then a demand for some philosophical accounting of the writing is, awkwardly, hard to lose.

I describe what I am after as the *Investigations*' everyday aesthetics of itself to register at once that I know of no standing aesthetic theory that promises help in understanding the literariness of the *Investigations* – I mean the literary conditions of its philosophical aims – and to suggest the thought that no work will be powerful enough to yield this understanding of its philosophical aims aside from the *Investigations* itself. Does this mean that I seek an aesthetics within it? I take it to mean, rather, that I do not seek an aesthetic concern of the text that is separate from its central work. My idea here thus joins the idea of an essay of mine, "Declining Decline," which tracks the not unfamiliar sense of moral or religious fervor in the *Investigations* and finds that its moral work is not separate from its philosophical work, that something like the moral has become for it, or become again, pervasive for philosophy. (As Emerson words the idea in "Self-Reliance": "Character teaches above our wills [the will of the person and of the person's writing]. Men imagine that they communicate their virtue or vice only by overt actions, and do not see that virtue or vice emit a breath every moment.")

There is something more I want here out of the idea of an ordinary aesthetics. The *Investigations* describes its work, or the form its work takes, as that of perspicuous presentation (§122), evidently an articulation of a task of writing. And it declares the work of its writing as "lead[ing] words back from their metaphysical to their everyday use" (§116), a philosophically extraordinary commitment not only to judge philosophy by the dispensation of the ordinary, but to place philosophy's conviction in itself in the hands, or handling, of ordinary words. But we also know that Wittgenstein invokes, indeed harps on, the idea of the perspicuous as internal to the work of formal proofs. Then is his use of the idea, in this one section of the *Investigations* that explicitly invokes it, meant to signal an ideal of lucidity and conviction that he cannot literally expect in a work made of returns to ordinary words? Yet he goes on in the next paragraph to insist: "The concept of perspicuous presentation is of fundamental significance for us. It earmarks our form of presentation, how we look at things." So is the idea that the writing of the *Investigations* contains the equivalent, or some analogy or allegory, of proofs? Or that it is meant to project arguments of formal rigor, even though its surface form of presentation does not, to say the least, spell them out? How else could we account for the influence of this work, such as it is, in institutions of professional philosophy?

My somewhat different proposal is that Wittgenstein is claiming for the ordinary its own possibility of perspicuousness, as different from that of the mathematical as the experience of an interesting theorem is from the experience of an interesting sentence. But how can this be? Doesn't Wittgenstein's idea of the perspicuous just *mean*, as it were, the look of a formal proof? My proposal is rather to conceive that Wittgenstein once hit off an experience of the convincingness, perhaps of the unity, of a proof, with the concept of perspicuousness; and for some reason, later (or earlier), he hits off an experience of a unity, or a reordering, of ordinary words with the same concept, as if discovering a new manifestation of the concept in discovering something new about the ordinary. He had said, in the section in question: "A perspicuous presentation is a

means to just that understanding which consists in 'seeing connections'." Understanding a proof surely requires seeing connections. So
does understanding a unity among sentences. Is there an interesting
connection to be seen between these?

I am encouraged to look for a specific manifestation of perspicuousness
in the ordinary by the passage (§89) in which Wittgenstein asks: "In what
sense is logic something sublime?" His answer, as I understand it, expresses one way of seeing his turn from the thoughts of the *Tractatus* to
those of the *Investigations*. I almost never allow myself an opinion about
the *Tractatus*, in which I do not know my way about. But I cannot avoid
just this instance now. The *Investigations* answers: "For there seemed to
pertain to logic a peculiar depth. Logic lay, it seemed, at the bottom of
all the sciences." And then appears one of those dashes between sentences in this text, which often mark a moment at which a fantasy is allowed
to spell itself out. It continues: "For logical investigation explores the
essence of all things. It seems to see to the ground of things and is not
meant to trouble itself over whether this or that actually happens." Is
Wittgenstein fighting the fantasy or granting it? Then a larger dash, and
following it: "[Logic] takes its rise, not from an interest in the facts of
nature, nor from a need to grasp causal connections; but from a striving to understand the foundation, or essence, of everything empirical."
But again, is this good or bad, illusory or practical? Then finally:
"Not, however, as if to this end we had to hunt out new facts; it is much
more essential for our investigation that we want to learn nothing *new*
from it. We want to *understand* something that is already open to view.
For *this* is what we seem in some sense not to understand." So something
in this philosophical fantasizing turns out to be practical after all, and
something that winds up sounding like a self-description of the *Investigations*.

More such self-descriptions are concentrated in the ensuing several
dozen sections of the book (§§90–133). Logic, however, drops out – that
is, as a formal ideal, not to say as the ultimate formal systematization of
the unity of knowledge. But the *aim* of philosophy expressed by that
fantasy of logic remains, if transformed, the mark of philosophy's intellectual seriousness. It demands an extraordinary understanding, but not
of something new; it is not in competition with science. And the aim is
still essence, the ground of everything empirical, but the means to this
ground is as open to view, and as ungrasped, as what there is to be
grasped essentially. The means is the ordinariness of our language. And
there is no single or final order in which ordinariness and its articulation
of essence is to be ordered, or presented, or formed – we might even say,
reformed. The new route to the old aim Wittgenstein calls the grammatical investigation. What is its form, or order?

Wittgenstein says (§123): "A philosophical problem has the form: 'I cannot find myself' " (as I might translate "Ich kenne mich nicht aus"). And I have said this is kin to the loss Dante suffers (loss of way) faced with the dark wood in the middle of life's journey, as he begins to narrate the journey. The implication of the connection is that Wittgenstein is here marking the beginning of something, to which it gives a certain form. Religion calls a similar beginning perdition. Such a moment marks the place from which Emerson, beginning "Experience," calls out, "Where do we find ourselves?" It is, accordingly, as the philosophical answer to this disorientation that Wittgenstein proposes the idea of perspicuousness – outside the realm of proof, and by means of a return to what he calls the ordinary, or "home" (I place the quotes to remind ourselves that we may never have been there). The section that names perspicuous presentation mentions "intermediate cases," hence suggests that the idea of understanding as "seeing connections" is one of supplying language games – as in the string of cases of "reading" (§156–178), or in comparing the grammar of the word "knows" to that of "can" or "in a position to" and also to "understands" (§150), or, more generally, in showing grammatical derivation, as of the grammar of "meaning" in part from "explaining the meaning," or in showing grammatical difference, as between "pointing to an object" and "pointing to the color of an object." Perspicuous representation is accordingly the end of a philosophical problem that has *this* form of beginning.

But the methods of language games, though perhaps the most famous form in which the *Investigations* is known, at least outside the precincts of professional philosophy, put no more literary pressure on language – they pose no greater problem for aesthetics – than Austin's appeal to what we should say when (not that his prose is easy to characterize – I have said something about that in taking up Derrida's treatment of *How To Do Things with Words*). I mean, it is not in this precinct of the perspicuous that the sense arises of accounting philosophically for the genius of this writing. What the provision of language games requires is apparently no more than the common mastery of a language. (It is a matter of asking for and providing, for example, the difference between doing something by accident and by mistake, or between seeing bread and seeing all the signs of bread, or between knowing the other from his or her behavior and knowing the other *only* from his or her behavior.) The genius would come in seeing how this mastery, and equally the loss of mastery, calls for philosophy. If writing of a certain character is essential to displaying what is thus seen, then this writing is essential to the philosophical work of the *Investigations*. And it, too, then would have to fall under the concept of perspicuous presentation.

Sometimes the movement from being lost to finding oneself happens at a stroke – of a pen, of genius – in any case without the means or intermediary methods of grammatical investigations. Here I adduce moments expressed in the words of such gestures as these: "What is your aim in philosophy?" "To show the fly the way out of the fly-bottle" (§309); "Why can't my right hand give my left hand money?" (§268); "We have got on to slippery ice where there is no friction and so in a certain sense the conditions are ideal, but also, just because of that, we are unable to walk" (§107); "If I have exhausted my grounds I have reached hard rock, and my spade is turned" (§217); "The human body is the best picture of the human soul" (p. 178); "If I am inclined to suppose that a mouse has come into being by spontaneous generation out of grey rags and dust, I shall do well to examine those rags very closely to see how a mouse may have hidden in them, how it may have got there and so on. . . . But first we must learn to understand what it is that opposes such an examination of details in philosophy" (§52); "(Uttering a word is like striking a note on the keyboard of the imagination)" (§6); "But if you are *certain*, isn't it that you are shutting your eyes in front of doubt?" "They are shut" (p. 224). These are patently, all but ostentatiously, "literary" gestures of the *Investigations*, outstanding in the sense of that work as cultivating its literary grounds. How precisely?

I note that there is pleasure to be taken in them; and a shock of freedom to be experienced; and an anxiety of exposure (since they treacherously invite false steps of the reader: I have heard the observation about the keyboard of the imagination taken as Wittgenstein's own opinion about words, not as the spelling out of a fantasy); and they are at once plain and sudden, especially in context – let us say brilliant. But our question is whether they are essential to the work of the *Investigations*, which is before all to ask whether they represent work. So if we observe that the pleasure comes in being liberated from an unexpressed, apparently inexpressible, mood – call this being given expression – hence that it has required finding or inventing a specific order of words, then we have to ask whether providing expression is a form of work. The lines or gestures I just cited require a specific talent to compose, one perhaps dangerous to philosophy, or distracting; and they require a matching aesthetic effort to assess: for example, to see whether their pleasure and shock and anxiety are functions of their brilliance. Differences in the work philosophy does and the work that art does need not be slighted if it turns out that they cross paths, even to some extent share paths – for example, where they contest the ground on which the life of another is to be examined, call it the ground of therapy.

Let us approach the question of literary necessity in the *Investigations* by following out my suggestion just now that such lines are to be understood as further manifestations of what Wittgenstein calls perspicuousness and identifies as a distinguishing mark of his writing. To capture the pervasiveness and the specificity of the experience in question (the pleasure, liberation, anxiety), it will help to remember that text's recurrence to scenes of pain, especially those of what I call inexpressiveness, from whose fixation the order of words in the ostentatiously literary gestures I cited offer freedom. I took this tack in the course with Putnam I referred to earlier, prompted by my commitment to the class to go over, for the first time in such a setting, aspects of my own writing on the *Investigations* in Part One and Part Four of *The Claim of Reason*.

An air of pathos struck me – long before the description, near the opening of Part Four, of the fantasy of inexpressive privacy or suffocation – as gathering intensity at the close of both Chapters 4 and 5, which end Part One. There we find stifled screams in a Hemingway hospital ward; Keats's mourning for a dead poet; images of starving or abandoned children. My surprise was greeted with certain smiles of recognition from a number of the graduate students present, as though I was tardy in my literary self-observations. Naturally I attributed this pathos to the pathos of the *Investigations* itself, specifically to its portrait of – or its conviction that there is something to be seen as – the human condition, say the human as conditioned by the present stage of history.

Part of my sense of the *Investigations* as a modernist work is that its portrait of the human is recognizable as one of the modern self, or, as we are given to say, the modern subject. Since we are considering a work of philosophy, this portrait will not be unrelated to a classical portrait of the subject of philosophy, say that to be found in Plato's *Republic*, where a human soul finds itself chained in illusion, so estranged from itself and lost to reality that it attacks the one who comes to turn it around and free it by a way of speaking to it, and thus inciting it to seek the pleasures of the clear light of day. A difference of the modern self is that, no longer recognizing itself in Plato's environment, and subject to a thousand impertinent interventions, it no longer surmises its intelligibility or companionability. So the kind of work proposed in the text of the *Investigations* will at first seem to the one for whom it is addressed – the modern philosophical subject – obvious, uninteresting, remote. Then if for some reason it persists in considering the work, it may begin to divine its own voice there. Everything depends on the specificity with which its portrait is drawn.

I have begun specifying it in the philosophically recurrent sense – or the recurrence of philosophy in recognizing the sense – of lostness to oneself. This beginning of philosophy is related, I believe, to the feeling of philosophizing as an effort to achieve the indestructible (§55) but which perceives a Wittgensteinian experience of therapy initially as the destruction of everything great and important (§118), as if human self-destructiveness is at war with itself in philosophy. This is equally expressed in the sense that our ideal encloses us, suffocates us (§103). I have more than once noted the human sense of disappointment with the human, in the form of a disappointment with the language it is given ("A name ought really to signify a simple" (§39)); this pairs with human perverseness ("Why does it occur to one to want to make precisely this word into a name, when it evidently is *not* a name? – That is just the reason" (§39)). Then no wonder. "The philosopher's treatment of a question is like the treatment of an illness" (§255), which Wittgenstein articulates as a sickness of the understanding (*Remarks on Mathematics*, p. 157) as well as a sickness of the will ("Why does it occur to us to *want* to make this word . . .?"; "[Philosophical problems] are solved . . . through an insight into the workings of language [which takes place precisely] *despite* a drive to misunderstand them" (§109)). Yet philosophy itself – the human creature in its grip – remains tormented, and must learn to give itself peace, which means to break itself off (§133). Add to these features the *Investigations*' beginning with (apart from an unnoticed child, and a curiously mechanical errand) a succession of primitive builders, and the strangeness of the human to itself is always before us – epitomized in its philosophizing and in the uncertainty of its grip on itself, or on the concept of itself (is it a *language* the builders have? is it *words* they use? if I do not know such things about them, how can I know them about myself?).

How shall we place the farther shore of perspicuousness, the literary? Let us say it is, alluding to Kant, a standpoint from which to see the methods of the *Investigations*, their leading words home, undoing the charms of metaphysics, a perspective apart from which there is no pressing issue of spiritual fervor, whether felt as religious, moral, or aesthetic. Standpoint implies an alternative, a competing standpoint, a near shore. For professional philosophers this shore is that of philosophical "problems" – in the Preface to *Philosophical Investigations* Wittgenstein lists them as "[subjects such as] the concepts of meaning, of understanding, of a proposition, of logic, the foundations of mathematics, states of consciousness, and other things." Without this shore, the *Investigations* would not press upon, and not belong in, an academic philosophical curriculum. Because of the farther shore, its belonging is, and should be, uneasy.

I wish I could make the two shores equally palpable, and sufficiently so to make questions as to which shore is the more important seem as foolish to us as it must seem to the river of philosophy that runs between.

One without the other loses the pivot of the ordinary, the pressure of everyday life; one without the other thus loses, to my way of thinking, the signature of the *Investigations*.

There remains a question of priority. From each shore the other is almost ignorable, and each imagines itself to own the *seriousness* of the *Investigations'* work. When the farther ignores the rigors of the near, it consigns philosophy to the perennial, the perhaps customary eternal. When the near ignores the yearning for the farther, it merely conforms to the customary institutional demands of the university, hence risks consigning philosophy to present intellectual fashion. Each position has its advanced and its debased versions.

To count, as I do here, on a willingness to maintain a continuity between near and far, is to count on a certain way of following the continuities implied between the pleasures I claimed for certain literary gestures in the *Investigations* and the portrait of human pathos I sketched from it. The way of following requires a willingness to recognize in oneself the moments of strangeness, sickness, disappointment, self-destructiveness, perversity, suffocation, torment, lostness that are articulated in the language of the *Investigations*, and to recognize in its philosophizing that its pleasures (they will have to reach to instances of the ecstatic) will lie in the specific forms and moments of self-recovery it proposes – of familiarity (hence uncanniness, since the words of recovery were already familiar, too familiar), of soundness, of finitude, of the usefulness of friction, of acknowledgment, of peace.

But what kind of pleasure could be essential to philosophy, and worthy of it? I think it will help us find an answer if we pick up more concretely Wittgenstein's reiterated observation in the *Remarks on Mathematics* that "Proof must be perspicuous" (quoted in *This New Yet Unapproachable America*, p. 16), and look at a proof. Coming from me it had better be simple. I take an example remembered from Euclidean geometry, the earliest discourse in which I remember experiencing something like ecstasy in arriving at a conclusion. I assume it is to be proved that the sum of the inner angles of a triangle equals 180 degrees, the measure of a straight line. I draw a triangle and construct through its apex a line parallel to its base:

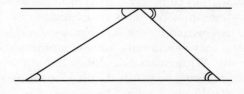

Fig. 1

Proof: Assuming that we have proven that opposite interior angles of a transverse are equal, we know that the lower left angle is equal to the upper left angle beneath the parallel, and that the lower right angle is equal to the upper right angle beneath the parallel. Now since the remaining angle at the vertex of the triangle is identical with the remaining angularity of the line, namely that between those upper left and right angles, the line's angularity is equal to the sum of the three angles of the triangle; which is to say, the sum is 180 degrees. Q.E.D. Look at it. The three angles precisely exhaust the line. This is perspicuous. It is a glimpse at the ground of everything empirical.

The obvious predicates of this experience remain, I find, pleasure of some kind, and a kind of liberation or relief, and, we might now specify, a sense of arrival, or completeness, as of relationship perfected, not finished but permanent. As well, therefore, as manifesting "the understanding which consists in 'seeing connections'," as in the section naming perspicuous representation (§122), the proof also manifests, it seems, what Wittgenstein calls, a few sections later, "the clarity that we aspire to," about which he says, "[it] is indeed *complete* clarity." Then he goes on to characterize this completeness in ways that no longer seem pertinent to such a proof as I have remembered from Euclidean geometry. "But this simply means that the philosophical problems" – that is, a certain sense of being at a loss – "should *completely* disappear . . . The real discovery is the one that makes me capable of breaking off philosophizing when I want to. The one that brings philosophy peace." We don't seem to require a background of philosophical torment to ask for such proofs and to receive their pleasure. This difference evidently goes with the fact that a proof is a structure that tells me something is over, a bottom reached; I do not have to consult my desire, there would be no intellectual pertinence in consulting it, to determine whether I may break off this thinking. The completed proof breaks it off. It affords me ecstasy not preceded by torment (but perhaps by the ups and downs of wonder). That is the beauty of it.

We seem to have rearrived at the question whether the concept of perspicuousness invited by the experience of certain formal proofs is further invited by a certain unity or reordering of ordinary words – supposing this to be something Wittgenstein means by his discovery of (non-formal) moments of complete clarity; ordinary words, that is, which are not meant to line up as premises to a conclusion. (Whatever structures of this kind are invited by the *Investigations*, and however welcome one may find them, they would raise no new problem about their source of clarity of the sort Wittgenstein describes himself as striving for.) Is there, perhaps, an ordering of words that is its own bottom line, sees to its own ground? Would we, I mean, be prepared to describe any such ordering in this way?

In answering affirmatively, I need a name for forms of ordinary words that I will claim partake of (satisfy the criteria of) completeness, pleasure, and the sense of breaking something off (the chief marks of perspicuous representation) – words that epitomize, separate a thought, with finish and permanence, from the general range of experience. To such a (non-formal) form of words I give the unsurprising name of the aphoristic. Having claimed that Wittgenstein's reconception of philosophy, or say of the form of a philosophical problem, required an extension of the discovery of formal perspicuousness to a discovery of non-formal perspicuousness, I extend this (or really just make explicit an extension within the insistence of Wittgenstein's writing) from the work of what Wittgenstein calls grammatical methods or treatments of language to the primitive fact of ordinary language, that it express desire, the point of language named by Augustine at the close of the citation with which Wittgenstein opens the *Investigations*.

So here's the surprising premise in my argument for taking Wittgenstein's writing as essential to his philosophizing, the manner to the method: The concept of the perspicuous, governed by the criteria of completeness, pleasure, and breaking off, is as surely invited by contexts of aphorism as it is by those of proof and of grammatical investigation.

Now this may seem, at best, to show only that the aphoristic belongs in *some* sense to the *Investigations*, not that it is essential to a manner of writing held to be essential to this philosophizing. I look at it somewhat differently. The power of grammatical investigations in *Philosophical Investigations* is a function of their leading a word back from its metaphysical capture by the appeal to its everyday use. The power of the aphoristic is a function of its granting the appeal, even in a sense the reality, of the metaphysical. It is a mode of reflecting the clarity brought by grammatical methods, one that in itself, as itself, exhibits this clarity, together with a satisfaction or acknowledgement of the obscurity from which clarity comes. To say that this exhibition is essential to the work of the *Investigations* is to say that appeals to the ordinary which fail this mode of reflection are not Wittgensteinian appeals, they do not take their bearing from the power to make philosophical problems completely disappear – hence appear. They do not, accordingly, express our interest in these problems, and so leave us subjected to them without understanding what kind of creatures we are, what our life form as talkers is, that we are thus fascinatable, that philosophy is seductive. (The philosophical sensibility here is radically different from Austin's.)

Since this claim for the aphoristic, say for its mode of expressiveness, rests upon experience, the claim's own perspicuousness depends upon attracting to itself sufficient pertinent experience. (The role of experience is critical. I am not supplying evidence for a hypothesis, but examples which call for a particular concept.) I will in the time left undertake to provide objects of this experience, noting that in the *Investigations* the aphoristic does not on the whole take the form of free-standing aphorisms (as in the cases of the fly and the fly-bottle or the body as the best picture of the soul), but is mostly directed, as I have indicated, to reflecting details of its methodicalness, its searching out criteria, articulating grammar, spelling out fantasies, calling attention to a fixated picture, presenting intermediate cases. To isolate the experience in independent aphorisms – to show that it is reliably housed in specific, recognizable linguistic structures – I will go outside *Philosophical Investigations* to Wittgenstein's aphorisms that find their way into Professor Von Wright's miscellany translated under the title *Culture and Value* and select ten of them to pair with ten aphorisms composed between the last years of the eighteenth century and the end of the first half of the nineteenth. This is where Wittgenstein, early in the entries of *Culture and Value*, places his aspiration:

> I often wonder whether my cultural ideal is new, i.e. contemporary, or whether it comes from the time of Schumann. At least it strikes me as being a continuation of that idea, though of course not the continuation that actually happened. Thereby the second half of the nineteenth century is excluded.

(The excluded half-century includes Frege, *Tristan* and the future of music, Nietzsche, and, for example, Helmholtz.)

I present the ten pairs without beforehand identifying which member is Wittgenstein's.

I.
- (a) One age misunderstands another; and a *petty* age misunderstands all the others in its own nasty way.
- (b) The age isn't ready for it, they always say. Is that a reason why it shouldn't happen?

II.
- (a) A mediocre writer must beware of too quickly replacing a crude, incorrect expression with a correct one. By doing so he kills his original idea, which was at least still a living seedling.
- (b) How many authors are there among writers? Author means creator.

III.
- (a) Each of the sentences I write is trying to say the whole thing.

(b) In poetry too every whole can be a part and every part really a whole.

IV.

(a) There is a pathos peculiar to the man who is happily in love as well as to the one who is unhappily in love.

(b) A so-called happy marriage is to love as a correct poem is to an improvised song.

V.

(a) The idea is worn out by now and no longer usable. . . . Like silver paper, which can never quite be smoothed out again once it has been crumpled.

(b) Isn't everything that is capable of becoming shopworn already twisted or trite to begin with?

VI.

(a) If in life we are surrounded by death, so too in the health of our intellect we are surrounded by madness.

(b) Like animals, the spirit can only breathe in an atmosphere made up of life-giving oxygen mixed with nitrogen. To be unable to tolerate and understand this fact is the essence of foolishness; to simply not want to do so is madness.

VII.

(a) Is this the sense of belief in the Devil: that not everything that comes to us as an inspiration comes from what is good?

(b) On my saying, "What have I to do with the sacredness of traditions, if I live wholly from within?" my friend suggested, – "But these impulses may be from below, not from above." I replied, "They do not seem to me to be such; but if I am the Devil's child, I will live then from the Devil."

VIII.

(a) My account will be hard to follow: because it says something new but still has egg-shells from the old view sticking to it.

(b) You're always demanding new ideas? Do something new, then something new might be said about it.

IX.

(a) One might say: Genius is *talent exercized with courage.*

(b) But one can never really have genius, only be one. . . . Genius is actually a system of talents.

X.

   (a)   It may be that the essential thing with Shakespeare is his ease
         and authority and that you just have to accept him as he is if you
         are going to be able to admire him properly, in the way you
         accept nature.

   (b)   The simplest and most immediate questions, like Should we
         criticize Shakespeare's works as art or as nature?

In each case the first member of the pair is from Wittgenstein; the
second is, with one exception, either from Friedrich or from August
Wilhelm Schlegel (from either the *Critical* or the *Atheneaum Fragments*).
That these figures take the preoccupations of Wittgenstein's sensibility
deep into, or into the origin of, German Romanticism fits my sense of his
continuing the Romantic's response to the psychic threat of skepticism.
(The exception to the Schlegel brothers is Emerson's declaration of
readiness to be, if need be, the Devil's child.)

Naturally I will not attempt to argue for the resemblance between the
members of the pairs; nor even argue here that the pairs present aphorisms, as opposed to adages, or maxims of practical wisdom – beyond
noting that they do not present standing, sociable responses to life's
recurrences, but rather new, eccentric, personal responses, to some
present crossroads of culture, characteristically marked by the recurrences of a word, as if the thought were turning on itself ("One age misunderstands another; and a petty age misunderstands all the others in its
own nasty way.") Nor shall I argue, on the basis of a score of examples,
that aphorisms with this particular sense of breaking off complete fragments, so to speak, are apt to take on just these subjects – those of genius
and talent, of life and death, of originality and banality, of human and
animal, of madness, music, misunderstanding, religion. *Philosophical Investigations* touches on, and so continues, in its way, all of these topics –
as, in its way, it continues to live on the sound of the fragment, the denial
of system (while by no means the denial of the systematic).

But there is a coincidence of insight between a moment from *Culture
and Value* and a moment from the *Investigations* which I find remarkable,
and to bear so precisely on recent work of mine on Emersonian Perfectionism, that I will end by citing it along with a thought or two about it.
It dates from 1949, four years after the Foreword to *Philosophical Investigations* was written, two years before Wittgenstein's death.

"Le style c'est l'homme," "Le style c'est l'homme même." The first
expression has cheap epigrammatic brevity. The second, correct
version, opens up quite a different perspective. It says that a man's
style is a *picture* of him.

The coincidence with the *Investigations* is – is it too obvious to mention, or too obscure to discuss? – with "The human body is the best picture of the human soul."

First let us venture a suggestion about what Wittgenstein finds cheap in the brief version – "Style is the man." Perhaps it is some resemblance to the saying "Clothes make the man," some unearned and cynical insight about the relation of social judgment to psychic reality, where the former is taken as open to view and the latter is taken to be of no interest even to the one in question. Or some resemblance to some such saying as "Life is the real work of art," which may at a stroke deny the seriousness and difficulty and beauty, such as they are, both of life and of art. How is the longer version different? – "Style is the man himself." Well, immediately it has the air of discovery in it, the winning through to an insight, both about what the man, in his way, has made out of something (a talent, a circumstance) and hence something about the character of the maker. This speaks to the image of the human body as a picture of the human soul. I do not think we need more out of the concept of the soul here than as a term for a subject's subjectivity, a thing possessed of mentality or mindedness or moodedness, one whose actions, as Heidegger roughly put it (making something of the German *Handlung* in his way), are ways of handling things (something Charlie Chaplin knew as well as Heidegger is not to happen on an assembly line). Do not need more, I mean, in order to note Wittgenstein's implied refusal of a metaphysical insistence that the body *is* the mind or the man. This insistence is ruled, in Wittgenstein's aphorism about the body as a picture, a kind of literary error, a case of poor reading. The insight of the aphorism is rather – along with an implied claim that an insight is necessary here – that every handling by the man (of an impulse or of a circumstance) is a signature, or a sketch that needs no signature for its attribution. I think this is something Nietzsche means, at the end of *The Genealogy of Morals*, when he speaks of man's being unable to empty himself of purpose and so finding a solution in taking emptiness as his purpose. The Hunger Artist conveys it somewhat differently, that being purely inexpressive is as exacting and unending a task as being purely expressive.

Allow me one further step. Prompted by Wittgenstein's reading of style as picturing the very man, I take his idea of the body's picturing to declare that his writing is (of) his body, that it is on the line, that his hand is in the manner of his text, in its melancholy accidents of reception (cf. *Walden*; I, 15) as well as in its successes with glad intentions. It is what you must expect of a perfectionist author, whose authority, such as it is, lies only in his example. Naturally, some find this attractive, others repellent; as some find it to be essential philosophy, others not.

Stanley Cavell: A Bibliography
1951–1995

Peter S. Fosl

Books (Chronologically)

Stanley Cavell (1926–), *Philosophical Passages: Wittgenstein, Emerson, Austin, Derrida*, Bucknell Lectures in Literary Theory 12, general editors Michael Payne and Harold Schweizer (Oxford: Blackwell, 1995). Includes:
1. Michael Payne, "Introduction," 1–11.
2. Stanley Cavell, "Emerson's Constitutional Amending: Reading 'Fate'," 12–41. Delivered at Bucknell University, 6 May 1993.

Acknowledgments: Special thanks to Richard Fleming. Thanks to Associated University Presses for permission to reprint material appearing in the *Bucknell Review* 32.1 (1989). Theresa Wenzke's library work at Bucknell University was invaluable to me. Thanks to Stanley Cavell, Tom Eisele, Leland Poague, Charles Bernstein, Kurt Fischer, Ludwig Nagl, and Gordon Bearn for additional references. I am also grateful to Linda Beard, Nancy Collins, and Holle Schneider (of the Fishburn Library at Hollins College) and to Eric Nitschke (of the Woodruff Library at Emory University) for help with DIALOG, telnet, and database searches and for assistance with interlibrary loans. Thanks to the *Bucknell Review*, Mohammed Azadpur, and Mitchell Pollack for their assistance with the first publication of the bibliography.

Notes: Please note that I have changed my surname from 'WASEL' to 'FOSL' and that I am the author of an earlier version of this bibliography appearing in *The Senses of Stanley Cavell: Bucknell Review* 32.1 (1989), 322–34.

Those who wish to inform me of errors or omissions or to correspond for other reasons may contact me through the following addresses: Department of Philosophy, Hollins College, Roanoke VA 24020-1513, U.S.A. Telephone: (703) 362-6000. Internet: 'foslp@-minnie.hollins.edu'. Fax: (703) 362-6642. Correspondents should include the most complete bibliographic information available to them as well as any annotations they think will be helpful.

3. Stanley Cavell, "What Did Derrida Want of Austin?" 42–65. Delivered at Bucknell University, 4 May 1993.
4. Seminar on "What Did Derrida Want of Austin?" 66–90. At Bucknell University, 5 May 1993. (Text revised December 1993.)
5. "The Self of Philosophy: An Interview with Stanley Cavell," 91–103. With Richard Fleming, Bucknell University, 6 May 1993.
6. Richard Fleming, "Continuing Cavell: Side Roads of the *Claim of Reason,*" 104–17. With "Appendix: The Source Text for 'Continuing Cavell'," 117–24.
7. Stanley Cavell, "Notes and Afterthoughts on the Opening of Wittgenstein's *Investigations,*" 125–86.
8. Peter S. Fosl and Michael Payne, "Stanley Cavell: A Bibliography 1958–1994," 187–97.

A Pitch of Philosophy: Autobiographical Exercises (Cambridge, MA: Harvard University Press, 1994). The Jerusalem-Harvard Lectures, delivered at the Hebrew University of Jerusalem 22, 24, and 26 November 1992 under the title "Trades of Philosophy." Includes:
Overture.
1. "Philosophy and the Arrogation of Voice."
2. "Counter-Philosophy and the Pawn of Voice."
"The Metaphysical Voice."
"Worlds of Difference."
"Pictures of Destruction."
"Derrida's Austin and the Stake of Positivism."
"Exclusion of the Theory of Excuses: On the Tragic."
"Exclusion of the Theory of the Non-Serious."
"Skepticism and the Serious."
"Two Pictures of Communication: Assigning."
"What (Thing) Is Transmitted? Austin Moves."
"Two Pictures of Language in Relation to (the) World."
"Three Pictures of My Attachment to My Words: Signing."
3. "Opera and the Lease of Voice."
Bibliography.
Acknowledgments.

Conditions nobles et ignobles, translation by Christian Fournier and Sandra Laugier (Paris: Editions de l'éclat, 1993). A translation of *Conditions Handsome and Unhandsome* (1990).

Le déni de savoir dans six pièces de Shakespeare, translation by Jean-Pierre Maquerlot, Chemins de pensée (Paris: Editions du Seuil, 1993). A translation of *Disowning Knowledge* (1987).

A la recherche du bonheur, translation by Christian Fournier and Sandra Laugier (Paris: Cahiers du Cinema, 1993). A translation of *Pursuits of Happiness: The Hollywood Comedy of Remarriage* (1981).

The Senses of Walden: *An Expanded Edition* (Chicago: University of Chicago Press, 1992). Previously appeared in 1981 on North Point Press.

Statuts d'Emerson: constitution, philosophie, politique, translation by Christian Fournier and Sandra Laugier (Combas, France: Editions de l'éclat, 1992). With an appendix including work by Ralph Waldo Emerson ("Destin," "Experience," "La loi sur les esclaves fugitifs"), Friedrich Nietzsche ("Fatum et histoire"), and Christian Fournier ("Note sur la situation politique d'Emerson").

Conditions Handsome and Unhandsome: The Constitution of Emersonian Perfectionism, The Paul Carus Lectures, 1988, Series 17 (Peru, Illinois: Open Court Inc., 1991).

Une nouvelle Amérique encore inapproachable, translation by Sandra Laugier-Rabaté (Combas, France: Editions de l'éclat, 1991). A translation of *This New Yet Unapproachable America* (1989).

Conditions Handsome and Unhandsome: The Constitution of Emersonian Perfectionism (Chicago: University of Chicago Press, 1990). The Paul Carus Lectures, delivered before the Pacific Division of the American Philosophical Association, April 1988.
Includes:
1. Preface and Acknowledgments.
2. Introduction: "Staying the Course." Addressing the pedagogical context in which the material for these essays was developed, namely a 1987 undergraduate course Cavell taught at Harvard University called "Moral Perfectionism."
3. "Aversive Thinking: Emersonian Representations in Heidegger and Nietzsche."
4. "The Argument of the Ordinary: Scenes of Instruction in Wittgenstein and in Kripke." Largely addresses Saul Kripke's *Wittgenstein on Rules and Private Language* (Cambridge: Cambridge University Press, 1982). See also, on this topic: G. P. Baker and P. M. S. Hacker, *Scepticism, Rules and Language* (Oxford, 1984) and *Rules, Grammar, and Necessity* (Oxford, 1985); and Colin McGinn, *Wittgenstein On Meaning* (New York, 1984).

5. "The Conversation of Justice: Rawls and the Drama of Consent." Largely addresses John Rawls's *A Theory of Justice* (Cambridge, MA: Harvard University Press/Belknap Press, 1971) and "Two Concepts of Rules" (*The Philosophical Review* 64 [January, 1965], 3–32).
6. Epilogue.
7. Appendix A: "Hope Against Hope."
8. Appendix B: "A Cover Letter." To members of the Jerusalem workshop on Institutions of Interpretation, at the Center for Literary Studies, the Hebrew University of Jerusalem, 15 May 1988.
9. Bibliography.

This New Yet Unapproachable America: Lectures after Emerson after Wittgenstein (Albuquerque, NM: Living Batch Press/Chicago: University of Chicago Press, 1989). The 1987 Fredrick Ives Carpenter Lectures, delivered at the University of Chicago. Includes:
1. "Work in Progress: An Introductory Report."
2. "Declining Decline: Wittgenstein as a Philosopher of Culture."
3. "Finding as Founding: Taking Steps in Emerson's 'Experience'."
4. Acknowledgments.
5. Works Cited.

In Quest of the Ordinary: Lines of Skepticism and Romanticism (Chicago: University of Chicago Press, 1988). Includes:
1. Preface and Acknowledgments.
2. At Berkeley
   The Mrs William Beckman Lectures (1983)
   "The Philosopher in American Life (Toward Thoreau and Emerson)."
   "Emerson, Coleridge, Kant (Terms as Conditions)."
   "Texts of Recovery (Coleridge, Wordsworth, Heidegger . . .)."
   "Recounting Gains, Showing Losses (A Reading of *The Winter's Tale*)."
3. At Stanford
   Conference: Reconstructing Individualism (1984)
   "Being Odd, Getting Even (Descartes, Emerson, Poe)."
   Postscripts
   "Skepticism and a Word Concerning Deconstruction."
   "Poe's Perversity and the Imp(ulse) of Skepticism."
   "The Skeptical and the Metaphorical."

4. At Stanford
   The Tanner Lecture (1986)
   "The Uncanniness of the Ordinary."
5. At Vienna
   Celebration Lecture (1986)
   "The Fantastic of Philosophy."
6. Bibliography.

Themes Out of School: Effects and Causes (Chicago: University of Chicago Press, 1988). Reprint of 1984 North Point Press edition.

Nach der Philosophie: Essays von Stanley Cavell, edited by Kurt Rudolf Fischer and Ludwig Nagl; Klagenfurter Beiträge zur Philosophie, series editors Thomas Macho and Christof Subik (Wien: Verlag des Verbandes der wissenschaftlichen Gesellschaften Österreichs, 1987). Includes:

1. "Vorbemerkung der Herausgeber," 5–7.
2. "Müssen wir meinen, was wir sagen?" 9–62.
3. "Der Zugang zu Wittgensteins Spätphilosophie," 63–93.
4. "Die Welt durch die Kamera gesehen" (from *The World Viewed*), 95–136.
5. "Denken – Was heißt das in der Fotografie?" 137–60.
6. "Danebenstehen, Gleichziehen: Bedrohungen der Individualität" (mit einem Nachtrag), 161–206 (trans. Herbert Hrachovec).
7. "Das Phantastische der Philosophie," 207–17. Cavell gave an English reading of this article at the Wittgensteinshaus in Vienna on 26 May 1986 on the occasion of the publication of the first volume of Wiener Reihe, *Themen der Philosophie: Wo Steht die Analytische Philosophie heute?* edited by Ludwig Nagl and R. Heinrich (Wien: Oldenbourg, 1986). First appeared in *American Poetry Review* 15.3 (1986). Reprinted in English in *In Quest of the Ordinary* (1988), 181–8.
8. "How can one inherit Europe? Stanley Cavell über Tradition und Neubeginn der amerikanischen Philosophie," Ein Interview mit Leonhard Schmeiser, 219–28. Broadcast on Österreichischen Rundfunks (Ö1) program "Dimensionen," 10 July 1986.

Rezensionsanhang:

9. "Kurt Rudolf Fischer über Stanley Cavell: *Must We Mean What We Say? A Book of Essays*," 231–9.
10. "Kurt Rudolf Fischer über Stanley Cavell: *The Claim of Reason. Wittgenstein, Skepticism, Morality, and Tragedy*," 240–7. First appeared in *Wiener Jahrbuch für Philosophie* VII (1974).

11. "Ludwig Nagl: Stanley Cavells Versuch, die Tiefengrammatik des Films zu entschlüsseln," 249–54.

Disowning Knowledge: In Six Plays of Shakespeare (Cambridge: Cambridge University Press, 1987). Includes:
1. Preface and Acknowledgments.
2. "The Avoidance of Love: A Reading of *King Lear*."
3. "Othello and the Stake of the Other."
4. "*Coriolanus* and Interpretations of Politics." Previously printed in *Themes Out of School* (1984), 60–96.
5. "Hamlet's Burden of Proof."
6. "Recounting Gains, Showing Losses: *The Winter's Tale*." Reprinted in *In Quest of the Ordinary* (1988), 76–101.

Themes Out of School: Effects and Causes (San Francisco: North Point Press, 1984). Includes:
1. Preface.
2. "The Thought of Movies."
3. "The Politics of Interpretation" ("Politics as Opposed to What?") (with "Postscript: A Reply to Gayatri Spivak").
4. "*Coriolanus* and Interpretations of Politics" ("Who does the wolf love?") (with a postscript). Reprinted in *Disowning Knowledge* (1987), 143–78.
5. "A Cover Letter to Molière's *Misanthrope*."
6. "On Makavejev on Bergman."
7. "A Reply to John Hollander."
8. "Foreword to Jay Cantor's *The Space Between*."
9. "North by Northwest."
10. "What Becomes of Things on Film?"
11. "The Ordinary as Uneventful: A Note on the *Annales* Historians."
12. "Existentialism and Analytical Philosophy."
13. "The Fact of Television."

Pursuits of Happiness: The Hollywood Comedy of Remarriage (Cambridge, MA: Harvard University Press, 1981). Includes:
1. Introduction: "Words for a Conversation."
2. "Cons and Pros: *The Lady Eve*."
3. "Knowledge as Transgression: *It Happened One Night*."
4. "Leopards in Connecticut: *Bringing Up Baby*."
5. "The Importance of Importance: *The Philadelphia Story*."
6. "Counterfeiting Happiness: *His Girl Friday*."
7. "The Courting of Marriage: *Adam's Rib*."

8. "The Same and Different: *The Awful Truth*."
9. Appendix: "Film in the University."

The Senses of Walden: *An Expanded Edition* (San Francisco: North Point Press, 1981). Includes *The Senses of* Walden (1972) plus:
1. "Thinking of Emerson."
2. "An Emerson Mood." Delivered as the Scholar's Day Address at Kalamazoo College, 1980.

The World Viewed: Reflections on the Ontology of Film (enlarged edition) (Cambridge, MA: Harvard University Press, 1979). Harvard Paperback no. 151 issued 1980. Includes all of the 1971 edition plus:
1. "Foreword to the Enlarged Edition."
2. "More of *The World Viewed*."

The Claim of Reason: Wittgenstein, Skepticism, Morality, and Tragedy (Oxford: Clarendon Press, 1979). Reissued on Oxford University Press 1982. Includes:
Part One: Wittgenstein and the Concept of Human Knowledge.
    I. Criteria and Judgment.
    II. Criteria and Skepticism.
    III. Austin and Examples.
    IV. What a Thing Is (Called)
    V. Natural and Conventional.
       Normal and Natural.
Part Two: Skepticism and the Existence of the World.
    VI. The Quest of Traditional Epistemology: Opening.
       The Reasonableness of Doubt.
       The Appeal to Projective Imagination.
       The Irrelevance of Projective Imagination as Direct Criticism.
       A Further Problem.
    VII. Excursus on Wittgenstein's Vision of Language.
       Learning a Word.
       Projecting a Word.
    VIII. The Quest of Traditional Epistemology: Closing.
       The Philosopher's Ground for Doubt Requires Projection.
       The Philosopher's Projection Poses a Dilemma.
       The Philosopher's Basis; and a More Pervasive Conflict with His New Critics.
       The Philosopher's Context Is Non-Claim.
       The Philosopher's Conclusion Is Not a Discovery.
       Two Interpretations of Traditional Epistemology; Pheno-

The Representative Case for Other Minds Is not Defined by the Generic.
The Passive Skeptical Recital Concerning Other Minds.
Skepticism and Sanity Again.
Asymmetries between the Two Directions of Skepticism.
Dr. Faust and Dr. Frankenstein.
Passiveness and Activeness; the Friend and the Confessor.
The Extraordinariness of the Ordinary; Romanticism.
Narcissism.
Proving the Existence of the Human.
The Vanishing of the Human.
The Question of the History of the Problem of Others:
  1. Distinctions of madness.
  2. The other as replacement of God.
  3. Blake and the sufficiency of finitude.
  4. The science and the magic of the human.
  5. Literature as the knowledge of the Outsider.
Bibliography.

The World Viewed: Reflections on the Ontology of Film (New York: Penguin Books, 1977).

Must We Mean What We Say? A Book of Essays (Cambridge: Cambridge University Press, 1976).

The Senses of Walden (New York: The Viking Press, 1972). Reissued by The Viking Press in 1974; Viking Compass edition also 1974. Includes:
  1. Preface.
  2. Acknowledgments.
  3. "Words."
  4. "Sentences."
  5. "Portions."

The World Viewed: Reflections on the Ontology of Film (New York: The Viking Press, 1971). Viking Compass edition also 1971. Reissued on The Viking Press in 1974. Includes:
  1. Preface.
  2. "An Autobiography of Companions."
  3. "Sights and Sounds."
  4. "Photograph and Screen."
  5. "Audience, Actor, and Star."

6. "Types: Cycles as Genres."
7. "Ideas of Origin."
8. "Baudelaire and the Myths of Film."
9. "The Military Man and the Woman."
10. "The Dandy."
11. "End of the Myths."
12. "The Medium and the Media of Film."
13. "The World as Mortal: Absolute Age and Youth."
14. "The World as a Whole: Color."
15. "Automatism."
16. "Excursus: Some Modernist Painting."
17. "Exhibition and Self-Reference."
18. "The Camera's Implications."
19. "Assertions in Techniques."
20. "The Acknowledgment of Silence."

Must We Mean What We Say? A Book of Essays (New York: Charles Scribner's Sons, 1969). Sections 1, 6, 7, 10, and 11 are published here for the first time. Includes:
1. Foreword: "An Audience for Philosophy."
2. "Must We Mean What We Say?"
3. "The Availability of Wittgenstein's Later Philosophy."
4. "Aesthetic Problems of Modern Philosophy."
5. "Austin at Criticism."
6. "Ending the Waiting Game: A Reading of Beckett's *Endgame*." Written in the summer and fall of 1964, this essay served as the basis for lectures delivered in Harvard College's Humanities course and for lectures delivered at Western Reserve University, the Case Institute, the University of Saskatchewan, and the University of North Carolina.
7. "Kierkegaard's *On Authority and Revelation*." Based on remarks prepared for a colloquium on this work held at the University of Minnesota's Department of Philosophy, January 1966.
8. "Music Discomposed."
9. "A Matter of Meaning It."
10. "Knowing and Acknowledging." An expanded version of remarks delivered at a colloquium at the University of Rochester, May 1966, responding to Norman Malcolm's paper, "The Privacy of Experience," later published in *Epistemology: New Essays in the Theory of Knowledge*, edited by Avrum Stroll, pp. 129–58 (New York: Harper and Row, 1967). Cavell's essay also addresses John W. Cook's "Wittgenstein on Privacy" (*The Philosophical Review* 74 [1965], 281–314);

this latter is reprinted in *Wittgenstein: The Philosophical Investigations*, edited by George Pritcher (New York: Doubleday Anchor Original, 1966) along with Cavell's "The Availability of Wittgenstein's Later Philosophy," 151–85.

11. "The Avoidance of Love: A Reading of *King Lear*." Part I was written in the summer of 1966 for Harvard College's Humanities course lectures; Part II was written in the summer and fall of 1967. Reprinted in *Disowning Knowledge* (1987), 39–124.

Stanley Louis Cavell. *The Claim to Rationality: Knowledge and the Basis of Morality* (Cambridge, MA: Photographic Department of the Harvard University Library, 1974). [Microfilm of typescript. 1 reel. 35 mm.] Submitted to Harvard University as Cavell's PhD dissertation in 1961. Much of this text was later incorporated into *The Claim of Reason* (1979). See especially Part Three of *The Claim of Reason* ("Knowledge and the Concept of Morality") and its subsection IX ("Knowledge and the Basis of Morality"). These texts were informed by a seminar Cavell jointly taught with Thompson Clarke in 1959–60 on Wittgenstein's *Philosophical Investigations*.

Articles and Anthology Contributions (Chronologically)

"Time after Time: Stanley Cavell on the Future Today." *London Review of Books* 17.1 (12 January 1995), 6–8. On Emerson, Nietzsche, and the future. An earlier version in French was delivered at the 1994 *Le Monde*/Le Mans conference on "The Future Today."

"Foreword" to Northrop Frye's *A Natural Perspective: The Development of Shakespearean Comedy and Romance* (New York: Columbia University Press, 1965), ix–xxiii. Frye's text was originally delivered as the Bampton Lectures in America (no. 15) in November 1963 at Columbia University; Columbia reissued the text with a foreword by Cavell in 1995.

"What Is the Emersonian Event? A Comment on Kateb's Emerson." *New Literary History* 25.4 (Autumn 1994), 951–8. Delivered 20 August 1993 before the American Political Science Association, addressing a selection entitled "Emerson's Philosophy of Self-Reliant Activity," from a then-forthcoming text by Kateb. See George Kateb, *The Inner Ocean: Individualism and Democratic Culture* (Ithaca, NY: Cornell University Press, 1994).

"Nichts versteht sich von selbst: Zur Sprache des Groucho- Marxismus." *Merkur-Deutsche Zeitschrift für Europaisches Denken* 48.4 (April 1994), 300–8. A translation by W. Winkler of "Nothing Goes Without Saying: Stanley Cavell Reads the Marx Brothers."

"Nothing Goes Without Saying: Stanley Cavell Reads the Marx Brothers." *London Review of Books* 16.1 (6 January 1994), 3 & 5. A review of a recently released edition of the scripts of three Marx Brothers films: *The Marx Brothers: "A Day at the Races," "Monkey Business," and "Duck Soup"* with an introduction by Karl French (London: Faber, 1993).

"Macbeth Appalled (II)." *Raritan: A Quarterly Review* 12.3 (Winter, 1993), 1–15.

"A la recherche du bonheur" (book excerpt). *Cahiers du Cinema* 466 (April 1993), 84–5. Translation by Christian Fournier and Sandra Laugier.

"Macbeth Appalled (I)." *Raritan: A Quarterly Review* 12.2 (Fall, 1992), 1–15.

"L'Humeur Emerson." *Critique: Revue générale des publications française et étranger* 48.541–2 (Juin–Juillet, 1992), 435–48. A French translation, by Sandra Laugier and Christiane Chauviré, of "An Emerson Mood," appearing in *The Senses of* Walden: *An Expanded Edition* (San Francisco: North Point Press, 1981). This volume of *Critique*, "La nouvelle Angleterre," is largely devoted to Emerson, and many of the articles presented cite Cavell.

"In The Meantime: Authority, Tradition, and the Future of the Disciplines." *The Yale Journal of Criticism* 5.2 (Spring, 1992), 229–37. From the Tenth Anniversary Symposium for the Whitney Humanities Center, 15–16 February 1991.

"Austin at Criticism." In *The Linguistic Turn*, edited by Richard Rorty, pp. 250–60 (Chicago: University of Chicago Press, 1992). First edition, 1967.

"Aversive Thinking: Emersonian Representations in Heidegger and Nietzsche." *New Literary History* 22.1 (Winter, 1991), 129–60.

"The Idea of Home." Social Research: An International Quarterly of the Social Sciences 58.1 (Spring, 1991), 9–10. This issue of the journal collects papers delivered at the New School for Social Research's conference, "Home: A Place in the World," held at the New School in October 1990. Cavell's piece serves as an introduction to the collection. The conference was part of a series of artistic and academic events on the same topic.

"Stella's Taste." In *Working Papers in Cultural Studies* 8, The Cultural Studies Project (Cambridge, MA: Massachusetts Institute of Technology Press, 1991). On microfilm: AS36.M414.A3, #8. Delivered at MIT, 4 May 1991.

"Emerson's Aversive Thinking." In *Romantic Revolutions: Criticism and Theory*, edited by Kenneth R. Johnstone, Gilbert Chaitin, Karen Hanson, and Herbert Marks (Bloomington: Indiana University Press, 1990), 219–49. First delivered at the Indiana Romanticism conference, March 1988. A subsequent version was delivered as the first of three Carus Lectures before the Pacific Division of the American Philosophical Association, April 1988. Revised and reprinted as "Aversive Thinking: Emersonian Representations in Heidegger and Nietzsche" in *Conditions Handsome and Unhandsome* (1990) and in *New Literary History* 22.1 (1991).

"Ugly Duckling, Funny Butterfly: Bette Davis and *Now, Voyager*." *Critical Inquiry* 16.2 (Winter, 1990), 213–47. Followed by a postscript.

"Postscript (1989): To Whom It May Concern." *Critical Inquiry* 16.2 (Winter, 1990), 248–89.

In "Editor's Notes." *Critical Inquiry* 17.1 (Fall, 1990), 238–44. A response to an Editorial Note by Tania Modleski addressing the character of "the unknown woman" in film, criticizing Cavell on feminist and scholarly grounds.

"What Photography Calls Thinking." In *Raritan Reading*, edited by Richard Poirier, pp. 47–65 (New Brunswick, NJ: Rutgers University Press, 1990).

"Who Disappoints Whom?" *Critical Inquiry* 15.3 (Spring, 1989), 606–10. Read on 8 December 1988 at Harvard's Kennedy School of Government on the occasion of a lecture by Allan Bloom entitled. "The Attack on Reason." This essay is also a reply to Bloom's *The Closing of the American Mind*.

"Sights and Sounds: From *The World Viewed*" (from chs. 2–6). In *Aesthetics: A Critical Anthology*, edited by George Dickie, Richard Sclafani,

and Ronald Roblin, pp. 560–75 (2nd edition; New York: St Martin's Press, 1989). Followed by Stanley Bates's "Movies Viewed: Cavell on Medium and Motion Pictures," 576–82. St Martin's issued an earlier edition of this volume in 1977 without Bates's essay. Includes:
1. "Photograph and Screen," 564–6.
2. "Audience, Actor and Star," 566–8.
3. "Types: Cycles as Genres," 568–73.
4. "Ideas of Origin," 573–5.

"Naughty Orators: Negation of Voice in *Gaslight*." In *Languages of the Unsayable: The Play of Negativity in Literature and Literary Theory*, edited by Sanford Budick and Wolfgang Iser, pp. 340–77. Irvine Studies in the Humanities (New York: Columbia University Press, 1989). Includes "Postscript (1988)," 373–7.

"Notes after Austin." In *Encounters*, edited by Kai Eridson, pp. 116–23 (New Haven, CT: Yale University Press, 1989).

"The Uncanniness of the Ordinary." *The Tanner Lectures on Human Values* VIII, edited by Sterling M. McMurrin, pp. 81–117 (Salt Lake City: University of Utah Press/Cambridge: Cambridge University Press, 1988). Delivered at Stanford University 3 & 8 April 1986. Reprinted in *In Quest of the Ordinary* (1988), 153–78.

"Two Cheers for Romance." In *Passionate Attachments: Thinking about Love*, edited by Willard Gaylin (M.D.) and Ethel Persons (M.D.), pp. 85–100 (New York: The Free Press (Macmillan), 1988). From remarks delivered at a symposium sponsored by the Columbia University Center for Psychoanalytic Training and Research and the Association for Psychoanalytic Medicine, 10 November 1984.

"Psychoanalysis and Cinema: The Melodrama of the Unknown Woman." In *Die Philosophen und Freud. Ein offene Debatte*, edited by H. Vetter and Ludwig Nagl, pp. 199–226 (Wien/München: Oldenbourg, 1988). A shortened version of Cavell's article appears in *Images in Our Souls: Cavell, Psychoanalysis, and Cinema* (1987); Cavell shortened this article himself.

"Psychoanalysis and Cinema: The Melodrama of the Unknown Woman." In *The Trial(s) of Psychoanalysis*, edited by Françoise Meltzer, pp. 227–58 (Chicago: University of Chicago Press, 1988). A revised and expanded edition of the 1987 article appearing in *Images in Our Souls: Cavell, Psychoanalysis and Cinema*, Psychiatry and the

Humanities 10, edited by Joseph H. Smith and William Kerrigan, pp. 11–43 (Baltimore: Johns Hopkins University Press, 1987).

"Declining Decline: Wittgenstein as a Philosopher of Culture." *Inquiry: An Interdisciplinary Journal of Philosophy and the Social Sciences* (Norway) 31.3 (Spring, 1988), 253–64.

"Notes after Austin." *The Yale Review* 76.3 (Spring, 1987), 313–22.

"Psychoanalysis and Cinema: The Melodrama of the Unknown Woman." In *Images in Our Souls: Cavell, Psychoanalysis and Cinema*, Psychiatry and the Humanities 10, edited by Joseph H. Smith and William Kerrigan, pp. 11–43 (Baltimore: Johns Hopkins University Press, 1987). This article incorporates material from "Freud and Philosophy: A Fragment" (*Critical Inquiry* 13.2 (Winter, 1987), 386–93).

"Freud and Philosophy: A Fragment." *Critical Inquiry* 13.2 (Winter, 1987), 386–93.

"Emerson, Coleridge, Kant. Emersons *Fate* und Coleridges *Biographia Literaria*." In *Romantik Literatur und Philosophie*, edited by Volker Bohn, pp. 183–212 (Frankfurt am Main: Suhrkamp Verlag, 1987). A translation of Cavell's article. "Genteel Responses to Kant? In Emerson's 'Fate' and in Coleridge's *Biographia Literaria*," *Raritan* 3.2 (Fall, 1983), 34–61. Translated by Oliver R. Scholz and Eckhard Lobsien.

"*North by Northwest*." In *A Hitchcock Reader*, edited by Marshall Deutelbaum and Leland A. Poague, pp. 249–64 (Ames: Iowa State University Press, 1986).

"Danebenstehen, gleichziehen: Bedrohungen der Individualität." In *Wo steht die Analytische Philosophy heute?* edited by Ludwig Nagl and R. Heinrich, translated by Herbert Hrachovec, pp. 116–49; Wiener Reihe, *Themen der Philosophie* 1 (Wien/München: Oldenbourg, 1986). First appeared as "Being Odd, Getting Even" in *Salmagundi: A Quarterly of the Humanities and Social Sciences* 67 (Summer, 1985), 97–128.

"In Quest of the Ordinary: Texts of Recovery." In *Romanticism and Contemporary Criticism*, edited and with a Preface by Morris Eaves and Michael Fischer, pp. 183–239 (Ithaca: Cornell University Press, 1986). Portions reprinted in *In Quest of the Ordinary* (1988) as "Texts of

Recovery (Coleridge, Wordsworth, Heidegger)," 50–75, and portions as "Poe's Perversity and the Imp(ulse) of Skepticism," 137–43.

"Denken – was heißt das in der Fotografie?" In *Camera Austria*, pp. 32–43 (Graz, Österreich: Forum Stadtpark, 1986). Delivered at a symposium in Graz, "Die Kraft (und die Herrlichkeit) der Fotografie," 1985. This is the first German translation of "What Photography Calls Thinking," *Raritan* 4.4 (Spring, 1985), 1–21. Translation by Klaus Feichtenberger.

"The Fantastic of Philosophy." *The American Poetry Review* 15.3 (May-June, 1986), 45–7. Reprinted in *In Quest of the Ordinary* (1988), 181–8; and *Nach der Philosophie* (1987), 207–17. From remarks prepared for a panel entitled "We Are Not Alone," part of a day-long symposium, "Fukiyose (Gathering): The Fantastic in Art and Literature," held by the Japan Institute at Harvard University on 25 May 1985. The remarks are, in part, comments on papers submitted to the panel by PhD candidates at the Institute.

"Hope Against Hope." *The American Poetry Review* 15.1 (January–February, 1986), 9–13. Reprinted in *Conditions Handsome and Unhandsome* (1991), 129–38. Delivered before a convocation at Iona College. Addresses Emerson and nuclear holocaust.

"Being Odd, Getting Even (Descartes, Emerson, Poe)." In *Reconstructing Individualism: Autonomy, Individuality, and the Self in Western Thought*, edited by Thomas C. Heller, Morton Sosna, and David E. Wellbery (with Arnold I. Davidson, Ann Swidler, and Ian Watt), pp. 278–313; cf. 13–14 (Stanford: Stanford University Press, 1986). From remarks delivered at an interdisciplinary conference at the Stanford Humanities Center, "Reconstructing Individualism," 18–20 February 1984. Reprinted in *In Quest of the Ordinary* (1988), 105–49, along with "The Skeptical and the Metaphorical," 144–9. See also *Salmagundi* 67 (1985), 97–128.

"Hamlet's Burden of Proof." *Hebrew University Studies in Literature and the Arts* 14 (Fall, 1986), 1–17. Reprinted in *Disowning Knowledge* (1987), 179–91, including a "Postscript," 189–91. Originally presented at Hebrew University, March 1986, and revised, often in the light of remarks by Ruth Nevo.
"A Capra Moment." *Humanities* 6.4 (August, 1985), 3–7.

"Philosophy's Two Myths of Reading." *The Agni Review* 22 (1985), 139–41. An excerpt from "The Philosopher in American Life (Toward

Thoreau and Emerson)," the first of Cavell's 1983 Beckman Lectures at the University of California/Berkeley as it appears in *In Quest of the Ordinary* (1988), 3–26.

"Being Odd, Getting Even: Threats to Individuality." *Salmagundi: A Quarterly of the Humanities and Social Sciences* 67 (Summer, 1985), 97–128.

"A Reply to Robert Mankin on *The Claim of Reason.*" *Salmagundi: A Quarterly of the Humanities and Social Sciences* 67 (Summer, 1985), 90–6. See Mankin's article in *Salmagundi* 67 (Summer, 1985), 66–89.

"The Division of Talent." *Critical Inquiry* 11.4 (June, 1985), 519–38.

"What Photography Calls Thinking." *Raritan: A Quarterly Review* 4.4 (Spring, 1985), 1–21.

" 'Who does the wolf love?' *Coriolanus* and Interpretations of Politics." In *Shakespeare and the Question of Theory*, edited by Patricia Parker and Geoffrey Hartman, pp. 245–72 (New York: Methuen, 1985).

"Emerson, Coleridge, Kant." In *Post-Analytic Philosophy*, edited by John Rajchman and Cornel West, pp. 84–107 (New York: Columbia University Press, 1985).

"Politics as Opposed to What?" In *The Politics of Interpretation*, edited by W. J. T. Mitchell, pp. 181–202 (Chicago: University of Chicago Press, 1983).

"Genteel Responses to Kant? In Emerson's 'Fate' and in Coleridge's *Biographia Literaria.*" *Raritan: A Quarterly Review* 3.2 (Fall, 1983), 34–61. Reprinted in *In Quest of the Ordinary* (1988), 27–49, as "Emerson, Coleridge, Kant (Terms as Conditions)."

" 'Who does the wolf love?' Reading *Coriolanus.*" *Representations* no. 3 (Summer, 1983), 1–20. Modified and expanded versions are reprinted in *Themes Out of School* (1984), 60–96, and *Disowning Knowledge* (1987), 143–78. Delivered as part of a colloquium on *Coriolanus* held at the Humanities Institute at Stanford University, 10–12 September 1982.

"The Thought of Movies." *The Yale Review* 72.2 (Winter, 1983), 181–200. Reprinted in *Themes Out of School* (1984), 3–26.

"Thinking of Emerson." In *Essays in Kant's Aesthetics*, edited by Ted Cohen and Paul Guyer, pp. 261–70 (Chicago: University of Chicago Press, 1982).

"The Fact of Television." *Daedalus: Journal of the American Academy of Arts and Sciences* 111.4 (Fall, 1982), 75–96. Reprinted in *Themes Out of School* (1984), 235–68.

"Politics as Opposed to What?" *Critical Inquiry* 9.1 (September, 1982), 157–78. This issue is devoted to *Critical Inquiry*'s symposium "The Politics of Interpretation," held at the University of Chicago's Center for Continuing Education, 30–31 October and 1 November 1981. The issue includes eight lectures delivered at the symposium plus panelists' subsequently written critical responses. Reprinted in *Themes Out of School* (1984), 27–59.

"Foreword" to Jay Cantor's *The Space Between: Literature and Politics*, pp. ix–xv (Baltimore: Johns Hopkins University Press, 1981). Reprinted in *Themes Out of School* (1984), 145–51.

"North by Northwest." *Critical Inquiry* 7.4 (Summer, 1981), 761–76. Reprinted in *Themes Out of School* (1984), 152–72.

"[An Afterimage–] On Makavejev on Bergman." In *Film and Dreams: An Approach to Bergman*, edited and with an introduction by Vlada Petric, pp. 197–220 (South Salem, NY: Redgrave Publishing Co., 1981). A collection of essays from the International Film Conference "Bergman and Dreams," held at Harvard University, 27–29 January 1978. Cavell's essay addresses Dusan Makavejev's *Sweet Movie* and *WR: Mysteries of the Organism*. Cavell delivered the opening paper. Reprinted in *Critical Inquiry* 6.2 (1979), 305–30, and in *Themes Out of School* (1984), 106–40.

With Hubert Dreyfus, Karsten Harries, John Haugeland, David C. Hoy, and Richard Rorty, "Being True to Heidegger." *New York Review of Books* 28.5 (1981), 45.

With M. Dickstein, R. Krauss, E. Goodheart, W. Phillips, P. Brooks, and E. Kurtzweil, "The Effects of Critical-Theories on Practical Criticism, Cultural Journalism, and Reviewing." *Partisan Review* 48.1 (1981), 9–35.

"Reflexions sur Emerson et Heidegger." *Critique: Revue générale des publications française et étranger* 36.399–400 (Juin–Juillet, 1980), 719–29. A translation of "Thinking of Emerson," first published in *New*

408 *Bibliography*

Literary History: A Journal of Theory and Interpretation 11.1 (Autumn, 1979), 167–76; reprinted in *The Senses of* Walden: *An Expanded Edition* (San Francisco: North Point Press, 1981). This issue of *Critique* is devoted to Anglo-American philosophy. Translated by Marie-Anne Lescourret.

"A Reply to John Hollander." *Critical Inquiry* 6.4 (Summer, 1980), 589–91. Reprinted in *Themes Out of School* (1984), 141–4.

"Knowledge as Transgression: Mostly a Reading of *It Happened One Night.*" *Daedalus: Journal of the American Academy of Arts and Sciences* 109.2 (Spring, 1980), 147–75. Addresses Frank Capra's *It Happened One Night* (1934). From remarks presented at a symposium at Emory University in October 1979 entitled "Intellect and Imagination: The Limits and Presuppositions of Intellectual Inquiry." A revised version appears in *Pursuits of Happiness* (1981), 71–110.

"Die Welt durch die Kamera gesehen." In *Theorien der Kunst*, edited by Dieter Henrich and Wolfgang Iser, pp. 447–90 (Frankfurt am Main: Suhrkamp Verlag, 1979). Translation by Lore Iser.

"Epistemology and Tragedy: A Reading of *Othello*" (together with a cover letter to Molière's Alceste). *Daedalus: Journal of the American Academy of Arts and Sciences* 108.3 (Summer, 1979), 27–43. See also *The Claim of Reason* (1979), Part Four, and *Disowning Knowledge* (1987), 39–124.

"Thinking of Emerson." *New Literary History: A Journal of Theory and Interpretation* 11.1 (Autumn, 1979), 167–76. Reprinted in *The Senses of* Walden: *An Expanded Edition* (1981), 121–38.

"Aesthetic Problems of Modern Philosophy" (selection). In *Art and Philosophy: Readings in Aesthetics*, 2nd edition, edited by W. E. Kennick, pp. 333–41 (New York: St Martin's Press, 1979). The first edition does not include Cavell.

[Excerpt from *The Claim of Reason*.] *L=A=N=G=U=A=G=E* 8 (New York: June, 1979).

[Selections from *The World Viewed*, chs 2–6.] In *Film Theory and Criticism*, edited by Gerald Mast and Marshall Cohen, 2nd edition, pp. 306–20 (New York: Oxford University Press, 1979). Oxford University Press issued the first edition in 1974. Includes:

1. "Photograph and Screen," 306–7.
2. "Audience, Actor, and Star," 308–10.
3. "Types: Cycles as Genres," 311–17.
4. "Ideas of Origin," 318–20.

"On Makavejev on Bergman." *Critical Inquiry* 6.2 (Winter, 1979), 305–30.

"Pursuits of Happiness: A Reading of *The Lady Eve*." *New Literary History: A Journal of Theory and Interpretation* 10.3 (Spring, 1979), 581–601. Addresses Preston Sturges's *The Lady Eve* (1941). Originally presented at the annual Eastern Division meeting of the American Philosophical Association, December 1978, in Washington D.C. A revised version appears in *Pursuits of Happiness* (1981), 45–70.

"The Avoidance of Love" (selection). In *Twentieth Century Interpretations of* King Lear, edited by Janet Adelman, pp. 70–87 (Englewood Cliffs, NJ: Prentice-Hall, Inc., 1978).

"What Becomes of Things on Film?" *Philosophy and Literature* 2.2 (Fall, 1978), 249–57. Addresses Ingmar Bergman's *Persona*, Luis Buñuel's *Belle de Jour*, Alfred Hitchcock's *Vertigo*, and Frank Capra's *It's a Wonderful Life*. Reprinted in *Themes Out of School* (1984), 173–83.

"Sights and Sounds" (selections from *The World Viewed*, chs 2–6]. In *Aesthetics: A Critical Anthology*, edited by George Dickie and Richard J. Sclafani, pp. 366–83 (New York: St Martin's Press, 1977). St Martin's issued a second edition in 1989. Includes:
1. "Photograph and Screen," 371–3.
2. "Audience, Actor, and Star," 373–5.
3. "Types: Cycles as Genres," 375–81.
4. "Ideas of Origin," 381–3.

"Film in the University or Leopards in Connecticut." *Quarterly Review of Film Studies* 2.2 (May, 1977), 141–58. A revised version of the essay previously appearing in the *Georgia Review* 30 (Summer, 1976), 233–62. Originally presented at the CUNY-NEH Conference on Film and the University, organized by Marshall Cohen and Gerald Mast; held at the Graduate Center of the City University of New York, 15–18 July 1975.

"Leopards in Connecticut." *The Georgia Review* 30 (Summer, 1976), 233–62. Addresses Howard Hawks's *Bringing Up Baby* (1938). A revised version appears in *Pursuits of Happiness* (1981), 111–32.

"Mussen wir meinen, was wir sagen?" In *Linguistik und Philosophie*, edited by Günther Grewendorf and Georg Meggle, pp. 168–219 (Frankfurt: Athenaüm Verlag, 1974).

"More of *The World Viewed*." *The Georgia Review* 28.4 (Winter, 1974), 571–631. Expanded and added as an appendix to the enlarged edition of *The World Viewed* (1979).

"Types: Cycles as Genres" (from *The World Viewed*). In *Film Theory and Criticism*, edited by Gerald Mast and Marshall Cohen, pp. 359–65 (New York: Oxford University Press, 1974). A second edition, issued in 1979, contains additional work by Cavell.

"Ideas of Origin" (from *The World Viewed*). In *Film Theory and Criticism*, edited by Gerald Mast and Marshall Cohen, pp. 579–82 (New York: Oxford University Press, 1974). Oxford issued a second edition in 1979 containing additional material by Cavell.

"Must We Mean What We Say?" In *Philosophy and Linguistics*, Controversies in Philosophy, edited by Colin Lyas, pp. 131–65 (London: Macmillan and Co. Ltd./New York: St Martin's Press, 1971).

"The Availability of Wittgenstein's Later Philosophy." In *Philosophy and Linguistics*, Controversies in Philosophy, edited by Colin Lyas, pp. 166–89 (London: Macmillan and Co. Ltd./New York: St Martin's Press, 1971).

"Some Reflections on the Ontology of Film." *New American Review* 12 (1971), 140–59.

"Austin at Criticism." In *Symposium on J. L. Austin*, International Library of Philosophy and Scientific Method, edited by K. T. Fann, pp. 59–75 (London: Routledge & Kegan Paul New York: Humanities Press, 1969).

"Austin at Criticism." In *Philosophy Today No. 1*, edited by Jerry H. Gill, pp. 81–101 (New York: Macmillan Company, 1968).

"Der Zugang zu Wittgensteins Spätphilosophie." In *Über Ludwig Wittgenstein*, edited by Ulrich Steinworth, pp. 119–53 (Frankfurt am Main: Suhrkamp Verlag, 1968). A translation of Cavell's "The Availability of Wittgenstein's Later Philosophy," *The Philosophical Review* 71 (January, 1962), 67–93. Translated by Rolf-Albert Dietrich. Also includes essays by Norman Malcolm, Peter Fredrick Strawson, and Newton Garver.

"Music Discomposed." In *Art, Mind, and Religion* (proceedings of the April 1965, Sixth Annual Oberlin Colloquium in Philosophy), edited by W. H. Capitan and D. D. Merrill, pp. 69–97 (Pittsburgh: University of Pittsburgh Press, 1967). Reprinted in *Must We Mean What We Say?* (1969), 180–212. Originally read as the opening paper at this symposium. Most of sections V, VI, and VII was presented as part of a symposium at the University of California/Berkeley, December 1960. Called "Composition, Improvisation, Chance," the symposium was held at a joint meeting of the American Musicological Society, the Society for Ethnomusicology, and the College Music Society. Accompanying this article are comments by Joseph Margolis (98–102), Monroe C. Beardsley (103–9), and a rejoinder by Cavell (110–32), which was later published in *Must We Mean What We Say?* as "A Matter of Meaning It," 213–37.

"Austin at Criticism." In *The Linguistic Turn*, edited by Richard Rorty, pp. 250–60 (Chicago: University of Chicago Press, 1967). Second edition, 1992.

"The Availability of Wittgenstein's Later Philosophy." In *Wittgenstein: The Philosophical Investigations*, edited by George Pitcher, pp. 151–85 (Garden City, NY: Doubleday & Co., Inc., 1966).

With Alexander Sesonske. "Logical Empiricism and Pragmatism in Ethics." In *Pragmatic Philosophy: An Anthology*, edited by Amelie Rorty, pp. 382–95 (Garden City, NY: Anchor Books, 1966).

"Austin at Criticism." *The Philosophical Review* 74.2 (April, 1965), 204–19. Reprinted in *Must We Mean What We Say?* (1969), 97–114. Largely written while Cavell was in residence in 1962–3 at the Institute for Advanced Study at Princeton University.

"Aesthetic Problems of Modern Philosophy." In *Philosophy in America*, edited by Max Black, pp. 74–97 (Ithaca, NY: Cornell University Press, 1965). Reprinted in *Must We Mean What We Say?* (1969), 73–96. A volume collecting original essays by younger American philosophers. The first half of the essay was delivered at a meeting of the American Society for Aesthetics in October 1962. It was largely written in 1962–3 while Cavell was in residence at the Institute for Advanced Study at Princeton University.

"Existentialism and Analytical Philosophy." *Daedalus: Journal of the American Academy of Arts and Sciences* 93.3 (Summer, 1964), 946–74. Reprinted in *Themes Out of School* (1984), 195–234.

"Must We Mean What We Say?" In *Ordinary Language*, edited by Vere Claiborne Chappell, pp. 75–112 (Englewood Cliffs, NJ: Prentice-Hall, Inc., 1964). Includes Benson Mates's essay "On the Verification of Statements about Ordinary Language."

"The Availability of Wittgenstein's Later Philosophy." *The Philosophical Review* 71 (January, 1962), 67–93. Reprinted in *Must We Mean What We Say?* (1969), 44–72.

"Must We Mean What We Say?" *Inquiry* 1.3 (Autumn, 1958), 172–212. Reprinted as the first essay in *Must We Mean What We Say?* (1969), 1–43. From a paper read at the Pacific Coast Division of the American Philosophical Association, 19 December 1957, for a symposium in part addressing Benson Mates's "On the Verification of Statements about Ordinary Language."

With Alexander Sesonske. "Moral Theory, Ethical Judgments and Empiricism." *Mind* 61.244 (October, 1952), 543–63.

With Alexander Sesonske. "Logical Empiricism and Pragmatism in Ethics." *The Journal of Philosophy* 48 (4 January, 1951), 5–17.

Interviews and Discussions (Chronologically)

With Giovanna Borradori, "An Apology for Skepticism." In Giovanna Barradori, *The American Philosopher: Conversations with Quine, Davidson, Putnam, Nozick, Danto, Rorty, Cavell, MacIntyre, and Kuhn*, translated by Rosanna Crocitto (Chicago: University of Chicago Press, 1993), 118–36. Originally published as *Conversazioni americane con Willard Van Orman Quine, Donald Davidson, Hilary Putnam, Robert Nozick, Arthur C. Danto, Richard Rorty, Stanley Cavell, Alisdair MacIntyre, Thomas S. Kuhn* (Gius: Laterza & Figli, 1991).

With Richard Fleming, "The Self of Philosophy: An Interview with Stanley Cavell." In Stanley Cavell, *Philosophical Passages: Wittgenstein, Emerson, Austin, Derrida*, Bucknell Lectures in Literary Theory 12, general editors Michael Payne and Harold Schweizer (Oxford: Blackwell, 1995), 91–103. Bucknell University, 6 May 1993.

Seminar on "What Did Derrida Want of Austin?" In Stanley Cavell, *Philosophical Passages: Wittgenstein, Emerson, Austin, Derrida*, Bucknell Lectures in Literary Theory 12, general editors Michael Payne and Harold Schweizer (Oxford: Blackwell, 1995). Recorded 5 May 1993 at Bucknell University; text revised December 1993.

With James Conant, "An Interview with Stanley Cavell." In *The Senses of Stanley Cavell*, edited by Richard Fleming and Michael Payne, 21–72. *Bucknell Review: A Scholarly Journal of Letters, Arts and Sciences* 32.1 (Lewisburg, PA: Bucknell University Press/London: Associated University Presses, 1989). This volume is a special edition of the *Bucknell Review* devoted to Cavell's work.

With Michael Payne and Richard Fleming, "A Conversation with Stanley Cavell on Philosophy and Literature." In *The Senses of Stanley Cavell*, edited by Richard Fleming and Michael Payne, 311–21. *Bucknell Review: A Scholarly Journal of Letters, Arts and Sciences* 32.1 (Lewisburg, PA: Bucknell University Press London: Associated University Presses, 1989). This volume is a special edition of the *Bucknell Review* devoted to Cavell's work.

With Daniel Callahan, Denise Carmody, Michael Fishbane, Stephen Richard Graubard, James Gustafson, Timothy Healy (S.J.), Robert Kiely, George Lindbeck, Robert Lynn, Frank Manuel, John Padberg (S.J.), and Theodore Sizer. "Conference on Religion and Education." *Daedalus: The Journal of the American Academy of Arts and Sciences* 117.2 (Spring, 1988), 1–146. From a conference discussion sponsored by *Daedalus* and Georgetown University.

With Leonhard Schmeiser, "How can one inherit Europe? Stanley Cavell über Tradition und Neubeginn der amerikanischen Philosophie." An interview in *Nach der Philosophie: Essays von Stanley Cavell*, edited by Kurt Rudolf Fischer and Ludwig Nagl (Wien: Verlag des Verbandes der wissenschaftlichen Gesellschaften Österreichs, 1987). Broadcast on Österreichischen Rundfunks (Ö1) program "Dimensionen," 10 July 1986.

"Observations on Art and Science." *Daedalus: The Journal of the American Academy of Arts and Sciences* 115.3 (Summer, 1986), 171–7. Under the same title, *Daedalus* collects remarks by Leon Cooper, Samuel Y. Edgerton, Jr., and Victor F. Weisskopf. See also: "Observations on Art and Science." In *Art and Science*, The Daedalus Library, edited by Stephen Richard Graubard, pp. 171–7 (Lanham, MD: University Press of America, 1986).

"Questions and Answers." In *Romanticism and Contemporary Criticism*, edited by Morris Eaves and Michael Fischer, pp. 225–39 (Ithaca: Cornell University Press, 1986).

Recorded Lectures

"His Girl Friday." In *Pursuits of Happiness: A Reading of Three Hollywood Comedies*. Patten Lectures, v. 1979–1980 (Bloomington: University of Indiana, 1980). Recorded 10 April 1980.

"The Philadelphia Story." In *Pursuits of Happiness: A Reading of Three Hollywood Comedies*. Patten Lectures, v. 1979–1980 (Bloomington: University of Indiana, 1980). Recorded 9 April 1980.

"It Happened One Night." In *Pursuits of Happiness: A Reading of Three Hollywood Comedies*. Pattern Lectures, v. 1979–1980 (Bloomington: University of Indiana, 1980). Recorded 8 April 1980.

Index of Themes and Concepts

Index of Names and Titles